PAUL AND RABBINIC
JUDAISM

PAUL AND RABBINIC JUDAISM

SOME RABBINIC ELEMENTS IN PAULINE THEOLOGY

BY

W. D. DAVIES, D.D., F.B.A.

Duke University

FORTRESS PRESS   PHILADELPHIA

Dedicated to My Wife

The introduction "Paul and Judaism since Schweitzer" is reprinted from *The Bible in Modern Scholarship*. Papers read at the 100th Meeting of the Society of Biblical Literature, December 28–30, 1964, edited by J. Philip Hyatt, copyright © 1965 by Abingdon Press.

Appendix D contains a review of H. J. Schoeps, *Paulus*, reprinted from *New Testament Studies* by permission of the Cambridge University Press.

First published in 1948
Second edition, with additional notes, 1955
Third edition, with new introduction and additional appendix, 1970
Third printing, 1979
Fourth edition, with new preface, by Fortress Press, 1980

Library of Congress Cataloging in Publication Data

Davies, William David, 1911–
Paul and rabbinic Judaism.

Bibliography: p.
Includes indexes.
1. Bible. N.T. Epistles of Paul—Theology.
2. Christianity and other religions—Judaism.
3. Judaism—Relations—Christianity. I. Title.
BS2651.D3 1980   230'.12   80-8049
ISBN 0-8006-1438-0

8293F80   Printed in the United States of America   1–1438

CONTENTS

Introduction: Paul and Judaism since Schweitzer   vii
Preface   xvii
Preface to the Second Edition   xix
Preface to the Fourth Edition   xxi
Principal Abbreviations   xxxix

Chap. 1 Introduction: Palestinian and Diaspora Judaism   I

    2 The Old Enemy: The Flesh and Sin   17

    3 The Old and the New Humanity: The First and Second Adam   36

    4 The Old and the New Israel: 'Nationalism'   58

    5 The Old and the New Man: I. Paul as Preacher to the Individual   86

    6 The Old and the New Man: II. Paul as Teacher of the Individual   III

    7 The Old and the New Torah: Christ the Wisdom of God   147

    8 The Old and the New Obedience: I. The Lord the Spirit   177

    9 The Old and the New Obedience: II. The Death of Jesus   227

   10 The Old and the New Hope: Resurrection   285

      Conclusion   321

App. A Dr Karl Barth's Interpretation of Romans I. 2   325

    B The Imperative Participle in Tannaitic Hebrew   329

    C Passages referred to in the Text, outside Talmudic Sources and the *Midrash Rabbah*, in the Order of their Occurrence   330

    D A Review of H. J. Schoeps, *Paulus*   342

Bibliography   *page* 353

Periodicals referred to in the Text   361

Commentaries consulted   362

Additional Notes   363

Index I   Quotations from the Old Testament   379

     II   Quotations from the Apocrypha and Pseudepigrapha   382

    III   Quotations from the New Testament   384

    IV   Quotations from the Targums   391

     V   Quotations from Rabbinical Literature   391

    VI   References to Classical and Hellenistic Authors and to Extra-Canonical Christian Writings   394

   VII   References to Rabbis cited   395

  VIII   Index of Authors   395

    IX   Subject Index   400

INTRODUCTION

PAUL AND JUDAISM SINCE SCHWEITZER

NOTE: *In order to set this work,* Paul and Rabbinic Judaism, *in its recent perspective, I have thought it wise to reprint the following paper on* Paul and Judaism since Schweitzer, *which was communicated to the Society of Biblical Literature and Exegesis in 1964. It can serve as a prelude to the present edition.*

The theme divides itself naturally into two parts with each of which we shall deal in turn.[1]

I. JUDAISM AS THE BACKGROUND OF PAUL

In the first place, the theme can be made to refer to the background of Saul of Tarsus. To what world did he most belong? Out of what current or currents in Judaism did he emerge? It is to the changes in our understanding of Paul's Jewish background since Schweitzer that we turn first. These changes have been radical and enriching. They can be clarified in the light of two main assumptions that governed the work of Schweitzer both on the Gospels and on Paul.

The first of these assumptions was made by most scholars and informed most treatments of the background of the NT in Schweitzer's day. The assumption was that it is possible to make a clear distinction between what was Semitic or Palestinian Judaism and Hellenistic or Diaspora Judaism in the first century. On the basis of this distinction Schweitzer set Paul, who was dominated by Palestinian categories, over against John, who was dominated by Hellenistic ones.[2] On the other hand, the same assumption led Montefiore to interpret Paul as a Diaspora Jew, who, had he known the superior Judaism of Palestine, would

---

[1] For surveys of Paulinism, see A. Schweitzer, *Paul and His Interpreters*, tr. W. Montgomery (London, 1912); B. Rigaux, "L'interprétation du paulinisme dans l'exégèse récente," *Littérature et Théologie Pauliniennes, Recherches Bibliques*, V (Bruges, 1960), 17–46; E. Earle Ellis, *Paul and His Recent Interpreters* (Grand Rapids, Michigan, 1961); Hans Joachim Schoeps, *Paulus: Die Theologie des Apostels im Lichte der jüdischen Religionsgeschichte* (Tübingen, 1959), pp. 1–42. On methodology, see Samuel Sandmel, "Judaism, Jesus and Paul: Some Problems of Method in Scholarly Research," in R. C. Beatty, J. P. Hyatt, and M. K. Spears, eds., *Vanderbilt Studies in the Humanities*, I (Nashville, 1951), pp. 220–50,
[2] See his *The Mysticism of Paul the Apostle*, tr. W. Montgomery (London, 1931).

never have embraced the gospel.[1] The dichotomy between Palestinian and Diaspora Judaism made it possible to localize Paul conveniently, according to one's approach, either within or without Palestinian Judaism. This dichotomy, while not universal (Schürer had long voiced a caveat against it[2]), was widely accepted when Schweitzer wrote. Its vitality is still evident. It informed, for example, the programme of the Society in its centennial meeting. Professor Koester and I were assigned to deal with what are, subconsciously at least, presumed to be separate, perhaps watertight compartments, Hellenism and Judaism in their relation to Paul.

But it is precisely this sharp separation which so much work since Schweitzer has made increasingly impossible. Historical probability alone should have warned against it. Judaism for a long period before the first century had been open to Hellenizing forces of an aggressive kind. These forces impinged upon it both from within and from without the borders of Palestine. And what historical probability suggests has been confirmed from Jewish literary sources and archaeological discoveries. Rabbinic sources have been more and more revealed to reflect Hellenistic influences in both their vocabulary and ideology.[3] Conversely, Hellenistic sources have often betrayed the influence of Semitic concepts and even documents.[4] Daube[5] suggested, with much probability, that even the methods of rabbinic exegesis, which at first encounter seem so peculiarly Jewish, were inspired by Greek models: Aristotle begat Akiba. On the archaeological side, the evidence has been overwhelming that Judaism was open to and receptive of Hellenistic influences on all sides.[6] It is not necessary to labour the obvious. The old dichotomy between Palestinian and Diaspora Hellenistic

---

[1] C. J. G. Montefiore, *Judaism and St. Paul* (London, 1914); the position is also represented by Joseph Klausner, *From Jesus to Paul*, tr. W. F. Stinespring (London, 1942); S. Sandmel, *A Jewish Understanding of the New Testament* (New York, 1956), pp. 37-51. *et alia*.

[2] E. Schürer, *The Jewish People in the Time of Jesus Christ*, tr. Sophia Taylor and Peter Christie (5 vols. and Index; Edinburgh, 1885); see Vol. I, Division II, pp. 29-50, (The 4th German ed. should be consulted). For a brief survey of the problem, A. D. Nock, *Early Gentile Christianity and Its Hellenistic Background* (Harper Torchbook; New York, 1964), pp. ix-x and the whole introduction, pp. vii-xxi, including a bibliography.

[3] See ch. 1 and now my article on "Reflexions on Tradition: The Aboth revisited" in the *Festschrift for John Knox* (Cambridge, 1967).

[4] See C. H. Dodd on the *Hermetica* in *The Bible and the Greeks* (London, 1935).

[5] *HUCA*, XXII (1949), 239 ff.; in *Festschrift Hans Lewald* (Basle, 1952), pp. 27 ff. on "Alexandrian Methods of Interpretation and the Rabbis." Cf. W. F. Albright, *From the Stone Age to Christianity* (Baltimore, 1946), pp. 274 f., 337, n. 26.

[6] See especially the monumental work of E. R. Goodenough, *Jewish Symbols in the Greco-Roman Period* (New York, 1953-65). (As an example of Hellenistic penetration,

Judaism is no longer tenable. At this point American scholarship in
particular deserves the greatest credit. The work of Morton Smith[1] and
Liebermann[2] on documents deserves our grateful recognition. But,
above all, the monumental works of E. R. Goodenough on Jewish symbols in the Greco-Roman world claim attention. It would be an im-
pertinence to praise these works: their full significance for the study of
Christian origins has still to be recognized.

The area in which Schweitzer particularly drew a contrast between
Hellenistic and Semitic concepts was that of mysticism, which is closely
related to *gnosis*. But since the publication of *The Mysticism of Paul the
Apostle* (English translation, 1931) the understanding of so-called mystical elements in first-century Judaism has been largely transformed.
The work of Gershom Scholem[3] in particular has compelled the recognition of mystical and proto-Gnostic currents within Palestinian
Judaism, so that Schweitzer's confidence in drawing rigid distinctions
between Pauline and Johannine forms of mysticism can no longer be
justified. Here the Dead Sea Scrolls are highly significant: they confirmed the awareness which was already growing before their discovery
that pre-Christian Judaism, although it does not reveal a fully developed

see Benjamin Mazar, "Excavations at the Oasis of Engedi," in *Archaeology*, XVI [1963],
99–107.) Goodenough postulates a widespread Hellenistic Judaism, represented particularly
by Philo, which he sets over against rabbinic Judaism, which sought at first to control all
Jewry. But it failed to do so. The Judaism of the rabbis did not become normative for all
Jews. It would be impertinent to discuss Goodenough's work here; we may be permitted
a few comments. First, we should go further than Goodenough in recognizing that first-
century "legalistic" or Pharisaic Judaism was itself Hellenized, so that the gulf between
Hellenism and Judaism of a rabbinic kind is not so sharp as he proposes. Secondly, whatever the variety of Judaism in the first century and subsequently (and this Goodenough
and others have established beyond doubt) the historically significant force in first-century
Judaism was the Pharisaic. And it was this force that the Church, and especially Matthew,
had to oppose. That the extent and depth of Pharisaic-rabbinic authority has been exaggerated, we may admit, but that it asserted itself we must also admit. For discussions of
Goodenough's work, see the following: Morton Smith, "The Image of God: Notes on
the Hellenization of Judaism, with Especial Reference to Goodenough's Work on Jewish
Symbols," *BJRL*, XL (1958), 473–512; Cecil Roth, *Judaism*, III (1954), 129–35; *ibid.*,
179–82; S. S. Kayser, *Review of Religion*, XXI (1956), 54–60; A. D. Nock reviewed vols.
I–IV and vols. V–VI in *Gnomon*, XXVII (1955), 558–72 and XXIX (1957), 524–33; E. J.
Bickerman, *HTR*, LVIII (1965), on "Symbolism in the Dura Synagogue," 127 ff.

[1] Most conveniently in *Israel*, ed. M. Davis (New York, 1956), pp. 74 ff. on "Palestinian Judaism in the First Century."

[2] *Greek in Jewish Palestine* (New York, 1942); and an article, "How Much Greek in
Jewish Palestine," in *Studies and Texts*, Vol. I: *Biblical and Other Studies*, ed. A. Altmann
(Cambridge, 1963), pp. 123–41.

[3] G. G. Scholem, *Major Trends in Jewish Mysticism* (Jerusalem, 1941); *Jewish Gnosticism,
Merkabah Mysticism, and Talmudic Tradition* (New York, 1960). See also his article on
"Religious Authority and Mysticism," *Commentary*, (November, 1964), pp. 31 ff.

Gnosticism, did emphasize *da'ath* and exhibit incipient tendencies towards later Gnosticism: they have made it luminously clear that much
that has often been labelled Hellenistic may well have been Palestinian
and Semitic.[1]

To sum up. While there is an unmistakable difference between
figures such as Hillel and Philo, this difference must not be made
absolute.[2] The lines between Hellenism and Judaism, by the first
century, were very fluid. Consider how difficult it is to define what
forces mould a figure such as President Lyndon Johnson. Is he a Southerner with a northern veneer, or is he a northern liberal who happens to
have been born in the South, or is he a Southern Texan? To define
what went into the making of a Paul is infinitely harder. In Paul Athens
and Jerusalem are strangely mixed, not because he was a Tarsian (if Van
Unnik be right, Tarsus can have influenced him very little[3]), but
because the Judaism within which he grew up, even in Jerusalem, was

---

[1] W. D. Davies, " 'Knowledge' in the Dead Sea Scrolls and Matthew 11: 25-30," in
Christian Origins and Judaism (Philadelphia, 1962), pp. 119 ff.; Bo Reicke, "Traces of
Gnosticism in the Dead Sea-Scrolls?" *NTS*, I (1954), 137-41; K. G. Kuhn, "Die in Palästina
gefundenen hebräischen Texte und das Neue Testament," *ZTK*, XLVII (1950), 192 ff.;
Helmer Ringgren, *The Faith of Qumran* (Philadelphia, 1963), pp. 114 ff. On "Gnostic
Themes in Rabbinic Cosmology," see A. Altmann in *Essays in Honour of J. H. Hertz*
(London, 1942), pp. 19 ff. "The early stages of Tannaitic thought are already under the
spell of Gnostic ideas" (p. 20). On Mysteries and Judaism, see A. D. Nock in *Mnemosune*,
S. 4, V (1952), 190 ff.; R. E. Brown, "The Pre-Christian Semitic Concept of 'Mystery,' "
CBQ, XX (1958), 417-33; see also W. C. van Unnik, *Die jüdische Komponente in der
Entstehung der Gnosis, Vortrag im katholischphilosophischen Seminar der Universität Frankfurt
am Main,* 4-2-1960, pp. 65-82. On Gnosticism, see F. C. Burkitt, *The Church and Gnosis*
(Cambridge, 1932); R. P. Casey on "Gnosis, Gnosticism and the New Testament," in
The Background of the New Testament and Its Eschatology: Studies in Honour of C. H. Dodd,
W. D. Davies and D. Daube, eds. (Cambridge, 1956), pp. 27 ff.; Hans Jonas, *The Gnostic
Religion* (Boston, 1958); R. McL. Wilson, *The Gnostic Problem* (London, 1958); J. Dupont,
Gnosis (Louvain, 1949); C. Colpe, *Die religionsgeschichtliche Schule* (Göttingen, 1961).

[2] See the suggestive statement of this in Richard N. Longnecker, *Paul, Apostle of
Liberty* (New York, 1964), p. 28. The geographic span of Judaism must be given due
weight and within this span variety. After the New York meetings, Professor Koester
urged the importance of geographic differences. With this I fully agree; see, for example,
The Setting of the Sermon on the Mount (Cambridge, 1964), appendix VII, "Galilean and
Judaean Judaism," pp. 450 ff. I may be permitted to mention that I often warn beginning
American students against thinking in an American—that is, in this context, a "continental"
manner—about the world of the NT, a manner which tends to ignore the almost "infinite"
variety which is possible in older cultures within a little space. I can recall a time, for
example, when I could detect not only from what county certain of my fellow countrymen came merely by their use of idioms and accents, but from what valleys in their various
counties.

[3] *Tarsus or Jerusalem* (London, 1952); for a summary of this, see G. Ogg, *Scottish
Journal of Theology*, VII (1955), 94-97.

largely Hellenized, and the Hellenism he encountered in his travels largely Judaized.

But Schweitzer made a second assumption which had important implications for his own work and has coloured most interpretations of Paul. Within Judaism itself he drew a sharp distinction between apocalyptic and Pharisaism and other aspects of Judaism. In his work *Von Reimarus zu Wrede* (English translation as *The Quest of the Historical Jesus*), Schweitzer insisted that Jesus is "simply the culminating manifestation of Jewish apocalyptic thought."[1] But this apocalyptic thought is to be utterly divorced from that of the Rabbis: it was the product of popular circles opposed to the learning of the Scribes. Rudolf Otto carried the matter further by connecting apocalyptic especially with Galilee from whose religious aberrations official Judaism had turned away.[2]

From this point of view Schweitzer was able to isolate Paul, as he had previously isolated Jesus, and place him in a purely eschatological context, divorced from Pharisaism and other first-century currents.

But this assumption of Schweitzer's has again been questioned and must now be most emphatically rejected. Studies and discoveries since Schweitzer's work have made it clear that apocalyptic and Pharisaism —differing as they did in emphases—were not alien to each other but often, if not always, enjoyed a congenial coexistence. Such a figure as Akiba alone should have warned us that this was the case, and now the Dead Sea Scrolls, which reveal a people fiercely dedicated to the Law and yet ardent in their eschatological hopes, have put the matter beyond any possible doubt.[3]

But the dominance of Schweitzer in Pauline studies has been such that the old dichotomy between apocalyptic and Pharisaism upon which he insisted still invades this field. The approach to Paul along almost exclusively apocalyptic lines and the rigidity of Schweitzer's dogmatic Paul re-emerges again and again. We note the two most recent significant, large-scale treatments of the apostle. The late Professor Johannes Munck, whose passing we all mourn, has forcefully, and with a disarming and insidious charm, done for Paul what Schweitzer did for

[1] *The Quest of the Historical Jesus* (London, 1910), pp. 365 ff.

[2] *The Kingdom of God and the Son of Man*, tr. F. V. Filson and B. L. Woolf (London, 1938), pp. 13 ff.

[3] See my *Christian Origins and Judaism*, on "Apocalyptic and Pharisaism," pp. 19–30; J. Bloch, *On the Apocalyptic in Judaism* (Philadelphia, 1953); E. Stauffer, *Die Theologie des Neuen Testaments* (4th ed.; Stuttgart, 1948), pp. 3 ff.; D. S. Russell, *The Method and Message of Jewish Apocalyptic*, 200 B.C.–400 A.D. (Philadelphia, 1964); T. F. Glasson, *Greek Influence in Jewish Eschatology* (London, 1961). Contrast D. Rössler, *Gesetz und Geschichte im Judentum*, 1960.

Jesus—that is, placed him in an eschatological straitjacket or an eschatological isolation, even though we now realize that the pre-conditions
for such an isolation did not exist.[1] With Schoeps we move forward,
because, although he still emphasizes the eschatological framework of
Paulinism chiefly in the manner of Schweitzer, he does insist that
Rabbinism and other factors have to be exploited for the interpretation
of Paul.[2] And his work forms a convenient bridge to the next section of
this Pauline report. Before we go on to it, let us sum up the problem of
Paul's background. What has happened since Schweitzer is that the
simple picture of a normative Pharisaic Judaism standing over against
apocalyptic and Hellenism has vanished. Its fast colours have become
blurred and mixed. Judaism has emerged as more varied, changing,
and complicated than Schweitzer could have appreciated. In particular,
the Dead Sea Scrolls have triumphantly confirmed the suspicions of
those who had already suspected Schweitzer's neat dichotomies.[3]

II. JUDAISM IN THE THEOLOGY OF PAUL

But let us move on to the second section of this report. Our subject
has another aspect: it relates not only to Judaism, as his background,
but to Paul's treatment of Judaism as a man "in Christ". How did the
apostle interpret Judaism in the light of the gospel? In his great work
The Mysticism of Paul the Apostle, true to his eschatological emphasis,
Schweitzer found the heart of Paul in a quasi-physical solidarity of the
baptized believer with Christ. To support this view he appealed exclusively to the concept of the solidarity of the elect with the Messiah,
a concept frequently found in apocalyptic sources. It is this that lies at
the root of his interpretation of Paul in terms of a cosmic mysticism
"in Christ."[4] This eschatological approach is Schweitzer's permanent
contribution to Pauline studies and, as we saw, it has informed the work
of all who followed him. To recognize the eschatological character of
Jesus Christ in the full light of Jewish eschatological expectations and
to pursue this insight with a ruthless logic has been the hallmark of
Schweitzer's work and it has been immensely enriching.

[1] See my critique of Munck in *Christian Origins and Judaism,* pp. 179–98, on "A New
View of Paul—J. Munck *Paulus und die Heilsgeschichte,*" reprinted from *NTS,* II (1955),
60–72.
[2] See my review printed below as Appendix D.
[3] The literature on the Scrolls and the NT is immense: to set the matter in perspective,
see the volume edited by K. Stendahl, *The Scrolls and the New Testament* (New York,
1957) and articles by Herbert Braun, *ThR,* N. F., XXIX (1963), 142 ff., XXX (1964),
89 ff., "Qumran und das Neue Testament."
[4] *The Mysticism of Paul the Apostle,* pp. 101 f.; *Paul and His Interpreters,* p. 225.

But it has also raised many questions. Two are pertinent here. First, in the light of Pauline eschatology and the cosmic mysticism "in Christ," which Schweitzer declared to be the heart of Paulinism, in what relation does Paulinism stand to Judaism? Before Schweitzer, Protestant scholarship, by and large, had given a clear answer to this question. Under the influence of Luther, it had found the heart of Paul and, indeed, of all the NT in justification by faith. And as long as this doctrine was regarded as the essence of Paulinism, in the last resort, the relation of Paul to Judaism could only be one of opposition or antithesis. But Schweitzer relegated justification by faith to a secondary position.[1] By insisting in a thoroughgoing way on the eschatological context and content of Paul's thought, he inevitably introduced a new perspective. He opened the way for the interpretation of Paul's understanding of Judaism in terms, not of opposition, but of fulfilment or finality. To root Paul seriously in Jewish eschatology, as did Schweitzer, was to remove the centre of gravity of Paulinism from justification by faith to a cosmic act involving the destiny of the totality of nature and of man: it was to shift the essential direction of the Pauline salvation from being primarily the alleviation of the pangs of conscience (a term not found in the OT and borrowed in the NT from popular Hellenistic "philosophy")[2] to being the redirection of the cosmos. The Pauline concept of salvation included, but was not exhausted by, a new self-understanding. Indeed, it has recently been urged by Kasemann[3] and Stendahl[4] that even the doctrine of justification by faith itself has to do, not so much with the individual conscience, as with the inclusion of Gentiles in the true Israel. What Kasemann and Stendahl affirm is, in my judgment, right; what they deny is not so altogether convincing. Did the inclusion of the Gentiles in "Israel" so shake the very "foundations" of Paul that his moral awareness was spurred into a new sensitivity, just as the current struggle for civil rights in the United States has "awakened" many who previously "slept."[5] There are, in any case, many—perhaps they are the majority of scholars—who still find the essence of Paulin-

---

[1] *The Mysticism of Paul the Apostle*, p. 225. "The doctrine of righteousness by faith is therefore a subsidiary crater. . . ." See pp. 221 ff. below.

[2] See my article on "Conscience" in *IDB*.

[3] "Gottesgerichtigkeit bei Paulus," *ZTK*, LVIII (1961), 367–78.

[4] "The Apostle Paul and the Introspective Conscience of the West," *HTR*, LVI (1963), 199–215, reprinted in S. H. Miller and G. Ernest Wright, eds., *Ecumenical Dialogue at Harvard* (Cambridge, 1964), pp. 236–56. In our view, for Paul what was a crisis of eschatology became a crisis of conscience.

[5] On sociological influences on Paul, see Ernest Benz, "Das Paulus–Verständis in der morgenlandischen und abendländischen Kirche," *Zeitschrift für Religions- und Geistesgeschichte*, IV (1951), 289–309.

ism in justification by faith, interpreted in terms of self-understanding. Bultmann has stated this position with moving brilliance in his treatment of Paul—surely the richest portion of his *Theology*. But it is significant that Bultmann, unlike Schweitzer, has emphasized Paul's affinities with the Hellenistic world, not with Judaism. The debate continues. But it was Schweitzer who radically reopened it, and in doing so he has, in the mind of some, helped to deliver us from Protestant and Western provincialism.

But this leads to the second question raised by Schweitzer's work. He enlarged our perspectives and delivered us from provincialisms, but did he also introduce into his interpretation of eschatology mechanical and even magical categories which deprive it of full moral seriousness? For example, does not baptism, the act whereby the believer already has participated in the cosmic redemption, become a magical rite for Schweitzer?[1] As Professor Louis Martyn suggested to me, Schweitzer's description of Paulinism is often reminiscent of the thought of those whom the Paul of the NT opposed, that is, those who felt that they had already been enriched and had already attained. The fact is that Schweitzer's Paul is so exclusively eschatological that he cannot participate in the full richness of Judaism. Schweitzer so isolated apocalyptic from other currents in Judaism that he deprived Paul of much of his Jewish heritage, even while insisting on his Jewishness. The nemesis of Schweitzer's approach was that it became difficult for him to do justice to other than strictly eschatological aspects of the apostle's thought. For example, the whole Pharisaic dimension in Paul could be neglected. In *Paul and Rabbinic Judaism*, I sought to do justice to elements in the apostle that are derived from Pharisaism. I ventured to suggest that the Paul revealed in the epistles was far more complicated than can be exhausted in purely eschatological categories. The Judaism which Schweitzer found fulfilled "in Christ" was an emasculated, apocalyptic Judaism, not the varied Judaism of Pharisaism, Qumran, and other currents. From the essential emphasis of Schweitzer there is no possibility of escape. But his emphasis must be related to aspects of Judaism which he ignored.[2] It is this process that is now going on—the exploitation of the fullness of Judaism, Hellenistic, Pharisaic, Essene (Qumran), Septuagintal and classically Hebraic, in the interests of a deeper under-

---

[1] See below, pp. 98 ff., where I quote V. Taylor, *Forgiveness and Reconciliation* (London, 1941), p. 138: "What is described by Schweitzer is not personal communion conditioned by faith, but a mode of being effected by eschatological rites."

[2] An interesting, forcefully argued example of this came to my notice after the above comment was communicated to the Society, in James Kallas, *The Significance of the Synoptic Miracles* (London, 1961), pp. 103 ff. His words apply *mutatis mutandis* to Paulinism.

standing of Paulinism. In short, the rooting of Paul not only in apocalyptic but in the whole complex of Judaism as an integral part of the
ancient Greco–Roman–oriental world is the way of advance beyond a
Schweitzer, who in his rightful concern to emphasize the "strangeness"
of primitive Christianity endangered its relations with the continuities
of history.[1] Recent scholarship is already revealing that the relation
between Paul and Judaism cannot adequately be expressed in terms of
the simple antitheses so long customary in Pauline scholarship. If
Schweitzer rightly revolted against the "liberal" psychological concentration of the nineteenth-century scholars, the time is now ripe for
a revolt against the "dogmatic" eschatological concentration of their
twentieth-century successors.

[1] Most recently there has been a salutary return to the study of the Targumim in
relation to the NT. It is exemplified in the brilliant work of R. Le Déaut, *La Nuit Pascale*,
(Rome, 1963) and of his pupil Martin McNamara, M.S.C., *The New Testament and the
Palestinian Targum to the Pentateuch* (Rome, 1966). Both are of importance for the study
of Paul. Recently Antoine Duprez in an article on "La Piscine Probatique" in *Bible et Terre
Sainte*, No. 79, Jan. 1966, pp. 5–14, has argued for the presence of a pagan cult—tolerated
by the Pharisees—in Jerusalem itself. This now should be noted in connection with
footnote 6 on p. viii above. Add to the same footnote 6 p. viii E. J. Bickerman, *From Ezra
to the last of the Maccabees*, 1962; M. Hengel, *Judentum und Hellenismus*, 1969. To footnote 1
p. xiii add: Compare J. A. Fitzmyer, *Pauline Theology*, 1967, p. 51.

PREFACE

As is indicated by its sub-title, the present work aims at presenting neither a complete examination of the relations of Paul to Rabbinic Judaism, nor an exhaustive account of Pauline theology: and, in particular, it does not deal with a subject, which will probably be of increasing importance and was recently exhaustively treated by Bonsirven,[1] namely, Paul's varying methods of dealing with the Old Testament—a subject which would demand the discipline of a lifetime. The work is rather an attempt to set certain pivotal aspects of Paul's life and thought against the background of the contemporary Rabbinic Judaism, so as to reveal how, despite his Apostleship to the Gentiles, he remained, as far as was possible, a Hebrew of the Hebrews, and baptized his Rabbinic heritage into Christ. The studies are governed by the desire to do justice to Paul as a Pharisee who had become a Christian; and concentrated as they are on different elements in his life and thought, they are nevertheless linked together, and it is hoped that they may not be without some value as a contribution to the deeper understanding of Pauline Christianity as a whole.

I have now to record my debt to those who have made this work possible. It is a pleasure to acknowledge what I owe to Dr J. S. Whale, now Headmaster of Mill Hill School, and formerly President of Cheshunt College, Cambridge. It was he who first encouraged me to labour in this field, and throughout the years his enthusiastic interest never flagged. To him and to the Governors of Cheshunt College, Cambridge, who made a generous grant towards this work, I am deeply grateful, and to the Rev. E. C. Blackman, M.A., Tutor at Cheshunt College, for much encouragement.

To two scholars in particular I owe more than can adequately be expressed. The supervisors of my research were Professor C. H. Dodd and Dr David Daube, Fellow of Gonville and Caius College and member of the Faculties of Divinity and Law, Cambridge. Both read my work in MS. and gave unstintingly of their time and learning in suggestions and criticisms. To sit at their feet was in itself an education, and their guidance has been invaluable. My debt to them will be apparent at every stage in the following pages, and my gratitude remains.

What I owe to the works of other scholars I have sought, albeit inadequately, to acknowledge in the footnotes. I have leaned most

[1] See J. Bonsirven, *Exégèse Rabbinique et Exégèse Paulinienne*. Paris, 1939. Unfortunately, I was unable to make use of this book.

heavily upon the monumental work of (Strack-)Billerbeck, but I have
verified all the references in the original sources. The translations of
different Rabbinic passages are culled from Dr Danby, from the
Soncino translation of the *Babylonian Talmud* and of *Midrash Rabbah*,
from the *Rabbinic Anthology* of Montefiore and Loewe, from Cohen's
Everyman's Talmud, from the *J.E.*, from the works of Büchler and
Marmorstein, from Lauterbach's edition of the *Mekilta*, and from Friedlander's edition of the *Pirḳê de Rabbi Eliezer*: the context usually indicates
the source of the translation. In most of the passages in Appendix C
I have used my own translations which aim at a 'literal' rendering rather
than elegance. I was greatly helped in the checking of Rabbinic references
by the Rev. J. Israelstam, B.A., of Bradford, a contributor to the Soncino
translation of the *Babylonian Talmud* and of the *Midrash Rabbah*, who
also made numerous useful suggestions.

I have been helped at various points by the following: Dr J. W.
Parkes, my former neighbour, who generously placed his books at my
disposal and gave me much stimulus; Professors S. A. Cook, H. H.
Rowley and T.W. Manson, Dr R. Newton Flew, and Miss Olive Wyon,
who kindly allowed me to consult them. The Rev. C. Whitworth,
M.A., B.D., and Miss Dorothy Gill helped with the indices as also did
my wife. To the printers of the University Press I am grateful for
the unfailing and humbling accuracy of their work, and to the
editorial staff at S.P.C.K. House for their courtesy.

Finally, I must refer to my parents; to my mother, the memory of
whose life of self-giving has been a constant source of strength, and
to my father, my first teacher in theology, who taught me in word
and deed to revere the Apostle Paul before I could begin to understand
him: few can have loved Paul more than he.

The blemishes in the following pages are mine, but I send the work
forth with the earnest desire that it should above all help to lead toward
a deeper understanding of Judaism among Christians, and of Pauline
Christianity among Jews.

W. D. DAVIES

3 February 1947
Bradford

PREFACE TO THE SECOND EDITION

THE appearance of a second edition of my work enables me to thank the many reviewers and readers who gave it such a generous reception. It has not been possible to introduce any significant changes in the text, but some notes are added on pp. 352–66.

Debate in the field covered by the volume still centres chiefly around methodology in the use of Rabbinic sources for the illumination of the Apostle, as of the New Testament generally; see, e.g., J. Jeremïas, *Nuntius*, Uppsala, Vol. i, No. i, 1949. In this connection a distinction should be made, especially in such traditional sources as the Rabbinic, between those concepts which are peripheral or again peculiar to certain individual teachers, and those which have been well defined in Judaism both before, during, and after our period. It is largely with these latter concepts that this volume has to deal and it is seldom that it has drawn upon any that cannot be traced to an early date. In addition we have further to notice that Professor W. F. Albright has stated recently that the discovery of the *D.S.S.* necessitates the re-writing of all works dealing with the background of the New Testament (see *The American Scholar*, Winter, 1952–3, p. 85), and his statement should serve the important purpose of compelling students of the New Testament to reckon very seriously with the *D.S.S.* A brief note on their bearing upon Pauline studies appears on p. 352, but this subject can only be touched upon in such a note and demands a special study. On the whole, however, as far as the present work is concerned, the *D.S.S.*, where they are directly relevant, have not introduced a revolution so much as confirmation of positions already suggested or maintained.

W. D. DAVIES

1 March 1953
Duke University
Durham, U.S.A.

PREFACE TO THE FOURTH EDITION

MANY developments in Pauline studies have taken place since 1948 when this volume first appeared. Some of these have been indicated in previous impressions in 1955, 1962, 1967, 1971, and 1979.[1] Here we merely indicate others. The interaction of all the explosive (not too strong an adjective!) developments indicated below in footnote 2— in the field of Apocrypha and Pseudepigrapha, Qumran writings, Rabbinic and Gnostic documents and in the data provided by innumerable disciplines now drawn upon for Biblical interpretation—has placed the study of Paul and Judaism in a far wider and more intricately complex context.[2] This complexity is compelling us to give up

[1] See pp. vii–xv; 146, n. 1; 342–52; 363–78.

[2] The New Testament sources have not ceased to be re-assessed. Dominant tendencies, if not unanimity, have emerged. As for Ephesians, many regard its authenticity as an open question, and others still defend its secondary authenticity, that is, its origin among Pauline circles reflecting the Apostle's mind. But its use for the interpretation of Paul has been questioned more and more, possibly by the majority of scholars. The authenticity of Colossians, either in its entirety or in parts, has also very often been rejected, but not as unequivocally as that of Ephesians. So, too, although its most recent commentators point to its increasing acceptance, the question of the authorship of 2 Thessalonians remains open. Certainly, however, we are now less confident in going outside the Epistles generally accepted as genuine. The caution thus generated is to be welcomed if not always succumbed to. The historical value of Acts, long under a cloud, is now in some quarters being more sympathetically reconsidered and urged, but the primacy of the Epistles cannot but remain unchallenged. (See M. Hengel, *Acts and the History of Earliest Christianity*, trans. J. Bowden; London, 1979; Philadelphia, 1980.)

Other Christian sources long neglected have recently been coming increasingly into their own. We note particularly the use being made of the Pseudo-Clementine documents. (See H. D. Betz, *Galatians*, Philadelphia, 1979.) This is very salutary. We made tentative use of them in this work (see p. 51) in connection with Adamic speculation. It is now clear that they have to be much more exploited than has been customary for illumination on the question of the Law and the relationship among Paul and the other apostles and Jews. Their late compilation—and their difficulty have too long been allowed to hide their relevance, particularly that of those sections which can almost certainly be traced back to the late first century.

To our great enrichment, archaeological work has uncovered two new literatures that impinge on Pauline as on other New Testament studies. Texts from the sectarians gathered at Qumran and its environs (see J. A. Fitzmyer, *The Dead Sea Scrolls: Major Publications and Tools for Study*, Missoula, 1977) and from Nag Hammadi (see now *The Nag Hammadi Library*, ed. J. M. Robinson, New York, 1977; D. Scholar, *Nag Hammadi Bibliography*, Leiden, 1971), though in the latter case more indirectly perhaps, have opened up new possibilities for the understanding of the world of Paul. These are being intensively examined and are constantly shedding new, if not revolu-

the customary simplicities and dichotomies of Pauline studies, at least
in their cruder forms. Were we to offer one phrase to characterize

tionary, light on the Apostle himself—by way both of contrast and of comparison.

There are, in addition, three developments of significance which have burgeoned
during the last three decades. Two are strictly literary and textual; the third is more the
outcome of the general academic history of our time. As for the strictly literary and
textual developments, it is to be emphasized that two previously known, generally
(though in the case of the first to be mentioned not exclusively) non-Christian sources
have attracted increasingly scholarly attention. First, documents constituting what used
to be called "The Inter-Testamental Literature"—the Apocrypha and Pseudepigrapha
—have been and are being studied in new dimensions of depth and breadth. Texts
already known are being re-edited and interpreted, as are others, previously unknown or
little known and certainly unexamined. The results of such work cannot be predicted,
and uncritical exaggeration is all too easy, but at the very least they are certain to deepen
very considerably our understanding of the Judaism that Paul knew. See J. H. Charles-
worth, *The Pseudepigrapha in Modern Research*, Missoula, 1976.

And, secondly, simultaneously (and, although doubtless mutually stimulating,
largely independently) there has been going on what some consider a revolution in the
approach to early Rabbinic sources which have been used for the illumination of Paul.
When this volume was being written in the forties, although there did exist critical
editions of isolated texts, especially in Germany, and to a lesser extent in the United
Kingdom, the textual and historical-critical study of Rabbinic sources was still comparatively little developed. Since that time, there have been major developments.
Critical editions of Rabbinic texts are in process (many have already been published).
The nature of the Rabbinic traditions has been more and more assessed and methods of
form and redaction criticism consciously applied to them in a more deliberate way than
previously. It is probably no exaggeration to claim that under Louis Finkelstein, Saul
Lieberman, Jacob Neusner and others in this country especially, the sources of Rabbinic
Judaism are now being exposed to critical scholarship with an intensity without precedent. Meanwhile, more customary critical methods have also been followed in Israel in
the wealth of the works of scholars such as Ch. Albeck, J. N. Epstein, D. Flusser, S. Safrai,
and E. E. Urbach, along with the more recent methods of form criticism and redaction
criticism which they have often employed less systematically without using such terms
for them. See the various studies by Jacob Neusner and two volumes by G. Stemberger,
who edited Herman L. Strack, *Einleitung in Talmud und Midrasch* (6th ed.), Munich,
1976, and published *Das klassische Judentum: Kultur und Geschichte der rabbinischen
Zeit*, Munich, 1979.

And, finally, during the period referred to, especially in this country but also in the
United Kingdom, departments of religion officially unattached to the Christian
churches have been organized. These often branch out beyond the confines of the
disciplines traditionally concentrated on in the older, more church-related divinity
schools and seminaries, with very tangible effects. These departments have brought
secular disciplines—classical, literary, historical, sociological, psychological, and phe-
nomenological—to bear more directly and deliberately upon the study of religion,
including the theme of this volume. This is to be welcomed wholeheartedly. The results
cannot but be stimulating, corrective, and enriching. At the same time they are likely
sometimes to occasion a healthy, if bewildering, confusion and a creative, if chaotic,
complexity out of which in time new insights will emerge. Any isolation of Biblical and
related literary studies is no longer possible.

the present situation, it would be "the eclipse of dichotomies." An eclipse may be temporary, and doubtless the dichotomies we shall question will return. But if they do, they will be described with a more refined scholarly sensitivity than in the past.

I.

On pp. vii–xv we dealt with the now long familiar discussions of the sharp dichotomy between Judaism and Hellenism, taking the geographic form of contrasting Palestinian and Diaspora Judaism. Evidence since those pages were re-published in 1971 has increased almost endlessly to confirm that to make such a sharp distinction was too simplistic: it was to ignore the unmistakable interpenetration of the two cultures both outside and inside Palestine. In an examination of the Pirqe Aboth we supplied evidence in addition to what we gave on pp. vii–xii and 1–16 and elsewhere for that interpenetration.[3] And now we need refer only to the overwhelmingly magisterial work of Martin Hengel.[4] The thesis of chapter 1 of this work can now be regarded as established. To speak simply in terms of Jewish and Hellenistic elements in Paul without qualification has become anachronistic. Certain factors which have become even clearer since we wrote before, however, are noteworthy. The evidence of the Xenon papyri[5] and of the Daliyeh papyri,[6] dating from the third and fourth centuries B.C.E. respectively, indicates that the Hellenization of Palestine was proceeding strongly before Alexander the Great. The presence of Hellenistic literary influences on Paul has become increasingly clear in his epistolary usages, as in the structuring of the Epistles, and in his use of Hellenistic rhetorical forms and phrases.[7] Whether the claims put forward for the significance of these strictly literary influences for the

[3] "Reflexions on Tradition: The Aboth Revisited", *Christian History and Interpretation: Studies Presented to John Knox,* Cambridge, 1967, pp. 127–60.

[4] *Judentum und Hellenismus: Studien zu ihrer Begegnung unter besonderer Berücksichtigung Palästinas bis zur Mitte des 2 Jhrs. v. Chr.,* Tübingen, 1973; E.T., *Judaism and Hellenism*; London, 1974; Philadelphia, 1974.

[5] See *Corpus Papyrorum Judaicorum*, vol. 1, ed. V. A. Tcherikover, Alexander Fuks, Cambridge, Mass., 1957.

[6] See F. M. Cross, Jr., "Papyri of the Fourth Century B.C. from Dâliyeh", in *New Directions in Biblical Archaeology,* ed. D. N. Freedman and J. C. Greenfield, New York, 1971, pp. 45–69.

[7] See H. D. Betz, *Galatians,* op. cit.; Wilhelm Wuellner, "Greek Rhetoric and Pauline Argumentation", *Early Christian Literature and the Classical Intellectual Tradition: in Honorem Robert M. Grant,* ed. W. R. Schoedel and R. L. Wilken, Théologie Historique, Paris, 1979, pp. 177–88; and "Paul's Rhetoric of Argumentation in Romans", *Catholic Biblical Quarterly* (1976), vol. XXXVIII, no. 3, pp. 330–51.

interpretation of the Apostle are always convincing does not here concern us. They have at least recalled us forcibly again to the effect of Hellenism upon him. Pharisees could be deeply influenced by Hellenistic literary usages.[8] We now know also that the Septuagint was being used in Palestine *by persons who knew Hebrew* as early as the second century B.C.E.[9] That a first-century Pharisee such as Paul should use the Septuagint should occasion no surprise and need not, even must not, of itself be taken to suggest that he did not know Hebrew.

Connected with the use of the Septuagint is the question of the canon. It was not too long ago suggested that there was an Alexandrian canon of Scripture different from that of Palestine. This was a most serious claim. It implied not only that there were authoritative documents used as Scripture by the Diaspora which significantly differed from those thus used in Palestine, but that Jews in Alexandria could and did claim an independent authority commensurate with that of the authorities in Palestine to fix such canonical Scriptures. If this were the case, the gulf between Palestinian and Hellenistic Judaism would have been religiously deep. For reasons we cannot supply here, the existence of a separate Alexandrian canon is almost certainly to be rejected. The care taken by the translators of the Septuagint to be faithful to the Hebrew text and to provide an equivalent for the Hebrew Torah in a Greek form supports this view, and there are textual and historical considerations that serve to explain the differences between the so-called Alexandrian canon and the Palestinian.[10]

The force of one other fact has become more appreciated. In the past, it had always been conceded that the ubiquitous and interconnected synagogues supplied a degree of unity to Judaism everywhere. But there was also at certain places a unity provided by the erection of temples which seem to have been recognized by the Palestinian authorities (despite the insistence of the tradition on the central place that the Temple in Jerusalem always enjoyed and that there alone was there valid sacrifice). The existence of such temples[11] and their relation

[8] See especially D. Daube, *Hebrew Union College Annual*, vol. XXII, pp. 239ff., and further p. 354 (note on p. 16) below.

[9] Fragments of Eupolemos, a Palestinian who used the LXX in the middle of the second century B.C.E., reveal that he was familiar with the Hebrew Bible.

[10] See A. C. Sandburg, Jr., *The Old Testament of the Early Church*, Cambridge, 1964; M. E. Stone, *Scriptures, Sects and Visions*, Philadelphia, 1980, pp. 95–97.

[11] At Arad near Beersheba in the sixth century B.C.E.; at Elephantine in Upper Egypt in the fifth century B.C.E.; at Araq-el-Emir in Transjordan and at Leontopolis, near Alexandria, in the second century B.C.E., and probably (see Josephus, *Antiquities*) at Sardis in Asia Minor in the first century B.C.E.

to the Jerusalem Temple again tends to blur the distinction between life in and outside Palestine.

The evidence for almost all these temples comes from archaeological data. We cannot be certain of the artistic forms employed on them. But the kind of ambiguity which we encounter in the presence of such temples outside Palestine in contradistinction to the insistence on the sole legitimacy of the Temple at Jerusalem emerges in the history of Jewish art in our period. The question of the influence of Hellenistic art on Judaism in the first century is extremely complex. The Second Commandment forbidding sculptured images and likenesses (Exod. 20. 4f.) was variously interpreted at different times and not always taken literally. Exod. 35. 31–35 elevates the artist. Solomon's Temple reflected ancient Near Eastern art, and later the art of the synagogue at Dura Europas was in the Greco-Roman tradition. One of the greater services of E. R. Goodenough was to make it reasonably clear that there was a visual dimension to Judaism.[12] The thesis of the first chapter of this volume that no rigid distinction is to be drawn between Palestinian and Diaspora Judaism seems to have architectural support also.

Yet there is still one point of debate. Granted the interpenetration of Hellenism and Judaism in Palestine, at what level was it? Certainly in varying degrees it did exist on the commercial, military, architectural, literary, artistic levels. But was it on the intellectual or conceptual level? There were always elements in Jewry resistant to Hellenism, and the undeniable difference between a Philo and a Hillel or an Akiba cannot be overlooked. As we have noted elsewhere, they cannot without qualification be classified in the same category of Judaism. But apart from evidence even in Philo, the difficulty of separating Palestinian from non-Palestinian documents in the Apocrypha and Pseudepigrapha suggests real conceptual fusion in certain circles at least. The intermingling of architects and builders shaped by Hellenistic tradition and working in Jerusalem in the construction of the Temple and of the men of letters and of philosophers in the courts of Herod, who cannot have been totally isolated however much Herod desired this, cannot have been without effect. And, again, sages of Judaism who traveled through the Greco-Roman world would have been in contact with intellectual currents of that world. Certainly we can claim this in the case of a Paul who moved between Jerusalem and the Greco-Roman world so freely and so perceptively. Pharisee as he was, he could also be Greek to the Greeks.

---

[12] *Jewish Symbols in the Greco-Roman Period* (13 vols.), New York, 1953–1968.

II.

Next, the dichotomy traditionally made between Pharisaism and Apocalyptic, recently re-emphasized by Rössler, must now be laid to rest,[13] especially in the period before 70 C.E. What made such a dichotomy possible was both a failure to recognize the loyalty of the Apocalyptists to the Law[14] and the retrojection of later negative Rabbinic attitudes toward Apocalyptic speculation, as they were generally understood, to that period.[15] That Paul was a Pharisee did not exclude him from an extraordinarily rich apocalyptic tradition. In recent work on the Apocrypha and Pseudepigrapha, parts of Enoch are dated to the late third and early second centuries B.C.E. This means that there was a pre-Maccabean speculative and pseudo-scientific interest which is not reflected in the Bible but which was widespread in the last two centuries B.C.E. The literature in which this appears (the ultimate origins of which we need not deal with here) was spurred into intense life by the conflict against Antiochus Ephiphanes and the Maccabean revolt and is unlikely, on those grounds alone, to have been anti-Pharisaic or to exhibit opposition to the Law: Apocalyptists no less than the sectarians at Qumran could combine fervent devotion to the Law with speculation about the End. To understand Paul's relation to Pharisaism is not to exclude him from a context of Apocalyptic. One of the pitfalls to be avoided in the interpretation of the Apostle is the neglect of the wholly eschatological, messianic situation in which he stood, neglecting both his participation in such a situation and his recoil from certain of its uncontrolled revolutionary aspects and excesses. The treatment of Paul as an apostle of freedom is both accurate and potentially misleading. He opposed both those who overemphasized the Law and those who would do without it. From the point of view of the former he was a libertarian and from that of the latter, a disciplinarian. The contradiction of attitudes which his epistles reveal is rooted in both his Apocalyptic and Pharisaic background which are inseparable.[16]

---

13 See Dietrich Rössler, *Gesetz und Geschichte: Untersuchungen zur Theologie der jüdischen Apokalyptik und der pharisäischen Orthodoxie*, WMANT 3, Neukirchen, 1960 (1st Ed.), 1962 (2nd Ed.).

14 This was long ago fully recognized by R. H. Charles. See his introduction to *The Apocrypha and Pseudepigrapha of the Old Testament*, Oxford, 1913, p. vii in the volume on the Pseudepigrapha.

15 That Apocalyptic did not "disappear" in Judaism after 70 C.E. is now clear.

16 We see no reason to retract the position we embraced in *The Expository Times* (1947–48), vol. LIX, pp. 233–37, on "Apocalyptic and Pharisaism." Recent studies by

III.

This leads to the chief dichotomy which recent scholarship has re-opened and even questioned: that between Gospel and Law. In this volume and elsewhere we have urged that, despite his polemic, to understand Paul as a figure primarily standing in opposition to the Law is questionable. The centre of his theology lay not in justification by faith as opposed to works, important as that was, but in participation in the life, death, and resurrection of Jesus the Christ. Christ crucified (*Christos estaurômenos:* both terms to be given their full paradoxical or contradictory weight) was his point of departure. Engagement with this question has been intense ever since. Criticism against the formulation given in this work has concentrated on several points. In view of the strong tradition in Protestant scholarship espe-cially, there was an understandable insistence that the question of justification by faith apart from the Law was the central clue to Paul's understanding of the Gospel and a suspicion and rejection of any attempt to find the notion of Christ as a New Law in the epistles. Nor has the insistence referred to diminished. We shall return below to these criticisms. Here we merely note that it is this dichotomy between Law and Gospel that seems most difficult to abandon. The ingrained Christian antipathy to the very word "Law" persists, despite the increasing number of Old Testament studies that have changed the understanding of the role and nature of Law in Judaism.[17] It is still ex-tremely difficult in Protestant exegesis to give full weight, for example,

Professor Mary Boyce on Zoroastrianism should, indeed, lead us even to expect affinities between Pharisaism and Apocalyptic. (See, for example, *Zoroastrians: Their Religious Beliefs and Practices*, London, 1979.) Prof. Boyce's work reveals how both the laws of purity, which came to mark Pharisaism, in Judaism and its apocalyptic schematizations may have, in part at least, a common origin in the same faith, Zoroastrianism, when it inevitably influenced Jews in the post-exilic period.

[17] See, for example, F. Leenhardt, *Two Biblical Faiths: Protestant and Catholic* (E.T. by Harold Knight, Philadelphia, 1964). One of the most illuminating developments in Old Testament studies has been the rehabilitation of the Law. Through the work of Alt, Von Rad, Martin Noth, Buber, Zimmerli, Clements, and others, the influence of the covenant tradition, with its Law, on the prophets has become clear. And just as the prophets have been connected with the Law that preceded them, so Finkelstein in a brilliant study has connected them with the Law that followed them in Judaism. The old antithesis of Law and Prophet has been challenged. The prophets are emerging as "teachers." On the above, see Albrecht Alt, *Die Ursprünge des Israelitischen Rechts* (Leipzig, 1934); Gerhard Von Rad, *Das Formgeschichtliche Problem des Hexateuch* (Stuttgart, 1938); reprinted in *Gesammelte Studien zum A.T.* (Munich, 1958), pp. 9–86; and his *Old Testament Theology* (2 vols.): Martin Noth, *Die Gesetze im*

to Paul's use of the phrase "the Law of Christ," a technical phrase in Jewish eschatology.

In very different ways two comparatively recent developments have dealt with this dichotomy. Prof. J. A. Sanders in a series of penetrating articles has taken up the notion of Christ as Torah.[18] Carrying further his understanding of the Old Testament as expressed in his *Torah and Canon* (Philadelphia, 1972), Sanders applies to the New Testament the distinction he makes between the two elements which he distinguishes within Torah: *mythos* (gospel-story-identity-*haggadah*) and *ethos* (law-ethic-life-style-*halakah*). For Sanders also, as for us, the early Church up to 70 C.E. was a daughter of Judaism: only after that date did it leave its nest. After 70 C.E., "Rabbinic Judaism, following the emphasis of Pharisaism, stressed the *ethos* or *halachah* aspect of Torah, while Christianity emphasized the *mythos* or *haggadah* aspect."[19] Sanders writes, "Paul's conversion may be seen . . . as a move on his part from emphasis on the *ethos* aspect of Torah to the *mythos* aspect," and again, "It was Paul's conviction that if one read the Torah story, emphasizing it as a story of *God's* works of salvation and righteousness for ancient Israel, one could not escape seeing that God had wrought another salvation and committed another righteousness, in Christ, just like the ones of old but an even greater one!"[20] For Paul the Torah remains authoritative and canonical, but the interpretation of it differs in Pharisaism and in Paul because the latter has elevated the "story" of Jesus to the norm of understanding it. With justice, Sanders notes this position as similar to that proposed here (see pp. 147–76, where we have urged that Christ became Torah for Paul),

---

Pentateuch (Munich, 1958), pp. 9–141. Walther Zimmerli in a series of lectures, *The Law and the Prophets: A Study of the Meaning of the Old Testament* (New York, 1965), gives a fascinating account of the theme in scholarship; see also R. E. Clements, *Prophecy and Covenant* (London, 1965). On the prophets in Judaism, see my article "Reflexions on Tradition: The Aboth Revisited" in *Christian History and Interpretation: Studies presented to John Knox* (Cambridge, 1967), pp. 127ff. Martin Buber in his work *The Prophetic Faith* (New York, 1960), pp. 24ff., puts great emphasis on the influence of the Sinai tradition on the prophets.

[18] "Torah and Christ", *Interpretation* (1975), vol. XXIX, no. 4, pp. 372–90; "Torah and Paul", in the Festschrift for Nils A. Dahl, *God's Christ and His People*, ed. W. A. Meeks and J. Jervell, Oslo, 1977, pp. 132–40. Compare our work in *H.T.R.* (1968), vol. LXI, pp. 87–105, "Torah and Dogma: A Comment", reprinted in *Papers from the Colloquium on Judaism and Christianity*, Harvard Divinity School, Oct. 17–20, 1963, Harvard University Press, 1964. See also *New Testament Studies*, vol. XXIV, 1977, p. 38, n. 1.

[19] *Interpretation*, op. cit., pp. 373, 375.

[20] Ibid., p. 380.

but he has modified, refined, and enriched that claim by placing it firmly and directly in the interpretative activity of first-century Judaism. He rightly urges that "Paul . . . was no more anti-Semitic than Amos, Micah, Hosea . . . had been."[21]

Simultaneously with the studies of J. A. Sanders, who found, as we do, continuity between Paul and Judaism, there appeared a work of immense learning and penetration, a major milestone in Pauline scholarship, Professor E. P. Sanders' *Paul and Palestinian Judaism* (London, 1977; Philadelphia, 1977). In the very brief space available we hesitate to discuss this work not only for fear of certain distortion but also because of our relationship to its author: *koina ta philôn*. As far as we know, *Paul and Palestinian Judaism* is the most thorough-going and direct challenge to the dominant and, it must be admitted, generally pejorative understanding of Judaism, certainly among most Protestants and probably among most Christians and through them Gentiles, ever to have been written. Jewish and Christian scholars qualified to judge—and there are very few such to match his learning and dedication—have accepted Sanders' assessment of first-century Judaism.[22] Jacob Neusner offered very forceful criticism which, finally, amounts to a radical questioning of the methodology of Sanders as reflecting Christian theological concerns rather than those native and central to Judaism itself.[23] Neusner urges a more stringent methodology concentrating on the expression of Judaism in the *halakah*. This is not surprising; it is in line with the engrained, traditional *halakic* approach of Rabbinic scholarship to the sources. (Professor Lieberman made the same criticism of our own monograph on *Torah in the Messianic Age*.) The force of this kind of criticism must be fully recognized. But whether the strictly *halakic* is the only possible approach may be questioned. In any case, despite his criticism, Neusner accepts Sanders' understanding of Judaism as "a covenanted nomism" as valid. It may be well first to quote Sanders' description of the common pattern of "covenantal nomism." It reads:

The "pattern" or "structure" of covenantal nomism is this: (1) God has chosen Israel and (2) given the law. The law implies both (3) God's promise to maintain the election

[21] In a letter dated April 1, 1977.
[22] See especially N. A. Dahl and S. Sandmel in *Religious Studies Review*, published by the Council on the Study of Religion (1978), vol. IV, no. 3, pp. 153-60. With Professor Dahl's judicious and extremely careful and positive review, I only differ in that I am unconvinced that Sanders has adequately faced the role of Apocalyptic in Paul (contrast Dahl, p. 155, line 12). G. B. Caird's forthcoming review in *J.T.S.* deserves pondering.
[23] "Comparing Religions" in *History of Religions*, vol. XVIII, pp. 177-91.

and (4) the requirement to obey. (5) God rewards obedience and punishes transgression. (6) The law provides for means of atonement, and atonement results in (7) maintenance or re-establishment of the covenantal relationship. (8) All those who are maintained in the covenant by obedience, atonement, and God's mercy belong to the group which will be saved. An important interpretation of the first and last points is that election and ultimately salvation are considered to be by God's mercy rather than human achievement.[24]

On this Neusner writes: "Anyone familiar with Jewish liturgy will be at home in that statement."[25] He finds Sanders' claim that "The covenant was presupposed, and the Rabbinic discussions were largely directed toward the question of how to fulfill the covenantal obligations" a "wholly sound and to me self-evident proposition."[26]

Of the importance of Sanders' work in the re-assessment of first-century Judaism—particularly the so-called doctrine of salvation by works, its function and relative importance in the total pattern (to use Sanders' preferred term)—there can be no question. In consequence, *Paul and Palestinian Judaism* is of potentially immense significance for the interpretation of Paul and of the relationship between the early Christian communities and Judaism. How does he deal with our own present volume?

Sanders admits that we are justified in refusing to regard the doctrine of justification by faith as the center of Paulinism and, *ipso facto* (especially within the context of most previous traditional Christian interpretation), in approaching Judaism not over against Judaism but within it. He endorses this volume fully and magnanimously in the framework of an outspoken attack on the customary Protestant, particularly Lutheran, approach to Judaism, in which Christian salvation in Paul is primarily understood as the antithesis to salvation by works in Judaism. But when he goes on to examine our book in detail, although at numerous points he finds it, with qualifications, acceptable and positive, he rejects our dominant approach to Paul which he rightly designates as covenantal nomism in Christ. We understand the Apostle as a Pharisee who accepted Jesus of Nazareth, crucified and raised from the dead, as the Messiah (not to the exclusion of other titles). In Paul's response to Christ, the Messiah, he came to understand the Christian life as patterned after that of Judaism: it was for him not the antithesis but the full flowering of that Faith, having its own Exodus, Torah, and community, the Israel of God, the Church.

[24] *Paul and Palestinian Judaism*, p. 422.
[25] Op. cit., p. 178.
[26] Op. cit., p. 177.

Sanders criticizes us especially on two fundamental points: (1) our emphasis on the Christian dispensation as an Exodus in Paul; and (2) above all, our concentration on the Messiahship of Jesus, our insistence that Jesus was more "Messiah" than "Lord" for Paul (though we never so explicitly express the matter).[27] With this second criticism there goes the rejection of the apocalyptic, or better, eschatological tradition of Judaism. For Sanders the category of the Lordship of Christ in Paul supercedes that of Messiahship and thus makes Apocalyptic less significant for the Apostle. Sanders accepts our criticism of Schweitzer as having placed Paul too much in an eschatological-dogmatic "straight-jacket," so that Schweitzer makes the eschatological scheme of Judaism, as he understood it, determinative of Paul's theology. But Sanders goes further than we do. He refuses to consider the possibility that apocalyptic speculation has influenced Paul to any considerable degree in his interpretation of Jesus. For example, our effort to apply contemporary first-century expectations about the role of the Law in the Messianic Age or the Age to Come—for changes in it, for its renovation as a New Torah or even for its abolition—he rejects.[28] Not only do these expectations not illumine Paul: every effort to apply them to him is mistaken. The implication is that it is an error to move from Paul's Jewish milieu to his Christianity, just as it is an error to think that Paul began with the human condition of alienation and then came to the Gospel.[29] Rather the Apostle—and this might seem paradoxical in view of Sanders' endorsement of our emphasis on his relationship to Judaism—by implication stands apart. His Christ, as Lord, is antithetically related to Judaism. We presume that this is how we are to understand such sentences as "This is what Paul finds wrong in Judaism: it is not Christianity."[30] Or again, "Faith . . . represents a more general theological conception than is generally realized: Christianity versus Judaism."[31]

First, as to the figures of the Exodus, the Covenant, the New Torah, which are the pillars of covenantal nomism in Christ: in explaining why the term "covenant" so rarely occurs in the Rabbinic sources, Sanders rightly urges that what is assumed need not be mentioned.[32]

---

[27] *Paul and Palestinian Judaism*, p. 497. See on the Messiahship of Jesus in Paul especially N. A. Dahl, *The Crucified Messiah*, Minneapolis, 1974, pp. 37–47; and also C. E. B. Cranfield, *Romans, I.C.C.*, Part II, Edinburgh, 1980, pp. 836–37.

[28] *Paul and Palestinian Judaism*, pp. 478–490.

[29] See ibid., pp. 474, 479, 484.

[30] Ibid., p. 522.

[31] Ibid., p. 491.

[32] Ibid., pp. 420–21.

Assumptions are usually unexpressed. We suggest that the same applies to the comparative rarity of references to Exodus, Covenant, New Torah (which is wholly absent) in Paul. (Had there been no disorders at Corinth, we should not have had the account of the Eucharist in 1 Cor. 11: but it was, we may be fairly certain, assumed by Paul.) As Sanders rightly insists, the argument from silence, though admittedly precarious, is not always to be rejected. The interpretation of the Christian dispensation as an Exodus is well attested in sources outside Paul and was probably part of the tradition he received from those who were Christians before him.[33] But Sanders tends to isolate Paulinism not only from Judaism but also from the tradition of the Churches, surely a precarious procedure. (It is highly significant that he does not deal with what was for Paul himself extremely important, his persecution of the Church in his pre-"conversion" days; the word "Church" does not occur in his index.) Sanders creates here another untenable dichotomy. The exact role of Moses in Paul *is* difficult to assess. The Apostle downplays the role of Moses, as did Judaism. It is important to note that he compares Moses not so much with Jesus as with Paul himself.[34] But this does not mean that the motif of the Exodus, as a totality, was unimportant for him. Are we to divorce such terms as "redemption," "liberty," "adoption," and even "new creation" from their traditional connection with the Exodus? In any case, Paul's treatment of Moses does reveal him as engaged in precisely the kind of eschatological speculation which Sanders does not consider important for the Apostle.[35] In the messianic climate of early Christianity, the motif of the correspondence between the first redemption and the last was surely operative and for Paul inescapable.

Still more attacked, however, as by so many others, has been the concept of Christ as the New Torah. The term itself does not occur in Paul: the substance of it does, in his understanding of Christ as the Wisdom of God.[36] With the absence of the term, two criticisms have

[33] See, for example, our work *The Setting of the Sermon on the Mount*, Cambridge, 1963, pp. 28–93; and "The Moral Teaching of the Early Church", *The Use of the Old Testament in the New and Other Essays: Studies in Honor of William Franklin Stinespring*, ed. J. M. Efird, Duke University Press, 1972, pp. 310–32, especially p. 312, nn. 6, 7.

[34] See 2 Cor. 3, where Moses is compared not with Jesus but with Paul. The force of the comparison of the Exodus with the Christian dispensation is less easy to assess in this respect in 1 Cor. 10. 1 and following.

[35] See Gal. 3. 16, 19; Rom. 4. 15, 5. 13, 10. 4. See our forthcoming chapter on "Paul from the Jewish Point of View" in *The Cambridge History of Judaism*.

[36] See herein, pp. 146–76. Unfortunately, the emphasis in the title of chapter 7 in "Christ the Wisdom of God" is frequently overlooked and concentration placed

been levied against the concept of this "New Torah." First, the weight of the evidence for it (itself susceptible to a different explanation) is largely derived from Colossians. But leaving aside the question of the authenticity of Colossians, which we regard as *at the least* open, we can claim that there are at least anticipations of the Wisdom Christology in the indisputably genuine Pauline epistles.[37] The second criticism is that the words of Jesus play far less a role in Paul than our notion of his words and person as constituting a New Torah demands. As to the significance of the words of Jesus for Paul, it is to be admitted that we would now more restrainedly express ourselves than we did on pp. 136–46. On p. 136 particularly, we should omit the adjective "primary", which we used of Jesus' words as a source for Paul's teaching. But it is also to be noted that some urge that we have not done sufficient justice to the place of the moral teaching of Jesus in Paul.[38] Be this as it may, it is often overlooked that in speaking of Christ as the New Torah, we emphasized that it was not simply the words of Jesus that constituted this concept but the totality of his life, death, and resurrection, the Living Person, who constituted the New Torah.

But even if the express notion of Christ Himself as constitutive of a New Torah be questioned, what cannot be doubted is that, within the new covenant which Paul understood to have been inaugurated by Christ through His death, the element of demand, expressed sometimes in explicit commandments stemming from Jesus Himself, is present. Paul's use of the phrase "The Law of Christ" even in Galatians is a stumbling block to those who set Paul in total opposition to the Law and even all law.[39] That phrase is probably to be understood within, as well as against, the expectations of Judaism. The "incarnation" of the Law is an idea not unfamiliar to the Judaism of Paul's day: it is explicit in Hellenistic Jewish sources and implied in the Temple Scroll, where the "author" amazingly assumes the right to pronounce Law in the name of God Himself.[40] Sanders in dismissing the importance of the Messiahship of Jesus for Paul does not do justice to the immense ferment in the early Christian messianic communities,

---

on the phrase "The Old and New Torah," Torah being then understood as commandments only.

[37] 1 Cor. 10. 1–4; Rom. 10. 6ff.; 1 Cor. 1. 24, 30.

[38] See a forthcoming paper by Dale Allison on "The Pauline Epistles and the Synoptic Gospels: The Pattern of the Parallels." He supplies bibliographical data on the theme.

[39] H. D. Betz, *Galatians*, pp. 298ff. on Gal. 6. 2 is very instructive and significant at this point.

[40] See Deut. 17. 14–20 as represented in the Temple Scroll, Column 56.

where doubtless some argued for an exodus from the Law, others, in reaction, for a return to the Law, and still others, like Paul himself, for the subordination of the Law to Christ as in Himself a New Torah—new not in the sense that He contravened the old but that He revealed its true character, or put it in a new light—although so to call Christ would have closed the door of his own people to Paul. What is increasingly clear is that first-century Judaism (as indeed Judaism at all times, but especially, as Gershom Scholem has taught, in times of messianic crisis) was inevitably engaged with the question of the Law.[41] Sanders is not wholly wrong in suspecting the *subordination* of Paul to the Jewish messianic ideas that he had inherited in his formulation of his theology. (We agree with Sanders that though not systematic, this was coherent, although it should not be overlooked that Paul could also be "all things to all men," and had the conceptual nimbleness of "a trimmer.")[42] We ourselves have urged that Paul was a marked reductionist in his approach to eschatology.[43] To read Paul after being immersed in apocalyptic documents is to move to a cleaner and leaner world; after the speculative fecundity of those documents even the "tortuous" epistles of Paul present "a blessed simplicity." But to believe that Paul, who was active within what we cannot cease to insist was a messianic movement, was not under the necessity to come to terms with the traditional expectations both among Christians and Jews, and was not influenced by them in his theological formulations, is to consign him to a vacuum. The outcome is to underestimate the messianic dimension of his thinking which was not submerged by Paul's use of the term "Lord" for Christ.

With Sanders' diminution of the significance of the intensely messianic context within which the Apostle laboured and thought, there goes his underestimation of notions of corporate solidarity with the Messiah. In our judgement, despite recent claims that it has been grossly overemphasized,[44] the notion of corporate solidarity should be treated with far greater seriousness than is done by Sanders. Perhaps

41 See especially *Sabbatai Sevi: The Mystical Messiah, 1626-1676*, Princeton, 1973, and our review in *J.B.L.* (1976), vol. XCV, no. 4, pp. 529-58, on "From Schweitzer to Scholem: Reflections on Sabbatai Svi."

42 See especially H. Chadwick, "All things to all men", *New Testament Studies* (1954-55), vol. I, pp. 261ff.

43 In "Paul and Jewish Christianity according to Cardinal Jean Daniélou: A Suggestion", *Judéo-Christianisme: volume offert au Cardinal Jean Daniélou, Recherches de Science Religieuse* (1972), vol. LX, no. 1, pp. 69-79.

44 Contrast C. E. B. Cranfield, *Romans I.C.C.*, vol. 2, p. 837, n. 4. But what are we to do, for example, with 1 Cor. 12. 13, where the word "Christ" can stand for the Church? Is not this a clear case of the notion of "corporate personality"?

this accounts for, or is related to, his failure to deal more thoroughly with the whole Passover motif in Paul which undergirds the position of covenantal nomism which he finds it necessary to reject.

That position, finally, finds support from what we had justifiably but only tacitly assumed when this volume was first written (see p. xvi) but must now in response to Sanders' radical separation of Judaism from Pauline "Christianity" make explicit. That is the simple but fundamental fact that Paul himself understands the Christian dispensation to be "according to the Scriptures" and in this he was not alone in the Early Church.[45] Sanders does deal with Paul's use of Old Testament passages in an instructive way. But he so deals with them as to leave the impression that the Apostle is using the Old Testament for his own ends, as it were, without radical seriousness, if Paul be governed in his treatment of Scripture by the dogmatic stance that salvation is only in Christ.[46] We may be unjust to Sanders at this point, but we have been unable to avoid this impression. However, Paul's appeal to the Old Testament for support seems to make the radical dichotomy between Pauline "Christianity" and "Judaism," in our judgement, untenable. If the Apostle conceived of his Christian faith simply as something that was not "Judaism", and held that what was wrong with the latter was that it was not "Christianity", his intense involvement (it is not merely for illustrative purposes but for the penetration of their meaning) with the Scriptures of his people becomes puzzling. Romans 9–11 in particular becomes a difficulty for this position, because there the history and destiny of the Jewish people, as understood in the Scriptures, is under discussion. Extremes often meet: like Bultmann, Sanders nowhere deals with this section in depth.[47]

To have done so would surely have modified his position. Sanders'

---

[45] The evidence for this need not be repeated. See, for example, Cranfield, op. cit., pp. 862–70.

[46] See E. P. Sanders, op. cit., p. 482. Since the publication of *Paul and Palestinian Judaism*, Sanders has, however, dealt with Rom. 9–11 in *Union Seminary Quarterly Review* (1978), pp. 175–181, in "Paul's Attitude towards the Jewish People."

[47] Extremes also meet in Sanders' suspicion of development in Paul (see pp. 432f., n. 9), which is generally typical of those who find justification by faith the centre of Paul's theology from the beginning. Recent work by R. Jewett, *A Chronology of Paul's Life*, Philadelphia, 1979 (published in London as *Dating Paul's Life*, 1979), and Gerd Lüdemann, *Paulus der Heidenapostel*, vol. I, *Studien zur Chronologie*, Göttingen, 1980, may compel modifications of our understanding of development in Paul. Not unrelated to this is the criticism made by B. R. Gaventa of the methodology of Sanders. In her view that methodology, which searches for a common pattern in all Paul's writings, does not allow each epistle to speak for itself in its own context, and therefore

understanding of the concern of both Jews and Christians as that of
being in and remaining in the community of God we find illuminating and convincing. But these two communities understood as
"Judaism" and "Christianity" respectively, for Paul were not completely distinct. Paul never refers to a New Israel. It is certain that the
community of Israel "after the flesh", not simply the Christian community, was a major concern of the Apostle, although not, as Stendahl
claims,[48] *the* major concern. Sanders' opposition of "Judaism" and
"Christianity" in Paul makes such a concern, which reached agonizing
proportions, inexplicable. We refer to our treatment of "Paul and the
People of Israel" elsewhere.[49] It agrees with all this that it is unlikely
that Paul thinks of what we call "Christianity" as a distinct religion
rather than as a form of his ancestral religion or as a further stage of its
development, however "new." Sanders assumes that Paul thinks of
Christianity as distinct, that is, he uses the verb "to convert" for the
Apostle's transition from Judaism to faith in Christ. But the vocabulary of conversion is absent from the epistles. One cannot resist the
suggestion that—in his minimizing of the Apocalyptic tradition, and
to some extent of the Old Testament, as of real significance for the
understanding of Paul, and in his failure to recognize the Apostle's
struggle over the meaning of "Israel" and the role of the Jewish
people even in the Christian dispensation—Sanders has presented
Paul as a solitary colossus in the Early Church, a colossus whose solitari-
ness the sources do not endorse. Paul was, indeed, a colossus. He was
such, however, not because his theology was totally new, but precisely
because he had integrated and reinterpreted (not ignored) the rich
traditions—Old Testament, Apocalyptic, Pharisaic—of his people in
the light of Christ. We learnt long ago from a Paulinist of the Vic-
torian era, George B. Stevens, that originality does not consist of
thinking new things but of thinking for ourselves. That is precisely
what Paul did "in Christ." Despite his very positive, and amazingly
informative, treatment of Judaism, is Sanders not, very paradoxically
(and despite occasional caveats of his), *mutatis mutandis*, somewhat
reminiscent of Marcion?

And so his work ends by placing this present volume between two
criticisms. One criticism—an old one—is governed by the conviction
that the true centre of Paulinism is justification by faith alone as

makes it difficult for Sanders to recognize changes and developments in the Apostle's
thinking. See her review "Comparing Paul and Judaism: Rethinking our Methods,"
in *Biblical Theology Bulletin* 10 (1980), pp. 37–44.

[48] K. Stendahl, *Paul among Jews and Gentiles*, Philadelphia, 1976.

[49] *New Testament Studies* (1966), vol. XXIV, pp. 4–39.

opposed to works, understood even by Professor Käsemann ultimately (although his understanding of the righteousness of God does open the door, it seems to us, to a reconciliation with those who have emphasized the incorporation in Christ in death and resurrection) in individual terms. According to this criticism—and who can ignore the immense and devoted industry and penetration with which their case is supported[50]—this volume overemphasizes the continuity between Paul and Judaism (a continuity which we would now insist is rooted in the faithfulness of God).[51] For example, Professor Kingsley Barrett with typical restraint wrote that "the discontinuity in Paul's thought is perhaps greater" than we have suggested.[52] On the other side are those like the late Samuel Sandmel[53] and now Professor Sanders (here grouped together) who, for different reasons, insist that this volume underestimates the discontinuity between Paul and Judaism, the former because it does not sufficiently recognize Paul's Hellenism, the latter by implication because we have overemphasized his dependence on Jewish categories. Both the fires of criticism to which we refer burn with great clarity. Herein lies their power but also, we suggest, their weakness. To repeat what we have already written, if anything has become evident in recent studies, it is the impossibility of drawing clear-cut lines in dealing with a first-century figure such as Paul in whom many cultures met. The cross-cultural interpenetration does not permit this. Both those who find the clue in his struggle over justification by faith, and Sanders, who opposes Paul unequivocally to Judaism, or Sandmel, who largely finds the clue in Paul's Hellenistic affinities, intricate and often brilliant as are their presentations, all in the end are in danger of a kind of reductionism. No single theme or motif can do justice to the mystery of Paul. To attempt to find such a key is to fall victim to those dichotomies which recent scholarship is transcending. Between the two faiths of his concern, Sanders is reintroducing a dichotomy (even a chasm) deeper than those other dichotomies of which we have written, at the very time when such dichotomies are suffering an eclipse. In this sense, though certainly not in others,

[50] The recent commentaries on Romans by C. K. Barrett, Matthew Black, F. F. Bruce, C. E. B. Cranfield, E. Käsemann, O. Kuss, and U. Wilckens, not to speak of others on other epistles such as that of H. D. Betz, on *Galatians*, compel unstinted admiration and point to the vitality of the position to which I refer.

[51] "Paul and the People of Israel," op. cit., pp. 14–29. That the climate of Pauline scholarship in its treatment of Judaism is more and more open to change appears in the important and very rich volume by.F. Mussner, *Traktat über die Juden*, Munich, 1979, which unfortunately reached us too late for use here.

[52] *The Epistle to the Romans*, New York, 1957.

[53] See his review referred to in n. 22 above.

despite its immense learning and stimulating challenge, in its interpretation of Paul, Sanders' work is to be questioned. In the last resort,
perhaps we differ in our approach to historical probability. The
Pauline faith was not primarily an antithesis to Judaism. But like great
art and music and literature also in their spheres, it could not be other
than a live interchange of tradition and freedom "in Christ." The very
name "Christ" evokes both continuity and, because Paul links it with
the adjective "crucified," revolution. Paul experienced newness in
continuity: the new creation, like the new moon, is the old creation
in a new light.

In concluding this very brief response to *Paul and Palestinian
Judaism*, be it noted that its concentration (a very reluctant one) on
differences, important as they are (the agreements are assumed), in no
way at all diminishes our deep appreciation and gratitude. Seldom can
a teacher have had such cause for pride in the creative independence
and achievement of one whom he once regarded as his pupil, but who
has long since far transcended any such category.

The space allowed is by now exhausted. Other matters which cry for
attention in various chapters we shall attempt to deal with in what we
hope may be a new, fully revised edition later and in an accompanying
work by Professor Gerd Lüdemann.

It remains to thank Norman Hjelm, the Director of Fortress Press,
for insisting on this preface and his editorial colleague John Hollar for
much help. Those on both sides of the Atlantic from whom I have
continued to learn I cannot enumerate, but I must thank my friends,
Professors David Daube for nourishing my penchant for continuity in
the theme of this work, and C. K. Barrett for refusing to indulge me
in it, and Dr. J. S. Whale for constantly delivering me from the temptation to intellectual complacency. As elsewhere, I have drawn on my
colleagues at Duke University, and especially in this preface on the
learning and sagacity of Professors J. L. Price and F. W. Young, and
on the skills of Mrs. Sarah Freedman. The original dedication remains,
enhanced by further years of common labour.

W. D. D.

3 February 1981
Duke University

PRINCIPAL ABBREVIATIONS

Ap. and Ps.	*The Apocrypha and Pseudepigrapha of the Old Testament,* ed. R. H. Charles.
B.D.B.	*Hebrew and English Lexicon of the Old Testament,* Francis Brown, S. R. Driver, C. A. Briggs.
Beginnings	*The Beginnings of Christianity,* F. J. Foakes Jackson and Kirsopp Lake.
Danby	*The Mishnah,* Herbert Danby.
Eschatology	*A Critical Study of the Doctrine of a future life in Israel, in Judaism and in Christianity,* R. H. Charles.
E.T.	English translation.
H.D.B.	*Dictionary of the Bible,* ed. J. Hastings.
H.Z.N.T.	*Handbuch zum Neuen Testament.*
I.C.C.	*International Critical Commentary.*
J.B.L.	*The Journal of Biblical Literature and Exegesis,* Philadelphia.
J.D.P.B.	*Authorized Daily Prayer Book of the United Hebrew Congregations of the British Empire,* S. Singer, 13th ed., 1925.
J.E.	*The Jewish Encyclopedia.*
J.Q.R.	*Jewish Quarterly Review.*
J.T.S.	*Journal of Theological Studies.*
LXX	*The Septuagint.*
M.N.T.C.	*The Moffatt New Testament Commentary.*
Moore	*Judaism in the First Centuries of the Christian Era,* G. F. Moore.
R.A.	*A Rabbinic Anthology,* selected by C. G. Montefiore and H. Loewe.
Ryl. Bull.	*The Bulletin of the John Rylands Library,* Manchester University Press.
Str.-B.	*Kommentar zum Neuen Testament aus Talmud und Midrasch,* Hermann L. Strack und Paul Billerbeck. München 1928.
Z.A.W.	*Zeitschrift für die alttestamentliche Wissenschaft.*
D.S.S.	*The Dead Sea Scrolls,* ed. by M. Burrows, J. C. Trever, and W. H. Brownlee. (I.e., *The Dead Sea Scrolls of St Mark's Monastery,* I: *The Isaiah Manuscript and the Habakkuk Commentary,* 1950; II, Fasc. 2: *Plates and Transcriptions of the Manual of Discipline,* 1951.)
D.S.H.	*The Dead Sea Habakkuk Commentary.*
D.S.D.	*The Dead Sea Manual of Discipline.*

Most of the Rabbinic abbreviations will be familiar. Certain common conventional spellings have been retained, e.g., *Aboth* (not *'Abot*), Bath Qol, *Derek Eretz Zuta, Akiba,* etc., but transliteration generally follows that of the *R.A.* We need only note that *R.* after *Pesikta* denotes *Pesikta Rabbati; Pesikta* by itself denotes *Pesikta de Rab Kahana; R.* or *Rabba* after *Gen., Exod., Lev., Num., Deut., Eccles., Cant.,* refers to the *Midrash Rabbah. J.* before a tractate denotes the *Jerusalem* or *Palestinian Talmud, b.* the *Babylonian Talmud,* and *Tos.* the *Tosefta.*

1

INTRODUCTION: PALESTINIAN AND DIASPORA JUDAISM

IT has long been a matter of controversy among New Testament scholars how best we should interpret the theology of Paul. On the one hand it has been claimed by scholars such as Holtzmann, Morgan, Bousset and Reitzenstein that he had been very deeply influenced by the syncretistic religious movements of his period, and that he is best understood in the light of his Hellenistic environment. On the other hand Paul has been interpreted by Schweitzer in exclusively Jewish terms.[1] To-day it has become clear, however, that Paul was influenced not only by the religion of his fathers, but also by the religious movements of the Hellenistic world of his day; that both Hellenism and Judaism were his tutors unto Christ. The extent, however, to which he was indebted to the one or to the other will probably always be a matter of conjecture and debate, because in the fusions of the first century we cannot split Hellenistic, Jewish and other factors. In the present work we shall not seek to deny all Hellenistic influence upon him; we shall merely attempt to prove that Paul belonged to the main stream of first-century Judaism, and that elements in his thought, which are often labelled as Hellenistic, might well be derived from Judaism.

That Paul belonged to the main stream of first-century Judaism has been denied by C. G. Montefiore, and for our purpose his work forms a convenient starting-point. In his book, *Judaism and St Paul*, the Apostle is presented to us as a Jew of the Dispersion unacquainted with the best Rabbinic Judaism of Palestine, and familiar only with Diaspora Judaism, "which was colder, less intimate, less happy because it was poorer and more pessimistic",[2] than the former. Many elements in Paul's thought are claimed to be due to religious influences that are not Jewish at all, and which certainly make it impossible to regard him as belonging to the typical Rabbinic Judaism of the first century. They can only be explained on the assumption that Paul knew only the Judaism that had been contaminated by Hellenism in the Dispersion.[3]

---

[1] See for a survey of the literature, A. Schweitzer, *Paul and his Interpreters* (E.T.).
[2] *Judaism and St Paul*, p. 93.
[3] Ibid. p. 93. This position has been further popularized by J. W. Parkes in *Jesus, Paul and the Jews*. In a less pronounced form this is also the thesis of J. Klausner in *From Jesus to Paul* (E.T.), e.g. Klausner writes of Paul: "...in spite of all his zeal and

Let us first examine certain assumptions that Montefiore has to make in order to reach this position. These are three in number. First, he assumed that certain statements in the New Testament cannot be regarded as historical. He writes: "I am...disposed to look with suspicion upon the statement in Acts (22. 3) that Paul was brought up in Jerusalem at the feet of Gamaliel, instructed according to the strict manner of the Law of our fathers." The passage in Philippians 3. 5 ff. he describes as "having no genuine Jewish ring". It is significant that scholars, who have emphasized the Hellenistic aspects of Paul's thought, generally find it necessary to reject much New Testament evidence. Montefiore refers to Loisy's words that "Tout ce que racontent les Actes au sujet de Paul avant sa conversion est grandement suspect".[1] Rawlinson points out that, "in the first edition of *Kyrios Christos*, Bousset was disposed to deny altogether that St Paul had been brought up at the feet of Gamaliel or had persecuted the Christians of Jerusalem, and to suggest that he was already domiciled at Damascus, and began his career as an opponent of Christianity there". In *Jesus der Herr* [2] he retracts these judgements, and in the second edition of *Kyrios Christos* contents himself with remarking that "the relations of the Apostle Paul with Jerusalem were of the scantiest kind" (op. cit. p. 75).[3] In all this one cannot help feeling that the New Testament is being manipulated in the interest of theories. There seems to be no adequate reason for rejecting the evidence of Acts, and of the Epistles, that Paul was trained in Rabbinic Judaism at Jerusalem,[4] and "profited in the Jews' religion above many [his] equals being more exceedingly zealous of the traditions of [his] fathers".[5] Commenting on 2 Corinthians 11. 22 and Philippians 3. 5 f. Rawlinson writes: "St Paul's emphatic claim in Philippians 3. 5 and 2 Corinthians 11. 22, to be a Hebrew suggests that his opponents had attempted to deny his affinities

extremeness he was not completely at home, either in his first religion or in his second, after his conversion. His soul was torn between Palestinian Pharisaism, the teachings of which he learned particularly in Jerusalem...and Jewish Hellenism—and in a certain measure also pagan Hellenism, in the midst of which he was born and educated in his childhood in pagan and half-Hellenistic Tarsus. This twofold state, or rather, this half-and-half condition was the cause of the complete overthrow of historic Judaism brought about by Paul—who was much more denationalized and divided in soul than was Jesus—the latter being a Jew of Palestine only, and hence not affected by foreign and conflicting influences." (Op. cit. p. 312.)

[1] *Judaism and St Paul*, p. 90. A. Loisy, *Revue d'histoire et de littérature religicuses* (1913), vol. IV, p. 490.

[2] *Jesus der Herr*, p. 31.

[3] A. E. J. Rawlinson, *The New Testament Doctrine of the Christ*, p. 93, n. 1.

[4] Acts 22. 3. See W. L. Knox, *Some Hellenistic Elements in Primitive Christianity*, p. 31, n. 2.

[5] Gal. 1. 14.

with Aramaic speaking Judaism and to rank him exclusively as a Hellenist."[1] Many modern scholars would apparently find Paul's opponents very congenial company.

In the second place, Montefiore drew a very pleasing picture, which we shall describe later, of the Palestinian Judaism of the first century. He could do so only on the bold assumption that that Judaism was like that of the fourth century, "that there are no signs of improvement in the teachings of the famous Rabbis of the fourth century over those of the first".[2] It is clear, however, that our sources for Rabbinic Judaism do not warrant such a definite conclusion. Thus the *Mishnah* was not compiled till the end of the second century, and most of the other Rabbinic sources are later than the third century.[3] While it is clear that the Rabbinic sources do preserve traditions of an earlier date than the second century, and that it is legitimate to define the *Mishnah* as a "deposit of four centuries of Jewish religious and cultural activity in Palestine beginning at some uncertain date possibly during the earlier half of the second century B.C. and ending with the close of the second century A.D.",[4] it must never be overlooked that Judaism had made much history in that period. It follows that we cannot, without extreme caution, use the Rabbinic sources as evidence for first-century Judaism.[5] Especially is it important to realize that our Rabbinic sources represent the triumph of the Pharisean party, and moreover of a 'party' within the Pharisean party as it were, that of Johanan ben Zakkai.[6] Pharisean opinions alone are recorded; parties, movements and opinions contrary to these were naturally excluded. Thus, for example, as Danby[7] points out, "in the Mishnah the Sadducees figure only as an insignificant, discredited and heretical sect" although we know that they played a large part both in first-century and earlier Judaism. It is almost certain therefore, and this will appear as our work proceeds, that many aspects of first-century Judaism find no place in our Rabbinic sources, and that

---

[1] *The New Testament Doctrine of the Christ*, p. 85, n. 4. See J. Klausner, *From Jesus to Paul*, p. 309, who cites evidence which, although not conclusive, is strong that Paul was a pupil of Rabban Gamaliel. Klausner, however, is more sceptical of Paul's claim to be a Benjamite because, so he claims, books of genealogy would hardly exist, for an obscure family like Paul's at least, at the end of the period of the Second Temple. (Op. cit. pp. 304f.)

[2] *Judaism and St Paul*, p. 87.

[3] For a discussion on the use of Rabbinic sources, see J. Bonsirven, *Le Judaïsme Palestinien*, vol. I, pp. xiiiff. See also Moore, vol. I, pp. 125ff.; M. J. Lagrange, *Le Judaïsme avant Jésus-Christ*, pp. xvff.

[4] Danby, p. xiii.   [5] Ibid. p. xiv.

[6] See Moore, vol. I, pp. 83ff.; Danby, p. xiii.

[7] P. xv, n. I.

that Judaism was much more variegated than such sources would lead us to expect.[1] Montefiore has himself pointed out that the first century was an age of transition and many cross-currents,[2] and it is hardly credible that the advent of Christianity, and the tragic experiences of the first and second centuries A.D., did not greatly modify and influence Judaism. In any case we cannot accept the convenient identification of first-century Judaism with the normative Judaism of later centuries which Montefiore assumes.[3]

Finally, we have seen that Montefiore draws a very sharp distinction between the Judaism of Palestine and that of the Diaspora; the one is to the other as white is to black. The picture which he draws of Palestinian Rabbinic Judaism is, indeed, attractive. To the typical and even to the average Jew, we are told, God was intensely personal, great and awful, but also merciful and loving;[4] the Torah was "in no wise a burden",[5] but a means "of joy on earth and joy in the life to come",[6] the source of spiritual blessedness and also of intellectual activity and development;[7] "greater than God's anger at failure to fulfil the Law was his compassion";[8] "this world is not bad but good"; "God has given the means of happiness even upon earth and through earthly and material things".[9] Apart from the great and outstanding fault of Rabbinic Judaism, its particularism,[10] we find in the Rabbinic Judaism of the first century in Palestine "... a joyous simple religion yet also an intellectual and rational religion in its own special way, a happy, spiritual and even ardent religion".[11]

Over against this Palestinian Judaism Montefiore sets Diaspora Judaism. To the Hellenistic Jew, so he claims, "God was less intimate, near and affectionate than the God of Rabbinic Judaism: a small contact with philosophy seems to have made God more distant and less approachable";[12]

---

[1] Cf. G. H. C. Macgregor and A. C. Purdy, *Jew and Greek Tutors unto Christ*, pp. 103 ff.

[2] *The Synoptic Gospels*, vol. I, p. ci; A. S. Peake's *Commentary on the Bible*, p. 618.

[3] Referring to the use of Tannaitic material for the early first century, Bonsirven writes: "Il est certain que ces textes, même anonymes, recèlent des materiaux anciens, et on admet communément que les doctrines juives ont peu évolué. Mais justement vers 70 peu avant et après, nous discernons une evolution: avant le grand soulèvement contre l'empire romain, nous constatons chez les Juifs une grande fermentation, qui a certainement provoqué des innovations et modifications dans la discipline et dans les doctrines; d'autre part la réaction contre le christianisme naissant a conduit à supprimer des coutumes, telles la récitation du décalogue, ou à prendre de nouvelles positions doctrinaires; enfin les catastrophes de 70 et de 135 ont provoqué dans le Judaïsme reserrement et unification." (*Le Judaïsme Palestinien*, vol. I, p. xv.)

[4] *Judaism and St Paul*, p. 26.   [5] Ibid. p. 31.   [6] Ibid. p. 28.
[7] Ibid. pp. 46–8.   [8] Ibid. p. 42.   [9] Ibid. p. 43.
[10] Ibid. p. 53.   [11] Ibid. p. 48.   [12] Ibid. p. 95.

the world was evil; pessimism and despair were never very far away;[1]
sin appeared in a more sinister light than it did to the Palestinian Rabbis;[2]
human repentance and divine forgiveness were less prominent; the Law
itself was often a source of doubt—questions about it naturally offered
themselves; it often ceased to be a source of joy.[3] Diaspora Judaism
was altogether colder and more sombre than Palestinian Rabbinic
Judaism. It is from this Hellenistic Judaism that Paul derived what
Montefiore has called his pre-Christian pessimism,[4] his 'mysticism',[5]
and his dualistic conception of the flesh and the spirit.[6] In addition it
is only on the assumption that his pre-Christian religion was of this
inferior Diaspora type that we can understand what Montefiore calls
"his almost complete omission of the twin Rabbinic ideas of Repentance
and Forgiveness",[7] his opposition of faith and works, and his attitude
to the Law.

We have now to examine this distinction drawn by Montefiore between the Judaism of Palestine and that of the Diaspora. Naturally it
is not to be expected that they should not present variations, but there
are certain significant facts which suggest that it is erroneous to over-
emphasize the differences between them as does Montefiore. In the first
place, certain geographical and historical factors are to be noted. Palestine[8] was dominated since 333 B.C. by the Greeks and from 63 B.C. by
the Romans. This domination was not merely political. Under the
Seleucids (198–168 B.C.) Palestine was subjected to a definite propaganda
for its Hellenization, and throughout our period it was open to strong
Hellenizing influences. Thus it came about that, although the common
people spoke Aramaic, Greek was also known at least to the learned,
so that Palestine was bilingual.[9] Greek terms were used to designate
such essentially Jewish institutions as the Sanhedrin, and it has been
claimed that more than 1100 Greek terms are used in the Talmud.[10]
Hellenistic manners, customs and amusements were inevitably assimilated.[11] Secondly, it must not be overlooked that frequent wars had

[1] *Judaism and St Paul*, p. 96.   [2] Ibid. p. 97.   [3] Ibid. p. 98.
[4] Ibid. p. 69.   [5] Ibid. p. 83.   [6] Ibid. p. 79.   [7] Ibid. pp. 75 ff.
[8] See W. O. E. Oesterley, *A History of Israel*, vol. II, pp. 175 ff., 217 ff.; M. J. Lagrange,
Le Judaïsme avant Jésus-Christ, pp. 35–46; J. Bonsirven, *Le Judaïsme Palestinien*, vol. I,
pp. 35 ff.; Schürer, *A History of the Jewish People in the Time of Jesus Christ* (E.T.)
Division II, vol. I, pp. 1 ff.
[9] *Antiquities*, 20, 11 (Whiston's translation, p. 426). See G. Kittel, *Die Probleme des
palästinischen Spätjudenthums und das Urchristentum*, pp. 35 ff.
[10] J. Bonsirven, *Le Judaïsme Palestinien*, vol. I, p. 36. See S. Krauss, *Griechische und
lateinische Lehnwörter im Talmud, Midrasch und Targûm*, Teil I.
[11] E.g. it has been suggested that Hillel's concern for his body is a Greek trait.
Cf. N. Bentwich, *Hellenism*, p. 225.

greatly decreased the numbers of the Jews in Palestine. According to Klausner [1] in the thirty years preceding Herod's capture of Jerusalem in 37 B.C. more than 200,000 Jews were killed. This meant that the Jews were reduced to a tiny political unit about the city of Jerusalem. In the rest of Palestine they were a dispersion surrounded on every side by Hellenistic influences. It is possible that its mountainous isolation preserved Jerusalem itself for some time against the 'contamination' of Hellenism,[2] but in the first century the flood of Hellenism had reached Jerusalem. There were Hellenistic synagogues in Jerusalem itself.[3] Paul, who had been taught by Gamaliel, apparently preferred the LXX[4] to the Hebrew text and it was claimed by the Rabbis that the Torah could only adequately be translated in Greek. It was allowed to recite the Shema in Greek and likewise grace after meals and the Eighteen Benedictions.[5] According to b. Soṭah 49 b R. Simeon b. Gamaliel II had 500 lads learning the wisdom of the Jews in his house and another 500 learning the wisdom of the Greeks.[6] The fact that after A.D. 70 it was necessary to forbid the teaching of Greek to one's son shows that previous to that date this was customary.[7] Even after Judaism had felt compelled to close its ranks against the influences of Hellenism we find that Judah the Prince (died A.D. 219),[8] to whom we owe the compilation of the *Mishnah*, received a Greek education as had his father Simeon b. Gamaliel II and Elisha b. Abuyah.[9]

In addition to the above, Palestinian Judaism had contacts with all parts of the Hellenistic world. The annual half shekel tax which every Jew paid to maintain the Temple cult bound him to Jerusalem wherever he was and pilgrims from the Diaspora visited the city in large numbers annually.[10] Moreover, by the time of the Christian era every large city of the Roman Empire had its synagogue or synagogues,[11] and while it is obvious that the Judaism of the Diaspora was more heavily and directly

---

[1] *Jesus of Nazareth* (E.T.), p. 167; *Beginnings*, vol. I, p. 147.

[2] M. J. Lagrange, *Le Judaïsme avant Jésus-Christ*, p. 50.   [3] Acts 6. 9.

[4] J. Bonsirven, *Le Judaisme Palestinien*, vol. I, p. 37. See A. Edersheim, *The Life and Times of Jesus the Messiah*, vol. I, p. 23 for the popularity of the LXX in Palestine itself.

[5] *J. Megillah* 1. 71 a. The scrolls of the Law could be written in Greek: so too a Bill of Divorce, *M. Megillah* 1. 8. See N. Bentwich, *Hellenism*, p. 252; J. Rabbinowitz, *M. Megillah*, ad loc.

[6] We need not accept the figures, but the fact to which they point is unmistakable. Cf. *Tos. Soṭah* 15. 8, p. 3-2.

[7] *b. Soṭah* 49a. See N. Bentwich, *Hellenism*, pp. 280f.

[8] A. Cohen, *Everyman's Talmud*, p. xxvi.

[9] A. Edersheim, *The Life and Times of Jesus the Messiah*, vol. I, p. 22. For Elisha b. Abuyah, *J.E.* vol. v, p. 138.

[10] *The Wars of the Jews*, 6, 11. 3. *Antiquities*, 14, 7. 2, for Temple Tax.

[11] Cf. E. Bevan, *A New Commentary on Holy Scripture*, Part II, p. 24. See *Antiquities*, 14, 7. 2, where Josephus quotes Strabo.

exposed to Hellenistic pressure than that of Palestine, it is noteworthy that the synagogue both in Palestine and the Diaspora gave to Judaism an unmistakable unity and coherence. "When neither language nor geographical location ensured the solidarity of Judaism the synagogue and devotion to the Law, both written and oral, guaranteed unity."[1] It seems that only in very remote synagogues was there any real syncretism between Judaism and pagan religion.[2] This coherence, which the synagogue and other factors lent to Judaism wherever it appeared, was strengthened by the fact pointed out by Knox.[3] The latter writes: "It was customary to invite visitors to address the synagogues of the Dispersion; it may already have been customary for emissaries to be sent from Palestine to visit those synagogues and to encourage them to persevere in their faith." He goes on: "The prestige of Jerusalem would demand that such emissaries should be able to speak in a style which educated Jews and interested Gentiles would regard as reasonably good, and Jewish interests would demand speakers who could represent them attractively before Gentile magistrates. Jewish preachers would further need a smattering of popular philosophy, particularly of that mixture of Stoicism and Platonism which was peculiarly congenial to Jewish missionary propaganda, and a knowledge of Greek literature so far as it could be derived from popular handbooks; it would seem that Judaism had its own compilations of this type...."[4] This being the case we may

[1] G. H. C. Macgregor and A. C. Purdy, *Jew and Greek Tutors unto Christ*, p. 147. See also *Beginnings*, vol. I, pp. 159ff.

[2] Cf. W. L. Knox, *Judaism and Christianity*, vol. II, pp. 88f. Knox finds syncretism in Phrygia. See W. M. Ramsay, *Cities and Bishoprics of Phrygia*, pp. 670ff. See also for a pagan-Jewish θίασος in Tanais in the second century B.C., C. Roberts, T. C. Skeat and A. D. Nock, in *Harvard Theological Review*, vol. XXIX (1936). Knox is critical of this being taken as evidence for syncretism, *Judaism and Christianity*, vol. II, p. 89, n. See also the discussion in *Beginnings*, vol. V, pp. 88ff.

[3] *Some Hellenistic Elements in Primitive Christianity*, pp. 30f. Acts 13. 15, 17. 2, 18. 4.

[4] Cf. W. L. Knox, op. cit. vol. II, p. 74. See also Str.-B. vol. IV, pp. 405ff. Str.-B. point out that the Rabbinic teachers knew of the books of Homer (ספרי המירם), cf. *M. Yadaim* 4. 6, and suggest that the teaching on Adam as ἀνδρόγυνος came from Plato via Philo to Palestinian Judaism. This latter is unlikely (see below, chapter 3) and it is to a certain Hermetic cosmogony that the term המירם refers according to Knox who reads הירמם (cf. *Judaism and Christianity*, vol. II, p. 105). Bentwich would also trace the cosmological speculations of the Rabbis in *Ma'aseh Bereshith* and *Ma'aseh Merkabah* to Hellenistic influences. It is doubtful, however, if this hypothesis is necessary, although it must be admitted that Hellenistic and Rabbinic speculation were reciprocally stimulating. We know that the Rabbis discussed philosophic matters with their Greek contemporaries, cf. *Gen. Rabba* 1. See also Str.-B. vol. IV, p. 405; *Gen. Rabba* 10. The Rabbis were familiar with the four primary elements of Greek philosophy, cf. J. Bonsirven, *Le Judaïsme Palestinien*, vol. I, pp. 163ff.

assume that there was a considerable reciprocal interchange of thought between the Judaism of Palestine and that of the Diaspora. It would prolong our discussion too much to inquire here whether and how far first-century Palestinian Judaism was modified by Hellenistic ideas.[1] That some Jews succumbed to Epicureanism appears from references to this in the Rabbinic literature.[2] Both Knox[3] and Bentwich[4] have urged that Hellenistic cosmology of the type found in Philo, and ultimately derived from the Timaeus, has supplied the Rabbis with much material for speculation. Stoicism has also been claimed as one of the influences on Rabbinic Judaism in our period.[5] Moreover, as our discussion will reveal, there are many points where the distinction between what is Hebraic and Hellenistic is very attenuated.[6] Where scholars have hesitated to do so,[7] it would be presumptuous to pass judgement; and it may be that Bonsirven[8] is right in seeing a series of tentative approaches towards Hellenism on the part of Rabbinic Judaism and then again and again a withdrawal into itself to preserve the central core of its being. Two things stand out clearly, however, first, that Palestinian Judaism is not to be viewed as a watertight compartment closed against all Hellenistic influences: there was a Graeco-Jewish 'atmosphere' even at Jerusalem itself, and, secondly, we can be certain that Judaism in the period before A.D. 70 was not as reserved and cautious as it afterwards became.[9] There is thus no justification for making too rigid a separation between the Judaism of the Diaspora and that of Palestine, and particularly is this true in the case of a man like Paul whose home was, most probably, a bit of Jerusalem outside Palestine.[10]

For our introductory purposes we have shown sufficiently that the assumptions which lie behind Montefiore's thesis are precarious. We have now to examine the Judaism of the first century to see whether there are elements in it that might account for those things which Montefiore feels compelled to derive from Paul's Hellenistic background.

---

[1] See J. Bonsirven, op. cit. vol. I, pp. 38f.

[2] *P. Aboth* 2. 18; J. Bonsirven, op. cit. vol. I, p. 37; W. L. Knox, op. cit. vol. II, p. 74.

[3] W. L. Knox, op. cit. pp. 75f.   [4] N. Bentwich, *Hellenism*, pp. 255ff.

[5] See J. Bonsirven, op. cit. vol. I, p. 39, n. 6. A. Marmorstein has found the influence of Stoicism in a saying of Ben Zoma: see *Revue des Études Juives* (1928), vol. LXXXVI, p. 38.

[6] See below, chapters 7 and 10.

[7] W. L. Knox, op. cit. vol. II, p. 109; E. Bevan, *The Legacy of Israel*, p. 67.

[8] Op. cit. vol. I, p. 40.

[9] See J. Bonsirven, op. cit. vol. I, p. 40; P. Wendland, *Die Hellenistische-römische Kultur* (1912), p. 208.

[10] Cf. A. Schweitzer, *Paul and his Interpreters*, p. 87.

There can be no question that the orthodox or normative Judaism of later centuries had its roots firmly planted in the first century, for the Rabbinical tradition was well fixed. Moreover, it is clear that it was Pharisaism, and that of the Shammaite kind, that dominated first-century Judaism. But it was not the only factor; it was only 'a movement within' Judaism.[1] Here we shall not attempt any exhaustive survey of Judaism in the first century; we shall discuss very briefly only those factors which the ultimate triumph of Pharisaism either suppressed or obscured and which are significant for the understanding of Paul. The Pharisees themselves, the Sadducees and others we shall pass by.

There was, in the first place, a great deal of apocalyptic speculation within Judaism. We need not enter here into a description of the apocalyptic literature,[2] and we are only concerned with that which can be used as evidence for Palestinian Judaism. Scholars have, moreover, differed greatly as to the extent to which the apocalyptic 'movement' formed an integral part of Rabbinic Judaism. On the one hand we find the view expressed by Moore[3] that apocalyptic interests lay outside the main current of Judaism, and consequently he would have us draw our picture of the latter from those Rabbinic sources which Judaism itself has always regarded as normative. On the other hand C. C. Torrey[4] writes: "The Jewish apocalyptic writings were not the property of any sect or school. Their point of view in general was that of Palestinian orthodoxy of which the Pharisees were the best representatives." Porter[5] has also referred to the absence of any sectarian tendency in the apocalyptic writings as an indication that they arose out of the main stream of Jewish life. On the same side is Charles, who claims that "Apocalyptic Judaism and legalistic Judaism were not in pre-Christian times essentially antagonistic. Fundamentally their origin was the same. Both started with unreserved recognition of the supremacy of the Law."[6] Charles also maintains that although "even before the Christian era each of these

---

[1] G. H. C. Macgregor and A. C. Purdy, *Jew and Greek Tutors unto Christ*, p. 87. For the supremacy of the school of Shammai in the time of Jesus see B. H. Branscomb, *Jesus and the Law of Moses*, p. 54. He writes: "Apparently then during the lifetime of Jesus the party of Hillel was not yet in control. The significance of this is obvious. It means that an active and rapidly growing party within the ranks of the scholars was at the time in vigorous protest against the currently accepted interpretation of the Torah...." In *Antiquities* 17, 2. 4 (Whiston's translation, p. 358), the Pharisees are referred to as a sect.

[2] See C. H. Charles, *Eschatology*, pp. 162ff.; M. J. Lagrange, *Le Judaïsme avant Jésus-Christ*, pp. 70ff.

[3] Vol. I, pp. 127ff.   [4] *J.E.* vol. I, p. 673b.

[5] *The Journal of Religion*, vol. VIII, no. I, pp. 41-4.

[6] *Ap. and Ps.* vol. II, p. vii.

two sides of Pharisaism necessarily tended to lay more and more emphasis on the chief factor in its belief and study to the almost complete exclusion of the other",[1] it was not till after A.D. 70 when the Jewish state fell, and when Christianity had adopted apocalyptic for its own purposes, that Judaism disowned the latter. Bonsirven finds a community of doctrine in the apocryphal and rabbinical literature[2] and Kautzsch[3] regards the Palestinian apocryphal literature as an expression of Pharisaic Judaism.

It is probable that the truth lies between the position taken by Moore and Torrey. Just as it would be difficult to define exactly the position which the doctrine of the Second Advent holds in the Christian Church to-day, because that position varies from communion to communion and even within the same communion, so was it probably with regard to apocalyptic in first-century Judaism. Doubtless to the Sadducees the apocalyptic teaching was slightly ridiculous, but there are certain considerations that make it probable that Pharisaism did not treat it thus cavalierly. Pharisaic emphasis on the doctrine of the resurrection (a doctrine which grew up in the apocalyptic schools), the Pharisaic interest in the Age to Come and in King Messiah,[4] these make it hard to believe that the Pharisees were wholly outside apocalyptic influences. The Pharisees would not carry their interests to extremes, as the Zealots did, but nevertheless they would not only be cognisant of apocalyptic speculation but in varying degrees doubtless attracted by it.[5]

Having now recognized that apocalyptic was by no means alien to Pharisaic Judaism, we go on to point out the familiar fact that apocalyptic is especially important in any study of the background of Paul. Schweitzer[6] indeed would isolate apocalyptic from the rest of Judaism and regard it as a separate and independent phenomenon, which supplies the key to Paul's thought. This, as we have seen, is to isolate apocalyptic too much from other elements in Judaism, but nevertheless the truth in Schweitzer's position has been acknowledged by other scholars. Dr Dodd[7] has written: "It seems clear that Paul started with eschatological beliefs of the type best represented by such Jewish writings as

[1] *Ap. and Ps.* vol. II, p. vii.

[2] *Le Judaïsme Palestinien*, vol. I, p. xxii.

[3] *Die Apokryphen und Pseudepigraphen des Alten Testaments*, vol. I, pp. xvf.

[4] With each of these points we shall deal below.

[5] I am indebted to Dr H. H. Rowley for much in the above. See also G. H. C. Macgregor and A. C. Purdy, *Jew and Greek Tutors unto Christ*, pp. 140-2. See also especially *Encyclopaedia Judaica, Das Judenthum im Geschichte und Gegenwart: zweiter Band*, vol. II, pp. 1154ff.

[6] *St Paul and his Interpreters*, p. 241.

[7] *Ryl. Bull.* (1934), vol. XVIII, no. 1, p. 27.

the Book of Enoch, the Apocalypse of Baruch, and the Apocalypse of
Ezra (2 Esdras) especially the last named.''[1]

To acknowledge this is to shed a great light on the points raised by
Montefiore. There is, first, Paul's attitude to the Law. In the Apocalypse
of Ezra the Law is regarded as a special divine gift to Israel,[2] but it
cannot redeem the sinner:[3] "to a race doomed to sin the promises of
the Law are a mockery".[4] "The utmost that the seer can hope from the
Law is that while the many are born to perish...few shall be saved."
Box writes that there is here "an approach to the mind of St Paul and
it is clear that this attitude of mind was by no means so rare and isolated
a phenomenon in contemporary Judaism as is sometimes supposed".[5]
The important point is that in their attitude to the Law, despite their
recognition of its impotence, both Paul and the author of 4 Ezra are
typically Rabbinic. For both the Law was to be obeyed literally, it was
not merely symbolic of the great principles of Judaism as to so many
Hellenistic Jews.[6] We cannot therefore vaguely assume that such discontent with the Law as we find in Paul, often indeed by the application
of a subjective psychology and not by fidelity to the sources,[7] was due
to his experience in the Diaspora, for discontent was not unknown in
Palestine.[8] This, of course, does not explain the extreme development
of Paul's criticism of the Law, as outlined by Montefiore, but it might
point to its origin.

Secondly, it is here that we can best deal with the idea of God in
first-century Judaism. Montefiore, as we saw, made much of the fact
that "the God of many Hellenistic and apocalyptic Jews seems to have
been a less intimate, near and affectionate God than the God of Rabbinic
Judaism". "A small contact with philosophy seems to have made God
more distant and less approachable."[9] Moore[10] also draws a sharp distinction between the idea of God held by Palestinians and that held by
Hellenistic Jews. "How innocent were the Palestinian masters", he
writes, "of an abstract or transcendent or any other sort of philosophical
idea of God." Of Philo, the chief representative of Hellenistic Judaism,
Abelson[11] writes: "His God is too impersonal. He is too much of

[1] Cf. C. W. Emmet, *Expository Times* (1916), vol. xxvii, p. 551. G. H. Box,
The Ezra-Apocalypse, p. xlii, who writes: "the author of the Salathiel Apocalypse is
our best representative of the kind of Jewish thought with which St Paul must have
been acquainted in his pre-Christian days."
[2] 4 Ezra 3. 19f.; 9. 31f.	[3] Ibid. 9. 36; cf. Rom. 3. 20.
[4] G. H. Box, *Ap. and Ps.* vol. ii, p. 554; cf. 4 Ezra 7. 116–31.
[5] *Ap. and Ps.* vol. ii, p. 555.	[6] See Moore, vol. ii, pp. 28f.
[7] See A. E. J. Rawlinson, *The New Testament Doctrine of the Christ*, p. 89.
[8] See *R.A.* p. 302.	[9] *Judaism and St Paul*, p. 95.	[10] Vol. i, p. 421.
[11] *The Immanence of God in Rabbinical Literature*, p. 72.

a metaphysical entity." Now it is naturally and inevitably true that Hellenistic philosophical conceptions did influence Judaism at such cultural centres as Alexandria, and it was this that gave birth to Hellenistic Judaism as we find it in Philo. But often the philosophic terminology, which Philo is compelled to use for his purpose, obscures the similarity of his religion with that expressed so naïvely in the literature of Palestinian Jewry. Abrahams,[1] criticizing Abelson, writes: "Does not Philo again and again compare God to a Father? Philo is full of warmth." Edwyn Bevan [2] has emphasized the same truth. All that "was so central in Old Testament religion was also central in the religion of Philo. The mode by which he thought to come into contact with God was Greek, but the God with whom he desired to come into contact was the God of Israel." "Before his God", writes Bentwich [3] of Philo, "he retains the childlike simplicity of the most un-Hellenic rabbi, and the perfect humility of the Hasid."

Moreover, in any case, every Jew of the Diaspora was not a Philo and it is not known how far Hellenistic philosophical ideas did influence all Greek-speaking Jews. What acquaintance the ordinary Jew, who had received little education, had with the speculative ideas of the Greek world must always be a matter of conjecture.[4] It is particularly important to remember this when we deal with Paul as we have already implied above. Not all Jews of the Diaspora were brought up in a home such as his to speak Aramaic and to excel in the Law. For example, how different Paul must have been from a Jew like Philo can be measured by the fact that Philo never even discovered that the Κύριος of the LXX represented the Hebrew *Yahweh*.[5] It has also been shown that Paul was acquainted only in the slightest degree with both Greek literature and philosophy.[6] Vague generalizations about the influence of Hellenistic philosophy upon the idea of God in Paul as opposed to ideas held by Palestinian Jews are, therefore, worthless. Moreover, we have seen that apocalyptic played an important part in Paul's religious background. The idea of God in apocalyptic leans mostly to the side of transcendentalism.[7] If, therefore, there be an element of transcendence in Paul's

[1] *The Immanence of God in Rabbinical Literature*, p. 72, n.
[2] *The Legacy of Israel*, p. 98.
[3] *Philo-Judaeus of Alexandria*, p. 139. Cf. H. A. A. Kennedy, *Philo's Contribution to Religion*, pp. 179 ff.
[4] Moore, vol. II, pp. 298–9.
[5] Cf. E. Bevan, *The Legacy of Israel*, p. 40.
[6] A. E. J. Rawlinson, *The New Testament Doctrine of the Christ*, pp. 99 f.
[7] Cf. G. H. C. Macgregor and A. C. Purdy, *Jew and Greek Tutors unto Christ*, p. 140. For the spirit and message of the apocalyptists, see H. H. Rowley, *The Relevance of Apocalyptic*, pp. 140 f.; for the emphasis on transcendence, pp. 153 ff.

conception of God it need not necessarily be traced to any Hellenistic philosophical influences.

We now come to what Montefiore called Paul's pre-Christian pessimism. Gilbert Murray has familiarized us with the 'failure of nerve' that prevailed in the Hellenistic age: but the Hellenistic world had no monopoly in pessimism; it was not unknown in Palestine. Knox[1] writes: "The temper of the age was tending increasingly to the belief that the universe was controlled by fate, a relentless power ordering all things through the planets and their course through the fixed stars." That Rabbinic Judaism knew of this kind of pessimism and had to deal with it severely appears from the sources.[2] But apart from the kind of pessimism that seemed to saturate the Mediterranean world, the slightest acquaintance with the apocalyptic literature reveals a despair of the present world, and in the case of 4 Ezra a sense of the universality and devastating effects of sin, which is almost Pauline. We read that "The creation hath already grown old and the vigour of her youth is past."[3] "For all who are born are defiled with sins and are full of iniquities and upon them their offences weigh heavily."[4] In addition we find the Rabbis discussing the question whether it was good that man had been created.

The Schools of Hillel and Shammai disputed two and a half years whether it would have been better if man had or had not been created. Finally they agreed that it would have been better had he not been created, but since he had been created, let him investigate his past doings, and let him examine what he is about to do. [The meaning is: "Let him live a righteous life."][5]

This passage is not alone and it seems clear that we need not go outside Judaism to account for 'pessimism' in Paul.

Finally, just as he derived Paul's pessimistic estimate of this world from Hellenistic sources, so too Montefiore refers his 'mysticism' to the same sources.[6] Rabbinic Judaism he asserts was not a religion which passed constantly and rapidly into 'mysticism': "its fervour, its ethics, its religious temper and its spiritual tone are generally other than those of the mystic who feels himself in God and God in him".[7] 'Mysticism'

---

[1] *Judaism and Christianity*, vol. II, p. 94.
[2] See *b. Shab.* 156a; *Tos. Sukk.* 2. 6, p. 194; *Gen. Rabba* 44. 4. 5. See W. L. Knox, op. cit. vol. II, p. 100.
[3] 4 Ezra 5. 55.   [4] G. H. Box, *Ap. and Ps.* vol. II, p. 555.
[5] *b. 'Erub.* 13b; cf. *Exod. Rabba* 48. See R.A. p. 539. It should not be forgotten also that political conditions must have led to much despair in first-century Palestine. See J. Klausner, *Jesus of Nazareth*, pp. 135ff.
[6] *Judaism and St Paul*, p. 48.   [7] Ibid. pp. 50f.

is a vague term, and discussions around this subject are apt to be lost in the bog of terminology, but waiving for the present the exact meaning which we are to ascribe to so-called Pauline 'mysticism' let us examine Montefiore's contention.

Every religion usually develops its own peculiar form of 'mysticism', and it is clear that any 'mysticism' which would be found on Jewish soil would differ in certain important respects from that of Hellenism. Hellenistic 'mysticism' aims at union with God; its climax is conceived as 'a being deified'. As Schweitzer [1] has pointed out, this is the kind of 'mysticism' that is impossible to Judaism; within Judaism the distinction between the Creator and the creature is never lost. But this does not mean that 'mysticism' was alien to Judaism. That the latter had its 'mystics' has been shown by Abelson,[2] and more recently by G. G. Scholem.[3] Both these scholars have shown that first-century Judaism was not only acquainted with the joy of the Law,[4] but also with the more ecstatic joy of the mystic. Here we can only briefly summarize what Abelson and Scholem have described at length. Scholem traces elements of Jewish mystical religion in apocalyptic works like the Ethiopic Book of Enoch and 4 Ezra,[5] and in the three centuries preceding the advent of Christianity esoteric doctrines were taught in Pharisaic circles. Ecclesiasticus[6] warns against the doctrine, but what the latter was we do not know. We cannot be certain how far the Book of Enoch or the Apocalypse of Abraham and such books reproduce the essentials of the esoteric doctrine. It has been claimed that Jewish 'mysticism' was fostered by the Essenes, and Abelson has produced evidence "that there existed as early as the first Christian centuries either a distinct sect of Jews or individual Jews here and there who combined mystical speculation with an ascetic mode of life".[7] There cannot be any doubt that organized groups fostered and handed down a certain esoteric doctrine or tradition or that there was a school of mystics who were not prepared to reveal their 'gnosis' to the public. Our ignorance of these groups is easily explained by the fact that "the editor of the Mishnah, the patriarch Jehudah the Saint, a pronounced rationalist, did

---

[1] *The Mysticism of Paul the Apostle*, p. 37. We shall deal fully with Paul's 'mystical' experiences below in chapter 8.

[2] See *Jewish Mysticism* and *The Immanence of God in Rabbinical Literature*.

[3] *Major Trends in Jewish Mysticism*.

[4] S. Schechter, *Some Aspects of Rabbinic Theology*, pp. 148 ff. See also M. J. Lagrange, *Le Judaïsme avant Jésus-Christ*, pp. 127 ff.

[5] G. G. Scholem, *Major Trends in Jewish Mysticism*, p. 39.

[6] 3. 22; cf. *J.E.* vol. III, p. 456.

[7] *Jewish Mysticism*, p. 28; see also pp. 17 f.

all he could to exclude anything that might savour of mysticism from the Mishnah".[1]

It is important for our purpose to notice that there were mystics among the Pharisees. Mysticism and legalism and loyalty to outward observances and institutions could coexist in Jewish as in medieval mysticism.[2] Scholem has shown that the 'mystical' groups were anxious to develop their 'gnosis' within the framework of orthodox Judaism.[3] That some of the Rabbis had 'mystical' experiences is proved by a reference in b. Ḥagigah 14b:

> Four sages entered paradise: Ben Azzai, Ben Zoma, Aher and Akiba.... Ben Azzai looked and died: Ben Zoma went mad: Aher destroyed the plants: Akiba alone came out unhurt.[4]

If what we have written be true, then Paul had no need to look wistfully towards the Mystery religions of the Hellenistic world for a warmth and emotion that Judaism lacked as Montefiore suggests.[5] Moreover, Schweitzer has convincingly shown, and we shall find so later in our discussion, that Paul's 'mysticism' cannot be Hellenistic. Paul never speaks of being deified as the Hellenistic mystics do. The distinction between Creator and creature always remains for Paul, a fact which shows his affinities to Jewish not Hellenistic 'mysticism'.

We have now considered the main positions advanced by Montefiore. The latter did not produce any evidence for his thesis but was content with a clear but very general statement of his interpretation of Paul which involved many vague generalizations. In this introductory chapter we have not sought to refute Montefiore at all points, such an effort would clearly demand an exhaustive study of Palestinian and Hellenistic Judaism in the first century, but we have merely questioned his assumptions and generalizations in order to show that those elements, dissatis-

---

[1] G. G. Scholem, *Major Trends in Jewish Mysticism*, p. 41. On the varieties of groups within first-century Judaism see Ch. Guignebert, *The Jewish World in the Time of Jesus Christ* (E.T.), pp. 191 ff. Guignebert writes, p. 203: "...we can now no longer doubt that there actually existed a Jewish gnosis from which the various sects drew their nourishment. In all probability, these sects sincerely believed themselves to be entirely orthodox with regard to the Torah; nevertheless, they occupied themselves with esoteric doctrines which fostered their illusion by seeming to be in accord with genuine legalism, while they falsified its spirit by interpretations wholly alien to it. Moreover, in addition to sects proper, all the great movements of contemporary Jewish thought, whether Pharisaism or Essenism owed something to this gnosis...."

[2] J. Abelson, *Jewish Mysticism*, p. 31.

[3] G. G. Scholem, op. cit. p. 47.

[4] *J.E.* vol. v, p. 138. See also Ch. Guignebert, *The Jewish World in the Time of Jesus Christ* (E.T.), pp. 204f. and references there given.

[5] *Judaism and St Paul*, p. 116.

faction with the Law, transcendentalism, pessimism and 'mysticism', which Montefiore found it necessary to derive from Hellenistic influences, might well emanate from Pharisaic Judaism itself and we have suggested that there is no need of Montefiore's hypothesis to account for them. It will be readily admitted, however, that it is not by such general assertions as those made by Montefiore and such broad counterassertions as we have made in this introductory chapter that the issue raised by Montefiore is to be decided. Only an examination of the basic elements in Pauline thought can reveal whether Paul was rooted in Rabbinic Judaism or not, and it is to such an examination that we shall apply ourselves in the following pages. It will not be our purpose to give a complete statement of Pauline theology but, beginning with his conception of sin, we shall endeavour to show that in the central points of his interpretation of the Christian dispensation Paul is grounded in an essentially Rabbinic world of thought, that the Apostle was, in short, a Rabbi become Christian and was therefore primarily governed both in life and thought by Pharisaic concepts, which he had baptized 'unto Christ'.

2

THE OLD ENEMY: THE FLESH AND SIN

WE now turn to the element in Paul's thought which more than any other, perhaps, has been claimed to be due to Hellenistic influences, his distinction between the σάρξ and πνεῦμα. Until recently two main views were prevalent. Pfleiderer,[1] Holtzmann[2] and Bousset[3] have all held that while there is an Old Testament element in the Pauline anthropology the predominant factor in it is Hellenistic. On the other hand the view that has most commended itself to British scholars is that while there is a sporadic introduction of Hellenistic terms and concepts Pauline anthropology rests entirely on an Old Testament basis.[4] It is well here to remind ourselves also of Montefiore's view. He wrote: "The Rabbis... did not oppose flesh and spirit in the same way as they are opposed in the writings of St Paul; and, above all, they did not make a distinction between the spiritual man on the one hand and the merely psychic (or natural) man on the other. Here most decidedly we touch un-Rabbinic ground.... The spirit and flesh doctrine of the eighth chapter of the Epistle to the Romans could not have been devised by anyone who to his Rabbinic antecedents merely added a conviction that the Messiah had appeared in the person of Jesus."[5] It is our contention, however, that the Pauline distinction between the σάρξ and πνεῦμα is not a replica of Hellenistic dualism, nor again simply to be explained from the Old Testament. It is rather the complex product of Paul's Old Testament background and his Rabbinic training. It is indeed the latter that affords us the best clue to much in his thought on the flesh and sin.[6]

---

[1] Cf. Otto Pfleiderer, *Paulinism* (E.T.), vol. I, pp. 47–68. Pfleiderer modified his position under the influence of Weber's *System der Altsynagogalen Palästinischen Theologie*, and adopted the view that Paul's doctrine of the flesh and spirit was based on the Rabbinic doctrine of the good and evil impulses. In this he was misled by Weber: for an examination of the latter, cf. F. C. Porter, "Biblical and Semitic Studies", in *Yale Bicentennial Publications*, pp. 98–107.

[2] H. J. Holtzmann, *Lehrbuch der Neutestamentlichen Theologie*, vol. II, pp. 12–24.

[3] W. Bousset, *Die Religion des Judenthums*, p. 386 (1st ed. 1903).

[4] W. Sanday and A. C. Headlam, *Romans* (I.C.C.), pp. 183 ff.; H. Wheeler Robinson, *The Christian Doctrine of Man*, pp. 104 f.

[5] C. G. Montefiore, *Judaism and St Paul*, pp. 79 f.

[6] Cf. also N. P. Williams, *The Ideas of the Fall and of Original Sin*, pp. 150 f.; W. F. Howard, *Christianity according to St John*, p. 86.

The view that in his use of σάρξ Paul reveals that he had virtually departed from his Jewish faith and accepted the typical Hellenistic dualism, which opposed matter to mind, and that he regarded sin as innate in the empirical nature of man need not detain us long. Three considerations sufficiently refute it. First, it is legitimate to apply a theological test to the theory.[1] N. P. Williams has forcefully pointed out that the ascription of Hellenistic dualism to Paul involves us in a psychological, ethical and spiritual impossibility.[2] It would be to make Paul's faith in the real coming of Christ into the world an absurdity. To Paul Christ was of the seed of David, a figure in history, a man after the flesh. If the latter was intrinsically evil, as Hellenistic dualism maintained, then Paul's faith in the historic Christ was vain. Secondly, there is an important lexical point. The term σάρξ was not used in the prevailing Hellenistic literature to express the material as opposed to the ideal. We find ὕλη opposed to νοῦς but never σάρξ. Liddell and Scott can give no instance of σάρξ being so used.[3] Now if Paul was seeking consciously to express the opposition of the material to the ideal in Hellenistic fashion, it is singular that he should use the word σάρξ which conveyed no dualistic associations to the Hellenistic world. Philo[4] used ὕλη and οὐσία of matter; surely if Paul moved in the same world of thought he too would have employed these terms. Thirdly, these two considerations are reinforced by a detailed examination of the Pauline use of σάρξ. It is clear that in his anthropology generally Paul is dependent on the Old Testament. The use of ψυχή, καρδία and πνεῦμα in the Epistles corresponds closely enough to that of *nephesh*, *lêb*, *ruach* in the Old Testament to prove that Paul draws on the latter. When we turn to the Old Testament word for 'flesh', *bâsâr*, it is clear that in the later literature, as H. Wheeler Robinson has shown, "it is used of man or man's essential nature in contrast with God or with 'Spirit', to emphasize man's frailty, dependence or incapacity. (Is. 31. 3, 40. 6; Ps. 56. 5, 78. 39; Job 10. 4, 34. 15; Jer. 17. 5; cf. also Ps. 103. 14; Job 4. 17, 25. 4f.) The contrast does not occur before Is. 31. 3 and must not be read into the earlier

---

[1] On the principle "if in difficulty enlarge your categories".

[2] Cf. N. P. Williams, *The Ideas of the Fall and of Original Sin*, p. 149. Williams also makes much of the fact that Paul's acceptance of the Fall theory in Rom. 5 would make it impossible for him to accept dualism: "The Fall theory and dualism are in principle... exclusive hypotheses" (p. 149). For Philo's awareness of the inconsistency between dualism and the traditional faith, see J. Drummond, *Philo Judaeus*, vol. 1, p. 300.

[3] It is only in Plutarch that there is anything corresponding to Paul's use of σάρξ. See Liddell and Scott. According to Liddell and Scott οὐσία in Stoic philosophy = ὕλη. In the *Hermetica*, however, οὐσία is distinguished from ὕλη; cf. *Herm.* IX. 11 and XI. 3

[4] Cf. James Drummond, *Philo Judaeus*, vol. 1, pp. 297f. For οὐσια, cf. *De Opif* §21; Cohn-Wendland, 1. 6.

Hebrew thought."[1] The same scholar goes on to add: "its importance
consists in its being the point of departure for the development of the
Pauline doctrine of the flesh, with distinct ethical reference."

That this is so, a brief recapitulation of the use of σάρξ in Paul will
show. In fifty-six cases σάρξ is used in a purely material sense either of
physical structure, or kinship, or sphere of present existence, or fleshly
weakness; in thirty-five cases it has an ethical significance.[2] This twofold
connotation which the term has for Paul leads him to apparent inconsistencies. In contexts where the ethical element predominates, for
example, he hesitates to say that Jesus came in the flesh but says that he
came in the 'likeness of sinful flesh'. Elsewhere, where the term could
only refer to the physical constitution of Jesus and could create no misunderstanding, he speaks of the body of his flesh.[3] The Apostle can at
one and the same time desire to be free from the flesh and yet recognize
that it is his duty to remain in the same.[4] In his flesh and in that of others,
of all, there is no good thing,[5] and yet he pleads that the flesh should be
sanctified.[6] One conclusion only emerges; the term σάρξ denoted for
Paul the material element in man which is morally indifferent; it has,
however, become the basis from which sin attacks man;[7] has, in short,
passed under the dominion of sin; it was a corrupted not a corrupting
element; the involuntary accomplice to the act of sin but not the criminal.
It is clear that Paul took over the Old Testament conception of bâsâr
as being weak and prone to sin. His use of σάρξ does not imply that
the physical element in man is of necessity evil as is implied in Hellenistic
dualism. We may accept Wheeler Robinson's conclusion that "Paul
finds in man's physical nature the immediate foe of the higher principle,
though this does not of course prove that the flesh is the ultimate enemy
as is implied when Hellenistic dualism is applied to Paul...we are
entitled to say that the ultimate enemy of the Spirit of God is not flesh
but the Sin of which the flesh has become the weak and corrupted
instrument".[8] [See Additional Notes.]

The use that Paul then makes of the term σάρξ can be adequately
explained as an accentuation of the ethical connotation that the term
already had in certain late documents in the Old Testament and his

[1] H. Wheeler Robinson, *The Christian Doctrine of Man*, p. 25.
[2] The evidence is summarized by H. Wheeler Robinson, op cit. p. 114.
[3] Cf. Rom. 8. 3 and Col. 1. 22. Cf. also C. H. Dodd, *Romans* (M.N.T.C.), p. 120.
[4] Phil. 1. 23. Such a verse could not have been written by one who believed in the
doctrine that σῶμα σῆμα.
[5] Rom. 7. 18.   [6] 2 Cor. 6. 14, 7. 1.   [7] Rom. 7.
[8] *The Christian Doctrine of Man*, p. 117; *Mansfield College Essays*, pp. 267 ff.

contrast between flesh and spirit is a natural evolution of the anthropology of the latter. Can we also trace a strictly Rabbinic influence in
his thought at this point? One thing is perfectly clear. Rabbinic Judaism
did not, as did Paul, take over the term *bâsâr* from the Old Testament
to express that side of human nature which is prone to moral weakness.[1]
The Aramaic *bĕnê bisrâ* signifies simply 'Sons of men' or 'men' without
any ethical nuance. Strack-Billerbeck refer to the Jerusalem Targum
on Is. 40. 6 and Zech. 2. 13 where *Kol-habâsâr* is rendered by *Kol-rashî'ayâ'*
as an apparent exception. In reality, however, they are no exception
because, as Strack-Billerbeck also point out, the Targum on Is. 66. 24,
renders the same expression by *Kol-tzadîqīyâ'*. The evidence they give
is conclusive that the Rabbis did not develop the ethical connotation
that *bâsâr* had in the Old Testament.[2] There are no expressions in
Rabbinic Judaism which literally correspond to the use of σάρκινος and
σαρκικός and πνευματικός and ψυχικός in Paul.[2]

It is equally certain and, of course, natural, that the contrast between
the lives which were σαρκικοί and those which Paul would call πνευματικοί was known to the Rabbis; but they spoke of the former as those
in which the evil impulse (*ha-yêtzer hâ-râ'*) and of the latter as those in
which the good impulse (*ha-yêtzer ha-tôb*) prevailed.[2] To this conception
we now turn. As early as Ecclesiasticus we find the view expressed
that there is implanted in man a sinful desire, impulse, inclination or
urge. We quote from that book:

11. Say not: "From God is my transgression",
    For that which he hateth he made not.
12. Say not: "(It is) he that made me to stumble",
    For there is no need of evil men.
13. Evil and abomination doth the Lord hate,
    And he doth not let it come nigh to them that fear him.
14. God created Man from the beginning,
    And placed him in the hand of his *yêtzer* (διαβούλιον).[3]

So too in 4 Ezra we read: "For the first Adam clothed himself with the
evil heart and transgressed and was overcome and not only so but also

---

[1] It may be worth mentioning, however, that בסרא may denote the private
parts and, as we shall see below, the latter were regarded as the most inferior (and
therefore the most immoral) aspects of the body. The association of sex with sin will
also occupy us later. See *R.A.* pp. 289f.
[2] For all this the notes in Str.-B. on 1 Cor. 3. 3 are most valuable; cf. also Str.-B.
on 1 Cor. 2. 14, 9. 11. Str.-B. vol. III, pp. 330f. See also pp. 329, 400.
[3] Cf. Ecclus. 15. 11–14. The discussion of this passage and of the whole teaching
of Ecclesiasticus on sin by F. C. Porter, "Biblical and Semitic Studies", in *Yale
Bicentennial Publications*, is very convincing. He there justifies the view above given
that 4 Ezra contains the conception of the יצר הרע, pp. 146f.

all who were begotten from him."[1] In the later Rabbinic literature the conception of the *yêtzer hâ-râ'* in man becomes the dominant description of sin.[2] The earliest reference to the *yêtzer ha-ṭôb* occurs in the Testament of Asher 1. 6, "Therefore if the soul take pleasure in the good (impulse) all its actions are in righteousness."[3] We can be sure, then, that in contemporary Rabbinic circles Paul would be made familiar with the doctrine of the *yêtzer hâ-râ'* and the *yêtzer ha-ṭôb*. It was the evil impulse that first attracted the Rabbis and indeed it was with this that they were always chiefly concerned;[4] and here too it is the *yêtzer hâ-râ'* which is most relevant to our purpose.

We cannot here enter into a detailed survey of Rabbinic teaching on the *yêtzer hâ-râ'*: the following brief summary must suffice. First, then, according to one view the good impulse was located on the right side and the evil impulse on the left side of a man;[5] according to another the two had their dwelling place in the kidneys;[6] but the overwhelmingly prevailing view was that the sphere where the struggle for mastery between the evil and good impulses occurred was the heart.[7] The association of the evil impulse with the heart as we have seen is at least as early as 4 Ezra: there is no specific evidence that it was earlier. The heart, of course, would stand for the volitional and intellectual elements in man.[8] We should say that the evil impulse then attacked man's will and mind. Secondly, the nature of the evil impulse is to urge or incline man to all sorts of sins. It seems, moreover, that it was especially, though not exclusively, connected with sexual sins,[9] sexual passion or lust; it was

---

[1] 4 Ezra 3. 21, 4. 30f.

[2] Cf. Str.-B. vol. IV, I, pp. 466f. and F. C. Porter, "Biblical and Semitic Studies", in *Yale Bicentennial Publications*, pp. 93 f. for the teaching on the יצרים: in the main, Porter and Str.-B. give the same picture.

[3] Cf. the whole passage, The Testament of Asher 1. 3–9 and Charles' note, *Ap. and Ps.* vol. II, p. 343.

[4] N. P. Williams, *The Ideas of the Fall and of Original Sin*, pp. 60f. does not find it necessary to mention the יצר הטוב at all.

[5] Cf. Str.-B. vol. III, p. 94; *Num. R.* 22. 9.

[6] Cf. Str.-B. vol. III, p. 95; *b. Ber.* 61a.

[7] Cf. Str.-B. vol. IV, I, pp. 467, 470, and F. C. Porter, "Biblical and Semitic Studies", in *Yale Bicentennial Publications*, p. 110. Cf. also *Sifre Deut.* on 6. 5, §32, and *M. Ber.* 9. 5, i.e. "Man is bound to bless [God] for the evil as he blesses [God] for the good, for it is written, 'And thou shalt love the Lord Thy God with all thy heart....' With all thy heart (לבב)—with both thine impulses thy good impulse and thine evil impulse." Cf. Danby, p. 10.

[8] Cf. H. Wheeler Robinson, *The Christian Doctrine of Man*, p. 22; F. C. Porter, "Biblical and Semitic Studies", in *Yale Bicentennial Publications*, p. 110; and *B.D.B.* p. 523.

[9] So much so that the majority of instances quoted in *A Rabbinic Anthology* by C. G. Montefiore and H. Loewe deal with sex. The יצר is "largely identified with sexual passion". Cf. *R.A.* pp. 304–5, and Str.-B. vol. IV, p. 466.

the force that led men particularly to unchastity and to idolatry.[1] Nevertheless, although some passages present God as repenting that he had made the evil inclination,[2] the latter is also regarded as being somehow good; it is not evil in itself, one is reminded of Paul's teaching on the flesh, but only in so far as man is impelled by it to evil acts. It is the urge to self-preservation and propagation in a man and can therefore be mastered and put to a good use. We may quote Moore: "the impulses natural to man are not in themselves evil. When God looked upon the finished creation and saw that it was all very good (Genesis 1. 31), the whole nature of man is included in this judgement, as R. Samuel ben Nahman observes: 'And behold it was very good.' This is the evil impulse! Is then the evil impulse good? Yet, were it not for the evil impulse no man would build a house, nor marry a wife, nor beget children nor engage in trade. Solomon said 'All labor and all excelling in work is a man's rivalry with his neighbour' (Ecclesiastes 4. 4)."[3] The appetites and passions are an essential element in the constitution of human nature and necessary to the perpetuation of the race and to the existence of civilization. In this aspect they are, therefore, not to be eradicated or suppressed, but directed and controlled. In the third place, the chief means of protection against the evil impulse was the study of the Torah;[4] and, in addition, it was wise to adjure the evil impulse by

---

[1] Cf. Str.-B. vol. IV, pp. 466–7 (cf. *Mekilta Nezikin* 17 on Exodus 20. 5). "So sehr hat Gott den bösen Trieb (nämlich zum Götzendienst) verfolgt, um keine Veranlassung zu geben, dass man irgendwo Raum fände fur ein erlaubtes Abbild." The importance of this for Rom. 1 will appear later.

[2] Cf. evidence in *R.A.* pp. 300–1, eg. *b. Sukk.* 52*b*. R. Ḥana b. Aḥa (A.D. 80–120) said: "In the school of Rab it was said, 'There are four things which God regretted to have made, The Exile, The Chaldeans, The Ishmaelites and The Evil Inclination'"; cf. Moore, vol. I, pp. 480–1.

[3] *Gen. R.* 9. 7. Moore, vol. I, pp. 482–3. If it be objected that R. Samuel b. Naḥman belongs to the fourth century we may refer to *b. Sanh.* 107*b*: "It was taught R. Simeon b. Eleazar [A.D. 165–200] said: 'Human nature (Hebrew, יצר), a child and a woman— the left hand should repulse them, but the right hand bring them back.'" On this H. Freedman comments (*The Talmud*, Nezikin VI. Sanhedrin II, 107*b*. Soncino Press, p. 736, n. 5): "One must not attempt to subdue his desires altogether, which is unnatural but to regulate them." See also N. P. Williams, *The Ideas of the Fall and of Original Sin*, pp. 66f., especially p. 69. If it be insisted that since the adjective רע is applied to the יצר then it must be evil, we must accuse the Rabbis of a lack of clarity at this point, since good could certainly come from the evil impulse as the above quotations show.

[4] Cf. *b. Kidd.* 30*b*. R. Ishmael (A.D. 140–65): "In the school of R. Ishmael it was taught: If this abomination meet you, drag it to the House of Study; if it is hard as stone it will be crushed; if it is hard as iron, it will be broken in pieces." Cf. *R.A.* pp. 296, 302, and Str.-B. vol. III, p. 332 (*Sifre Deut.* on 11. 18, § 45) on 1 Cor. 3. 3. The Evil impulse is sometimes personified as an evil spirit. This is illustrated by the

an oath in the name of the Lord.[1] Furthermore: "if a man has yielded
to the evil impulse, there is still a remedy—repentance. 'There is no
malady in the world for which there is not a cure. What is the cure for
evil impulse? Repentance.'"[2] Fourthly, it was held that in the Age to
Come the evil impulse to unchastity and idolatry would be destroyed.
One quotation, traced to R. Judah (A.D. 150) will suffice: "In the world
to come God will bring the Evil Impulse and slay it in the presence of
the righteous and the wicked."[3] Lastly, for our purpose it will be good
to quote Moore's words: "The opportunity or the invitation to sin may
come from without, but it is the response of the evil impulse in man to
it that converts it into a temptation. It pictures in imagination the
pleasures of sin, conceives the plan, seduces the will, incites to the act.
It is thus primarily as the subjective origin of temptation or more
correctly as the tempter within, that the yêtzer hâ-râ' is represented in
Jewish literature. Since it compasses man's undoing by leading him into
sin, it is thought of as maliciously seeking his ruin, a kind of malevolent
second personality.... Hence it is not strange that in parallel passages in
the Midrash evil impulse may be found in one and sin in another, with
the same things said about them. It is hardly necessary to say that the
interchangeableness of the terms does not imply that the impulse is
identified with sin."[4]

Can we relate this doctrine of the Two Impulses to the teaching of
Paul? There are three passages in particular where the Apostle deals
with the problem of Sin, all in the Epistle to the Romans,[5] namely,
Romans 1, 2, 5. 12f., and Romans 7. In the latter of these passages we
are justified in tracing a direct connection with the doctrine of the
Two Impulses. Paul's description of his moral experience in that chapter

following: "R. Meir used to mock at sinners. One day Satan appeared in the likeness
of a woman on the other side of the river. As there was no ferry boat, he seized the
rope bridge, and went across. When he was halfway, Satan vanished saying, 'If they
had not called out from heaven, "Beware of R. Meir and his Torah," I would not have
assessed your blood at two farthings'." (b. Ḳidd. 81a.) Cf. R.A. p. 298; cf. also Moore,
vol. I, p. 489.

[1] Moore, vol. I, p. 489; cf. Sifre Deut. on 6. 6, § 33; Bacher, Die Agada der Tannaiten,
vol. II, p. 360.

[2] See Moore, vol. I, pp. 491, 520; cf. Tanḥuma Bereshith, § 38, p. 25.

[3] The importance of this for Paul once he conceived Jesus as the Messiah will be
obvious. Cf. for the details Str.-B. vol. IV, pp. 482f.; b. Sukk. 52a.

[4] Moore, vol. I, p. 481. Also pp. 492f. and Str.-B. vol. IV, p. 466. The relevance of
this to Paul's teaching on the flesh will be clear. This paragraph might well have been
written of the φρόνημα τῆς σαρκός of Paul.

[5] We need not here discuss the phrase "the children of wrath by nature" in Eph. 2. 3;
cf. F. R. Tennant, The Fall and Original Sin, p. 252.

is probably an account of his struggle against his evil *yêtzer*. To this view we now turn.

The words that we quoted above from Moore make it clear that the doctrine of the Two Impulses is not an explanation of sin, but merely a description of the way in which sin acts within man. The mystery of sin remains. Similarly in Romans 7 Paul's aim is psychological, he is merely describing the activity of sin within his own soul. As to the Rabbis sin was a power from without man which utilized the *yêtzer hâ-râ'* to lead man to sinful acts, so also to Paul sin is equally an external power that comes to dwell in the flesh and utilizes the φρόνημα τῆς σαρκός[1] to work its havoc. We shall now point out that by the latter Paul meant what the Rabbis referred to as the *yêtzer hâ-râ'*: and we can assume at once from what has been written above that while the *yêtzer hâ-râ'* was not essentially evil so too for Paul the flesh was not evil of itself.[2]

In Romans 7 Paul divides his life into three periods: roughly they are as follows. First, a period when although sin was latent in him, it was 'dead', and he was able to live a full life without restraint,[3] the age of innocence as we should call it. Secondly, the period when the commandment came and with it sin sprang to life. Hitherto sin was not known as sin; it was revealed as such by the Law. The latter, moreover, not only brought into being the awareness of the sinfulness of sin but also, on the principle that forbidden fruits are sweetest, actually gave an impetus towards sin.[4] Paul is driven into the painful state that Aristotle called ἀκρασία (incontinence) in which a man knows what is right and desires it and yet cannot do it. He becomes a Jekyll and Hyde.[5] The third stage in the Apostle's life is that in which the Spirit comes to deliver him. With this we are not now directly concerned.[6]

It was customary among the Rabbis to discuss the different ages of a man. In *Pirkê Aboth* 5. 24, Judah ben Tema (A.D. *c.* 150) said: "At five years the Scriptures; at ten years the Mishnah; at thirteen the commandments; at fifteen the Talmud etc...." This saying is regarded as an addition to the *Aboth* but at the age of thirteen it was generally recognized that a boy is made a "son of commandment"—*bar-mitzwâh*,

---

[1] Cf. Rom. 8. 6.   [2] Cf. above, p. 22.

[3] Cf. Rom. 7. 8, 9. For the significance of ἔζων here, cf. C. H. Dodd, *Romans* (*M.N.T.C.*), pp. 110–11: "I lived—with faculties at full stretch."

[4] Cf. Rom. 7. 8, 9; cf. also C. H. Dodd, *Romans* (*M.N.T.C.*), pp. 108 f.

[5] Cf. Rom. 7. 15 f.; compare the words of Moore of the יצר הרע as a 'malicious second personality' above; C. H. Dodd, *Romans* (*M.N.T.C.*), p. 113; Aristotle, *Nicomachean Ethics*, 7. 4. 2.

[6] Cf. Rom. 7. 25 f. and 8.

i.e. he becomes morally responsible and is received into the community.[1] There were discussions also as to when the *yêtzer hâ-râ'* entered a man; was it before or after birth?[2] Most of the Rabbis held that it was at birth. What is significant is that the *yêtzer hâ-râ'* was thought to be thirteen years older than the *yêtzer ha-ṭôb* in the life of every man; for that period it reigned alone when man was not morally responsible.[3] It was at the age of thirteen that the struggle between the Two Impulses began. It was, then, with the coming of the Law that the *bar-mitzwâh* would become aware of the exceeding sinfulness of sin, and suffer the pangs of ἀκρασία. Moreover, from what we have said about the largely sexual nature of the *yêtzer hâ-râ'*, it would be the commandment which worried Paul, which would generally worry any sensitive *bar-mitzwâh*.[4] From the age of thirteen onwards the struggle between the Two Impulses is unceasing: "From this warfare there was no discharge";[5] and, as we have already seen, the chief remedy proposed by Judaism was the Torah.[6]

When we compare such speculations with what Paul describes in Romans 7 the similarity is obvious. It is difficult not to believe that the Apostle is there describing his experience as a Jew suffering under the

[1] On *P. Aboth* 5. 24, W. O. E. Oesterley writes: "This saying is omitted by several authorities: it is a later addition." But Strack suggests that it was excluded from the book on account of its melancholy conclusion; cf. R. Travers Herford in *Pirkê Aboth* in *Ap. and Ps.* vol. II, p. 710. The boy at thirteen although responsible, i.e. able to fulfil the Law—is not held to be 'fully' responsible: this latter comes when he is twenty; cf. also A. Cohen, *Everyman's Talmud*, pp. 77f.

[2] Cf. Moore, vol. I, p. 481. To support the view that it was at birth the verse Gen. 4. 7: "Sin croucheth at the door" was quoted. *b. Sanh.* 91b reads: "Antoninus also enquired of Rabbi [A.D. 200], 'From what time does the Evil Tempter hold sway over man; from the formation [of the embryo] or from [its] issuing forth [into the light of the world?]' 'From formation,' he replied. 'If so,' he objected, 'it would rebel in its mother's womb and go forth. But it is from when it issues.' Rabbi said: 'This thing Antoninus taught me, and Scripture supports him, for it is said, At the door [i.e. where the babe emerges] sin lieth in wait.' (Genesis 4. 7)." See also *Genesis R.* 34. 10. On Antoninus see *J.E.* vol. I, pp. 656f.

[3] For this see Str.-B. vol. IV, p. 470; cf. *Aboth R.N.* I. פרק טז, p. 62; Str.-B. on Rom. 2. 15, vol. III, p. 95.

[4] Rom. 7. 7, "Thou shalt not covet"; cf. C. H. Dodd, *Romans* (M.N.T.C.), pp. 110f.

[5] Cf. Str.-B. vol. IV, pp. 471, 482–3; *R.A.* pp. 302f.; not only "the bigger a man's whole nature the more powerful too is the *yêtzer* within him" but "even the righteous are never completely secure from the solicitations of the *yêtzer*". Every man is to crush his evil impulse: thus, R. Simai (c. A.D. 200) said: "The evil *yêtzer* is like a big rock, which stands at the cross-roads, and people stumble against it. The king said, 'Crush it little by little, till I come and remove it altogether'; so God says 'The Evil Inclination is a great stumbling block; crush it little by little, till at the last I remove it from the world'" (*Pesikta* 165a). (*R.A.* p. 296.)

[6] See above, p. 22.

yêtzer hâ-râ'. There is, it is true, no exact equivalent in Romans 7 to the rabbinical idea of the *yêtzer ha-ṭôb*;[1] but it would not be going too far to claim that Paul is here directly contesting the Rabbinic view that the Law gives deliverance from the tyranny of the evil impulse. It may be argued that when the Rabbis speak of the Torah as the remedy for the evil impulse, they mean the study of or the occupation with the revelation, whereas Paul in Romans 7 is thinking of the actual commands of the Torah which, he claims, bring about a consciousness of sin, and that therefore the Torah as a remedy for the evil impulse and the Torah in Paul's mind in Romans 7 refer to different things. This, however, does not appear convincing to us. Surely Paul too, when he referred to the commandment as inciting to sin, was thinking of the occupation with the commandment or concentration upon it rather than of the commandment *in vacuo* as it were. The juxtaposition of the *yêtzer hâ-râ'* and the divine remedy the Torah is, we feel, reproduced in Paul's antithesis of the σάρξ or the φρόνημα τῆς σαρκός and the Spirit. N. P. Williams is probably right then in saying, at least generally, that 'sin', 'the old man', 'the sinful body', 'the body of this death', 'the sinful passions aroused by the Law', 'the mind of the flesh' are all so many picturesque and paraphrastic names for the *yêtzer hâ-râ'*.[2] It is a likely conjecture of his also that φρόνημα τῆς σαρκός almost amounts to a literal translation of the *yêtzer hâ-râ'*.[3]

The phrase φρόνημα τῆς σαρκός leads us to a difficulty that is often

---

[1] Cf. F. C. Porter, "Biblical and Semitic Studies", in *Yale Bicentennial Publications*, p. 134. Though we do not accept Porter's main position, he is right in saying that Paul's conception of the Spirit has almost nothing in common with the relatively unimportant rabbinical idea of the good *yêtzer*. See also the following sentence: "On the other hand there is a closer, though still remote, parallelism between his contrast of flesh and spirit and the Jewish conception of the Law as the divinely given remedy for the evil nature of man, the power before which it must yield."

[2] Cf. N. P. Williams, *The Ideas of the Fall and of Original Sin*, p. 150.

[3] F. C. Porter's note is worth quoting in full. "It is important to observe that there was no Greek word with which the various meanings of the Hebrew יצר could be rendered. In its literal meaning the verb was commonly rendered in the LXX by πλάσσω and the noun by πλάσμα in Isa. 29. 16; Hab. 2. 18; Ps. 103. 14. Aquila and Sym. use it also in Deut. 31. 21; Isa. 26. 3. But this word could not bear the figurative meaning of the Hebrew. In Gen. 8. 21 'יצר of the heart' is rendered by ἡ διάνοια; so in 1 Chron. 29. 18 'in the יצר of the thoughts of his heart' = ἐν διανοίᾳ καρδίας; while in Gen. 6. 5 ('every יצר of the thoughts of his heart') πᾶς τις διανοεῖται ἐν τῇ καρδίᾳ αὐτοῦ. But in 1 Chron. 28. 9 'every יצר of the thoughts' becomes πᾶν ἐνθύμημα. The word is rendered by ἡ πονηρία in Deut. 31. 21 and is passed by in Isa. 26. 3, unless indeed our Hebrew text itself is corrupt." "Biblical and Semitic Studies", in *Yale Bicentennial Publications*, p. 136. See also N. P. Williams, *The Ideas of the Fall and of Original Sin*, p. 150.

pointed out. We saw that the *yêtzer hâ-râ'* was located generally in the heart, whereas Paul clearly regards the σάρξ as the base of operations for sin. The question is inevitable whether, had Paul been describing the conflict with his *yêtzer*, he too would not have spoken of 'the heart' rather than 'the flesh'? It has been suggested that the Apostle regarded the σάρξ as the seat of sin because he was thinking more particularly of sins in the 'flesh' in a restricted sense; but that the sins of the flesh included for Paul not merely sexual sins but also such things as pride is clear from Galatians 5.[1] The probable explanation, however, of why Paul used σάρξ is not far to seek. There was no scientific fixity or accuracy about the use of psychological and anthropological terms in his day and the Old Testament use of σάρξ (*bâsâr*), which we have already discussed, would naturally and suitably suggest itself to him. In addition to this the location of the *yêtzer* in the heart, while dominant in Rabbinic thought, must not be too hard pressed. The *yêtzer hâ-râ'* as we saw, had a long start over the *yêtzer ha-tôb* in man, and some passages suggest that it had gained dominion over the whole 248 members of the human body: it would not be difficult then for Paul to envisage sin as invading all his members and having its base in all his flesh.[2]

We may assume then that in Romans 7 Paul reflects and possibly actually has in mind the Rabbinic doctrine of the Two Impulses. We now turn to the thought of Romans 1, where there is a view of sin which is apparently quite un-Rabbinic, far removed from Romans 7. We cannot agree with Tennant[3] that we can ignore the discussion of human sinfulness in the early chapters of Romans "because they contain no theory or doctrine to account for the absoluteness of the universality of sin". There is, indeed, a clearly defined theory of the origin of sin in Romans 1. It is that sin arose because men turned from the worship of the True God, whom of themselves they could know, to idolatry of the creature. In Paul's own words, men "changed the glory of the incorruptible God into an image made like to corruptible man"…"they changed the truth of God into a lie and worshipped and served the creature more than the Creator who is blessed for ever". It is "for this cause that God gave them up to vile affections…".[4]

What is the relation, if any, between this theory and the Rabbinic one we have already outlined? Are we to assume that here Paul is drawing upon ideas remote from the Rabbinic world or can we still

---

[1] Cf. N. P. Williams, op. cit. p. 153.
[2] Cf. Str.-B. vol. IV, pp. 470, 472; e.g. *Aboth R.N.* I. פרק טז, p. 63.
[3] Cf. F. R. Tennant, *The Fall and Original Sin*, p. 252.
[4] Rom. I. 20, 26.

trace the influence of the Rabbis? Many scholars have traced in Romans 1 the influence of the Alexandrian Book of Wisdom.[1] The evidence seems to justify the conclusion drawn by Sanday and Headlam that "while on the one hand there can be no question of direct quotation, on the other hand the resemblance is so strong both as to the main lines of the argument (i. natural religion discarded, ii. idolatry, iii. catalogue of immorality) and in the details of thought and to some extent of expression, as to make it clear that at some point in his life St Paul must have bestowed on the Book of Wisdom a considerable amount of study".[2] The views of the Stoics, of Plato and of Heracleitus have been traced in the latter book and the argument that Paul uses in Romans 1 has been designated a Stoic one, derived by the Apostle either directly from the Book of Wisdom or otherwise.[3] It will be our present task to show that in his treatment of sin in Romans 1, Paul, although using Hellenistic terminology, is still within the Rabbinic tradition.[4]

In the first place, the idea that God's existence can be derived from the mere contemplation of His works in creation is a familiar theme in Judaism. A passage in The Testament of the Twelve Patriarchs reads:

> Sun and moon and stars change not their order; so do ye also change not the law of God in the disorderliness of your doings. The Gentiles went astray, and forsook the Lord, and changed their order, and obeyed stocks and stones, spirits of deceit. But ye shall not be so, my children, recognizing in the firmament, in the earth, and in the sea, and in all created things, the Lord who made all things, that ye become not as Sodom, which changeth the order of nature.[5]

Nature is here obviously regarded as a possible way to God. Cohen begins his chapter on the Rabbinic doctrine of God with the words: "As in the Bible so throughout the literature of the Rabbis, the existence of God is regarded as an axiomatic truth. No proofs are offered to convince the Jew that there must be a God. To avoid the profane use of the sacred name, in accordance with the third commandment various designations were devised, common among them being 'The Creator' and 'He who spake and the world came into being'. They indicate the view that the existence of God follows inevitably from the existence of the Universe."[6] Thus there is a tradition recorded that Abraham dis-

---

[1] Cf. W. Sanday and A. C. Headlam, *Romans (I.C.C.)*, pp. 51 f.; C. H. Dodd, *Romans (M.N.T.C.)*, pp. 26 f. A very good summary of Paul's relation to the Book of Wisdom in scholarship is given in *Ap. and Ps.* vol. 1, pp. 526 f.

[2] W. Sanday and A. C. Headlam, *Romans (I.C.C.)*, pp. 51 f.

[3] Cf. *Ap. and Ps.* vol. 1, pp. 531, 526.   [4] See below, chapter 6.

[5] Test. Naphtali 3. 2 f.   [6] A. Cohen, *Everyman's Talmud*, p. 2.

covered the existence of God by reasoning back to a first cause. When
he refused to accept idolatry, so the tradition runs, King Nimrod
demanded that he should worship fire. The following argument is then
recorded:

> Abraham replied to him: "We should rather worship water which ex-
> tinguishes fire." Nimrod said to him: "Then worship water." Abraham
> retorted: "If so we should worship the cloud which carries water!" Nimrod
> said: "Then worship the cloud." Abraham retorted: "If so, we should
> worship the wind which disperses the cloud!" Nimrod said: "Then worship
> the wind." Abraham retorted: "Rather should we worship the human being
> who carries the wind."[1]

A. Cohen comments on this: "Such a line of reasoning leads to the
hypothesis of an ultimate Creator."[2] The same kind of argument will
also be found in the Apocalypse of Abraham[3] and elsewhere. We see,
therefore, that Paul's statement in Romans 1. 20 ("For the invisible
things of Him from the creation of the world are clearly seen, being
understood by the things that are made, even His eternal power and
Godhead; so that they are without excuse") would be sound Rabbinic
doctrine. In their intercourse with Gentiles the Rabbis would probably
often argue as Paul does in Romans 1.[4]

It is further part of Paul's teaching in Romans 1, as we saw, that it
was the idolatry of the Gentile world that was responsible for its sinful
condition. Here again Paul is reproducing Rabbinic teaching. The
quotation cited above from Test. Naphtali 3. 2f., shows clearly how
idolatry is connected with immorality, and idolatry was, indeed, identified by the Rabbis with immorality. As in the Old Testament, so
among the Rabbis belief in God was not merely a matter of intellectual
import; it concerned the whole personality—the man who denies the
existence of God is morally corrupt.[5] It is significant that in Galatians 5. 20 Paul enumerates idolatry as one of the fruits of the flesh,
calling fornication, uncleanness, inordinate affection, evil concupiscence
and covetousness, simple idolatry.[6] It is clear that the Apostle regarded
idolatry as the expression of the evil impulse: his similarity to the
Rabbis in this matter will be clear from two quotations. In b. Shab. 105 b

---

[1] Gen. R. 38. 13.   [2] A. Cohen, Everyman's Talmud, p. 2.
[3] This belongs to the first century A.D.
[4] Cf. A. Cohen, Everyman's Talmud, p. 3; J. Bonsirven, Le Judaïsme Palestinien,
vol. I, pp. 162 ff.
[5] A. Cohen, Everyman's Talmud, p. iii.
[6] Cf. Col. 3. 5; 1 Cor. 5. 10, 6. 9.

we read: "This is the device of the evil impulse: To-day it says 'Do this', to-morrow 'Do that', till at last it says 'Worship an idol' and the man goes and does it."[1] According to this, idolatry is the last condition to which the *yêtzer hâ-râ'* will reduce a man, so that, by implication, where idolatry is all other evils are present. Again another Rabbi said: "He who hearkened to his evil impulse is as if he practised idolatry: for it is said, 'There shall no strange God be within thee: thou shalt not worship any God.'" Here idolatry is identified with any and every obedience to the *yêtzer hâ-râ'*.[2] The thought that idolatry is the root of all evil would easily suggest itself: to fall down to worship Satan would mean submission to the *yêtzer hâ-râ'*.

Enough has been written to show that however much Paul may have been indebted to Alexandrian ideas in the thought of Romans 1, he was still moving strictly within the realm of Rabbinic ideas. We may state the relationship between Romans 1 and Romans 7 somewhat as follows. The *yêtzer hâ-râ'* was regarded as expressing itself chiefly in two directions; it led to idolatry and to unchastity. Within the nation of Israel it was believed generally that the impulse to idolatry had ceased; it only remained in the Gentile world.[3] In Romans 1 Paul is describing that Gentile world, and in true Rabbinic fashion finds the root of its evil in the most glaring of all the fruits of the evil impulse, idolatry; his first picture of sin is on a large scale in order to show the problem in its true light. Unconsciously of course, he follows Plato, who in order to understand justice in the soul drew a large-scale picture of justice in the State. He gives in Romans 1 the large-scale view of sin and then in Romans 7 draws the picture of his own soul where the *yêtzer hâ-râ'*, that had led to idolatry in the pagan world, was reducing him to impotence and "all manner of concupiscence". In both chapters he has the activity

---

[1] *b. Shab.* 105 *b*. The saying is attributed to Johanan b. Nuri (A.D. 120–40).

[2] *J. Ned.* 9. 41. *b*. The saying is attributed to R. Yannai (A.D. 200–20). The connection between Idolatry and Social Evil was a common theme in contemporary literature. The following references in the *Ap. and Ps.* are worth mentioning: 3 Macc. 6. 11, Wisd. 13–15, Letter of Aristeas, §§ 134 f., Jubilees 9. 4–7, Epistle of Jeremy 4–73, 2 Enoch 10. 6.

[3] Cf. Str.-B. vol. III, pp. 111–12. The Rabbinic teachers regarded it as established that in their time idolatry had no place in Israel, e.g. Judith 8. 18–20 reads: "18. For there arose none in our age, neither is there any now in these days, neither tribe, nor family, nor people, nor city among us, which worship gods made with hands, as hath been aforetime. 19. For the which cause our fathers were given to the sword, and for a spoil, and had a great fall before our enemies. 20. But we know none other God, therefore we trust that he will not despise us, nor any of our nation." It was assumed that either during the exile or soon after, the impulse to idolatry was removed utterly from the people. Cf. Moore, vol. I, p. 222.

of the same power in mind, the activity of the *yêtzer hâ-rẫ*, an activity, moreover, which in the Messianic Age as we saw was destined to be uprooted, and, since Paul had accepted Christ as the Messiah, for him was actually being uprooted. He himself was being delivered from "the body of this death"[1] and the Gentiles were being "turned to God from idols to serve the living and true God".[2]

There remains one other passage (Romans 5. 12f.) with which we have to deal. In the latter sin is connected with the transgression of Adam. "...by one man sin entered into the world and death by sin: and so death passed upon all men for that all have sinned...." Into the various explanations of these words that have been suggested we cannot here enter.[3] The passage does not aim at explaining the existence of sin: it merely asserts the fact that there is a connection between the first man, Adam's transgression and the sinfulness of the world. Paul clearly implies that Adam's sin produced certain effects; it led to death and also had sinful consequences. The sin of the first man meant that not only

---

[1] Cf. Rom. 7. 24.   [2] 1 Thess. 1. 9.

[3] For discussions of this problem, see H. Wheeler Robinson, *The Christian Doctrine of Man*, pp. 112f.; F. R. Tennant, *The Fall and Original Sin*, pp. 253f.; N. P.Williams, *The Ideas of the Fall and of Original Sin*, pp. 124f. We cannot here recapitulate the arguments brought forward by various scholars. H. Wheeler Robinson and F. R. Tennant both deny that Paul asserts a causal relation between the sin of Adam and that of all men: they very largely agree that it is the thought of Adam as the 'corporate personality' which is the clue to Paul's thought. "The moral defilement of man is represented as contracted in and with the sin of Adam" (G. B. Stevens, *The Pauline Theology*, p. 37). On the other hand N. P. Williams, in *The Ideas of the Fall and of Original Sin*, p. 131, claims that there is a causal connection between the transgression of Adam and claims "that the conception which is struggling for expression in St Paul's mind is that of a hereditary disease, somehow introduced into the human stock by Adam's sin", p. 132. The position we have adopted in our discussion lies between that of H. Wheeler Robinson and F. R. Tennant on the one hand and N. P. Williams on the other. Rom. 5. 19 seems to demand a causal connection between Adam's sin and that of his posterity, but the nature of this causal connection is undefined in Paul. We have avoided making Paul too Rabbinic because of this causal connection: if we hold with H. Wheeler Robinson and F. R. Tennant that there is no causal connection, then Paul's thought is purely Rabbinic. According to Moulton-Milligan, καθίστημι in contemporary Greek means 'to give rank as'. Possibly that is Paul's meaning in Rom. 5. 19, that men through the sin of Adam were given rank as sinners, "given facilities for sin, and made apt to sin". This would mean that nothing Paul has written here "suggests that Adam's transgression *compelled* his descendants to sin, and so doomed them inevitably to the penalties of sin". (See K. E. Kirk, *The Clarendon Bible, Romans*, p. 100.) Nevertheless, the distinction between 'causing' and 'making apt to' must be very small, and one doubts if Paul drew this distinction in Rom. 5. 19.

were all subsequent generations born into a world where sin had been committed and would, therefore, inevitably meet with the objective fact of sin, but that through Adam's sin they themselves were made sinners (ὥσπερ γὰρ διὰ τῆς παρακοῆς τοῦ ἑνὸς ἀνθρώπου ἁμαρτωλοὶ κατεστάθησαν οἱ πολλοί, οὕτω καὶ διὰ τῆς ὑπακοῆς τοῦ ἑνὸς δίκαιοι κατασταθήσονται οἱ πολλοί (Romans 5. 19)).[1] Nevertheless, every man fell because of his own sin as is clearly implied in Romans 7; and some scholars have claimed that this is the significance of ἐφ' ᾧ πάντες ἥμαρτον in Romans 5. 12.[2] To infer, however, from the latter that Adam's transgression injected a kind of virus into man's system which made him sin inevitably is to read into the text ideas borrowed from later theological speculation. It is best to find in the words ἐφ' ᾧ πάντες ἥμαρτον the concept of the representative character of Adam's sin. This concept of a solidarity of all mankind in Adam enables Paul to say that in Adam all sinned.[3] This comes out clearly in Paul's treatment of his experience in Romans 7 which, although intensely personal, nevertheless echoes the account of Adam's fall in Genesis. Paul there pictures his own moral struggle in terms of that of Adam. The words in Romans 7. 11, "for sin taking occasion by the commandment, deceived me", are reminiscent of 2 Corinthians 11. 3, where the same verb ἐξαπατάω is used of the deception of Eve, and surely reflect Genesis. There is throughout the chapter, in the words of Dr Dodd, "a side glance at the story of the Fall of Man". For Paul the sin of Adam is the sin of everyman.

In all this Paul was interpreting current Rabbinic thought. The teaching of 4 Ezra and 2 Baruch[4] is closely allied to that of the Apostle. In both Adam's transgression is held to have certain well-defined consequences, and yet every man sins by himself.[5] Thus in 2 Baruch 54. 15-19, we read:

For though Adam first sinned
And brought untimely death upon all,

[1] Cf. N. P. Williams, *The Ideas of the Fall and of Original Sin*, p. 131; Hans Lietzmann, *H.Z.N.T. An die Römer*, p. 64. For death as the result of Adam's fall, Wisd. 2. 23f., Ecclus. 25. 24, 4 Ezra 3. 7, etc.

[2] So H. St J. Thackeray, *The relation of St Paul to Contemporary Jewish Thought*, p. 37. Also Hans Lietzmann, *H.Z.N.T. An die Römer*, p. 61; W. Sanday and A. C. Headlam, *Romans (I.C.C.)*, p. 134; contrast G. B. Stevens, *The Pauline Theology*, pp. 36f.; F. R. Tennant, *The Fall and Original Sin*, p. 257.

[3] For this cf. G. B. Stevens, *The Pauline Theology*, p. 37; C. H. Dodd, *Romans (M.N.T.C.)*, pp. 78f.; and references above given to the works of H. Wheeler Robinson and F. R. Tennant.

[4] Cf. W. O. E. Oesterley, *2 Esdras*, pp. xxvif.

[5] The Introduction to 2 Baruch and 4 Ezra in *Ap. and Ps.* vol. ii, pp. 477f, 555f. should also be consulted.

Yet those who were born from him
Each one of them has prepared for his own soul torment to come,
And again each one of them has chosen for himself glories to come.
Adam is, therefore, not the cause save only of his own soul
But each of us has been the Adam of his own soul.

In the above the responsibility of each individual is emphasized. In 4 Ezra 3. 21–2, however, we read as follows:

For the first Adam, clothing himself with the evil heart, transgressed and was overcome; and likewise also all who were born of him. Thus the infirmity became inveterate; the Law indeed was in the heart of the people, but (in conjunction) with the evil germ; so what was good departed and the evil remained.

Again in 4. 30–2:

For a grain of evil seed was sown in the heart of Adam from the beginning, and how much fruit of ungodliness has it produced unto this time, and shall yet produce until the threshing-floor come!

Again in 7. 116f.:

And I answered and said: This is my first and last word; better had it been that the earth had not produced Adam, or else having produced him, (for thee) to have restrained him from sinning (117). For how does it profit us all that in the present we must live in grief and after death look for punishment? (118). O thou Adam, what hast thou done! For though it was thou that sinned, the fall was not thine alone, but ours also who are thy descendants! For how does it profit us that the eternal age is promised to us, whereas we have done the works that bring death?

In this last passage Adam is accused of having somehow involved the race in perdition. Nevertheless, in verses 127–9 and in 8. 56, the author recognizes human free will, as does the author of 2 Baruch and there is an evident incongruity in his thought. It is difficult not to find this same incongruity although in a less pointed form in all the Rabbinical teaching on Sin. That Adam's sin involved all his posterity, the righteous as well as the wicked, is sound Rabbinical doctrine; but the Rabbis were always anxious to safeguard human freedom, and so could not regard the relation between Adam's sin and the sinfulness of mankind as directly causal. As F. C. Porter has pointed out, "the Jews never regarded the idea that the yêtzer became evil solely through man's sin as adequate. It must rather have explained his sin".[1] The Rabbis do not make it

---

[1] F. C. Porter, "Biblical and Semitic Studies", in *Yale Bicentennial Publications*, p. 118.

clear exactly how, apart from the infliction of death, the sin of
Adam affected all men, but as Moore writes: "there is no notion
that the original constitution of Adam underwent any change in consequence of the fall, so that he transmitted to his descendants a vitiated
nature in which the appetites and passions necessarily prevail over
reason and virtue, while the will to good is enfeebled or wholly
impotent."[1]

The similarity of all this to what we find in Paul will be obvious. It
was what made Adam sin that also made Paul to sin[2] and yet Paul's
sin is related to that of Adam as well; for Paul every man sins both
because of his own submission to the *yêtzer* and also because of the sin
of the first man, Adam. As we saw, Paul no less than the Rabbis would
reject the view that Adam had injected a kind of virus into the human
stock which contaminated all men, but in asserting a direct causal
relation, which he does not describe, between the Fall of Adam and the
sin of all men in Romans 5. 19, he goes beyond the teaching of the
Rabbis, who were careful to insist on the full responsibility of every
individual for his sin despite the effects of Adam's fall. It is possible that
in the sharp contrast that he has drawn between Christ, the Second
Adam, and the first Adam, Paul has been led to a more radical statement
of the significance of the latter than is found in the Rabbis, and it must
be remembered that Paul was not primarily concerned with precise
theological definitions in Romans 5. 12f.[3] Moreover, the Apostle also,
as we saw, by implication at least, insists on the responsibility of the
individual for his sin in Romans 7. If therefore it is claimed that Paul
does emphasize the causal relation between the Fall of Adam and the sin
of his posterity more than do the Rabbis, nevertheless we cannot doubt
that his thought on sin is governed by essentially Rabbinical concepts.
Niebuhr[4] has recently written: "The Christian doctrine of sin in its
classical form offends both rationalists and moralists by maintaining the
seemingly absurd position that man sins inevitably and by a fateful
necessity, but that he is nevertheless to be held responsible for actions
which are prompted by an ineluctable fate. The explicit scriptural foundation for the doctrine is given in Pauline teaching. On the one hand
Paul insists that man's sinful glorification of himself is 'without excuse'.
'So that they are without excuse because that, when they knew God,
they glorified Him not as God.' And on the other hand he regards
human sin as an inevitable defeat, involved in, or derived from, the sin
of the first man. 'Wherefore as by one man sin entered into the world

---

[1] Moore, vol. 1, p. 479.   [2] Cf. Rom. 7.
[3] Cf. N. P. Williams, *The Ideas of the Fall and of Original Sin*, p. 124.
[4] *The Nature and Destiny of Man*, vol. 1, p. 256.

and death by sin and so death passed upon all men for that all have sinned.'" This paradox which Niebuhr refers to in Paul's teaching is a heightened form of what we have found in Rabbinic Judaism, and the assertion both of inevitability and responsibility is an accentuation of the Rabbinic doctrine of sin. Paul is far removed from any Hellenistic dualism where there can be no real responsibility. His teaching on the Second Adam, who to the fight and to the rescue came, will occupy us in the next chapter.

3

THE OLD AND THE NEW HUMANITY:
THE FIRST AND SECOND ADAM

IS experience on the road to Damascus led to a tremendous
deliverance and transformation in the life of Saul of Tarsus.
On the one hand it meant for him redemption from the power
of sin,[1] from the bondage of the Law[2] and from the dominion of unseen
forces of evil, what we might call the demonic element in life.[3] The
terms he uses to proclaim the same truth are familiar, justification to
describe his freedom from guilt before God,[4] remission to express the
cancelling of his debts to God,[5] and reconciliation to mark the removal
of his enmity towards God.[6] These words do not refer to distinct acts
or effects, they are different ways of expressing the one truth, that in
Christ Paul had been freed from what had formerly frustrated him. But
not only had Christ broken for him the dominance of evil, He had also
supplied him with new power. The deliverance of Paul had a positive
content. His Epistles are full of antitheses setting forth the difference
that Christ has made. He refers to an old man who was crucified with
Christ,[7] to the new man put on through Christ;[8] bondage has given
place to liberty;[9] life in the flesh to life in the Spirit.[10] He had been
delivered from the power of darkness and translated into the Kingdom
of His dear Son;[11] delivered from the present evil age into the new age.[12]

Henceforth, it was Paul's primary task in life and thought to interpret
this experience in terms which would be understood by his contemporaries. How was he to express this deliverance and power that had
come to him through Christ? He could not use the terminology that
his Lord had used. Jesus Himself had explained His advent as the arrival
of the Kingdom of God.[13] But Paul's experience at Thessalonica soon
proved to him that however suitable the term βασιλεία had been in
Palestine, its political connotation made it equally unsuitable for use
in the Graeco-Roman world, for the announcement of the arrival of
another βασιλεία, however spiritual, might and actually did lead to
trouble with the Roman authorities.[14] Political considerations, therefore,

[1] Rom. 8. 3.   [2] Ibid. 10. 3; Gal. 3. 13.
[3] Rom. 8. 15; Col. 2. 15; Eph. 6. 10–16.   [4] Rom. 3. 21.
[5] Col. 1. 14.   [6] 2 Cor. 5. 18.   [7] Rom. 6. 6.
[8] Col. 3. 10.   [9] Gal. 4. 3, 9 and 5. 1.   [10] Rom. 8.
[11] Col. 1. 13.   [12] Gal. 1. 4.   [13] Mark 1. 15.
[14] W. L. Knox, *St Paul and the Church of Jerusalem*, p. 271, nn. 7 and 8. See Acts 17. 7–8.

compelled Paul to seek other ways to describe what the Synoptics called "the arrival of the Kingdom of God". We have seen that he used the terminology of the two ages, a concept that was perfectly familiar to the Rabbinic Judaism of his day.[1] In the coming of Christ *hâ-'ôlâm ha-bâ'*, on which the eyes of the Jewish world were set, had suddenly moved from the distant horizon and become present fact. But he also described the advent of Christ in another striking figure that was also familiar to his Jewish contemporaries—it was a new creation. The radical character of his experience in Christ he described as καινὴ κτίσις;[2] all things have become new;[3] the light which he saw in the face of Jesus he compares with the light at creation;[4] when he speaks of the groaning of the whole creation and its travailing in pain together, he is almost certainly thinking of the account of creation given in Genesis as the counterpart of the new creation in Christ.[5]

In describing the Christian Dispensation as a New Creation Paul, as we have said, was using terms familiar to Judaism. There are passages in the Old Testament where the Messianic Age is pictured in cosmological terms, as a return to the perfection of the beginning,[6] but Judaism generally discouraged speculation of a cosmological kind. The discussion of Gen. 1. 2 and Ezekiel 1. 4ff. was forbidden: they were considered subjects suitable only for the few. Because certain mystical and esoteric groups within Judaism had made these chapters the object of study, and many had been corrupted thereby, cosmological speculation was regarded as a menace to religious faith. Even as early as Ecclesiasticus such studies were suspect: the reader is warned ". . .in what is permitted to thee instruct thyself, thou hast no business in secret things".[7] Nevertheless, one factor made it inevitable that Messianic speculation should

---

[1] For the Doctrine of the Two Ages, cf. Str.-B. vol. IV, pp. 799f.

[2] Gal. 6. 15.

[3] 2 Cor. 5. 17. For the meaning of καινός here, cf. A. Plummer, 2 Cor. 3. 6, p. 85. *Second Corinthians (I.C.C.)* ". . .καινός always implies superiority to that which is not καινός, whereas what is νέος may be either inferior or better than what is not νέος." Cf. also J. B. Lightfoot on Col. 3. 10 in *The Epistles of St Paul, Colossians and Philemon*, p. 213.

[4] 2 Cor. 4. 6.

[5] Rom. 8. 22, 23, 26; cf. C. H. Dodd, *The Bible and the Greeks*, p. 106.

[6] Isa. 11. 6, 65. 25. (Note the addition of the reference to the serpent in Isa. 65. 25.)

[7] Ecclus. 3. 21–4; cf. M. *Ḥagigah* 2. 1; Danby, pp. 212f.; *b. Ḥagigah* 13a; and A. Cohen, *Everyman's Talmud*, pp. 29f. The Rabbis were generally practical and not speculative in their interests; cf. P. *Aboth* 1. 17; G. G. Scholem, *Major Trends in Jewish Mysticism*, pp. 41f. See on *Ma'aseh Bereshith* and *Ma'aseh Merkabah* Moore, vol. I, pp. 383f. and pp. 411f. respectively.

pursue the cosmological turn given to it as early as Isaiah. This was the growth within Judaism of interest in the doctrine of the Fall of Adam depicted in Genesis.

It is clear that the Exile had burnt the sense of sin into the very being of the Jewish nation.[1] The clear but too facile prophetic or Deuteronomic interpretation of Israel's tragic history no longer satisfied.[2] Judaism had to seek for new explanations of the origin and prevalence of sin and its consequences. F. R. Tennant and N. P. Williams have both shown how it first fixed on the legend of the descent of the watchers in Gen. 6. 1–4 as the explanation of the origin of sin. Later, however, attention was more and more fixed on Gen. 3, which by the first century A.D. played the predominant part in all mythological speculation on the origin of sin.[3] What was originally merely a warning of a primitive kind against the dangers of knowledge became of primary importance in Jewish thought.[4] Genesis 3 was first taken as teaching merely that death came into the world through Adam's sin.[5] In the Book of Jubilees the effects of the Fall of Adam are extended to the animal creation;[6] and in the Apocalypse of Baruch and 4 Ezra and the later Midrashic literature the cosmical disarrangements caused by the sin of Adam are more and more emphasized.[7] We are not here concerned with the moral or spiritual results attributed to Adam's Fall but merely with the fact that it had cosmological significance.

The evidence that this was so is amply given by Strack-Billerbeck in their commentary on Rom. 8. 20f.[8] The world had been created for the sake of man;[9] it had been created for man's service.[10] When Adam sinned, therefore, the whole creation became involved in corruption.[11]

[1] W. O. E. Oesterley and T. H. Robinson, *Hebrew Religion*, p. 296.

[2] Ibid. pp. 308f.

[3] Cf. F. R. Tennant, *The Fall and Original Sin*, pp. 235f.; N. P. Williams, *The Ideas of the Fall and of Original Sin*, pp. 20f.

[4] Ibid. pp. 49f.

[5] Ecclus. 24. 24; cf. F. R. Tennant, op. cit. pp. 119f.

[6] Jubilees 3. 28–9.

[7] Cf. F. R. Tennant, op. cit. pp. 238f.

[8] Here Paul describes the creation as subject unto vanity, etc., and is clearly reflecting current Rabbinic speculation upon creation (cf. C. H. Dodd, *The Bible and the Greeks*, p. 106). Str.-B. vol. III, pp. 247f.

[9] Cf. 4 Ezra 8. 44, 6. 55, 59, 7. 11, 8. 1; *Gen. R.* 28. 6; *M. Sanhedrin* 4. 5; cf. Danby, p. 388.

[10] Cf. 4 Ezra 6. 45; *Gen. R.* 8. on 1. 26; *Pesikta* 36b—referring to a saying by R. Simeon (c. A.D. 180).

[11] Cf. 4 Ezra 8. 11: "For their sakes I made the world and when Adam transgressed my commandments, that which had been made was condemned"; Apoc. Baruch 23. 4; *M. Sanhedrin* 4. 5; *Gen. R.* 28. 6, 23. 6.

Opinions differed as to whether the physical world had lost its pristine perfection through its own sin, e.g. because the earth had allowed unfruitful trees to grow rather than fruitful ones, or had become involved in corruption willy-nilly because of man's sin (Paul in Rom. 8. 20 seems to accept the latter view). Similarly some held that the beasts had themselves, like man, disobeyed their Creator, all except the Phoenix, and so entered into corruption. In any case various cosmic disorders followed Adam's sin, the circulation of the planets was affected, fruit took longer to ripen on the trees, vermin appeared on the earth, wild beasts acquired their ferocity and obstinacy and lost their speech.[1] Six things in particular followed the Fall: the earth lost its fruitfulness, as did the trees, and the atmosphere ceased to be clear; while as for man he lost the glory of his appearance, the eternity of his life, and the magnitude of his form.[2]

It was over against this background of a Fall which had involved the cosmos that the Messianic Age was conceived: it would have to undo the evil consequences of that Fall.[3] Schürer has long since traced clearly how the older Messianism of the Old Testament, which was national, had given place in our period to a wider Messianism which included all mankind in its scope: "even the irrational creation, heaven and earth and the whole universe" would be transformed.[4] There was, of course, no one fixed orthodox view on such matters as this, but it was generally recognized that the Messianic Age would correspond to the beginning of all things. This is explicitly set forth in 4 Ezra 7. 29, 32: "And the world shall return to its first silence seven days, as it was at the beginning so that no man is left."[5] It follows that the Messiah would have to be a figure of cosmic significance, capable of restoring the whole universe to its original condition, the master not only of man but of nature. It further follows that once Paul had become convinced that Jesus was the Messiah it was natural that he should have assigned to him cosmic functions, and regarded the Christian Dispensation as a new creation that redressed the balance of the old. Inevitably "the Christian conception of Redemption is the counterpart of the Jewish conception of Creation".[6]

[1] Cf. Str.-B. vol. III, p. 250; Jubilees 3. 1-35.
[2] Cf. Str.-B. vol. IV, pp. 799f. and F. R. Tennant, *The Fall and Original Sin*, pp. 150f.
[3] Cf. Str.-B. vol. IV, pp. 799f.
[4] Schürer, *The Jewish People in the Time of Jesus Christ*, vol. II, Div. II, pp. 130f.
[5] 4 Ezra 8. 29-32; also 2 Baruch 3. 7; cf. Moore, vol. II, p. 303. The passage quoted from 4 Ezra refers to a period at the end of the Messianic Age, but the principle discussed applies to all the Messianic Period.
[6] Cf. C. H. Dodd, *The Bible and the Greeks*, p. 106. It is worth referring here to Manson's words: "the end corresponds to the beginning because the purpose of God, which runs through and determines the whole process is one and homogeneous

C. F. Burney has convincingly pointed out this truth. He writes:[1] "There is an essential unity in the teaching of St Luke, St Paul and St John as to the mode and meaning of the Incarnation which ought not to be overlooked. All go back in thought to the appearance of Jesus Christ on earth as a new creation to be compared and contrasted with the first creation of the world and of mankind, and all therefore drew on Gen. 1. 2, in working out their theme." We have already referred to passages in Paul's Epistles which support this view.[2] In Luke 1. 35 there is a clear reference to Gen. 1. 2, where, to quote Burney again: "the spirit of God is pictured as brooding or hovering over the face of the waters in the initial process of creation, which issues in the production of light. So for St Luke the Divine Birth means the dawning of ἀνατολὴ ἐξ ὕψους, ἐπιφᾶναι τοῖς ἐν σκότει καὶ σκιᾷ θανάτου καθημένοις (Luke 1. 78, 79) and φῶς εἰς ἀποκάλυψιν ἐθνῶν (Luke 2. 32)." For the relation of the Incarnation to Creation in the Fourth Gospel we have only to refer to the Prologue.[3] Finally we may see, though indeed less pointedly, in Matt. 1. 23: "Behold a virgin shall be with child and shall bring forth a son, and they shall call his name Emmanuel, which being interpreted is, God with us", the awareness of the inauguration of a new epoch such as God had called into being at creation.

It is not fantastic to trace the same thought of Jesus as the Lord of Creation in other passages in Mark and Luke. Thus in Mark 4. 35f. we find the story of the storm followed in Mark 5. 1-20 by the healing of the Gerasene demoniac. The description of the storm is reminiscent of Ps. 113. 3f. In the latter God is pictured as the One who is above the "voice of many waters", and who also can save his people "from the tumult of evil and oppression".[4] Again all the Synoptists in their descriptions of the End refer to certain physical phenomena which clearly imply the cosmic significance of Jesus; and in Luke 21. 25, after a description of the distress at the End such as we get in Matthew and Mark, there is a reference to "the sea and the waves roaring". What are we to make of this? Turning again to Mark 4. 35 and 5. 1-20, which we compared with Ps. 113. 3f., we note that there are many passages similar to Ps. 113. 3f. in the Old Testament, e.g. Isa, 5. 30; Ps. 64. 8; Ps. 93. 3f. Jer. 5. 22; 38. 36 (31. 35), where the LXX reveals clear traces of cosmo-

---

throughout. The end answers to the beginning because all things are in the hands of God who sees the end from the beginning." T. W. Manson, *The Teaching of Jesus*, p. 247, n. 2.

[1] Cf. *The Aramaic Origin of the Fourth Gospel*, p. 43.
[2] Cf. Gal. 6. 15; 2 Cor. 5. 17; Rom. 8. 22f.
[3] Cf. C. F. Burney, *The Aramaic Origin of the Fourth Gospel*, p. 44.
[4] Cf. E. Hoskyns and N. Davey, *The Riddle of the New Testament*, pp. 86f.

logical mythology, and we cannot doubt that in Mark 4. 35 and 5. 1–20 the Incarnation is thought of as a new creation. Christ commands the storm as God did the cl aos at the beginning. This thought cannot have been far away in this passage from Mark. Furthermore, however, it is to be remarked that the noise at creation is far more emphasized in those passages in the LXX, to which we referred, than in the account of creation in Genesis where only the onomatopoeic root *hûm* suggests noise in the Hebrew text and even this is lost in the LXX rendering, and Dr Dodd has pointed out that "Gunkel is probably right in deriving all such passages from the early creation mythology of Israel lying behind the restrained and sober creation narrative of Genesis",[1] and it is probable that when Luke 21. 25 refers to συνοχὴ ἐθνῶν ἐν ἀπορίᾳ ἤχους θαλάσσης καὶ σάλου we are to find an allusion to the primeval chaos: Luke's thoughts turn to the beginning of all things as he thinks of his Lord.

We conclude from all this that the ascription of Messiahship to Jesus implied from the first that He had cosmic significance, and that for Christians His Advent was a new creation.

In view of the interpretation of His Advent as a new creation the transition to the thought of Christ as the Second Adam was easy and ultimately almost inevitable. Paul we know made this transition and explicitly called Jesus 'the Second Adam'—the counterpart of the Adam whose creation was described in Gen. 1. 2.[2] We have now to inquire whether Paul originated this conception or received it from the Church, because there are certain elements in the New Testament which might suggest that the identification of Christ with the Second Adam is pre-Pauline.

We begin with Phil. 2. 6f. Dealing with this passage as a pre-Pauline Christian hymn', Hunter writes:[3] "Its theme is Jesus, the Second Adam, who, conquering the temptation to which the first Adam fell, chose the role of the suffering servant and for his obedience unto death was highly exalted by God and made Lord of the whole cosmos." Rawlinson explains the passage in the same light, as the deliberate contrast of Christ with the first Adam.[4] Hunter, moreover, goes on to infer that Paul's conception of Christ as the Second Adam (Rom. 5. 12–21; 1 Cor. 15. 45–9)

---

[1] Cf. C. H. Dodd, *The Bible and the Greeks*, p. 106. See H. Gunkel, *Schöpfung und Chaos*, and W. O. E. Oesterley, *The Evolution of the Messianic Idea*, for the treatment of this whole question.

[2] Cf. 1 Cor. 15. 22, 45; Rom. 5. 12f. Actually Paul speaks of the *last* Adam.

[3] In *Paul and His Predecessors*, p. 46.

[4] Cf. A. E. J. Rawlinson, *The New Testament Doctrine of the Christ*, p. 134.

goes back to the pre-Pauline Christian tradition.¹ But this does not necessarily follow. Philippians was written nearly at the end of Paul's life, so that the hymn he quotes might well be the work, if not of the Apostle himself, at least of a disciple of his. We do not know enough about the authorship of this hymn to base any argument upon it as to Paul's derivation of the category of the Second Adam. There is nothing in the text to indicate that Paul is quoting the work of any other person; he employs the hymn as if it were part and parcel of his customary exhortation.²

We next notice that if the identification of Christ with the Second Adam was pre-Pauline we should expect it to have left its mark on the Synoptic Gospels and especially in the accounts of the Temptation where there would be obvious occasion for contrasting Christ with Adam. There are differences between the accounts of the Temptation in Matthew, Mark and Luke. It is likely that those in Matthew and Luke which are derived from Q are to be regarded as imaginative expansions of a midrashic kind. The latter "need not originally have referred to the same occasion as Mark 1. 12–13: they might equally well have been a comprehensive picture of the temptations to which Jesus was exposed throughout his ministry (cf. Mark 8. 33)".³ It is by no means possible to connect the Q version of the Temptation with the contemporary teaching about the Temptation of Adam. But when we turn to the Marcan version, which is the most original, there are elements that are very difficult to explain. The phrase καὶ ἦν μετὰ τῶν θηρίων is peculiar to Mark. What is its significance? Can it be that Mark here has the first Adam in mind who was tempted along with the wild beasts?⁴ The presence of the angels is easily explicable on this assumption also. It was part of Rabbinic tradition that the angels had been asked by God to worship Adam and led by Satan they had refused.⁵ In contrast to this Christ was ministered to by the angels. It does seem that in the Marcan account of the Temptation the scenery is the Garden of Eden and Christ is placed against the same background as was the first Adam. The Marcan narrative, however, although it possibly lends itself to the view

¹ A. M. Hunter, *Paul and His Predecessors*, p. 51.
² Cf. Eph. 5. 14, where διὸ λέγει introduces the hymn "and indicates an express citation"; A. M. Hunter, op. cit. pp. 44–5.
³ *Transactions of C. H. Dodd's Seminar* (Cambridge, 1938), privately circulated.
⁴ Cf. Mark 1. 13; Gen. 2. 18f. The relations of Adam and the wild beasts are often mentioned. The fall involved the beasts—Str.-B. vol. III, pp. 250f. See also 2 Enoch 53. 6, *Ap. and Ps.* vol. II, p. 464 n. 5.
⁵ Cf. W. Bousset, *Hauptprobleme der Gnosis*, pp. 198f; b. Sanh. 59b; Slavonic—Enoch 31. 3. See also *Pirkê de Rabbi Eliezer*, § xiii, p. 91, n. 3.

that Christ was here conceived as the Second Adam, victorious over temptation, is so meagre that nothing can be built on it for our purpose. Moreover, since the Q version of the Temptation has no allusions to Adam's experience, and since Hebrews which makes the Temptation of Christ central has no reference to Adam,[1] it is natural to infer that the juxtaposition of Christ and Adam was not prevalent.

Before leaving this question as to the origin of Paul's doctrine we have to consider also the view set forth by Burney in *The Aramaic Origin of the Fourth Gospel*.[2] In his treatment of 1 Cor. 15. 45 he comes to the conclusion that the whole verse from οὕτω καὶ γέγραπται down to ζωοποιοῦν is a quotation:

Whence was it derived? There can be no doubt that the form in which Paul's argument is cast is influenced by Rabbinic speculation and that the Rabbinism of Palestine.... But prior to St Paul's conversion the earliest circle of Christian believers at Jerusalem was drawn not merely from the peasant class, but embraced (according to Acts 6. 7) "a great company of priests" who would scarcely have been unversed in Rabbinic teaching but may be supposed to have applied such learning as they had acquired to the service of the new Faith. It is by no means improbable, therefore, that the passage as a whole may have been drawn from a collection of Old Testament Testimonia composed with the object of meeting Rabbinic Judaism upon its own ground. ...If then this interpretation of 1 Cor. 15. 45 as wholly a quotation be correct, the implication is that some time before St Paul wrote his epistle in A.D. 55-6 the antithesis between the first Adam and Christ as the Second Adam had been worked out in Christian Rabbinic circles and was used in argument.[3]

Two things make us question this presentation of the case by Burney. First, he implies that the priests who became Christians had speculative interests such as would lead them to the thought of Christ as the Second Adam. We only hear of these priests in Acts,[4] and as far as our evidence goes, they played no influential part in the life of the Early Church. The leading priests were usually Sadducean, i.e. they did not generally belong to the reflective section of Judaism; they were usually more concerned with liturgical minutiae and with ecclesiastical politics than with theology. The latter was chiefly the preserve of the Pharisees, to whom Paul belonged.[5] Secondly, since the labours of J. Rendel Harris[6] in this field, it is agreed that there were Testimonia, passages

---

[1] Cp. Heb. 4. 15.   [2] Pp. 43-8.
[3] Cf. pp. 45 f.   [4] Cf. Acts 6. 7.
[5] Cf. N. H. Snaith, *The Priesthood and the Temple; A Companion to the Bible* (ed. T. W. Manson), pp. 431 f. In fairness to Burney, however, it must be noted that a number of Pharisees did join the Church. Cf. Acts 15. 5; Lev Gillet, *Communion in the Messiah*, p. 5.
[6] Cf. *Testimonies* (with Vacher Burch).

of Scripture collected together, which might be used as quotations in the defence of the Faith. Indeed, it is possible that the Testimonia were composed not merely from verses of Scripture but also from Midrashic expansions upon these. Certain well-defined blocks of Scripture were used by Christians, but there is no evidence that Gen. 1, 2 formed part of such Testimonia. We know that the verse quoted by Paul in 1 Cor. 15. 45, i.e. Gen. 2. 7, was not a favourite one for discussion among the Rabbis[1] and the New Testament only makes use of it at this point. Had it been part of the Testimonia of the early Church and had it been used for the Christ as the Second Adam there would surely be traces of it elsewhere. This tells very strongly indeed against Burney's hypothesis.[2]

We may conclude from the foregoing that whereas the idea of the Christian Dispensation as a new creation was pre-Pauline, the conception of Christ as the Second Adam was probably introduced into the Church by Paul himself. What it meant to him we have now to enquire. We shall first deal with speculations about Adam or the First Man in the contemporary world and then discuss their relevance to Paul's interpretation of Christ as the Second Adam.

We have seen that the deepened sense of sin which the experience of the Exile produced within the nation of Israel eventually led to speculation on the story of the Fall in Gen. 3, and so it is that whereas the idea of the Fall played little, if any, part in the Old Testament,[3] a marked feature of Judaism in the centuries preceding the Christian era was the

---

[1] Cf. Str.-B. vol. III, p. 477. The readings of the Targums are given by Str.-B. Dr D. Daube makes the following suggestion: "Targum Onkelos translates Gen. 2. 7 by a 'speaking' creature (ממלל) not a 'living', i.e. he interprets חיה as חוה. The Jerushalemite Targum goes further and refers to speech, sight and hearing. I just wonder whether they were out to make impossible the Christian, Pauline use of this passage as referring to 'life' in an exalted sense; and whether they tried to insist that 'living creature' meant simply a creature that speaks, sees and hears." (In a private communication.)

[2] It is significant, for example, that E. Hoskyns and N. Davey, in dealing with the interweaving of the Old Testament with the New Testament to show that it was the Old Testament context that gave redemptive significance to the life and death of Jesus, do not need to refer to Gen. 1, 2 at all; cf. *The Riddle of the New Testament*.

C. F. Burney's further point that Luke carries the genealogy of Jesus back to Adam because he is comparing the birth of Adam, by an act of God, with that of Christ, which happened in the same way, does not concern us here, because, as he himself points out, it is likely that Luke may have owed this conception to Paul's doctrine of the Christ as the Second Adam: or Luke's speculation may be derived from Hellenistic sources.

[3] Cf. H. Wheeler Robinson, *The Christian Doctrine of Man*, pp. 58f.; W. O. E. Oesterley, 2 Esdras, p. xxv.

growth of speculation about the Fall and about the First Man, Adam. It has been held that the impetus for this came from Iranian and ulti- mately Aryan and Babylonian mythology;[1] but such a hypothesis is not necessary. The myth of the *Ur-mensch* it is true was in the air throughout the period, but Jewish preoccupation with the problem of sin and its relation to Adam is enough to account for the growth of tradi- tions about the latter.[2] Passages in Ezekiel and possibly in the Book of Job show that the First Man had early exercised the minds of Jewish thinkers. Thus in Job 15. 7ff. "there is an obvious allusion to a legend that the first man was a kind of demi-god, created before the hills, who had access to the council of God and acquired extraordinary knowledge of the mysteries of the world".[3] And again in Ezek. 28 "we find what is undoubtedly an account of the expulsion from Eden applied in a figurative manner to the downfall of the King of Tyre". (This was so interpreted by the Rabbis.)[4] It is probable, though not certain, that both these passages refer to Adam, they at least point to traditions about the First Man in which the latter appears in a far more glorious guise than in the J document of the Pentateuch.[5] As time went on and the consequences of the Fall were more and more dwelt upon it was natural that the pre-fallen condition of Adam should be more and more glorified in order to heighten the tragedy of the Fall.[6] To his glorification we now turn.

First, then, Adam as created by God was no ordinary man; he was of an enormous size extending from one end of the earth to the other,[7] and from heaven to earth.[8] At the Fall he was reduced to 100 yards, the first authority to attribute this length to him being R. Meir[9] (c. A.D. 150).

[1] See J. M. Creed in *J.T.S.* vol. XXVI, pp. 113–36; W. Manson, *Jesus the Messiah*, pp. 174–90, Appendix D; W. Bousset, *Hauptprobleme der Gnosis*, pp. 160ff.

[2] Cf. C. H. Dodd, *The Bible and the Greeks*, p. 146, n. 1: "In view of the state of the evidence it seems probable that even if Iranian mythology gave an impetus to such speculations, the Ἄνθρωπος doctrine in its familiar Hellenistic forms owes much to direct reflection by Jewish thinkers and others influenced by them, upon the mysterious story of man's origin told in Genesis, and possibly to more fantastic forms of that story handed down in Jewish tradition. Adam is probably more directly the ancestor of the Hellenistic Ἄνθρωπος than Gayomard." Contrast W. Manson, *Jesus the Messiah*, p. 178.

[3] Cf. F. R. Tennant, *The Fall and Original Sin*, pp. 61f.

[4] Ibid. p. 63; and Str.-B. vol. III, p. 478; *Pesikta* 36b.

[5] Cf. F. R. Tennant, op. cit. pp. 61ff.; N. P. Williams, *The Ideas of the Fall and of Original Sin*, p. 56.   [6] Cf. N. P. Williams, op. cit. p. 56.

[7] Cf. Str.-B. vol. III, p. 325. The view is traced back to R. Eliezer b. Azariah (A.D. 100), *Pesikta* R. 115a.

[8] Cf. Str.-B. vol. IV, p. 946; *Gen. R.* 8. 1.

[9] *Pesikta* 1b. See Str.-B. vol. IV, p. 947.

Although there is nothing to that effect in Genesis, Adam was conceived as being created immortal,[1] one day in his life might correspond to a thousand years.[2] Adam was also possessed of a glory derived from God Himself. There was an indescribable brightness in his face, the brightness of the sole of his foot darkened the Sun, how much brighter was his face![3] The light which he possessed enabled him to see throughout the world.[4] His difference from ordinary mortals is emphasized also by his bisexuality.[5] Moreover Adam was worthy of the worship of angels.[6] They had been 'best-men' at his wedding and had served him at table.[7] Finally, the wisdom of Adam was continually praised. His wisdom exceeded that of the angels in that he was able to name all the beasts of the earth, while the angels could not.[8]

The First Man was therefore altogether glorious; his fall was correspondingly disastrous. As we have seen, according to R. Meir his size was reduced as a result of the Fall to 100 yards;[9] he lost also the glory of his appearance, whether on the Sabbath or on the day previous authorities differed,[10] and, of course, his immortality was lost.[11] There is a sharp distinction drawn between Adam before and after the Fall, but there is no justification for saying with Tennant that "we meet in the Midrash, as in the writings of Philo, with the distinction between

[1] Cf. Str.-B. vol. IV, p. 887. 4 Ezra 3. 7; 2 Baruch 17. 3, 23. 4. (See *Ap. and Ps.* vol. II, p. 495, n. 4); *Sifre Deut.* on 32. 32, § 323, which traced this view to R. Judah (c. A.D. 150); cf. Str.-B. vol. III, p. 227.

[2] Cf. Jubilees 2. 23. Also W. L. Knox, *St Paul and the Church of the Gentiles*, p. 7; cf. Str.-B. (on 2 Pet. 3. 8), vol. III, p. 773.

[3] Cf. Str.-B. vol. IV, p. 887. The view is derived from R. Simeon b. Menasya (c. A.D. 180), but that the tradition is early is proved by the fact that it is found in Sirach 49. 16; cf. Charles, *Ap. and Ps.* vol. I, p. 507: "The thought implicit here seems to be that Adam, in virtue of having been directly created by God, without human parentage, enjoys a glory which is not shared by any other member of the human race (cf. Luke 3. 38). This idealization of Adam is a notable feature and occurs here for the first time in Jewish literature...." Cf. *Pesikta*, 36b.

[4] b. Baba Bathra 58a; cf. W. Bousset, *Hauptprobleme der Gnosis*, p. 198.

[5] Cf. Str.-B. vol. I, p. 802; *Gen. R.* 8. 1. There was a tradition traceable to A.D. 260 that when God created the first man the latter had two faces: he was later sawn asunder to form two persons; cf. W. Bousset, *Hauptprobleme der Gnosis*, p. 198.

[6] Cf. Adam and Eve 12. 1 (*Ap. and Ps.* vol. II, p. 137).

[7] Cf. Str.-B. vol. II, p. 702, traced to R. Judah b. Tema (c. A.D. 165); b. Sanh. 59b.

[8] Cf. Jubilees 3. 1-35; *Pesikta* 34a; Str.-B. vol. III, p. 681; *Pirkê de Rabbi Eliezer*, § xiii, p. 91.

[9] See above, p. 45.

[10] Cf. Str.-B. vol. IV, pp. 887, 940; *Pesikta Rabbati* 115a.

[11] Ibid. p. 887; 4 Ezra 3. 7; 2 Baruch 17. 3, 23. 4; *Sifre Deut.* on 32. 32, § 323.

a celestial Adam made in the image of God and the earthly Adam".[1] Judaism knew no such distinction. There was one Adam who was made from the earth,[2] whose life was sharply divided into two parts by the Fall, but there was no difference in kind between Adam before and after his fall.

Paul would naturally be familiar with this often fantastic speculation about the First Man within Judaism. But he would also be brought into contact with other developments of the 'Adamic' doctrine. Whilst within Rabbinic Judaism itself speculation about the First Man and his Fall had led to the glorification of Adam—in Hellenistic circles it had been modified by Platonism. Philo in particular shows this development. His treatment of Genesis is familiar.

Recognizing that there were two accounts of the creation of man in Gen. 1, 2 he assumed that the two chapters dealt with two different men. In true Platonic fashion he distinguished between a Heavenly Man whose creation is described in Gen. 1 and an earthly man whose formation is described in Gen. 2. He writes: "There are two kinds of men. The one is Heavenly Man, the other earthly. The Heavenly Man being in the image of God has no part in corruptible substance, or in any earthly substance, whatever; but the earthly man was made of germinal matter which the writer calls 'dust'. For this reason he does not say that the Heavenly Man was created (πεπλάσθαι) but that he was stamped with the image of God (κατ' εἰκόνα τετυπῶσθαι θεοῦ), whereas the earthly man is a creature (πλάσμα) and not the offspring (γέννημα) of the Creator."[3] That the Heavenly Man is after the image of God is not to be understood in a physical sense. "He says that man was made in the image and likeness of God; and he says well, for there is no earthly being liker God than man. But no one must suppose that this similarity is in bodily shape: for God is not anthropomorphic nor is the human body God-shaped. But the word 'image' refers to the mind which is the governor of the soul."[4] He further describes the Heavenly Man thus: "Man after God's image is a (Platonic) idea, a genus, a type (σφραγίς), noumenal, incorporeal, neither male nor female, by nature immortal."[5]

As Bousset has pointed out,[6] Philo deals more fully with the earthly than with the Heavenly Man, and shares in the glorification of Adam which we met in Rabbinic Judaism. The earthly man is very glorious

---

[1] Cf. F. R. Tennant, *The Fall and Original Sin*, p. 149.
[2] Cf. Gen. 2. 7 עָפָר מִן הָאֲדָמָה.
[3] *Leg. Alleg.* I. 31; C. H. Dodd's translation; Cohn-Wendland, vol. I, p. 69.
[4] *De Opif.* § 69; Cohn-Wendland, vol. I, p. 23.
[5] Ibid. p. 46.
[6] W. Bousset, *Hauptprobleme der Gnosis*, pp. 194 f.

because "the copy of a supremely beautiful model must itself of necessity be beautiful".[1] Drummond[2] has accurately paraphrased Philo's picture:

The first earth-born man, the founder of our whole race, had the noblest endowments of both mind and body and was in very truth beautiful and good. The fairness of his bodily form may be conjectured from three considerations. Since the earth was newly created, the material out of which things were made was unmixed and pure. Moreover, God was not likely to have selected any common portion of the earth out of which to mould this statue in the human form, but to have taken from pure material the purest and best sifted part; for the body was contrived as a house or sacred temple of rational soul, which it was to bear as the most God-like of images. And, lastly, the Creator was good, not only in other respects, but in knowledge, so that each part was both excellent in itself and exactly adapted to the entire organism.... He (the earthly man) was anxious to say and do everything to please the Father and King, following him in the paths of virtue... he passed his time in unmingled blessedness... he excelled in every noble quality and reached the very limit of human bliss.

Philo could not attribute all the qualities that the Rabbis attributed to Adam to his earthly man. We have seen, for example, that asexuality was ascribed by him, not to the earthly, but to the Heavenly Man. Similarly, he refers some things in Gen. 1. 2 to the latter and others to the former. Thus, Gen. 2. 15, "the Lord took the man whom he made and set him in paradise to work and to keep," he refers to the Heavenly Man because he could 'keep' virtue intact, i.e. persist in it, while the earthly man could not.[3] It is the earthly man who receives the commandment, the Heavenly Man had no need of such.[4]

To attempt, however, to distinguish Rabbinic and Platonic elements in Philo is precarious. A writer in the *Jewish Encyclopedia*[5] traces the idea of the Heavenly Man as ἀνδρόγυνος to an ancient midrash: he refers to b.'Erub. 18a and Gen. R. 8 according to which Gen. 1. 27 implies bisexuality. But Strack-Billerbeck have pointed out that the idea is found in the *Symposium* of Plato[6] and that Philo may have derived it from there. The same applies to the statement that the idea of the Heavenly Man in Philo is derived from a Pharisaic Midrash on Psalm 139. 5.[7] Apart from the date

[1] De Opif. § 139; Cohn-Wendland, vol. I, pp. 48f.; 2 Enoch 30. 10–18.
[2] James Drummond, *Philo Judaeus*, vol. II, p. 278.
[3] Ibid. p. 276.
[4] *Leg. Alleg.* 1. 30; Cohn-Wendland, vol. I, p. 85.
[5] Vol. I, pp. 176f. (K. Kohler).
[6] Cf. Str.-B. vol. IV, pp. 405f.; *Symposium*, § 189: one wonders, however, how serious was Plato at this point.
[7] Gen. R. 8. 1.

of the midrash (fifth century) it seems easier to account for the Heavenly Man in Philo along Platonic lines.[1] What we can be sure of is that Philo reveals an interweaving of Jewish and Platonic speculation on the First Man. That he was not alone in this is clear from the Hermetic writings, especially from the Poimandres, which probably dates from the early second or even late in the first century. Dr Dodd has shown that here, too, Platonic, Stoic and Jewish doctrines are combined.[2] It is fair to infer that in Paul's day throughout the cultured Mediterranean world the Heavenly Man or the First Man, however he might be termed, was the source of a perpetual interchange of thought and discussion. This had resulted in a twofold development; within Rabbinic Judaism in the glorification of Adam, and in Hellenistic Judaism in the distinction between a Celestial and an earthly Adam; and there were doubtless many varieties of these developments in which now the Rabbinic and now the Platonic emphasis prevailed.

What relation has all this to Paul's doctrine of the Second Adam as it occurs in 1 Cor. 15? From the latter we gather that there were two main controversial issues with which the Apostle had to deal—the fact and the manner of the Resurrection[3] from the dead.[4] It has been claimed that throughout the chapter Paul has to fight a battle on two fronts, against a Hellenistic denial of all Resurrection of the Dead in the interests of a mistaken 'spirituality', and against a too crass Rabbinic materialism as to the method of the Resurrection.[5] He has to assert the reality and centrality of the Resurrection against those who claimed that the soul could exist without a body, and also to re-interpret the Resurrection in such a way as to show that it was not the flesh and blood that was to be raised but a body new in kind, 'a spiritual body'.

We shall examine this view later when we shall have occasion to enter into the detailed examination of 1 Cor. 15. What is important to notice at this point is that it is the principle that the *Endzeit* corresponds to the *Urzeit* that governs Paul's thought, and hence in thinking of the Risen Lord he is led naturally to contrast Him with the first Adam. Just as the first Adam had introduced the order of animate life on the physical or earthly plane, so Christ the Second Adam had introduced a new order of life in the spirit.[6] The reference to Adam is abrupt. Rawlinson writes:

[1] C. H. Dodd, *The Bible and the Greeks*, p. 209.
[2] Ibid. pp. 209 and 100.
[3] The Resurrection of Jesus was not in question.
[4] Cf. in this connection the notes on 'Body' in Moffatt's Commentary on 1 Cor. 7. 1–3.
[5] Cf. J. Weiss, Meyer, *Kommentar zum Neuen Testament, Der Erste Korintherbrief*, ad loc. p. 345.   [6] Cf. 1 Cor. 15. 45 f.

"I believe that the true exegesis of the passage depends upon recognizing that the expanded quotation from Gen. 2. 7 in 1 Cor. 15. 45 is a parenthesis which should be printed in brackets and that verses 44, 46 should be read together as a continuous sentence.... The reference all through is to the antithesis between the 'natural' and the 'spiritual' body, not to the contrast between the 'earthly' and the 'heavenly' man."[1] But if this is so it is difficult to understand why Paul should have explicitly referred to the two Adams in this way at all. There must have been something in the situation at Corinth to call for such a reference.

It is not unimportant to remember the nature of the Church to which Paul was writing. A Church situated in a cosmopolitan commercial centre like Corinth was sure to be cognisant of all the popular intellectual speculations of the day;[2] and that the Corinthian Church was intellectually alive we gather from the Apostle himself.[3] We also gather that it was grievously divided.[4] Paul merely mentions the different parties in the Church and it is with the mere fact of 'cliqueishness', with the scandal of disunion, that he is primarily concerned. But we can be quite sure that the parties were divided not merely in their preference for this or that 'star' preacher, as it were, but also and possibly more radically in matters of doctrine.[5] What each party stood for we can only guess. But we do know that there must have been a considerable Jewish element in the Church at Corinth; the use of Rabbinic methods in the Epistle points to this.[6] Moreover, it is tempting to infer that it was the Peter party which was most strongly Jewish. Moffatt writes of the latter: "Probably some of his [Peter's] adherents at Corinth belonged to the group which doubted the Apostolic credentials of Paul, if they did not belong to the Palestinian Christians by whom Peter's authority was viewed as supreme."[7] The thought suggests itself that there may have been a party, probably the Peter party, which was a nursery for Adamic traditions. Despite all this, however, the above temptation to ascribe to any particular party any special interest in the Adamic speculations must be resisted. We can only insist that the Church at Corinth must have been familiar with such ideas about Adam as we have outlined above.

Nevertheless, we do know that the *Clementine Homilies*, which have been variously dated but which probably contain documents

---

[1] Cf. A. E. J. Rawlinson, *The New Testament Doctrine of the Christ*, p. 129, n. 1.

[2] Cf. W. L. Knox, *St Paul and the Church of the Gentiles*, p. 125.

[3] Cf. 1 Cor. 1. 18f. On Corinth, cf. A. Plummer, *First Corinthians* (*I.C.C.*), pp. xxif.   [4] Cf. 1 Cor. 3. 3.

[5] Cf. J. Moffatt, *First Corinthians* (*M.N.T.C.*), on 1 Cor. 9.

[6] Cf. W. L. Knox, *St Paul and the Church of Jerusalem*, p. 311.

[7] Cf. J. Moffatt, *First Corinthians* (*M.N.T.C.*), p. 10.

of the late first century,[1] ascribed the apostleship to the Gentiles to Peter and not to Paul and made violent attacks upon the latter. It is significant that in the *Homilies*, which as stated are pro-Petrine and anti-Pauline, the glorification of Adam is carried to great lengths. He was conceived as possessing the Spirit of God and, therefore, incapable of sin;[2] he was ignorant of nothing.[3] The view they present of Adam and Christ was, to quote Lightfoot:[4] "that the Word or Wisdom of God had been incarnate more than once and that there had been more Christs than one, of whom Adam was the first and Jesus the last." Christ had been incarnate in Adam, Enoch, Noah, Abraham, Isaac, Jacob, Moses and, lastly, in Jesus (sometimes Moses is omitted from this list in order to make Jesus the seventh of the series).[5]

It is very dangerous to argue from documents uncertainly dated to the Church in Corinth in the first century; and it is indeed possible that the *Clementine Homilies* emphasize the glory of the first Adam only because Paul emphasized the glory of the Second Adam. This may have been a convenient and, perhaps, popular method of attacking the Apostle in the second century. But it is also possible that the *Homilies* reflect traditions of controversies in the first century in which Paul was accused of calumniating the first Adam. If views in any way similar to those found in the *Homilies* had 'privily entered' into the Church at Corinth we can see how Paul would seek to counteract them. True, Christ was to undo the evils of the Fall and was indeed the counterpart of the first Adam and might be called a Second Adam; but he was not a mere second edition of the first Adam in his unfallen state; he was a new creation, unique. The first Adam, however glorious, was of the earth earthy; Jesus was the Lord from heaven, the inauguration of a new era of the Spirit, who had appeared ἐφάπαξ, not as one of a series. He was different in kind from the first Adam.

It must be admitted, however, that all this is very conjectural. We are on more solid ground when we turn to the Hellenistic-Jewish ideas that would meet Paul at Corinth. That Christians at the latter place were familiar with Alexandrian developments is rendered certain by the fact that Apollos had preached and attracted a following there,[6] and it is probable that Hellenistic-Jewish ideas, such as are best known to us in Philo, were circulating in most of the chief cities of the Mediterranean

---

[1] See Additional Notes, p. 356.
[2] *Hom.* 3. 7.
[3] *Hom.* 3. 18.
[4] Cf. J. B. Lightfoot, *The Epistle to the Galatians*, p. 326.
[5] See W. Bousset, *Hauptprobleme der Gnosis*, p. 173; *Hom.* 3. 20, 13. 14.
[6] I Cor. 3. 4f.; Acts 18. 24f., 19. 1.

world and were even studied at Jerusalem itself. Certainly Corinthian
Christians would be familiar with Philo's distinction between the
Heavenly and the earthly man and would doubtless be tempted to
identify their Lord with the former, in an attempt to accommodate
their faith to contemporary thought. While it is improbable, though
not impossible, that Paul was directly acquainted with Philo's works,[1]
he too would certainly be familiar with the ideas about the Heavenly
Man with which the Corinthian Christians were occupied. Indeed, in
true missionary fashion he was prepared to use terminology such as we
find in Philo in the service of the Gospel, and to allow the Corinthian
Christians to call Jesus the Heavenly Man, the Lord from Heaven. But
herein lurked a danger; accommodation might go too far. Philo had
claimed that the Heavenly Man was a pre-existent incorporeal Idea and
Christians might think of Christ as such. In 1 Cor. 15 Paul enters the
fray claiming that Jesus is indeed the Lord from Heaven, but He is not
a mere idea, and incorporeal, but one who has appeared in history. He
reverses the order found in Philo and identifies the Heavenly Man not
with a pre-existent Idea, who was chronologically prior to the earthly
Adam of Genesis, but with Jesus, the Son of David, who was later[2]
than the Adam of Genesis in time and therefore might be called a Second
Adam. For Philo the Heavenly Man belonged to another realm of
being, a realm that could never come to terms with matter; for Paul
the Heavenly Man is Christ, who has introduced that other realm into
this, into time, space and sense. Paul, in his doctrine of the Second Adam,
asserts the same truth that the Fourth Gospel proclaims in its insistence
that the Word became flesh, in another, Rabbinic way, that the particular is not a scandal. He was impelled to assert this not from any
philosophical motives but from the mere fact of Christ in history.

We can be fairly certain, therefore, that there was a polemical motive,
possibly motives, behind Paul's use of the term, the Second Adam, for
Christ. But he was also influenced by other considerations. The other
passage besides that in 1 Cor. 15 where Paul introduces the conception
is in Romans. There he is dealing with the difficulty, how is it possible
for one to die for all, for the death of one man Jesus to be efficacious for
others? "How can His conquest over sin and His achievement of the
human ideal be effective for other individuals?"[3] In answering this

---

[1] See H. St J. Thackeray, St Paul and Contemporary Jewish Thought, p. 231. J. Weiss,
Meyer, Kommentar zum Neuen Testament, Der Erste Korintherbrief, pp. 374f., thinks
Paul independent of Philo at this point.

[2] This does not mean that Paul did not believe in the pre-existence of Christ: but
we cannot here enter into that question.

[3] Rom. 5. 12-21; C. H. Dodd, Romans (M.N.T.C.), p. 79.

question Paul has recourse to the current Rabbinic doctrine[1] that through the Fall of the First Man, Adam, all men fell into sin. Similarly, he argues: "through the moral achievement of Jesus all men may rise to goodness".[2] We cannot be certain whether it was the polemical motive or the doctrinal necessity of explaining how Christ could die 'for' others, that first led Paul to think of Christ as the Second Adam. Probably, however, this conception played a far more important part in his thought than the scanty references to the Second Adam in 1 Corinthians and Romans would lead us to suppose. In particular, in his development of the idea of the Church as the Body of Christ, Paul is largely influenced by Rabbinic ideas about Adam.

As we have seen, Rabbinic speculation about the creation of the physical body of Adam was very varied and often even grotesque. But it seems that two dominant interests were served by it, the need for emphasizing the unity of all mankind and the duty of love; while, of course, much of the haggadic material on Adam is playful fantasy and not serious theology. First, then, the fact that all men are derived from one ancestor Adam means that in him all men are one. There is a real unity of all men in him; all belong to each and each belongs to all. Thus in *M. Sanhedrin* 4. 5[3] we read: "Therefore but a single man was created in the world to teach that if any man has caused a single soul to perish from Israel, Scripture imputes it to him as though he had caused a whole world to perish, and if any man saves alive a single soul from Israel, Scripture imputes it to him as though he had saved alive a whole world." It was in order to emphasize that in Adam all people were one that such strange stories were circulated as to the formation of Adam's body. According to a tradition going back to R. Meir[4] (c. 150), God made Adam out of dust gathered from all over the earth. "It has been taught: R. Meir used to say: 'The dust of the first man was gathered from all parts of the earth', for it is written, 'Thine eyes did see mine unformed substance' [Ps. 139. 16], and further it is written, 'The eyes of the Lord run to and fro through the whole earth' [Zech. 4. 10]." (Epstein comments: "This is perhaps another way of teaching the equality of man, all men having been formed from one and the same common clay."[5])

---

[1] Cf. W. Sanday and A. C. Headlam, *Romans* (*I.C.C.*), pp. 136f. We need not here recapitulate the evidence there given for the Rabbinic doctrine. Cf. also Str.-B. vol. III, pp. 227, 250f.

[2] C. H. Dodd, *Romans* (*M.N.T.C.*), p. 79.

[3] Cf. Danby, pp. 387f.

[4] Cf. *b. Sanh.* 38a; *Gen. R.* 8; Str.-B. vol. III, p. 479; also *J.E.* vol. I, p. 176.

[5] *The Babylonian Talmud, Seder Nezikin*, Ed. I. Epstein, *Sanhedrin*, vol. I, p. 241. Soncino Press.

Later speculation claimed that his head was formed from the earth of the Holy Land, the trunk of his body from Babylonian soil and his various members from the soil of different countries.[1] "R. Oshaiah said in Rab's name: 'Adam's trunk came from Babylon (38*b*), his head from Eretz Israel, his limbs from other lands, and his private parts according to R. Aha from Akra di Agma.'" Epstein, in the page referred to above, explains that Adam's head, the most exalted part of his body, comes from Eretz Israel "the most exalted of all lands, while Akra di Agma was a place notorious on account of its immorality". Because of this cosmopolitan physical structure of Adam it followed that a man from the East and a man from the West were of the same material formation, and therefore one. In the deepest sense "there was neither Jew nor Greek".[2] Thus in *Pirkê de Rabbi Eliezer* we read:

The Holy One, blessed be He, spake to the Torah: "Let us make man in our image, after our likeness" (Gen. 1. 26). (The Torah) spake before Him: Sovereign of all the worlds! The man whom Thou wouldst create will be limited in days and full of anger; and he will come unto the power of sin. Unless Thou wilt be long-suffering with him, it would be well for him not to have come into the world. The Holy One, blessed be He, rejoined: And is it for nought that I am called "slow to anger" and "abounding in love"? He began to collect the dust of the first man from the four corners of the world; red, black, white and "pale green" (which) refers to the body....[2]

Why (did He gather man's dust) from the four corners of the world?

Thus spake the Holy One, blessed be He: If a man should come from the east to the west or from the west to the east, and his time comes to depart from the world, then the earth shall not say, The dust of thy body is not mine, return to the place whence thou wast created. But (this circumstance) teaches thee that in every place where a man goes or comes, and his end approaches when he must depart from the world, thence is the dust of his body, and there it returns to the dust, as it is said, "For dust thou art and unto dust shalt thou return" (ibid. 3. 19).

In addition to all this of course Adam was bisexual,[3] so that in him there was neither male nor female. The phrase "This is the book of the generations of Adam" (Gen. 5. 1) was interpreted to mean that God revealed to Adam all the generations to come,[4] this really means that all subsequent generations were in him as it were. How naïvely physical

---

[1] Cf. *b. Sanh.* 38*a*; *Gen. R.* 8; Str.-B. vol. III, p. 479. Also *J.E.* vol. I, p. 176.

[2] *Pirkê de Rabbi Eliezer*, § XI, pp. 76f. With reference to the colours Friedlander asks: "Might the four colours indicate the different colours of the skin of man?" Ibid. p. 77, n. 2. See Str.-B. vol. III, p. 479. The Jerusalem Targum on Gen. 2. 7 claims that God created Adam red, brown and white.

[3] *Gen. R.* 8. 1; *b. 'Erub.* 18*a*; *b. Ber.* 61*a*. See Str.-B. vol. I, p. 802.

[4] Cf. *Gen. R.* 24. 1ff.; *Aboth R.N.* I. פרק לא, p. 91; Str.-B. vol. II, p. 174.

was all this speculation is seen from the fact that different individuals
were conceived as being derived from or attached to different parts of
Adam's body; one might belong to his hair, another to his ear, another
to his nose, they literally formed different members of his body.[1] There
was speculation also on the meaning of Adam's name; the latter was
found to suggest universality or the unity of all mankind in him. We
read in 2 Enoch 30. 13: "And I appointed him a name from the four
component parts, from East, West, South and from North." A stood
for Ἀνατολή, D for Δύσις, A for Ἄρκτος, and M for Μεσημβρία. The
same idea meets us in the Sibylline Oracles[2] where we read: "Yea it
is God Himself who fashioned four lettered Adam, the first man
fashioned who completes in his name morn and dusk, antarctic and
arctic."

Adam, then, stands for the real unity of mankind in virtue of his
creation. There is also another factor. The nature of Adam's creation
is made the basis of the duty of love, equality and peace among men.
To quote again *M. Sanhedrin* 4. 5: "Again but a single man was created
for the sake of peace among mankind that none should say to his fellow,
My Father was greater than thy Father...." Furthermore, R. Simeon
b. Azzai (A.D. 120–40) deduced the principle of love from Gen. 5. 1,
which reads, "This is the book of the generations of Adam...":

> Thou shalt love thy neighbour as thyself [Lev. 19. 18]. R. Akiba said:
> "That is the greatest principle in the Law." Ben Azzai said: "The sentence
> 'this is the book of the generations of man' [Gen. 5. 1] is even greater than
> the other."[3]

Gen. 5. 1 teaches that all men are the offspring of him who was made
in the image of God.

The relevance of all this to an understanding of Paul's doctrine of the
Body of Christ is evident. Christians are according to Paul united with
one another and with Christ; they share with one another and with
Christ in one corporeity. This comes out clearly in Paul's treatment of
the Last Supper. In 1 Cor. 11. 29 he writes: "For he that eateth and
drinketh unworthily, eateth and drinketh damnation to himself, not
discerning the Lord's body." He here refers to those who in their conduct
at the Holy Communion forgot their unity with their fellow Christians
and with Christ, who failed to recognize that to partake in the Lord's
Supper was not merely to participate in Christ but also in their fellow
Christians who are one with Christ. Irregularities at the Table of the

---

[1] Cf. Str.-B. vol. II, p. 174; *Ex R.* 40. 3.   [2] Sib. Or. 3. 24–6.
[3] *Sifra* 89 פרק ד; cf. *Gen. R.* 24. 7. See Bacher, *Die Agada der Tannaiten*, vol. II,
pp. 418 f. and also p. 285.

Lord such as prevailed at Corinth denied the solidarity of all Christians with each other and with their Lord.[1] As Dr Dodd puts it, "there is a sort of mystical unity of redeemed humanity in Christ",[2] "a new corporate personality is created in Christ".[2] In a quite physical sense Christians are all one in Christ. This unity Paul calls the Body of Christ.[3] He goes on to develop this concept: the Body is animated by the Spirit[4]—a kind of life-force that manifests itself in different ways so that there are many members in the One Body, unity in diversity.[5]

Now we may agree with Schweitzer that the concept of the solidarity of all Christians with Christ is necessarily derived from Paul's eschatological background. He writes: "Since both Jesus and Paul move in an eschatological world of thought, the concept of this community of the saints in which, by the predestination of God, the saints are united with one another and with the Messiah as the Lord of the Elect, is to them perfectly familiar".[6] Dr Moffatt also writes: "There is more than half a truth in Dr Schweitzer's contention that the so-called Mysticism of Paul really amounts to his statement of the truth that the pre-existent Church is manifested in appearance and reality through the death and Resurrection of Jesus."[7] The real problem, however, is why Paul should use the term 'Body' to express the unity of the saints with one another and with their Lord. "How could a thinker come to produce this conception of the extension of the body of a personal being? How can Paul regard it as so self-evident that he can make use of it without ever explaining it?"[8] We suggest that more satisfying than Schweitzer's view, which while it does help us to understand the community of the Messiah with His followers does not elucidate the expression 'body', and also more satisfying than those views advanced by A. E. J. Rawlinson[9]

---

[1] J. Moffatt, *First Corinthians* (*M.N.T.C.*), p. 173. J. Moffatt's interpretation of 1 Cor. 11. 27f. is followed by A. Schweitzer, Armitage-Robinson, C. A. Anderson Scott and G. H. C. Macgregor. See references in J. Moffatt, ibid. p. 173, n. 1.

[2] C. H. Dodd, *Romans* (*M.N.T.C.*), pp. 79f.

[3] The extremely physical or literal nature of the relation comes out particularly in the discussion on marriage. A Christian husband or wife can make his or her partner Christian. Cf. 1 Cor. 7. 14.

[4] See below, chapter 8.   [5] 1 Cor. 12. 11f.; Rom. 12. 4.

[6] A. Schweitzer, *The Mysticism of Paul the Apostle*, p. 104. See also R. N. Flew, *Jesus and His Church*, pp. 73f.; also G. Johnston, *The Doctrine of the Church in the New Testament*, p. 50, for criticism of Flew.

[7] J. Moffatt, *First Corinthians* (*M.N.T.C.*), p. 188.

[8] A. Schweitzer, op. cit. p. 116.

[9] See *Mysterium Christi*, pp. 225ff. A. E. J. Rawlinson closely connects the idea of the σῶμα τοῦ Χριστοῦ with the Eucharist.

and W. L. Knox,[1] is the answer suggested by our discussion of the
Adamic speculations of first-century Judaism. T. W. Manson[2] has pointed
out one example of the term σῶμα being used of a body corporate in
6/7 B.C.[3] but this example only affords a partial parallel to the New Testament usage. Manson writes: "It is thus no longer possible to say that
σῶμα is never used in pre-Christian Greek for a 'body' of people or
society. The uniqueness of the New Testament phrase resides not in the
word σῶμα but in the qualifying genitive. The body is not τὸ σῶμα τῶν
Χριστιανῶν but τὸ σῶμα τοῦ Χριστοῦ." In the light of our discussion,
however, this becomes intelligible. Paul accepted the traditional Rabbinic doctrine of the unity of mankind in Adam. That doctrine implied
that the very constitution of the physical body of Adam and the method
of its formation was symbolic of the real oneness of mankind. In that
one body of Adam east and west, north and south were brought together,
male and female, as we have seen. The 'body' of Adam included all
mankind. Was it not natural, then, that Paul when he thought of the
new humanity being incorporated 'in Christ' should have conceived
of it as the 'body' of the Second Adam, where there was neither Jew
nor Greek, male nor female, bond nor free.[4] The difference between
the Body of the First Adam and that of the Second Adam was for Paul
that whereas the former was animated by the principle of natural life,
was *nephesh*, the latter was animated by the Spirit. Entry upon the
Christian life is for the Apostle the putting off of the old man with his
deeds and the putting on of the new man. The purpose of God in Christ
is "in the dispensation of the fullness of times" "to gather together in
one all things in Christ",[5] i.e. the reconstitution of the essential oneness
of mankind in Christ as a spiritual community, as it was one in Adam
in a physical sense.

[1] W. L. Knox, *St Paul and the Church of the Gentiles*, pp. 160 ff. He regards the σῶμα
idea, in its form at least, as derived from Stoic sources. See also *J.T.S.* (1938), vol. XXXIX,
pp. 243 f. and G. C. Richards, *J.T.S.* (1937), vol. XXXVIII, p. 165.

[2] *J.T.S.* (1936), vol. XXXVII, p. 385.

[3] In an Edict of Augustus.

[4] In the Old Testament the term Adam was used generically for all mankind and
though the Rabbis did not use Adam generically in this way he remained the typical
representative of mankind (cf. *J.E.* vol. I, p. 174). It would therefore be natural for
Paul to use the term Christ generically to stand for the new humanity, i.e. Christians,
and so he could speak of τὸ σῶμα τοῦ Χριστοῦ when he meant τὸ σῶμα τῶν
Χριστιανῶν. Cf. D. Daube, *J.Q.R.* vol. XXXV, pp. 227 ff.

[5] Eph. 1. 10.

4

THE OLD AND THE NEW ISRAEL:
'NATIONALISM'

WE closed our treatment of the conception of Christ as the
Second Adam with a reference to what is called the Universalism of Paul, his assertion of the universal scope and
efficacy of the work of God in Christ. In its fully developed form this
implies not only that sexual, class and national barriers are broken down
for those who are 'in Christ',[1] but that the universe in its entirety,[2]
which is at present under the dominion of evil forces, will ultimately
be reconciled to God. It is not merely all men, Greek and Jew, Scythian
and barbarian,[3] who are made at one with themselves and with God but
also all things, that God may be all in all.[4] Paul's universalism of course
derives from his experience of the grace of God in Christ. The universality of sin he knew, apart from any proofs that Scripture might
supply, through his knowledge of his own heart and of the ways of
men, both Jewish and Gentile;[5] the universality of forgiveness and
reconciliation burst upon him with the light of the knowledge of the
glory of God in the face of Jesus Christ.[6] It is not insignificant that to
be converted had meant for Paul to be a missionary to the Gentiles.
Universalism was involved in his conversion.[7]

Nevertheless, although the universalism that we have noticed was
implicit in the depth of Paul's experience of God in Christ from the
first, its explicit formulation in thought was a slow process, and its
strict logical expression in life was never achieved. In fact, both in life
and thought, the Book of Acts and the Epistles of Paul reveal a conflict
in the latter which was never completely resolved, a conflict between
the claims of the old Israel after the flesh and the new Israel after the
Spirit, between his 'nationalism' and his Christianity. It is, indeed, from
this tension that there arise most of the inconsistencies that have puzzled

[1] Cf. Gal. 3. 28; Col. 3. 11.　　　　　　　　　　[2] 1 Cor. 15. 23-4.
[3] Col. 3. 11; cf. also 2 Cor. 5. 19; Rom. 8. 19-23; Col. 1. 20.
[4] 1 Cor. 15. 25-8; cf. Rom. 11. 32. Here A. Schweitzer takes 'all' to refer to the
Elect; cf. *The Mysticism of Paul the Apostle*, p. 185, but C. H. Dodd rightly takes Paul
to mean exactly what he says, cf. *Ryl. Bull.* vol. XVIII, no. 1, p. 40 and *Romans*
(*M.N.T.C.*), pp. 183-6.
[5] Rom. 1. 18f. and Rom. 2; see also Rom. 7.　　　　[6] 2 Cor. 4. 6.
[7] Cf. C. H. Dodd, *Ryl. Bull.* vol. XVIII, no. 1, p. 36; contrast A. Schweitzer, *The
Mysticism of Paul the Apostle*, p. 181.

interpreters of Paul; and it is only in the light of the Judaism of the first century A.D. that this is to be understood.

Montefiore has rightly suggested that the factors that led to the rise of universalism in Jewish thought in the Old Testament were chiefly two, namely, the rise of the great empires which laid claim to world dominion, and also religion.[1] The separation of these two factors, however, is really artificial, because politics and religion, life and thought, cannot be separated into distinct watertight compartments. It was in and through their contacts with the great Assyrian and Babylonian empires that the people of Israel, tutored by their prophets, were gradually led to recognize in the tribal deity of their small hilly state the Lord of the whole universe. It was what Yahweh proved to be as the God of Israel that led the prophets to worship Him as the Lord of all the nations. Thus Deutero-Isaiah could "drop the keystone of the monotheistic arch into its place"[2] because he had become aware of Yahweh the God of Israel as also the God whose presence could be experienced in Babylon and who could deliver his people from Babylon, and from this paradox there emerged within Judaism both an extremely narrow nationalism and a noble universalism.[3]

As early as Habakkuk[4] (605–600 B.C.) the tendency had arisen to set the hostile Gentile nations over against the 'Israel' of God, and to regard the former as godless and the latter at least as comparatively righteous.[5] Later in Ezekiel (593–571 B.C.) this had grown to great dimensions. Like their predecessors, both Jeremiah and Ezekiel had proclaimed the coming of a Day of Yahweh;[6] for both this would be a day of judgement on Judah, but it would issue finally in the restoration of 'Israel' to its

---

[1] C. G. Montefiore, 4 Ezra: A Study in the Development of Universalism.

[2] H. Wheeler Robinson, The Religious Ideas of the Old Testament, p. 60; Theodore H. Robinson, Prophecy and the Prophets, p. 165; R. H. Charles, Eschatology, pp. 84f.

[3] C. G. Montefiore, The Hibbert Lectures (1892), "On the Origin and Growth of Religion as Illustrated by the Religion of the Ancient Hebrews"; R. H. Charles, Eschatology, pp. 103f.; Moore, vol. I, pp. 219f. The penetrating remarks of H. Wheeler Robinson deserve quotation: "Israel's service was unique and indispensable. Its particularity was the condition of its intensity. The true universality is not reached by thinning out our convictions so as to make them spread over as wide a surface as possible. It is reached by so intense a devotion to them that we penetrate nearer to the centre of things and so draw nearer to each other. That is the characteristic of Israel's religion at the best and in the best of her representatives." See Redemption and Revelation, p. 91.

[4] Cf. R. H. Charles, Eschatology, pp. 95f.

[5] Cf. Hab. I. 4, 13. The Gentile is רשע; Judah צדיק, cf. Pss. 9. 5, 17; 10. 2, 3, 4; 58. 10; 68. 2; 125. 3; and Isa. 26. 10.

[6] R. H. Charles, Eschatology, pp. 84f.

own land and the establishment of the Messianic kingdom.[1] But whereas
in Jeremiah all the nations, even those hostile to 'Israel', would finally
be converted to the true faith,[2] in Ezekiel no hope is extended to them.[3]
While for Jeremiah the 'Israel' of God will be the instrument of saving
others, in Ezekiel it is itself saved to the exclusion of others.[4] In the
subsequent centuries Judaism has representatives of both these attitudes,
Ezekiel's point of view did not immediately win the field. According
to the great prophet of the Exile, the so-called Deutero-Isaiah (545–
539 B.C.), through the instrumentality of the 'Israel' of God all the
nations are to be converted and included in the Messianic kingdom.
'Israel' was given, not merely "to raise up the tribes of Jacob and to
restore the preserved of Israel", but also "to give light to the Gentiles
to make God's salvation known to the ends of the earth".[5] There are
also various isolated passages of a late date that attest the ultimate salvation of all nations. Thus in Isa. 2. 2–4 (=Mic. 4. 1–3) we read of all the
people coming to walk in the light of the Lord, and the same thought
occurs in many Psalms.[6] In a truly remarkable passage in Isa. 19, Egypt
and Assyria are promised equality in 'spiritual blessedness' with 'Israel'.
"In that day shall Israel be the third with Egypt and with Assyria, even
a blessing in the midst of the land, whom the Lord of hosts shall bless
saying, Blessed be Egypt my people and Assyria the work of my hands,
and Israel mine inheritance."[7] We can trace this universalism down
through the second century B.C.[8] In the Sibylline Oracles[9] (200–100 B.C.)

[1] R. H. Charles, *Eschatology*, pp. 103 f.
[2] Ibid. pp. 104 f.; also Jer. 16. 19, 12. 16, 17.
[3] Ibid. pp. 106 f.   [4] Cf. T. W. Manson, *The Teaching of Jesus*, p. 181.
[5] Isa. 49. 6; cf. R. H. Charles, *Eschatology*, p. 108.
[6] Cf. Pss. 22, 65, 86, 87.
[7] Cf. C. G. Montefiore's treatment of this in *The Hibbert Lectures* (1892), pp. 147 f.;
he regards it as being pre-exilic, the work of the prophet Isaiah himself; so Kuenen
and Stade. Cheyne places it in the time of the Ptolemies (*Origin and Religious Contents
of the Psalter*, p. 190).
[8] It is customary to refer to Mal. 1. 11: "from the rising of the sun even unto the
going down of the same my name is great among the nations: and in every place
(or sanctuary) smoke is made to arise in my name, even a pure offering". Browne's
treatment of this, however, is convincing; cf. *Early Judaism*, p. 142. He writes: "As the
offering here referred to is made in the name of Yahweh, it cannot be, as some have
suggested, that the prophet in an outburst of universalism regarded the offerings of
the heathen to their gods as being acceptable to Yahweh, nor would such a view be in
agreement with the writer's estimate of other religions (2. 11, 12). Rather it means
that the Jews of the Dispersion, by the purity of their offerings at such sanctuaries
as Elephantine and Casiphia, commended the worship of Yahweh among the nations;
and this the prophet contrasted with the conduct of the sacrifices at Jerusalem."
[9] Sib. Or. 3. 772, 773; cf. R. H. Charles, *Eschatology*, p. 177 and *Ap. and Ps.* vol. II,
p. 392.

we read: "And from every land they shall bring frankincense and gifts to the house of the great God": and in the Book of Tobit[1] (170 B.C.): "Many nations shall come from afar, and the inhabitants of the utmost ends of the earth unto thy holy name." In the Book of Enoch[2] and in the Testaments of the Twelve Patriarchs,[3] both dated from 200–100 B.C., the same note is struck.

But on the other hand the influence of Ezekiel had not been dormant in the centuries succeeding the Exile. Circumstances had favoured the growth of a narrow nationalism in line with that prophet's thought, some indeed would say that they had made it inevitable. It is at least arguable that just as some form of monasticism was probably a necessity to the Christian Church in the tumult and disruption of the fifth century A.D., so too some form of isolationism was a necessity for Judaism in the centuries following the Exile. We who have known the optimism with which Woodrow Wilson[4] introduced his Fourteen Points after the War of 1914–18, and the tragic failure of the nations to implement them, should find no difficulty in recognizing that it was one thing for Deutero-Isaiah in the first thrill of enthusiasm at the prospect of the return, to visualize Israel as the missionary of Yahweh to the nations, while it was quite another thing for the exiles who returned to Palestine and who had to translate dreams into realities.[5] This is not the place to trace the history of post-exilic Judaism, but we have previously pointed out the fatal ease with which Palestine was exposed to foreign influences. At every point the returned community felt the pressure and attraction of its Gentile neighbours. Surely segregation alone could preserve it from extinction; a splendid isolation was the only policy possible! "If the Jewish nation was to be preserved", writes Cohen, "it must be ringed round by a burning faith as by a frontier of fire."[6] So thought Nehemiah and Ezra; and the post-exilic history of Judaism became the

---

[1] Tobit 13. 11.   [2] Enoch 10. 21, 48. 4.

[3] Test. Dan. 6. 7; Test. Levi 2. 11, 4. 4, 8. 14; Test. Simeon 6. 5; Test. Naphtali 2. 5, 8. 3; Test. Benjamin 9. 2, 10. 5; Test. Asher, 7. 3; Test. Judah 25. 5. See especially R. H. Charles, *Ap. and Ps.* vol. II, pp. 294, 358. He traces prophetic influence in The Testaments of the Twelve Patriarchs; and also suggests that the triumph of the Maccabees led to a hope of a general conversion of the Gentiles; cf. also W. L. Knox, *St Paul and the Church of Jerusalem,* p. 26, n. 57.

[4] See particularly H. G. Wells' account of the Peace Conference in *The Outline of History,* vol. II, pp. 732 ff.

[5] Cf. A. C. Welch, *Post-Exilic Judaism,* p. 11; S. A. Cook, *The Truth of the Bible,* p. 41. "We cannot say that the prophets had failed or that the reactionaries have won. We have to recognize the vast difference between the more individualistic teachers and the rank and file, between the spiritual experts so to say and the ordinary men."

[6] A. Cohen, *Everyman's Talmud,* p. xvii.

history of a 'fenced' community. But a fence while it preserves, also excludes. The Torah, which differentiated the Jew from others, also separated him from them. Moreover, the cruel persecutions of Antiochus Epiphanes established the belief that the nations were the conscious and designed enemies of God.[1] It was no mere superiority complex[2] nor any especial obstinacy in the Jewish people[3] that led to particularism, and we can understand, though we do not therefore condone, the fact that the missionary challenge thrown down by Deutero-Isaiah was not taken up. In any case, despite the protests of people like the authors of the Book of Ruth and the Book of Jonah[4] (350 B.C.?) particularism or narrow nationalism prevailed. Browne has seen the first step in this direction in the rejection of the Samaritans[5] and by the first century B.C. there is an almost complete absence of any expression of universalism. In one passage, indeed, the Gentiles are spared in the Messianic Age, but they are spared merely in order that they may serve Israel, "He shall possess the nations of the heathen to serve him beneath his yoke";[6] in the books of the Maccabees and in the Book of Jubilees the note of universalism is completely lacking. Moreover, when we turn to the literature of the first century A.D., the attitude towards the Gentiles in some quarters has still further hardened. The most extreme expression of contempt towards the latter is found in 4 Ezra. Thinking of the Gentiles the author writes: "Thou hast said that they are nothing and that they are like unto spittle and Thou hast likened the abundance of them to a drop in a bucket."[7]

[1] C. G. Montefiore, *The Hibbert Lectures* (1892), p. 435.

[2] See G. Johnston, *The Doctrine of the Church in the New Testament*, p. 26.

[3] Cf. L. E. Browne, *Early Judaism*, p. viii.

[4] Cf. W. O. E. Oesterley and T. H. Robinson, *An Introduction to the Books of the Old Testament*, p. 84, and especially pp. 375f.

[5] Cf. L. E. Browne, *Early Judaism*, p. 112.

[6] Psalms of Solomon (first century B.C.) 17. 32; Ps. 72. 11. The note by H. E. Ryle and M. R. James in *The Psalms of Solomon* on 17. 32 deserves to be quoted: "This Messianic dominion over the Gentiles is dwelt upon in Ps. 72. 11 etc. (πάντα τὰ ἔθνη δουλεύσουσιν αὐτῷ), Isa. 56; Zech. 14; Dan. 7. 14. Compare for the language Zeph. 3. 9 τοῦ δουλεύειν αὐτῷ ὑπὸ ζυγὸν ἕνα.... In the later literature 4 Esdras 13, Apoc. Bar. 72 the fate of the Gentiles is far less mild. Most of them are to perish, and all who are left are to be enslaved..." (p. 140). The idea therefore that the Messiah should have dominion over the Gentiles is common before the first century B.C. But along with this, as we saw, there was a distinct recognition of the final inclusion of Gentiles in the blessedness of salvation. It should also be pointed out that Charles regards as from the first century B.C. certain passages in the Testaments of the Twelve Patriarchs which attest a universalism, but these are almost alone. Cf. *Ap. and Ps.* vol. II, p. 294.

[7] 4 Ezra 5. 23-7, 13. 37. Also Ass. Moses (A.D. 7-29) 10. 7-10; Ap. Baruch 83. 3, 6, 7; Jubilees 23. 29.

It is illegitimate, however, to suppose that this last sentence quoted from 4 Ezra adequately describes the attitude of Judaism to the Gentiles in the first century A.D. That century did possibly witness a growth of the particularist spirit,[1] but apart from the presence of such men as Hillel at its beginning and Ben Azzai a short time after its close, it also reveals what we might quite definitely call an 'uneasy conscience' on the Gentile question. In fact, as Montefiore has pointed out, 4 Ezra is a picture of an extremely sensitive soul in bitter conflict.[2] Brought up in a kind of first-century Chauvinism which condemned the Gentiles lock, stock and barrel, the author can only accept the traditional attitude towards the latter under protest. Far more human than the creed he professes, he agonizes over the fate of the majority of the human race, who on his theory are doomed to destruction.[3] We feel that it was really cold comfort for him to know that it is fitting that, as in nature, so in human affairs the many are lost and the few saved.[4]

We see the same symptoms of an uneasy conscience in the varying views prevalent on the subject of Proselytism. With the decline in the belief in the ultimate salvation of the Gentiles it came to be recognized that the only hope for the latter was to become Jews, i.e. to be naturalized into the Jewish people,[5] and it is this that accounts for the considerable activity shown in the gaining of proselytes. The New Testament supplies evidence for the latter;[6] and the large number of proselytes gained shows that Jewish propaganda was successful.[7] R. Eleazar of Modiim (A.D. 120–40) said that "God scattered Israel among the nations for the sole end that proselytes should wax numerous among them".[8] Generally, however, the Rabbis seem to have oscillated between a desire to keep off proselytes with one arm and the desire to draw them with the other.[9] Thus Shammai (A.D. 10–80) adopted a strict attitude towards proselytes, demanding that they should give assent to the Torah both written and oral before knowing its contents,[10] and R. Eliezer b. Hyrkanos

---

[1] Cf. a good note by W. L. Knox, St Paul and the Church of Jerusalem, p. 26, n. 27.

[2] 4 Ezra: A Study in the Development of Universalism.

[3] 4 Ezra 7. 62f.; cf. C. H. Dodd, "The Mind of Paul", in Ryl. Bull. vol. XVIII, no. 1, p. 36; G. H. Box, The Ezra-Apocalypse, p. xi.

[4] 4 Ezra 8. 41f., 9. 21.

[5] Cf. A. Schweitzer, The Mysticism of Paul the Apostle, pp. 178f.; Moore, vol. I, pp. 232f.; W. L. Knox, St Paul and the Church of Jerusalem, p. 120, n. 37.

[6] Matt. 23. 15.

[7] Cf. W. L. Knox, op. cit. p. 120, n. 37; Beginnings, vol. I, pp. 164f. and vol. V, pp. 74f., and especially Schürer, History of the Jewish People, Div. II, vol. II, pp. 291f. and particularly pp. 297f. The success of Jewish proselytizing led to legislation to hinder it. Cf. J.E. vol. X, p. 224; J. Juster, Les Juifs dans l'Empire Romain, vol. I, pp. 259–63.

[8] b. Pes. 87b. See R.A. p. xliv.

[9] Cf. Moore, vol. I, pp. 341f.

[10] b. Shab. 31a.

(A.D. 80–120) was suspicious of all proselytes.[1] On the other hand one of the sayings of Hillel (A.D. 10–20) recorded in Aboth 1. 12 reads: "Be one of the disciples of Aaron a lover of peace, following after peace, loving mankind and drawing them to the Law." It is also worth referring to the story of how "a foreigner came to Shammai saying, 'Make a proselyte of me on condition that you teach me the whole of the Law while I stand on one foot.' Shammai drove him off with a measuring stick that he had in his hand. Thereupon he repaired to Hillel with the same proposition. Hillel received him as a proselyte and taught him: 'What you do not like to have done to you do not do to your fellow. This is the whole of the Law: the rest is the explanation of it. Go learn it.'"[2] It is, indeed, clear that the Rabbis fall far short of accepting Deutero-Isaiah's missionary call, and that there is no great enthusiasm for seeking and saving that which was lost in their midst,[3] but nevertheless, they are not indifferent to the Gentiles—indeed, they are obviously disturbed by them.[4]

Further evidence that this was so is found in the fact that theories were formulated within Rabbinic Judaism to prove that the Gentiles had been given the same chance as Israel. (Had the 'Gentile question' been utterly closed such a justification or defence of Jewish teaching would have been unnecessary!) It was the Gentiles themselves who were responsible for their miserable lot: they too had had the opportunity of accepting the Torah but had refused it.[5] R. Jose b. Simeon said

---

[1] *Mekilta Nezikin* 18 on Exod. 22. 20f.; *Eccles. Rabbah* on 1. 8. See W. G. Braude, *Jewish Proselytizing in the First Five Centuries of the Common Era*, pp. 39f.

[2] *b. Shab.* 31 a. Consideration for the feelings of the Proselyte is urged, e.g. in *M. Baba Metzia* 4. 10. *Mekilta*, ibid. A prayer for proselytes was included in the Eighteen Benedictions. See Singer, *J.D.P.B.* p. 48.

[3] Cf. *R.A.* p. xliv; Moore, vol. I, p. 342.

[4] Many of the extreme anti-Gentile statements often quoted in descriptions of Rabbinic Judaism owe their origin to the bitter experience of persecution in the second century and later, e.g. the words of Simeon b. Yoḥai (c. A.D. 140) "kill the best of the Gentiles: Crush the head of the best of snakes" (*Mekilta Beshallaḥ* 2 on Exod. 14. 7) are those of a man who had lived through the Hadrianic persecutions and spent thirteen years of his life hiding in a cave. (Cf. A. Cohen, *Everyman's Talmud*, p. 70.) In such periods of persecution proselytes often turned into informers and were a menace to the Jewish community: anti-proselyte utterances are therefore to be expected. (A. Cohen, ibid. p. 68.) But they are not to be taken as typical of all Rabbinic Judaism (in the first century A.D.). The whole question of proselytizing is dealt with very clearly in W. G. Braude, *Jewish Proselytizing in the First Five Centuries of the Common Era*, above referred to. According to Braude "all the rabbis spoke enthusiastically of proselytizing and idealized converts and their makers", p. 7. But see Dr Daube's review in *J.T.S.* vol. XLII (Jan.–April 1942), pp. 127f.

[5] Cf. 4 Ezra 7. 72. See S. Schechter, *Some Aspects of Rabbinic Theology*, p. 131.

(A.D. 120–90): "Ere you stood at Sinai and accepted my Torah you were called Israel, just as other nations, e.g. Sabtekhah, Raamah, are called by simple names without addition. But after you accepted the Torah at Sinai you were called 'My people', as it says, Hearken O my people and I will speak."[1] Moreover, not only had the Gentiles failed to keep the Torah revealed on Mount Sinai. Adam had been given six commandments that were to be binding on all nations. One other commandment had been added to these and all seven were again given to Noah so that his descendants—the Gentiles—should obey them, but all in vain: the Gentiles did not accept even these.[2] It should further be pointed out how it was claimed by the Rabbis that the Gentiles had not only been offered the Law but had also been given prophets.[3] On the basis of the references to Balaam in the Old Testament it was held that the latter had been sent as a prophet to the Gentiles just as Moses had been sent to Israel; indeed it was thought by some that Balaam was superior to Moses.[4] In all, seven prophets had been given to the Gentiles. Thus R. Simeon b. Gamaliel[5] (A.D. 140–65) said: "I was once on a journey and a man came up to me with outstretched arm and he said to me, 'You say that seven prophets have arisen among the nations and they warned them [but they hearkened not] and they went down into hell'. I said to him, 'My son, so it is'." The view remains to be noticed also that proselytism itself was intended for a warning to the Gentiles. This appears from the following:[6] "And many nations shall be joined to the Lord on that day" (Zech. 2. 11). R. Haninah b. Papa [A.D. 120–40] said:

This refers to the day when God will judge all the nations in the time to come. Then He will bring forward all the proselytes in this age and judge the nations in their presence and say to them, 'Why have you left me to serve idols in which there is no reality.' The nations will reply, 'Sovereign of the universe, had we come to Thy door, Thou wouldst not have received us.' God will say to them, 'Let the proselytes from you come and testify against you.' At once will God bring forward all the proselytes who will judge the nations and say to them, 'Why did you abandon God and serve idols that are unreal? Was not Jethro a priest of idols, and when he came to God's door, did not God receive him? And were we not idolaters, and when we came to God's door, did not God receive us?' At once all the wicked will be abashed at the answer of the proselytes.

[1] Tanḥuma, וארא, §1, p. 19; cf. Num. R. 14. 10; Sifre Deut. on 33. 2, §343. See also R.A. p. 166.
[2] See Moore, vol. I, p. 274, and below, pp. 114f. for the Noachian commandments.
[3] Cf. H. Loewe, R.A. p. 653, n. 7.   [4] Cf. R.A. p. 575.
[5] Lev. R. 2. 9.   [6] Pesikta R. 161a.

To summarize we quote Montefiore:

> The particularist doctrine of the Rabbis was that the heathen nations could not be 'saved'. They were doomed to hell. Yet sometimes the heart of the Rabbis smote them for this cruel doctrine, even as the heart of some Christian theologians smote them for a similar teaching. For if the heathen knew no better and had never heard of the one true God how could their doom be justified?...Hence the theory of the 'seven prophets' who 'warned' them. But these prophets had ceased long ago. What then? Well, then came the Law which arranged for the reception of proselytes. Ever since, the nations could become Jews if they chose. The proselytes of each generation are a warning to all their contemporaries. The warning is unheeded; therefore the doom of hell is justified.[1]

We have recorded all the above details in order to show the reality of what we may call the Gentile Problem within Rabbinic Judaism and that it was 'in the air' as it were in the Judaism of Paul's time. That Paul himself was troubled by this problem we can be certain. Born in no mean city, a Roman citizen,[2] he would early have been brought into contact with Gentile life. Despite its sensuality and idolatry the varied and colourful life of the Hellenistic world would appeal to him as we know that it attracted other Jews throughout the post-exilic period: it would have been quite unlike the Paul revealed to us in the Epistles and in Acts to disregard the life and fate of the majority of the people around him. But at the same time, of course, the very fascination of Hellenism would make him more intensely aware of his Jewishness. All that we know of Paul, his utter devotion to the Law, his fanatic zeal[3] and fiery temperament[4] would lead us to expect to find him as a disciple of the gloomy Shammai.[5] Actually we know that he sat at the feet of a disciple of the gentle Hillel, Gamaliel, of whose tolerance we learn in Acts.[6] But though he was thus a student under 'liberal'[7] tutors it is difficult to believe that Paul would accept their attitude on many questions. (Glover has indeed plausibly suggested that indignation at the caution of Gamaliel in dealing with the young Christian movement helped to make Paul a persecutor.)[8] In any case Paul, like the author of 4 Ezra, must in his

---

[1] R.A. p. 576.   [2] Cf. Acts 21. 39.

[3] Cf. Acts 9. 1; Gal. 1. 13 f.

[4] Cf. 2 Cor. 6 and 7; T. R. Glover, *Paul of Tarsus*, p. 58: "Paul had plenty of human nature and was quick to respond to its promptings."

[5] C. H. Dodd, *Ryl. Bull.* vol. xviii, no. 1, p. 36.   [6] Cf. Acts 5. 33 f.

[7] For the relation of Hillel's school to that of Shammai's, cf. W. L. Knox, *St Paul and the Church of Jerusalem*. See index. On their different attitudes towards proselytes, W. G. Braude, *Jewish Proselytizing*, p. ii.

[8] T. R. Glover, *Paul of Tarsus*, p. 57.

studies as in his personal contacts, have been compelled to consider 'the lesser breeds without the Law' and to wonder at the fate of 'the many' who were doomed to destruction. His very extreme devotion to the Law may have been the shadow of an agony he felt for those without the Law: his human sympathies would be in conflict with his creed.[1]

It is from this conflict that Paul was released when he became a Christian. The release came to him with the realization that it was no longer devotion to the Torah which was primary but faith in Christ;[2] and because this faith in Christ or personal relationship to Christ was possible for anyone he could become the friend of sinners and publicans and of those who were afar off, the strangers and foreigners, the Gentiles, and they could become joint heirs with him in the blessings of God.[3] The religion of the Torah was essentially a national religion. To accept the Torah meant not merely initiation into a religion, as did, for example, the acceptance of Mithraism, but incorporation into a nation,[4] and "naturalization in the Jewish people was the only way by which an alien could hope to share in its glorious future".[5] Christ was, however, a revelation of God apart from the Law. This meant that one could be a Christian without being a Jew, and so the doors were open to the Gentiles. In Judaism all had to be Jews, there could be no Greek nor Scythian. In Christ there could be both Jew and Greek and Scythian, the national principle had been transcended.[6]

The discovery that the Gentile was his brother 'in Christ' came to Paul then as the solution of an inner conflict: it was a thrilling mystery.[7] Throughout his Epistles there is a sense of barriers long standing being broken down.[8] Whether Paul became immediately aware of the significance of Christ for the Gentiles is a matter of doubt. Acts gives us three accounts of his conversion and in each of these the call to preach to the Gentiles is connected with his conversion;[9] but unfortunately our knowledge of Paul's practice for the first thirteen or fourteen years after his conversion must be a matter of conjecture. However, we do know that when Barnabas had visited Antioch to inquire into the results of

---

[1] Cf. C. H. Dodd, *Ryl. Bull.* vol. xviii, no. 1, p. 36; also T. R. Glover, op. cit. p. 59.

[2] Rom. 3. 21 f.   [3] Cf. Eph. 2.   [4] Cf. Moore, vol. 1, p. 233.

[5] Ibid. vol. 1, p. 231. Moore quotes Juster with approval: "Il faut avoir present à l'esprit le caractère ethnico-religieux des Juifs et ne pas essayer de diviser des choses indivisibles."

[6] Gal. 3. 26–9; Rom. 10. 12.

[7] Eph. 1. 9; 3. 3, 4.   [8] Eph. 2; Gal. 5. 1.

[9] The three accounts are in Acts 9. 1 f., 22. 4–16, 26. 12–18. They are possibly from three different sources. Cf. C. H. Dodd, *The Apostolic Preaching and its Developments*, pp. 30 f.; *Beginnings*, vol. iv, pp. 99 f., vol. v, pp. 188 f.

preaching the Word to the Gentiles there and saw 'the gracious power of God' and therefore approved of it, he naturally turned for help in such work to Paul who was at Tarsus.[1] It is probable, therefore, that the latter had already won some kind of reputation in work connected with the Gentiles, and that it was during these 'silent' years that he faced the implications of his acceptance of Christ.[2] At any rate we know from his Epistles and from Acts that he regarded himself and was regarded by others as the Apostle to the Gentiles *par excellence*. Paul preached peace to those afar off and ultimately, as we saw, reached a complete universalism.

So far we have emphasized the fact that for Paul the acceptance of Jesus as the Christ meant the universalizing of religion. In the words of Dr Dodd: "for Paul to accept Christ meant that he was outside the Law and therefore on common ground with Gentiles and hence that the true Church of Christ must rest upon the principle, 'there is no distinction', in Christ there is neither Jew nor Greek."[3] But when we examine the Acts and Pauline Epistles further we discover what seem to be inconsistencies. It is, of course, true that missionaries must always be adepts at adaptation, and we should not expect a strict logical consistency in a man who spent his life not in a study but in the maelstrom of religious controversy and missionary labours. Nevertheless, there are aspects of Paul's life and thought that call for explanation.

1. A survey of Paul's practice in preaching on his missionary journeys reveals that he was at least as much concerned with preaching to the Jews as to the Gentiles, this despite his strong assertion that he had been set apart as a minister of the uncircumcision.[4] It is a familiar fact that the Apostle presented the Gospel first to the synagogues of the different places he visited.[5] It was his declared policy to preach first to the Jews and it was his custom always so to do.[6] Now the synagogue would naturally be the base of any missionary enterprise to the Gentiles, because of the number of adherents from among the latter that most synagogues seemed to have,[7] and it may be urged that this entirely accounts for Paul's practice of first approaching the synagogues. But

---

[1] Acts 11. 22f.

[2] A. D. Nock, *St Paul*, pp. 87f.; W. L. Knox, *St Paul and the Church of Jerusalem*, p. 159.

[3] *Ryl. Bull.* vol. XVIII, no. 1, p. 37.

[4] Gal. 2. 7; Gal. 1. 16; Acts 9. 15, 26. 17.

[5] Acts 13. 5 (at Salamis); 13. 14 (Antioch in Pisidia); 14. 1 (Iconium); 17. 1 (Thessalonica); 17. 17 (Athens); 18. 4 (Corinth); 18. 24ff. (Ephesus).

[6] Acts 13. 46; cf. J. W. Parkes, *Jesus, Paul and the Jews*, pp. 97f.

[7] W. L. Knox, *St Paul and the Church of Jerusalem*, p. 122, n. 54, p. 123, n. 55.

THE OLD AND THE NEW ISRAEL: 'NATIONALISM' 69

it is clear from the Book of Acts that it was with the Jews that Paul wrestled most. He seems incapable of leaving the latter to themselves. Thus we read that in 'Antioch in Pisidia' "Paul and Barnabas waxed bold and said, It was necessary that the word of God should first have been spoken to you: but seeing ye put it from you, and judge yourselves unworthy of everlasting life, lo, we turn to the Gentiles".[1] Yet in the next place to which they came, Iconium, "they went both together unto the synagogue of the Jews".[2] Again it is surely remarkable that in Acts 28 the author takes leave of his readers with a scene in which Paul on arrival at Rome calls together for consultation not the Christians but the Jewish elders, who welcomed the Apostle and argued with him as one of themselves.[3] It is this 'preoccupation' of Paul with the Jews in the Book of Acts that has led many to doubt the historicity of the latter.[4] Could the Paul who wrote so vehemently to the Galatians have been so sedulously careful to give the first place in his labours to the Jews? And again it is this that has added force to the view that Paul became a missionary to the Gentiles only because the Jews had first rejected the Gospel, i.e. his universalism is a secondary product of his missionary experience and not an integral element in his faith from the beginning.[5] For our purpose, however, what is noteworthy is that the Apostle to the Gentiles was throughout his journeys strangely and persistently concerned with his own kinsmen after the flesh.

2. We next turn to Paul's attitude towards the Law. We have seen that for Paul faith in Christ had ousted obedience to the Law as the way of salvation. In consonance with this there are passages in Paul's Epistles where the Law is not only relegated to a very inferior position but actually declared to be a 'yoke of bondage' of which Christ was the end.[6] Christ has superseded the Law and in one place Paul suggests apparently that he is no longer bound to the Law.[7] Nevertheless, the same man who wrote that "Christ is the end of the Law" also wrote: "Do we then through faith cancel the Law? Not at all; we establish the Law."[8] Despite passages such as Phil. 3. 2–3: "Beware of dogs! Beware of evil workers! Beware of the concision; for we are the circumcision, we who pray in the Spirit of God and boast in Christ and put no trust in the flesh", where Paul is attacking those who would impose the Law on all Christians, Dr Dodd has found in the Apostle an increasingly

---

[1] Acts 13. 45 f., 18. 6.   [2] Acts 14. 1.
[3] Acts 28. 17 f.
[4] See Johannes Weiss, *The History of Primitive Christianity*, vol. I, p. 210.
[5] Cf. A. Schweitzer, *The Mysticism of Paul the Apostle*, p. 181; see C. H. Dodd, *Ryl. Bull.* vol. XVIII, no. 1, p. 41, n.
[6] Rom. 7. 6; Gal. 5. 1.   [7] 1 Cor. 9. 21.   [8] Rom. 3. 31.

irenic attitude towards the Law.[1] Moreover, Paul observed the Law, and that in the pharisaic manner, throughout his life.[2] In 1 Cor. 7. 18 he implies that obedience to it is his duty; to conciliate the Jews he even agreed to the circumcision of Timothy, who was born of a Greek father, and Acts 21. 21 f. make it clear that he regarded the observance of the Law as incumbent upon all Jewish Christians.[3] We are faced with a dilemma. The Apostle who first turned to the Gentiles on the ground that salvation could be received apart from the Law, himself lived and died 'a Pharisee'.

Various explanations of this 'inconsistency' have been proposed. Anderson Scott has claimed that the Law for Paul meant two things, "the Law as a system whereby men could secure or thought they could secure righteousness by merit, and the contents of the Law, the divine requirements as to the character and conduct of men". In the former sense the Law had come to an end. In the latter sense it remained valid for Jews and Christians, though not valid in quite the same sense for both.[4] This is not stated so baldly by Dr Dodd, but in his examination of Paul's use of the term νόμος the latter has also pointed out that "he betrays by such expressions as ὁ νόμος τῶν ἐντολῶν ἐν δόγμασιν and τὰ δικαιώματα τοῦ νόμου a consciousness that there was a wider sense of νόμος = Tôrâh within which fell the narrower sense of commandments, statutes and judgements. . . . A further indication in the same direction is the fact that Paul cites 'ὁ νόμος' when the actual passages quoted are not of the nature of commandments and are not even found in the Pentateuch."[5] At the same time Dr Dodd points out that such passages

[1] Ryl. Bull. vol. XVIII, no. 1, p. 41; contrast A. Schweitzer, The Mysticism of Paul the Apostle, p. 201. Cf. J. Weiss, The History of Primitive Christianity (E.T.), vol. II, pp. 549 f.

[2] Acts 16. 3, 21. 26, 23. 6; W. L. Knox, St Paul and the Church of Jerusalem, p. 122, n. 54: "Obedience to the Law was a life-long matter."

[3] W. L. Knox, St Paul and the Church of Jerusalem, ibid. writes: "It is clear that Paul throughout his life continued to practise Judaism: and that he expected Jewish converts to do so, cf. 1 Cor. 7. 18; Acts 16. 3, 21. 26, 23. 6, where it is incredible that Paul should have been guilty of the dishonesty of proclaiming himself a Pharisee and the son of a Pharisee if his only claim to the title was that he believed in the resurrection of the dead; for this belief was widely held by Jews who had no claim to be regarded as Pharisees. The only objection that can be brought against this view is the language of 1 Cor. 9. 21, where St Paul seems to imply that when dealing with Gentiles he behaved as if not bound by the Law. On the other hand this interpretation of the passage is impossible. St Paul could not both behave as a Jew when dealing with Jews and as free from the Law when dealing with Gentiles . . . ."

[4] C. A. A. Scott, Christianity According to St Paul, p. 42; also J. Weiss, The History of Primitive Christianity, vol. II, p. 550.

[5] The Bible and the Greeks, p. 35. This distinction which Dr Dodd finds in Paul is familiar to Rabbinic Judaism. See Moore, vol. I, p. 263.

are not frequent in Paul.[1] Moreover, even if such a distinction as Anderson Scott suggests could be proved beyond question, the problem would still remain, why, if he regarded the Law as a system as no longer valid, should Paul himself still observe it?

On this question again Schweitzer has insisted on apocalyptic as supplying the clue. Briefly stated, his position is as follows: For Paul the End will come when the number of those who are elect is completed,[2] i.e. when the Elect are brought to being 'in Christ'. The all important thing is the 'being in Christ'; once this is achieved it becomes a matter of indifference whether a person observes the Law or not but "whatever the external condition in which a man has made his election a reality, that is to say, has become a believer, in that condition he is, as a believer, to remain".[3] So if a man is called under the Law he is to be under the Law still, and hence it would be legitimate for Paul to practise the Law. This, of course, does not do justice to Schweitzer's theory but it will be seen that his position rests on what he calls the theory of the *status quo*. But the interpretation of the passages which he quotes in favour of this view is not convincing. Thus it is not at all clear that I Cor. 7. 21-2 means that a slave should never accept freedom even if it is possible for him to do so:[4] and in I Cor. 7. 3-5 ff., the counsel that the married and the unmarried and the widowed should continue in their present state can be adequately accounted for by the two facts that Paul regarded the End as imminent, and therefore all changes as unnecessary, and also that to him the unmarried and the widowed were better able to attend to Christ's demands.[5] We do not need the elaborate theory of Schweitzer to elucidate these passages. Moreover, that theory also implies that for Paul the Torah had really become a matter of indifference.[6] But this is precisely what the whole life of Paul forbids us to believe. It is the seriousness with which the Apostle to the Gentiles still remained a Pharisee which is to be explained and it is this that Schweitzer's theory really overlooks.

It appears that Paul's contradictory attitudes towards the Torah become explicable only when we look at his life from the Rabbinic point of view. First, we have seen that Paul throughout his life might be described as a Pharisee who had accepted Jesus as the Messiah, i.e. he

---

[1] *The Bible and the Greeks*, p. 36.
[2] *The Mysticism of Paul the Apostle*, pp. 181 f.
[3] A. Schweitzer, op. cit. pp. 193 f.
[4] Cf. C. H. Dodd, *Ryl. Bull.* vol. xviii, no. i, p. 31 and *J.T.S.* (1924), vol. xxvi, no. 101, p. 77. So J. Moffatt, *First Corinthians* (*M.N.T.C.*), p. 87.
[5] See the treatment in J. Moffatt, *First Corinthians* (*M.N.T.C.*), pp. 73 f.
[6] A. Schweitzer, op. cit. p. 194.

was living in the Messianic Age which preceded the Age to Come.[1] If then we inquire what the Pharisees thought about the position of the Torah in the Messianic Age we may find light on Paul's attitude to the Torah. As far back as Jeremiah we find the view that in the Messianic Age the Torah would be spontaneously obeyed by every individual.[2] So too in the pre-Christian pseudepigrapha it was taught that the Messiah when he came would be wise and an exponent of the Torah. Thus in 1 Enoch 49. 1-3 we read:

1. For wisdom is poured out like water,
   And glory faileth not before him for evermore.
   For he is mighty in all the secrets of righteousness,

2. And unrighteousness shall disappear as a shadow,
   And have no continuance
   Because the Elect One standeth before the Lord of Spirits,
   And his glory is for ever and ever,
   And his might unto all generations.

3. And in him dwells the spirit of wisdom,
   And the spirit which gives insight,
   And the spirit of understanding and of might....[3]

Later Rabbinic literature reveals the same attitude, and although those passages which explicitly speak of the Messiah as the bringer of a New Torah, Tôrâh ḥᵉdâshâh, are late, we cannot doubt that they reflect earlier beliefs, because there must have been controversies among the Rabbis as to the role of the Torah in the Messianic Age at all periods. Moore writes: "Inasmuch as the days of the Messiah are the religious as well as the political consummation of the national history, and, however idealized, belong to the world we live in, it is natural that the Law should not only be in force in the Messianic Age but should be better studied and better observed than ever before; and this was indubitably the common belief."[4] When the Rabbis taught, moreover, that the Messiah when he came would bring a new Law, they thought of that Law as new not in the sense that it would be contrary to the Law of Moses but that it would explain it more fully.[5]

[1] For the distinction of the Messianic Age from the Age to Come in later apocalyptic, cf. R. H. Charles, *Eschatology*, pp. 200f. We shall return to this in chapter 10, which does not invalidate the above.   [2] Jer. 31. 33.

[3] Cf. Isa. 11. 9. Other passages containing the same idea are 1 Enoch 51. 3; Psalms of Sol. 17. 35, 17. 48. In the former (17. 35) the Messiah is διδακτὸς ὑπὸ θεοῦ. Str.-B. wrongly refers to 17. 43 instead of 17. 48; Str.-B. vol. IV, p. 2.

[4] Moore, vol. I, p. 271; also Schürer, *The Jewish People in the Time of Jesus Christ*, Div. II, vol. II, p. 174.

[5] On all this see Str.-B. vol. IV, p. 1, Erster Exkurs: "Zur Bergpredigt Jesu". Passages referring to a New Torah or Teaching in the Messianic Age are *Lev. R.* 13. on 11. 1; Targum Jonathan on Isa. 12. 3. See Str.-B. ibid. p. 2.

True to this expectation Jesus had come and preached a new Torah from the mount[1] and had yet remained loyal to the old Torah, displaying "universalism in belief and particularism in practice".[2] In view of all this, it would not be unnatural for Paul also to believe that loyalty to the new law of Christ[3] did not involve disloyalty to the Torah of his fathers, while at the same time holding that the latter, in its full sense, had also predicted that the Gentiles should share in the glories of the Messianic Age. There was no reason why Paul should not reject the view that Gentiles should be converted to Judaism before entering the Messianic Kingdom and at the same time insist that for him as a Jew the Torah was still valid. In so doing he was being true both to the universalist tradition of Judaism and at the same time showing his identification with the Israel according to the flesh: he was being true to the 'new' and the 'old' Israel.

There is another practical consideration to notice. That it would be to Paul's advantage to observe the Law becomes evident in Acts 18. 18, 21. 23f., where Paul joined with four men in ritual purification according to the Law that all might know that "he walked orderly and kept the Law". This is in keeping with what we know of Judaism. The latter was very tolerant of ideas; it could comprehend the greatest variety of beliefs; Gamaliel's attitude to the early Christian movement is typical of Rabbinic tolerance.[4] This is also attested of course by the numerous groups and movements within Judaism.[5] But on the other hand Judaism was equally intolerant of any neglect of the Law.[6] The career of Elisha b. Abuyah (first century A.D.) (Acher) illustrates this. His knowledge was beyond question, and he was regarded as an authority on religious questions, and yet his opinions carried no weight with the Rabbis because he did not practise the Law. The sins which made the Pharisees hate Acher were the "fact that he rode through the streets of Jerusalem in an ostentatious manner on a Day of Atonement which fell on a Sabbath and that he was bold enough to ignore the *tehum*, the limits of the Sabbath Day journey". It is these facts that both the Jerusalem Talmud and the Babylonian Talmud cite as proofs that Elisha had forsaken Pharisaism, they are facts which show contempt of the Law.[7]

We may assume that Paul would be fully aware that once he forsook the observance of the Torah Judaism would close its door against him;

---

[1] Matt. 5.   [2] A. Schweitzer, *The Mysticism of Paul the Apostle*, p. 178.

[3] Gal. 6. 2.   [4] Acts 5. 34f.

[5] See above, pp. 8 f.; also Moore, vol. I, pp. 110f.

[6] This is sometimes expressed by saying that it was orthopraxy not orthodoxy that was emphasized in Judaism; cf. D. Winton Thomas' review of J. Bonsirven's, *Le Judaisme Palestinien*, in *J.T.S.* (1936), vol. XXXVII, p. 85.

[7] *J.E.* vol. v, pp. 138f.; R. T. Herford, *Pirqê Aboth* (2nd ed.), p. 120.

that he could propound theories about the Law which were anathema to his Jewish co-religionists; that he could even accept Jesus as the Messiah and yet retain their respect, but that once he deliberately gave up the practice of the Torah he would for ever forfeit the right to be seriously listened to by the other Rabbis. The observance of the Law in short was Paul's passport with Judaism. Had he ceased to be faithful to the former, for example, such a meeting as that of the Council of Jerusalem[1] would have been impossible, because a non-practising Paul would not have been taken seriously.[2] On the other hand it is clear that Paul's repute as a strict Pharisee gave him a considerable influence over Christians. Thus a Galilean Jew, like Peter, who had only lived up to the standards of ordinary Judaism, would always be consciously at a disadvantage in any argument over interpretation with a trained Pharisee like Paul, and would always be more ready to yield to such a one than to others. With a view both to his prestige within the Church and to his relations with Judaism, it was expedient for Paul to maintain his devotion to the Law.

For our purpose, however, whether the explanation we have given above of Paul's devotion to the Law be satisfactory or not, the significant point is that throughout a life that suffered greatly at the hands of Jewry, the Apostle, surely at great inconvenience[3] to himself, honoured and observed the mark of his people, the Torah, never separating himself from Israel after the flesh.

3. Again, in the third place, we come to an inconsistency in the Apostle's theology, or rather in what has been called his philosophy of history. As a result of his encounter with Christ on the road to Damascus Paul had been introduced into a fellowship or community constituted in the name of Jesus as the Christ. The dominant characteristic of this community, as we shall see later, was the possession of the Spirit. It could be composed of people from all nations and classes and from both sexes, the one condition of inclusion within it being faith in Christ. The way in which Paul came to interpret this community has been often described and the briefest outline will suffice here. For Paul it was God who was in Christ,[4] and therefore the community constituted in

[1] W. L. Knox, *St Paul and the Church of Jerusalem*, p. 159. Had Paul ceased practising the Law there would have been an end to his prospects among Jews—and, resulting from this, an end to his prospects among Gentiles, because a man regarded as an outcast by his own group usually has little prestige among members of another group.

[2] Ibid.

[3] How difficult it must have been for Paul to observe the Law when he was a prisoner, for example, will be realized when we remember that he could accept food only from his practising Jewish friends.

[4] 2 Cor. 5. 19.

Him became for Paul the 'people of God' and "the life 'in the Spirit' marked the Church as being the true 'Israel of God' in its 'eschatological' manifestation Gal. 6. 15–16".[1] Paul saw in the emergence of the Church that the 'Israel of God' had entered upon a new phase in its history. The Church fulfils the functions of the faithful remnant, and is interpreted by Paul in terms of the remnant doctrine of the Old Testament. In the death of Jesus the old Israel had come to an end, and yet in the Resurrection it had begun anew, and there was therefore a real continuity between the Israel of the Old Testament and the Christian Church, and in the latter Paul sees the world-wide growth of the true Israel, an Israel formed of those who had accepted the claims of Jesus as Messiah.[2]

But Paul had been brought up to believe that the people whom God had called to be His own was the nation of Israel. True, like other Pharisees, Paul could not but have recognized that not all Jews were true Jews[3] and that the people of God was not coterminous with Jewry. Nevertheless, he would still have thought that salvation was of the Jews. The recognition that the Christian Church, therefore, was the true Israel constituted a stumbling-block for Paul, because if the Church has taken over the functions of 'Israel' then in the words of Dr Dodd "there is no ground for assigning any special place in the future to the Jewish nation as such".[4] The logic of his conception of the Church demanded that Paul should not think of Israel after the flesh as having any special office, but this is somehow what he could not conceive. The fact that when the Messiah came to his own, his own received him not, was a shattering blow to him, and he reels under the emotional tension caused by the rejection of Jesus by Jewry. He yearns over his people: "I have great heaviness and continual sorrow in my heart. For I could wish that myself were accursed from Christ for my brethren, my kinsmen after the flesh."[5] Despite his noble universalism he finds it impossible not to assign a special place to his own people. The Jews' rejection of Jesus is in the purpose of God,[6] i.e. it is for good: it will be the means of bringing in the Gentiles: but it does not mean that God has cast off his

---

[1]   C. H. Dodd, *The Apostolic Preaching and its Developments*, p. 140.

[2]   I have not deemed it necessary further to enlarge on this in view of C. H. Dodd's treatment in *The Apostolic Preaching and its Developments*, pp. 138f., and in *History and the Gospel*, pp. 130f., and *Romans (M.N.T.C.)*, pp. 162–87 on Rom. 9. 30f.; and see R. Newton Flew, *Jesus and His Church*, p. 209; George Johnston, *The New Testament Doctrine of the Church*, pp. 76f.

[3]   Rom. 2. 28–9; cf. Jer. 4. 4; Deut. 10. 16, 30. 6; *P. Aboth* 5. 19. See Str.-B. vol. III, pp. 124f.

[4]   *Romans (M.N.T.C.)*, p. 183.   [5]   Rom. 9. 1.

[6]   For all this see C. H. Dodd, *Romans (M.N.T.C.)*, pp. 176–83 (Rom. 11. 1–32).

people in the process: when all the Gentiles are saved then all Israel will be saved.[1]

Our brief examination of Paul's missionary activity, of his religious practice and of his thought has shown that in all these things the Apostle reveals a consuming desire not only to please but to win over his own people after the flesh to the Faith. It is customary to explain this as a product of his patriotism or nationalism. "Once a Jew, always a Jew" would be pre-eminently true of a nature such as Paul's and the claims of Israel after the flesh would naturally occupy him. We cannot of course deny the force of this: nationalism has rightly been called 'man's other religion'. But, nevertheless, this is not the full explanation of Paul's intense longing for the conversion of the Jews. The explanation of this lies in the religious aspirations of contemporary Judaism. To this we now turn.

W. R. Smith has written: "that the doctrines and ordinances of the Old Testament cannot be thoroughly comprehended until they are put into comparison with the religions of the nations akin to the Israelites."[2] He substantiated this claim by his work on the religion of the Semites. In his lecture on "The nature of the religious community and the relation of the gods to their worshippers" he pointed out how in the Semitic world there was a solidarity of gods and their worshippers. He writes:

Every human being without choice on his own part, but simply in virtue of his birth and upbringing, becomes a member of what we call a 'natural' society. He belongs, that is, to a certain family and a certain nation, and his membership lays upon him definite obligations and duties which he is called upon to fulfil as a matter of course and on pain of social penalties and disabilities, while at the same time it confers upon him certain social rights and advantages. In this respect the ancient and modern worlds are alike; but there is this important difference, that the tribal or national societies of the ancient world were not strictly natural in the modern sense of the word, for the gods had

---

[1] Related to all this, though we need not elaborate it, is Paul's inconsistency in trying to prove that there is an advantage in being born or having at some time been a Jew. He is at great pains to prove such an advantage (cf. Rom. 3. 1 f, 9. 1–5. See C. H. Dodd, *Romans* (*M.N.T.C.*), pp. 43 f. 151). Why? Logically he ought not to be. Dodd writes on Rom. 3. 1 f.: "The Jewish objector is thus driven from his last ditch. 'Then what is the Jew's superiority?' he exclaims; 'What is the good of circumcision?' The logical answer on the basis of Paul's argument is, 'None whatever'. But the trouble is that the 'Jewish objector' is in Paul's own mind. His Pharisaism—or shall we say his patriotism?—was too deeply engrained for him to put right out of his mind the idea that somehow the divine covenant with mankind had a 'most favoured nation clause'," p. 43; also W. Sanday and A. C. Headlam, *Romans* (*I.C.C.*), pp. 232 f.

[2] W. R. Smith, *The Religion of the Semites*, p. xiv.

their part and place in them equally with men. The circle into which a man was born was not simply a group of kinsfolk and fellow citizens, but embraced also certain divine beings, the gods of the family and of the state, which to the ancient mind were as much a part of the particular community with which they stood connected as the human members of the social circle. The relations between the gods of antiquity and their worshippers were expressed in the language of human relationship and this language was not taken in a figurative sense but with strict literality. If a god was spoken of as father and his worshippers as his offspring, the meaning was that the worshippers were literally of his stock, that he and they made up one natural family with reciprocal family duties to one another.[1]

A god then would be bound up with his people and even with the land they occupied; people, god and land formed one inseparable unity:[2] to change one's god would be equivalent to changing one's nationality:[3] the destruction of a people would mean the disappearance of its god.[4]

The Old Testament of course transcends this primitive Semitic ideology.[5] Yahweh came to be regarded as the father of Israel not because of any natural connection between them but because of the 'Grace' of Yahweh expressed in certain acts of redemption. The relationship of Yahweh and His people was deemed to rest, not upon necessity, but upon the former's free choice of Israel and the latter's recognition and acceptance of that choice. As Oesterley and Robinson have written: "The early Israelite may have thought of Yahweh much as the Moabite thought of Chemosh but the relationship rested on a different basis. Chemosh always had been a Moabite and never could be anything else; Yahweh had existed as a God independently of Israel, and, if need be, could so exist again, or could, on the other hand, extend His interests and His influence to others than the original Israel. The connection

---

[1] W. R. Smith, *The Religion of the Semites*, pp. 29 f.
[2] Cf. S. A. Cook, *The Old Testament: a Reinterpretation*, pp. 115 f. and especially p. 119; T. H. Robinson, *Prophecy and the Prophets*, p. 143; W. O. E. Oesterley and T. H. Robinson, *Hebrew Religion*, p. 170. Cook writes: "People and land are essentially one (cf. Hosea 1. 2), each is Yahweh's inheritance (1 Sam. 26. 19, cf. Zech. 2. 12) and Israel is sown or planted (Hosea 2. 23, Amos 9. 15) in a land which Yahweh gave his servant Jacob (Ezek. 28. 25).... There is a strong sense of soil (Prov. 10. 30): the land is inalienably Israel's (Lev. 25. 23)...Naaman must take away with him Israelite soil in order to worship Yahweh fitly in his own land (2 Kings 5. 17) and strangers entering the sacred land must learn the cult of the God of the land" (17. 26 f.) (Cook, op. cit. p. 120).
[3] W. R. Smith, *The Religion of the Semites*, p. 36.
[4] Cf. W. O. E. Oesterley and T. H. Robinson, *Hebrew Religion*, p. 140; T. H. Robinson, *Prophecy and the Prophets*, p. 135.
[5] Cf. R. H. Charles, *Eschatology*, pp. 14 f.; W. R. Smith, *The Religion of the Semites*, p. 42; W. O. E. Oesterley and T. H. Robinson, *Hebrew Religion*, p. 199.

between God and people was not 'natural' but...artificial."[1] It was this 'unique' character of the relationship between Yahweh and Israel that enabled the prophets of the Old Testament to develop what we may call the doctrine of the Remnant, a peculiar conception of 'Israel'. Insisting on Yahweh's freedom to choose Israel in the beginning and recognizing that Israel as a whole had not been faithful to its covenant, the prophets maintained that Yahweh could exist without His people, that indeed it might be His purpose to destroy His own people or nation if they were not faithful. In Isaiah we find the idea that only a remnant of the people would be saved;[2] in Jeremiah that the national relationship between Yahweh and Israel is to be replaced by a personal one between Yahweh and the individual Israelite;[3] the prophet, indeed, seems to have felt at times that the "whole cause of Yahweh in the world hung on his individual life".[4] The figure of the servant of Yahweh in Deutero-Isaiah points to the same belief that all are not true Jews who are born of Abraham but only such as are included in the personal bond with Yahweh.[5] Hence arises the problem that S. A. Cook has emphasized as to the meaning of the term 'Israel' in the Old Testament.[6] In certain places, of course, it stands for the northern kingdom, it can also apparently stand for Israel and Judah; and again for the 'ideal' or 'true' Israel that has responded to God. Cook writes: "The prophets virtually introduce a new conception: it is no longer the group's god but the god and a new group, not Israel's Yahweh but Yahweh's Israel. It is as though Yahweh started afresh, replacing an old association, such as that to which Amos refers (Amos 3. 2, 'you only have I known') by a new Israel."[7] We can easily understand why Paul could so convincingly appeal to the prophets in his interpretation of the Church. He, like them, was re-discovering the meaning of the term 'Israel'.[8]

But there is another side to Judaism than that with which we have

---

[1] W. O. E. Oesterley and T. H. Robinson, *Hebrew Religion*, p. 140.

[2] Isa. 4. 3-5. Contrast Ezek. 37. 12-14. See Mal. 3. 16-17; Dan. 7. 13-14. 22-7.

[3] Cf. R. H. Charles, *Eschatology*, p. 58; J. Skinner, *Prophecy and Religion*, pp. 27f., 223ff.   [4] Cf. J. Skinner, *Prophecy and Religion*, p. 223.

[5] See H. Wheeler Robinson, *The Cross of the Servant*; A. S. Peake, *The Servant of Yahweh and Other Lectures*; also J. Skinner, *Isaiah XL-LXVI*, pp. xxxiii f. and pp. 233 f. (Cambridge Bible for Schools) and *Prophecy and Religion*, pp. 233 f.; S. A. Cook, *The Old Testament: a Reinterpretation*, pp. 178 f.

[6] See references in his index to *The Old Testament: a Reinterpretation*, and N. W. Porteous, *Record and Revelation* (ed. H. W. Robinson), p. 220.

[7] S. A. Cook, *The Old Testament: a Reinterpretation*, pp. 184 f.; *The Truth of the Bible*, p. 67. For the idea of Israel after the flesh nationally and historically limited as being historically unjustified, cf. S. A. Cook, *The Truth of the Bible*, p. 71.

[8] See above, pp. 74 f.

up till now been concerned. Concentration on the development of such a doctrine as that of the Remnant in the Old Testament[1] lays us open to one grave danger, the danger of under-estimating the tenacity of universal primitive conceptions which the Semites have shared with other peoples. Oesterley and Robinson have pointed out that the idea of the choice of Israel by Yahweh is only explicitly set forth in the end of the seventh century:[2] it was the interpretation that the prophets gave to Israel's history. It may be true that like priest like people, but it is certainly not true that like prophet like people. The Jews would be singularly unlike other people if they had understood their prophets and accepted their teaching, i.e. if they had accepted the view that their relationship with Yahweh was not natural and national but ethical and personal.[3] W. R. Smith writes: "The mass of the Hebrews before the exile received with blank incredulity the prophetic teaching that Jehovah was ready to enforce his law of righteousness even by the destruction of the sinful commonwealth of Israel. To the prophets Jehovah's long-suffering meant the patience with which he offers repeated calls to repentance and defers punishment, while there is hope of amendment; but to the heathen and to the healthy minded in Israel, the long-suffering of the gods meant a disposition to overlook the offences of their worshippers."[4] In other words the conception of Yahweh as Israel's God rather than of Israel as Yahweh's people persisted; Israel after the flesh is still unsupplanted by Israel as an idea. Not only was this true among the masses. Inconsistently enough the prophets themselves did not draw the full implications of their teaching. True they gave birth to Israel as an 'idea' or an 'ideal', but they also invariably cling to Israel as a nation as still somehow the people of Yahweh. This paradoxical nationalism in their religion we can clearly trace, the survival of the primitive Semitic conception of the solidarity of a god and his people. Moreover, the extra-canonical literature of the post-exilic period reveals what we can possibly describe as a recrudescence of the doctrine of the necessary connection between Yahweh and Israel. To the examination of this we now turn. There are three elements in the late passages of the Old Testament and in the Apocrypha and Pseudepigrapha which for our purpose are significant.

1. First, a persistent yearning for the ingathering of the dispersed of Israel into one national entity.

[1] This is the danger of the survey of Old Testament Theology in T. W. Manson's *The Teaching of Jesus*, pp. 175 f.

[2] Cf. W. O. E. Oesterley and T. H. Robinson, *Hebrew Religion*, p. 114.

[3] Cf. J. Skinner, *Prophecy and Religion*, pp. 180–1.

[4] Cf. W. R. Smith, *The Religion of the Semites*, p. 61.

We saw that the prophets had interpreted the exodus from Egypt as leading to a covenant whereby a heterogeneous group of tribes had become the people of Yahweh, they had become one people and they had one God.[1] (The idea that Israel should be one explains why throughout the Old Testament and in the Pseudepigrapha the disruption of the kingdom was regarded with such horror;[2] the division was a denial of that oneness which should characterize the people of Yahweh.) However widely the Jews came to be dispersed, their awareness of their essential oneness remained; it was not their loyalty to a common land of which they were perforce deprived, not the cement of a common language that sustained this awareness, but their sense of being the One people of the One God. Throughout the later prophets and in the Apocrypha and Pseudepigrapha the theme recurs that all Israel must again be gathered from the four corners of the earth: its divisions must be healed: the Lord is to be One and His people One. The evidence for this is abundant.

We begin with Jeremiah. Born in Anathoth,[3] which is situated in the territory of Benjamin, it was perhaps natural that Jeremiah should have been concerned not merely with his own kingdom of Judah but also with the fate of the northern kingdom exiled in 722 B.C.,[4] because ethnologically Benjamin belonged to Israel.[5] At any rate his prophecies reveal an absorbing interest and a constant love for the Rachel tribes; it is his heart's desire that northern Israel as well as Judah should ultimately return from exile.[6] His purchase of a portion of his family inheritance is symbolic of his belief in the ultimate salvation of all his people and their establishment upon their own soil.[7] If we accept Jer. 31. 2-6, 18–20, 21–2, 25, 26 as being authentic and accept the literal interpretation that Skinner favours,[8] they reveal the same longing. This means that for Jeremiah the nation was still the sphere if not the unit of religion; as Skinner puts it: "the main point is that in some sense a restoration of the Israelite nationality was the form in which Jeremiah

---

[1] W. O. E. Oesterley and T. H. Robinson, *History of Israel*, vol. i, pp. 88 f.; *Hebrew Religion*, pp. 139f.

[2] Cf. 1 Enoch 89. 51; Test. Zebulun 9. 1 f.: "Observe, therefore, the waters, and know when they flow together, they sweep along stones, trees, earth and other things. But if they are divided into many streams, the earth swalloweth them up, and they vanish away. So shall ye also be if ye be divided."

[3] Jer. 1. 1.   [4] Cf. S. A. Cook, *The Truth of the Bible*, p. 44.

[5] Cf. J. Skinner, *Prophecy and Religion*, p. 19.

[6] Ibid. Jer. 3. 12f., 31. 4–16, 31. 9, 15–20; Skinner regards 3. 14–18 which also speaks of the restoration of Israel and Judah as post-exilic; cf. p. 82: they are the work of a post-exilic editor.

[7] Cf. J. Skinner, *Prophecy and Religion*, p. 298; Jer. 32. 6ff.   [8] Ibid. pp. 300f.

conceived the Kingdom of God."[1] In Ezekiel we find the idea that Yahweh is a jealous god[2] who can brook no rivals and who therefore inflicts punishment on Israel because of her apostasy;[3] but the restoration of Israel is assured, because Yahweh's name must be upheld among the nations; the failure of His people would bring dishonour upon Himself.[4] The ingathering of all scattered Israelites then is a constant theme in Ezekiel; the reassembled nation will be purified in heart and spirit, there will be one flock under Yahweh as the shepherd.[5] The same motif runs through Deutero-Isaiah; true 'Israel' is to be a missionary to the Gentiles, but its first task, before turning to the latter, is to seek the return of the lost sheep of the house of Israel; there is a core of nationalism in the most universal of the prophets.[6] G. A. Cooke has collected the evidence for the longing for the restoration in his commentary on Ezekiel; we need only refer to his work for the later prophets.[7] As for the Apocrypha and Pseudepigrapha there is abundant material to show that the idea grew in intensity that Yahweh must indicate His choice of His people by restoring them to their land according to their tribes as a united people; perhaps the most well-known expression of this idea is found in the Psalms of Solomon. Speaking of the Son of David whom the Lord shall raise up the author writes:

And he shall gather together a holy people, whom he shall lead in righteous-
ness,
And he shall judge the tribes of the people that has been sanctified by the Lord
his God.
And he shall not suffer unrighteousness to lodge any more in their midst
Nor shall there dwell with them any man that knoweth wickedness,
For he shall know them, that they are all sons of their God.
And he shall divide them according to their tribes upon the land
And neither sojourner nor alien shall sojourn with them any more.[8]

The literature of the first century A.D. contains the same idea,[9] and our Rabbinic sources reveal the hope and longing for the coming of the day when Israel shall be restored to its true position. The liberation of Israel

---

[1] Ibid. p. 308.
[2] Ezek. 16. 38, 20. 9, 22, 36. 5f., 39. 25.
[3] Ezek. 5. 13.   [4] Ezek. 39. 25f.
[5] Ezek. 36. 16–38, 37. 24; see G. A. Cooke, Ezekiel (I.C.C.), p. 372.
[6] Isa. 43. 5, 54. 7.
[7] G. A. Cooke, Ezekiel (I.C.C.), p. 125, and see index to same under 'Restoration';
cf. Mic. 2. 12, 4. 6f.; Zeph. 3. 19; Zech. 10. 8–10; Neh. 1. 9. See also Amos 9. 1–15.
[8] Psalms of Sol. 17. 28f.
[9] The evidence may be grouped thus:
    (1) For the period 200–100 B.C. cf. Ecclus. 36. 11, 48. 10f.; Tobit 13. 6f., 14. 7;

from oppression and the ingathering of the dispersed to their own land
has a place in the oldest prayers of the synagogue: "Sound the great
horn (as a signal) for our freedom;[1] lift up the standard[2] for the
assembling of our exiles" with the response "Blessed art Thou, O Lord,
who gatherest the dispersed of his people Israel."[3]

2. Secondly, the growth of belief in the eternal relation between Israel
and God.

This grew alongside of the intense desire that we have traced for
national unity. We saw that, despite his individualism, Jeremiah still
regarded the nation of Israel as peculiarly Yahweh's; the latter could
not utterly forsake his people.[4] So too in Ezekiel the relation between
Israel and Yahweh is regarded as being ultimately indestructible.[5] So
close is the relation that the prophet uses the figure of marriage to
describe it, the figure that most brings out the essential unity of any two
partners.[6] The same thought is more and more stressed in Deutero-
Isaiah: "Can a woman forget her suckling child that she should not have
compassion on the son of her womb? Yea, she may forget, yet will not
I forget thee. Behold, I have graven thee upon the palms of my hands,
thy walls are continually before me. For thy Maker is thine husband,
the God of the whole earth."[7] In the Apocrypha and Pseudepigrapha
we can trace an ever-increasing emphasis on the unique relation between
Israel and her God. Israel is the Lord's portion;[8] the sole abode of
Wisdom (Law);[9] the chosen of Yahweh,[10] which will never be cut off;
the everlasting heritage of Yahweh;[11] his first-born;[12] and the same ideas
persist down to the first century A.D. Thus in Psalms of Solomon we
read:

Thou didst choose the seed of Abraham before all the nations
And didst set Thy name upon us O Lord
And Thou wilt not reject us for ever.[13]

---

1 Enoch 90. 30; Test. Reuben 6. 8; Test. Levi 16. 5; Test. Asher 7. 4; Test. Benjamin 9. 2;
Jubilees 1. 15.
    (2) For the period 100–1 B.C., 2 Macc. 1. 6, 18; *Ap. and Ps.* vol. I, p. 133;
1 Enoch 57; Psalms of Sol. 8. 27, 11. 1, 17. 1f., 56.
    (3) For the period A.D. 1–100, 2 Baruch 77f., 78. 4f.; 4 Ezra 5. 41.
[1] Isa. 27. 13; cf. Zech. 9. 14.   [2] Isa. 11. 12.
[3] See Moore, vol. II, p. 367; cf. *b. Meg.* 17b–18a.
[4] See above, Jer. 11. 7, 20. 34, 41.
[5] Cf. Ezek. 37. 26; G. A. Cooke, *Ezekiel* (*I.C.C.*), pp. 29f.
[6] Ezek. 16.   [7] Cf. Isa. 49. 15, 16.
[8] Cf. Ecclus. 17. 17f.; *Ap. and Ps.* vol. II, p. 376.   [9] Ecclus. 24. 4–10.
[10] Ecclus. 47. 22; Judith 7. 30.   [11] Susanna 16. 5.
[12] Susanna 19. 29.   [13] Psalms of Sol. 9. 17f.

According to the Assumption of Moses[1] God created the world for the sake of Israel and henceforth this became the prevailing attitude of Judaism.[2] In Rabbinic literature God's love for Israel and Israel's love for God are constant themes; we need only refer to the Rabbinic Anthology to prove this.[3] All this, as we saw, may be interpreted as an unconscious return to primitive Semitic ideology: for our purpose, however, it is the fact that matters that there was in Paul's day a renewed emphasis on the eternal relationship between his nation and God.[4]

3. Finally, there is one other aspect of Judaism which calls for brief mention in this connection, that is the growth and nature of the belief in resurrection. The contrast between the Jewish conception of resurrection and the Greek desire for immortality has often been drawn. It was their sense of the value of the individual personality that led the Greeks to their doctrine of immortality. On the other hand the Jewish sense of the oneness of the nation made the idea of a merely individual immortality unattractive, and the attitude of Judaism towards the future was determined more by the sense of national solidarity than by individual aspirations.[5] Just as Moses preferred to be blotted out of God's book rather than persist without the people, people who "had sinned a great sin",[6] so, too, without his brethren, his kinsmen after the flesh, no Jew could ultimately enjoy immortality however justly deserved, and however delectable. Throughout the history of Judaism the sense of community, the awareness that the individual can only attain to his highest in the life of the community both now and hereafter is dominant, and it is

[1] 1. 11, 12. Also 4 Ezra 6. 55, 59, 7. 11; 2 Baruch 14. 18; created for sake of righteous in Israel 2 Baruch 14. 19, 15. 7, 21. 24; *Ap. and Ps.* vol. I, p. 415.
[2] The following is a list of references for the peculiar relation which is eternal between Israel and Yahweh:
(1) 200–100 B.C.: Ecclus. 17. 7f., 24. 4–10, 47. 22; Judith 7. 30; Song of the Three Children 1. 12; Susanna 6. 23, 16. 5f.; Test. Levi 14. 3; Test. Judah 23; Jubilees 1. 17, 2. 19ff., 15. 1, 19. 18, 19, 28, 22. 9, 33. 20.
(2) 100–1 B.C.: 2 Macc. 7. 32, 14. 15; 3 Macc. 6. 3; Psalms of Sol. 7. 5f., 9. 17.
(3) A.D. 1–100: 2 Baruch 48. 20, 78. 7f.; 4 Ezra 3. 17, 4. 25, 5. 23, 32, 6. 55, 58
[3] *R.A.* pp. 58f.; S. Schechter, *Some Aspects of Rabbinic Theology.* See also W. O. E Oesterley, 2 *Esdras*, p. 40, who dismisses the idea of the eternal relation of Israe and Yahweh in the Old Testament too easily.
[4] Cf. Moore, vol. II, p. 367; A. Cohen, *Everyman's Talmud*, p. 376.
[5] Cf. Moore, vol. II, pp. 311f. See R. H. Charles, *Eschatology*, chapter III, pp. 81f. especially pp. 129f.
[6] Exod. 32. 31f.

this that lies at the root of the doctrine of resurrection. Moore's words deserve quotation at length:

> What the Jew craved for himself was to have a part in the future golden age of the nation as the prophets depicted it, the Days of the Messiah, or in the universal Reign of God, or in the Coming Age—always in the realization of God's purpose of good for his people. The idea of salvation for the individual was indissolubly linked with the salvation of the people.... Most naturally it was felt that, of all men, the martyrs who had laid down their lives for their religion in the persecution, and the heroes who had fallen in the final conflict with heathenism, had earned a part in the salvation that was at hand, and it was easy to believe that God who must also recognize their desert, would bring them to life to enjoy it.[1]

With the various details of resurrection we shall be concerned in a later chapter.[2] Here the point to notice is that the community of the resurrection, those who would share in the final blessedness was always primarily conceived as a community of Israelites. Thus each of the patriarchs would be raised at the head of his tribe,[3] and, while it is possible to exaggerate this, the popular belief undoubtedly was that the dead of Israel would be raised because of a solidarity of Israelites past, present, and to come that could not be broken. There are, indeed, passages which speak of personal resurrection; thus in the second benediction in the *Shemoneh 'Esreh*[4] the emphasis unmistakably lies on personal resurrection. Furthermore, we also find the view that the wicked in Israel would perish never to be raised again.[5] Nevertheless, there is always the awareness of the unity of all Israelites and that the relation of Israel to God cannot be annulled even by sin. Thus Rabbi Meir[6] could say that the Jews "whether or not they carry on as children are always children", and when we read in *Mishnah Sanhedrin* 10. 1, that "all Israel has a part in the world to come" we are probably to take it to mean that all Jews after the flesh are destined to share in that world.[7]

Our brief survey of these three currents, the yearning for the ingathering of the dispersed of Israel, the growth of the belief in the eternal relation of Israel and Yahweh and the hope of a resurrection of Israel to share in the Age to Come, in the Judaism of Paul's day, helps us to under-

---

[1] Moore, vol. II, pp. 312f. The concept of 'solidarity' will engage us in the next chapter and need not be further elaborated at this point.

[2] See chapter 10 below.

[3] Test. Judah 25. Also Test. Zebulon 10. 2; Test. Benjamin 10. 7.

[4] See *J.D.P.B.* pp. 44 f.

[5] *Cant. R.* 2. 13; *Pesikta Rabbati*, 74 a.

[6] *b. Kidd.* 36 a; cf. Jer. 4. 22; Deut. 32. 20; Isa. 4. 4; Hos. 2. 1.

[7] See on the whole question Str.-B. vol. IV, pp. 1167f.; cf. Moore, vol. II, p. 387.

stand the tenacity with which Paul clung to his fathers' ways and the emotional intensity of his concern for the salvation of Jewry. True, Paul could appeal to the prophets[1] in justification of his universalism, but the latter, and all the best thought of his day, attested another fact, that salvation must be of and to the Jews. When the Apostle claimed that it was the being 'in Christ' that was fundamental, and not the being 'in Israel', for sharing in the Age to Come, and that it was the dead 'in Christ' who were to be raised up to share in its glories,[2] and therefore that it was not Israelites as such but only those 'in Christ' who were being ingathered into the people of God, he was running counter to an integral part of the message of the great prophets as well as of his Rabbinic contemporaries. Doubtless Paul, like Jeremiah, and indeed like every true man, felt that there was something unnatural in shedding the religious traditions of his nation, but it was not merely what we should call nationalism or patriotism that led Paul to seek throughout his life to conciliate and convert the Jews first; it was the whole religious impetus of Judaism; his emotional reaction to the exclusion of the greater part of the Old Israel after the flesh from the New Israel after the Spirit, only becomes fully intelligible in the light of the expectation of a restored and united people and a passionate belief in an eternal bond uniting the Old Israel and her God, together with a sense of national solidarity that is possibly, in its intensity, unique in world history, and these three elements as we saw could call to their aid the genius and warmth of Semitic religion. That the Apostle did agonize over Jewry and lived and died a Pharisee shows how near to the heart of first-century Judaism he must have been; it certainly gives the lie to any attempt at minimizing his essential Jewishness.

The conflict that Paul faced between the claims of the Old and the New Israel must be faced again and again wherever the claims of 'nationalism' conflict with those of Christ. Paul's refusal utterly to sacrifice his nation to logical consistency points to the truth that it is not the suppression but the sublimation of nationalism that is to be desired. There can be no Jew nor Greek 'in Christ' and yet both Jew and Greek must be brought captive to Him.[3]

[1] On this see C. H. Dodd, *Romans* (*M.N.T.C.*), p. 50.
[2] See below, chapter 10.
[3] See W. B. Griffith, "Fy Nghenedl fy hun", in *Y Dysgedydd*, vol. cxxx, no. 12, pp. 269ff.

5

THE OLD AND THE NEW MAN: I. PAUL AS
PREACHER TO THE INDIVIDUAL

HITHERTO we have been concerned with Paul's discovery of a new hope for mankind as a whole, and with his wrestling over the fate of his own nation, in short with what it has become customary to call the horizontal problems of life, the problems of human relations, international and national. Vital as these were, however, there was another problem with which Paul was even more painfully concerned, that of his personal relation to God, the vertical problem. The distinction between a man's outward relation with his fellowmen and his inward relation to God is, of course, unreal and psychologically indefensible; nevertheless it is for our purpose convenient. It enables us to concentrate on the intensely personal or individual and inward implications of that acceptance of Christ by Paul which led to peace with God.[1] In this section, therefore, we shall deal with Paul's treatment of the individual.

The formula which Paul most frequently used to describe the nature of the Christian man was that he was 'in Christ'.[2] We have already seen that by this Paul meant that the individual who accepted Christ was part of a new humanity of which He was the head;[3] that he was being ingathered into the true Israel of God.[4] It agrees with this that there are passages where to be 'in Christ' is clearly to be in the Church.[5] In short ἐν Χριστῷ is a social concept, to be ἐν Χριστῷ is to have discovered the true community. This interpretation has rightly been emphasized by recent scholars.[6] Paul knows nothing of solitary salvation; to be 'in Christ' is not for him the mystic flight of the alone to the

---

[1] Rom. 5. 1.

[2] Cf. A. Deissmann, St Paul (E.T.), pp. 138ff. It might equally be said, of course, that a Christian is also ἐν πνεύματι 'in the Spirit'; we are not here concerned with this. Cf. C. A. A. Scott, Christianity According to St Paul, pp. 150f. See below chapter 8.

[3] Cf. above, pp. 53f.   [4] Cf. above, pp. 74f.

[5] Cf. 1 Cor. 12. 12. Here Paul writes: "As the human body is one and has many members all the members of the body being one body in spite of their number—so also is Christ"; though the conclusion which anyone familiar with Paul's use of the metaphor of the body would anticipate would be "so also is the Church": C. A. A. Scott, Christianity According to St Paul, p. 154.

[6] Cf. C. H. Dodd, Romans (M.N.T.C.), pp. 86f.; R. N. Flew, Jesus and His Church, pp. 212f.; C. A. A. Scott, Christianity According to St Paul, pp. 151f.; V. Taylor, Forgiveness and Reconciliation, p. 135.

alone; he quite definitely assigns such ecstatic mystical experiences as he had, and they were evidently very real ones, to a secondary place in his religious life.[1]

Nevertheless, like all mortal men, Paul too in the deepest things had to journey alone, and while we admit the social content of the formula ἐν Χριστῷ there can be no question that to be 'in Christ' signified for Paul the most intensely personal relation with Christ. In the words of Deissmann it denotes "the most intimate possible fellowship of the Christian with the living Christ".[2] Despite his strong sense of community in religion, of "the common life in the Body of Christ",[3] Paul throughout his life laboured and thought under the cherished conviction that God had separated him from his mother's womb in order to reveal Christ to him;[4] that Christ had loved him and died for him and lived in him.[5] The experience by which Paul was delivered from what Kierkegaard has taught us to call *die Angst* was of necessity a lonely one, and its issue in a deep awareness of a universal community which led Paul to "brother all the souls of earth" must never be allowed to rob it of its essentially personal character.[6] It is no accident that Paul, through Luther, could be claimed as the father of modern individualism.

When, however, we seek to understand the exact nature of this personal union with Christ we are in difficulty. The formula ἐν Χριστῷ only becomes fully intelligible in the light of certain other passages where Paul speaks of having died and risen with Christ.[7] The passages are numerous; the following are typical:

Rom. 6. 5: For if we have been planted together in the likeness of his death, we shall be also in the likeness of his resurrection.

[1] Cf. 2 Cor. 12. 2. The whole context makes it clear that for Paul the experience there described is not of first rate importance. Cf. C. H. Dodd, *History and the Gospel*, p. 31. See below.

[2] Cf. *St Paul* (E.T.), p. 140. Also V. Taylor, *Forgiveness and Reconciliation*, p. 138.

[3] Cf. L. S. Thornton's book: *The Common Life in the Body of Christ*.

[4] Gal. 1. 15. Paul speaks of 'I in Christ' and 'Christ in me'. We shall deal with this latter conception in our discussion on the Spirit in chapter 8.

[5] Gal. 2. 20; cf. A. E. J. Rawlinson, *The New Testament Doctrine of the Christ*, p. 150. "It has been noticed that St Paul is unique among Apostolic writers in specifically applying the idea of our Lord's self oblation on behalf of mankind to himself as an individual—'He loved *me*, and gave himself up for *me*.'"

[6] Vincent Taylor writes *à propos* of the communal and personal emphasis in the phrase ἐν Χριστῷ: "There does not seem to be any necessary antagonism between this communal interpretation...and the view of Deissmann; but, as between the two explanations, the emphasis upon personal faith-union or fellowship with Christ Himself marks the more fundamental element in the experience." *Forgiveness and Reconciliation*, pp. 137f.

[7] Cf. V. Taylor, *Forgiveness and Reconciliation*, p. 139.

Rom. 6. 4: We are buried therefore with him by baptism into death.

Rom. 6. 6: Knowing this, that our old man is crucified with him.

Rom. 8. 17: If so be that we suffer with him, that we may be also glorified together.

Gal. 2. 20: I am crucified with Christ.

Col. 2. 12: Buried with him in baptism....

Col. 3. 1: If ye then be risen with Christ....

It is clear from the above that to be 'in Christ' involves an identity of experience with Christ. The union of the individual with Christ is such that the experiences of Christ are re-enacted in the experience of the individual Christian. The life, death, resurrection and glorification of Jesus cease to be mere external facts of history but living realities in the Christian's own life. The latter appropriates to himself the past events of the historical and risen life of Jesus so that they become his own. Thus it is that Paul could speak of Christ being formed in a person[1] and carrying on his life in that person.[2] The Christian shares in the sufferings of Christ.[3] Paul would have much sympathy with the view expressed in the old poem:

> Though Christ in Bethlehem
> A thousand times were born,
> Unless He's born in thee
> He was never born at all.

But this must not be taken to mean that Paul[4] was indifferent to the actual events of the life of Jesus. Again and again he holds up the historical Jesus for imitation;[5] he could not ignore that life even for homiletical reasons. To him every Christian, like his Lord, was to have his Olivet and Calvary and Easter.[6] Moreover, all this, of course, does not refer to any pietistic or imaginative absorption of the individual in Christ, but to the facing of the harsh realities of the actual situations of life in His Spirit; it is in other words to have the mind of Christ and His obedience.[7]

Various interpretations of this Christ-mysticism, as it has been called, have been proposed. Particularly the attempt has been made to prove that here Paul is manifestly influenced by the mystery religions. Loisy[8] and Lake[9] went so far as to claim that under the influence of Paul

---

[1] Cf. Gal. 2. 20.   [2] Rom. 8. 17; Phil. 3. 10; 2 Cor. 1. 5f.

[3] Phil. 3. 10.

[4] Cf. A. E. J. Rawlinson, *The New Testament Doctrine of the Christ*, p. 117; H. A. A. Kennedy, *The Theology of the Epistles*, pp. 98 ff.

[5] Cf. C. H. Dodd, *History and the Gospel*, pp. 64 ff.

[6] V. Taylor, *Forgiveness and Reconciliation*, p. 142.   [7] Phil. 2. 5f.

[8] Cf. *Hibbert Journal* (October 1911), p. 51.

[9] Cf. *The Earlier Epistles of St Paul*, p. 215.

Christianity was transformed into a mystery. Bousset[1] has forcefully argued that Paul was converted to the Christianity of a Gentile church, and that his religion is the cult of the Risen Christ whom he conceives after the pattern of the gods of contemporary mysteries. Reitzenstein[2] has also found in the latter the key to the understanding of Paul. With the details of the views of these scholars we need not stay, but it will be well briefly to state their explanation of the conception of the dying and rising with Christ that we find in Paul.

In all the mysteries there is the figure of a god, an Attis, Osiris or Dionysus, who died and rose again.[3] Their aim was to enable the initiate to achieve union with the god, a union that is often called deification.[4] This was achieved by ritual acts and often very sensuous ceremonial designed to convey impressively the passage from death to life.[5] The union thus effected between the believer and the god issued in σωτηρία which consisted chiefly in escape from cruel fate, and especially from death.[6] Now there is an obvious superficial resemblance between such ideas and those found in Paul about dying and rising with Christ. Loisy concluded that the latter's conception of salvation through death and resurrection is wholly analogous with that found in the mystery religions: he found in the Eucharist and in Baptism the Christian replicas of ritual elements in the mysteries.[7] Reitzenstein has further pinned down the Iranian myth of the Primal Man as that which offers the nearest parallel to the thought of Paul.[8]

It will be clear that these theories imply that Paul had turned his back upon his Jewish inheritance, and virtually accepted the Hellenistic outlook.[9] It is not surprising, therefore, that most British scholars, while they recognize the minute researches that lie behind the above theories, have been sceptical of the conclusions drawn from them. On several grounds the latter have failed to convince. First, the sources to which

[1] Cf. *Kyrios Christos.* See A. E. J. Rawlinson, *The New Testament Doctrine of the Christ*, pp. 92 f.

[2] R. Reitzenstein, *Die Hellenistischen Mysterienreligionen*; cf. J. M. Creed, *J.T.S.* vol. XXVI, pp. 113-36; W. Manson, *Jesus the Messiah*, pp. 174 f.

[3] Cf. H. A. A. Kennedy, *St Paul and the Mystery Religions*, pp. 206 f.

[4] H. A. A. Kennedy, op. cit. pp. 199 f.

[5] H. A. A. Kennedy, op. cit. pp. 91 ff.; cf. A. D. Nock, *Conversion*, p. 37.

[6] H. A. A. Kennedy, op. cit. pp. 199 f. For the whole subject, see A. D. Nock, *Conversion*; chapter VII deals with the appeal of the Mystery cults and is illuminating. See also A. D. Nock in *Essays on the Trinity and the Incarnation* (ed. A. E. J. Rawlinson), pp. 57 f.

[7] *Hibbert Journal* (October 1911).

[8] See J. M. Creed, *J.T.S.* vol. XXVI, and W. Manson, *Jesus the Messiah*, pp. 174 f.

[9] Cf. A. E. J. Rawlinson, *The New Testament Doctrine of the Christ*, p. 97.

appeal has been made are of a late date, and our ignorance of the actual
nature of the ceremonies performed in the mysteries makes any comparison with Christian practice precarious.[1] Secondly, there is the almost
complete silence of Christian writers to the end of the second century
on the question of the mysteries.[2] Thirdly, there are lacking in the
mysteries certain elements that are fundamental to Paul's view of dying
and rising with Christ. It is necessary to enlarge on this point. We have
recognized at the outset that there is a social aspect to the Pauline concept
of the being 'in Christ'; union with Christ however personal had meant
incorporation into a community that could be described as one body.
As far as we know, however, the mysteries were individualistic. Born
of the individualism of the age[3] the mysteries offered to the solitary an
experience of apparent deification but not of real brotherhood. Edwyn
Bevan has written: "In the Hellenistic Mystery religions the man who
received initiation was simply lifted out of the lower sphere individually
into the higher sphere: there was so far as we know no common purpose
which the society set to achieve in the real world."[4] It is, moreover,
clear that there is a profound difference between the gods of the mysteries
and Christ, the Saviour of Paul. The latter's interest in the Jesus of
history excludes the idea that Jesus was for him merely the counterpart
of what Osiris and Attis and the other gods were to their devotees: these
were originally merely "mythological personifications of the processes
of vegetation";[5] they were not rooted and grounded in history as was
the Jesus whom Paul knew as the Risen Lord. It cannot be over-

[1] Thus the Mithras Liturgy which is often cited cannot be quoted with any certainty.
Apuleius' *Metamorphoses* is placed in the middle of the second century A.D. by
H. A. A. Kennedy, *St Paul and the Mystery Religions*, p. 69; cf. also C. A. A. Scott,
Christianity According to St Paul, p. 124.

[2] According to C. A. A. Scott, op. cit. p. 125, the only exceptions are the *Didache*,
Ignatius and Justin Martyr, and they are not weighty. It is particularly important to
note that Edwyn Bevan's claim that the figure of the Redeemer does not appear in
any non-Christian Gnostic system has not been answered; cf. Essay V, "The Gnostic
Redeemer", in *Hellenism and Christianity*. Cf. also A. E. J. Rawlinson, *The New Testament Doctrine of the Christ*, p. 125, n. 3. A. D. Nock sums up as follows: "We know
them [i.e. the Mysteries] best from sources of the second century A.D. and later, and
it is fairly clear that they rose in importance in the second century, but there can be
little doubt that much of what is then characteristic of them had taken shape earlier."
See *Essays on the Trinity and Incarnation* (ed. A. E. J. Rawlinson), p. 58.

[3] H. A. A. Kennedy, *St Paul and the Mystery Religions*, pp. 72f.; A. D. Nock, *Conversion*, p. 101.

[4] *The Hellenistic Age* (ed. J. B. Bury), pp. 105f.

[5] H. A. A. Kennedy, *St Paul and the Mystery Religions*, p. 213; A. E. J. Rawlinson,
The New Testament Doctrine of the Christ, p. 271; S. H. Hooke, *Judaism and Christianity*,
vol. I, pp. 213f.

emphasized that Jesus for Paul was not the creation of human imagination, no projection of his religious experience, but a fact in recent history.[1]
Moreover, his union with Christ was for Paul no absorption into the
divine such as is fundamental to the mystery religions. Indeed, the
Apostle would have been horrified at such a thought.[2] Nor was it by
any celebration of outward rites such as Baptism or the Eucharist that
the union and dying and rising with Christ was achieved. The attempt
to trace the influence of mystery religions on his teaching on these
sacraments has failed.[3] On the contrary it is faith, "a joyful self committal
of the whole personality to God"[4] in Christ, that always determines his
being 'in Christ'. Taylor and Manson[5] have both pointed this out
recently. The critical verse is the familiar one: "I am crucified with
Christ: nevertheless I live; yet not I, but Christ liveth in me: and the
life which I now live in the flesh I live by the faith of the Son of God,
who loved me, and gave himself for me."[6] Here there is no loss of
personal identity in mystical absorption, but the firm maintenance of
the 'I—Thou' type of religion. There is nothing corresponding to Pauline
'faith' in the mysteries. This is, indeed, what we should expect. Paul's
faith in Christ, although it may not have been born out of his experience
of moral failure, nevertheless was the source of moral strength. On the
other hand, while it would be wrong to deny all ethical significance to
the mysteries, it was not their strong point; the deaths of Osiris and
Attis were not meant to achieve spiritual redemption and their devotees
were not so much conspicuous for their virtue as for their esoteric
experiences.[7] Finally, the attempt to show that much of Paul's language
is derived directly from the mysteries has not been successful. The chief
terms in question were σωτηρία, μυστήριον, τέλειος, σοφία, γνῶσις. We
need only refer to the convincing treatment of these terms by Kennedy
and Scott.[8] Moreover, a glance at the kind of experience which was

---

[1] See C. H. Dodd's study, *History and the Gospel*, pp. 53–4; for Paul Jesus came
'in the flesh', Rom. 8. 3.

[2] A. Schweitzer has rightly insisted upon this in his book *The Mysticism of Paul the
Apostle*. See his chapter ii, "Hellenistic or Judaic?", pp. 26f.

[3] Cf. H. G. Marsh, *The Origin and Significance of the New Testament Baptism*, pp. 1f.;
G. H. C. Macgregor, *Eucharistic Origins*, pp. 27f.; also A. D. Nock, *Conversion*, p. 204.

[4] C. A. A. Scott, *Christianity According to St Paul*, p. 133.

[5] W. Manson, *Jesus the Messiah*, pp. 189f.; J. Weiss, *The History of Primitive
Christianity*, vol. II, p. 470; V. Taylor, *Forgiveness and Reconciliation*, p. 141.

[6] Gal. 2. 20.

[7] H. A. A. Kennedy, *St Paul and the Mystery Religions*, p. 213.

[8] C. A. A. Scott, *Christianity According to St Paul*, pp. 127f.; H. A. A. Kennedy,
St Paul and the Mystery Religions, pp. 115f. On the Pauline use of μυστήριον, see
J. A. Robinson, *St Paul's Epistle to the Ephesians*, p. 240. According to the latter it

engendered by the mysteries will add conviction to the criticism already made of the theory that Paul derived his conception of dying and rising with Christ from that source. Nock has summarized the experience of Lucius described in the *Metamorphoses* of Apuleius, Book XI, which gives the experience of conversion into the mysteries at its best. We cannot here enter into details; we merely refer to Nock's statement of Lucius' experience on the day when his initiation began and subsequently:

Lucius, though it was barely dawn, hastened to the priest. And as soon as the priest saw him, he said, "O Lucius, happy are you, blest are you, whom the majestic deity honours so greatly with her gracious goodwill. Why do you now stand idly and keep yourself waiting? This is the day for which your steadfast prayers have asked, the day on which at the divine commands of Her of many names [i.e. Isis] you are by these hands of mine to be led into the most holy secrets of her rites?" The priest did the morning ceremonies, produced his hieroglyphic book of ritual, and told Lucius what he must procure for the initiation. He did as he was commanded and then was led among the band of pious to the nearest baths. There he was washed as usual and the priest prayed and besprinkled him, set him before the feet of the goddess and gave certain teaching in private and also instructions in public to abstain from meat and wine and to curtail all enjoyment of food for ten days.

Lucius obeyed, and the sun sank and brought on evening. In accordance with ancient custom the faithful came together from every side, honouring him with their several gifts. All who were not holy were removed, and the priest clothed him in a linen garment and led him to the holy of holies.

"You, O zealous reader, will perhaps ask eagerly enough, what was then said and done. I would tell you if I might, but ear and tongue would incur the same guilt of rash inquisitiveness. Yet I will not torture you with long suspense, when you are perhaps aglow with pious yearning. So hear, yes, and believe the things which are true. I visited the bounds of death: I trod Proserpina's threshold: I passed through all the elements and returned. It was midnight, but I saw the sun radiant with bright light. I came into the very presence of the gods below and the gods above and I adored them face to face. Well, I have told you things of which though you have heard them you must not know.

denotes "the great truths of the Christian religion, which could not have become known to men except by Divine disclosure or revelation. A mystery in this sense is not a thing which *must* be kept secret. On the contrary, it is a secret which God wills to make known, and has charged His Apostles to declare to those who have ears to hear it." When therefore Paul in 1 Cor. 4. 1 writes: "Let a man so account of us, as of the ministers of Christ, and stewards of the mysteries of God", he is not thinking of himself as the priest of a Mystery, "as a 'hierophant' charged with the custody of secret rites, etc., but as an evangelist entrusted with the preaching of the Gospel". See A. E. J. Rawlinson, *The New Testament Doctrine of the Christ*, pp. 283f. On "mystery" see now R. E. Brown, *The Semitic Background of the Term "Mystery" in the New Testament*, Philadelphia, 1969 (Facet Books).

"Therefore I will relate the one thing which can without sin be proclaimed to the minds of those outside. It was morning: the rites were done and I came forth consecrated in twelve robes. The dress is sacred in truth, but there is nothing which bids me to be silent concerning it, for very many were then present and saw it. As I was bidden, I stood on a wooden platform set in the very centre of the temple before the image of the goddess. I was before all eyes, in a linen garment, but one decorated with patterns of flowers. A costly cloth hung on my back from my shoulders to my heels. For whichever side you beheld me I was adorned with animals marked out in various colours: here were Italian dragons.... In my right hand I bore a blazing torch; my head was duly bound with a wreath of gleaming palm, the leaves standing out like rays. So when I was arranged in the fashion of the Sun and set there like an image the veils were suddenly drawn back, and the people streamed in to see me. Then I kept the most joyous birthday of the rite: there was a charming feast and merry banquet. The third day also was celebrated with a similar ceremonial rite: there was a solemn breakfast and legal completing of the initiation. I remained there for a few days and drew a pleasure which cannot be told from the divine image, to which I was bound by a favour for which no return of gratitude could be made. Still at length, at the bidding of the goddess, having paid humble thanks, not indeed fully, but to the best of my abilities, I at length made preparations to go home, slow in all conscience, for I found it hard to break the chains of most eager desire which held me back!"[1]

No comment is further needed; the whole atmosphere in which Lucius lived and moved is far removed from that of him who had died and risen with Christ.

Considerations such as the above confirm what after all we would expect on *a priori* grounds, because much in the practice of some at least of the mysteries must have disgusted and revolted any serious-minded Jew, that Paul did not borrow directly from the mysteries, and that, therefore, we should not look to the latter for the explanation of his so-called 'mysticism'. Recently, however, a fresh turn has been given to the discussion of the relation of Paul to the mysteries.

It is, of course, a familiar fact, that will also have become clear from our previous chapter, that Paul's contacts on his missionary journeys would be chiefly with Gentiles who already had considerable sympathy with Judaism, with proselytes and others attracted to the religion of the Torah. It cannot be over-emphasized, that while his direct contacts with Hellenistic paganism would be few, his relations with Hellenistic Judaism would be peculiarly close throughout his life. If the mysteries were confined to the former, we can, as we saw, dismiss the idea that Paul consciously borrowed from them, they would have been for him

[1] A. D. Nock, *Conversion*, pp. 144 f.

part of the abominations of the heathen. But what if the mysteries had already gained a foothold within Judaism? What if the synagogues had themselves become homes of mysteries? It is this that is asserted by E. R. Goodenough. It is necessary to summarize his argument.[1]

Fundamental is Goodenough's insistence that it was "the passionate desire of the Hellenistic man to experience emotionally the concepts he had learnt from Greek rationalism".[2] In accordance with this, Hellenism absorbed the various oriental mythologies not for their own sake, but for the purpose of transforming them into mystic symbols of metaphysical truth. It was thus that it dealt with Isis and Attis. "The mystery is not a path to Isis or Attis; it is a path to reality, existence, knowledge, life, of which Isis or Attis is the symbol."[3] It was in the same way that it used Mithraism and Christianity and, not least, Judaism; the traditions of the latter were made the handmaidens of the intellectual concepts of Hellenism. Gradually the Jews of the Dispersion were led captive to Greek religion. To some, we know that the synagogue assumed the character of a philosophic school,[4] to many, says Goodenough, it assumed the character of a θίασος, and Judaism came to be interpreted as the greatest mystery. How, when or through whom, this development took place can never be known, but it is Goodenough's claim that there existed in the first century a long-established Jewish mystery; he has found in Philo its best representative.

With the details of his analysis of Philo's thought we cannot linger. Philo has forsaken the comparatively simple idea of God found in Judaism and formulated a doctrine of God as the absolute, like that of later Neoplatonism.[5] The supreme God is wholly other and His contact with the world of matter is by means of a 'Light-stream'. Here Philo is at one with the prevailing Hellenism of his day. Moreover, the latter commonly interpreted the Light-stream either after the Persian conception of the πλήρωμα or after that of the female-principle in the Egyptian cult of Isis, i.e. the supreme God could be conceived after the analogy of a great king and his satraps (the powers) or after that of Osiris who had Isis—the female principle in nature, as his wife. It is this that forms the background of Philo's thought. It was his aim to find within the traditions of Judaism effective symbols by which he could express the process by which the soul came to see the greatest God, an experience that meant death and rebirth to the mystic, an ascent from the "toils of the body into immaterial and immortal life". The Jewish

---

[1] E. R. Goodenough, *By Light, Light, The Mystic Gospel of Hellenistic Judaism.*
[2] Ibid. p. 2.   [3] Ibid. p. 1.
[4] Cf. Moore, vol. I, pp. 284 f., 324; A. D. Nock, *Conversion,* pp. 61 f.
[5] *By Light, Light,* pp. 11 ff.

mystery by which this ascent could be achieved was twofold. There was, first, the mystery of Aaron, the lesser mystery, which was the way of those who obeyed the Torah of Judaism literally. In this the service of the Jewish temple and High-priesthood was interpreted as the mystery of the cosmos in which the initiate could join in the hymn of the universe to its Maker. It is important to notice that Gentiles were not asked to join the mystery of Aaron; it was no part of Philo's purpose to get Gentiles to obey the literal Law, because the mystery of Aaron, cosmic as it was in its significance, could only lead a person to His powers, not to the supreme God Himself. The higher mystic union with the supreme Deity belonged only to those initiated into the greater mystery, the mystery of Moses. For Philo, the patriarchs of the Old Testament, Enos, Enoch, Noah, Abraham, Isaac, Jacob and Moses had lived in such a way that their lives revealed the higher and direct way to union with the supreme God; living before the Torah had been given, they in themselves were incarnations of the higher Law of which the Jewish Torah was merely a material copy, as it were. The patriarchs were types of mystical perfection. The life of Abraham especially revealed the true way of ascent to God and the events of his life are interpreted in that light, e.g. his departure from Chaldaea at the call of God signifies that he had left all erroneous opinion about the character of God, and his marriage with Sarah is symbolic of his mystic union with Sophia. But greater than Abraham was Moses, himself a type of the higher Law of God, he is ideal King, Priest and Prophet and is, indeed, the Divine Logos. His life typifies the perfect mystic way, and the Exodus becomes an allegory of the way in which Moses can lead the soul from slavery to the corporeal to a vision of God. Pictorial representation of the three stages of this mystery—the leaving of Egypt, the destruction of the passions at the Red Sea, and the consummation at the Well, are preserved for us according to Goodenough in the Dura frescoes.[1] Moreover, this mystery is not merely a mystic gnosis of the Hermetic type, i.e. a mystery without external rites of initiation; it had a fully organized cultus with initiation rules, baptism and a sacred table.

What justifies this long summary of his theory for our purpose is that in the course of his treatment of Philo Goodenough has occasional references to Paul. He implies that, while it is unthinkable[2] that Paul should have directly taken over practices and ideals from Hellenistic

---

[1] It is not clear yet what Goodenough's full case will be, because he has not dealt fully with the frescoes. In *The Hebrew Bible in Art* J. Leveen rejects his view of the frescoes, cf. pp. 32 ff., and his view seems far more convincing than that of Goodenough.

[2] *By Light, Light*, p. 10.

mysteries, he would inevitably be greatly influenced by Jewish Hellenistic mysteries of the type represented, on his theory, in Philo. Paul, we infer, merely transferred to Jesus the interpretation that this mystic Judaism had imposed upon Moses. Thus for Paul, Jesus was not merely an ethical ideal but also a present power to save, just as Moses was to Philo,[1] and both Moses and Jesus formed ἐκκλησίας.[2] The corollary of all this, of course, is that for Paul dying and rising with Christ was an experience essentially mystical in the Hellenistic sense. The force of this must be admitted, if Goodenough's case could be accepted. At the risk of very great presumption we now point out criticisms that have been rightly made against the latter.

In the first place to approach Philo as if he regarded the traditions of Judaism merely as convenient pegs on which to hang a Hellenistic metaphysic is surely to misunderstand him. We may quote W. L. Knox:

He [i.e. Goodenough] writes of "the passionate desire of the Hellenistic man to experience emotionally the concepts he has learnt from Greek rationalism", the opposite seems to me to be the case; the passionate desire of the Hellenistic man in so far as he cared for these things, was to find a philosophic basis which would justify him in continuing a form of religion which attracted him or which he had inherited.... Philo's object was to justify Judaism in terms of contemporary thought and to read into it as much of the conventional theology of the Hellenistic world as he could drag in by hook or by crook.[3]

This is borne out when we consider the details of Philo's practice. Despite his obvious familiarity with, and understanding of, the philosophic movements of his day, he himself observed the Torah with all the zeal of an orthodox Jew. He roundly condemned those Jews who ignored the literal meaning of the Law as being worthless in favour of a symbolic meaning. Thus circumcision might be interpreted as a "sign of the excision of pleasure and all passions", etc., but nevertheless it had to be observed literally.[4] So great was the respect in which Philo was held that he was ethnarch of his community and chosen to represent his fellow-countrymen in an important delegation to Rome.[5] We cannot believe that such a man could ever have regarded the Torah as

---

[1] *By Light, Light*, pp. 232 ff.

[2] *Ibid.* p. 205. For further parallels also, cf. p. 267.

[3] *St Paul and the Church of the Gentiles*, p. x; cf. also A. D. Nock, *Gnomon* (March 1937), p. 156; G. C. Richards, *J.T.S.* (1937), vol. XXXVIII, pp. 415 ff.

[4] Cf. *De Migratione Abrahami*, § 92. See §§ 89–94; Cohn-Wendland, vol. II, p. 286. For condemnation of those who did not practise the Law, *De Exsecrationibus*, §§ 138 f.; Cohn-Wendland, vol. V, p. 368, περι 'Αρων, § 4.

[5] See *J.E.* vol. X, p. 6, for details of his life.

merely a secondary version of a higher Law, or that to such a one the practice of Judaism was a matter only for the spiritually immature; his whole life contradicts this. Moreover, Philo's references to the mysteries make it incredible that he himself was favourable to a Jewish mystery.[1] He denounced the mysteries in no uncertain terms. His use of the metaphor of initiation, which Goodenough takes literally, can be paralleled in Plato's descriptions of the apprehension of philosophic truth and does not necessarily imply initiation into a mystery.[2] Nock has further pointed out that, "Philo sketches what he regards as two ideal forms of Jewish existence when he describes the Therapeutae in *De vita contemplativa* and the Essenes in *Quod omnis probus liber*, pp. 75ff. and in a fragment *ap. Euseb. P.E.* 8, 11, 1–18." He goes on to ask: "How could he fail here at least to allude to cultus of the type of his mysteries if it existed in such circles?"[3] We must add that Paul's references to Abraham and Moses do not suggest the elaborate mysticism and symbolism that Goodenough traces in Philo.[4] We may conclude with Nock's words that Philo's "contacts are with pagan speculation, both such as gives to religious tale and practice a philosophic content and such as gives to philosophy a religious form, not with pagan rites or popular piety. From that he is as far removed as from Jewish apocalyptic."[5]

In view of all this the case put forward by Goodenough cannot be accepted. A far more balanced view of the relations between Judaism and Hellenistic religions is that given by Knox.[6] He has shown how Judaism not only in the Dispersion but even more so in Jerusalem itself was eager to adopt any convention of Hellenistic religion in order to exalt the one God and His Torah; Judaism could indeed be assimilated to a mystery cult to a remarkable degree—for missionary ends.[7] It is this that has misled Goodenough; as we have already pointed out it is not the case that Philo used Judaism for the sake of expressing a mystic theology, but rather that he used the ideology of the mysteries for the

---

[1] Cf. especially G. C. Richards, *J.T.S.* vol. xxxviii, who points out that τερθρεία, the term used by Philo of the mysteries, might be translated 'humbug'. *De Spec. Leg.* I, §§ 319ff.; Cohn-Wendland, vol. v, p. 77. He condemns the mysteries for keeping secret, what, if true, would benefit all mankind.

[2] See *Gnomon* (1937), p. 162.

[3] *Gnomon* (1937); Cohn-Wendland, vol. vi, for 'De vita contemplativa' and 'Quod omnis probus liber sit'.

[4] Cf. Rom. 4.   [5] *Gnomon* (1937).

[6] Cf. *St Paul and the Church of the Gentiles*, especially chapter ii, "The Synagogue and the Gentiles".

[7] He even points out that Palestinian Judaism, because it felt more secure, could and did adopt Hellenistic modes more than Diaspora Judaism. *St Paul and the Church of the Gentiles*, pp. 53f.

sake of Judaism. All that we can safely assume as to the impact of the mysteries on Judaism and Paul is that the mysteries quite definitely formed part of the milieu into which Paul brought his gospel; that Paul undoubtedly would therefore be open to their influence, and that many of the terms he used would have an undertone of meaning which would strengthen the appeal of the gospel to the Hellenistic world.[1] Further than this, however, we cannot go; the attempt to make Paul the κῆρυξ of a new mystery offering a mystic death and rising again has failed.

We now, at the other extreme, have to deal with A. Schweitzer's interpretation of dying and rising with Christ. His position is familiar and the briefest summary will suffice. Pauline mysticism then, according to Schweitzer, is determined by the conception, often found in apocalyptic literature, of a solidarity of the elect with the Messiah: "it is derived from the eschatological concept of the community of God in which the elect are closely bound up with one another and with the Messiah".[2] Because Christ had passed into the resurrection mode of existence, and because Christians share in His corporeity, the latter had also died and risen with Christ into the life of the resurrection. Schweitzer emphasizes that it is not by belief in Christ that this quasi-physical solidarity was achieved; he criticizes severely the view that belief in Christ determines the 'being in Christ'.[3] The union of the Christian with Christ is achieved by Baptism while the Eucharist is a pledge that the believer will partake of the future Messianic feast. Schweitzer even writes that "in Paul it is not a question of an act which the believer accomplishes in himself; what happens is that in the moment when he receives baptism the dying and rising again with Christ takes place in him without any co-operation or exercise of will or thought on his part".[4]

There are glaring weaknesses in this approach to Pauline teaching. Kennedy has called it grotesque,[5] and it is difficult not to agree. The mechanical conception of the Christian life it involves does not do justice to the centrality of Faith in Paul.[6] The man who could write that he strove towards the mark of the high calling of God in Christ Jesus, who

---

[1] For a convenient summary, cf. A. D. Nock's essay in *Essays on the Trinity and the Incarnation* (ed. A. E. J. Rawlinson), pp. 53–156.

[2] A. Schweitzer, *The Mysticism of Paul the Apostle*, pp. 101f.

[3] Ibid. p. 117.

[4] A. Schweitzer, *Paul and his Interpreters*, p. 225. It is curious that the 'Mystery-theory' and Schweitzer's here meet. Schweitzer assumes what we can only call a magical effect of baptism which would be precisely what the 'Mystery-theory' would welcome.

[5] H. A. A. Kennedy, *St Paul and the Mystery Religions*, p. 295.

[6] Ibid. pp. 285, 288, 289.

urged all to work out their own salvation, was unlikely to entertain such 'magical' ideas as Schweitzer ascribes to him.[1] Taylor's criticism is apt: "What is described by Schweitzer is not personal communion conditioned by Faith, but a mode of being effected by eschatological rites."[2] Apart then from the necessarily speculative character of the eschatological doctrine of Schweitzer his interpretation of Pauline emphasis on rising and dying with Christ is very unsatisfying.

Nevertheless, despite all this, this much at least must be said of Schweitzer's theory, that it does not lead us to a cul-de-sac as did that of the influence of mystery religions on Paul. Particularly did the latter imply a discontinuity between Jesus and Paul, because obviously Jesus was not influenced by the mysteries. Schweitzer, on the other hand, has shown that there is a real continuity between the so-called Pauline 'mysticism', and elements in the teaching of Jesus. His concept of the solidarity of the Messiah with the Elect, too mechanically applied by himself, does provide us with a key to the real meaning of Paul's thought on the individual. To this we now turn.

Schweitzer points out that there is a peculiar intimacy in the relation between Jesus and those who accept Him. He writes: "It is simply not the fact that Jesus' preaching dealt with nothing but the nearness of the Kingdom of God, and the ethic to be practised during the period of waiting. He also declared that in the fellowship with Him on which they had entered His followers had already the guarantee of future fellowship with the Son of Man."[3] Thus those who accept the disciples whom He sent accept Him:[4] the places that refuse them will suffer a worse fate than Sodom and Gomorrah[5]—unwittingly they have rejected Christ. He who receives a child in His Name receives Him. He, who offends against one of the least of those who believe in Him, prepares for himself a fate so terrible that it would have been better for him if he had never been born.[6] To give to one of the least of the brethren of Christ is to give to Him.[7] The followers of Christ can suffer with Him[8] and truly represent Him—they are as it were an extension of His personality. The explanation of this solidarity, we saw, was found in the eschatological conception "...that of the pre-ordained union of those who are elect to the Messianic Kingdom with one another and with the Messiah which is called the community of saints".[9] It is now

---

[1] Cf. Phil. 2. 12, 3. 13, etc.
[2] V. Taylor, *Forgiveness and Reconciliation*, p. 138.
[3] *The Mysticism of Paul the Apostle*, p. 105.
[4] Matt. 10. 40.
[5] Matt. 10. 14–15.
[6] Matt. 18. 5–6.   [7] Matt. 25. 31–45.
[8] Matt. 5. 11–12.
[9] *The Mysticism of Paul the Apostle*, p. 101.

generally accepted that the idea of a Messiah in apocalyptic did involve the idea of a community of the Messiah; and whether we trace this conception, as it is found in Jesus, to the Book of Enoch[1] or to Dan. 7, or to Isa. 53,[2] it is a fact that Jesus was aware that he was gathering around Himself a community of people pledged to loyalty to Him above all else.[3] We must clear up one misconception as to this community at the outset. Schweitzer speaks of the community of the Elect as being predestined to fellowship with Christ. But it is apparent that even he does not adhere logically to this view. Because this is a point of considerable importance for our thesis we quote his words: "If election is not confirmed by entering into fellowship with Him, it becomes invalid. On the other hand one who is not actually elect but through his conduct enters into fellowship with Jesus, can thus acquire the right of an elect person to be with the Son of Man in the Messianic Kingdom. Thus in the ultimate result everything depends upon the realization of fellowship with Jesus."[4]

Surely this is to cut the root of all predestination. Flew is right in saying: "The predestination does not predestinate. The election of the saints only becomes a reality if they believe in the preaching of Jesus and their election, he says, 'is not an unalterable fact'."[5] Fellowship with Christ is, then, a challenge to the individual, it calls for decision; it is no mechanical election of a community; the individual stands in terrible loneliness to accept or to reject.[6] Kierkegaard's insistence on 'the *category of the individual*' is in line with the mind of Jesus.

Further for our purpose it is essential to emphasize that the community gathered by Jesus was for Him the nucleus of a new Israel. This has often been demonstrated.[7] Jesus regarded Himself as the Messiah, i.e. the representative leader and head of Israel, and He concentrated His attention during His ministry on Israel.[8] Moreover, His appeal was

[1] So R. Otto, *The Kingdom of God and the Son of Man* (E.T.), pp. 176ff. See also A. Schweitzer, *The Mysticism of Paul the Apostle*, pp. 101–2.

[2] T. W. Manson, *The Teaching of Jesus*, p. 227. See R. N. Flew, *Jesus and His Church*, pp. 74ff.   [3] R. N. Flew, cit. op. p. 78.

[4] A. Schweitzer, *The Mysticism of Paul the Apostle*, p. 107.

[5] R. N. Flew, op. cit. p. 77.

[6] It is this that gives urgency to the preaching of Jesus; the passages are many where the element of choice is emphasized. Matt. 6. 24, 7. 13. See C. H. Dodd, *The Parables of the Kingdom*, p. 201; cf. S. A. Cook, *The Truth of the Bible*, p. 38.

[7] See especially C. H. Dodd, *History and the Gospel*, pp. 130f.; R. N. Flew, op. cit. pp. 48f.

[8] Matt. 19. 28. See C. H. Dodd, *History and the Gospel*, pp. 130f.: "He accepted an historic destiny as the Messiah, the representative leader and head of Israel. Whether or not He used the express words, 'I am not sent but unto the lost sheep of the House

to Israel as a corporate body,[1] and the twelve disciples He chose corresponded to the twelve tribes of Israel. That this was so is substantiated by the two acts of prophetic symbolism which accompanied His last visit to Jerusalem, the Triumphal Entry,[2] and the Cleansing of the Temple,[3] and also by the third act of prophetic symbolism, the institution of the Eucharist at the Last Supper.[4] The 'great refusal' of Jesus by Israel meant the death of the 'Old Israel', a doom is pronounced on the Temple,[5] the fig-tree will no longer bear fruit.[6] Nevertheless, the 'Temple' will be raised[7] up, a 'New Israel' will be established, and in the Eucharist the disciples are being treated as the nucleus of the 'New Israel'.[8]

Scholars are divided as to whether we should apply the term Church to the community that Christ gathered round Him while He was on earth or whether we should reserve the term to the post-Resurrection community.[9] In any case we can assume that Paul's conception of the Church as the New Israel has its roots in the teaching of Jesus, and that his conception of the solidarity of Christians with their Lord is no innovation of his. It is this that will help to explain his conception of dying and rising with Christ. Flew's words are pertinent:

Here we shall find the link between the original teaching of Jesus, on the one hand, and, on the other, the thought of the primitive community in

of Israel' (Matt. 15. 24), those words describe the limitations which He actually accepted. The Church must have been extremely anxious to show that His mission was both to Jews and to Gentiles, yet even Paul describes Him as διάκονος περιτομῆς (Rom. 15. 8) and our earliest evangelical sources, Mark and Q, can produce only two cases of contact with Gentiles—the Centurion and the Syro-Phoenician woman—while even the later sources can add only the case of the Greek proselytes at the Feast in John 12. 20, along with two examples of friendly contact with Samaritans. Such cases were obviously sporadic and almost accidental. His concentration upon Israel is the more marked because, according to a well-attested saying, He divined that He would have found a more ready response in Tyre and Sidon."

[1] Cf. C. H. Dodd, ibid. pp. 131f.

[2] Luke 13. 33: "for it cannot be that a prophet perish out of Jerusalem"—only in the centre of the nation's life could he fittingly die.

[3] Mark 11. 5 and parallels.

[4] Mark 14. 22; 1 Cor. 11. 23. For the Eucharist, see below. G. Johnston regards the institution of the Eucharist as described in Mark and Paul as "the real proof that Jesus had a renewed Israel in mind". The New Testament Doctrine of the Church, p. 48.

[5] Matt. 26. 60b–1; cf. Acts 6. 14; Mark 13. 2, 15. 58.

[6] Mark 11. 13. See also Mark 12. 1f. for the figure of the vineyard.

[7] Mark 14. 58; Matt. 26. 60b–1; John 2. 19.

[8] C. H. Dodd, History and the Gospel, p. 137. We have not deemed it necessary to enlarge on the above section in view of the admirable discussions referred to by C. H. Dodd and R. N. Flew.

[9] See G. Johnston, The New Testament Doctrine of the Church. Johnston would reserve the term Church for the post-Resurrection community. See pp. 50–7.

Jerusalem and the profounder Christianity of St Paul. The preaching of the βασιλεία involves the gathering of the true Israel of God, the little flock. Jesus Himself as the destined Messiah gathered this community in close companionship with Himself. In fellowship with Him now, they have their guarantee of fellowship with the Son of Man hereafter. St Paul takes up this conception of a corporate relationship of the community with Christ Himself and interprets it by what is misleadingly called his Christ-Mysticism.[1]

Now it will be clear that if for Paul, as for Jesus, the community of Christians was a New Israel, then entry into it would have some analogy with entry into the Old Israel. In other words, the process by which a man became ἐν Χριστῷ, and died and rose again with Christ, may be illuminated for us by the process through which membership in the Jewish community was, ideally at least, achieved. The best guide to the essence of any religion is its liturgy, and to understand the real significance of being a Jew it will be necessary for us to refer to the liturgy of Judaism, and, for our purpose, especially to that of the Passover.[2] The whole character of the festival of the Passover stamps it as being originally a festival of the home, and after the cessation of Temple worship it resumed its original character. Although the Paschal meal, however, was a family meal, the mere fact that as long as the Temple at Jerusalem stood, the lamb could only be slain at the central sanctuary served as a reminder that the family was part of a larger unit, the nation.[3] It was only the circumcised who could partake of it, and it was always the festival *par excellence* which marked the oneness of the people of Israel, and also the way in which the individual Jew became truly united with his people. The significance of the Passover for the individual is unmistakable. This becomes clear from a study of the ritual: the latter is preserved for us in the *Haggâdâh shel pesaḥ* and in *Mishnah Pesaḥim*.[4] The date of the Haggadah is uncertain; it was probably arranged, however, by Gamaliel II (A.D. 80–120), and the fact that he did arrange a ritual implies that it had long been in use in some form. Moreover, the parts of the ritual that most concern us are regarded as the oldest. On the basis of Exod. 13. 8 ("And thou shalt shew thy son in that day, saying, This is done because of that which the Lord did unto me when I came forth out of Egypt") it was deemed necessary to narrate the story of the Exodus on the eve of the Passover. The following passages especially are to be noted. The youngest competent at the table says:

"Wherefore is this night different from all other nights?"

[1] *Jesus and His Church*, p. 80.
[2] For details with regard to the Passover, cf. *J.E.* vol. VI, p. 141, and *Mishnah Pesaḥim*; Str.-B. vol. IV, pp. 41 ff.; Moore, vol. II, pp. 40f.
[3] See *M. Pesaḥim* 5. 5.　　　　[4] *M. Pesaḥim* 10.

The response is given:

"We were slaves to the Pharaoh in Egypt, and the Lord our God brought us forth from thence with a strong hand and outstretched arm. If the most holy, blessed be He, had not brought our fathers from Egypt then we, our children and our children's children would have been slaves to the Pharaohs in Egypt...."

The significance of the rite for the individual will be clear from the following:

Four times does the Bible refer to the enquiring son. This indicates that the Bible thought of four kinds of enquiring sons—the wise son, the wicked son, the simple son, and the one that is too young to enquire himself.... Which is the wise son's question? "What mean the testimonies and the statutes and the judgements which the Lord our God hath commended you?" (Deut. 6. 30.) Thou must answer him by telling him of the laws of the Passover down to the law that no *aficoman* may follow the Paschal lamb. Which is the wicked son's question? "What mean you by this service?" (Exod. 12. 26.) When he thus says You he *purposely excludes himself and so rejects one of the principles of Judaism.* Therefore mayest thou retort upon him by quoting (Exod. 13. 8): "This is done because of that which the Lord did for ME when I came forth from Egypt."

Or again:

In every generation *each one of us* should regard himself as though *he himself* had gone forth from Egypt, as it is said (Exod. 13. 8): "And thou shalt shew thy son in that day, saying, This is done because of that which the Lord did unto ME when I came forth out of Egypt." Not our ancestors alone did God redeem then, but he did US redeem with them as it is said (Deut. 6. 23): "And he brought US out from thence that he might bring US in to give US the land which he sware unto our fathers."[1,2]

Therefore we are in duty bound to thank, to praise, to glorify, to exalt, to honour, to bless, to extol, and to give reverence to Him who performed for US, as well as for our forefathers, all these wonders. He has brought US forth from bondage to freedom, from sorrow to joy, from mourning to festival, from darkness to bright light, and from slavery to redemption. Now, therefore, let us sing before Him a new song, Hallelujah!

[1] We have printed the personal pronouns in heavy type in order to show how the present reality of a past event was conceived.

[2] The quotations are taken from הגדה של פסח: *The Revised Haggada*, trans. and ed. by Rev. A. A. Green, Minister of Hampstead Synagogue (London 1897), pp. 27, 31, 51; cf. also *M. Pesaḥim* 10. 6, Danby, p. 151, who points out that the whole sentence beginning with "In every generation", etc., is omitted in older sources. Nevertheless, the theme is constant throughout the Haggadah and underlies the whole rite.

These quotations will make it clear that the real member of the Old Israel is he who has appropriated to himself the history of his people: he has himself been in bondage in Egypt, has himself been delivered therefrom. We may also add that he has himself received the Torah. Moore's[1] words will make this clear:

The Law is not to be regarded as an antiquated edict (διάταγμα) to which nobody pays any attention, but as a new one which everyone must read.[2] Every day when a man busies himself with the study of Torah he should say to himself, it is as if this day I received it from Sinai[3]...in what seems to us fanciful forms the rabbis sought to impress on themselves and others that the student is himself receiving the Law from the Lawgiver as really as if he stood at the foot of Sinai amid the awe-inspiring scenery depicted in Exodus 19. 1, and Deuteronomy 10 ff.

It is the same idea that Büchler really finds in Gen. 17. 14; Deut. 31. 16, 20; and Jer. 11. 10, 31. 33; on which he comments:

All the three passages take it for granted that the covenant made by God with Israel at Sinai continued to be binding throughout the centuries though not renewed; and the same is stated explicitly in Genesis 17. 9, 12; when God imposed circumcision upon Abraham and his descendants throughout their generations expressly as an everlasting covenant (13), and so also the Sabbath in Exodus 31. 16, "to observe the Sabbath throughout their generations, for a perpetual covenant".[4]

It was not only one generation that was to stand at the foot of Sinai to receive the Law but all subsequent generations. The person who fails to read the national experience into his own experience thereby excludes himself from the community. The external facts of history have to become living, present realities: the realization of one's own personal participation, as it were, in these external acts of history *ipso facto* makes one a member of the nation. The individual must himself make the appropriation, he can choose to regard himself as a slave brought out of Egypt or he can refuse to do so, but his very appropriation or refusal involves him in community or isolation.

Turning again to Paul, it is highly significant that in several places in the Epistles, once explicitly and elsewhere by implication, the Apostle

[1] Cf. Moore, vol. II, pp. 242f.

[2] Cf. *Sifre Deut.* on Deut. 6. 6, § 33.

[3] *Tanḥuma, Yitro*, § 7, p. 73. This reads: "On this day Israel came to Mount Sinai (Exod. 19. 1). Why on *this* day? Because, when thou learnest Torah, let not its commands seem old to thee, but regard them as though the Torah were given *this* day. Hence it says, 'On *this* day', and not 'On that day'."

[4] Cf. A. Büchler, *Studies in Sin and Atonement*, p. 10.

compares the Christian life to the Passover Festival: he obviously regards the great deliverance at the Exodus and its accompaniments as the prototype of the mighty act of God in Christ. The relevant passages are (in Moffatt's translation):

(1) 1 Cor. 5. 6–8:

Your boasting is no credit to you. Do you not know that a morsel of dough will leaven the whole lump? Clean out the old dough that you may be a fresh lump. For you are free from the old leaven; Christ our paschal lamb has been sacrificed. So let us celebrate our festival, not with any old leaven, not with vice and evil, but with the unleavened bread of innocence and integrity.

Here the consciousness is expressed that Christians form a 'New' Israel—they are the real people of God and the whole Christian life, because of the crucified Christ, can be thought of as a Passover festival of joy.[1]

(2) 1 Cor. 10. 1f.:

For I would have you know this, my brothers, that while our fathers all lived under the cloud, all crossed through the sea, all were baptized into Moses by the cloud and by the sea, all ate the same supernatural food, and all drank the same supernatural drink (drinking from the supernatural Rock which accompanied them—and that Rock was Christ) still with most of them God was displeased; they were laid low in the desert. Now this took place as a warning for us, to keep us from craving for evil as they craved. You must not be idolaters, like some of them; as it is written,

> The people sat down to eat and drink
> And they rose up to make sport.

Nor must we commit immorality, as some of them did—and in a single day twenty-three thousand of them fell. Nor must we presume upon the Lord as some of them did—only to be destroyed by serpents. And you must not murmur, as some of them did—only to be destroyed by the Destroying angel.

Here again the story of the 'Old Israel' is treated as parallel and yet continuous with the 'New Israel'. The Exodus of the 'Old Israel' is re-enacted in the experience of the 'New', and 1 Cor. 10. 1–5 is to be regarded as a midrash.[2]

---

[1] Cf. J. Moffatt, First Corinthians (M.N.T.C.), chapter lviii; see also J. Weiss, Meyer, Kommentar zum N.T., Der Erste Korintherbrief, p. 136. Weiss writes: "...dem P. und der Gemeinde vor ihm die typologische Betrachtung vertraut war, dass die 'Erlösung' durch Christus der Erlösung aus Aegypten entspreche...." It is noteworthy here how in Deutero-Isaiah 43. 14ff. the return from the Exile in Babylon is compared to a new Exodus. Cf. S. A. Cook, The Truth of the Bible, p. 26.

[2] Cf. J. Weiss, Meyer, Kommentar zum N.T., Der Erste Korintherbrief, p. 250; J. Moffatt, First Corinthians (M.N.T.C.), pp. 129f. See also L. S. Thornton, The Common Life in the Body of Christ, pp. 325, 333.

(3) 1 Cor. 15. 20:

Christ did rise from the dead, he was the first to be reaped of those who sleep in death.

Here again the reference to the 'firstfruits' may have Passover significance, because the ceremony of the firstfruits occurs in Passover week.[1] In Deuteronomy the firstfruits are commanded to be given with a profession of gratitude to God for deliverance from Egyptian bondage and the possession of the fruitful land of Palestine;[2] Christ is the firstfruits of a new redemption.

(4) 2 Cor. 3. 1–11:

Am I beginning to commend myself? Do I need, like some people, to be commended by written certificates either to you or from you? Why, you are my certificate yourselves, written on my heart, recognized and read by all men; you make it obvious that you are a letter of Christ which I have been employed to inscribe, written not with ink but with the Spirit of the living God, not on tablets of stone but on tablets of the human heart. Such is the confidence I possess through Christ in my service of God. It is not that I am personally qualified to form any judgement by myself; my qualifications come from God, and He has further qualified me to be the minister of a new covenant—a covenant not of written law but of spirit; for the written law kills but the Spirit makes alive. Now if the administration of death which was engraved in letters of stone, was invested with glory—so much so, that the children of Israel could not gaze at the face of Moses on account of the dazzling glory that was fading from his face; surely the administration of the Spirit must be invested with still greater glory. If there was glory in the administration that condemned, then the administration that acquits abounds far more in glory (indeed, in view of the transcendent glory, what was glorious has thus no glory at all); if what faded had its glory, then what lasts will be invested with far greater glory.

The obvious contrast between the Christian Exodus and that of the 'Old Israel' needs no emphasis in the above passage and we shall return to it later.

From these passages Carrington has concluded that Paul in the two Corinthian Epistles is using a definite midrash something like that found in the *Mekilta*.[3] He writes:

A study of *Mekilta* suggests that the original narrative of Exodus 12–24 had itself an instructional and initiatory character; it was certainly so regarded in

---

[1] See *H.D.B.* vol. II, p. 10; G. Buchanan Gray, *J.T.S.* (July 1936), vol. XXXVII, pp. 24 f.; cf. J. Moffatt, *First Corinthians* (*M.N.T.C.*), p. 58; H. Lietzmann, *H.Z.N.T.*, *An die Korinther*, pp. 11, 45.

[2] Cf. Deut. 26. 1–11.

[3] For the *Mekilta*, see Moore, vol. I, pp. 135 f.

the New Testament period. Beginning with the Passover ritual and the blood of the covenant, *Mekilta* develops the thought of Israel turning from idolatry, and by the Red Ṣea baptism, becoming the Son of God; it stresses the faith of Israel and the gifts of the Holy Spirit through which Israel was enabled to sing the song of triumph.... St Paul in 1 and 2 Corinthians is clearly working from a midrash of this character.[1]

This generalization is far too sweeping,[2] but the references in the Epistles do clearly show that Paul did think of the Passover in connection with the Christian life and clearly employed its underlying thought in his Christian exhortation. It is not impossible then, that his conception of the dying and rising with Christ by which the Christian individual re-enacts in his own experience the life of Christ as it were, is derived from the same world of thought as is indicated for us in the liturgy of the Passover, where the historical event calls for personal appropriation by the individual Israelite, i.e. just as the true Jew is he who has made the history of his nation his own history, so the Christian is he who has made the history of Christ his own. Knox's comment on Rom. 6 is interesting in the light of this:

> In Romans 6...the death and Resurrection of Jesus replace the Exodus from Egypt. The proselyte through circumcision and the proselyte's bath was enabled to come out of Egypt and pass through the Red Sea into the promised land of Israel. This original salvation of the people was re-enacted in every Gentile who was prepared to come out of Egypt, the natural type of evil in a religion whose literature was dominated by the utterances of the prophets who had counselled submission to Babylon. Paul transfers the argument to the death and Resurrection of Jesus. Those who share in it through faith pass through the waters of Baptism, are delivered from the old Egyptian bondage to sin and pass instead into a new slavery to righteousness, which results in sanctification. Here the union of the Christian with Jesus is stated in terms of an exchange from one slavery to another on the strength of the Christian conception of the passion and Resurrection as the new Passover.[3]

---

[1] Cf. P. Carrington, *The Primitive Christian Catechism*, pp. 6f.

[2] Comparison with Str.-B. vol. III does not make it at all probable that in 1 Corinthians Paul is definitely following a particular midrash. If this were so, we would expect to find many more parallels from the *Mekilta* quoted by Str.-B. As it is there are only very faint echoes of the *Mekilta* in 1 Cor. 6: 1, 7. 3, 23, 8. 5, but these are so tenuous that nothing should be built thereon. Similarly, while in 2 Cor. 3 it is remotely possible that Paul is using a fixed midrash, it is far more likely that he is following his own fancy, improvising as it were. W. L. Knox doubts whether his readers would follow him in his haggadic excursions, for this reason presumably. Cf. *St Paul and the Church of the Gentiles*, p. 130; also R. H. Strachan, *Second Corinthians (M.N.T.C.)*, ad loc.

[3] W. L. Knox, *St Paul and the Church of the Gentiles*, pp. 87f.

We now see what kind of κῆρυξ Paul was: he was the κῆρυξ not of a new mystery but of a new Exodus[1] and all that that implied. Dr Dodd has made us familiar with the nature of the κήρυγμα of the Apostle as of the early Church; it was the proclamation of certain events; but no mere events, rather events charged with meaning; and Paul's doctrine of the individual Christian is that he is one who has made his own these external events that he proclaims. This comes out clearly in the Eucharist where the rite is designed not merely 'in memory' of Christ but εἰς τὴν ἐμὴν ἀνάμνησιν with a view to recalling Him, i.e. appropriating Him as present reality.[2] It is in the light of this that we are to understand the dying and rising with Christ.

We have, however, to face one difficulty. Knox has claimed that the mode of thought, which we have been discussing, by which external historical events are to be re-enacted in a man's soul is Hellenistic. We quote his words (referring to the method of argument, he writes): "a past event of history (or mythology) embodied in a ritual action became an 'effective symbol' for producing a change in the character of the believer. This conception had passed from Hellenistic religion into the devotional language of the synagogue. Paul transferred it to the faith of the Church."[3] He regards such language as we have quoted above from the Passover Liturgy as due to the gradual approximation of Judaism to Hellenistic religion; the Hellenistic element is traced back by him to a period previous to the close of the Old Testament canon.[4] We shall now very briefly point out that we need not go outside Judaism to account for the conception with which we now deal. We may refer to Pedersen's[5] illuminating study of Israel's life and culture, and his emphasis on the sense of community within Israel. As we previously saw, the community of Israel is a unity of past, present and future.

Community goes deeper than one generation: it extends backwards as well as forwards through history. We see this whenever we consider the family. From father to son the same soul grows through time; it is the same in preceding and succeeding generations, just as at any time it is common to the whole family.... The relation to the fathers cannot be decided merely by the sons

[1] Cf. L. S. Thornton, *The Common Life in the Body of Christ*, p. 325.
[2] Cf. C. A. A. Scott, *Christianity According to Paul*, p. 191.
[3] W. L. Knox, op. cit. p. 98.
[4] W. L. Knox, op. cit. p. 28. This page should also be consulted as showing how in Judaism "the canonical account of the Exodus, with a superficial colouring drawn from the religious language of the Hellenistic world, became a regular form of preaching addressed to the Gentiles".
[5] *Israel: its Life and Culture*, I–II.

deriving the substance of their souls from them. It is true that the fathers form a long succession through the generations but the differences in point of time are not decisive.... The fathers are constantly present and take part in the life of the family. Therefore the relation between fathers and descendants is mutual. Just as the blessing of the fathers is inherited by the sons, in the same manner the greatness of the sons reacts upon the fathers. In face of this view of history it is of no importance to distinguish sharply between what has been done by each generation. The Israelites to whom Amos spoke had come up from Egypt (3. 2); this can be said because every Israelite shared in this experience.[1]

Another excellent example of this method of thought occurs in the Book of Joshua.[2] The aged leader tells a generation that had not actually come out of Egypt, "And I brought your fathers out of Egypt: and *ye* came into the sea; and the Egyptians pursued after your fathers with chariots and horsemen unto the Red Sea, and when they cried unto the Lord, he put darkness between *you* and the Egyptians, and brought the sea upon them, and covered them; and *your eyes have seen* what I have done in Egypt, and ye dwelt in the wilderness a long season." It is this same mode of thought that we have found in the Rabbinic literature, and we conclude that the concept under notice is to be explained in the light of the Israelite conceptions of personality and community.[3] Just as the Church for Paul was an extension of the personality as it were of Christ, so also was the individual Christian; it follows that the experience of Christ can be re-enacted in the latter: the Christian man can die and rise with his Lord. With the depth of moral and spiritual meaning in such words for Paul, we have not dealt, but only with the background of thought from which they come. One thing, however, is noteworthy; we saw in our discussion of Paul's conception of sin, that there was both a corporate and an individual aspect to it; in Rom. 1 and 2 the corporate aspect and in Rom. 7 the individual is to the fore. There is a parallel twofold strain in Paul's view of redemption; the individual 'dies and

---

[1] Johs. Pedersen, *Israel: its Life and Culture*, 1–11, .p. 276. See especially pp. 263ff. There is a remarkable expression of this in 4 Ezra 5. 41f. which reads, "41. And I said, But lo, O Lord, thou art ready to meet (with blessing) those who survive in the end. But what shall our predecessors do, or we ourselves or our posterity? 42. And he said unto me: I will liken my judgement to a ring; just as there is no retardation of them that are last, even so there is no hastening of those that are first." On verse 42 G. H. Box comments: "i.e. just as in the case of a ring or circle there is neither beginning nor end, so God's judgement will reach all generations at one and the same time". (*Ap. and Ps.* vol. ii, p. 573.)

[2] Joshua 24. See also Deut. 26. 5f.

[3] H. Wheeler Robinson, *Z.A.W.* Beiheft 66 (1936), pp. 49ff.: S. A. Cook, *The Old Testament: a Reinterpretation*, pp. 115ff.; cf. *The One and the Many in the Israelite Conception of God* and references there given by A. R. Johnson.

rises' with Christ, but this experience is also of necessity a corporate one in that it involves participation in the death and resurrection of a community, the Israel of God.[1]

[1] The mysticism of the Johannine writings provides some parallel to that of Paul. V. Taylor, in *Forgiveness and Reconciliation*, p. 145, writes: "In substance the Johannine mysticism closely resembles the Pauline mysticism, the principal differences being that the former also discloses itself as a God-mysticism and does not make use of the dying and rising with Christ." The mysticism expressed by μένειν ἐν in John occurs chiefly in the section John 13–17. In a paper discussing this section, J. Macpherson (Dr Dodd's *Seminar*, 1939) has claimed that these discourses are "the εὐχαριστική προφητεία of the greatest prophetic celebrant of the Eucharist that the Christian *ecclesia* has ever known". "Moreover the only really relevant formal parallel to John 13–17 is the Jewish rite of the paschal meal." The dialogue in the discourses he compares to the questions asked by the sons of the house in the Passover Liturgy. G. H. C. Macgregor (*Eucharistic Origins*, p. 48), has claimed that Paul does not draw much on the Passover Rite in his teaching. Macgregor writes: "There is in fact no evidence that Paul himself regarded the Last Supper as a Passover meal. It is the 'new covenant' rather than any link with the old covenant that interests him; and when he looks for an Old Testament type of the Eucharist he finds it not in the Passover but in the 'spiritual meat' provided in the manna" (1 Cor. 10. 1–4). But Macpherson, rightly we believe, has claimed that Passover motifs became part and parcel of the early Christian liturgies. In any case we can be sure that the Passover Rite must have loomed large in Christian circles in any attempt at expressing the new religion. This gives us added justification for seeking to elucidate Pauline thought by reference to his strictly Jewish background.

6

THE OLD AND THE NEW MAN: II. PAUL AS
TEACHER OF THE INDIVIDUAL

IN our last section we dealt with that background of thought from
which Paul derived his conception of the dying and rising of the
Christian man with his Lord. It is now our concern to discuss what
we have previously ignored, namely, the profound ethical significance
for the individual of this experience. There were certain things, indeed,
that made it perilously easy for early Christians to ignore this significance.
Mere emotional enthusiasm expressed in groanings that could not be
uttered, and phenomena such as the mere ecstatic speaking with tongues,
which clearly characterized the life of the early Church, could so often be
plausibly mistaken for spirituality;[1] and among Gentiles, who lacked any
deep acquaintance with Judaism, antinomianism was always crouching
at the door ready to enter in under the cloak of grace.[2] So much the
Epistles of Paul reveal.

In addition to this there was one element in the κήρυγμα of the Apostle,
as of the early Church generally, which is of especial importance in this
connection. That κήρυγμα implied a belief in the return of Jesus with
power, and the coming of the 'End'.[3] How far this belief dominated
Christian thought in the earliest days we need not determine;[4] suffice it
to say that it was sufficiently strong to have profound ethical reper-
cussions. The First Epistle to the Thessalonians shows how emphasis on
the expected return of Jesus had led some Christians to neglect their
work and to ignore the demands of society,[5] and we may reasonably
infer that Thessalonica was not the only place where Second Adventism
became an excuse for indolence and moral indifference. Paul's 'robust
common sense', as it has been called, immediately sensed the danger and
in his Epistle to the Church he reveals his concern for the moral well-
being of his converts; he seeks to show them "that a passionate expectation of a tremendous change" should not "disturb and destroy the

[1] I Cor. 12–14.   [2] Rom. 6. 1f.
[3] Cf. C. H. Dodd, *The Apostolic Preaching and its Developments*; I Thess. 1. 10;
Rom. 2. 16.
[4] Cf. W. L. Knox's review of Dr Dodd's book *J.T.S.* (1937), vol. xxxviii, p. 75,
and also *St Paul and the Church of the Gentiles*, p. 55, n. 3, where Knox writes: "I am
inclined to think that he [Dr Dodd] underestimates the importance of eschatology in
the form of an imminent Second Coming." But see his recent book, *Sources of the
Synoptic Gospels*, vol. i, p. 2 (Cambridge, 1953).
[5] I Thess. 4. 11f.

interests of the present".[1] It is not suggested, of course, that it was the menace of crude eschatology to morality that first led Paul to emphasize the moral duties of the Christian man; it is indeed clear from his First Epistle to the Thessalonians that at his first visit to the latter he had already given certain moral instructions.[2] Nevertheless, just as it is fair to claim that the delay in the 'Second Coming' was a principal cause in the development of Christian theology,[3] so too it is this that necessitated concentration on Christian ethics and that conditioned the development of the latter.[4] It meant that a gospel that was largely eschatological in its emphasis was compelled to withdraw its gaze from the future and adapt itself to this world of time and space, that Christianity had to come to terms with society and with culture. It was not sufficient for Paul as κῆρυξ to proclaim that the individual Christian had died and risen with Christ, and that his life was hid with Christ in God.[5] He had also to reckon with the fact that though ἐν Χριστῷ the individual Christian was also ἐν σαρκί and confronted by the tensions that this inevitably involved. In short, Paul the κῆρυξ had to become διδάσκαλος, the father of his converts in life as well as in faith, their trainer in 'the race' or 'boxing contest' of the Christian discipline.[6] Dr Dodd has made it clear that the early Christian preachers drew a distinction between the κήρυγμα through which converts were won to the Church, and the διδαχή on which they were nourished. This διδαχή included what we should call apologetics and also theological exposition, but chiefly ethical instruction.[7] As is seen in the First Epistle to the Corinthians, problems continually arose in the Pauline, as in other Churches, which demanded solution and provoked ethical thought, and fortunately the διδαχή that Paul taught his converts is amply preserved for us in his Epistles.[8] We shall now endeavour to show how some of this didactic material derives from a Rabbinic tradition.

Before we turn, however, to the more precise definition of the sources

[1] Cf. 1 Thess. 4. 5. H. Scott Holland quoted by R. N. Flew, *Jesus and His Church*, p. 62.

[2] Cf. 1 Thess. 4. 1: "ye have received of us how ye ought to walk...."

[3] Cf. C. H. Dodd, *The Apostolic Preaching and its Developments*, p. 73.

[4] Cf. 1 Cor. 7. 26, 29, where Paul's treatment of marriage is conditioned by eschatology. Cf. also M. Dibelius, *H.Z.N.T.* (1927), vol. XII, on Ephes. 4. 1; 1 Cor. 1. 8; J. Weiss, *The History of Primitive Christianity*, vol. I, p. 254.

[5] Cf. Col. 3. 1 f.

[6] Cf. Phil. 3. 14; Gal. 2. 2; (2 Tim. 4. 7, possibly Pauline); also 1 Thess. 5. 8; Eph. 6. 10–17; Rom. 13. 12; 1 Cor. 9. 7; 2 Cor. 10. 3–6; Phil. 2. 25. Also Philemon, verse 2 for the Christian life as a battle.

[7] Cf. C. H. Dodd, *The Apostolic Preaching and its Developments*, pp. 3 f.

[8] Ibid. p. 8.

of ethical material that Paul may have used, there is a preliminary question that immediately rises to our minds, the question whether, as we might expect, the Pauline approach to the moral education of Gentile converts is influenced to any degree, great or small, by the Rabbinic teaching on the moral duties of Gentiles summarized in the Noachian commandments.[1] In order to answer this question let us recall the situation in the early Church as it appeared to Paul.

As we have previously written, Paul was a Pharisee who was convinced that he was living in the Messianic Age. In that Messianic Age, according to the universalist tradition within Judaism, the Gentiles would come to share in the worship of the true God; this expectation Paul saw being fulfilled in the life of the Christian Church. That this was the light in which Paul regarded the influx of the Gentiles into the true Israel is clear. The following passage from Ephesians we may take as an expression of his views:

Wherefore remember, that ye being in time past Gentiles in the flesh, who are called Uncircumcision by that which is called the Circumcision in the flesh made by hands; That at that time ye were without Christ, being aliens from the commonwealth of Israel, and strangers from the covenants of promise, having no hope, and without God in the world: But now in Christ Jesus ye who sometimes were far off are made nigh by the blood of Christ....Now, therefore, ye are no more *strangers* and *foreigners*, but fellowcitizens with the saints, and of the household of God....[2]

In short, the Gentiles 'in Christ' had ceased to be strangers and foreigners and had become Israelites in the true sense. The Greek words used for the terms 'strangers' and 'foreigners' are respectively ξένοι and πάροικοι; it is important to remember their significance.[3] The latter term πάροικος is regularly employed in the LXX to translate the Hebrew *gêr* (another term so used is προσήλυτος). As to the meaning of *gêr* in the Old Testament scholars have been divided. According to some it simply meant a non-Israelite living in Israelite territory; according to others, in the later books of the Old Testament, it meant a convert to the religion of Israel. But whatever view we take of the meaning of *gêr* it is clear that when it is translated by πάροικος it signifies a foreigner living among Israelites as a resident alien. The other term ξένος (and also ἀλλότριος[4])

[1] For the Noachian commandments, cf. *J.E.* vol. VII, pp. 648f. and Moore, vol. I, pp. 274f., 339.

[2] Eph. 2. 11f.

[3] Cf. *Beginnings*, vol. V, pp. 80f. for discussion of this question. See also W. G. Braude, *Jewish Proselytizing in the First Five Centuries*, p. 136. Note on *Gêr Tôshâb* and God-fearer. Our argument is not affected by his conclusions.

[4] Cf. ἀπηλλοτριωμένοι of Eph. 2. 12.

is used in the LXX to describe any foreigner, translating the Hebrew *nokrî*. Thus Ruth asks Boaz:[1] τί ὅτι εὗρον χάριν ἐν ὀφθαλμοῖς σου τοῦ ἐπιγνῶναί με, καὶ ἐγώ εἰμι ξένη;

Now it will be obvious that for any strict Jew his relations with the *gêrîm* and *nokrîm* was a matter of importance. Judaism had early to formulate teaching to regulate the intercourse of the faithful with all such. The *gêr* was to be treated with kindness and was not to be oppressed, because he had no legal machinery which could protect him.[2] On the other hand the *gêr* was expected to fulfil certain demands. He was to abstain from offering sacrifice to strange gods,[3] from marriage within the forbidden degrees,[4] from work on the Sabbath,[5] from blood,[6] and from eating leavened bread during Passover week.[7] Judaism came to make the assumption in time that there were certain ethical demands which could reasonably be regarded as binding on Jews and non-Jews: laws such as those proclaimed by Sophocles in the *Antigone* "that are not of to-day nor yesterday but are for ever".[8] It was, perhaps, too much to expect the non-Jews to recognize the relevance of all the Torah of Judaism, but on the other hand there were certain elementary ethical precepts which all mankind should instinctively recognize. There were certain things which ἡ φύσις αὐτὴ διδάσκει[9]—as the Stoics would put it—and, although doubtless there were 'Barths' as well as 'Brunners'[10] in the first no less than in the twentieth century, the Rabbis generally, in accordance with this assumption, reckoned certain laws as binding upon every living soul, laws which had been given to men before the special revelation to Israel on Mount Sinai. These laws came to be formulated into what were called the Noachian commandments, a name which, since all men were regarded as having descended from the three sons of Noah, indicated the universality of the Laws. Six of these were believed to have been given to Adam and a seventh was added to these, according to some authorities, after the flood. These rules, however, are not all derived, as we might expect, from the earlier chapters of the Pentateuch; some of the laws found in the latter are ignored by the Rabbis, while others not found therein were introduced into the Noachian laws by the manipulation of certain hermeneutic rules. It is precarious to speak in detail concerning these Noachian laws. Some authorities refer to thirty such, and it is clear that there was no fixed scheme of

---

[1] Cf. Ruth 2. 10.
[2] Cf. *Beginnings*, vol. v, pp. 80f. and Moore, vol. i, pp. 328f.
[3] Cf. Lev. 17. 7–9.   [4] Lev. 18. 6–26.
[5] Exod. 20. 10f.   [6] Lev. 17. 10ff.
[7] Exod. 12. 18f.   [8] Sophocles, *Antigone*, lines 455ff.
[9] Cf. 1 Cor. 11. 14.   [10] See Appendix A.

commandments which was universally recognized. We may, however, state that most authorities came to regard them as being seven in number.[1]

The relevance of all this to an understanding of Paul's approach to his converts will be apparent. To him the Gentile Christians had once been *gêrîm* and *nokrîm*,[2] but now 'in Christ', without observance of the Torah, they were to be considered full members of the true Israel; there was to be no distinction between Jew and Gentile. But the 'being in Christ' unfortunately did not always signify any ethical seriousness as we saw; indeed, some Gentile converts seemed to regard themselves as "beyond good and evil".[3] Paul was faced increasingly with the problem of moral discipline, and here the question arises whether in laying ethical demands on these erstwhile *gêrîm* and *nokrîm* Paul was guided by those demands that Judaism had always placed upon them, in short whether in his work as ethical διδάσκαλος he had recourse to the Noachian laws in the form in which they were prevalent in his day.

Now, that Paul was familiar with the Noachian commandments cannot be doubted; we can quite definitely trace the conceptions underlying those commandments in his Epistle to the Romans. In the first chapter of the latter Paul is dealing with the moral condition of the Gentile world. In verses 18 ff. it is his contention that there is "a revelation of God to all men", ἀπὸ κτίσεως κόσμου, and that man's mind in its natural state, through the things that are created, can recognize the Creator. He does not expressly state it in Rom. 1, but he also implies in that chapter that God's moral demands are apparent to all men in their natural state, man's natural recognition of his Creator would have naturally led to his recognition of that Creator's moral laws, that is Paul's implicit logic; and in the second chapter this is made explicit in his recognition of a law written in the hearts of the Gentiles, who are

---

[1] Cf. above references to Noachian Laws, also S. Krauss, *Revue des Études Juives* (1903), vol. XLVII, pp. 34 ff. The six commandments enjoined on Adam were: (1) not to worship idols, (2) not to blaspheme the name of God, (3) to establish courts of justice, (4) not to kill, (5) not to commit adultery, (6) not to rob. A seventh commandment was added after the Flood, not to eat flesh that had been cut from a living animal (cf. Gen. 9. 4). See *Gen. Rabba* 16. 6; b. *'Abodah Zarah* 64 b; b. *Sanhedrin* 56 a; b. *Sanhedrin* 56 b.

[2] We believe that we are justified in thinking that Paul is here using these terms in the sense they originally bore in the Old Testament. The term גֵּר underwent changes: it came to denote in Rabbinic Judaism a proselyte and the resident alien came to be called גֵּר תּוֹשָׁב. See Moore, vol. I, pp. 328–41. Paul is not using a strict terminology in his thought of the Gentile Christians as having been once ξένοι and πάροικοι, but merely expressing the fact of their original 'foreignness'.

[3] Cf. C. H. Dodd, *The Evolution of Ethics* (ed. Dr Sneath), p. 304.

called by him "a law unto themselves" for this reason.[1] The fearful vices which beset the Gentile world are due to the rejection of τὴν φυσικὴν χρῆσιν for τὴν παρὰ φύσιν χρῆσιν.[2] It is, of course, clear that the form in which Paul's argument is cast in these chapters is Hellenistic. J. Weiss writes:

We find in Paul's positive teaching about God, as it is indicated in this passage (Rom. 1. 18–23), unmistakable traces of his acquaintance with wide-spread Greek ideas which to be sure may have come to him through Jewish sources. Especially is this true of the statement "that the invisible things of him since the creation of the world are clearly seen, being perceived through the things that are made, even his everlasting power and divinity; that they might be without excuse". In this terse and comprehensive sentence, almost every word and the whole train of thought can be demonstrated from Hellenistic sources.[3]

There are very close parallels in Wis. 13. 1–7 and Philo, De Monarch. §§ 34f., and the thought is a Hellenistic commonplace. Similarly Paul's conception that every man by nature knows something of God recalls the Stoic doctrine that the divine reason, Logos, or as the Book of Wisdom says, the divine wisdom, has planted a seed of itself in the souls of men and that out of it there grows a secret relationship, an affinity for and an attraction toward God.[4] Paul's idea of conscience is also Stoic.[5] Nevertheless, although the outward form of these chapters is Hellenistic their inner substance is also Jewish. Paul is here both Jew and Greek and it is difficult not to trace here the Rabbinic teaching on what is morally natural and, therefore, incumbent on every man, and that in the catalogue of vices given by Paul the latter sees the rejection by mankind of those demands that God in Rabbinic teaching had placed on the conscience of all men. Thus Klein[6] has pointed out that τὰ μὴ καθήκοντα, the comprehensive Stoic[7] phrase used by Paul to describe the immoral activity of the Gentile world, corresponds to the Hebrew sheˈlôˈ keˈhôgân, an expression which is of great import in the Derek 'eretz literature with which we shall soon be concerned. Thus in the 'ôrchôth ḥayyîm, in a passage from the work of Eliezer b. Hyrkanos (A.D. 80–120), Klein finds that one of the weightiest rules refers to "that which is unseemly". He writes: "One of the most important of the Derek 'eretz rules ran thus: 'Keep thee far from what is unseemly and from what

[1] Cf. Rom. 2. 14.   [2] Cf. Rom. 1. 26f.
[3] Cf. J. Weiss, The History of Primitive Christianity, vol. I, p. 240.
[4] Cf. J. Weiss, op. cit. vol. II, p. 511; also C. H. Dodd, The Bible and the Greeks, p. 36.
[5] C. H. Dodd, op. cit. p. 36, and references there given.
[6] Cf. Der älteste christliche Katechismus, p. 72.
[7] Cf. W. Sanday and A. C. Headlam, Romans (I.C.C.), p. 47.

resembles it.'"[1] Also in the midrash called *Tanna debe Eliahu*,[2] which, however, most scholars regard as very late, there are three standards by which the moral demands to be placed on all men are to be judged, namely, that which is useful, and honest and also that which is fitting: on these three things the world and society are deemed to rest.[3] While, therefore, we do not deny that the thought of Rom. 1, 2, has Stoic affinities and reflects the type of thought familiar to us in the Book of Wisdom, there can be little doubt that Paul is here employing Stoic terms and Hellenistic modes to expound those conceptions in Rabbinic Judaism which had led to the formulation of the Noachian commandments; to speak metaphorically, the dress in Rom. 1, 2 is Hellenistic but the body Rabbinic.

Having established Paul's familiarity with the Rabbinic conception of the Gentiles expressed for us in the Noachian commandments, we have now to go on to inquire whether we can go further and claim that these commandments played any large or normative part in Paul's work as διδάσκαλος. This brings us to a consideration of the Apostolic decree of Acts 15. There can be no doubt that that decree was immediately concerned with the problem of social intercourse between Jews and Gentiles within the Church. In Burkitt's words, "there was a demand for a minimum of common decency and behaviour from these Gentile newcomers if they were to be received as fellow-worshippers...",[4] because apparently many of the Gentile converts "had no intention of ordering their life in accordance with the law of Moses or indeed, so far as the older Jewish believers could make out, in accordance with any rules whatever".[5] The solution reached was that suggested by James that the Gentiles should be forbidden (three or) four things, namely, εἰδωλόθυτα, αἷμα, πορνεία, πνικτά.[6] We need not agree with Burkitt that the decree had only to deal with the problem of social intercourse and was not meant to help to ensure the salvation of Gentile Christians.[7] There were certain requirements, as we saw above, that James and every Rabbi would have no hesitation in demanding from all men, moral requirements the rejection of which, *ipso facto*, kept one outside the pale

---

[1] G. Klein, op. cit. pp. 72, 134. Most scholars regard ארחות חיים as a very late collection; but the phrase *shᵉlô' kᵉhôgân* is early: Akiba used it; see *b. 'Abodah Zarah* 55a.

[2] Cf. *J.E.* vol. XII, pp. 46f.   [3] Cf. G. Klein, op. cit. pp. 66f.

[4] Cf. F. C. Burkitt, *Christian Beginnings*, p. 111.

[5] F. C. Burkitt, op. cit. p. 110.

[6] Into the question of the text at this point we need not here enter. Cf. *Beginnings*, vol. V, p. 195, for the whole subject.   [7] F. C. Burkitt, op. cit. p. 115.

of salvation.[1] It is tempting and probably correct to see in the Apostolical decree an expression of these demands, a version of the Noachian commandments possibly abbreviated or in the form current in the first century. It is incredible that in any discussion on the status of Gentiles within the Church those commandments should not have been the subject of discussion, and the meaning of the decree is probably that those responsible for it, knowing themselves to be living in the Messianic Age, while they did not insist on circumcision for all Christians, did insist on their observing those fundamental demands which the Rabbis assumed to be binding on all men.[2]

We have next to examine Paul's attitude to this decree. We note three interpretations that are relevant. According to Burkitt, Paul, although the fact is not expressly stated, accepted the decree. The Apostle he claimed would have understood the alarm felt in the Church at Jerusalem at the thought of social intercourse with some Christians of the type, let us say, that we can imagine in the Corinthian Church. He writes: "St Paul did not mind issuing ordinances on occasion. If, therefore, the recommendations in the Apostolical Decrees happened to be such as in St Paul's eyes 'nature itself teaches' (1 Cor. 11. 14) then I do not think he would have felt it inconsistent with 'his' gospel to recommend, even to enforce them."[3] Manson[4] regards Acts 15 as the answer of the Church to the problem of social intercourse set forth by Paul in Gal. 2. 11–14 and claims, with Burkitt, that Paul was probably present at the meeting, and that as a working compromise he accepted the decree.[5] Later, however, when Paul's mission field was invaded by Judaizers he refused to regard the decree as binding, and came to regard all regulations of such a character as 'irrelevant to Christianity'. Weiss,[6] in the third place, holds that Paul was not present at the meeting recorded in Acts 15 and that there was a complete break between Paul and the Church at Antioch before Judas and Silas had brought the decree from Jerusalem. We cannot here enter into details on a notoriously difficult problem. Certain considerations, however, make Burkitt's view difficult of ac-

---

[1] Cf. also Paul in 1 Cor. 6. 9: "Know ye not that the unrighteous shall not inherit the Kingdom of God? Be not deceived: neither fornicators nor idolaters, nor adulterers, nor effeminate...nor extortioners shall inherit the Kingdom of God."

[2] Cf. P. Carrington, *The Primitive Christian Catechism*, pp. 14f.; also *Beginnings*, vol. IV, ad loc.; T. W. Manson strongly dissents: see reference below.

[3] Cf. F. C. Burkitt, op. cit. p. 123.

[4] T. W. Manson, *Ryl. Bull.* (April 1940), vol. XXIV, no. 1, pp. 21f.

[5] T. W. Manson, op. cit. p. 23.

[6] Cf. *The History of Primitive Christianity*, vol. I, pp. 275f.

ceptance. First, in the church at Corinth, where the 'food' question was acute and where a decree such as that formulated by the Jerusalem council would have been invaluable, Paul makes no reference to it. Indeed, his advice to Christians that they were to eat what was set before them without question actually contradicts it.[1] Secondly, it is to be noted that the decree is directed only to the churches of Antioch, Syria and Cilicia and not to the strictly Pauline churches.[2] Thirdly, the idea that Paul merely demanded a minimum of good conduct from his converts is in flat opposition to the evidence of his Epistles where he places upon them the full law of Christ.[3]

Without, therefore, passing judgement on the date and circumstances of the Jerusalem decree, it has become clear that we cannot claim that the Noachian commandments were in any sense normative for Paul in the ethical teaching of his converts. We can claim, however, that the conceptions which gave them birth became an integral part of his theology and must have often guided his thoughts in discussions on the Gentile question. Our next task will be to point to other more specific directions in which Paul found guidance from Rabbinic Judaism in his work as διδάσκαλος.

We begin with Paul's conception of the Christian man who was once afar off, a gêr and a nokrî, as a new creation. The man who is 'in Christ' is καινὴ κτίσις.[4] This phrase is no invention of the Apostle's; it is derived by him from the Rabbinic thought of his day. The words b'riyyâh h'dâshâh are used in many senses, but for our purpose we note particularly that the metaphor is used to describe a proselyte to Judaism. Thus Gen. R. 39. 4 reads: "Whoever brings a heathen near to God and converts him is as though he had created him."[5] Again, in a closely related metaphor, the proselyte is often likened to a new-born child. In the Babylonian Talmud in Yebamoth 48 b, R. Hananiah claimed that proselytes were grievously afflicted because in the time previous to their conversion they had failed to observe the seven Noachian commandments. But R. Jose (A.D. 150) rejected this view by saying that 'a proselyte converted to Judaism is like a newborn child' (k'qâtôn nôlâd), and God, therefore, could not punish him for deeds done before his birth, i.e. in his pagan days.[6] There was a halakic rule to this effect as

---

[1] Cf. 1 Cor. 10. 27.
[2] Cf. J. Weiss, The History of Primitive Christianity, vol. I, p. 314.
[3] Cf. T. W. Manson, Ryl. Bull. (April 1940), vol. XXIV, no. 1, pp. 18 f.
[4] Cf. 2 Cor. 5. 17; Gal. 6. 15; Eph. 4. 24; Col. 3. 10.
[5] Cf. F. C. Burkitt, Christian Beginnings, p. 109.
[6] Cf. Str.-B. vol. II, pp. 421 f.

is pointed out in Strack-Billerbeck: 'The proselyte is like a newly born child.'[1]

From this it follows that the language of 'new birth' or 'new creation' in connection with converts to Christianity would naturally suggest itself to its preachers. Thus in 1 Peter,[2] we read that Christians are 'begotten again', and in James the two metaphors are combined: "Of his own will he *begat* us with word of truth, that we should be a kind of firstfruits of his creatures (κτισμάτων)."[3] Paul, however, avoids the conception of a new birth and prefers that of a new creation. Schweitzer has seen in this Pauline rejection of the metaphor of rebirth evidence of the non-Hellenistic character of Paul's thought;[4] there may be some force in this view because the prevalence of the conception of rebirth in Hellenistic religious circles is so noticeable. It must not, however, be pressed too far because the conception is also found, as we saw above, in Rabbinic circles. It is safer to say that the metaphor of a new creation harmonizes better than that of rebirth with that conception of the whole Christian Dispensation as a new creation which we have already found in Paul.[5] Just as Paul in a corporate sense had spoken of an old humanity and a new humanity represented by the first Adam and the Second Adam, so in an individualization of the same thought the metaphor of a new creation enabled him to speak of an old man and a new man. This is borne out by the fact that where Paul writes in these terms there can be no doubt that he has the old Adam and the Second Adam in mind. Thus in the Epistle to the Colossians we read: "Seeing that ye have put off the old man with his deeds; and have put on the new man which is renewed in knowledge *after the image of him that created him.*"[6] We may further add that what gave depth to the Pauline conception of the Christian as a new creation was that he was a new creation in a new

---

[1] Cf. Str.-B. vol. II, pp. 423 f.; F. Gavin, *The Jewish Antecedents of the Christian Sacraments*, pp. 51 f.; b. *Yebamoth* 62 a.

[2] Cf. 1 Pet. 1. 3, 2. 2.   [3] Cf. James 2. 18.

[4] Cf. A. Schweitzer, *The Mysticism of Paul the Apostle*, pp. 14 f. "The Pauline assertion that he who is in Christ is a new creature (καινὴ κτίσις) has nothing to do with the notion of rebirth. That Paul, in view of his familiarity with the Greek language must have known the term rebirth and its significance for Hellenistic personal religion is doubtless to be assumed. But he is unable to make use of it because his thought follows logical and realistic lines." Also F. C. Burkitt, *Christian Beginnings*, pp. 108 f. For Regeneration see W. L. Knox, *Some Hellenistic Elements in Primitive Christianity*, note 1, pp. 90 ff.; W. F. Howard, *Christianity According to St John*, note 8, pp. 197 ff. These two scholars evaluate the significance of the passages on a 'new birth' in Rabbinic Judaism differently.

[5] Cf. above, chapter 3.

[6] Cf. Col. 3. 9. The words in italics show where Paul's thought lies. Of course, the linguistic link, man=Adam (אדם), is also of some importance in all the above.

world, because Jesus had had cosmic significance, whereas the proselyte to Judaism was still living in an old world; Judaism could not, like Paul, think in terms of a new order that had arrived.[1]

To resume our argument, however, it will be evident from the above that the Jewish treatment of proselytes may enlighten us as to the way in which Paul, and others, dealt with converts to Christianity. Now the process by which a man was made a proselyte was threefold: it consisted of circumcision, immersion in water (i.e. baptism), and the presentation of an offering in the Temple.[2] Of these rites baptism assumed a growing importance. Thus, "towards the end of the first century R. Joshua and R. Eliezer b. Hyrkanos could debate whether baptism or circumcision be the essential rite of initiation into Judaism".[3] Moreover, from the Rabbinic sources it is clear that the baptism of a proselyte was the occasion of his instruction. In b. Yebamoth 47a we read that after the presentation and examination of the candidate: "Then they are to instruct him in some of the lighter and weightier commandments. . . ." So too in the extra-canonical tractate Gerim, baptism involved instruction.[4] As to the exact content of the instruction given to proselytes at baptism we cannot speak with certainty: those scholars are probably right who find underlying the Two Ways enshrined in the Didache and the Epistle of Barnabas, and also underlying the Mandata of Hermas, early Jewish catechetical material.[5] It is probable that in our period there was much hortatory and ethical material which every Rabbi used probably at his own discretion.[6] For our immediate purpose, however, we point out that if, as seems likely, Christian baptism is probably closely related in origin to Jewish proselyte baptism, we should expect it to be the occasion of moral instruction like its counterpart in Judaism.[7]

[1] Cf. R. H. Strachan, Second Corinthians (M.N.T.C.), p. 113.

[2] Cf. Moore, vol. I, p. 331.

[3] Cf. F. Gavin, Jewish Antecedents of the Christian Sacraments, p. 31.

[4] Cf. F. Gavin, op. cit. p. 33.

[5] Cf. Beginnings, vol. v, p. 79; G. Klein, Der älteste christliche Katechismus, pp. 157f.; also P. Carrington, The Primitive Christian Catechism (1940), p. 9; C. Taylor, Teaching of the Twelve Apostles; contrast Armitage-Robinson, Barnabas, Hermas and the Didache, criticized by Maclean, The Doctrine of the Twelve Apostles. See B. H. Streeter, The Primitive Church, pp. 279f.

[6] Beginnings, vol. v, p. 77.

[7] See F. Gavin, op. cit. pp. 26–58. He writes: "for the interpretation of early Christian belief and practice in regard to Baptism we need look no further than contemporary Rabbinic Judaism", p. 58. See also H. G. Marsh, The Origin and Significance of the New Testament Baptism, who accepts the same point of view, p. 81. See Beginnings, vol. I, pp. 332 ff. for the suggestion that it was the seven deacons, who represented the Hellenistic Jews, that first introduced baptism in the name of Jesus following the Jewish practice for the initiation of proselytes and making use of the

That this was so will become clear from the Pauline Epistles. Thus
Paul in Rom. 6 is enlarging upon the union of the Christian with Christ
in death and resurrection; to explain the meaning of this, he writes:
"Surely you know that all of us who have been baptized into Christ
Jesus have been baptized into His death,"[1] and later on he makes it
obvious that this meant that the baptized person was to consider himself
'dead unto sin'.[2] Paul's manner of referring thus to baptism in order
to enforce the ethical implications of dying and rising with Christ
implies that it had ethical significance for the baptized, that the Christian
at baptism had been made aware of the moral nature of the new life
upon which he was entering. The inference is fully justified that in the
early Church, as in Judaism, baptism was an important occasion for ethical
teaching. This fact has recently been emphasized in an illuminating
study by Carrington,[3] and in what follows we shall be indebted to him.

It has, of course, long been recognized that the ethical or hortatory
sections of the Pauline Epistles, which usually follow doctrinal exposi-
tions, are generally parallel to similar sections of other New Testament
Epistles, namely, 1 Peter, James and Hebrews. We may compare the
following passages: Col. 3. 8–4. 12; Eph. 4. 20–6. 19; 1 Pet. (A) 1. 1–4. 11;
1 Pet. (B) 4. 12–5. 14; Jas. 1. 1–4. 10; and also Heb. 12. 1f. and
Rom. 12. 1f. Now the suggestion has been favourably received that in
1 Pet. 1. 3–4. 11, we have preserved for us material used at the baptism
of converts. Streeter[4] writes as follows:

H. Gunkel in his Introduction to the Epistle mentions a recent conjecture of
Perdelwitz...that this section of the Epistle (i.e. 1. 3–4. 11) was originally an
address given by the bishop to a group of newly baptized persons—presumaby
at some great festival....In the early Church, candidates for baptism were
normally adults converted from heathenism, and would include persons of
very different classes—slaves, married women, fathers of families (2. 18–3. 7).
Read as an address given on such an occasion the exhortations are extraordinarily appropriate—an inspiring description of the new life into which
they have been reborn, followed by encouragement to face alike the respon-
sibilities involved and the hostility of the outside world.

In view of this attitude towards 1 Pet. 1. 3–4. 11, it is natural that we
should seek for traces of baptismal catechetical material in the other
hortatory sections both Pauline and non-Pauline in the New Testament,

formula 'in the name of Jesus' "to indicate that their converts were not merely
proselytes to Judaism, but to that special sect which recognized the claims of Jesus",
p. 342.
[1] Rom. 6. 3.   [2] Rom. 6. 11.
[3] *The Primitive Christian Catechism.*
[4] Cf. *The Primitive Church*, pp. 122 f.

and we are not disappointed. A close examination of the passages to which we have referred above reveals in some at least a common order which is largely observed by Paul in the arrangement of his material in Colossians and Ephesians, and which is followed also in 1 Peter and James, and less completely in Hebrews. The following tables will make this clear: in the first we have written out in full the relevant passage in Colossians and Ephesians to make the position perfectly straightforward.

ORDER IN COL. 3. 8–4, 12

(1) *Putting off*

3. 8. *But now ye also put off all these*; anger, wrath, malice, blasphemy, filthy communication out of your mouth: 9. Lie not one to another, . . .

(2) *The New Creation*

seeing that ye have put off the *old man with his deeds*; 10. And *have put on the new man, which is renewed in knowledge after the image of him that created him*: 11. Where there is neither Greek nor Jew, circumcision nor uncircumcision, Barbarian, Scythian, bond nor free: but Christ is all, and in all. 12. Put on therefore, as the elect of God, holy and beloved, bowels of mercies, kindness, humbleness of mind, meekness, longsuffering; 13. Forbearing one another and forgiving one another, if any man have a quarrel against any: even as Christ forgave you, so also do ye. 14. And above all these things put on charity, which is the bond of perfectness. 15. And let the peace of God rule in your hearts, to the which also ye are called in one body; and be ye thankful.

ORDER IN EPH. 4. 22–6. 18

(1) *The New Creation*

4. 22. *That ye put off concerning the former conversation the old man*, which is corrupt according to the deceitful lusts; 23. And be renewed in the spirit of your mind; 24. And *that ye put on the new man, which after God is created in righteousness and true holiness.*

(2) *Putting off*

25. *Wherefore putting away lying*, speak every man truth with his neighbour: for we are members one of another. 26. Be ye angry, and sin not: let not the sun go down upon your wrath: 27. Neither give place to the devil. 28. Let him that stole steal no more; but rather let him labour, working with his hands the thing which is good, that he may have to give to him that needeth. 19. Let no corrupt communication proceed out of your mouth, but that which is good to the use of edifying, that it may minister grace unto the hearers. 30. And grieve not the holy Spirit of God, whereby ye are sealed unto the day of redemption. 31. Let all bitterness, and wrath, and anger, and clamour, and evil speaking, be put away from you, with all malice: 32. And be ye kind one toanother, tenderhearted, forgiving one another, even as God for Christ's sake hath forgiven you.

5. 1. Be ye therefore followers of God, as dear children; 2. And walk in love, as Christ also hath loved us, and hath given himself for us an offering and a sacrifice to God for a sweetsmelling savour: 3. But fornication, and all uncleanness or covetousness, let it not be once named among you, as becometh saints; 4. Neither filthiness, nor foolish talking, nor jesting, which are not convenient; but rather giving of thanks. 5. For this ye know, that no whoremonger, nor unclean person, nor covetous man, who is an idolater, hath any inheritance in the kingdom of Christ and of God. 6. Let no man deceive you with vain words: for because of these things cometh the wrath of God upon the children of disobedience. 7. Be ye not therefore partakers with them. 8. For ye were sometimes darkness, but now are ye light in the Lord: walk as children of the light: 9. (For the fruit of the Spirit is in all goodness and righteousness and truth;) 10. Proving what is acceptable unto the Lord. 11. And have no fellowship with the unfruitful works of darkness, but rather reprove them. 12. For it is a shame even to speak of those things which are done of them in secret. 13. But all things that are reproved are made manifest by the light: for whatsoever doth make manifest is light. 14. Wherefore he saith, Awake thou that sleepest, and arise from the dead, and Christ shall give thee light: 15. See then that ye walk circumspectly, not as fools, but as wise. 16. Redeeming the time, because the days are evil. 17. Wherefore be ye not unwise, but understanding what the will of the Lord is.

(3) *The Worship of God*

16. *Let the word of Christ dwell in you richly in all wisdom; teaching and admonishing one another in psalms and hymns and spiritual songs*, singing with grace in your hearts to the Lord. 17. And whatsoever ye do in word or deed, do all in the name of the Lord Jesus, giving thanks to God and the Father by him.

(4) *Submit yourselves*

18. *Wives, submit yourselves unto* your own husbands, as it is fit in the Lord. 19. *Husbands*, love your wives, and be not bitter against them. 20. *Children*, obey your parents in all things: for this is well pleasing unto the Lord. 21. *Fathers*, provoke not your children to anger, lest they be discouraged. 22. *Servants*, obey in all things your masters according to the flesh; not with eyeservice, as menpleasers; but in singleness of heart; fearing God:

(3) *The Worship of God*

18. And be not drunk with wine, wherein is excess; but be filled with the Spirit; 19. Speaking to yourselves in psalms and hymns and spiritual songs, singing and making melody in your heart to the Lord; 20. Giving thanks always for all things unto God and the Father in the name of our Lord Jesus Christ;

(4) *Submit yourselves*

21. Submitting yourselves one to another in the fear of God: 22. *Wives* submit yourselves unto your own husbands, as unto the Lord. 23. For the husband is the head of the wife, even as Christ is the head of the church: and he is the saviour of the body. 24. Therefore as the church is subject unto Christ, so let the wives be to their own husbands in everything. 25. *Husbands,* love your wives, even as Christ also loved the church, and gave himself for it; 25. That he might sanctify and cleanse it with the washing of water by the word, 27. That he might present it to himself a glorious church, not having spot, or wrinkle, or any such thing; but that it should be holy and without blemish. 28. So ought men to love their wives as their own bodies. He that loveth his wife loveth himself. 29. For no man ever yet hated his own flesh; but nourisheth and cherisheth it, even as the Lord the church: 30. For we are members of his body, of his flesh, and of his bones. 31. For this cause shall a man leave his father and mother, and shall be joined unto his wife, and they two shall be one flesh. 32. This is a great mystery: but I speak concerning

Christ and the church. 33. Nevertheless let every one of you in particular so love his wife even as himself; and the wife see that she reverence her husband.

6. 1. *Children*, obey your parents in the Lord: for this is right. 2. Honour thy father and mother; which is the first commandment with promise; 3. That it may be well with thee, and thou mayest live long on the earth. 4. And, ye *fathers*, provoke not your children to wrath: but bring them up in the nurture and admonition of the Lord. 5. *Servants*, be obedient to them that are your masters according to the flesh, with fear and trembling, in singleness of your heart, as unto Christ; 6. Not with eyeservice, as menpleasers; but as the servants of Christ, doing the will of God from the heart; 7. With good will doing service, as to the Lord, and not to men: 8. Knowing that whatsoever good thing any man doeth, the same shall he receive of the Lord, whether he be bond or free. 9. And, ye *masters*, do the same things unto them forbearing threatening: knowing that your Master also is in heaven; neither is there respect of persons with him.

(5) Watch and Pray

4. 2. *Continue in prayer, and watch in the same with thanksgiving*; 3. Withal *praying* also for us, that God would open unto us a door of utterance, to speak the mystery of Christ, for which I am also in bonds: 4. That I may make it manifest, as I ought to speak. 5. Walk in wisdom toward them that are without, redeeming the time. 6. Let your speech be alway

(5) Stand and Resist

10. Finally, my brethren, be strong in the Lord, and in the power of his might. 11. Put on the whole armour of God, that ye may be able to stand against the wiles of the devil. 12. For we wrestle not against flesh and blood, but against principalities, against powers, against the rulers of the darkness of this world, against spiritual wickedness in high places.

with grace, seasoned with salt, that ye may know how ye ought to answer every man.... [Personal details follow here.]

13. Wherefore take unto you the whole armour of God that ye may be able to withstand in the evil day, and having done all, to stand. 14. Stand therefore, having your loins girt about with truth, and having on the breastplate of righteousness; 15. And your feet shod with the preparation of the gospel of peace; 16. Above all, taking the shield of faith, wherewith ye shall be able to quench all the fiery darts of the wicked. 17. And take the helmet of salvation, and the sword of the Spirit, which is the word of God:

(6) Stand

12. Epaphras, who is one of you, a servant of Christ, saluteth you, always labouring fervently for you in prayers, that ye *may stand perfect* and complete in all the will of God.

(6) Pray and Watch

18. Praying always with all prayer and supplication in the Spirit, and watching thereunto with all perseverance and supplication for all saints.

We note that both in Ephesians and Colossians the exhortations can be grouped under the same headings and that apart from the fact that in Colossians the reference to the New Creation comes second and not first in order and that the counsels 'to watch and pray' and 'to stand' vary in their position in Colossians and Ephesians, there is discernible a certain sequence of thought. This sequence moreover is also found in 1 Peter and James. Here we will only indicate this fact briefly:

I PET. (A) I. 1–4. II
(1) The New Birth

1. 22. ...in obeying the truth...: 23. Being born again, not of corruptible seed, but of incorruptible, by the word of God, which liveth and abideth for ever.

JAS. I. 1–4. 10
(1) The New Birth

1. 18. Of his own will begat he us with the word of truth, that we should be a kind of firstfruits of his creatures.

(2) Putting off

2. 1. Wherefore laying aside all malice, and all guile, and hypocrisies, and envies, and all evil speakings,

(2) Putting off

1. 21. Wherefore lay apart all filthiness and superfluity of naughtiness, and receive with meekness the engrafted word....

(3) *Worship*

2. 5. Ye also, as lively stones, are built up a spiritual house, an holy priesthood, to offer up spiritual sacrifices, acceptable to God by Jesus Christ.

(3) *Worship*

1. 26. If any man among you seem to be religious and bridleth not his tongue, but deceiveth his own heart, this man's religion is vain. 27. Pure religion and undefiled before God and the Father is this, To visit the fatherless and widows in their affliction, and to keep himself unspotted from the world.

(4) *Submit yourselves* (cf. also 1 Pet. B, 5. 5, 6.)

2. 13. Submit yourselves to every ordinance of man for the Lord's sake: ... 18. Servants,...
3. 1. Likewise, ye wives,... 7.... husbands,...

(4) *Submit yourselves*

4. 7*a*. Submit yourselves therefore to God.

(5) *Watch* (cf. also 1 Pet. B 5. 8)

4. 7. ...be ye therefore sober, and watch unto prayer.

(5) *Resist*

4. 7*b*. Resist the devil.

(6) *Resist: Stand*

5. 8–12 (1 Pet. B). ...your adversary the devil, etc.

This remarkable similarity in order and in content in the hortatory sections of the Epistles calls for the assumption that the various authors drew upon a common storehouse of material.[1] The variations both in order and in matter prevent us from assuming the existence of a single fixed source which was regarded as universally authoritative; and, as suggested already, that interpretation of the above passages is best which sees in them baptismal catechetical material that was used by the early Church. Moreover, the common order that we have observed is marked by the prominence given to certain words: ἀποτίθεσθαι, ὑποτάσσειν, γρηγορεῖν, ἀγρυπνεῖν, νήφειν, στῆναι, ἀντιστῆναι, which suggests that there was possibly a catechetical pattern or formula which was followed by our authors in which these words were pivotal. It is significant that an examination of the incidence of these words in the New Testament reveals that they belong to a hortatory tradition; they cannot be regarded as being part of the customary vocabulary of any of the New

[1] Cf. P. Carrington, *The Primitive Christian Catechism*, pp. 23 f.

Testament authors.[1] Further, the appropriateness of such terms in connection with baptism is apparent. The putting off of evil would be fitly symbolized by the stripping off of the garments before immersion; the command to stand morally would correspond to standing up in the baptismal service after prostration in prayer and the references to the taking of the milk of the word is probably connected with the ritual act of giving the baptized a drink immediately after immersion.[2] To confirm the baptismal associations of the passages under discussion we may also refer to Dibelius' suggestion that in Eph. 5. 14, "Awake thou that sleepest and arise from the dead and Christ shall give thee light", Paul is quoting a baptismal hymn.[3]

In view of what we have written it will have become clear that Paul, like other writers of the New Testament, was indebted to baptismal catechetical material and that he used this material in his role as διδάσκαλος. There was a common storehouse of baptismal hortatory material, probably oral, on which he could draw. Moreover, it is equally clear that in his catechizing of baptized Christians he was following the custom of Jewish Rabbis when they baptized proselytes. To Paul, as to the Rabbis, the convert was a new creation, to be instructed and warned. We may probably rightly surmise that much of Paul's activity in his dealings with converts must have been indistinguishable to outsiders from that of Jewish Rabbis in their proselytizing. Finally, this comparison of Paul with the Rabbis as a catechist has another aspect. As we saw above it is probable that the instruction given at baptism was left to the discretion of the individual Rabbis who may or who may not have followed a set scheme of instruction. This was probably so in the early Church and it would explain why we find such variations in the catechetical material that we have dealt with above, and how, for example, Paul could apply to his converts the concept of a new creation, because it harmonized more with his thought, rather than that of a new birth, which others preferred.

Strange as it might seem then, Paul the Apostle of the freedom of the Christian man from the bondage of legalism has turned out to be a catechist after the manner of a Rabbi. But instruction given in connection with baptism did not exhaust the paraenetical duties of the early Christian leaders, and Paul himself has expressly told us that he did not regard baptismal activity as his *forte*.[4] He must have had many more things to

[1] P. Carrington, *The Primitive Christian Catechism*, pp. 47f.   [2] Ibid. pp. 81f.
[3] *H.Z.N.T.* vol. XII, p. 69. Also A. M. Hunter, *Paul and His Predecessors*, p. 44. (We note that the thought of this hymn has many parallels in the Hermetic literature; cf. C. H. Dodd, *The Bible and the Greeks*, pp. 170f.)
[4] Cf. 1 Cor. 1. 17.

teach his converts than could be pushed into a catechism at baptism. We can gather from his Epistles in what light he regarded the Christian community. Paul's advice to the Thessalonian Christians[1] not to walk as the Gentiles, to refrain from fornication, not to overreach each other in business, to have regard 'to those without' and other references in other Epistles reveal that he thought of Christians as forming a community that was 'holy', apart from the world and dedicated to God, which had therefore to observe certain rules. The Church was for him, in Carrington's phrase, a 'neo-levitical community',[2] and despite its freedom in the Spirit it had to know moral order also, it had to regulate its life. The Church, like every new sect within Judaism, had to draw up rules for the moral guidance of its members and had to define its position. Moreover, there is solid evidence that in doing this Paul and the other Christian leaders drew upon certain Jewish codes or regulations.

There are certain sections of the hortatory material used by Paul and others which present an important grammatical problem; we refer to those sections where the participle is used for the imperative. This is frequently found in 1 Peter and also in Rom. 12. 9–19, 13. 11, Eph. 4. 2f., Col. 3. 12f. and possibly in Col. 3. 16. As examples we may quote from Rom. 12. 9–19: ἀποστυγοῦντες τὸ πονηρόν, κολλώμενοι τῷ ἀγαθῷ, τῇ φιλαδελφίᾳ εἰς ἀλλήλους φιλόστοργοι, τῇ τιμῇ ἀλλήλους προηγούμενοι, τῇ σπουδῇ, μὴ ὀκνηροί, τῷ πνεύματι ζέοντες, τῷ κυρίῳ δουλεύοντες, τῇ ἐλπίδι χαίροντες. . . .

How are we to account for this strange use of the participle? Dr Daube has dealt with this question in an article entitled *Participle and Imperative in 1 Peter*. Rejecting the view that we can assume an anacoluthon with an imperative such as ἐστε implied,[3] and also Moulton's[4] view that the use of the participle for the imperative was a genuine Hellenistic development, he very convincingly suggests that the participle in question may be due to Hebrew or, less probably, Aramaic influence. Into the details of Dr Daube's argument we cannot enter here.[5] He points out that in the New Testament the usage occurs solely in the Haustafeln and similar rules; it occurs solely in rules concerning the social behaviour of Christians within their community and within their families, and that this is precisely one of the kinds of rules in which

---

[1] Cf. 1 Thess. 4. 1–12.

[2] Cf. P. Carrington, *The Primitive Christian Catechism*, p. 21.

[3] Cf. W. Sanday and A. C. Headlam, *Romans (I.C.C.)*, p. 360.

[4] *A Grammar of New Testament Greek*, vol. 1, pp. 180ff., 232ff.

[5] Dr Daube's work has since been published as an appendix to the Dean of Winchester's commentary on 1 Peter. Macmillan (1946).

post-Biblical Hebrew used the participle. With a wealth of detail this position is so consolidated that the conclusion becomes inevitable that wherever in the Epistles of Paul we find the participle used instead of the imperative there Paul is certainly using material derived from Jewish sources, probably from some kind of Jewish codes of rules that had established themselves within Judaism as useful for the purpose of moral education.

When we ask, however, what kind of code or codes were used by Paul we are in difficulty. It is impossible to give a cut-and-dried answer. Nevertheless, we do know that the Church was not without precedent in drawing up moral rules and we can point to the kind of material upon which Paul drew. We refer to three sources.

1. The most familiar of all Rabbinic ethical tractates occurs to us first—the *Pirkê Aboth*. But Dr Daube observes that there is not a single rule with the imperative participle in the *Pirkê Aboth*. The reason he gives for this is that the latter is not a code in the strict sense, but a collection of sayings through which the Tannaites expressed their deepest thoughts, and the cold impersonal participle form is unsuitable for such a work. Moreover, the *Aboth* belongs in some respects to the Wisdom literature where the participle was not used to express duties, the warmer form of personal address: "My son..., etc." being used. While, therefore, the matter of the codes drawn upon by the New Testament writers would be similar to much in the *Aboth*, the form would be different.

2. Secondly, we refer to the fact that it was customary and necessary for different sects or parties within Judaism to draw up rules and codes to regulate their intercourse with outsiders both Jewish and Gentile. Thus in the Zadokite Fragment we see the rules of a sect—'Torah' designed to safeguard the purity of a community. A 'New Covenant' formed the basis of the community, faithfulness to it was rewarded by love for God,[1] disloyalty to it by the visitation of "the sword that avengeth with the vengeance of the Covenant".[2] Among other things the Covenant implied the rejection of idolatry, fornication, murder and unjust acquisition of gain.[3] The words describing the treatment to be meted out to the faithless, "And as for him who abhors doing precepts of upright men...he shall be expelled from the congregation",[4] recall those of Paul in 1 Corinthians. The date of the Zadokite Fragment is uncertain, but whether we regard it as pre-Christian or post-Christian

[1] Cf. *Ap. and Ps.* vol. II, pp. 785ff.; 9, verses 24-7.
[2] Cf. 9 (B), verse 11.   [3] Ibid. verses 15f.
[4] Ibid. verse 30; cf. 1 Cor. 5. 1f.

it reveals the process of moral fencing which every community had to undergo in order to preserve its identity.[1]

An example of a more detailed codification of rules where the participial imperative is common, is found in *Mishnah Demai*.[2] Originating in the community of the Ḥaberim, the Associates, in its dealings with the *'am hâ-'âretz* it contains rules to be observed by scrupulous persons in their trading relations with less scrupulous persons; the first half of it goes back to the second temple. We might say, with Dr Daube, that the codes used by Paul would differ in matter from the technicalities of *Mishnah Demai*, but would be similar in form.

3. Lastly, we turn to what is known as the *derek 'eretz* literature. We are chiefly concerned with *Derek Eretz Zuta* and the *Derek Eretz Rabba*. According to the *Jewish Encyclopedia*[3] we can date *Derek Eretz Rabba* at least from A.D. 160. Moreover, there was a collection of ethical sayings in the school of Akiba called *Hilkot Derek Eretz* on which it is highly probable that the *Derek Eretz Rabba* was based, so that the rules and customs of behaviour contained in the latter can possibly go back to the first century. The work contains, among other things, rules of conduct in matters of eating and drinking and for different walks of life. So too *Derek Eretz Zuta*, chapters 1–4 of which are Tannaitic, is a collection of ethical maxims arranged in the manner of *Aboth* except that they are anonymous. Both Klein and Dr Daube have independently referred to this literature as important for the understanding of Paul's work as διδάσκαλος. It will be well first to present Klein's approach to the subject. It is the great interest of his book *Der älteste christliche Katechismus* that it has concentrated attention on the Rabbinic recognition of a natural ethical standard and on the way in which this was made the *point d'appui*, as it were, for Judaism in its missionary appeal to the heathen; and it is in the light of this conception that he has traced the rise of the *derek 'eretz* literature. According to Klein[4] just as the priests in Israel served as a medium whereby the ethical truths of the great prophets of Israel were made popular and palatable, whereby the gold of prophecy, as it were, was minted into common currency, so there grew up a literature to popularize the good life among the heathen. It described the way of life that all men should lead, seeking by means of saws and aphorisms, narratives and rules, to guide men

[1] H. H. Rowley, *The Relevance of Apocalyptic*, p. 72, dates it in the last century and a half B.C. See pp. 71–2 for references. See also E. Meyer, *Ursprung und Anfänge des Christentums. Zweiter Band: Die Entstehung des Judenthums und Jesus von Nazaret*, pp. 47 ff.; *Ap. and Ps.* vol. II, pp. 785 ff.

[2] Cf. Danby, p. 20.   [3] *J.E.* vol. IV, p. 526.

[4] G. Klein, *Der älteste christliche Katechismus*, p. 62.

into the right way. Judaism, as indeed we saw above, recognized that mankind as a whole could not accept the Torah in its fullness but in the *derek 'eretz* literature it offered to all a way that they could follow, a signpost to the desirable goal. It was, of course, hoped that the knowledge of the *derek 'eretz* would whet the appetite of a convert for the whole Torah later on.[1] Klein referred to the *Tanna debe Eliahu*[2] passages of which, following Friedmann, he dates back to the pre-Talmudic Age regarding them as a missionary appeal to the heathen; these reveal a concept of *derek 'eretz*—a natural law to be followed by all. In addition to this Klein appealed to the *'orchôth ḥayyîm* which he regarded as a collection chiefly of ethical rules but also of ritual and hygienic requirements which Eliezer b. Hyrkanos was supposed to have given to his son in his last hour. Pointing out Eliezer's great enthusiasm for the conversion of the heathen Klein found in the *'orchôth ḥayyîm* his teaching to the latter.[3]

Now we know that outside Palestine such an ethical appeal was made to the heathen world. There is a striking passage in the Sibylline Oracles where an appeal is made to the heathen to amend their ways:

Happy shall those men be throughout the earth who shall truly love the Mighty God, blessing him before eating and drinking, staunch in their godliness, Who, when they see them, shall disown all temples and altars, vain

[1] G. Klein, op. cit. pp. 137 f., holds that sayings such as the Golden Rule were meant to be potted versions of the essential Torah which should be offered to the heathen. He maintains that, on the basis of Ps. 34. 12 ff., a catechism was formed which developed into the Two Ways which we find in the *Didache* and elsewhere; catalogues of virtues were added and catalogues of vices, and later an eschatological conclusion was given to the catechism. It is Ps. 34. 12 f. that Klein claims to underlie Rom. 12, but his interpretation seems very forced. One thing is of interest: referring to the famous passage in Josephus, *Antiq.* 20. 2, 3 (cf. Whiston (E.T.), p. 415), where a trader obviously acts as missionary, Klein holds that Jewish traders often acted thus. Under pretence of selling *Lebensbalsam*, סם חיים, they offered the description of the good life found in Ps. 34. 15—סם was a pun on סור מרע of that Ps. 34. 12, the *Lebensbalsam* was 'Turning from evil', etc. It is tempting to suggest that the use of καπηλεύοντες by Paul in 2 Cor. 2. 17, may have as its background this trading missionary activity of which Klein speaks. Cf. also J. Weiss, *The History of Primitive Christianity*, vol. i, p. 212. It is also worth noting that Klein regards the Noachic commandments as a missionary minimum designed to attract the heathen. Dr Daube on the other hand, in a review of W. G. Braude's book, *Jewish Proselytizing in the First Five Centuries*, writes: "it would be interesting to know whether this and similar rules (Noachian Laws) were not to some extent the result of a feeling of resignation as regards conversion proper." Cf. *J.T.S.* (1942), vol. XLIII, p. 128.

[2] It is only fair to point out that the *J.E.* dates this in the tenth century.

[3] Cf. G. Klein, *Der älteste christliche Katechismus*, p. 133. On the date of this see above, p. 117.

erections of senseless stones, befouled with constant blood of living things and sacrifices of four footed beasts. But they shall look to the great glory of the true God, neither committing murder nor bartering dishonest gain, which things are altogether evil. Nor do they set their foul affection on another's bed....[1]

And again we read:

O ill starred mortals, let not these things be and drive not the great God to divers deeds of wrath, but have done with swords and moanings and killing of men and deeds of violence and wash your whole bodies in ever running rivers and stretching your hands to heaven seek forgiveness for your former deeds and with praises ask pardon for your bitter ungodliness. God will grant repentance and will not slay: He will stay his wrath once more if with one accord ye practice precious godliness in your hearts.[2]

Lake's words are relevant here:

It is noteworthy that here...besides the recognition of the true God, abstention from idolatry and idolatrous sacrifices, murder, theft and immorality is inculcated as necessary in the first passage and from violence and murder and immorality (ὕβρις) in the second. This is very similar to the Apostolical Decrees if they be interpreted as moral requirements. Of course the writer of the Oracula does not actually say that he was willing to associate with Gentiles who accepted his precepts but he certainly indicates that God would receive them and the greater may be supposed to include the less.[3]

In addition we have also to notice the poems of Pseudo-Phocylides. In the latter there is no condemnation of idolatry in any polemic[4] fashion, but ethical demands culled from Leviticus and the Pentateuch are set forth, so as to appeal to the natural understanding of men. Klein saw in these poems a tactful missionary appeal on moral grounds to the heathen world and he has pointed out numerous parallels from the derek 'eretz literature. If we follow Klein then, not only outside Palestine but within its borders, there had grown up a literature setting forth the demands that Judaism made on the heathen, and the influence of this literature had permeated all Christian exhortation, as Klein shows in the case of the Didache.[5] The probability then would be very great that Paul would naturally have turned to this missionary ethical material in dealing with his converts.

We cannot, however, accept all Klein's thesis. In saying that the derek 'eretz literature formed a point d'appui for Judaism in its missionary work, Klein gives to that literature a significance that it never could have had. Dr Daube seems nearer to the truth when he regards many

---

[1] Cf. Sib. Oracles 4, lines 24–34.   [2] Ibid. 162–70.   [3] Cf. Beginnings, vol. v, pp. 209f.
[4] Cf. G. Klein, Der älteste christliche Katechismus, pp. 143f.; P. Carrington, The Primitive Christian Catechism, p. 15.   [5] G. Klein, op. cit. pp. 184f.

regulations found in the *Derek Eretz Rabba* and *Zuta* as regulations intended to guide a superior group of scholars, which could never have been used in a missionary capacity.[1] Nevertheless, Klein has performed a great service in calling attention to the *derek 'eretz* literature as a possible source for the hortatory material used by Paul. Thus Dr Daube has rightly written: "It is a work of this kind [*Derek Eretz, Zuta*] a guide for the elect, that we may suspect behind the admonitions in the epistles. . . . The ideals proclaimed in *Derek Eretz Zuta* are similar to those found in the epistles." Unfortunately, however, we cannot certainly pin down the *derek 'eretz* literature as a direct Pauline source because the date of the extant material is uncertain (although as we saw it is probably Tannaitic), and in *Derek Eretz Rabba* and *Zuta*, as Dr Daube notes, the participle for the imperative, although found, is rare. It is essential, however, to remember that there was much *derek 'eretz* material that was orally transmitted. Klein is probably right in claiming that every Rabbi had a collection of such material, ethical and social maxims, rules for conduct. It is of course true that these collections are omitted from the *Mishnah*; but we do not therefore deny their existence, because we know that the *Aboth* itself, which is somewhat like the *derek 'eretz* literature, was included in the *Mishnah* not because of its ethical character, but because of its significance in establishing the continuity and longevity of Jewish tradition. We can be sure that Paul would be familiar with ethical maxims and social conventions which the Rabbis propagated and that he used these in his training of Christians. From such material he possibly derived those codal elements which we have observed in his exhortations. Examples of the participial imperative in Rabbinic literature will be found in Appendix B.[2]

We have referred to the *Pirḳê Aboth*, the literature of the sects,[3] and to the *derek 'eretz* tradition. While we may have been unable definitely to point to specific Jewish codes used by Paul and the other New Testament writers, we have shown that there was a tradition well defined and familiar within Judaism of ethical exhortation, which would and probably did supply precedents for the early Christian leaders in their work of moral education. Dr Daube may be right in suggesting that if we combine *Aboth*, *Demai*, and *Derek Eretz Zuta* we can get some idea of

[1] Cf. *Participle and Imperative in* 1 *Peter*. [2] Contrast with Daube, A. P. Salom in *Australian Biblical Review*, vol. xi (1963), pp. 41ff on "The Imperative Use of the Participle in the N.T.".

[3] Cf. G. Johnston, *The Doctrine of the Church in the New Testament*, p. 29: "Now the existence of these groups in Judaism is very significant. The nation was never thoroughly homogeneous and Pharisaism had to struggle for its triumph. . . . For its [the Church's] organization in congregations or assemblies there were precedents."

the kind of code material that lies behind the hortatory sections of the Pauline and other New Testament epistles. The variations in the various epistles may be due to the fact that Paul, and the others, used different versions of the same code or codes or different translations of them. What is important for our purpose is that Paul again has been proved to have appealed to a didactic tradition with Judaism.

If the view of the source of much of the Pauline ethical teaching above presented, as derived from catechetical and code material of Jewish origin, be correct, certain results naturally follow. It is clear that what is found in the hortatory sections of the Epistles of Paul arises largely from a didactic habit, from a tradition of exhortation which Paul held in common with the other apostolic leaders. Moreover, in the light of all this, these exhortations are not necessarily to be regarded as having any immediate or especial relevance to the Churches addressed; they are composed of general requirements, not of specific directions.[1] It is illegitimate to argue for example—as did the older exegetes—that the words in Col. 3. 22: "Servants, obey in all things your masters according to the flesh; not with eyeservice, as menpleasers; but in singleness of heart, fearing God..." are of necessity inserted because of a possible misunderstanding of Paul's intervention in the case of Onesimus; this may or may not have been the case, but is not a foregone conclusion. Nevertheless, A. M. Hunter[2] has gone too far when he writes that in view of the traditional character of the exhortatory material used by Paul it "has nothing to do with the theoretic foundations of the ethics of the Apostle". On the contrary, all the traditional material has been baptized by Paul unto Christ. Thus in Col. 3. 18-4. 1, as elsewhere, Paul has Christianized material of a 'foreign' origin by the addition to it of a formula ἐν κυρίῳ, this being added to show that all the exhortations were regarded as inspired by the Spirit of the Lord.[3]

While, however, we are justified in pointing out that Paul borrowed from a pre-Christian tradition of exhortation, this must not be allowed to make us overlook the fact that it was the words of Jesus Himself that formed Paul's primary source in his work as ethical διδάσκαλος. To this, the ethical teaching of Jesus in its impact upon Paul, we now turn.

A fact which has been insufficiently recognized is the large extent to which the Pauline Epistles are reminiscent of the Synoptic Gospels. In his exhaustive survey of the relationship between Paulinism and the

[1] Cf. M. Dibelius, *From Tradition to Gospel* (E.T.), pp. 238f.
[2] A. M. Hunter, *Paul and His Predecessors*, p. 64.
[3] Cf. M. Dibelius, *From Tradition to Gospel*, p. 241; also *A Fresh Approach to the New Testament Literature* (E.T.), p. 220; C. H. Dodd, *The Evolution of Ethics* (ed. Sneath), pp. 296ff.; and especially *Ryl. Bull.* (January 1934), vol. XVIII, no. 1, p. 33.

Logia of Jesus, Resch has pointed out the amazing number of places where Paul echoes or offers parallels to the Evangelists.[1] The following table reveals this:

Numbers of Parallels to the Synoptics		Parallels to the Agrapha
In 1 Thessalonians	63	8
2 Thessalonians	25	1
1 Corinthians	214	21
2 Corinthians	99	9
Galatians	88	11
Romans	270	35
Colossians	81	4
Ephesians	127	14
Philemon	10	—
Philippians	58	4
Acts	61	3
Total	1096	110

It must be admitted that Resch has overstated his case; his parallels are often the fruit of his wishes rather than of his thought.[2] Nevertheless, the evidence that he has gathered is very impressive and the question arises, what accounts for all these parallels? Now just as the parallels between 1 Peter and the Pauline Epistles were explained as due to the influence of 'Paulinism' upon the former,[3] so too it has been suggested that the same influence is traceable in Mark and Luke.[4] Scholars, however, are by no means convinced of the Paulinism of Mark and Luke, and moreover we not only have to account for parallels in Mark and Luke but also in Matthew, the Gospel of Christian Rabbinism, where surely we cannot suspect 'Paulinism' as the *Tendenzkritik* understands it.[5] In fact, just as the similarities between 1 Peter and the Pauline Epistles are now seen to derive from the use of a common source of hortatory

---

[1] *Der Paulinismus und die Logia Jesu*, by D. Alfred Resch in *Texte und Untersuchungen zur Geschichte der altchristlichen Literatur*: Gebhardt u. Harnack. Neue Folge, Zwölfter Band (1904).

[2] Thus it is surely an overstatement to cite the first words he gives from 1 Thess. 1. 2—εὐχαριστοῦμεν τῷ θεῷ—as a parallel to Luke 10. 21, Matt. 11. 25. One might note many such a forcing of the issue.

[3] Cf. H. A. A. Kennedy, *The Theology of the Epistles*, pp. 166 f.; see C. Bigg, *St Peter and St Jude (I.C.C.)*, pp. 15 ff.

[4] See Vincent Taylor, "Note on the Alleged Paulinism of Mark" in *The Gospels*, p. 64; also p. 78: "There is no Paulinism in Luke."

[5] Cf. A. Resch, *Der Paulinismus und die Logia Jesu*, pp. 635 f.

material,[1] so we must assume that only the use of a common source, the words of Jesus, can account for the parallels that Resch has pointed out between Paul and the Synoptic Gospels and also the Agrapha of Jesus.

Ignoring the more doubtful parallels that Resch appeals to, we shall now refer to those places in the Pauline Epistles where Paul is clearly dependent upon the words of Jesus. Two factors are relevant:

(a) There is clearly traceable in the Epistles a process whereby reminiscences of the words of the Lord Jesus Himself are interwoven with traditional material. Thus:

(1) Rom. 12. 14: "Bless them which persecute you: bless, and curse not." A clear echo of the words of Jesus, Matt. 5. 44.

(2) Rom. 12. 17: "Recompense to no man evil for evil." Cf. Matt. 5. 39 ff.

(3) Rom. 12. 21: "Be not overcome of evil, but overcome evil with good." Cf. Jesus' teaching on non-resistance.

(4) Rom. 13. 7: "Render therefore to all their dues: tribute to whom tribute is due; custom to whom custom; fear to whom fear; honour to whom honour." Cf. Mark 12. 13–17; Matt. 22. 15–22; Luke 20. 20–6.

(5) Rom. 13. 8–10: "Owe no man any thing, but to love one another: for he that loveth another hath fulfilled the law. 9. For this, Thou shalt not commit adultery, Thou shalt not kill, Thou shalt not steal, Thou shalt not bear false witness, Thou shalt not covet; and if there be any other commandment, it is briefly comprehended in this saying, namely, Thou shalt love thy neighbour as thyself. 10. Love worketh no ill to his neighbour: therefore love is the fulfilling of the law." Cf. Mark 12. 28–34; Matt. 22. 34–40; Luke 10. 25–8.

(6) Rom. 14. 10: "But why dost thou judge thy brother?" Cf. Matt. 7. 1; Luke 6. 37.

(7) Rom. 14. 13: "Let us not therefore judge one another any more: but judge this rather, that no man put a stumblingblock or an occasion to fall in his brother's way."

On this passage Dr Dodd comments: "This emphasis on the danger of putting a stumbling-block in the way of the weak recalls certain sayings in the Gospels—Matthew 18. 7; Mark 9. 42; Luke 17. 1–2. It can hardly be doubted that sayings like these were in Paul's mind.... The key word is σκάνδαλον translated 'hindrance'. It is not a good or usual Greek word and the very fact that Paul uses it here suggests that he knew it in the tradition of the sayings of Jesus."[2]

(8) Rom. 14. 14: "I know, and am persuaded by the Lord Jesus, that there is nothing unclean of itself...." Cf. Mark 7. 15; Matt. 15. 11.

---

[1] Cf. M. Dibelius, *A Fresh Approach to the New Testament and Early Christian Literature*, pp. 217f., especially p. 220. Also H. A. A. Kennedy's emphasis on the common Church consciousness in *Theology of the Epistles*, pp. 170f.

[2] *Romans* (*M.N.T.C.*), p. 218, n. 1.

The same knowledge of the words and spirit of Jesus is revealed interwoven with exhortations in 1 Thess. 4–5. Thus:

(1) 1 Thess. 4. 8: "He therefore that despiseth, despiseth not man, but God, who hath also given unto us his holy Spirit." Cf. Luke 10. 16.

(2) 1 Thess. 4. 9b: "...for ye yourselves are taught of God to love one another."

(3) [For 1 Thess. 4. 16f., see below.]

(4) 1 Thess. 5. 2: "The day of the Lord so cometh as a thief in the night." Cf. Luke 12. 39; Matt. 24. 43.

(5) 1 Thess. 5. 3: "For when they shall say, Peace and safety; then sudden destruction cometh upon them, as travail upon a woman with child; and they shall not escape." Cf. Luke 12. 39 ff., 21. 34.

(6) 1 Thess. 5. 6: "Therefore let us not sleep, as do others; but let us watch and be sober." Cf. Matt. 24. 42; Mark 13. 37; Luke 21. 34, 36.

(7) 1 Thess. 5. 13: "And be at peace among yourselves." Cf. Mark 9. 50.

(8) 1 Thess. 5. 15: "See that none render evil for evil unto any man." Jesus' teaching on non-resistance.

(9) 1 Thess. 5. 16: "Rejoice evermore." Cf. Luke 6. 23, 10. 20.

We may also refer to:

(1) Col. 3. 13: "Forbearing one another, and forgiving one another, if any man have a quarrel against any: even as Christ forgave you, so also do ye."

Of this E. F. Scott writes:[1] "We can hardly doubt, with a verse like this before us that it [the Lord's Prayer] was familiar to Paul...."

(2) Col. 3. 5: "Mortify therefore your members which are upon the earth." Cf. Matt. 5. 29, 30; Mark 9. 43, 47; Matt. 18. 8, 9.

(3) Col. 3. 12: "Put on therefore, as the elect of God, holy and beloved, bowels of mercies, kindness, humbleness of mind, meekness...." Cf. Luke 6. 38.

(4) Col. 4. 2 f.: "Continue in prayer, and watch," etc. Cf. Matt. 26. 41; Mark 14. 38; Luke 22. 40, 46.

(5) Col. 4. 3: "To speak the mystery of Christ." Cf. Luke 8. 10; Mark 4. 11; Matt. 13. 11.

(6) Col. 4. 6a: "Let your speech be always with grace, seasoned with salt." Cf. Luke 14. 34, 35; Mark 9. 49, 50; Matt. 5. 13.

(7) Col. 4. 6b: "...that ye may know how ye ought to answer every man." Cf. Luke 12. 12; Matt. 10. 19; Mark 13. 11; Luke 21. 14.

---

[1] Colossians (M.N.T.C.), ad. loc.; cf. also A. M. Hunter, Paul and His Predecessors, p. 59. The latter, following Zahn, finds an allusion to the Lord's Prayer also in Rom. 8. 15: "But ye have received the Spirit of adoption, whereby we cry, Abba, Father"—"the phrase 'whereby we cry, Abba, Father' refers to the corporate recitation of the Pater-noster by the newly baptized as the first exercise of their Christian privileges." He also finds the same thing in 2 Thess. 3. 3.

(8) Col. 4. 12: "...always labouring fervently for you in prayers, that ye may stand perfect." Cf. Luke 21. 36, 13. 24; Matt. 5. 48.

This brief survey of the hortatory sections in Romans, 1 Thessalonians and Colossians has revealed how Paul is steeped in the mind and words of his Lord; he is obviously familiar with the latter and unconsciously mingles them with the hortatory material he has derived from other sources. But we go on to the second point.

(b) Not only do we find words of Jesus used without differentiation along with other hortatory material, there is also clear evidence that there was a collection of sayings of the Lord to which Paul appealed. We note the following explicit references to words of Jesus:

(1) 1 Cor. 7. 10: "And unto the married I command, yet not I, but the Lord, Let not the wife depart from her husband." Cf. Mark 10. 12.

(2) 1 Cor. 9. 14: "Even so hath the Lord ordained that they which preach the gospel should live of the gospel." Cf. Luke 10. 7; Matt. 10. 10.

(3) 1 Cor. 11. 23 ff.: "For I have received of the Lord that which also I delivered unto you", etc.[1]

(4) 1 Thess. 4. 15 f.: "For this we say unto you by the word of the Lord, that we which are alive and remain unto the coming of the Lord shall not prevent them which are asleep", etc.

(5) Acts 20. 35: "...remember the words of the Lord Jesus, how he said, It is more blessed to give than to receive."

(6) 1 Cor. 14. 37: "If any man think himself to be a prophet, or spiritual, let him acknowledge that the things that I write unto you are the commandments of the Lord."

The most instructive instance of Paul's appeal to the words of Jesus is found in 1 Cor. 7. 25: "Now concerning virgins I have no commandment of the Lord: yet I give my judgment, as one that hath obtained mercy of the Lord to be faithful." Dibelius' words on this deserve quoting:

When in 1 Cor. 7. 25, Paul remarks 'concerning virgins I have no directions of the Lord' we may probably deduce that he had received a number of such 'directions of the Lord', and that the two sayings of Jesus which he cites in this letter belong to him. Amongst these directions he finds no words about virgins, and we may hear a tone almost of regret as he confirms his lack. Hence he voices either the sayings which he has in his memory...or else he looks through the leaves of papyrus which he carries. Thus there were not only words of Jesus alongside of other sayings contained in the framework of exhortation but also collections which contained exclusively sayings of Jesus, and which were given to the missionaries orally or fixed in writing. Naturally such collections serve the purpose of exhortation but of course the sense of

[1] For this see below, chapter 9.

their authority operated in the fact of their composition. It was desired to hand down certain directions not only in the spirit or in the name of the Lord —as would hold good in the end of every Christian exhortation—but also of His authoritative sayings.[1]

From the above survey we gather that in addition to any traditional material that Paul used he had also the words of Jesus to which he turned for guidance, and he makes it clear that when there is an explicit word uttered by Christ on any question, that word is accepted by him as authoritative. Weiss,[2] however, has claimed that it is only in matters of a strictly legislative character that this appeal to the words of Jesus as a norm is made, and that where Paul deals with problems of the personal life of the individual his appeal is to the direct guidance of the Spirit. Now it is of course true that it is in 1 Corinthians (along with Romans), as the lists drawn up by Resch show, that Paul makes most use of the words of Jesus, but we have seen that those words permeate all his ethical exhortations. Moreover, at the most personal point of all his Epistles we cannot help tracing the impact of the teaching of Jesus. In Rom. 7 in illustration of his moral failure Paul chooses that commandment which more than any other deals with the inner life. It is, as Dr Dodd has written, "highly significant that Paul has chosen for his example the one prohibition of the Decalogue which deals with the inner life and not with overt action".[3] It is surely from the words of his Lord that he had made the shattering discovery of the supreme importance of the motive behind any act and of a thought even without any act: he had learnt of Christ.[4] Further Weiss has claimed that "the word 'commandments' (ἐντολαί) is never used by Paul of the sayings of Jesus".[5] But nevertheless, in 1 Cor. 7. 25, Paul refers to a word of the

---

[1] M. Dibelius, *From Tradition to Gospel*, p. 242. Resch would have us see in several places the direct use of Jesus' words by Paul; he thus regards 1 Thess. 4. 16; 1 Cor. 4. 6, 5. 6, 9. 10, 10. 24, 33, 13. 5, 14. 34, 35, 37, 15. 52; Gal. 5. 9; Rom. 12. 3, 13. 1; Col. 3. 18. This, however, it seems to us he can only do by a *tour de force*; cf. A. Resch, *Der Paulinismus und die Logia Jesu*, pp. 153 f., 459 f.

[2] Cf. *The History of Primitive Christianity*, vol. II, p. 554.

[3] *Romans* (*M.N.T.C.*), ad loc.

[4] Unless we recognize the place that the impact of the teaching of Jesus had on the mind of Paul, his conversion descends to something very much like magic, at least so it seems to us.

[5] There is an apparent exception to this in 1 Cor. 14. 37 (εἴ τις δοκεῖ προφήτης εἶναι ἢ πνευματικός, ἐπιγινωσκέτω ἃ γράφω ὑμῖν, ὅτι κυρίου ἐστὶν ἐντολή. εἰ δέ τις ἀγνοεῖ, ἀγνοείτω), but the word ἐντολή is probably not to be taken as part of the original text; cf. C. H. Dodd, *History and the Gospel*, p. 57, n. 3. So J. Weiss, Meyer, *Kommentar z. Neuen Testament, Der Erste Korintherbrief*, p. 343, and H. Lietzmann, *H.Z.N.T.*, pp. 9, 75, who gives the various readings. D. and G. have the original text probably, i.e. ὅτι κυρίου ἐστιν.

Lord as an ἐπιταγή, and most important of all in two places Paul explicitly refers to the Law of Christ. To this we now turn.

The explanation that Weiss offers of the conception of a νόμος τοῦ Χριστοῦ in Paul he expresses as follows: "Here appears the old pre-Pauline mode of thought according to which the life of the Christian is a life after the words and commandments of the Lord."[1] In short, Paul's use of the words of Jesus is merely an overhang from the very early legalistic days of the Church. But it is difficult to believe that in the earliest days of the Church the words of Jesus did play any crucial part in the life of Christians. W. Manson has recently pointed out rightly that "in the primitive statement of the case for Christianity the tradition of the words of Jesus does not appear to have figured with any prominence".[2] The chief reason for this, he suggests, was that Christianity brought not primarily a new ethic, however exalted, but a Messianic faith; the person of Christ, not his words, first formed the arena of conflict so that the latter assumed a secondary significance. In other words, the centrality of the κήρυγμα for a time obscured the significance of the διδαχή. But only for a time was this so. We know that one of the most important events in the history of the early Church was the formation of the 'document' called Q,[3] in which the words of Jesus are gathered together. This 'document' has been variously dated, but it can hardly be later than A.D. 60 and Streeter assigns it to A.D. 50. This means that in the period of Paul's activity the Church was occupied, indeed we may say was preoccupied, with preserving the words of Jesus. So great was this preoccupation that we may probably regard the Gospel of Mark which is kerugmatic rather than didactic in its emphasis as possibly written in reaction to the over-emphasis that was placed in Q on the διδαχή of Jesus.[4] Later on, however, the balance was restored and in Matthew and Luke the words of Jesus are again given prominence. Manson has rightly claimed that

The incorporation of the Q material in our Gospels of Matthew and Luke brings with it a certain qualification of the Christological standpoint of Mark, if not an entire displacement of the Markan emphasis. More firmly than Mark the two latter evangelists have drawn around Jesus the mantle of the teacher, the revealer of the deep things of God....While Matthew and Luke have taken over from Mark the early emphasis upon signs and wonders, they have qualified the epiphany doctrine of Mark by didactic supplementations and

[1] Cf. *The History of Primitive Christianity*, vol. II, p. 554.
[2] Cf. *Jesus, the Messiah*, pp. 51 f.
[3] Cf. B. H. Streeter, *The Four Gospels*, p. 150 for the date of Q.
[4] Ibid. pp. 186 f. for the relation of Mark and Q.   Also C. H. Dodd, *The Apostolic Preaching and its Developments*, pp. 104–17.

revisions which signify the re-entrance into the picture of the original historical lineaments of Jesus the teacher of religion.[1]

Lest, however, Manson's words might leave the impression that it is only in Matthew and Luke that Jesus appears as teacher, we quote the opening words of Dr Dodd's essay on "Jesus as teacher and prophet":[2] "It is not the least remarkable feature of the Gospels as historical documents that although they all—even Mark—are written under the influence of a 'high' Christology, yet they all—even John—represent Jesus as a teacher with His school of disciples." Throughout the Gospels friend and foe give to Jesus the title of Rabbi—"the courtesy title commonly given to Jewish teachers of the Law"—(the Talmud knows him as a Rabbi of the Tannaitic period)[3] the teaching of Jesus is handed down in a Rabbinic form[4] and he is represented to us as disputing with Rabbis upon points arising out of "the interpretation of the Torah or the unwritten tradition". Moreover, there is apparent in Jesus a reverent attitude towards the Law and a substantial agreement with the Pharisees that love to God and neighbour are the two great commandments of the Law.[5] The conviction of the importance of Jesus as teacher shines clear; there is scarcely room to doubt that it came to be seen that in the *teaching* of Jesus, as Manson puts it, "We are brought face to face with God", that the *words* of Jesus are at the heart of the Gospel, an integral part of it.

So far then from accepting Weiss' view that Paul's conception of a νόμος τοῦ Χριστοῦ is merely a return to or a survival of primitive legalism, we have to recognize a growing emphasis within the Church on the historical Jesus as teacher and an increasing recognition of the value of His words which culminates in what has been called the Rabbinism of Matthew. On the other hand, however, this appreciation of the διδαχή of Jesus has been claimed to be a reaction against the Pauline emphasis on the exalted Christ, whom Paul preferred not to know after the flesh. This has been urged especially by Dr Strachan.[6] But if our thesis be correct, we cannot doubt that to Paul, from the first, the teaching of Jesus was of momentous significance and that His exalted Lord was never divorced from the Jesus of Nazareth, the 'Rabbi'. The developments that led to the formation of Q during the period (we repeat this

---

[1] *Jesus, the Messiah*, p. 53.

[2] *Mysterium Christi* (ed. A. E. J. Rawlinson), pp. 53 f.

[3] b. *'Abodah Zarah* 16b–17a.

[4] R. Bultmann, *Geschichte der Synoptischen Tradition*, pp. 20–3.

[5] Mark 12. 28–34; Luke 10. 25–8.

[6] Cf. *The Historic Jesus in the New Testament*, also *Second Corinthians* (M.N.T.C.), pp. 111 f.

because of its importance) of Paul's activity cannot have been alien to his mind; indeed, he must have shared in and contributed to that development. We have above noted the extreme deference with which he refers to the words of the Lord, and his almost unconscious references to them show that his mind was permeated with His sayings; his converts are they who have learnt Christ, the *talmidê* of Jesus the Rabbi.[1] Above all, we must see in his profound sense of sin, that enabled him to write Rom. 7, the result of standing under the judgement of that ethical absolute which we, like him, have found in the words of Jesus. The cumulative result of what we have written above is that Paul must have regarded Jesus in the light of a new Moses, and that he recognized in the words of Christ a νόμος τοῦ Χριστοῦ which formed for him the basis for a kind of Christian Halakah.[2] When he used the phrase νόμος τοῦ Χριστοῦ he meant that the actual words of Jesus were for him a New Torah. It has of course been frequently urged upon us that for Paul Christianity is not a moral code but a life in the spirit, and that for Paul each individual must be fully convinced by his own reason on moral questions. It agrees with this approach to Paul that Dr Dodd[3] has interpreted the phrase νόμος τοῦ Χριστοῦ "not of the Torah of Jesus, i.e. His teaching conceived as legislation for His Church but (as) νόμος τοῦ πνεύματος τῆς ζωῆς ἐν Χριστῷ Ἰησοῦ; the νόμος τοῦ πνεύματος...is an immanent principle of life like the Stoic Law of nature, but determined by the Spirit of Christ". We have seen, however, that we can accept Paul's use of νόμος τοῦ Χριστοῦ quite simply as a description of the New Torah that Jesus supplied in His words. It would, of course, be foolish to belittle the centrality of the conception of the Spirit in the Pauline ethic,[4] but this must not be taken to mean that the ethical teaching of Jesus as such has no significance for Paul, or that there is no room in his teaching for the recognition of the moral supremacy of Christ and the need for submission to His moral authority. Strangely enough, it is Dr Dodd who has also best clarified this for us:

That Christ loved us and died to save us is the most moving fact in Paul's universe. And he so died "that those who live should no longer live for

[1] Cf. W. Manson, *Jesus the Messiah*, p. 54.
[2] See an important article by D. Daube, *J.T.S.* (1938), vol. XXXIX, pp. 45ff. on ἐξουσία in Mark 1. 22, 27. There it is pointed out that it was quite usual to speak of different Torahs, e.g. the Torah of the Hillelites, the Torah of the Shammaites, etc.; cf. *b. Soṭah* 47b; *b. Megillah* 3a; and it is argued convincingly that Mark 1. 21–8 records how Jesus was regarded as the author of a new Torah or of new Halakôth such as only authorized Rabbis could lay down (cf. Mark 1. 27).
[3] *The Bible and the Greeks*, p. 37.
[4] Cf. J. Weiss, *The History of Primitive Christianity*, vol. II, p. 556.

themselves". His love puts a moral constraint upon us. Accordingly the stamp of Christ will be upon the whole of the Christian's daily activity. The 'law of Christ' is binding upon him in all things. That law is apprehended inwardly by the activity of the indwelling Spirit of Christ, for it is the Spirit that gives us 'the mind of Christ'. But it would be a mistake to divorce this thought from a direct reference to the historic teaching of Jesus Christ. Paul, in fact, not only allows that teaching to mould and colour his own thought to a greater extent than is commonly realized, but he also definitely cites the words of Christ as morally authoritative.[1]

The upshot of all this is that it is possible to make too much of the contrast between Pauline Christianity as a religion of liberty and Judaism as a religion of obedience. Indeed, it is not improbable that Paul would not find it strange to regard himself as a Christian Rabbi charged to be a steward not only of a κήρυγμα but of a διδαχή, a New Torah to be applied, expounded and transmitted. Carrington[2] has suggested that early Christianity developed along the same lines as Rabbinic Judaism, which in the first century created a distinction between elders capable of handling Torah (the *Tannaim*) and those who were not. To examine his thesis would take us into the maze of early Christian organization, but there can be little question that he is justified in saying that "there is evidence that one element of great importance in the Christian ecclesia was the propagation of Torah by teachers who had received it in true succession", and it is not leading us astray to make us think of Paul, in one aspect at least, as the great *Tanna* of the Gentiles.

It may not be altogether irrelevant to point out also that the view of Paul here presented has at least the advantage of historical probability. The interpretation of 'Paulinism' in terms of the Exalted Christ and the 'mystical' relation of the believer to him has made it necessary for historians of primitive Christianity to picture Paul as an isolated genius whose religion was far too lofty to be understood by the generality of the Church.[3] A Marcion and an Augustine had to rediscover him before his influence could be felt. In short, Paul is cut off from any vital connection with the development of Christian thought. The recognition, however, that Paul regarded the words of his Lord as a νόμος τοῦ Χριστοῦ lessens the gulf between him and the other teachers of the Church in the second century, and makes the development of Christian thought more reasonably credible.[4]

[1] *The Evolution of Ethics* (ed. Sneath), p. 301.
[2] *The Primitive Christian Catechism*, pp. 67f.
[3] Cf. A. C. McGiffert, *A History of Christian Thought*, vol. 1, p. 30.
[4] See, for example, the chapter on Irenaeus in A. C. McGiffert, op. cit. pp. 132ff., especially p. 148.

We have wandered far from the title of this chapter, "The Old and the New Man", but we have not wandered aimlessly. We are now better able to understand that subject in its entirety. The Christian man for Paul, we wrote in the previous chapter, is one who has died and risen with Christ; he has undergone a New Exodus. We now see that he has also stood at the foot of a New Sinai, which implies that he is confronted with the teaching of Jesus. It is the latter that helps to give ethical content to the dying and rising with Christ. In other words, 'mysticism' and morality, Gospel and Law are inseparable in the Christian man's experience.[1]

[1] V. P. Furnish, *Theology and Ethics in Paul*, 1968, has argued against Paul's dependence on Jesus's words or moral teaching: he allows only eight convincing parallels to the Synoptic Gospels in the Epistles; see pp. 51–65. I have urged in a forthcoming *Festschrift* for W. F. Stinespring, ed. J. M. Efird, Duke University Press, that Furnish's treatment of the evidence is too mathematical, and does not allow for the "living" character of tradition. The other "allusions" usually referred to he does not find persuasive. He dismisses the work of Alfred Resch, *Der Paulinismus und die Logia Jesu in ihrem gegenseitigen Verhaltnis untersucht*, in *Texte und Untersuchungen zur Geschichte des altchristlichen Literatur*, Vol. xxvii, 1904, as "imaginary" (p. 59), as he criticizes C. H. Dodd's treatment of the phrase *Ennomos Christou* in *Studia Paulina*, 1953. Furnish's treatment is salutary; but it does not convince me that the words of Jesus were not highly significant for Paul if not "his primary" source for moral teaching. Does Furnish deal justly with the richness of the oral tradition which prevailed in the early Church which finally coalesced, in part, in the Gospels? Here the method employed by H. Riesenfeld, in his articles "Parabolic Language in the Pauline Epistles", and "Paul's 'Grain of Wheat' Analogy and the Argument of 1 Cor. 15", and "The Parables in the Synoptic and in the Johannine Traditions", all to appear in a forthcoming volume, *The Gospel Tradition* (Fortress Press), is more appropriate or sensitive in dealing with tradition. The detection and dismissal of allusions is not as simple as Furnish suggests, particularly in a milieu where the reception and transmission of tradition was so living. The work of A. M. Hunter, *Paul and His Predecessors* (London 1940) and P. Carrington, *The Primitive Christian Catechism* (Cambridge 1940) Furnish refers to only in bare footnotes. See pp. 38n, 261n. A very useful and balanced discussion by David L. Dungan under the title *Logia Kyriou and Community Regulations* is forthcoming under the imprint of the Fortress Press. As for the imperative participle the evidence of the Scrolls demands more attention than is given to it in 39n 33. The role of Jesus as moral teacher is less difficult to understand in the light of the recent brilliant work of L. Finkelstein, *New Light from the Prophets* (Valentine Mitchell, London, 1969). Dr. Finkelstein writes that "To the magnificence of the poetry of the Prophets and the inspiration of their rhetoric, must now be added the greatness of their academic teaching which raised disciples who became teachers of succeeding generations of teachers" (p. 1). They are the precursors of the Sages of Israel (*ibid*). His work should warn us against thinking that the prophetic, charismatic, eschatological aspects of Jesus's ministry precluded his role as patient teacher. See *The Setting of the Sermon on the Mount*, pp. 415ff. R. Bultmann recognized Jesus as Rabbi, *Jesus and the Word* (New York & London 1934), *ad rem*. This is questioned by M. Hengel in his fascinating study *Nachfolge und Charisma: Eine exegetischreligionsgeschicht-liche Studie zu Mt. 8 : 21f und Jesu Ruf in die Nachfolge* (Berlin 1968), pp. 41ff. But he does recognize a continuity between the teaching of Jesus and that of the early Church. The whole matter is bound up with the question of the relation between Jesus and Paul which is surveyed by Furnish in *The Bulletin of the John Rylands Library*, Vol. 47, No. 2 (March 1965), pp. 243 in "The Jesus – Paul Debate: From Baur to Bultmann". I remain unconvinced that Paul was not interested in the historical Jesus: it does not seem to me that the interpretation of 2 Cor. 5. 16 and Gal. 1. 11f and the argument from silence appealed to, demand such a conclusion.

7

THE OLD AND THE NEW TORAH:
CHRIST THE WISDOM OF GOD

IN the preceding chapter the attempt was made to show that in the words of Jesus Paul had found a New Torah. The exclusive attention which was there paid to the teaching of Jesus, legitimate as it was for our purpose, must not, however, be allowed to imply that there was any departmentalism in the mind of Paul whereby the teaching of Jesus was artificially separated from the person of Jesus. That any such dichotomy was alien to the Apostle, becomes evident when we remember that in his work as ethical διδάσκαλος he not merely referred to the words of Jesus, but also to His character. Thus he holds up certain qualities of the historic Jesus which were to be imitated. He points to the Jesus "who pleased not Himself",[1] and to His meekness and gentleness.[2] It is a commonplace of New Testament studies that Paul's greatest doctrinal statements subserve his ethical exhortations; when Paul had to impress certain ethical duties upon his converts he appealed to what Jesus essentially was and did. In writing to the Philippians to inculcate humility he urges: "Let this mind be in you, which was also in Christ Jesus: who, being in the form of God,...took upon Him the form of a servant, and was made in the likeness of men, and being found in fashion as a man He humbled Himself, and became obedient unto death, even the death of the Cross."[3] Similarly, liberality is commended to the Corinthians through a reminder of Him who "though He was rich, yet for your sakes became poor".[4] It has often been plausibly suggested that the exhortation to, and description of, ἀγάπη in 1 Corinthians is based upon the life of Jesus, is in short a kind of character sketch of the Lord.[5] Moreover, when Paul calls himself a μιμητής τοῦ Χριστοῦ and urges others to follow him in so far as he follows Christ[6] we cannot fail to realize that for him every Christian is pledged to an attempted ethical conformity to Christ; the imitation of Christ is part and parcel of Paul's ethic.[7]

In the mind of the Apostle, therefore, the teaching and character of

---

[1] Rom. 15. 3.   [2] 2 Cor. 10. 1.   [3] Phil. 2. 5f.

[4] 2 Cor. 8. 9; cf. C. H. Dodd, *History of the Gospel*, pp. 65f. The moral ideal that Paul has, "is embodied in the character of Jesus".

[5] See C. H. Dodd, op. cit. p. 66. Only from the life of the historic Christ could such a picture of ἀγάπη as is found in 1 Cor. 13 have arisen.

[6] 1 Cor. 11. 1; 1 Thess. 1. 6.

[7] Contrast C. A. A. Scott, *The Fellowship of the Spirit*, pp. 93 f.; see J. Weiss, *The History of Primitive Christianity*, vol. II, p. 555. C. A. A. Scott writes: "It is true that

Jesus were inextricably bound together, and we may be sure that it was
the actualization of the teaching in the life of Jesus that impressed Paul
as it has always impressed men. For our purpose, however, what is
significant is the simple fact that the life of Jesus and His words are for
Paul an inseparable unity. This, of course, is consonant with what we
have already written in the two previous chapters, where we saw that
to be a Christian is to re-live, as it were, in one's own experience the
life of Jesus, to die and to rise with Him, and also at the same time to
stand under the moral imperative of His words; and it is possible to
infer from this the important consequence that not only did the words
of Jesus form a Torah for Paul, but so also did the person of Jesus. In
a real sense conformity to Christ, His teaching and His life, has taken the
place for Paul of conformity to the Jewish Torah. Jesus Himself—in
word and deed or fact is a New Torah.

It is true that at no point in the Pauline Epistles is the recognition of
Jesus as a New Torah made explicit in so many words. This fact, however, is clearly implied in the famous passage in which Paul contrasts
the Christian ministry with that of the Old Covenant in 2 Corinthians.
Here Paul, a minister of Christ, assumes "that he himself is no less
a distinguished person than Moses",[1] for whereas the glory which shone
in Moses' face because he had been entrusted with the Torah of Israel
was a fading glory, the Christian minister had received a glory that was
not fading because he had looked into the face of Jesus Christ and found
there a new knowledge. Paul and the other Christian ministers had
found the Light which had come into being at creation, in the face of
Jesus. The significance of this is only fully realized when it is recalled
that in Rabbinic Judaism the Torah was associated with light,[2] and as

there are some phrases which look in that direction (i.e. towards the imitation of
Christ). Paul says, 'Be ye imitators of me, as I also am of Christ.' But it has been well
pointed out that the reference in these cases is not to the details of character and conduct
manifested in the historical Jesus, but to that central act of self-devotion to His mission
with all its consequences, which was the act of love." He goes on to quote J. Weiss:
"In both cases (i.e. 1 Cor. 11. 1 and 1 Thess. 1. 6) it is not a matter of external
imitation, nor of the inculcation of teaching, but of complete inward adhesion of the
personality to that of the teacher in conception of life, disposition and behaviour."
This, however, is surely invalidated by the fact that Christ is an object of imitation
in the same sense as Paul himself is. Cf. C. H. Dodd, op. cit. p. 56, n. 6.

[1] Cf. R. H. Strachan, *Second Corinthians* (*M.N.T.C.*), p. 86; also A. Menzies, *The
Second Epistle to the Corinthians*, p. 23.

[2] Cf. Prov. 6. 23. Apoc. Bar. 59. 2, 77. 16; 4 Ezra 14. 20f. *Sifre Numbers* on
6. 25, § 41: 'The Lord make his face to shine upon thee....' "It refers to the light of
the Torah, as it says Prov. 6. 23, 'The Torah is a light'." Cf. Str.-B. vol. III, p. 357;
Deut. R. 7. 3: "Just as oil gives light to the world, so too do the words of the Torah
give light to the world."

Knox has written of this passage: "The original light created by God in the beginning had been equated not with the Torah, the mere reflection of the light which had been vouchsafed to Moses, but with the true knowledge of God revealed in the person of Jesus who...was Himself that primal light...." The object of the argument was to prove that Jesus, not the Torah, was the true revelation of the divine glory and the divine light.[1] This probably means that Jesus was a New Torah. Perhaps for the sake of clarity it is necessary to remind ourselves, in calling Jesus a New Torah, of the essential meaning of the word Torah. It is unfortunate that its rendering in the LXX by the Greek νόμος should have over-emphasized its legal connotation: the legal is only one aspect of Tôrâh—it is Tôrâh as mitzwâh only.[2] By Tôrâh Judaism meant as Moore has written: "all that God has made known of his nature, character and purpose and of what he would have man be and do".[3] It is not merely to be understood in the restricted sense of legislation. It is clear, then, that this may be taken to mean that Paul would think of Jesus as the Torah of God not only in the sense that His words were a νόμος but that He Himself in toto was a full revelation of God and of His will for man.

The fact that Jesus has replaced the Torah at the centre of Paul's life has, of course, been amply recognized by scholars.[4] The importance of this for the understanding of Paul's thought, however, has not been sufficiently emphasized. It was inevitable that to regard Jesus as the Torah of God meant that Paul would be influenced in his interpretation of Jesus by those conceptions which Rabbinic Judaism cherished about the old Torah. We should expect on a priori grounds that attributes ascribed to the Torah revealed on Sinai would by the Apostle be transferred to Christ. We may illustrate what we mean by reference to the gospel of Christian Rabbinism, St Matthew. We have had occasion previously to point out a fact, that has been emphasized by Windisch,[5] that in this Gospel especially, Jesus is deliberately set before us as a new law-giver who is greater than Moses; the 'Sermon' on the Mount is the counterpart of the 'Sermon' on Sinai. In consonance with this at different points in the Gospel, in passages peculiar to it, we read of

---

[1] Cf. W. L. Knox, St Paul and the Church of the Gentiles, p. 133.

[2] So in Some Aspects of Rabbinic Theology, S. Schechter devotes a special chapter to "The Torah in its Aspect of Law" (Mitzwoth). Cf. R.A. p. 683, and especially C. H. Dodd, The Bible and the Greeks, pp. 25 f.; J. Bonsirven, Le Judaïsme Palestinien, vol. I, p. 248.

[3] Cf. Moore, vol. I, p. 263.

[4] Cf. for example, W. L. Knox, St Paul and the Church of the Gentiles, p. 55; J. Klausner, From Jesus to Paul, p. 516.

[5] Cf. H. Windisch, Der Sinn der Bergpredigt, pp. 97 ff. Also Str.-B. vol. IV, p. I.

Christ what might well have been written of the Torah. Thus in Matt. 18. 20 we read: "For where two or three are gathered together in my name, there am I in the midst of them." With this we may compare the saying in *Pirkê Aboth*: "When they sit together and are occupied with the Torah, the Shekinah is among them."[1] Again in Matt. 11. 29, 30: "Take my yoke upon you", etc., we are probably right in finding a contrast between the yoke of Christ's teaching or law and that of the Torah. Taking the yoke of the Torah was a familiar Rabbinic expression.[2] In Matthew clearly there is a substitution of Christ for the Torah, and Christ, we may say, is pictured after the image of the Torah.[3] Windisch has contrasted this Matthaean Gospel of a New Law with the Pauline Gospel of Grace and Faith.[4] But if our thesis be correct this contrast is not justifiable, and we should expect to find in Paul the same process that we found in Matthew, the interpretation of Christ in terms of the old Torah. That this was so will be proved when we find that this approach supplies a key to what we may call the problem of the Wisdom Christology of the Pauline Epistles. To this we now turn.

We shall first examine those passages where it has been claimed that Paul is influenced by the speculation on Wisdom in the Old Testament and in Rabbinic Judaism. We begin with one of the most disputed Christological passages in all the Pauline Epistles, namely, Col. 1. 15f., which reads: ὅς ἐστιν εἰκὼν τοῦ θεοῦ τοῦ ἀοράτου, πρωτότοκος πάσης κτίσεως· ὅτι ἐν αὐτῷ ἐκτίσθη τὰ πάντα, ἐν τοῖς οὐρανοῖς καὶ ἐπὶ τῆς γῆς, τὰ ὁρατὰ καὶ τὰ ἀόρατα, εἴτε θρόνοι εἴτε κυριότητες εἴτε ἀρχαὶ εἴτε ἐξουσίαι· τὰ πάντα δι' αὐτοῦ καὶ εἰς αὐτὸν ἔκτισται· καὶ αὐτός ἐστι πρὸ πάντων, καὶ τὰ πάντα ἐν αὐτῷ συνέστηκε. On account of its strangeness the speculation here found on the nature of the person of Christ has been regarded by many as an interpolation into the text. The Baur school used it as a proof that the Colossian Epistle was not Pauline, and Holtzmann omitted this passage in his treatment of the Christology of Paul.[5] Similarly, Porter has recently passionately rejected verses 15–17 as being incompatible with Paul's thought as a whole and irrelevant to

---

[1] Cf. *P. Aboth* 3. 7.

[2] Cf. for example, *P. Aboth* 3. 6; *R.A.* p. 117; *M. Ber.* 11. 2; Moore, vol. 1, p. 465.

[3] In the *Didache* 6. 2, the commandments of Jesus are called ζυγὸς τοῦ κυρίου. See A. Büchler, *Studies in Sin and Atonement*, pp. 36ff. Also especially *Theologisches Wörterbuch zum Neuen Testament*, vol. II, pp. 902f.

[4] Cf. *Der Sinn der Bergpredigt*, pp. 96f.

[5] Cf. M. Dibelius, *H.Z.N.T.* vol. XII, p. 9; H. J. Holtzmann, *Lehrbuch der Neutestamentlichen Theologie*, pp. 73ff.

the context in which they occur. According to Porter they are an insertion into the text by someone whose religion had been that of the Logos type of Hellenistic Judaism.[1] Textually, however, there is no justification whatever for accepting the views of any of these scholars and to solve our difficulties by recourse to the knife is to violate the objectivity which should characterize our study. We therefore accept these verses as being Pauline.

Now Paul's first assertion in this passage, that Christ is the image of God, would by itself cause no difficulty, because apart from every other consideration this would be a natural designation of one who had already been called the Second Adam, a being who like his counterpart would of course be in the image of God.[2] It is the other statements, those which assert the pre-cosmic generation of Christ and his agency in creation that occasion questioning. Lightfoot,[3] Johannes Weiss[4] and recently E. F. Scott,[5] have turned for illustration of the doctrine here enunciated by Paul to Alexandrian Judaism, to the Logos doctrine of Philo. On the other hand appeal has been made to Stoicism in the elucidation of the passage.[6] But there is clearly one figure in the Old Testament which bears a striking resemblance to the Christ depicted here by Paul. Judaism had ascribed to the figure of Wisdom a pre-cosmic origin and a part in the creation of the world. It becomes probable therefore that Paul has here pictured Christ on the image of Wisdom. This was suggested by Windisch[7] but it has been convincingly proved by the work of Dr C. F. Burney.[8]

According to the latter the phrase in Col. 1. 15, πρωτότοκος πάσης κτίσεως, is a direct allusion to Prov. 8. 22, יְהוָה קָנָנִי רֵאשִׁית דַּרְכּוֹ which is translated: "The Lord begat me as the beginning of His way." But as Burney pointed out, and as we shall state more fully later on,[9] the term *rêshîth* in Prov. 8. 22 was used by Rabbinic Judaism as the key to the *bᵉrêshîth* which begins the Hebrew Bible. This latter *bᵉrêshîth* of Gen. 1. 1 was correspondingly interpreted as meaning 'by wisdom'. It is natural to infer that when in the Epistle to the Colossians Paul calls

---

[1] Cf. F. C. Porter, *The Mind of Christ in Paul*, pp. 179f.

[2] See above, chapter 3.

[3] J. B. Lightfoot, *The Epistles of St Paul: Colossians and Philemon*, pp. 141f.

[4] *The History of Primitive Christianity*, vol. II, pp. 482f.

[5] Cf. *Colossians, Philemon and Ephesians* (M.N.T.C.), pp. 20f.

[6] See A. E. J. Rawlinson, *The New Testament Doctrine of the Christ*, p. 162 and references there. Also J. Weiss, *The History of Primitive Christianity*, vol. II, p. 479; E. Norden, *Agnostos Theos*, pp. 240f.

[7] *Untersuchungen z. Neuen Testament. Die Weisheit und die Paulinische Christologie*, pp. 220f.

[8] Cf. *J.T.S.* (January 1926), vol. XXVII, pp. 160f.   [9] See p. 172.

Christ the πρωτότοκος πάσης κτίσεως he is thinking of him as the *rêshîth* of creation. Moreover, although it is idle to deny the Stoic colouring in the phrases ὅτι ἐν αὐτῷ ἐκτίσθη τὰ πάντα... καὶ τὰ πάντα ἐν αὐτῷ συνέστηκε..., etc., it has been clearly shown that these can be adequately explained in the light of Rabbinic usage. To quote Burney:

Here we have an elaborate exposition of *Bĕrêshîth* in Gen. 1. 1, in the Rabbinic manner. Three explanations are given of the preposition *bĕ*: then four explanations of the substantive *rêshîth*; and the conclusion is that in every possible sense of the expression, Christ is its fulfiller.... Putting the argument in tabular form for the sake of lucidity, it appears as follows—

Prov. 8. 22 ff., where Wisdom (i.e. Christ) is called *rêshîth* gives the key to Gen. 1. 1, "Bereshith God created the heavens and the earth":

Bĕrêshîth	— in *rêshîth*	—	ἐν αὐτῷ ἐκτίσθη τὰ πάντα...
„	— by „	—	πάντα δι' αὐτοῦ ἔκτισται...
„	— into „	—	πάντα εἰς αὐτὸν ἔκτισται...
Rêshîth	— Beginning —		αὐτός ἐστι πρὸ πάντων...
„	— Sum-total —		τὰ πάντα ἐν αὐτῷ συνέστηκε...
„	— Head	—	αὐτός ἐστιν ἡ κεφαλὴ τοῦ σώματος.
„	— Firstfruits —		ὅς ἐστιν ἀρχή, πρωτότοκος ἐκ τῶν νεκρῶν.

Conclusion: Christ fulfils every meaning which may be extracted from *Rêshîth*—ἵνα γένηται ἐν πᾶσιν αὐτὸς πρωτεύων.[1]

We can now see the significance of all the passage in Col. 1. 15–18. In a later treatment of Prov. 8–9 we shall have occasion to observe that the function of Wisdom was twofold, it operated both in the cosmos, in creation, and also in the world of men, in what we might call the work of redemption. The twofold function is here transferred to Christ, who is not only the agent in creation in a physical sense but also the agent of the moral recreation of mankind. Dibelius is surely justified in finding here what we have repeatedly found elsewhere, the correspondence between creation and redemption.[2] Christ is the Wisdom of God in both spheres.

We are not, however, confined to the passage in the Epistle to the Colossians in our attempt to trace the lineaments of the figure of Wisdom in the Christology of Paul. There are other indications elsewhere that there were such. We refer, first, to a passage in 1 Cor. 10. 1–4:

Moreover, brethren, I would not that ye should be ignorant, how that all our fathers were under the cloud, and all passed through the sea; and were all

[1] Cf. *J.T.S.* (January 1926), vol. XXVII, pp. 175f.
[2] Cf. M. Dibelius, *H.Z.N.T.*, *An die Kolosser*, vol. xii, p. 6f; also H. R. Mackintosh, *The Person of Jesus Christ*, p. 71. Contrast F. C. Porter, *The Mind of Christ in Paul*—who criticizes Dibelius on this account.

baptized unto Moses in the cloud and in the sea; and did all eat the same
spiritual meat; and did all drink the same spiritual drink: for they drank of
that spiritual Rock that followed them: and that Rock was Christ.

Here Paul warns his Corinthian converts against the danger of pre-
suming on their privileges. To emphasize this he appeals to the experience
of their 'fathers', the people of Israel, in the wilderness. Although all
the Israelites had had manna and had all drunk of the Rock, yet with
most of them God was displeased. So too mere participation in the
Christian sacraments was not enough to secure that he that stood should
never fall. In passing, Paul strangely equates the Rock, which had
followed the Israelites and from which they had been supplied with
water, with Christ.[1] Moffatt points out that "there is no indication
that Jewish piety attached any Messianic significance to the Rock".[2]
Philo, however, interpreted the passage in Deut. 8. 15: "who brought
forth water out of the Rock", as a reference to the Wisdom of God.
He writes: "The rock of flint is the Wisdom of God from which
he feeds the souls that love Him."[3] The same idea also occurs in the
Book of Wisdom where there is a vivid picture of Wisdom as the
helper of Israel in the wilderness. There also Wisdom is connected
with the giving out of "water out of the flinty rock".[4] It is not
impossible, therefore, that Paul in equating Christ with the Rock
was thinking of Him as the Divine Wisdom according to a familiar
convention of interpretation.

Secondly, the suggestion has been made that we are to find a connection with Wisdom in Rom. 10. 6 ff.

But the righteousness which is of faith speaketh on this wise, Say not in
thine heart, Who shall ascend into heaven? (that is, to bring Christ down
from above:) or, Who shall descend into the deep? (that is, to bring up Christ
again from the dead). But what saith it? The word is nigh thee, even in thy
mouth, and in thy heart: that is, the word of faith, which we preach....

Sanday and Headlam[5] pointed out that these words are not a direct
quotation from the Old Testament—from Deut. 30. 11–14; Paul is here

---

[1] For the legend, cf. Str.-B. vol. III, pp. 406 f.
[2] J. Moffatt, First Corinthians (M.N.T.C.), p. 130; A. Bugge, Das Gesetz und Christus,
claims that Christ is here equated with the Rock because the Rock was in Rabbinic
thought equated with the Torah and Christ had become the Torah for Paul. This
would be useful for our thesis, but Bugge does not give any evidence in support of
his statement. See Zeitschrift für die Neutestamentliche Wissenschaft (1903), p. 96.
[3] Philo, Leg. Alleg. 2. 21. Cohn-Wendland, vol. I, pp. 107 f. See Str.-B. vol. III, ad loc.
[4] Wisd. of Sol. 2. 4.   [5] Romans (I.C.C.), p. 289.

using words which had become proverbial. It is possible that they were
proverbially used in connection with Wisdom because in Baruch 3. 29 ff.
they are applied to Wisdom. Thus we read:

> Who hath gone up into heaven, and taken her [i.e. Wisdom]
> And brought her down from the clouds?
> Who hath gone over the sea, and found her
> And will bring her for choice gold?

On the basis of this passage Windisch has claimed that Paul in Rom. 10.
6f. has the figure of Wisdom in mind.[1] Here, however, it must be
admitted that the appeal to this passage in proof of Paul's Wisdom
Christology does not carry conviction. The words in Baruch refer to
the undiscoverability of Wisdom whilst Paul uses them in Rom. 10. 6ff.
to describe the essential accessibility or nearness of Christ in order to
prove that the Jews who reject Him are without excuse.[2] In any case
the mere fact that Baruch uses a passage in the description of Wisdom
cannot be regarded as proof that Paul could only have used it in the
same connection.

In the third place, we are on much firmer ground when we turn to
the familiar places where Paul actually calls Christ the Wisdom of God.
These are:

(1) 1 Cor. 1. 24: "But unto them which are called, both Jews and Greeks,
Christ the power of God,[3] and the wisdom of God."

(2) 1 Cor. 1. 30: "But of him are ye in Christ Jesus, who of God is made
unto us wisdom, and righteousness, and sanctification, and redemption."

It will be remembered that Paul is here concerned with curbing what
we may well call the intellectual and spiritual snobbery of certain
elements in the Corinthian Church, and the main burden of these
passages is that no philosophical subtlety nor intellectual acumen can
arrive at the true Wisdom. The latter is found in what the philosophy
of this world would call folly, the folly of the Cross of Christ where
God Himself reveals a Wisdom that He has foreordained. This Wisdom
which is contrasted with the wisdom of this world is constituted not
of intellectual knowledge but of righteousness, sanctification and re-

---

[1] Cf. *Die Weisheit und die Paulinische Christologie*, pp. 223 f.

[2] Cf. C. H. Dodd, *Romans (M.N.T.C.)*, p. 165. As will appear as our discussion
proceeds, however, what is highly significant for our purpose is that the passage quoted
by Paul from Deut. 30. 12–14 refers to the Torah in Deuteronomy, whereas Paul
applies it to Christ.

[3] Paul's neglect of the conception of Christ as power may be due to the fact that
this might lead to a doctrine of a plurality of 'powers' (δυνάμεις), whereas there could
be no plurality of 'Wisdoms'.

demption.[1] Here again we see Paul's twofold emphasis in his ascription of the title Wisdom to Christ—it is a pre-cosmic Wisdom and a morally recreative Wisdom that he finds in His Lord.

In view of the evidence which we have recapitulated above, we may assume that Paul has pictured Jesus in terms of the Wisdom of the Old Testament and contemporary Judaism. But this clearly constitutes a great problem. How was it that the Jesus whom Paul regarded as a man born among men, about whom he knew personal details, should be interpreted as the pre-cosmic and creative Wisdom of God? Whence are we to derive or how are we to account for this speculative development in the Apostle's thinking about his Lord? To this question several answers have been given which now fall to be considered.

The first answer that naturally suggests itself is that Paul is here directly dependent upon Jesus, because Jesus during His earthly ministry had already identified Himself with the Divine Wisdom. Many passages in the Synoptic Gospels might be quoted in support of this view and we shall now briefly deal with these in an order inverse to their cogency. In the first place, there are words in Luke 11. 49, which reads: διὰ τοῦτο καὶ ἡ σοφία τοῦ θεοῦ εἶπεν, Ἀποστελῶ εἰς αὐτοὺς προφήτας. The words here ascribed to ἡ σοφία τοῦ θεοῦ are in Matt. 23. 34f., placed on the lips of Jesus Himself. Are we then to conclude that in the Lukan passage the phrase ἡ σοφία τοῦ θεοῦ stands for the ἐγώ of Jesus, i.e. that Jesus is here the Divine Wisdom? It is unlikely that this is so. We may possibly have here a quotation from a lost apocryphal book or we may more plausibly paraphrase the phrase into something like "God in His Wisdom said", but whatever view we take of the strange use of ἡ σοφία τοῦ θεοῦ here it is precarious to base any conclusions upon it as to Jesus' interpretation of His own person.[2]

Secondly, attention has been called to the passage Matt. 11. 16–19 = Luke 7. 31–5 which ends with the words καὶ ἐδικαιώθη ἡ σοφία ἀπὸ τῶν ἔργων αὐτῆς. We may reject the view that ἀπό here means 'against' representing the Aramaic min-q°dâm (Hebrew mipp'nê); this would give the very improbable translation that Wisdom is vindicated against her

---

[1] The translation of 1 Cor. 1 30 has occasioned difficulty; should 'righteousness, sanctification and redemption' be regarded as explanatory of Wisdom or not? The evidence suggests that the above translation is the best. So T. C. Edwards, *The First Epistle to the Corinthians*, p. 30; J. Moffatt, *M.N.T.C.* ad loc.; H. Lietzmann in *H.Z.N.T.*, *An die Korinther*, ad loc. ignores the difficulty and regards all the terms as co-ordinate. Contrast A. Plummer, *First Corinthians (I.C.C.)*, p. 27.

[2] Cf. J. M. Creed, *The Gospel According to St Luke*; W. Manson, *Luke (M.N.T.C.)*, ad loc. The idea that here we are to assume some lost apocryphal book is the least convincing by far of the two alternatives above discussed.

works (i.e. against the faithless Jews).[1] We have to note, however, the difference of reading in the text of Luke where we find τέκνων for the ἔργων of Matthew. It is possible that both readings derive from the same underlying Aramaic, but attempts to prove this have not been convincing.[2] Two interpretations of the verse are possible. First, the majority of scholars have accepted the reading of Luke, i.e. τέκνων, as the original one and have taken the verse to mean that while the Divine Wisdom is condemned by the generality of Israel in that they rejected both John the Baptist and Jesus, nevertheless she is vindicated by her true children, i.e. those who accepted the Baptist, the ascetic, and also those who accepted the friend of publicans and sinners, since John the Baptist and Jesus were alike sent by the Divine Wisdom.[3] According to this interpretation it cannot of course be maintained that Jesus here regards Himself as the Divine Wisdom. But, secondly, if we accept the reading ἔργων the meaning is that while the actions of Jesus on earth were slandered and rejected by the Jews yet at the bar of history those ἔργα were vindicated and Jesus was proved to be the Wisdom of God.[4] But if this interpretation be true it is difficult to regard the words as those of the historic Jesus, and it seems probable that we are here to read the experience of the early Church which came to equate Jesus with the personified Wisdom of God. We prefer, on this interpretation, to take the words as evidence of the faith of the early Church not of the mind of Jesus.

Thirdly, there remains to be considered the saying in Matt. 11. 25–30 (cf. Luke 10. 21–22). Attention has long been drawn to the similarity between this saying and Ecclus. 51. According to E. Norden[5] the sequence of thought found in both Matthew and Ecclesiasticus, namely:

Thanksgiving to God	Matt. 11. 25, cf. Ecclus. 51. 1–12
The Revelation of a Mystery	Matt. 11. 27, cf. Ecclus. 51. 13–22
The appeal to men	Matt. 11. 28–30, cf. Ecclus. 51. 23–30

is a common traditional scheme belonging to the "mystical philosophical literature of the East", so that though Matt. 11. 25–30 and Ecclus. 51

---

[1] Cf. A. H. McNeile, *The Gospel According to St Matthew*, ad loc. and T. H. Robinson, *Matthew* (*M.N.T.C.*); Wellhausen regards ἀπό here as = מן קדם.

[2] P. de Lagarde, cited by McNeile, suggested that τέκνα and ἔργα both represent the Aramaic עבדיא. But as McNeile points out παῖδες or δοῦλοι would be a more natural rendering for this.

[3] So A. H. McNeile, *The Gospel According to St Matthew*; A. Plummer, *An Exegetical Commentary on the Gospel According to St Matthew*; W. Manson, *Luke* (*M.N.T.C.*), pp. 82f.; E. Klostermann in *H.Z.N.T.* vol. IV, *Das Matthäusevangelium*.

[4] T. H. Robinson, *Matthew* (*M.N.T.C.*), ad loc.

[5] *Agnostos Theos.* pp. 227f.

are similar they can be quite independent of one another. Moreover, since we cannot regard Jesus as a "mystical theosophist of the East", the passage in Matthew cannot be a genuine utterance of his. P. W. Schmidt,[1] however, regards the passage as genuine and, emphasizing the parallelism between the Matthaean saying and Ecclesiasticus, has claimed that here Jesus is consciously drawing on chapter 51. He also points out that this saying of Jesus follows closely on another passage, Matt. 11. 16-19, where Jesus is represented as the Divine Wisdom. In view of all this Schmidt holds that in Matt. 11. 25-30 Jesus is deliberately identifying Himself with the Divine Wisdom; the words afford authentic testimony to a Wisdom Christology emanating from Jesus Himself.

What shall we say to this? In the first place we may admit the authenticity of this saying. Its language is not at all Hellenistic but is throughout Semitic.[2] Its thought also is thoroughly Hebraic;[3] the idea of knowing and being known of God is found in the Old Testament.[4] Further, although of course it is not impossible that a saying which is not authentic should have crept into Q, nevertheless the fact that the saying does occur in Q affords it good attestation.[5] The mere fact, moreover, that the passage has a Johannine ring should not weigh the scales against authenticity; the correct inference from its presence in the Synoptics is that drawn by Howard who writes: "its presence in that early stratum of Gospel tradition should warn us against assuming too readily that the mystical teaching of the Fourth Gospel is foreign to the historical situation when placed upon the lips of Jesus".[6] In the second place we may agree that those scholars are right who have traced a connection between the saying and Ecclus. 51. The parallelism between Matt. 11. 28 ff. and Ecclus. 51. 23 f. is particularly close.

At this point, however, we must call a halt. We cannot postulate a deliberate dependence upon Ecclus. 51 and the conscious expression

---

[1] P. W. Schmidt, *Menschheitswege zum Gotterkennen*, pp. 195 ff. I failed to procure a copy of this book and have drawn upon A. E. J. Rawlinson, *The New Testament Doctrine of the Christ*, p. 260.

[2] Cf. W. L. Knox, *Some Hellenistic Elements in Primitive Christianity* (Schweich Lectures 1941), pp. 6 f.

[3] A. E. J. Rawlinson, *The New Testament Doctrine of the Christ*, p. 263.

[4] Jer. 31. 34; Hos. 4. 1, 6. 6; Amos 3. 3; Deut. 34. 10.

[5] This of course cannot be written of the 'Come unto Me' utterance of Matt. 11. 28-30, which since it was not in Luke cannot be proved to be in Q, though Harnack accepts it as possibly from Q because of its Q affinities; cf. *Sayings of Jesus*, pp. 307 f. See also W. Manson, *Jesus the Messiah*, p. 73.

[6] W. F. Howard, *The Fourth Gospel in Recent Criticism and Interpretation*, pp. 221 f.

of a Wisdom Christology in this saying, for several reasons. First, we note that not all are agreed that Ecclus. 51 can be tripartitely divided as Norden suggested;[1] but more important still is the fact that verses 28–30 in Matt. 11 have no parallel in Luke and we can recognize that if they stood in Q following verses 25–7 it is inexplicable that they should have been omitted by Luke. But if verses 28–30 do not integrally belong to verses 25–7 then the neat parallelism pointed out by Norden and Schmidt is disturbed, and the case for direct dependence upon Ecclus. 51 falls to the ground. In the second place it seems clear that the emphasis in the Matthean passage is on the unique relation between Jesus and God, in other words, on the Sonship of Jesus. As Vincent Taylor[2] has written: "What is expressed is the consciousness of a unique filial relationship";[3] it is this rather than a Wisdom Christology that we should most properly read into this great saying. Obviously, Jesus might have used the language of Wisdom in His invitation to the weary without thereby identifying Himself with Wisdom.

Our review of the most important relevant passages in the Synoptic Gospels is now complete. Our examination has revealed that while it is clear that the early Church regarded Jesus as the personified Wisdom of God and that Jesus Himself may have regarded Himself as speaking in the name of the Holy Wisdom of God, nevertheless, the evidence does not warrant the view that Jesus Himself had entertained a Wisdom Christology. The view that Paul had received such a Christology as a legacy from his Lord cannot therefore be substantiated.

We next proceed to examine the second answer given to the question as to the origin of Paul's Wisdom Christology, namely, that already in Judaism the figure of the Messiah had become merged with that of Wisdom, so that once Paul had become convinced that Jesus was the Messiah he would automatically regard Him as the Wisdom of God.

---

[1] Cf. A. H. McNeile, The Gospel According to St Matthew; McNeile regards Ecclus. 51. 1–12 as merely a thanksgiving for deliverance from danger, which does not form one whole with the rest of the chapter.

[2] Jesus and His Sacrifice, p. 37.

[3] "The prophets themselves say that they 'saw' that Jehovah, the Holy One is a God of righteousness; that they 'heard' Him say that He desires mercy and not sacrifice" (C. H. Dodd, The Authority of the Bible, p. 95), but no prophet claimed that he knew Jehovah. Full knowledge was always an object of desire, not of attainment, a mark of the Messianic Age, not of present experience, cf. for example, Jer. 31. 31–4. It is this fulness of knowledge that Jesus claims for Himself in Matt. 11. 28f. (see R. Bultmann in T.W.Z.N.T., vol. 1, pp. 688 f. for γινώσκω, especially pp. 700 f.), and this unique relationship is expressed by saying that Jesus knew God fully— claimed a knowledge of God that before not even the prophets had claimed.

Messianic speculation is the key to his Christology. His equation would be simple. Thus:

The Messiah = The Wisdom of God,
but Jesus = The Messiah,
∴ Jesus = The Wisdom of God.

This is the solution favoured by Windisch[1] and it falls to us now to examine those passages to which he appeals in order to prove that the Messiah was already connected with Wisdom within Judaism. These are as follows:

(1) Certain verses in the Book of Enoch (1 Enoch):

(a) 48. 1–7. The verses especially relevant are:

1. And in that place I saw the fountain of righteousness
   Which was inexhaustible....
   And around it were many fountains of wisdom....
2. And at that hour that Son of Man was named....
3. Yea before the Sun and the signs were created
   Before the stars of the heaven were made,
   His name was named before the Lord of Spirits....
6. And for this reason hath he been chosen and hidden before Him
   Before the creation of the world and for evermore.
7. And the wisdom of the Lord of Spirits hath revealed him to the holy
   and the righteous.

(b) 49:

2. And in him dwells the spirit of wisdom.

We need not cavil at the fact that these words are written of the Son of Man and not of the Messiah. The figure of the latter was highly complex and in Judaism as in the thought of Jesus and of the early Church the lineaments of the Son of Man and of the Messiah had become inextricably merged.[2] In the above passages, however, while it is clear that the Son of Man is thought of as pre-existent and is brought into close proximity to wisdom, there is no identification with the latter. Indeed, in verse 7 the Son of Man is distinguished from the wisdom of the Lord of Spirits.[3] It is questionable whether 48. 1–7 implies more than

---

[1] *Die Weisheit und die Paulinische Christologie*, pp. 227f. See also W. L. Knox, *Some Hellenistic Elements in Primitive Christianity*, p. 39.

[2] This is the view favoured by A. E. J. Rawlinson in *The New Testament Doctrine of the Christ*; and J. Bonsirven, *Le Judaïsme Palestinien*, vol. I, p. 360, regards the term 'Son of Man', etc., as a name for the Messiah. So Moore, vol. II, pp. 323f. This is not the view of the editors of *Beginnings*; cf. vol. I, pp. 345f., especially pp. 365f. See the discussion by Rawlinson, op. cit. pp. 12f.

[3] Of this verse Windisch writes in a footnote: "Nicht ganz deutlich ist die Bedeutung der 'Weisheit' in 48. 7."

is expressed in 49. 2 which is based on Isa. 11. 9, that the Son of Man would be characterized by wisdom much as he would be characterized by righteousness and other qualities. Windisch surely goes too far when he claims that here the Son of Man and Wisdom are related as are Christ and the πνεῦμα in Paul.[1] In addition, the reference that Windisch makes to Enoch 42, where Wisdom is depicted as failing to find a dwelling-place on earth and therefore returning to heaven to dwell among the angels, as showing that Wisdom is here to be compared with the Messiah who is also unknown on earth and dwells in heaven among the angels, falls far short of proof. That chapter appears to be an isolated fragment of Wisdom speculation which it is very difficult if not impossible to connect with its context—a fragment without any Messianic or Apocalyptic significance.[2]

(2) The next passage where Windisch has traced the possible identification of Wisdom with the Messiah is in Micah 5. 1. The Hebrew is as follows:

וְאַתָּה בֵּית־לֶחֶם אֶפְרָתָה צָעִיר לִהְיוֹת בְּאַלְפֵי יְהוּדָה

מִמְּךָ לִי יֵצֵא לִהְיוֹת מוֹשֵׁל בְּיִשְׂרָאֵל

וּמוֹצָאֹתָיו מִקֶּדֶם מִימֵי עוֹלָם :

The interpretation of this verse has occasioned difficulty: does it imply a pre-existent Messiah or does it merely mean that the Messiah would belong to one of the oldest families, namely, the Davidic? The weight of the evidence is against the former and in favour of the latter view, i.e. we are not to understand a pre-existent Messiah in this verse.[3]

When we turn to the LXX, however, we find that the Hebrew:

וּמוֹצָאֹתָיו מִקֶּדֶם מִימֵי עוֹלָם

is translated by

καὶ ἔξοδοι αὐτοῦ ἀπ' ἀρχῆς ἐξ ἡμερῶν αἰῶνος.

In this translation Windisch claims that the LXX translator is seeking to ascribe to the Messiah the qualities of the figure of Wisdom and that he has here been influenced by Prov. 8. 22 which reads:[4] κύριος

---

[1] *Die Weisheit und die Paulinische Christologie*, p. 228.
[2] Cf. *Ap. and Ps.* vol. II, p. 213.
[3] H. Schultz, *Old Testament Theology* (E.T.), vol. II, pp. 414f.; C. A. Biggs, *Messianic Prophecy*, p. 218, n. 1 and J. M. P. Smith in *I.C.C.* ad loc. agree with the view expressed. See, however, C. F. Burney, *J.T.S.* vol. X, pp. 580–4, who accepts the prophecy as being authentic and regards the Messiah as having existed in reality or in the mind of God from time immemorial.
[4] H. Windisch, *Die Weisheit und die Paulinische Christologie*, p. 228.

ἔκτισέ με ἀρχὴν ὁδῶν αὐτοῦ εἰς ἔργα αὐτοῦ. With this he also compares Sirach 24. 9: πρὸ τοῦ αἰῶνος ἀπ' ἀρχῆς ἔκτισέ με. . . . But surely this is to read too much into the LXX version of Mic. 5. 1. It is difficult to see how the LXX, which generally aimed at fidelity to the original rather than elegance, could have otherwise rendered the Hebrew. The use of ἀπ' ἀρχῆς to translate *miqqedem* does not prove dependence on Prov. 8. 22, because ἀρχή, although it usually translates *rō'sh* or *rēshîth* (as in Prov. 8. 22) or *t'hillâh* in the LXX, renders *qedem* in thirteen places.[1] There is no need therefore to postulate the influence of Prov. 8 in the LXX of Mic. 5. 1.

(3) Finally, Windisch suggests that again in the LXX of Ps. 110. 3 we are to find the merging of the figure of Wisdom with that of the Messiah.[2] Briggs, who regards the passage as a description of a Davidic Messiah, translates Ps. 110. 1–3 thus:

> Utterance of Yahweh to my lord: "Sit enthroned at my right hand,
> Till I make thine enemies a stool for thy feet.
> With the rod of thy strength rule in the midst of thine enemies."
> Volunteers on the sacred (mountains) are thy people, in the day of thy host:
> From the womb of the morn came forth to thee the dew of thy youth.

The Hebrew of verse 3 is as follows:

עַמְּךָ נְדָבֹת בְּיוֹם חֵילֶךָ

בְּהַדְרֵי־קֹדֶשׁ מֵרֶחֶם מִשְׁחָר לְךָ טַל יַלְדֻתֶךָ

This is translated by the LXX thus:

> μετὰ σοῦ ἡ ἀρχὴ ἐν ἡμέρᾳ τῆς δυνάμεώς σου,
> ἐν ταῖς λαμπρότησι τῶν ἁγίων σου·
> ἐκ γαστρὸς πρὸ Ἑωσφόρου ἐγέννησά σε.

This according to Windisch implies a Messiah who is pre-existent, an attribute which he would derive from the figure of Wisdom. Some other versions, we may add, understood the verse in this sense.[3] Moreover, the association of the Messiah with the throne of God in Ps. 110. 1, Windisch compares with the similar association of Wisdom with God's throne in the Book of Wisdom.[4] Over against Windisch, however, we note that it is surprising that the terms ἐκ γαστρός and πρὸ Ἑωσφόρου

---

[1] Cf. Hatch and Redpath, *Concordance to the Septuagint*.

[2] H. Windisch, op. cit. p. 229.

[3] See C. A. and E. G. Biggs, *Psalms (I.C.C.)*, vol. II, p. 380. The versions are the Vulgate and the Syriac.

[4] Cf. Wisd. of Sol. 9. 4, 10.

do not occur either in the descriptions of Wisdom either in Prov. 8 or in Ecclesiasticus. In this case again we feel that although the translator of Ps. 110. 3 in the LXX may have been influenced by Wisdom speculation, we are left with a mere possibility, not with proof.

We have now examined those passages brought forward by Windisch to prove that the Messiah had been interpreted as the Wisdom of God in Judaism, and in all cases we have found the evidence unconvincing. We would naturally expect the Messiah to be endowed with wisdom and there are several passages where it is stated that in the age of the Messiah Wisdom will return to earth. Moreover, although we have no concrete evidence of this it may of course be possible that the Messiah had been identified with the Divine Wisdom before the time of Paul, but such identification, if it had been made, certainly played no considerable part in Judaism.[1] In addition, there is one important point to notice. In all the cases mentioned by Windisch it is the pre-existence of the Messiah, a pre-existence borrowed from the figure of Wisdom according to him, that has to be considered. But there is clear evidence that the pre-existence of an object or of a person had no particular or unique significance for Rabbinic Judaism.[2] It was the activity of Christ in creation, not His pre-existence that Paul emphasized in his Wisdom Christology in the Epistle to the Colossians and with such activity none of the passages brought forward by Windisch deals. We are forced to conclude that we must look elsewhere for the link between Jesus and the Divine Wisdom in the mind of Paul. We shall now seek to prove that this link is to be found in Paul's conception of Christ as a New

[1] Cf. W. L. Knox, *St Paul and the Church of the Gentiles*, p. 118.

[2] Knox's words (op. cit. pp. 112f.) will illustrate this: "It was generally agreed that the Torah had existed from all eternity, it follows that Moses had existed in the same way, for it was hard to suppose that the Torah could be dissociated from him.... In the same way the Temple might have pre-existed from all eternity....Naturally Hellenistic Jewish writers associated this view with Plato's doctrine of ideas: here again he had borrowed from Moses. All this was a mere glorification of the religion of Judaism, it was not intended to be taken seriously, except in so far as it implies the unique character of God's revelation to Israel; or in the case of the Messiah it was a fanciful attempt to explain the problem of his sudden appearance as a full-grown man. It could never have led to an association of the Messiah with the work of creation, for this belonged to an entirely different aspect of Jewish thought. The unimportance of his pre-existence is shown by the ease with which the celestial pre-existences were at a later stage, perhaps in answer to Christianity, increased to seven by the addition to the Torah, the Temple and the Messiah of heaven, hell, repentance and the throne of God. By Himself the pre-existent Messiah could never have obtained a role in the cosmogony of Judaism." Cf. Moore, vol. I, p. 526, vol. II, p. 344; also J. Bonsirven, *Le Judaïsme Palestinien*, vol. I, pp. 370f. where there is a full discussion; S. Schechter, *Some Aspects of Rabbinic Theology*, pp. 127f.

Torah, who had replaced the old; and, since we are not merely concerned with the origin of Paul's Wisdom Christology, but with its significance, we shall have to trace the development of Wisdom speculation within Judaism.

Knox has argued that the personified figure of Wisdom in the Old Testament was introduced into the literature of the third century B.C. as a counter-attraction to the figure of Isis whose cult was widely diffused throughout the dominions of the Ptolemies, and was so popular that it might prove dangerously seductive to Jewry. Both in Proverbs and in Ecclesiasticus Knox finds a figure formed for polemic purposes, to counteract the charms of Isis and Astarte respectively (goddesses who had been practically merged into one another for centuries before this).[1] Other scholars have traced the figure of Wisdom to other non-Jewish sources.[2] We cannot examine such theories here, but it must be insisted that whatever its ultimate origin, and many scholars have claimed that we need not go outside Judaism itself to account for it,[3] the figure of Wisdom supplied a real need in the Judaism within which it is found.[4]

In lectures delivered recently at Cambridge Dr C. E. Raven quoted with approval the sentence that "the misfortune that has overtaken the spiritual outlook of man is that as his universe has expanded his conception of the deity did not expand with it".[5] These words refer to the modern situation in Christendom, but Dr S. A. Cook has forcibly reminded us again and again that in the sixth century B.C. Israel passed through a crisis similar to that now confronting the western world.[6] In one respect this is peculiarly true because the experience of the Exile in Babylon inevitably introduced the nation of Israel to a larger world than it had hitherto known, much as the amazing achievements of modern science have enlarged the horizons of modern man. But the Israel of the sixth century B.C. survived its crisis because, it is a familiar fact, its God expanded with its universe, a territorial conception of God gave place to a universal conception or as Dr T. H. Robinson has

[1] Cf. *St Paul and the Church of the Gentiles*, pp. 55 f.; also *J.T.S.* vol. XXXVIII, pp. 230 f.

[2] Cf. O. S. Rankin, *Israel's Wisdom Literature*, pp. 222 f. for the relevant literature.

[3] Cf. O. S. Rankin, op. cit. pp. 227 f. Rankin refers to E. Meyer and P. Heinisch as holding this view.

[4] With the general character of wisdom in the Old Testament we are not here concerned. For this see W. O. E. Oesterley and T. H. Robinson, *Hebrew Religion*, pp. 287 f., 333 f.; also S. A. Cook, *The Old Testament: a Reinterpretation*, p. 203, and O. S. Rankin, *Israel's Wisdom Literature*.

[5] *Science, Religion and the Future*, p. 64. The sentence is quoted from F. Wood Jones, *Design and Purpose*, p. 75.

[6] See his two books, *The Old Testament: a Reinterpretation* and *The Truth of the Bible*.

written: "Israel's God was no longer the tribal deity of a little hill people in a Western Asiatic State: He was the supreme end and the highest goal of human knowledge."[1] So it comes about that one of the marks of post-exilic Judaism is an increasing emphasis on what has been called the 'Transcendence of God'. The evidence for this has frequently been cited.

Already in Ezekiel[2] we have travelled far from the naive anthropomorphism of earlier times when Yahweh could take a walk in the cool of the evening[3] and dine with his friend Abraham.[4] For Ezekiel the throne of God is surrounded with mystery; in the vision vouchsafed to him at his call to the prophetic ministry he sees only "the appearance of the likeness of the glory of the Lord".[5] When we turn to Deutero-Isaiah it is the omnipotence of Yahweh which is emphasized and His omniscience. "It is He that sitteth upon the circle of the earth and the inhabitants thereof are as grasshoppers, that stretcheth out the heavens with a curtain", etc.[6] Bennett pointed out that the name Creator for Yahweh (from *bârâ'*) is distinctive of the post-exilic prophets[7] and in the latest books of the Old Testament names such as *êl 'elyôn, hâ-shêm*, occur with increasing frequency and they are all names, so it has been claimed,[8] that suggest the transcendence of God.[9] Similarly, it was emphasis on the uniqueness of Yahweh, the God who is One and not to be compared with any other, which led to the degradation of the gods of the heathen to the rank of angels, which play a great part in later Judaism.[10] Finally, the meticulous scrupulosity of the Law and the extreme punctiliousness with which the approach to God by sacrifice and in worship was regulated have been regarded as proofs of the extreme transcendentalism of the post-exilic idea of God.[11]

But as elsewhere so in Judaism transcendence, to use theological terms,

---

[1] Cf. T. H. Robinson, *Prophecy and the Prophets*, pp. 143, 152.

[2] Cf. W. H. Bennett, *The Post-Exilic Prophets*, pp. 30f.

[3] Gen. 3. 8.   [4] Gen. 18. 18.

[5] Ezek. 1. 28. (We miss the clear-cut outlines of Isa. 6, when Isaiah saw the Lord with his own eyes.)

[6] Isa. 40. 22f.

[7] Cf. *The Post-Exilic Prophets*, pp. 136, 164. "The use of ברא 'create', exclusively for the initiating energy of Yahweh, implies that He possesses a power to which there is nothing exactly corresponding in Man." For the importance of the doctrine of creation in Judaism see J. Bonsirven, *Le Judaïsme Palestinien*, vol. I, pp. 162f.

[8] Cf. for the *name* Lev. 24. 11–16; for עליון, cf. Num. 24. 16.

[9] Cf. A. Lods, *Les prophètes d'Israel et les débuts du Judaïsme*, p. 368. For the divine names, see J. Bonsirven, op. cit. pp. 116ff.

[10] Cf. W. H. Bennett, *The Post-Exilic Prophets*, p. 168.

[11] C. H. Dodd, *The Authority of the Bible*, p. 177.

made acute the problem of immanence.[1] The fact of God's nearness could not be denied; that Judaism could never doubt. But since the days when Yahweh could be conceived as a kind of enlarged man were now forever past, the question of the modes or manner of God's nearness became important, it had to be faced anew. As to the many ways in which Judaism faced these questions we cannot here inquire. Rankin's statement of the issue must suffice for us:

Under the necessity of connecting the world of men with the God, who in majesty and nature was so far above this world, there were two courses which Judaism could take and which it took. It transformed the deities of foreign worship into angels who, representing the functions of the Supreme Being, were more or less the equivalent of abstract ideas or divine attributes, and on the other hand it turned such abstract ideas as the Spirit of God (as world creating power, Job 33. 4; Apoc. Baruch 23. 5; as filling all things Wisd. of Sol. 1. 7; as ruling history Is. 43. 10) and the word of God (Ps. 107. 20, 119. 50) into what may be called hypostases or personifications of the divine activity and power.[2]

But more important than the word or the spirit in the speculations of the earlier Judaism was the figure of Wisdom. It is with this, especially in its relation to the creation of the world that we are concerned.

As was natural, since Yahweh was now proclaimed as the Creator of the Universe, the post-exilic period witnessed a great interest in the

[1] Here, however, one caution is to be voiced. In the description of the enlarged conception of God which the post-exilic period reveals, the use of the term transcendence may be misleading because it has certain philosophical connotations which are alien to the faith of the Old Testament. The transcendence of God in Judaism must not be taken to mean necessary inaccessibility. The God of Israel could never become the τὸ ὄν of philosophical speculation. It is to be noticed that in the works of all the prophets mentioned above Yahweh is not only the Creator but also the Redeemer. (For Ezekiel, cf. W. H. Bennett, *The Post-Exilic Prophets*, p. 140. He shows how anthropomorphic expressions persist in Ezekiel; cf. for Deutero-Isaiah, N. H. Snaith, *The Distinctive Ideas of the Old Testament*.) It is also salutary to remember Moore's criticisms of Christian interpreters of Judaism (cf. *H.T.R.* (1921) vol. xiv, pp. 197ff.; also Moore, vol. ii, pp. 423f.). Belief in angels, for example, can be quoted as proving either the nearness of God or His remoteness according to one's predilection: the meticulous precepts of the Torah can be claimed to prove God's concern with the minutest details of life quite as much as His awful holiness, and the use of certain names for God does not necessarily prove that these are to be taken to imply what they literally connote. Nevertheless, when we have admitted the force of all this, there can be no gainsaying the increasingly majestic character of the God of post-exilic Judaism, and it is legitimate to designate this by the term transcendence.

[2] O. S. Rankin, *Israel's Wisdom Literature*, p. 223.

manner of the creation of the world.[1] This interest was also no doubt stimulated by the fact, which we have previously noted, that the Exile led to a deepening of the sense of sin in Israel[2] and that this concentrated attention on the Fall of Adam the first man created; this in turn must have contributed something to the preoccupation of many thinkers with creation. Dr Dodd has defined the problem of creation thus: "Any theistic account of the universe which postulates at the beginning God on the one hand and formless matter on the other must meet the difficulty that there is nothing in mere matter which could ever respond to the will of God or else it must give account of the potential properties of matter which made possible the emergence of a cosmos; but in that case it is not mere matter."[3] It is to the necessity of meeting this difficulty that we owe the account of creation preserved for us in Gen. 1, where the universe comes into being at the word of God. The majestic qualities of the God of Gen. 1 have often been contrasted with the homely ones of Gen. 2; there is a clear attempt to safeguard the otherness of the Creator.[4] But Gen. 1 is not the only evidence of interest in the creation—it was a matter of speculation to many, for example, the author of Ps. 33 writes:

> 6. By the word of the Lord were the heavens made;
>   And all the host of them by the breath of his mouth.
> 8. Let all the earth fear the Lord....
> 9. For he spake, and it was done;
>   He commanded, and it stood fast.

We may assume that much as the origin of species has occupied the minds of Christians in our time so the problem of creation agitated post-exilic Judaism, and whatever foreign influences may have contributed to the development of the figure of Wisdom it is clear that the latter is part of the attempt made by Judaism to reconcile 'Transcendence' and 'Immanence' in the realms of creation and otherwise.[5]

---

[1] Cf. A. Lods, *Les prophètes d'Israel et les débuts du Judaïsme*, p. 367.

[2] See above.

[3] Cf. *The Bible and the Greeks*, p. 132. That this is the problem of Gen. 1 is clear; cf. J. Skinner, *Genesis (I.C.C.)*, pp. 13 f. for an important exegetical treatment of Gen. 1. 1. Later Rabbinism necessarily took Gen. 1 to mean creation *ex nihilo*. Cf. J. Bonsirven, *Le Judaïsme Palestinien*, vol. 1, p. 165. Cf. *Genesis R.* 1: "The philosopher said, 'Your God is a great Craftsman, but He found good materials which were of assistance to Him in the work of Creation, viz. TOHU, BOHU, darkness, spirit, water and the deeps.' The Rabbi answered, 'A curse alight upon you!' In connection with all of them Scripture mentions that they were created...."

[4] For a convenient account, cf. D. C. Simpson, *Pentateuchal Criticism*, p. 44.

[5] Cf. C. H. Dodd, *The Authority of the Bible*, pp. 178 f.

We first meet the figure of Wisdom in some sense personified in the 28th chapter of the Book of Job:

> 23. God knows the way to her
> And He has knowledge of her above.
>
> 25. When He fixed the weight of the wind
> And decreed for waters their measure.
>
> 26. When He made rules for the rain
> And paths for the lightning flash.
>
> 27. He saw her then and studied her
> He established her and proved her.[1]

Here clearly it is implied that the ground plan of the Creation is Wisdom which was examined by God in His creative activity. Davidson's words are relevant here: "Wisdom in this passage...is properly the idea or conception lying behind or under the fixed order of the Universe, the world plan. This fixed order itself with all its phenomena and occurrences is nothing but God fulfilling Himself in many ways, but these ways may be reduced to one conception and this is Wisdom, which is thus conceived as a thing having an objective existence of its own."[2]

The figure becomes more clearly marked in Prov. 8. 22f.:[3]

> Jahve begat me at the beginning of His ways,
> The first of His works, of old (He begat me).
> I was installed from everlasting, from the beginning.
> Or ever the earth was,
> When there were no depths I was born:
> When there were no fountains abounding with water.
> Before (the bases of) the mountains were sunk,
> Before the hills was I brought forth:
> While as yet He had not made the earth nor open places,
> "Nor the green" of the soil of the world.
>
> When He prepared the heavens I was there:
> When He drew the vault (circle) upon the surface of the deep,
> When He made the skies firm overhead,
> When He fixed firmly the fountains of the deep,
> When He set the sea its bound,
> That the waters should not transgress His commandment;

[1] O. S. Rankin's translation, *Israel's Wisdom Literature*, p. 240.
[2] Cf. A. B. Davidson, *The Book of Job (Cambridge Bible for Schools)*, pp. 199f.
[3] Cf. O. S. Rankin, *Israel's Wisdom Literature*, p. 241, for the translation. Also C. F. Burney, *J.T.S.* vol. XXVII (1926).

When He "made strong" the foundations of the earth
Then I was by Him as master-workman.
And I was His delight day by day;
Rejoicing before Him continually,
Rejoicing in the world of His earth,
And my delight was with the sons of man.

From the above we may deduce not only that Wisdom was begotten
of God before creation (verse 22) but that Wisdom was in some sense
actively concerned in creation. She is no longer merely a ground plan,
who was studied, but—the architect. Into the vexed question of the
exact nature of this figure we need not enter here. J. Lebreton's careful
statement may serve us: "It is difficult to see in this passage only poetical
personification and, in fact, the majority of commentators agree in the
view that Wisdom is presented here as already distinguished from God,
constituting a hypostasis or, at least, tending in that direction."[1] It will
be well also to point out that Wisdom has not only a part to play in
creation. She is also peculiarly concerned with mankind. She reveals
the way of life and righteousness to men. She confers Truth, Righteousness, Knowledge, Judgement, Justice and Law. We may briefly state
that in the Old Testament Wisdom is a means of expressing the Divine
Immanence in Creation and also the Divine Activity in morality and
knowledge, in short in what we may call the Redemptive activity
of God:

For whoso finds me finds life, . . .
All who hate me love death.[2]

One fact, however, will be evident from the above, namely, that
Wisdom as found in the Old Testament is in no sense a 'nationalistic'
figure. There is about all the Wisdom literature of the Old Testament
an international flavour, there is in it nothing that is specifically Israelite.[3]
It is not surprising, therefore, that there should grow up a tendency to
make the figure of Wisdom more distinctly Jewish. It is this that we
find in the Book of Ecclesiasticus. There the figure of Wisdom becomes
identified with the Torah, Wisdom takes up her abode in Israel and is
established in Zion. Perhaps the author thought that the Wisdom of
Proverbs was altogether too foreign.[4] At any rate for him it cannot be

---

[1] *Histoire du Dogme de la Trinité* (E.T.), p. 93.

[2] Prov. 8. 35a, 36b.

[3] Cf. S. A. Cook, *The Old Testament: a Reinterpretation*, p. 204.

[4] D. B. Macdonald, in *The Hebrew Philosophical Genius*, p. 36, claims that Ecclesiastes
is a criticism of the Wisdom school, it attacks the view that Wisdom can avail to solve
the difficulties of life. See O. S. Rankin, *Israel's Wisdom Literature*, pp. 45 ff.

compared with the Torah and must be displaced by the latter. The passage in Ecclesiasticus is as follows, from chapter 24:

> 3. I came forth from the mouth of the Most High
> And as a mist I covered the earth....
>
> 5. Alone I compassed the circuit of heaven
> And in the depth of the abyss I walked.
>
> 6. Over the waves of the sea, and over all the earth,
> And over every people and nation I held sway.
>
> 7. With all these I sought a resting-place
> And said: In whose inheritance shall I lodge?
>
> 8. Then the Creator of all things gave me commandment,
> And he that created me fixed my dwelling place (for me),
> And he said: Let thy dwelling place be in Jacob,
> And in Israel take up thine inheritance.
>
> 9. He created me from the beginning of the world....

In verse 23 the identification of Wisdom with the Torah is made explicit:

> All these things are the book of the Covenant of God Most High
> The Law which Moses commanded (as) an heritage for the assemblies of Jacob.

The Torah is regarded here as the expression of the Divine Wisdom. We need not follow Knox in claiming that this identification of the Torah with Wisdom is due to Stoic influences.[1] As early as Deuteronomy the Torah is associated with Wisdom; thus we read: "Keep, therefore, and do them (i.e. the commandments) for this is your wisdom and your understanding."[2] Moreover, the way in which Ben Sirach introduces this identification "makes the impression that it was a commonplace in his time when the study of the Law and the cultivation of wisdom went hand in hand, and as in his case were united in the same person".[3] The significance of this identification of the Torah with Wisdom has been well expressed by Edwyn Bevan: "The author of the commandments (the Torah) is the author of the world and the wisdom embodied in the commandments is the wisdom diffused through the world. Yes, the Hebrew sage feels vividly that this Law handed down among his people is no mere code of a single race not even merely of the earth, but the Incarnation if one may say so, of a cosmic principle and akin to the stars."[4]

[1] Cf. W. L. Knox, *St Paul and the Church of the Gentiles*, p. 60.
[2] Deut. 4. 6. [3] Cf. Moore, vol. 1, p. 265.
[4] Cf. E. Bevan, *Jerusalem under the High Priests*, pp. 60f.

In subsequent centuries in Rabbinic Judaism Ben Sirach's outlook
became commonly accepted. We cannot here trace the development of
the concept of Wisdom in Hellenistic Judaism,[1] a development which
culminated in the Book of Wisdom, but it is important to emphasize
that in the Judaism of Palestine in Paul's day and elsewhere the identification of the Torah with Wisdom was a commonplace. The evidence for
this is familiar and need not be exhaustively given here. In the Book of
Baruch we read that God "found out every way of knowledge, and
gave it to Jacob his servant and to Israel his beloved". "After that it was
seen upon earth and conversed among men. This is the book of the
commandments of God and the law which abideth for ever."[2] So too
in 4 Maccabees: "Wisdom (σοφία) is a knowledge of things divine and
human, and of their causes...", and "This Wisdom is the education
given by the Law."[3] Schechter has written: "As soon as the Torah was
identified with the Wisdom of Proverbs, the mind did not rest satisfied
with looking upon it as a mere condition for the existence of the world.
Every connotation of the term Wisdom, in the famous eighth chapter
of Proverbs was invested with life and individuality. The Torah by this
same process was personified and endowed with a mystical life of its
own which emanates from God yet is partly detached from him."[4] We
are here concerned, however, only with three characteristics which the
Torah acquired through its identification with Wisdom and we shall
enumerate them briefly as follows:

1. The Torah, like Wisdom, came to be regarded as older than the
world. Thus it is the first among the seven things which were created
before the world.[5] Again in *Sifre* on Deut. 11. 10, Prov. 8. 22 is taken to
mean that the Law was created before everything. "The Law because
it is more highly prized (literally, dearer) than everything, was created
before everything, as it is said, 'The Lord created me as the beginning
of his way.'"[6] (Prov. 8. 22.)

2. Secondly, the Torah is brought into connection with creation:
e.g. R. Akiba said: "Beloved are Israel to whom was given a precious
instrument wherewith the world was created. It was greater love that

[1] See W. L. Knox, *St Paul and the Church of the Gentiles*, chapter iii, especially pp. 62f.
[2] Cf. Ap. Baruch 3. 37f.   [3] Cf. 1. 17; also 7. 21-3, 8. 7.
[4] Cf. *Some Aspects of Rabbinic Theology*, p. 129.
[5] Ibid. p. 128; *R.A.* pp. 169f.; Moore, vol. 1, p. 526; *Genesis R.* 1. 4; *b. Pes.* 54a;
b. Ned. 39b; *b. Shab.* 88b–89a; *b. Zeb.* 116a. *Bereshith Rabba* 1 reads: "Six things
preceded the creation of the world; among them were such as were themselves truly
created, and such as were decided upon before the Creation; the Torah and the throne
of glory were truly created." See also J. Bonsirven, *Le Judaïsme Palestinien*, vol. 1,
pp. 250f.
[6] Cf. Moore, vol. 1, p. 266: *Sifre Deut.* on 11. 10, §37.

it was made known to them that there was given unto them a precious instrument whereby the world was created, as it is said: 'For a good doctrine have I given you; forsake not my Law.'"[1] (Prov. 4. 2.)

3. Thirdly, the world is claimed to be created for the sake of the Torah. Thus R. Yudan said: "The world was created for the sake (literally: because of the merit) of the Torah."[2] Moore also quotes a far earlier passage in this connection, the aphorism of Simeon the Just: "The stability of the world rests on three things, on the Law, on 'worship' and on deeds of personal kindness."[3]

For our purpose this bare catalogue must suffice; the significance of the equation of Wisdom with Torah, however, must not be overlooked. To what strange artificialities the necessity of connecting God with the universe could lead will be familiar to students of Gnosticism with its doctrine of emanations, intermediate beings and its pronounced dualism. From such aberrations, Judaism went a long way to preserve itself when it made the Torah the instrument of creation. It thereby gave cosmic significance to morality and gave also to cosmic speculation a sobriety which otherwise it might have lacked. Another noteworthy factor is the possibility that within Judaism there were conceptions not far removed from the Platonic doctrine of ideas albeit expressed much more naïvely than in Plato. Thus the Torah had a celestial existence before it came into being at Sinai, and we are reminded of Philo's doctrine of the λόγος ἐνδιάθετος and the λόγος προφορικός. In any case the Torah was regarded as existing in two places, first in what Plato would have called the realm of ideas and secondly in time, and it was not the Torah alone that had this twofold existence as we have previously seen.[4] Although we cannot discuss the many aspects of this question here, it is well to be on our guard against too sharp a distinction between what is 'Platonic', or 'Hellenistic', and Hebraic. We shall now proceed to relate all this Torah-Wisdom speculation to the Christology of Paul, where we have also found the ascription of a celestial or pre-cosmic existence to a person who appeared in time.

[1] P. Aboth 3. 23. See W. O. E. Oesterley, The Sayings of the Jewish Fathers, p. 42; cf. J. Bonsirven, op. cit. vol. I, p. 167.

[2] Cf. Gen. R. 12. 2.   [3] P. Aboth. I. 2.

[4] On this, see J. Bonsirven, op. cit. vol. I, p. 169, who writes: "Peut on déduire de ces données qu'il régnait en Israel, et depuis longtemps, une théorie des idées, semblable à celle de Platon, mais aucunement dérivée de la philosophie grecque? Ce serait mettre des modes fort métaphysiques dans des cerveaux tout concrets; cependant la notion de prédestination, si vivace en tout esprit Juif, devait conduire à penser qu'aucune créature ne venait à l'existence, qui n'ait été au préalable présente à la pensée et la volonté du Créateur." See also pp. 250ff. See Review by D. Winton Thomas in J.T.S. (1936), vol. XXXVII.

It is now necessary to recall our contention that for St Paul the person and teaching of Jesus had replaced the Torah as the centre of his religious life, and had assumed for him, therefore, the character of a New Torah. Once this step had been taken, however, that of substituting Jesus for the Torah of Judaism, Paul's mind would inevitably move forward to transfer to Jesus those attributes with which Judaism had honoured the Torah. We have seen, moreover, that the Torah had become identified in Judaism with the Wisdom of God and had been given the qualities of the latter, both pre-existence and participation in the creation of the universe as well as the moral discipline or redemption of mankind. The way was therefore open for Paul to identify Jesus with the same Wisdom of God and to ascribe to him pre-existence and creative activity. The immediate occasion that compelled Paul to develop the implications of his early equation of Christ with the Wisdom of God in 1 Cor. 1. 24, was the Colossian heresy, which it will be remembered contained a strong Jewish element,[1] but that the way in which he arrived at his interpretation of Christ in the Epistle to the Colossians is that suggested by us seems to be conclusively proved by the fact that the argument there used by Paul of Christ, that he is the *rêshîth* of creation, is used in Rabbinic Judaism of the Torah. For convenience we quote Burney:

In *Bereshith Rabba*, the great Midrashic commentary on Genesis, Rabbi Hoshaiah (*c.* third century A.D.) opens with a discussion of Prov. 8. 30, where Wisdom states, "Then I was with Him as *'āmôn* ('master-workman')."

After mentioning various proposed explanations of *'āmôn*, he continues as follows:

Another explanation of *'āmôn* is *'ōmên* 'workman'. The Law says, "I was the working instrument of the Holy One, blessed be He." In worldly affairs a human king who is building a palace does not build it by his own skill, but he has parchment plans (διφθέραι) and drawing tablets (πίνακες) that he may know how to make rooms and doors. In the same way the Holy One, blessed be He, was looking at the Law when He created the world. Now the Law says, "By *rêshîth* God created"; and there is no *rêshîth* except the Law; compare the passage "The Lord gat me as *rêshîth* of His way."[2]

This argument is dated late but we can probably assume that it was a familiar one: in any case Paul used it of Christ—the New Torah.

We have now dealt with the background of Paul's Wisdom Christology, and have found that no Hellenistic source or sources need be postulated for its explanation. Both Knox and Howard have again

---

[1] J. B. Lightfoot, *The Epistles of St Paul: Colossians and Philemon*, p. 70; cf. Col. 2. 16, 17, 21 f.

[2] Cf. C. F. Burney, *J.T.S.* (1926), vol. XXVII.

drawn attention to the fact that Paul, like the Auctor ad Hebraeos does not use the term Logos in his cosmological speculation. Knox would explain this on the grounds that Paul did not know the term. He writes: "It is interesting to observe as showing the gradual diffusion of language in the synagogues of the Dispersion that Paul is not acquainted with Philo's...word while the author of the Fourth Gospel is. The latter writer has even less contact with Philo's outlook than Paul himself, but Philo's term has become by this time a commonplace of the Syna-gogues."[1] It is difficult to accept this view. As to the term Logos, Howard comments that it "must have been known in Ephesus, especially when we remember that at that very time there had come to Ephesus a certain Jew named Apollos, an Alexandrian by race, who was mighty in the scriptures, to whom Priscilla and Aquila expounded the way of God more perfectly".[2] Howard argues that it was owing to the 'Gnostic' associations of the term Logos that Paul eschewed it, and that[3] "there is some internal evidence that an inhibition was imposed upon the use of the closely related term Wisdom. In 1 Corinthians Paul boldly proclaimed: 'But of him are ye in Christ Jesus, who was made unto us Wisdom from God, even righteousness and sanctification and redemption.'[4] But in his later letters he never repeats the title. Even in Colossians, where his language is evidently chosen from the vocabulary of the Wisdom books, and he writes of Christ as the 'image of the invisible God, the first born of all creation',[5] he does not make the expected declaration that Christ and Wisdom are one. But with a side glance at the shibboleths of Gnosticism he does say that in Christ 'all the treasures of knowledge and wisdom are hidden'[6]." All this may be true, but it should also be recognized that if, as we have main-tained, Paul's thoughts were centred on Christ as the New Torah he would have no need to employ the term Logos, and if even in Colossians it was of Torah that Paul was thinking this would help to explain his neglect of the explicit term Wisdom. In any case the essential ideas underlying his description of Jesus in cosmological terms are derived from Judaism.[7]

It remains to seek to understand the significance of the ascription to Christ of the attributes of Wisdom. Are we to find any profound

---

[1] Cf. W. L. Knox, St Paul and the Church of the Gentiles, p. 114, n. 4.
[2] Cf. W. F. Howard, Christianity According to St John, p. 42.
[3] Cf. W. F. Howard, op. cit. p. 43.
[4] 1 Cor. 1. 30.   [5] Col. 1. 15.   [6] Col. 2. 3.
[7] That the term Λόγος would be familiar to Palestinian Judaism comes out clearly in the Odes of Solomon. See J. H. Bernard, "The Odes of Solomon", in Texts and Studies, Contributions to Biblical and Patristic Literature, vol. VIII, p. 31.

religious truths in the doctrines of the pre-existence and of the creative activity of Christ, or are we to see in such conceptions what, following Knox, we might call a Christian fancy? We have already pointed out that in Judaism the conception of pre-existence was midrashic; we are to seek for no deep metaphysical truth in it. We may assume that for Paul too the pre-existence of Christ by itself had no profound significance. When we turn, however, to the idea that the Law was the instrument of creation we cannot believe that here Judaism was only exercising its playful imagination. On the contrary, it was deeply in earnest and by this idea it gives expression to one of its most fundamental convictions, that the universe conforms to the Torah, that Nature itself is after the pattern of the Torah; in short, to claim that the Torah was the instrument of creation was to declare that Nature and Revelation belonged together, that in theological terms there was a continuity not a discontinuity between Nature and Grace. To use Stoic terms, to live according to the Torah is to live according to Nature.[1]

To return now to Paul; in teaching that Christ was the agent of creation Paul too, we cannot doubt, was seeking to express a similar truth; that to live after Christ is the natural life, that the Creator is the Redeemer, that Nature and Grace are related not antithetical. Paul was essentially a townsman and hardly ever does he turn in Wordsworth fashion to Nature's 'old felicities' for parable or illustration, but, strange as it may seem, his doctrine of the agency of Christ in creation really sets forth a truth that Jesus always assumed in his Nature parables. To explain what we mean let us again read Dr Dodd's words:

There is a reason for this realism of the parables of Jesus. It arises from a conviction that there is no mere analogy, but an inward affinity, between the natural order and the spiritual order; or as we might put it in the language of the parables themselves, the Kingdom of God is intrinsically *like* the processes of nature and of the daily life of men. Jesus therefore did not feel the need of making up artificial illustrations for the truths He wanted to teach. He found them ready made by the Maker of man and nature. That human life, including the religious life, is a part of nature is distinctly stated in the well-known passage

[1] See the remarks of H. Loewe in *R.A.* p. lxix. He writes: "What is true in nature is true in religion: what is false in science cannot be true in religion. Truth is one and indivisible. God is bound by His own laws....It is indeed ironical to note that the unity of the 19th Psalm has been impugned by some people for the very reason that it asserts, first, God's supremacy alike in the natural and in the religious spheres and, secondly, the congruence of those spheres. The sun, in going forth on its daily round, is fulfilling Torah as much as is a human being who worships God, as much as is a Jew when he performs the commandments, which are 'pure and enlightening to the eyes' Ps. 19. 8." He refers to *Sifre Deut.* on 32. 1, § 306. See *R.A.* p. 208.

beginning "Consider the fowls of the air. . ." (Matt. 6. 26, 30; Luke 12. 24–8). This sense of the divineness of the natural order is the major premiss of all the parables. . . .[1]

With such an outlook upon the natural world Paul too, despite his affinities with apocalyptic, would agree, and it is not only in Rom. 1 that Paul recognizes the validity of natural theology. If our interpretation be correct, this is presupposed in his doctrine of Christ as the creative Wisdom of God.[2]

The relevance of all this to contemporary theology will be easily apparent. We have already compared the post-exilic period in Judaism with the present situation in Christendom. In the former period two things coincided, an increasing awareness of the transcendence of God and of the sin of man. The 'immanence' of God, however, was preserved in true perspective by the development among other things of the doctrine of Wisdom. Judaism never failed to believe that, however warped by human sinfulness, Nature was the expression of the Divine Wisdom. When we turn to modern Christendom two facts stare us in the face, a shattering awareness under the pressure of what has been called 'modern wickedness' of the reality of evil and also an increasing emphasis on the 'otherness' of God. Along with these salutary emphases, however, there has developed an insistence on the discontinuity between Nature and Grace, and we have witnessed what may perhaps with justice be called a contemptuous dismissal of natural theology. The revelation of God in Christ is set over against the knowledge of God that Nature gives not as its completion but as something wholly other. Thus Karl Barth has written: "Knowledge of grace in point of fact destroys the idea of an indirect revelation in Nature. . . ."[3] His view has not passed unchallenged. Thus for example Brunner writes: "The denial of this revelation through the creation in the latest theology empties the Biblical idea of creation of meaning—the Creation is a manifestation of the Wisdom and Godhead of God."[4] But we may go further than this and say that it ignores the doctrine of Christ as the Wisdom of God which we have found in Paul. When Christ is the agent of creation surely that creation must witness to Him; there is

[1] Cf. *Parables of the Kingdom*, pp. 21 f.
[2] It will be clear that there is in Paul something of an antinomy: there is on the one hand the belief that through the Fall creation itself has been affected, and, on the other, the belief that in creation is visible 'the eternal power of God'. Cf. J. Weiss, *The History of Primitive Christianity*, vol. II, p. 597. Both views are native to Judaism.
[3] Quoted by H. R. Mackintosh, *Types of Modern Theology*, p. 278.
[4] Cf. *Man in Revolt* (E.T.), p. 530.

continuity not discontinuity between God's work as Creator and as Redeemer. We cannot doubt that modern Christendom, if it is to survive the crisis of science, must like post-exilic Judaism, having rightly re-emphasized the transcendence of God and human sinfulness, and without sacrificing either truth, go on also to trace in the created universe the marks of the Wisdom of God, and thus claim the perilous new world of modern science as its own.

8

THE OLD AND THE NEW OBEDIENCE:
I. THE LORD THE SPIRIT

IT has been our contention in the preceding chapters that Jesus in the totality of His teaching and of His person, of His words, life and death and Resurrection, had not merely replaced the 'old Torah', but had assumed for Paul the significance of a 'New Torah'. Moreover, it was further suggested that the interpretation of Jesus in terms of a 'New Torah' illuminates for us both the origin and meaning of the cosmological significance that the Apostle ascribed to his Lord. Important as it was, however, to assert the cosmic functions of Christ, we saw that it was chiefly the exigencies of controversy that actually induced Paul to do so. Had it not been for the heresy at Colossae it is possible that we should never have had from the Apostle a fully articulated theory of Christ's agency in creation. Paul's interests lay elsewhere.[1] Polemics might lead him to speculation on creation, but he was primarily concerned with redemption: more a missionary or an evangelist to a world which he saw to be in desperate plight under the Wrath of God[2] than an apologetic theologian, it was with the moral and spiritual significance of Jesus that he would naturally be preoccupied. This explains why the concept of Wisdom, through which he came to expound the creative activity of Christ, plays a far smaller part in the Epistles of Paul than that of the Spirit, through which he expressed the ethical and redemptive and eschatological aspects of his faith, that newness of life now and in the future that had come through Christ.

The importance of the Spirit in the thought of Paul will be obvious even from a cursory reading of his Epistles; it becomes still more obvious when we notice the parallelism between the concept of the Spirit in Paul with that other concept which we saw to be central, that of 'being in Christ'. We have previously seen that the Christian for Paul is one who has died and risen with Christ, and who is therefore ἐν Χριστῷ. But through the Resurrection Christ had become the life-giving Spirit,[3] and so the Christian who is ἐν Χριστῷ can also be described in a parallel fashion as being ἐν πνεύματι.[4] On the other hand Paul had spoken of Christ being in the Christian (ζῶ δέ, οὐκέτι ἐγώ, ζῇ δὲ ἐν ἐμοὶ Χριστός·)[5]

---

[1] In this connection we may refer to F. C. Porter, *The Mind of Christ in Paul.*
[2] Cf. Rom. 1, 2.   [3] 1 Cor. 15. 45.
[4] Rom. 8. 9f.: ὑμεῖς δὲ οὐκ ἐστὲ ἐν σαρκί, ἀλλ' ἐν πνεύματι, εἴπερ Πνεῦμα θεοῦ οἰκεῖ ἐν ὑμῖν. εἰ δέ τις πνεῦμα Χριστοῦ οὐκ ἔχει, οὗτος οὐκ ἔστιν αὐτοῦ.
[5] Gal. 2. 20; Rom. 8. 10; Col. 1. 27.

and similarly the Spirit is said to be in him.[1] Just as to die and rise with Christ involved dying to sin and living to righteousness,[2] so also to be in the Spirit or to walk in the Spirit is to bear good fruit—love, joy, peace, long-suffering, graciousness, goodness, faithfulness, meekness, self-restraint.[3] Both Christ and the Spirit might also be said to be the life of the Christian.[4] Again we emphasized that to be ἐν Χριστῷ meant to belong to the Body of Christ, which implied an almost corporeal relation with Christ and with all other Christians, so too there is a unity of the Spirit[5] which is shared by all Christians, there is a fellowship created by the Spirit.[6] The Church is both the body of Christ and "the home of the Spirit", or "the sphere of the incarnating of the Spirit".[7] Finally, while Paul can describe the world to come as that sphere where we shall be with Christ,[8] it is also essentially the realm of Spirit.[9]

It has not been our intention in the above to attempt an exhaustive account of the Spirit in the Pauline Epistles. We have merely pointed out the centrality of this conception, and it is to the interpretation of it that we shall now turn. We shall seek to show that just as the conception of Christ as a 'New Torah' helped us to understand and interpret the cosmic activity of Christ in Paul's thought, so too it can help us to understand his teaching on the Spirit, at least in some of its aspects. But before we can proceed to deal with this we shall first have to examine certain theories that would account for the Spirit in Paul in terms of some aspect of Hellenistic philosophy or religion.

In the first place, it has been held that we are to understand the teaching of St Paul on the Spirit in the light of the Stoic conception of the world soul or *anima mundi*. It will be remembered that Stoicism was a thoroughgoing monism; it asserted, in the words of Edwyn Bevan, "that the whole universe was only one Substance, one Physis, in various states", and that "that one substance was Reason, was God".[10] It is true that two principles of Being were differentiated, namely, the material and the divine, the former being passive (τὸ πάσχον = ὕλη) and the latter active (τὸ ποιοῦν), but, "there was nothing which was not in its ultimate

---

[1] Rom. 8. 9f.; 1 Cor. 3. 16, 6. 19.
[2] Rom. 6. 1f., 8. 10.   [3] Gal. 5. 22f.
[4] Rom. 8. 2, 10; Gal. 6. 8; Col. 3. 4.
[5] Rom. 12. 4f.; 1 Cor. 12. 12; Eph. 4. 4.
[6] Phil. 2. 1; 2 Cor. 13. 13; cf. C. A. A. Scott, *The Fellowship of the Spirit*, p. 70. See also R. N. Flew, *Jesus and His Church*, p. 151.
[7] Cf. G. Johnston, *The Doctrine of the Church in the New Testament*, pp. 99f., 101, n. 2.
[8] Cf. Phil. 1. 23; 1 Thess. 4. 17.   [9] 1 Cor. 15. 44f.
[10] Cf. Edwyn Bevan, *Stoics and Sceptics*, p. 41.

origin, God: it was He in whom man lived and moved and had his being".[1] It follows from this that, although Reason is ascribed to God, the latter is conceived corporeally; and, following Heracleitus,[2] Zeno described God as a fiery substance or a fiery ether that surrounded and at the same time interpenetrated the whole universe.[2] But there was also another term to hand which was admirably suited to describe the one underlying φύσις of all things, the familiar term denoting 'breath' or wind, the most impalpable, ubiquitous and apparently the most refined of all substances, the term πνεῦμα. It is difficult, however, to define the exact status of πνεῦμα in Stoicism. It is often associated with fire so that it may have been considered as one of the four elements; thus Cleanthes called the ethereal fire πῦρ αἰθερῶδες the 'fiery Breath' (πνεῦμα).[3] Again fire and air are presented as its component parts,[4] and Stobaeus claimed that πνεῦμα was said to be 'air in motion' ἀὴρ κινούμενος.[5] But on the other hand Dr Dodd has written: "statements are made about it which are not applicable to air as an element."[6] Dr Dodd quotes Chrysippus[7] "that the self existent is πνεῦμα moving itself to itself and from itself or πνεῦμα moving itself to and fro" (εἶναι τὸ ὂν πνεῦμα κινοῦν ἑαυτὸ πρὸς ἑαυτὸ καὶ ἐξ αὐτοῦ, ἢ πνεῦμα ἑαυτὸ κινοῦν πρόσω καὶ ὀπίσω). Moreover, we find applied to πνεῦμα the adjectives νοερόν and ἀΐδιον,[8] while Posidonius described God as 'intelligent and fiery' (πνεῦμα νοερὸν καὶ πυρῶδες).[9] Hence W. Scott's definition of the Stoic πνεῦμα in which man lives and moves and has his being as a 'living and thinking gas' is singularly apt.[10]

That Paul would be acquainted to some extent at least with such Stoic conceptions can hardly be doubted. In this connection it is noteworthy that his native city was Tarsus in Cilicia, which was not merely a leading intellectual centre of the age but had been particularly the home of a number of Stoic philosophers.[11] We may agree with Knox, over against Ramsay, that Paul in his early education was not influenced 'to

---

[1] Ibid. p. 41.

[2] Ibid. p. 43. For Heracleitus, see J. Burnet, *Greek Philosophy*, pp. 57 ff. and *Early Greek Philosophy*, pp. 63 ff.; W. L. Davidson, *The Stoic Creed*, pp. 87 f.; F. Büchsel, *Der Geist Gottes im Neuen Testament*, pp. 47 f. gives an excellent summary of the Stoic concept of πνεῦμα.

[3] Cf. *Hymn to Zeus*.

[4] See F. Büchsel, op. cit.   [5] *Ecl.* 1. 17.

[6] Cf. *The Bible and the Greeks*, p. 122.   [7] *Ecl.* 1. 17.

[8] See F. Büchsel, op. cit. pp. 47 f.   [9] *Ecl.* 1. 17.

[10] *The Bible and the Greeks*, p. 122, n. 7.

[11] Cf. *H.D.B.* vol. IV, pp. 685 f., especially p. 687; W. M. Ramsay names the following Stoic philosophers from Tarsus: Athenodorus, Athenodorus Cananites and Antipater (c. 144 B.C.).

any considerable extent' by the atmosphere of Tarsus.[1] Nevertheless, we may be sure that the Apostle, who was clearly fond and proud of the city of his birth,[2] must have known something at least of the city's past, of its great men and of the peculiarities of their thought. Apart, however, from the Apostle's special connection with Tarsus, it must be realized that by the first century Stoic ideas in some form or other and in varying degrees had become part and parcel of the intellectual and religious currency of most thinking men. The time immediately preceding the Christian era has been rightly characterized by Edwyn Bevan as an age of eclecticism. Writing of it he says: "At a time when many men, not philosophers in any sense, wanted some guide for life which was raised above the old mythologies and which yet met their sense of some greater spiritual Reality encompassing the life of men, it was natural that a kind of body of popular philosophic doctrine should come into vogue, made of the commonplaces of the different schools, with a blurring of their distinctive peculiarities."[3] This philosophical (and religious) amalgamation was of course the work of many minds, but it was chiefly effected by Posidonius. With this encyclopaedic figure, "who stands behind the later philosophical literature of antiquity",[4] we cannot linger; but we emphasize that the basis of his 'amalgam' was Stoicism and that therefore through him and many others, whose names are lost, there filtered through into the popular mind the terms and concepts, blurred but nevertheless recognizable, of Stoic as of other thinkers. It was through the work of such men, for example, that Philo of Alexandria[5] acquired the acquaintance that he had with Stoicism, and it would have been more than strange if the nimble mind of Paul of Tarsus had not been affected by this popularization of philosophy.

According to some scholars, however, not only can we assume Paul's familiarity with those popular Stoic conceptions which were in the air as it were in his age, but there is evidence that he used these in his presentation of the Gospel. Thus Norden[6] has isolated certain doxological formulae in the Pauline Epistles which he regards as derived from Stoicism via Hellenistic Judaism.[7] He compares a saying of Marcus Aurelius: "Whatsoever is agreeable to you, O Universe, is so to me too.

---

[1] Cf. W. L. Knox, *St Paul and the Church of Jerusalem*, p. 124, n. 66.

[2] Cf. *H.D.B.* vol. IV, p. 688. Acts 21. 39.

[3] Edwyn Bevan, *Stoics and Sceptics*, p. 92.

[4] Ibid. p. 86. Also W. L. Knox, *St Paul and the Church of the Gentiles*, pp. 62f.

[5] Knox, op. cit. p. 95.

[6] Cf. *Agnostos Theos*, pp. 240f.: "Eine Stoïsche Doxologie bei Paulus: Geschichte einer Allmachtsformel."

[7] Cf. Sib. Oracles, Book III, v. 11; cf. R. H. Charles, *Ap. and Ps.* vol. II, p. 379.

Your things are never mistimed. Your methods are acceptable and your seasons all spring and summer to me O Nature, ἐκ σοῦ πάντα, ἐν σοὶ πάντα, εἰς σὲ πάντα",[1] with Rom. 11. 33 f., 1. Cor. 8. 6, Col. 1. 16f., Eph. 4. 5f. The relation of Christ and God,[2] as the case might be, to the universe is comparable to that of the World-Soul or Reason to the universe in Stoicism. Johannes Weiss has written of the passage Col. 1. 15 f.: "'In him all things consist', here Christ takes exactly the same position which the World-Soul has in the Stoic system; he is the innermost, animating cohesive principle of power in the natural universe and in the realm of spirit, and therefore identical with the life-creating Spirit of God which penetrates the entire world and pours into the souls of men."[3] "The fixed outlines of the personality", he also writes of Paul's idea of Christ, "had been softened and dissolved and replaced by the idea of a formless, impersonal all-penetrating being."[4] We are to understand Paul's language about the Spirit, so it is suggested, language in which he speaks of 'being in the Spirit' of walking 'in the Spirit', etc., in the light of these Stoic conceptions. In the same way, as we saw, Knox has claimed that the expression 'body' applied to the Church goes back to the Stoic idea that 'the cosmos was a body' and the divine mind either its 'head' or the spirit which animated it.[5] It further agrees with all this that the Spirit should be interpreted in materialistic terms. Johannes Weiss described the Spirit as "a fluid which surrounds us and also penetrates us",[6] an idea which he traced quite naturally to the Stoics. The Spirit he regards as almost a physical kind of life which Christians come to share by a 'symbiosis' with their Lord.[7] There are verses indeed which seem to suggest something of this kind, e.g. we read, "though our outward man is decaying, yet our inward man is renewed day by day",[8] or again: "But if the Spirit of him that raised up Jesus from the dead dwelleth in you, he that raised up Christ Jesus from the dead shall quicken also your mortal bodies through his Spirit that dwelleth in you."[9] It will be obvious also that, if accepted, this view of the Spirit

[1] Book 4, § 23; cf. also J. Weiss on 1 Cor. 8. 6, Meyer, *Kommentar zum Neuen Testament, Der Erste Korintherbrief*, pp. 223 f.
[2] In 1 Cor. 8. 6 it is of Christ and God that the formula speaks; in Col. 1. 15 f. of Christ alone and in Rom. 11. 29–36 of God alone.
[3] Cf. *The History of Primitive Christianity*, vol. II, p. 465.
[4] Ibid. p. 465.
[5] W. L. Knox, *St Paul and the Church of the Gentiles*, pp. 161 f.; also T. A. Lacey, *The One Body and the One Spirit*, pp. 54 f., 232.
[6] *The History of Primitive Christianity*, vol. II, p. 464.   [7] Ibid. p. 463.
[8] Cf. 2 Cor. 4. 16 f.; also for the same thought Col. 3. 3 f.; Rom. 8. 2; Eph. 1. 13 f.; 2 Cor. 1. 22, 5. 5 (Christ is the Spirit of life).
[9] Rom. 8. 11.

as a kind of material would greatly simplify our understanding of I Cor. 15. 44, where Paul contrasts the earthly body which the Christian has in this world with the σῶμα πνευματικόν of the world to come which will be his through the Resurrection. We could then give to that passage the straightforward meaning that the 'body',[1] the organ of personality, would have a 'material' of a 'spiritual' kind through which to express itself in the world to come just as it had 'material' of flesh and blood for the same purpose in this world.[2]

We are now in a position to examine the interpretation of the Spirit in Paul as the counterpart of the Stoic *anima mundi*. Let us begin with the last point, that Paul regards the Spirit as a kind of material or substance. Rawlinson dismisses this view summarily by saying "it would be absurd to infer... that St Paul thinks of the Spirit as being literally or semi-literally a fluid" in such verses as "in one Spirit were we all baptized into one body whether Jews or Greeks, whether bond or free and were all made to drink of one Spirit".[3] But this is gravely to over-simplify the matter. Büchsel[4] treats it more seriously, and we must agree with him that the essentially personal character of the Spirit must be preserved at all costs, the Spirit is so closely related to Christ[5] and to God[6] and the relation of the Christian to Christ, 'in the Spirit' is so

---

[1] For 'body', cf. C. H. Dodd, *Romans* (*M.N.T.C.*), p. 90, and also p. 194. He defines 'body' in Paul as "the organization of personality as an acting concrete individual".

[2] Contrast F. Büchsel, *Der Geist Gottes im Neuen Testament*, p. 396, n.; cf. Johannes Weiss, Meyer, *Kommentar zum Neuen Testament*, pp. 371 f. He writes: "Dass nun ein solches σῶμα πνευματικόν genannt werden kann, ist nur möglich, wenn πνεῦμα als eine Art Substanz gedacht ist.... Vielleicht hat auch auf. P. die Stoische Lehre eingewirkt, wonach πᾶν τὸ ποιοῦν σῶμά ἐστιν (*Diog. Laert.* VII, 38) und ein lebendiges Wirken ohne σῶμα überhaupt nicht gedacht werden kann." Cf. also C. H. Dodd, *Romans* (*M.N.T.C.*), p. 90; J. Moffatt, *First Corinthians* (*M.N.T.C.*), p. 260.

[3] Cf. A. E. J. Rawlinson, *The New Testament Doctrine of the Christ*, p. 159.

[4] Cf. *Der Geist Gottes im Neuen Testament*, pp. 396–410; for 'Geist als Stoff', pp. 396 f.

[5] F. Büchsel, op. cit. p. 398.

[6] F. Büchsel, op. cit. pp. 401 f.; Rom. 8. 9; 2 Cor. 3. 17; Gal. 4. 6; 1 Cor. 2. 16. Also Rom. 1. 4, 8. 2; 1 Cor. 10. 3, 4; 2 Cor. 3. 16–18. 'Now the Lord is that Spirit', etc. In 1 Cor. 2. 16 Paul apparently equates πνεῦμα and νοῦς. This implies, if we are to think of Paul as a metaphysician, that he cannot have accepted a Stoic metaphysic. In Stoicism the connection of πνεῦμα and νοῦς is not as close as that between air and fire and Spirit, and if Paul equated both he must have thought of πνεῦμα in a non-Stoic way. (See F. Büchsel, op. cit. pp. 47 f.) We may illustrate this from the Poimandres. The latter tractate ascribes the function of the πνεῦμα in Gen. 1 to what is called the πνευματικὸς λόγος. Dr Dodd comments that for the author "with his Stoic metaphysic, πνευματικὸς λόγος should mean a word which was in some sort material, consisting of the fire-like πνεῦμα which belongs to the higher elements. This, however, cannot be his meaning. In Chapter x the Λόγος is said to be 'of one substance' (ὁμοούσιος)

thoroughly of the 'I-thou type' based upon a personal act of faith that we must throughout think of the Spirit in personal terms.[1] It must also be admitted that of necessity, because of its material connotation, the use of such a term as fluid in the description of a personal being must seem to us peculiarly unfitting. But it cannot be sufficiently emphasized that it might not have been so for Paul. Not only was it difficult for Paul, as it is indeed for us, wholly to free himself from what we may call the 'fleshly screen' that hampers all language,[2] but in the first century "the idea of personality had not been defined or distinguished from substance or quality".[3] It might therefore have been possible for Paul to think of the Spirit in material terms and yet to preserve its essentially personal character.

We may then admit that the term πνεῦμα might have borne for Paul a certain physical nuance and that in 1 Cor. 15. 44 it is thought of as a kind of substance. But we now point out that this is not necessarily due to the influence of Stoic ideas. Thus it may be explained in the light of Jewish usage. Gunkel indeed has called the Spirit in Jewish thought a 'Lichtstoff'; he claimed that ruach in the Old Testament, even as applied to Yahweh, is materially conceived.[4] The fact that ruach means 'wind' as well as Spirit in the Old Testament is not to be taken to suggest, as Wendt held, that Spirit is immaterial like the wind: the wind is in fact 'material', and so also is Spirit.[5] Now although there are passages where the Spirit in the Old Testament seems to be materially conceived,[6] however, we must question Gunkel's emphasis. Surely it is not the 'materiality' of the ruach that is to the fore in the Old Testament, but its quality as power, vitality, activity or life;[7] its essence is power not substance. Much more to our purpose is the fact that in Rabbinic

with the Νοῦς Δημιουργός, who is the offspring of the primal Νοῦς....But νοῦς is essentially immaterial. The Λόγος therefore is not made of any material element, not even of the highest element, πνεῦμα. The writer would seem to have taken over the language of his biblical source without sufficiently considering whether it is strictly consistent with his own metaphysics." To confuse πνεῦμα and νοῦς for a Stoic is an inconsistency. (See *The Bible and the Greeks*, p. 125.) If we are to find Greek influences at all there it would be safer to find a 'Platonic' emphasis in Paul's use of νοῦς in 1 Cor. 2. 16 than a Stoic one. But for νοῦς in Paul, see H. W. Robinson, *The Christian Doctrine of Man*, pp. 104ff.; p. 194 below. For Greek usage, F. Büchsel, op. cit. pp. 37ff.

[1] Cf. C. A. A. Scott, *Christianity According to St Paul*, p. 144.
[2] Cf. Edwyn Bevan, *Symbolism and Belief.*
[3] Cf. Thomas Rees, *The Holy Spirit*, pp. 103f.
[4] H. Gunkel, *Die Wirkungen des heiligen Geistes*, p. 47.   [5] Ibid. p. 48.
[6] Cf. for example, Ezek. 37, where the Spirit is appealed to as if it were the Wind.
[7] Cf. especially N. H. Snaith, *The Distinctive Ideas of the Old Testament*, pp. 143f. See p. 156 where Snaith criticizes P. Volz (*Der Geist Gottes*, p. 23) for speaking of a '*ruach-Stoff*'.

Judaism the Spirit is often conceived in material terms. Abelson's[1] catena of passages has sufficiently demonstrated this and it will be well to recapitulate his evidence. This is as follows:

1. Places where the Holy Spirit is conceived as Light or Fire.

(a) B. Megillah 14a: "Iskah is Sarah; why was Sarah called Iskah? Because she looked by the Holy Spirit."

(b) Leviticus Rabbah 9. 9: "R. Meir looked by the Holy Spirit."

(c) Leviticus Rabbah 32. 4: "The Holy Spirit enlightened Moses" (in allusion to Lev. 24. 10–12).

(d) Genesis Rabbah 85. 9.

"These illustrations", writes Abelson, "are enough to make it clear that the Holy Spirit was somehow associated with some kind of visual sensation. The possessor of the Holy Spirit actually saw some kind of light."[2] Other passages, and more convincing ones, quoted by the same author are: (1) B. Makkoth 23a, which reads: "The Holy Spirit shone forth in three places; in the court of Shem: in the court of Samuel: in the court of Solomon." (2) Leviticus Rabbah 1. 1: "At the time when the Holy Spirit rested upon Phinehas the latter's face was burning like flames." (3) Genesis Rabbah 91. 6: "From the day that Joseph was stolen the Holy Spirit left him [Jacob]; as a consequence his sense of sight became imperfect and his sense of hearing also."

2. Places where the Holy Spirit is conceived as Sound or as some other material object.

(a) Leviticus Rabbah 8. 2: "As soon as the Holy Spirit began to knock Samson took two mountains and knocked them together just as a man knocks two pebbles together." Further on we read: "At the time that the Holy Spirit rested upon Samson his hairs stood up and knocked against one another like a bell and their sound was heard from Zarah to Eshtaol."

(b) B. Ḥagigah 15a: "Ben Zoma said unto him [i.e. to R. Joshua b. Ḥanania who was standing on an ascent of the Temple and was angry at Ben Zoma's failure to rise before him], I was gazing at the space between the upper and lower waters and I see there is only an interval of about three fingers' breadth between them, as it is said, And the Spirit of God was hovering upon the face of the waters, i.e. as a dove which hovers over her young, but does not touch them."[3]

(c) Genesis Rabbah 70. 8, speaks of the Holy Spirit being 'drawn up' like water from a well.

---

[1] J. Abelson, The Immanence of God in Rabbinical Literature, pp. 212f.
[2] Ibid. p. 216.
[3] See also Abelson, op. cit. p. 220, for further examples.

(d) *Leviticus Rabbah* 15. 2. The Holy Spirit has weight like a material object; we read: "Even the Holy Spirit which rests upon the prophets only rests by weight."

With such ideas of the Holy Spirit as are revealed to us in the above quotations Paul must have been familiar and it is from them rather than from Stoicism that we are to derive any 'materiality' that may attach to his concept of the Spirit.[1]

We now pass to those aspects of Paul's teaching on the Spirit where we not merely cannot trace any Stoic influence but find what has even been called a reaction against the latter. First, let us consider the Spirit in relation to man. It is well known that there is no consistency in Paul's use of the term πνεῦμα. Sometimes he employs the term to denote a normal element in human nature, e.g. "The Grace of our Lord Jesus Christ be with your spirit brethren";[2] or again: "For who among you knoweth the things of a man, save the spirit of a man which is in him";[3] or again: "The Spirit Himself bears witness with our spirit that we are God's children."[4] From these quotations it is clear that for Paul there is in all men, even the unregenerate, what he calls πνεῦμα. Without seeking to define this πνεῦμα which every man possesses we may think of it with Snaith as, "the controlling directive power in man".[5] On the other hand, however, Wheeler-Robinson has shown that out of 146 cases in which the term πνεῦμα occurs, it signifies in 116 places not a normal element in human nature but 'supernatural influences' or 'a divine invasion',[6] e.g. "God sent forth the Spirit of His Son into our hearts, crying, Abba, Father".[7] This double use of the term πνεῦμα in Paul to denote both a supernatural influence and a natural element in human nature is traced by Knox to a similar ambiguity of usage in Stoicism, where "the divine element in the Stoic wise man was with

---

[1] This would throw light on the experience of Paul on the road to Damascus. The Risen Lord whom he there encountered belonged to the realm of Spirit, and we have had occasion already to mention the close relation of the Spirit to Christ in Paul. The Risen Christ, the Lord the Spirit, appeared to Paul when "suddenly there shined round about him a light from heaven" (Acts 9. 3, 22. 11). Here von Hügel has suggested that "we get Christ or the Spirit conceived as an element as it were an ocean of ethereal light in which souls are plunged and which penetrates them" (*The Mystical Element in Religion*, vol. II, pp. 90f.). The whole of Paul's conversion fits naturally into a Rabbinic background, where the Spirit would naturally be conceived as Light; cf. J. Abelson, op. cit. p. 222, n. 5.

[2] Gal. 6. 18.　　　　　　　　　　　[3] 1 Cor. 2. 11.

[4] Rom. 8. 16.

[5] *The Distinctive Ideas of the Old Testament*, p. 183.

[6] Cf. H. W. Robinson, *The Christian Doctrine of Man*, pp. 109f.

[7] Gal. 4. 6; cf. Acts 2. 16f.: The Spirit is "poured forth."

difficulty differentiated from the divine element present in human nature as such; the distinction was made, but not very clearly maintained. . . ."[1] But we need not go outside the Old Testament to account for the Pauline usage. In the post-exilic passages of the Old Testament *ruach* "has come to denote the normal breath-soul as the principle of life in man", Ezek. 37. 5, 6, 8, whilst at the same time it retained its earlier connotation of 'supernatural influences', e.g. the prophetic consciousness was accredited to it, Ezek. 2. 2,[2] and it has been rightly emphasized that the "Old Testament doctrine of the Spirit of God is in closest genetic relation to the New Testament doctrine of man's renewal by the Spirit of Christ".[3]

For our purpose the significance of this is clear. Stoicism, despite its distinction, not very clearly maintained, between the human spirit and the Divine Spirit in its 'wise man', regarded the spirit of man as essentially part of the Divine Spirit so that man is a microcosm in the most literal sense of the macrocosm. True to his national inheritance, however, Paul on the other hand always maintained a qualitative difference between the spirit of man and the Spirit of God. For him the Spirit of God is not continuous with (or shall we say consubstantial with?) the spirit of man; it is the Spirit 'of God' and as such is necessarily other than the spirit of man—the creature of God. This becomes most clear from the passage: "For what man knoweth the things of a man, save the spirit of man which is in him? even so the things of God knoweth no man but the Spirit of God. . . . Now we have received. . . the spirit which is of God."[4] Here the Spirit of God and the spirit of man are set over against each other; the true Wisdom is not attainable through merely human means; the spirit of man, the normal element in human nature cannot achieve it; it is revealed by the Spirit of God. The character of the Spirit is therefore always transcendental. This of course is not to deny that it becomes in the Christian the immanent Divine. The famous words of Paul in Romans,[5] where the Spirit testifies along with our own spirit, enters into us and assists us in our weakness, pleading for us and searching our hearts, and other passages where the Spirit[6] inspires love in our hearts and gives the fruit of joy, peace, righteousness, etc., emphasize this truth. But the Spirit never ceases to be of God; it is never merely a property of man as such. The Spirit within us is never for Paul the fruition, refinement or development

---

[1] Cf. *St Paul and the Church of the Gentiles*, p. 117.
[2] H. Wheeler Robinson, *The Christian Doctrine of Man*, pp. 19, 64.
[3] Ibid. p. 15.
[4] 1 Cor. 2. 11 f.
[5] Rom. 8. 11, 16, 26, 27.   [6] Gal. 5. 22, etc.

to the utmost degree of our own spirit but the gift of God to us, and as such far removed from the kind of immanence which we have found in Stoicism.[1]

In the second place, we turn to the relation of the Spirit to the cosmos. We have already explained that for Stoicism the cosmos is, so to speak, saturated with πνεῦμα; the Spirit is the *anima mundi*. Now in the passage already referred to in 1 Corinthians, Paul draws a distinction between the spirit of the world and the Spirit of God, and it has been suggested by Lacey that he is here deliberately rejecting the Stoic concept of the spirit, since the phrase used by Paul τὸ πνεῦμα τοῦ κόσμου is characteristic of Stoicism. The argument is that at Athens Paul had been tempted to present the Gospel in terms of Stoic immanence, hence his quotation from Aratus, a Stoic poet of Cilicia.[2] The attempt, however, to interpret the Gospel in such terms proved a miserable failure. Paul was consequently cured of "any desire to accommodate the Gospel to modern thought", as it were, and when he arrived at Corinth, humbled by his experiences, he determined not to know anything save Christ and Him crucified; and rejecting the wisdom of this world, by which we are to understand the subtleties of philosophy, he no longer speaks of the πνεῦμα τοῦ κόσμου of the Stoics but reverts to the thoroughly Hebraic concept of the Spirit of God as transcendent.[3] It is doubtful if we are to follow Lacey in his reconstruction of the history of Pauline preaching. It is not clear that we are justified in finding an implied contrast between the preaching of Paul at Athens and at Corinth. There may be no allusion to his experiences at Athens in 1 Cor. 2. 1 f. Moffatt wrote:[4] "There is no hint that he had felt disillusioned by the Athenian experience. It is not of any such contrast between one method of his own and another that he thinks in the present passage, but of the difference between himself and other evangelists who had tried to be more ambitious and philosophic in the mission (3. 10) since he left." Moreover, it cannot certainly be assumed that Paul preached Stoic immanence on the basis

[1] The best treatment of this is in F. Büchsel's *Der Geist Gottes im Neuen Testament*, p. 399: "Dass ich Gottes Geist habe, heisst: in mir ist ein Denken, überhaupt ein geistiges Leben, das nicht nur aus Gott stammt sondern geistiges Leben ist....Für Paulus ist der Pneumatiker nicht durch ein drittes mit Gott verbunden, sondern er trägt Gottes Wesen in sich, er hat Anteil an Gott selbst." So too the Christian virtues are of God through the Spirit. So F. Büchsel, op. cit. p. 312, e.g. "Liebe ist etwas Göttliches im Menschen, nicht das ideal Menschliche."

[2] ἐν αὐτῷ γὰρ ζῶμεν καὶ κινούμεθα καὶ ἐσμεν. Lacey suggests that this is an echo of ἐκ σοῦ γὰρ γένος ἐσμεν in Cleanthes' Hymn, and that the latter was used by Paul, but that the author of Acts confused Cleanthes and Aratus.

[3] Cf. T. A. Lacey, *The One Body and the One Spirit*, pp. 62 f., 244.

[4] *First Corinthians* (M.N.T.C.), p. 22.

of one quotation in Acts.[1] Schweitzer[2] in particular has rejected this quotation as an indication of Paul's preaching on four grounds. First, that Acts 17 is the only place where we find Paul thinking of 'a being in God', elsewhere he always speaks of 'a being in Christ'; secondly, the speech is not strictly historical but an imaginative composition of the author after the manner of Greek historians; thirdly, the reference to an inscription of an unknown god betrays the unhistorical nature of the scene in Athens since there could never have been such an inscription;[3] and, finally, the Stoic quotation appears to be merely a literary device, an 'unmotived addition' to the passage with which Schweitzer contrasts the use of phrases such as ἐν Χριστῷ in the Epistles where the thought of being ἐν Χριστῷ dominates all else.

We need not here decide on the validity of Schweitzer's position, but it is obviously forceful enough to make Lacey's interpretation of 1 Cor. 2 as a deliberate rejection of Stoic immanence which he had preached at Athens if not untenable at least very uncertain.[4] Nevertheless, that Lacey is right in finding an essential difference between the Spirit in Paul and the πνεῦμα τοῦ κόσμου of Stoicism is substantiated by the fact that in no case does Paul, or any other New Testament writer, employ the concept of the Spirit in any cosmological context. "One notable limitation of the sphere assigned to the Holy Spirit in the New Testament... is that it is nowhere described as the agent of creation or as a cosmic principle."[5] The Spirit in Paul is confined in its activity to humanity. Rees has contrasted this limitation with what is found in Hebrew and Jewish literature. But it seems clear to us that in thus denying cosmic significance to the Spirit Paul is in direct agreement with the Rabbinic thought of his day. In this connection a brief glance at the idea of the Spirit in the Old Testament and Judaism will be instructive. It is frequently asserted that the Spirit in the Old Testament is given creative, cosmic functions, and it is true that there are passages where this is so. But this aspect can easily be over-emphasized. Thus Davidson has written:[6] "The operation of the Spirit of God upon the material world... is rarely emphasized (in the Old Testament)", and Rees[7] can only refer

---

[1] Acts 17. 28.   [2] Cf. *The Mysticism of Paul the Apostle*, pp. 6 ff.

[3] Cf. for the evidence, *Beginnings*, vol. v, pp. 240 f. K. Lake agrees that "it is doubtful whether there ever was an inscription which read exactly ἀγνώστῳ θεῷ", p. 245.

[4] How dangerous such reconstructions as Lacey's are can be seen from the fact that Knox sees in Paul's experience at Athens the occasion for his undertaking the Hellenization of the Gospel. Cf. *St Paul and the Church of the Gentiles*, p. 26. See also a criticism of Knox by A. D. Nock. *J.T.S.* (1940), vol. XLI, pp. 292 f.

[5] Thomas Rees, *The Holy Spirit*, pp. 84 f.

[6] A. B. Davidson, *The Theology of the Old Testament*, p. 120.

[7] Cf. Thomas Rees, *The Holy Spirit*, pp. 12 f. He refers to Gen. 1. 2; Job 27. 3; Isa. 44. 3, 4; Ezek. 37. 10; Job 26. 13, 33. 4; Ps. 33. 6, 104. 30. In Job 27. 3, "the spirit

to eight verses in which the Spirit is active in creation in the whole of the Old Testament. Still more illuminating is Wood's study,[1] in which he points out that in the pre-exilic literature the Spirit is always used of God acting directly or indirectly upon man, and that where the Spirit acts on external nature it is still for the sake of man. The exilic and post-exilic periods, however, saw a change. The growth of interest in cosmogony in those periods, which we have previously dealt with, led to the closer association of the Spirit with the work of creation, and it is significant that it is to these periods that all the passages quoted by Rees belong. When we come to later Judaism, to the apocryphal and pseudepigraphical literature, we find, however, a reversion to the pre-exilic emphasis. Again the Spirit is confined in its operation entirely to man; it no longer acts in nature at all, and Wood has written: "The seemingly simple fact of dropping the relation to external nature from the idea of the Spirit forms the greatest single crisis in its history."[2] The Rabbinical literature reveals the same standpoint as that found in the apocryphal and pseudepigraphical literature—the Spirit is almost entirely devoid of any cosmic significance. The Holy Spirit in Rabbinic literature is not conceived as the life-creating power of God. Thus in Gen. 1. 2, where, if anywhere, they could have found a cosmic significance for it, the *ruach* is interpreted by the Rabbis either of the wind or of the spirit of Adam or of the Messiah. In the Targum Jerusalem 1. 2, the spirit in Gen. 1. 2 is spoken of

---

is the principle of life in man". In Isa. 44. 3, 4 it is again concerned with man: and in Ezek. 37. 10 it is concerned with the revival of the nation. In Job 33. 4 it is concerned with man. Only in Gen. 1. 2 and Job 26. 13 and Ps. 33. 6 and 104. 30 is the Spirit concerned merely with nature. And as to Gen. 1. 2, the creative activity of the Spirit should not be pressed. Skinner's note on Gen. 1. 2 is significant: " *The Spirit of God was brooding*, not as has sometimes been supposed, a 'wind' sent from God to dry up the waters.... But the divine Spirit figured as a bird brooding over its nest and perhaps symbolizing an immanent principle of life and order in the as yet undeveloped chaos.... It is remarkable, however, if this be the idea, that no further effect is given to it in the sequel. (1) The idea of the Spirit as formative principle of the Kosmos, while in the line of the Old Testament doctrine that he is the source of life (Ps. 33. 6, 104. 29 f.) yet goes much beyond the ordinary representation and occurs only here (possibly Isa. 40. 13). (2) The image conveyed by the word brooding (מרחפת) is generally considered to rest on the widespread cosmogonic speculation of the world-egg (so even Delitzsch and Dillmann) in which the organized world was as it were hatched from the fluid chaos. If so we have here a fragment of mythology not vitally concerned with the main idea of the narrative but introduced for the sake of its religious suggestiveness." *I.C.C.* pp. 17f. ad loc.

[1] Irving F. Wood, *The Spirit of God in Biblical Literature*, p. 7; H. W. Robinson, *The Christian Doctrine of Man*, p. 6. "The term רוח is rarely used as in Gen. 1. 2 of influence on inanimate objects."

[2] Irving F. Wood, op. cit. p. 76.

as a spirit of mercy not as a creative spirit.[1] When Paul, therefore, thinks of the Holy Spirit as concerned exclusively with man he is being true to the Rabbinic outlook of his upbringing and is as far as possible removed from any Stoic conception of a πνεῦμα that penetrates the cosmos.

Before leaving this brief examination of Paul's doctrine of the Spirit in its relation to Stoicism it will not be amiss to refer to that conception of the Spirit that is suggested by Dr C. E. Raven. The latter has criticized the neglect in the theology of the Church of the creative function of the Holy Spirit and His activity in the world of nature. He writes: "that in our faith in the Holy Ghost as the Giver of Life we have warrant for believing that He is operative not only in the edifying of the saints but in the whole process of Evolution...that we should claim nothing less than the whole sphere of experience as the scene of His activity and that doing so should set our faces against the dualism of natural and supernatural."[2] We have already pointed out that such dualism as Dr Raven deplores is remote from the mind of Paul. But the latter expressed the divine activity, as did Dr Raven's precursor John Ray, not in terms of the Holy Spirit but in terms of Wisdom. Dr Raven would trace the activity of the Holy Spirit "not only in a comet's rush but in a rose's birth" whereas Paul would see in such things the marks of Divine Wisdom. Here we are not concerned with the question whether the doctrine of the Holy Spirit *should* be reinterpreted as Dr Raven suggests, but we are concerned to point out that Paul, and for that matter all the New Testament writers, would have felt that such a conception of the Spirit as Dr Raven's leans more to Stoicism with its πνεῦμα τοῦ κόσμου than to that energy from God full of power, strength, and life that he designated by τὸ πνεῦμα τὸ ἅγιον.[3] The Spirit in Paul is not "the manifestation of the Godhead in the cosmic process of which humanity is for us the consummation and Jesus the crowning glory";[4] it is, on the contrary, however unsatisfactory such language must be, a gift poured forth from on high; it is supernatural; it

---

[1] Cf. Str.-B. vol. II, p. 493. Vol. I, p. 48: πνεῦμα ἅγιον רוח הקדש "bezeichnet in Matt. I. 18 die lebenwirkende Schöpferkraft Gottes; in dieser Bedeutung scheint sich רוח הקדש in der alteren rabbin-Literatur nicht zu finden."

[2] Cf. *The Creator Spirit*, p. 18.

[3] Cf. C. E. Raven, *Science, Religion and the Future*, p. 73: "Bergson's own myth of an *Élan Vital*, reviving the ancient belief in an *Anima Mundi* and the careful and interesting theory of a Plastic Nature expounded by Ralph Cudworth, the Cambridge Platonist and John Ray the great naturalist, stresses both the continuity and the creativity of the evolutionary process, and has obvious links with the undeveloped but continuously held Christian doctrine of the Holy Spirit."

[4] *The Creator Spirit*, p. 28.

retains the sense in Paul as in the Old Testament of "a specially given energy".[1]

We now proceed to deal very briefly with another attempt to explain the Spirit in Paul, that which would do so in the light of Hellenistic mysticism. Reitzenstein[2] in particular has interpreted Paul in this way, and although, unlike Bousset,[3] he has not attempted to construct a system of Pauline theology in the light of Hellenistic mysticism it will be well to state his position. To do this clearly we must begin with the widespread desire of the Hellenistic world for what was called γνῶσις. Reitzenstein quotes the Λόγος Τέλειος as an illustration of this: (φωτὶ οὖν σου σωθέντες) χ[αίρομε]ν ὅτι σεαυτὸν ἡμῖν ἔδειξας (ὅλον),... [ἐ]γνωρί-σαμέ[ν (σε), ὦ φῶς] ἁπάσης γνώσεως...οὕτως οὖ[ν (σὴν) χάριν] προσκυ[ν]ήσαντες μ[η]δεμίαν ᾐτήσαμεν [χάριν πλὴν θ[έλησον ἡμᾶς δια[τ]ηρηθῆναι ἐν τῇ σῇ γν[ώ]σ[ει καί...η [πρὸς] τὸ μὴ σφαλῆναι[ι] τοῦ τοιούτου [βίου].[4] This desire for γνῶσις, which arose as a reaction against an arid rationalism, is not to be confused with the desire for an intellectual understanding of the meaning of things: γνῶσις is the vision (θεία) of God which gives an intimate personal insight into ultimate reality; it is an experience intense and highly emotional which delivers man from the tyranny of εἱμαρμένη.[5] It illumines its possessor[6] and gives him σωτηρία, and finally it is that which deifies him—τοῦτό ἐστι τὸ ἀγαθὸν τέλος τοῖς γνῶσιν ἐσχηκόσιν θεωθῆναι.[7] A person who possessed such γνῶσις might be called γνωστικός or πνευματικός, the most common term,[8] and such a person, the πνευματικός, was contrasted with the merely natural man who possessed no γνῶσις, the ψυχικός. This appears in the opening prayer of the Mithras Liturgy which reads: "For to-day I, a mortal born of mortal womb, exalted by Almighty power and incorruptible right hand, with immortal eyes shall behold by immortal

---

[1] Cf. H. Wheeler Robinson, *The Christian Experience of the Holy Spirit*, for a discussion of all that this involves.

[2] Cf. *Die Hellenistischen Mysterienreligionen*, especially pp. 308 f., 333 f.

[3] *Kyrios Christos*. See Rawlinson's treatment of Bousset's theory in *The New Testament Doctrine of the Christ*.

[4] Cf. *Die Hellenistischen Mysterienreligionen*, pp. 286 f., Λόγος Τέλειος, 41 b; also ibid. p. 66. See W. Scott, *Hermetica*, vol. I, p. 376.

[5] Cf. R. Reitzenstein, op. cit. p. 300. *Corp. Herm.* 12. 9, πάντων ἐπικρατεῖ ὁ νοῦς, ἡ τοῦ θεοῦ ψυχή, καὶ εἱμαρμένης καὶ νόμου καὶ τῶν ἄλλων πάντων, καὶ οὐδὲν αὐτῷ ἀδύνατον....

[6] Cf. H. A. A. Kennedy, *St Paul and the Mystery Religions*, p. 108.

[7] *Corp. Herm.* I. 26. Hermetic quotations follow Reitzenstein, but for convenience references are given to W. Scott, *Hermetica*.

[8] Cf. *Die Hellenistischen Mysterienreligionen*, pp. 70 f.

spirit the immortal Aeon and Lord of the crowns of fire, I who have been sanctified by sacred rites, while, for a little, my human natural powers (ἀνθρωπίνης μου ψυχικῆς δυνάμεως) stay behind.... Stand still, mortal nature of man."[1] There is in the πνευματικός a kind of double personality; through the πνεῦμα the πνευματικός is led to the vision of God while his human or 'psychical' nature—ἀνθρωπίνη καὶ ψυχικὴ φύσις—remains bound to the earth; even when his earthly body commits a sin the pneumatic is unconcerned[2] because his essential ἐγώ dwells above the strain and stress of this world; his earthly body may still be subject to the slings and arrows of outrageous fortune,[3] but he himself is divine. In illustration of such cases of double personality we may refer again to the opening of the Mithras Liturgy where the worshipper prays that he may be allowed to ascend up to heaven. Ἱλαθί μοι, πρόνοια καὶ Τύχη, τάδε τὰ πρῶτα παράδοτα μυστήρια, μόνῳ δὲ τέκνῳ ἀθανασίαν, ἀξίῳ μύστῃ τῆς ἡμετέρας δυνάμεως ταύτης, ἣν ὁ μέγας θεὸς Ἥλιος Μίθρας ἐκέλευσέν μοι μεταδοθῆναι ὑπὸ τοῦ ἀρχαγγέλου αὐτοῦ, ὅπως ἐγὼ μόνος αἰητὸς οὐρανὸν βαίνω καὶ κατοπτεύω πάντα.[4] Later on we find instructions given for the journey: ἕλκε ἀπὸ τῶν ἀκτίνων πνεῦμα τρὶς ἀνασπῶν, ὃ δύνασαι, καὶ ὄψει σεαυτὸν ἀνακουφιζόμενον καὶ ὑπερβαίνοντα εἰς ὕψος, ὥστε σε δοκεῖν μέσον τοῦ ἀέρος εἶναι· οὐδενὸς δὲ ἀκούσει οὔτε ἀνθρώπου οὔτε ζῴου ἀλλ' οὐδὲ ὄψει οὐδὲν τῶν ἐπὶ γῆς θνητῶν ἐν ἐκείνῃ τῇ ὥρᾳ πάντα δὲ ὄψει ἀθάνατα.[5] Or again we read in Corpus Hermeticum 10. 6, ἀδύνατον γάρ, ὦ τέκνον, τὴν ψυχὴν ἀποθεωθῆναι ἐν σώματι ἀνθρώπου κειμένην, θεασαμένη τοῦ ἀγαθοῦ (τὸ) κάλλος, (ἀλλὰ χωρίζεσθαι αὐτοῦ και μεταβάλλεσθαι ἐν) τῷ ἀποθεωθῆναι....[6] Reitzenstein also refers to the experiences of the alchemist Zosimos who has a dream and learns in a vision that οἱ γὰρ θέλοντες ἄνθρωποι ἀρετῆς τυχεῖν ὧδε εἰσέρχονται καὶ γίνονται πνεύματα φυγόντες τὸ σῶμα. He asks the man who is leading him καὶ σὺ πνεῦμα εἶ? and receives the answer καὶ πνεῦμα καὶ φύλαξ πνευμάτων.[7]

It is in the light of such pneumatic experiences that Reitzenstein would have us understand Paul. It would, however, take us too far afield to make a minute criticism of the detailed account of the way in which he

---

[1] Translation from H. A. A. Kennedy, St Paul and the Mystery Religions, p. 143. Cf. Eine Mithrasliturgie, p. 4: ἐπεὶ μέλλω κατοπτεύειν σήμερον τοῖς ἀθανάτοις ὄμμασι, θνητὸς γεννηθεὶς ἐκ θνητῆς ὑστέρας βεβελτιωμένος ὑπὸ κράτους μεγαλοδυνάμου καὶ δεξιᾶς χειρὸς ἀφθάρτου ἀθανάτῳ πνεύματι τὸν ἀθάνατον Αἰῶνα καὶ δεσπότην τῶν πυρίνων διαδημάτων ἁγίοις ἁγιασθεὶς ἁγιάσμασιν ἁγίας ὑπεστώσης μου πρὸς ὀλίγον τῆς ἀνθρωπίνης μου ψυχικῆς δυνάμεως....

[2] Cf. Die Hellenistischen Mysterienreligionen, p. 67.

[3] On Τύχη, cf. G. Murray, The Four Stages of Greek Religion, pp. 112–14.

[4] Cf. Eine Mithrasliturgie, p. 2.   [5] Cf. ibid. p. 6.

[6] Cf. Die Hellenistischen Mysterienreligionen, p. 289.

[7] Cf. ibid. pp. 312f.; also pp. 189ff. for another example.

attempts to establish this: a statement of the salient points must suffice.

First, then, Reitzenstein[1] refers to 1 Cor. 1-3. Here Paul emphasizes that his preaching is 'in the Spirit', and that he has received the Spirit of God which can reveal to him the deep things of God—His Wisdom. With this Spirit of God he contrasts the normal or natural spirit of man; this cannot comprehend the things of God and the man who possesses this natural πνεῦμα only is merely ψυχικός, he cannot sit in judgement upon him who possesses the divine πνεῦμα, the πνευματικός, and indeed, "Der ψυχικός ist Mensch schlechthin, der πνευματικός ist überhaupt nicht mehr Mensch".[2] In distinguishing between the spirit in the natural man or the ψυχικός and the Spirit of God in the πνευματικός Reitzenstein holds that Paul is presupposing the usage of the term πνεῦμα found in magical sources where it is used, among other ways, in this twofold sense, e.g. in one papyrus we read ἐπικαλοῦμαί σε τὸν κτίσαντα... πᾶσαν σάρκα καὶ πᾶν πνεῦμα;[3] in another we read of τὸ θεῖον πνεῦμα.[4] Not only so, but the threefold division of men into σαρκικοί, ψυχικοί, πνευματικοί in Paul is said to derive from the 'mystery religions' where already three classes of people were distinguished, namely, the unbelievers, the proselytes and the τέλειοι.[5] Moreover, Paul identifies πνεῦμα with νοῦς—an identification which was only possible because in the Hellenistic mysteries the πνευματικός was also considered to be ἔννους. For example in the Poimandres νοῦς signifies everywhere what is usually denoted by πνεῦμα.[6] In view of all this Reitzenstein claims that all the uses of πνεῦμα in Paul are paralleled in Hellenistic documents.[7]

Let us now examine the above in the same order. First, as to the use of the term πνεῦμα to signify both a quality of man and of God, we have already seen that this twofold usage is easily explicable in terms of the *ruach* of the Old Testament which is used in the same ways.[8] So too Paul's distinction of the σαρκικοί, ψυχικοί and πνευματικοί is best explained in the light of Old Testament anthropology. We have seen that Paul's conceptions of σάρξ and πνεῦμα correspond to those of the Old Testament on *bâsâr* and *ruach* and Wheeler Robinson has also shown how the Pauline ψυχή is parallel to the Old Testament *nephesh* which stands for 'the principle of life'. "The Old Testament usage had evolved

[1] Cf. *Die Hellenistischen Mysterienreligionen*, pp. 333 f.; 76 f.   [2] Ibid. p. 341.
[3] Cf. F. G. Kenyon, *Greek Papyri in the British Museum*, p. 180; *Die Hellenistischen Mysterienreligionen*, pp. 308 f.
[4] Cf. ibid. pp. 309 f.; cf. F. G. Kenyon, op. cit. pp. 102, 114.
[5] Cf. *Die Hellenistischen Mysterienreligionen*, p. 326.
[6] Cf. ibid. p. 338. Reitzenstein quotes κρατὴρ ἢ Μονάς, § 4 (*Corp. Herm.* 4) ὅσοι μὲν οὖν ἐβαπτίσαντο τοῦ νοός, οὗτοι μετέσχον τῆς γνώσεως....
[7] Cf. ibid. p. 312.   [8] See above, p. 186.

a psychological term *ruach*, with higher associations and was tending to confine the originally general term *nephesh* to the lower aspects of consciousness; hence the developed Pauline contrast of the corresponding Greek adjectives,"[1] i.e. πνευματικός and ψυχικός.

Moreover, it must be pointed out that Reitzenstein can only quote one example of the use of ψυχικός, the example we have above quoted; and he only refers to one instance of the use of πνευματικός, also when he cites Wessely, *Zauberpapyri*, where Eros is addressed as "Lord of all spiritual perception (πνευματικῆς αἰσθήσεως) of all hidden things" (πάσης πνευματικῆς αἰσθήσεως κρυφίων πάντων ἄναξ).[2] In the second place we notice that Reitzenstein gives no evidence for his statement that the mystery religions distinguished the three classes that he mentioned:[3] and in the third place, when we turn to the Pauline identification of πνεῦμα with νοῦς, we find that the two passages where this occurs are quotations from the LXX and therefore, according to Kennedy, "cannot form the basis of any general hypothesis".[4] Apart from this, however, it is to be noted that Reitzenstein is mistaken in claiming that νοῦς in the Poimandres signifies the πνεῦμα. The latter is one of the elements, whereas the Νοῦς is God.[5]

Secondly, then, Reitzenstein[6] points out that in 1 Cor. 15 and elsewhere, Paul bases his Gospel, as well as that of the other Apostles, on the fact of the Resurrection. The validity of his κήρυγμα rests upon the reality of his experience of the Risen Lord whom he has seen. His gospel is no merely human affair derived from tradition or evolved from any consultations with other apostles. No! once the light of the Risen Christ, who is Spirit, had broken in upon him he had no need to confer with flesh and blood as to the essentials of his Gospel; these he knew of himself through the Spirit. Such an attitude corresponds to the experience of the Hellenistic mystic.[7] Reitzenstein quotes: ὁ ποιμάνδρης,

[1] Cf. H. Wheeler Robinson, *The Christian Doctrine of Man*, p. 109; see also pp. 16f. for רוח and נפש in Old Testament; also pp. 105f.

[2] *Die Hellenistischen Mysterienreligionen*, p. 311; H. A. A. Kennedy, *St Paul and the Mystery Religions*, p. 143.

[3] Cf. *Die Hellenistischen Mysterienreligionen*, p. 326.

[4] The passages are 1 Cor. 2. 16, Rom. 11. 34; H. A. A. Kennedy, *St Paul and the Mystery Religions*, p. 159.

[5] See *The Bible and the Greeks*, pp. 117f., 123, 125; *Corp. Herm.* 1. 6.

[6] *Die Hellenistischen Mysterienreligionen*, pp. 77f.

[7] Ibid. p. 78: "Wer einmal Gott geschaut hat, muss nach der Anschauung seiner Gemeinden und seiner eigenen, Überzeugung weiterer Tradition nicht bedürfen, sondern aus sich selbst imstande sein, alles zu erkennen wie es von einem solchen Mann ausdrücklich in dem hermetischen Wiedergeburtsmysterium gesagt wird."

ὁ τῆς αὐθεντίας νοῦς, πλέον μοι τῶν ἐγγεγραμμένων οὐ παρέδωκεν εἰδὼς ὅτι ἀπ' ἐμαυτοῦ δυνήσομαι πάντα νοεῖν καὶ ἀκούειν ᾧ βούλομαι καὶ ὁρᾶν τὰ πάντα.[1] It follows that Paul no longer needs to know Jesus after the flesh—κατὰ σάρκα;[2] the historic Jesus is of no significance to him. It is the guidance of the Spirit that matters and Paul can be independent of the words and teaching of Jesus and as a πνευματικός he is undergoing a μεταμόρφωσις from glory to glory since he is not merely human but already subject to πνεῦμα.[3]

Here, however, Reitzenstein has gone far astray. His interpretation in the first place involves a misinterpretation of the phrase κατὰ σάρκα in 2 Cor. 5. 16. That phrase does not mean that the Jesus of history no longer interests Paul; the phrase should be taken with οἴδαμεν. As Rawlinson has written: "For St Paul there is only one Christ—Jesus of Nazareth. What he is repudiating is not a fleshly kind of Christ but a fleshly kind of knowledge. In virtue of the new life which he now lives in Christ Jesus, he no longer forms his judgements, whether about Christ or about anyone else κατὰ σάρκα, but in accordance with what he elsewhere describes as 'the mind of the Spirit' Romans 8. 4 sqq."[4] In addition to this Reitzenstein's view of Paul at this point ignores that conscious dependence on the example and words of Jesus for moral guidance which we have insisted upon in our chapter on Paul as διδάσκαλος; we need not repeat here what we there wrote, except to insist again that there is abundant evidence in the Pauline Epistles that the words and life of Jesus were normative for Paul. We will only notice further that the term which Paul employs in connection with the dictates of Christ is not such as would be suitable in descriptions of the inward promptings of the Spirit. The term is ἐπιταγή[5] which, while it could

---

[1] Corp. Herm. 13. 15.
[2] 2 Cor. 5. 16. Cf. Die Hellenistischen Mysterienreligionen, pp. 78, 373 f.
[3] 2 Cor. 3. 18. Cf. Die Hellenistischen Mysterienreligionen, pp. 357 f.
[4] Cf. The New Testament Doctrine of the Christ, p. 90, n. 5; cf. also F. Büchsel, Der Geist Gottes im Neuen Testament, pp. 275 f. for a convincing insistence upon this. "Aber Christus nach dem Fleisch kennen heisst nicht, Christus geschichtlich kennen" (pp. 278 f.); "...Das Fleisch Jesu und die geschichtliche Wirklichkeit Jesu decken sich nicht" (p. 279). For a concise summary of views on this verse R. H. Strachan, Second Corinthians (M.N.T.C.), pp. 111 f.; but Strachan writes: "to know Christ after the flesh means that the sayings and doings of Jesus of Nazareth however well known to and authoritative for Paul they must have been, possessed a religious and credal value subordinate to the 'revelation' (Gal. 1. 15) of the dying, risen and exalted Jesus, and the instruction given to Paul by the Spirit". In this he seems to over-emphasize the 'Spiritual' aspect in Paul. C. A. A. Scott, Johannes Weiss, J. H. Moulton, Bousset and Lietzmann interpret the verse to imply that Paul had seen Jesus. See Christianity According to St Paul, p. 12.
[5] Cf. 1 Cor. 7. 6, 7. 25; 2 Cor. 8. 8.

be used of the commandments of Christ, would be unsuitable if used of pneumatic revelations. To enter here into a discussion of the relation of the Spirit to Christ in Paul is not practicable, but without deciding whether Paul actually identified the Spirit with Christ or not, we can assert that they are at least brought into the closest possible relation.[1] This meant that in all his pneumatic experience, ecstatic and other, Paul was still governed by his knowledge of the Jesus of history. We may quote the words of Dr Dodd: "it is notorious that the conception of the indwelling Spirit is in Paul hardly separable from the conception of the living Christ. But this does not mean, as has been said, 'a certain depersonalizing of the idea of Christ'. It means that Paul, while accepting the truth 'that Spirit with Spirit can meet', will not recognize as a valid experience of guidance by the Spirit anything which is not continuous with the revelation of God in Jesus Christ, that is to say, with the Church's tradition of His work and teaching."[2] Even the enthusiasm of the Spirit in Paul is brought captive to the obedience of Christ; its jurisdiction was not autonomous.

We come thirdly to those instances of so-called double personality in Paul. First, Reitzenstein finds in the famous words "I am crucified with Christ; nevertheless I live, yet not I but Christ liveth in me", an instance of this; the second instance he finds in 2 Corinthians: "I will come to visions and revelations of the Lord; I knew a man in Christ above fourteen years ago, (whether in the body, I cannot tell; or whether out of the body, I cannot tell: God knoweth) such an one caught up to the third heaven. And I knew such a man (whether in the body or out of the body I cannot tell, God knoweth), How that, he was caught up into

---

[1] Cf. especially 2 Cor. 3. 17, 18: ὁ δὲ κύριος τὸ πνεῦμά ἐστίν· οὗ δὲ τὸ πνεῦμα κυρίου, ἐλευθερία. ἡμεῖς δὲ πάντες, ἀνακεκαλυμμένῳ προσώπῳ τὴν δόξαν κυρίου κατοπτριζό-μενοι, τὴν αὐτὴν εἰκόνα μεταμορφούμεθα ἀπὸ δόξης εἰς δόξαν, καθάπερ ἀπὸ κυρίου πνεύματος. C. H. Dodd, *The Apostolic Teaching and its Developments*, p. 47, favours the view that here the Spirit and Christ are identified; so also R. H. Strachan, *Second Corinthians (M.N.T.C.)*, p. 88; T. Rees, *The Holy Spirit*, pp. 98f.; others reject identification, e.g. E. F. Scott, *The Spirit in the New Testament*, pp. 180f. and the whole section, pp. 177f.; A. E. J. Rawlinson, *The New Testament Doctrine of the Christ*, p. 155, n. who thinks, along with the majority of the Greek Fathers, that Paul means only that in the previous passage the Lord denotes the Spirit; J. Lebreton, *Les Origines du Dogme de la Trinité*, p. 567, n. 2, gives the evidence for the Greek Fathers. C. A. A. Scott, *Christianity According to St Paul*, p. 258, thinks of 'equivalence' not of 'identity'. See for a survey of the views of English scholars, D. R. Griffiths, *Expository Times*, Dec. 1943.

[2] Cf. *History and the Gospel*, p. 56. The words in inverted commas are quoted from Holtzmann, *Neutestamentliche Theologie*, vol. II, p. 88. See also Baron von Hügel, *Eternal Life*, p. 69.

paradise, and heard unspeakable words, which it is not lawful for a man to utter."[1] The similarity of the experience described in this latter passage to that of other 'travellers beyond the bourne' which we have referred to above will need no comment, but let us examine the two passages further. When Paul writes in Gal. 2. 20, that he has been crucified with Christ, we have previously seen that by this he means that he has appropriated to himself the experience of Christ; the outward historical act of the crucifixion has been re-enacted in his own soul. The expression derives from Paul's experience that ἐν Χριστῷ his old life had died, his past ideals, ambitions and pride were all crucified. When therefore Paul goes on to speak of Christ living in him he is not referring to any ecstatic experiences whereby his own individuality is submerged: true, the old ἐγώ, by which he means not his individuality, but, in Lightfoot's phrase, his "natural man, the slave of the old covenant",[2] is dead, but he himself still lives in the flesh and his relation to Christ is determined by an act of personal commitment, by faith, so that his allegiance is now given to a new master.[3] It is not necessary to find there any connection with the kind of double personality that Reitzenstein referred to in Hellenistic circles. As Kennedy puts it: "the relation of the human individual Paul to Jesus the historic person is never lost in a vague and impalpable experience".[4]

When we turn to the other passage, 2 Cor. 12. 2–4, the case is different. Here we are clearly dealing with an authentic ecstatic experience in which St Paul believed that he had been to the third heaven, and indeed was not sure whether or not his material body had journeyed there with him. Moreover, there are various other details in the Epistles that confirm the view that Paul had ecstatic experiences. His conversion was described by him in such terms;[5] he could speak with tongues;[6] he heard God speak to him and so too Christ;[7] his preaching and his works are 'in the Spirit'.[8] Paul's visit to the other world in ecstasy then is no isolated phenomenon in his experience.[9]

---

[1] R. Reitzenstein, *Die Hellenistischen Mysterienreligionen*, pp. 84f., 369; cf. Gal. 2. 20 and 2 Cor. 12. 2–4.

[2] J. B. Lightfoot, *The Epistle to the Galatians*, p. 119.   [3] Ibid. p. 119.

[4] *St Paul and the Mystery Religions*, p. 146. G. S. Duncan, *Galatians* (*M.N.T.C.*), p. 71: "...undoubtedly the main strand in this conception of sharing Christ's crucifixion is the experimental one. It is altogether unnecessary to appeal to the influence or even the analogy of the pagan mystery-cults." For the 'I-thou' relationship in Gal. 2. 20, see also the exposition of H. Lovell Cocks, *By Faith Alone* (1943), pp. 171f.

[5] Cf. Acts 9. 3f. and parallels.   [6] 1 Cor. 14. 6, 18.

[7] 2 Cor. 12. 9; Acts 18. 9, 22. 17 (γενέσθαι με ἐν ἐκστάσει).

[8] 1 Cor. 2. 4; 2 Cor. 12. 11.

[9] Cf. H. Gunkel, *Die Wirkungen des heiligen Geistes*, p. 63.

There are, however, certain things to consider before we agree with Reitzenstein that Paul was a thoroughgoing *pneumatiker* such as we find in Hellenism, despite his ecstatic experiences. First, such experiences as Paul describes were known among the Rabbis of Palestine so that we need not postulate any Hellenistic influence here;[1] and secondly, it is important to emphasize that Paul does not claim that such experiences are of primary significance. His revaluation of the gifts of the Spirit in 1 Cor. 12. 1f., etc., where he clearly places the spectacular phenomena of Spirit-possession in subordination to the supreme gift of love, will be familiar; for Paul the true supernatural is never the supramundane visions of the pneumatic but ἀγάπη.[2] Thus, it is noteworthy that in describing his experiences in 2 Cor. 12, Paul is almost apologetic. He never makes a parade of his strange journey to Paradise, as the pneumatic in Hellenism must have done to some degree, and he never makes any vision he may have had, however helpful to him personally, the basis of any of his teaching.[3] This of course agrees with the view we have already put forward that it was not the guidance of the Spirit unchecked and uninformed that was regulative for Paul.

We turn next to the fourth point. It will be obvious that to deny to Paul any interest in the words of Jesus involves Reitzenstein in an explanation of those passages where Paul actually quotes the words of his Lord, and for our purpose, particularly, in an explanation of the words of Jesus quoted in the account of the institution of the Eucharist.[4] Reitzenstein overcomes the difficulty by claiming that in the latter the words of Jesus were necessary for the cultic practice of the Church. In short, he holds that for Paul Christianity is a mystery centring round the Lord Jesus who had died and risen again. It is in this light that he would explain those passages where Paul speaks of being baptized into Christ's death, etc., and that he would also explain the two sacraments of Baptism and the Eucharist, which he holds cannot be accounted for on any merely Jewish grounds.[5]

The relation of Paul to the mystery religions has already been

---

[1] *b. Ḥag.* 13 *b.* See above.

[2] 1 Cor. 13. 1f., on which see Meyer, *Kommentar zum Neuen Testament*, p. 312: "Die Charismen sind nichts wert ohne Liebe."

[3] Cf. Edwyn Bevan, *Sibyls and Seers*, p. 66. See the whole chapter for a clear estimate of the value of such experiences. It is to be noted that Paul did give a fundamental significance to his experience on the way to Damascus, but not to his ecstatic experiences.

[4] Cf. *Die Hellenistischen Mysterienreligionen*, p. 79. In view of our discussion in the chapter on Paul as διδάσκαλος we need not examine Reitzenstein's statements in detail.

[5] Ibid. p. 81.

discussed. The objections previously suggested to the theory of any dependence on account of the late date of the authorities quoted as evidence for the mystery religions and on other grounds, hold also against Reitzenstein's theory.[1] In addition, however, there arises the question whether the Hermetic literature, the Mithras Liturgy and magical papyri can be used as evidence for the mystery religions at all, as they are by Reitzenstein. The latter seems to assume that there was a kind of recognized Hellenistic mystery theology attached to the various kinds of cults and that this theology can be illustrated from the sources we have named. There seems, however, to be no justification for assuming that the teaching of documents such as the *Corpus Hermeticum* was bound up with cultus at all. Two quotations will make this clear; the first from Rawlinson, who wrote: "It would seem that we ought to recognize as having been, so to speak, in the air, side by side with the idea of salvation by 'mysteries' (in the sense of secret rites and initiations), the alternative idea of salvation by gnosis, that is to say, by revelation."[2] But Reitzenstein, as we have seen, would have us identify or conflate these two modes of salvation. Secondly, Dr Dodd has written: "Passages from the Hermetic writings are often cited, in a rather loose fashion, as evidence for the 'mystery religions'. But it should be clearly understood that we have no reason whatever for supposing that the writers of the Corpus at any rate were devotees of any of these religions in the sense of practising the ritual which was their essential feature."[3] All this has significance for our estimate of Reitzenstein's understanding of Paul as a *pneumatiker* who can be compared with an initiate in a mystery religion, who has died and risen again and received the πνεῦμα from the Lord of his cult. In the first place we have seen that we cannot assume because the Spirit plays an important part in the Mithras Liturgy[4] and in magical texts that the Spirit played an equally important role in the mystery religions. In fact, although we do read of prophets[5] in the latter, they do not appear to have been very significant and the piety

---

[1] See above, pp. 89 f.
[2] A. E. J. Rawlinson, *The New Testament Doctrine of the Christ*, p. 67; also p. 67, n. 1.
[3] *The Bible and the Greeks*, p. 245.
See J. M. Creed, *J.T.S.* (1913–14), vol. xv, pp. 513 f. on the Hermetic Writings, especially pp. 537 f. He quotes Dr W. Kroll and F. Cumont as supporting the criticisms above given of Reitzenstein: Kroll in *Pauly-Wissowa Realencyclopädie* (1912), vol. vIII, pp. 820–1 and Cumont in *Les Religions Orientales*, pp. 132, 340, n. 41.
[4] *Die Hellenistischen Mysterienreligionen*, pp. 169–85; *Eine Mithrasliturgie* (1903). F. Cumont has a low opinion of the Mithras Liturgy as evidence for mysteries: *The Oriental Religions* (E.T.), p. 260. So F. Büchsel, *Der Geist Gottes im Neuen Testament*, p. 101.
[5] F. Büchsel, op. cit. pp. 104–5.

of the mystery religions, so far as we can judge, does not appear to have been of a pneumatic character.[1] Secondly, it is clear again that those documents, e.g. the Mithras Liturgy and the magical texts where the idea of πνεῦμα is prominent, are post-Christian and we must not exclude the possibility that they reveal the influence of Christian pneumatology. While the idea of the Spirit in the Hellenistic world is undoubtedly pre-Christian, it will always be an open question whether the peculiarities of the πνεῦμα as we meet them in Hellenistic sources are untouched by that intensification of Spirit phenomena which came with primitive Christianity.[2] Thirdly, in view of the late date and limited nature of the magical texts, which are chiefly used as sources of evidence, it would be a grave mistake to give too great or too widespread significance to the pneumatic element in Hellenistic religion.[3]

Our examination of the four pivotal points of Reitzenstein's position has shown that his conception of Paul as a pneumatic after the Hellenistic pattern cannot be substantiated; this is so both because the evidence he adduces is not convincing and because the Paul who reveals himself in the Epistles will not fit into the frame made for him by Reitzenstein. Moreover, both in our discussion of Reitzenstein's position and of the alleged Stoic character of the Pauline πνεῦμα, we were compelled time and again to refer to Old Testament and Rabbinic conceptions of the Spirit. Thus the materiality of the Spirit (such as it was) in Paul and the non-cosmic character of its activity we found to correspond to what is taught in Rabbinic sources. In short, our discussion so far seems to point to the latter as the direction in which we should seek help for our understanding of Paul's teaching on the Spirit. To this we now turn.

We begin our attempt to interpret Paul's conception of the Spirit in the light of Rabbinic Judaism by referring to one aspect which sets it wholly apart from what we found in Hellenism, namely, its communal character. In the Hellenistic parallels that Reitzenstein offers to the Pauline idea of the Spirit, the latter is always regarded as being active in the life of individuals as such, the pneumatic always journeys alone. So too, of course, for Paul the Spirit is, or at any rate should be, profoundly the possession of every individual Christian. Thus in the case

---

[1] See F. Büchsel, op. cit. p. 111, and the whole chapter "Πνεῦμα in den Mysterien-kulten, im Zauber und in verwandten Erscheinungen des Hellenismus", pp. 100f.

[2] F. Büchsel, op. cit. p. 109.

[3] In addition it is legitimate to ask how much of the pneumatology of the magical texts is really not Hellenistic at all but derived from a debased Judaism. For the influence of Judaism on magical literature see W. L. Knox, *St Paul and the Church of the Gentiles*, note ii, pp. 208ff.

of Paul himself, the Apostle is convinced that he personally has been delivered from "the law of sin and death" by the Spirit;[1] his own preaching is in the power of the Spirit[2] and he can claim for himself that he has the Spirit of God.[3] The Epistles make it clear that it was the Spirit that led individual Christians to accept the message of the Gospel,[4] and that called them to personal sanctification.[5] The Spirit is poured forth into the heart of every Christian,[6] who is to regard himself as personally joined to Christ as is a wife to her husband;[7] his body has become a temple of the Holy Spirit.[8] Further, the Spirit differentiates between different Christians conferring upon them differing χαρίσματα.[9]

To isolate this individual nature of its activity, however, is to distort Paul's whole conception of the Spirit. It is not this which is most characteristic of his thought.[10] More noticeable is his emphasis on the Spirit as the source of Christian fellowship and unity.[11] At the risk of labouring the obvious, we point out that for Paul the Spirit is not only the life of the new man but of the New Israel, the Church. The latter is the Body of Christ and is animated by the Spirit;[12] the solidarity of all Christians with one another and with their Lord, through the one Spirit, is such that Christians as a Body no less than as individuals constitute a temple of the Holy Spirit.[13] It is wholly consonant with this that gifts of the Spirit are bestowed not for individual self-gratification but for the upbuilding or edification of the whole society of Christians.[14] Under the guidance of the Spirit all are for each and each is for all and the society is truly co-operative. Pneumatic phenomena of whatever kind are to subserve the common weal. This is, of course, what we should expect since, as we saw, the supreme expression of the Spirit is ἀγάπη,[15] and this by its very nature was constitutive not only of a community of the like but of the unlike; the Church, the fellowship created by the Spirit, knew neither Jew nor Greek,[16] bond nor free, male nor female, and membership in it involved a sharing of material no less than of spiritual

---

[1] Rom. 8. 2. [2] I Cor. 2. 4; I Thess. 1. 5. [3] I Cor. 7. 40.
[4] I Thess. 1. 6. [5] I Thess. 5. 3f.
[6] Gal. 4. 6; Rom. 5. 5; Eph. 3. 16f., 4. 30.
[7] I Cor. 6. 17. [8] I Cor. 12. 20f.
[9] I Cor. 12–14; cf. H. B. Swete, *The Holy Spirit in the New Testament*, pp. 185–6.
[10] Contrast E. F. Scott, *The Spirit in the New Testament*, pp. 124f.
[11] Eph. 2. 18f., 4. 3f., ἐν σῶμα καὶ ἐν πνεῦμα: I Cor. 12. 40f.
[12] I Cor. 12. 13.
[13] I Cor. 3. 16: οὐκ οἴδατε ὅτι ναὸς θεοῦ ἐστε, καὶ τὸ πνεῦμα τοῦ θεοῦ ἐν ὑμῖν οἰκεῖ;
[14] I Cor. 12. 14f.
[15] I Cor. 13. [16] Gal. 3. 28; Rom. 10. 12.

benefits.[1] In the light of this we may conclude that intensely personal as was the experience of the Spirit in Paul, he never regarded it as something peculiar to himself. The pronouns used by him in contexts dealing with the Spirit are almost always in the plural number, and it was ever more natural for the Apostle to speak of 'our' than of 'my' receiving the Spirit.[2] In short, the Spirit for Paul implies community: to be possessed of the Spirit was, in the words of Anderson Scott, to know "life of a new quality, life which awakened deeper levels of personality and related men to one another and to God in a bond which neither death nor life could break".[3]

This communal nature of the Spirit in Paul, which we have been discussing, could not but have received ample recognition, so conspicuous is it. It has been suggested, however, that we are to account for Paul's emphasis upon it chiefly because of his missionary experience. E. F. Scott has written:

As time went on, and the Christians were more and more cut off from the world around them, they were thrown back on their own fellowship and all action was judged by the standard of 'brotherly love'. Paul especially, by the nature of his work, was compelled to think in terms of the Church. His converts consisted of little groups which maintained themselves with difficulty in the midst of great alien populations. Only as they held together supporting one another in their new faith and practice, could the mission be kept alive.[4]

We must indeed agree with Scott, and we have previously noted this, that much of the theology of the Apostle is determined by his ethical and pastoral concern, and doubtless his emphasis on "the unity of the Spirit" owes something to this source. Nevertheless, it is misleading to regard this emphasis as primarily the outcome of missionary expediency. This is to make the Church account for his conception of the Spirit; it is to make the Spirit ancillary to the Church and not constitutive of it; it is to reduce the 'unity of the Spirit', as it were, to the level of the motto of a Co-operative Society. No interpretation of Paul's doctrine of the Spirit can be accepted which does not regard it as integral to the whole of his thought and not merely an aspect of his missionary strategy or pastoral technique.

We are on much safer ground, therefore, when we seek to relate Paul's teaching on the communal aspect of the Spirit to Old Testament

[1] Cf. Acts 2. 44–6, 4. 32–7; 2 Cor. 8. 7f.; Rom. 12. 13.

[2] Cf. the catena of passages in H. B. Swete, *The Holy Spirit in the New Testament*, pp. 169–71, 199–201, 224f.; e.g. to the question τίς γὰρ ἔγνω νοῦν κυρίου Paul answers ἡμεῖς δὲ νοῦν Χριστοῦ ἔχομεν.

[3] *The Fellowship of the Spirit*, p. 46.

[4] *The Spirit in the New Testament*, p. 124.

and Judaistic antecedents. Following Gunkel,[1] Newton Flew,[2] while fully recognizing that the Spirit is given to the community, has suggested that "this fact differentiates the New Testament belief from that of Israel and later Judaism, where the Spirit is only bestowed on certain special individuals, and where there is a hope of a general outpouring in the last days". But such a statement of the case does not do justice either to the Old Testament or to Judaism, and that the communal aspect of the Spirit in Paul is true to the thought of both the latter cannot be doubted. Thus I. F. Wood claimed that although in the Old Testament the Spirit is conferred upon individuals, the individuals are so endowed not for their own sake but for the sake of the nation. "The personal experiences of the private Hebrew", he writes, "are not ascribed to the Spirit of God but only those which bear directly or indirectly for good or ill upon the progress of national matters."[3] For example, the Spirit falls upon Samson, as upon other 'judges', merely that he may deliver 'Israel'. Wood overstates the issue and we need not postulate a national factor in the bestowal of the Spirit on such a figure as Samson in all the cases where this occurs,[4] but nevertheless even in its earliest forms it is clear that the Spirit in the Old Testament has a national reference. It is possession of the Spirit that equips the national leaders, the judges[5] and kings,[6] for their functions. Moreover, prophecy, itself the activity of the Spirit *par excellence*, is directed always not to the individual but to the nation as a whole; the appeal of the prophets is invariably to the 'House of Israel'.[7] It is in the prophet Ezekiel, however, that the communal aspect of the Spirit's activity appears most clearly. In his famous vision of the Valley of Dry Bones, the Spirit appears as the organizing principle of national unity. Despite his emphasis on the responsibility of the individual, Ezekiel desires the spiritual renewal of the individual Israelite only that the nation as a whole may be reintegrated.

Then he said unto me, Son of Man, these bones are the whole house of Israel: behold, they say, Our bones are dried, and our hope is lost: we are cut off for our parts. Therefore prophesy and say unto them, Thus saith the Lord God; Behold, O my people, I will open your graves, and cause you to come up out of your graves, and bring you into the land of Israel. And ye shall know that I am the Lord, when I have opened your graves, O my people, and

---

[1] *Die Wirkungen des heiligen Geistes*, p. 29.   [2] *Jesus and His Church*, pp. 150f.

[3] *The Spirit of God in Biblical Literature*, pp. 9f.

[4] E.g. Judges 14. 6 can hardly have any 'national' significance in itself (i.e. the killing of the young lion). See also 1 Sam. 19. 20f.

[5] E.g. Judges 15. 14 (Samson), 6. 34 (Gideon).

[6] 1 Sam. 10. 6 (Saul); 2 Sam. 6. 12f.

[7] Amos 3. 1, 4. 1, 5. 1; Hos. 4. 1, 5. 1, 9. 1, 14. 1; Isa. 1. 4; Jer. 1. 4; Ezek. 3. 1, etc.

brought you up out of your graves, and shall put my Spirit in you and ye shall live: and I shall place you in your own land: then shall ye know that I the Lord have spoken it, and performed it, saith the Lord.[1]

Again in Deutero-Isaiah this strictly communal activity of the Spirit appears. In Isa. 44. 3, we read:

> I will pour out my Spirit upon thy seed
> And my blessing upon thine offspring.

Skinner comments on the whole passage that "once more the gloom of the present is lighted up by the promise of a brilliant future: the Divine Spirit shall be poured out on Israel and strangers shall esteem it an honour to attach their selves to the people of Yahweh".[2] In addition to these passages, moreover, there is the well-known passage in Joel. 2. 28-9: "And it shall come to pass afterward, that I will pour out my Spirit upon all flesh; and your sons and your daughters shall prophesy, your old men shall dream dreams, your young men shall see visions. And also upon the servants and upon the handmaids in those days will I pour out my Spirit." Whether we interpret these words to mean that in the latter days prophetic inspiration, dreams, visions and prophecies will become democratized or, as did the Early Church, that in addition to such phenomena there would also be a spiritual change of heart among the people, the communal reference is unmistakable.[3] Finally, before we close this survey it is noteworthy that in descriptions of the ideal ruler of the latter days, the Messianic King, the Spirit is made to rest upon him as the source of all his regal virtues.[4] So too, the very different figure of the Servant in Deutero-Isaiah which is almost certainly communal is also endowed with the Spirit to fulfil his work.[5]

We have now clearly shown that there is traceable in the Old Testament teaching on the Spirit a persistently communal reference. Our

---

[1] Ezek. 37. 11-14; cf. F. Büchsel, *Der Geist Gottes im Neuen Testament*, p. 23: "In der Hoffnung des Ezekiels steht im Vordergrunde das Volk."

[2] J. Skinner, *Cambridge Bible for Schools and Colleges, Isa. XL-XLVI*, p. 45.

[3] See the discussion in R. N. Flew, *Jesus and His Church*, p. 145. Flew writes: "Against the view that Pentecost would be the fulfilment of the devout wish of the founder of Hebrew prophecy: 'Would God that all the Lord's people were prophets, that the Lord would put his spirit upon them' (Num. 11. 29) must be set the fact that a new order of prophets speedily developed in the Christian Church, distinct from Apostles, and distinct from those who possessed the gift of speaking with tongues. It is not likely that the author of Acts, who knew well what a Christian prophet was, would have intended us to infer that all those who received the Holy Spirit became prophets in this sense." Edwyn Bevan interprets it as merely referring to prophetic inspiration, not to a spiritual change of heart. *Symbolism and Belief*, p. 173.

[4] Isa. 11. 2f.; 59. 21.   [5] Isa. 42. 1.

next task is to inquire whether this aspect of the Spirit's activity prevailed in Judaism. It will already have been noticed that in the later books of the Old Testament this aspect although present is not very manifest; indeed, the quotations that we have given above exhaust the relevant references.[1] So, too, when we pass to the Apocrypha and Pseudepigrapha we can only trace the 'national' significance of the Spirit in that it will be plenteously bestowed upon the Messianic ruler of the nation. E.g. Enoch 62. 2:

> And the Lord of Spirits seated him (the Elect One) on the throne of His glory
> And the Spirit of righteousness was poured out upon him.

And Psalms of Solomon 17. 37f.:

> For God will make him mighty by means of His holy spirit, etc.

E. F. Scott has written in reference to these passages: "they show that Isaiah's conception of the Messiah as endowed with the whole power of the Spirit had now established itself as an integral element in the apocalyptic hope".[2] The paucity of references to any communal significance of the Spirit which we have found in the Apocrypha and Pseudepigrapha, however, is consonant with the fact that in the latter there is revealed a decline in the belief in the present activity of the Spirit and a tendency to relegate this activity both to the golden ages of the past and to the glorious age to come.[3] This was to become increasingly true of Judaism and shall claim our attention in the next section. For our present purpose, however, we need not stay with the Apocrypha and Pseudepigrapha but pass on directly to the communal aspect of the Spirit in Rabbinic Judaism.

We shall discover later that our Rabbinic sources present us with a grave contradiction in their teaching on the Spirit, but without staying to consider this now, we begin by pointing out certain passages in those sources which assume the essentially social nature of any experience of the Spirit. However saintly an individual might be, the Rabbis deemed that only if he lived in an equally 'worthy' environment could he receive the Holy Spirit; his milieu had to be such as to make possible his reception of the latter. Thus God had spoken to Moses, and the same was

---

[1] It is doubtful if we are to take Zech. 12. 10 ("And I will pour upon the house of David, and upon the inhabitants of Jerusalem, the spirit of...supplications", etc.) as meaning anything more than a change of heart in reference to a certain historical incident: it is not a hope of a general spiritual renewal.

[2] *The Spirit in the New Testament*, p. 51.

[3] Cf. T. Rees, *The Holy Spirit*, p. 23; F. Büchsel, *Der Geist Gottes im Neuen Testament*, pp. 56, 63 and the whole chapter.

also true of all the other prophets, only because of the merit of Israel; he was, in short, a 'worthy' man in a 'worthy' community. We read: "Not only with Moses alone did (God) speak because of the merit of Israel but all the prophets were spoken to by God as a result of the merit of Israel...." And again: "Under no circumstances did prophets prophesy but because of the merit of Israel."[1] Closely associated with this is the way in which the diminution of prophecy or the cessation of the Spirit, which we shall discuss later, was traced to the increasing sinfulness of Israel. It is no accident that it was in that post-exilic period when 'Israel' became increasingly conscious of the exceeding sinfulness of sin that the Spirit took wings and fled.[2] In *Sifre Deuteronomy* R. Eliezer (A.D. 80–120), when he came to the Scriptural verse: "And because of these abominations the Lord thy God is driving them out before thee" (Deut. 18. 12), used to remark: "What harm we cause ourselves! Since he who clings to impurities a spirit of impurity rests on him...", and he goes on to ask: "Why is the Holy Spirit so little in evidence in Israel?" and answers with the quotation: "But your iniquities have separated between you and your God" (Isa. 59. 2).[3] A sinful nation is no longer a suitable environment for the Holy Spirit. The same attitude helps us to understand those passages where the geographic incidence of the Holy Spirit is discussed. According to some Rabbis, since Palestine alone was sanctified, outside Palestine it was only on the seas that the Holy Spirit could be experienced. This view was held by some Rabbis who cited in support of it Ezek. 1. 3. According to other Rabbis, although God revealed himself everywhere it was only in Palestine that the Holy Spirit remained constantly.[4] Further, the activity of the Holy Spirit was still more closely limited to Jerusalem "because all the tribal patriarchs were born on foreign soil while Benjamin was born in the land of Israel"[5] (and Jerusalem was in Benjamite territory). "In order to understand the issue involved in this difference of opinion," writes Parzen, "we must bear in mind that Palestine is the Holy Land. Therefore it is the proper place for Revelation. Foreign lands are from the Rabbinic viewpoint 'impure'; consequently not suitable for Divine Revelation...."[6] It will be seen in the light of

---

[1] *Mekilta Pisha* 1.   [2] See above, pp. 217f.
[3] *Sifre Deut.* on 18. 12, § 173.
[4] Cf. *Targum Jonathan* on Ezek. 1. 3.
[5] *Mekilta Baḥodesh*, 4.
[6] Cf. H. Parzen, "The Ruaḥ Hakodesh in Tannaitic Literature", *J.Q.R.* (1929–30), vol. xx, p. 53; A. Büchler, *Studies in Sin and Atonement*, p. 297, quotes an anonymous statement from *Mekilta* on Exod. 12. 1: "God spoke to Moses in Egypt, outside the city: and why did he not speak to him in the city? Because it was full of abominations

this that the geographical limitation of the activity of the Holy Spirit is bound up with its communal character, it comes to a community and therefore to the abode of that community.

We have still, however, to mention the most illuminating passages. These are statements made about certain outstanding Rabbis that although they were personally worthy of the Holy Spirit they were nevertheless debarred from its enjoyments because of their sinful age. Thus: "When the sages entered the house of Guryo at Jericho, they heard the Bath Qol (the Heavenly Voice) announce 'One man is present here who is worthy of the *ruach ha-qôdesh* but his generation is not worthy of it'...."[1] "At another time the Sages were in session at Jabneh and they heard the Bath Qol announce 'There is one man present in this conclave who is worthy of the *ruach ha-qôdesh* but his generation is unworthy of it'."[1] Elsewhere it is stated of these two Rabbis, Hillel the Elder and Samuel the Small that they had received the Holy Spirit, but we are probably to see in statements to this effect legendary expansions of the view above referred to according to which the Rabbis are said to have been denied the Spirit although personally worthy of it.[2] It is fair to claim in the light of all that we have written above that for Rabbinic Judaism no individual in isolation, like the magician of the Hellenistic world, could receive the Spirit: it was necessary for him in order to do so to live in a particular milieu.[3]

The significance of this for our understanding of Paul will be clear. His insistence on the essentially social nature of the Spirit's activity falls into line with Rabbinic thought, where the communal reference of the Spirit has been demonstrated. It is doubtful if Paul would ever have claimed that he himself had the Spirit unless he had been convinced that he belonged to a peculiar community which was also experiencing the Spirit. That he did believe himself to belong to such a community

and idols. Though God spoke to some of the prophets outside Palestine, He spoke only in a clean place near water, as in Dan. 8. 2: 'And I was by the stream Ulai'; and in 10. 4: 'And I was by the side of the great river which is Tigris'; and Ezek. 1. 3: 'The word of the Lord came expressly unto Ezekiel the priest, the son of Buzi, in the land of the Chaldaeans by the river Chebar." See *Mekilta Pisḥa* 1.

[1] *Tosefta Soṭah* 13. 3, pp. 318-19; *J. Soṭah* 9. 24b,; b. Soṭah 48b; b. Sanh. 11a; cf. Str.-B. vol. I, p. 129.

[2] Cf. F. Büchsel, *Der Geist Gottes im Neuen Testament*, p. 124.

[3] In *Pesikta R.* 160a, we read: "When the Temple was rebuilt, the Shekinah did not rest upon it. For God had said, 'If *all* the Israelites return [from Babylon] the Shekinah shall rest upon it, but if not, they shall be served only with the Heavenly Voice.'" (R.A. p. 16.) H. Loewe comments on this: "This interesting passage implies that there can be no full revelation when Israel is divided..."—this confirms what we have written above: community is essential to the activity of the Holy Spirit.

we have seen, the New Israel had been brought to birth, the milieu suitable for the Spirit had arrived. As in other things so in his emphasis on the communal nature of the Spirit Paul, then, was a Hebrew of the Hebrews. Without seeking to explain this social or communal doctrine of the Spirit in Judaism, we will here merely recall that aspect of Hebrew thought, so strangely modern, which has been emphasized by Pedersen,[1] where man finds his true being only in community and where, therefore, the Spirit of God, which is essentially life-giving, must be creative of community.

We now proceed to another aspect of Rabbinic teaching on the Holy Spirit which is relevant to our understanding of Paul. We have seen that for the Rabbis the experience of the Holy Spirit demanded membership in a certain kind of community. But not only so. Our quotations showed that another way of expressing the same fact was that the Holy Spirit could only be experienced in a fitting 'age'. If we may borrow phrases from Carlyle, for the Rabbis the 'hero' needed his 'hour' no less than the 'hour' its 'hero'. This brings us to that contradiction in Rabbinic teaching on the Holy Spirit to which we have previously referred.

On the one hand we find the fact often stated that the Holy Spirit had ceased altogether from 'Israel'. In this connection there were three views. With the third of these, namely, that which traced the cessation of the Holy Spirit to the destruction of the Second Temple in A.D. 70, we need not stay.[2] As for the other two views, the first connected the cessation of the Holy Spirit with the destruction of the First Temple. We read:

Five things which existed in the first temple were lacking in the second. These were: (*a*) Fire from on high. (*b*) Anointing oil. (*c*) The Ark. (*d*) The Holy Spirit. (*e*) Urim and Thummim.[3]

These words, with slight variations, occur often. In the *Mekilta*, Simeon b. Azzai (A.D. 120–40) puts into the mouth of Baruch, Jeremiah's disciple: "Why should I be different from other disciples of the prophets? Joshua served Moses, and the holy spirit rested on him; Elisha served Elijah, and the holy spirit rested on him."[4] This complaint fits in with

---

[1] *Israel*, I–II, p. 263: "Loneliness, the lack of community, the Old Testament only knows as something unnatural."

[2] See A. Marmorstein in *Archiv für Religionswissenschaft* (1930), vol. 28: "Der heilige Geist in der Rabbinischen Legende", pp. 287f.

[3] Cf. *b. Yoma* 21 *b*; *Numbers Rabba* 15. 10; see also *Song of Songs Rabba* 8.

[4] *Mekilta Pisḥa* 1.

the view that with the destruction of the First Temple the Holy Spirit ceased. According to the second view it was claimed that the Holy Spirit had ceased with the death of the last prophets. This of course accords with that very close connection, which is found in Rabbinic thought, some would even call it an identification, between prophecy and the Holy Spirit,[1] a connection which made it difficult if not impossible to conceive of the active presence of the Holy Spirit without some form of prophecy. Of the belief in the cessation of prophecy there is evidence in the Old Testament where we read: "We see not our signs: there is no more any prophet: neither is there among us any that knoweth how long."[2] The same attitude is also expressed in 1 Macc. 4. 46, 9. 27, 14. 41, and also in Josephus.[3] For the Rabbinic view we quote: "When the last prophets Haggai, Zechariah and Malachi died the holy spirit ceased out of Israel; but nevertheless it was granted them to hear (communications from God) by means of a Bath Qol."[4]

On the other hand, however, attention has been drawn to passages in the Rabbinic sources which suggest that the Holy Spirit was still active in 'Israel'. The relevant passages are:

1. R. Hiyya (A.D. 200–20) said: "If a man learns the Law without the intention of fulfilling that Law, it were better for him had he never been born." And R. Johanan said: "If a man learns the Law without the intention of fulfilling the Law, it were better for him had he never seen the light." R. Aha (c. A.D. 300) said: "He who learns in order to do is worthy to receive the Holy Spirit."[5]

2. Words by R. Yudan (c. A.D. 350): "Whosoever openly makes known the words of Torah, he is worthy of the Holy Spirit."[6]

3. R. Nehemiah (A.D. 140–65) says: "Whosoever taketh upon himself one precept in faith is worthy that the Holy Spirit should rest upon him."[7]

4. The celebrated dictum of R. Phinehas b. Jair (A.D. 165–200): R. Phinehas b. Jair said: "The Torah leads to watchfulness, watchfulness to strictness, strictness to sinlessness, sinlessness to self-control, self-control to purity, purity to piety, piety to humility, humility to sinfearing, sinfearing to holiness, holiness to the Holy Spirit, and this last to the resurrection of the dead."[8]

---

[1] J. Abelson, *The Immanence of God in Rabbinical Literature*, pp. 228 f.; I. Abrahams, *Studies in Pharisaism and the Gospels* (2nd ser.), pp. 120 ff.; Moore, vol. 1, p. 237. Also Str.-B. vol. 1, p. 128.

[2] Ps. 74. 9.   [3] *Antiquities*, 13. 1. 1.

[4] *b. Yoma* 9 b; *b. Soṭah* 48 b; *b. Sanh.* 11 a; *M. Soṭah* 9. 12; *Tosefta Soṭah* 13. 2, p. 318.

[5] *Lev. Rabba* 35. 7.

[6] *Song of Songs Rabba*, 1. 8.   [7] *Mekilta Beshallaḥ* 7.

[8] *Mishnah Soṭah* 9. 15; *b. 'Abodah Zarah* 20 b. The Hebrew is as follows:

מיכן היה רבי פנחס בן יאיר זרידות טביאה לידי נקיות נקיות טביאה לידי טהרה טהרה
טביאה לידי קדושה קדושה טביאה לידי ענוה ענוה טביאה לידי יראת חטא יראת חטא
טביא לידי חסידות חסידות טביאה לידי רוח הקדש רוח הקדש טביא לידי תחיית המתים :

On the basis of such passages as these, as well as on other grounds which we shall discuss later, Abelson and Marmorstein have claimed that the Holy Spirit was regarded by the Rabbis as actively present in Israel. "The Rabbis", writes Abelson, "did not relegate the possibilities of the Holy Spirit to any one particular section of time. Although strongly particularist in many respects, there were others in which they were emphatically universalist. This is one of them. The possession of the Holy Spirit was not for them limited to the past, neither was it the exclusive property of their own time. It was a gift from God for all time, which everyone could attain to provided he used the right means."[1] Similarly, Marmorstein has denied any contradiction between πνεῦμα and νόμος. A succinct phrase sums up his position: "Gesetzes Frommig-keit ist die Vorstufe der Geistes Frommigkeit."[2]

It must, however, be pointed out that two of the Rabbis cited belong to the fourth century A.D.; and there has been much discussion as to the significance of R. Phinehas b. Jair's words. It has been suggested that they are Essene[3] and therefore not such as could strictly be quoted as evidence for Rabbinical Judaism. Büchler[4] rejects their Essene character; but, even if we follow Büchler, it is noticeable that this passage and all the others quoted make no claim to the actual possession of the Holy Spirit, but only to the possibility of this, among those faithful to the demands of Torah.

In addition, however, to the actual passages enumerated above, attempts have been made to show that despite the doctrine of the cessa-tion of the Spirit, the latter was often experienced in life. First, reference may be made to the work of Israel Abrahams.[5] In his view prophecy in the pre-Christian era had become degenerate; it had become merely oracular and, therefore, "the cessation of prophecy was gain not loss". Moreover the true prophetic spirit, despite the decay of the prophetic office, persisted. Abrahams quotes from the Prayer of Azariah[6] which, although it bears witness to the cessation of prophecy,[7] "is in the true

[1] The Immanence of God in Rabbinical Literature, p. 268.
[2] Archiv für Religionswissenschaft, pp. 286f.
[3] See Bacher, Die Agada der Tannaiten, vol. II, p. 497.
[4] A. Büchler, Types of Palestinian Piety, pp. 42f.: "The individual terms used by R. Phinehas b. Yair in their technical meanings were...familiar already to earlier Rabbis...the originality of R. Phinehas lay in the systematic gradation of the various moral qualities to lead up the pious, by a natural progress in self-education, to the highest perfection, the possession of the Holy Spirit" (p. 62). See also J.E. vol. v, p. 225.
[5] Studies in Pharisaism and the Gospels (2nd ser.), pp. 120f. See the remarkable passage in Zech. 13. 2ff.
[6] Cf. R. H. Charles, Ap. and Ps. vol. I.
[7] Prayer of Azariah, verse 15.

prophetic spirit". He goes on to claim that "the devotees of the Law had absorbed some features of prophecy at i.J best....Not everyone who opens 'Thus saith the Lord' is a prophet, just as not everyone lacks prophetic gift because he opens 'It is written'." "Not only so but it was explicitly maintained that the Pharisees were the successors of the prophets." R. Abdimi of Haifa (A.D. 279–320) said: "From the day whereon the Temple was laid waste, Prophecy was taken from the prophets and given to the Sages."[1] We may mention also along with this the possibility that the ordination of the Rabbis to their office implied the transmission therewith of the gift of the Holy Spirit even as Joshua and the Seventy Elders had received this from Moses; so too it has been pointed out that the High Priests of the First Temple had the Holy Spirit and that possibly this was true of the High Priests of our period.[2]

Secondly, Marmorstein pointed out that many of the Rabbis were pneumatic in the sense that they could exercise the gift of prediction. He refers to the High Priest John, John Hyrkanos (140–135 B.C.),[3] R. Johanan b. Zakkai (A.D. 10–80),[4] R. Eliezer b. Hyrkanos (A.D. 80–120)[5] as such. There were others of whom it was said that they saw in the Holy Spirit, e.g. R. Gamaliel II (A.D. 80–120),[6] R. Akiba (A.D. 120–40),[7] R. Simeon b. Yohai (A.D. 140–65).[8] In addition certain of the Rabbis, chief among whom was Rabbi Haninah b. Dosa (A.D. 10–80), possessed gifts of healing.[9]

Thirdly, Marmorstein has referred to the belief in the Shekinah as evidence that Rabbinic Judaism knew the active presence of the Holy Spirit.[10] He insists on the close parallelism between the two conceptions of the Holy Spirit and the Shekinah. Both expressions were used as metonymies for God; the sins that drove away the Holy Spirit also drove away the Shekinah; the virtues that qualify one for the Holy Spirit also qualify for the Shekinah. A religion that cherished the conception of

---

[1] b. Baba Bathra 12a; I. Abrahams, op. cit. pp. 126f. See also F. Büchsel, Der Geist Gottes im Neuen Testament, pp. 125f. and H. Parzen, J.Q.R. (1929–30), vol. xx on the connection between the Holy Spirit and Wisdom.

[2] F. Büchsel, Der Geist Gottes im Neuen Testament, p. 126, and especially n. 2.

[3] Tosefta Soṭah 13. 5. The בת קול foretells a victory of Jewish forces at Antioch; cf. Josephus, Antiquities, 13. 4.

[4] b. Giṭṭin 56a. [5] b. Sanh. 68a.

[6] Tos. Pes. 1. 27; b. 'Erub. 64b.

[7] Pesikta 176b.

[8] Pesikta 90a. See also J. Soṭah 1. 16d for Rabbi Meir.

[9] A. Marmorstein, Archiv für Religionswissenschaft, pp. 295f.

[10] Ibid. pp. 292f.; also A. Marmorstein, Doctrine of God, pp. 99f.; M. J. Lagrange, Le Judaïsme avant Jésus-Christ, pp. 446f.; J. Abelson, The Immanence of God in Rabbinical Literature, pp. 77f.; Moore, vol. I, pp. 434ff. and see Index.

the Shekinah cannot, so it is implied, have been devoid of the experience
of the Holy Spirit.

Finally, both in the life of the schools and in the experience of individuals the mind of God was still being revealed to Israel by the *bath qôl*,[1]
which therefore fulfilled the function of the Holy Spirit. Marmorstein
refers to two cases where the *bath qôl* gave decisions on questions of
Halakah. Thus according to R. Abba (A.D. 290) and R. Samuel (A.D. 254)
the schools of Hillel and Shammai had been at strife for two years: "The
one said The Halakah is according to our meaning: the other said
The Halakah is according to our meaning. Then there came forth the
bath qôl which said 'These words like those are the words of the Living
God but the true Halakah is after the school of Hillel'."[2] Again,
Marmorstein refers to the Halakah dispute between R. Eliezer b.
Hyrkanos (A.D. 80–120) and R. Joshua b. Hananiah (A.D. 80–120) in
which a *bath qôl* came and declared that R. Eliezer had the right standpoint.[3] Such utterances of the *bath qôl*, which Marmorstein compares
with the voices heard by Jesus at His baptism and by Stephen at his
martyrdom, were due, so he holds, to the activity of the Holy Spirit.[4]

We have now to ask how this contradiction, that between those
statements recording the cessation of the Holy Spirit and the evidence
adduced for its continuance within Rabbinic Judaism, is to be resolved.
We have already seen that the explicit passages appealed to by Marmorstein and Abelson are not very cogent, and we now suggest that only
by a *tour de force* can the four points mentioned immediately above be
taken to prove that the experience of the Holy Spirit was frequent in
Rabbinic times. Let us take the four points in order.

Although the fourth-century passage quoted from R. Abdimi of Haifa
is too late to be used as evidence for the first century, we need not cavil
at Abrahams' insistence that many of the Rabbis were worthy heirs of
the prophets. However, it is not the 'spirituality' of Rabbinic Judaism
that is in question but the 'form' in which it expressed itself, and we
cannot agree with Abrahams that this is not important. It surely is
significant that even the 'prophetic spirits' of Rabbinic Judaism did not
declare 'Thus saith the Lord' but appealed to a past revelation, 'It is
written'. It is no accident that the power, originality and driving force
of the Rabbis, to which Abrahams rightly refers, did not lead to immediate deliverances of their own personal certainties, but were canalized
within the framework of tradition. It is precarious also to assume that

[1] For בת קול, see Str.-B. vol. i, pp. 125f.
[2] b. 'Erub. 13b.   [3] b. Baba Metzia 59b.
[4] Cf. A. Marmorstein, *Archiv für Religionswissenschaft*, pp. 296f.; contrast Edwyn
Bevan, *Sibyls and Seers*, pp. 106–8.

Rabbinic ordination by the laying on of hands in the first century was meant to signify the transmission of the Holy Spirit, and the evidence is equally uncertain as to the acquisition of the Holy Spirit through the office of the High Priesthood.[1]

When we turn to those Rabbis, who because they could predict the future and perform miracles of healing, are regarded as pneumatics and as evidence for the activity of the Holy Spirit, certain considerations are noteworthy. It is doubtful if mere prediction such as is ascribed to R. Zadok, R. Johanan b. Zakkai, etc., would be taken to imply any profound prophetic gifts. We know that Rabbinic Judaism came to frown upon those who 'calculated the times' and prediction would scarcely differ from such calculation.[2] Miracles again were so common that the Rabbis were not impressed by them.[3] We also know that the ecstatic 'spiritual' experiences which some Rabbis claimed were looked upon as more dangerous than welcome;[4] they were in any case accorded a secondary place much as his visit to Paradise was by Paul. In addition we have already seen that the Rabbis, despite the occurrence of experiences such as we are discussing, do not reveal any awareness that they lived in an 'Age' of the Spirit; their deep consciousness of the sinfulness of their age was too marked for this. Passages have already been quoted referring to their 'unworthy' generation, and R. Akiba himself who 'saw by the Holy Spirit' gives expression to the same sense of sin.[5]

There remains to consider two things, the belief in the Shekinah and the *bath qôl* as evidence for the activity of the Holy Spirit. Since to enter into details would prolong our discussion inordinately, the broadest statement of our case must suffice. First, then, the Shekinah. "All worship", writes Moore, "demands a *praesens numen* and however men

[1] F. Büchsel, *Der Geist Gottes im Neuen Testament*, pp. 126f. For Rabbinic ordination see *J.E.* vol. IX, p. 428. Dr Daube has argued in *J.T.S.* (1938), vol. XXXIX, pp. 48f. that Rabbinic ordination meant more in the first century than later; but further than this we cannot go.

[2] Cf. I. Abrahams, *Studies in Pharisaism and the Gospels* (2nd ser.), p. 120; *b. Sanh.* 97b.

[3] Cf. *R.A.* pp. 340, 690, n. 97; cf. C. G. Montefiore, *Rabbinic Literature and Gospel Teachings*, pp. 205f. and pp. 247f. where *b. Sanh.* 90a is quoted: "If a prophet tells you to transgress the words of the Law, listen to him; but if he tells you to commit idolatry, do not listen to him, even if he made the sun stand still in the sky."

[4] *b. Ḥag.* 14b.

[5] Cf. F. Büchsel, *Der Geist Gottes im Neuen Testament*, p. 129: "Auf der andern Seite kommt das intensive Sündenbewusstsein der Rabbinen im Betracht." For Akiba, cf. *b. Sanh.* 65b; also *Sifre Deut.* on 18. 12, § 173. Again Büchsel writes: "Der Satz: Bemühung um die Tora macht des Geistbesitzes würdig, galt nur in abstracto. In concreto hiess es: wehe über uns: unsere Sünden machen uns unwürdig."

may entertain the idea of the omnipresence of God, they find it difficult to realize his specific presence in the particular place where they gather for religious service without some aid to faith or imagination."[1] This is the origin and meaning of the conception of the Shekinah. The Shekinah stands for the Presence of God Himself and is often a metonymy, as we saw, for God.[2] The term Holy Spirit is often interchanged with that of *Shekinah*, but although this is so the terms are not therefore identical.[3] The Holy Spirit has connotations of prophecy and power which are not suggested by the term *Shekinah*, which denoted the abiding presence of God among His people but did not indicate that character of invasive energy which always underlies the conception of the Holy Spirit. Secondly, when we turn to the *bath qôl* it seems that Marmorstein over-emphasized its significance. The sources make it abundantly clear that no deliverance of a *bath qôl* could supersede the authority of the Torah. In questions of Halakah the *bath qôl* was not to be accepted. Thus, indeed, one of the illustrations referred to by Marmorstein[4] himself shows that an utterance of a *bath qôl* was not regarded as binding. Although the *bath qôl* had pronounced against him, R. Joshua b. Ḥananiah (A.D. 80–120), in his dispute with R. Eliezer b. Hyrkanos, refused to accept its judgement. "In this case", Marmorstein merely remarks, "Rationalism was victorious over the *bath qôl*",[5] but had the *bath qôl* the significance of the Holy Spirit, such a refusal to acquiesce in its decision as R. Joshua's would have been unthinkable. It will be well to quote the lengthy passage in full:[6]

On a certain occasion R. Eliezer used all possible arguments to substantiate his opinion, but the Rabbis did not accept it. He said: 'If I am right, may this carob tree move a hundred yards from its place.' It did so. They said: 'From a tree no proof can be brought.' Then he said: 'May the canal prove it.' The water of the canal flowed backwards. They said: 'Water cannot prove anything.' Then he said: 'May the walls of this House of Study prove it.' Then the walls of the house bent inwards as if they were about to fall. R. Joshua rebuked the walls and said to them: 'If the learned dispute about the Halakah, what has that to do with you?' So, to honour R. Joshua, the walls did not fall down, but to honour R. Eliezer, they did not become quite straight again. Then R. Eliezer said: 'If I am right, let the heavens prove it.' Then a heavenly voice said: 'What have you against R. Eliezer? The Halakah is always with him.' Then R. Joshua got up and said: 'It is not in heaven' [Deut. 30. 12]. What did he mean by this? R. Jeremiah said: 'The Law was

[1] Moore, vol. I, p. 435. See also M. J. Lagrange, *Le Judaïsme avant Jésus-Christ*, pp. 446 ff.   [2] *b. Sukk.* 5a; *b. Sanh.* 39a; *b. Soṭ.* 17a.
[3] Moore, vol. I, p. 437.   [4] *Archiv für Religionswissenschaft*, p. 298.
[5] Ibid. p. 298: "In diesem Falle siegte der Rationalismus gegen die Tochterstimme."
[6] *b. Baba Metzia* 59b.

given us from Sinai. We pay no attention to a heavenly voice. For already from Sinai the Law said, "By a majority you are to decide"' (Exod. 23. 2).

After this necessarily brief examination we are in a position to draw certain conclusions: the evidence, both direct and indirect, of belief in the frequent activity of the Holy Spirit in Rabbinic Judaism is unconvincing. The weight of the evidence suggests that that activity was regarded as a past phenomenon in Israel's history, a phenomenon which had indeed given to Israel its Torah, its prophets and the whole of its Scriptures, but which had ceased when the prophetic office ended. This, however, does not mean that we are to regard Rabbinic Judaism as an arid desert scorched to barrenness by its belief in a transcendent God, who no longer revealed Himself to His people. On the contrary, the phenomena, which we have discussed above, are eloquent of the awareness of the near presence of God, and we need not deny that there may have been individuals who were conscious of the Holy Spirit as active in their lives. Nevertheless, as the whole method of Rabbinic teaching makes abundantly clear, it was the Torah given on Mount Sinai in a past age that was regulative for all life. However much the fact may have been exaggerated by Christian scholars, Rabbinic piety was essentially nomistic, and even Abrahams is constrained to admit that "in a sense it is true that the growing devotion to the Law was one of the causes of the cessation of Prophecy".[1] "The Rabbis...", so writes Cohen, "would have denied that they were originators of Jewish thought. All they would have admitted was they were excavators in the inexhaustible mine of the divine Revelation contained in the Scriptures and brought to light treasures that lay hidden beneath the surface."[2]

We may now pass on to an essential point for the understanding of Paul. If our preceding remarks are correct, we may assume that Paul was reared within a Judaism which, to use very moderate language, tended to relegate the activity of the Holy Spirit to the past. We now point out, however, that it was also a Judaism which cherished a strong expectation of the coming of the Holy Spirit in the future.[3] The quota-

---

[1] *Studies in Pharisaism and the Gospels* (2nd ser.), p. 120.

[2] *Everyman's Talmud*, p. 132. See T. Herford, *Pharisaism*, chapters 1 and 2; J. Bonsirven, *Le Judaïsme Palestinien*, vol. 1, pp. 248 f.

[3] Cf. A. Marmorstein, *Archiv für Religionswissenschaft*. He refers to an unknown teacher. "In dieser Welt gibt es weder einen Propheten noch einen heiligen Geist (cf. Ps. 74. 9) sogar die Schekina ist wegen unserer Sünden von uns gewichen (Jes. 59. 2) aber in der zukünftigen Welt wird ihnen eine neue Offenbarung zuteil werden" (cf. *Agadath Bereshith* (ed. Buber), §47, p. 68). "*Die letzte Vorstellung gehört zum eisernen Fond der Agada,*" p. 288 (our italics).

tions which we cited above from Ezekiel, Deutero-Isaiah and Joel showed how vital was this expectation in the Old Testament and it is traceable in the Psalms of Solomon, and we cannot doubt that the abundant Messianic speculation of Rabbinic Judaism utilized this expectation. In this connection we are probably justified in assuming that many Rabbinic references to the Holy Spirit have suffered conscious suppression because of the pneumatic emphasis of Christianity. We know that some Rabbis took a sarcastic attitude towards those who claimed possession of the Spirit[1] and such an attitude would doubtless lead to the exclusion of many pneumatic references from our Rabbinic sources. Bousset's[2] claim however that Joel had little influence on subsequent thought has been answered by Abrahams[3] who quotes *Numbers Rabba*:

The Holy One, blessed be He, said: In this world individuals were given prophetic power, but in the world to come all Israel will be made prophets, as it is said, (Joel 2. 28): And it shall come to pass afterward, that I will pour out my spirit upon all flesh; and your sons and your daughters shall prophesy, your young men shall see visions; and also upon the servants and the handmaids in those days will I pour my spirit. Thus did R. Tanḥuma son of R. Abba expound.[4]

We cannot doubt that the Rabbinic Judaism of the first century would have regarded the Messianic Age or the Age to Come as the Era of the Spirit.

Returning now to Paul, we have insisted that he is best understood as a Pharisee who believed that the Messiah had come. This being so, he would naturally expect certain accompaniments of this fact, and in this he was not disappointed. In becoming a Christian Paul entered a new community and in the pneumatic phenomena that marked the life of that community, in its enthusiasm and power he saw proof of the advent of the Age to Come. The active presence of the Spirit in power was a mark of the *Endzeit*, and, in the words of Gunkel, "the legitimization of the Gospel".[5] Indeed, we may go further. It is doubtful if the mere acceptance of the Messianic claims of Jesus in itself would have made much difference to Paul. We know that Akiba, for example, accepted the Messianic claims of Bar Kokba and that this did not seem to have

---

[1] *b. Baba Bathra* 12a.
[2] *Die Religion des Judenthums* (1903, 1st ed.), p. 229.
[3] *Studies in Pharisaism and the Gospels* (2nd ser.), p. 127.
[4] *Numbers Rabba* 15. 25.
[5] Of Jesus, H. Gunkel writes: "Er ist nicht Kind seiner Zeit. Zur Zeit Jesu und in den ersten beiden Jahrzeiten der apostolischen Zeit waren soweit wir wissen Geisteswirkungen im Judentum nur höchst sporadisch aufzuweisen.... Das auftreten des Geistes ist ein Zeichen der Zeit." See *Die Wirkungen des heiligen Geistes*, pp. 56–60.

any very extraordinary significance for him;[1] and it is clear that in time the title ὁ Χριστός was used by Paul, without any strictly Messianic connotation, merely as a proper name for Jesus.[2] What lent reality to the Messianic claims of Jesus was the presence of the Spirit, the advent of the power of the Age to Come, and Dr Dodd has made us familiar with the way in which this fits in with the life and thought of the early Church in his work on 'Realized Eschatology'.[3] For our purpose here, however, we merely emphasize that the awareness of a Supernatural Power at work in the community, which issued in ecstatic experiences and in a fruitful moral enthusiasm, phenomena which cannot be paralleled in the contemporary Judaism, at any rate to anything like the same degree, would be taken by Paul as evidence that he had arrived at the Age when it was bliss to be alive and very heaven to be young. We are far removed from the individualistic, esoteric pneumatology of the Hellenistic world and in the full stream of that Rabbinic thought which had looked forward to a community and an Age of the Spirit. For Paul, with the advent of Christ, this had arrived.

The Pauline doctrine of the Spirit, then, is only fully comprehensible in the light of Rabbinic expectations of the Age to Come as an Age of the Spirit and of the community of the Spirit. But we have now to face a difficulty: what was meant by an Age of the Spirit? It is to be remarked again that as in other respects so in its treatment of the Spirit Paul's mind reverted to the thought of Creation, to the origin of life. Christ is the Second Adam, who has become life-giving Spirit, and He is contrasted with the first Adam of whom we read in Genesis that "God breathed into his nostrils the breath of life, and man became a living soul".[4] The Spirit is essentially creative, life-giving, and it is a familiar fact that for Paul the whole of the Christian life in its ethical no less than in its 'ecstatic' aspects is the expression of the activity of the Holy Spirit. Love, joy, peace, righteousness, and 'every victory won' in the moral sphere are regarded by Paul as the fruit of the Spirit.[5] So trenchantly does Paul insist upon the Spirit as the source of Christian morality that it has been claimed, by Gunkel in particular,[6] that we find in the Pauline

---

[1] We have no details of Akiba's thought on the Spirit. Is this due to the suppression of such references in antagonism to Christianity, or did Akiba accept Bar Kokba as Messiah and yet develop no doctrine of the Spirit?

[2] A. E. J. Rawlinson, *The New Testament Doctrine of the Christ*, p. 74.

[3] *The Apostolic Preaching and its Developments*, pp. 133 ff.

[4] Cf. Gen. 2. 7; 1 Cor. 15. 45. Note that Paul goes back to Gen. 2 and not to Gen. 1.

[5] Gal. 5. 22f.

[6] *Die Wirkungen des heiligen Geistes*, pp. 72f. See T. Rees, *The Holy Spirit*, p. 79. A. M. Hunter accepts this view also, *Paul and His Predecessors*, p. 121. Contrast R. N. Flew, *Jesus and His Church*, p. 149, and references there given.

teaching what amounts to a transformation of the idea of the Spirit found in the early Church, where the Spirit is merely a wonder-working power, mysterious and non-ethical: it is customary to express this by saying that Paul ethicized the Spirit. In a somewhat similar fashion Lagrange[1] has insisted that when Paul made the Spirit the source of the ethical life in Christians and its sustainer he reversed what is found in Rabbinic Judaism where the Holy Spirit, so he claims, is never the source of the good life but always its reward. Many of those passages, which we quoted above, would seem to make reception of the Spirit dependent upon the 'worthiness' of the recipient, and Lagrange especially quotes the words of R. Phinehas b. Jair which we again reproduce:

R. Phinehas b. Jair said: "The Torah leads to watchfulness, watchfulness to strictness, strictness to sinlessnesss, sinlessness to self-control, self-control to purity, purity to piety, piety to humility, humility to sinfearing, sinfearing to holiness, holiness to the Holy Spirit, and this last to the resurrection of the dead."[2]

On these Lagrange comments: "The Holy Spirit should therefore be at the summit of this scale of virtues, acquired by an effort of perseverance in accordance with the Pharisaic methods." Later he writes: "It must be repeated: The Holy Spirit is not a principle of action but a recompense." He also points out that "The Holy Spirit is not even that in man which supplies the impulse to prayer".[3] Clearly if we are to follow Gunkel and Lagrange Paul's 'ethicized' conception of the Holy Spirit is to be sharply distinguished from those ideas of the Holy Spirit found both in the Early Church and in Rabbinic Judaism: it is a new departure in the history of the Spirit.

Such an approach to Paul's doctrine, however, is untenable. Gunkel's view that, within the Church, it was Paul who first ethicized the Spirit we need not refute here. This has been done effectively elsewhere. In this connection we need merely endorse the words of Newton Flew: "It is unjust to the evidence to declare that Paul ethicized the idea of the Spirit as though that idea had been non-ethical before. We do not minimize the spiritual and intellectual greatness of Paul, if we insist that he was not the first to discern what the Holy Spirit is and does."[4] Lagrange's position requires greater attention. We have already referred

[1] Le Judaïsme avant Jésus-Christ, p. 443.
[2] M. Soṭah 9. 15; b. ʿAbodah Zarah 20b.
[3] Lagrange, op. cit. p. 444; cf. Str.-B. vol. III, p. 243.
[4] Jesus and His Church, p. 144; cf. F. Büchsel, Der Geist Gottes im Neuen Testament, p. 252: "Aber dass erst Paulus religiöse und sittliche Wirkungen vom Geist abgeleitet habe, ist irrig."

to the dubiety of the use of R. Phinehas b. Jair's words as a source for
first-century Rabbinic Judaism on account of its Essene affinities, and,
moreover, the Hebrew does not obviously suggest the idea of reward
in that particular passage.[1] Nevertheless, the conception that loyalty to
the Torah, "the estimation of and obedience to the Torah, the development
and paraphrase of the contents of the Torah, the practical achievement
and the theoretical interpretation of its tenets and ideals",[2] made one
worthy of the Holy Spirit is well attested as we saw above: but this
surely must not be taken to mean that for the Rabbis the Holy Spirit itself
was not conducive of morality. There are indeed a few specific sayings,[3]
which present the Holy Spirit as the source of good works, the most
pertinent being, "All that the righteous do they do in the Holy Spirit";[4]
but this is of a very late date, belonging to the thirteenth century, and
therefore quite unconvincing for our purpose. We have already referred
to a passage from *Sifre Deuteronomy* where Rabbi Eliezer contrasted the
Holy Spirit with the spirit of impurity. Our case, however, does not
rest on such isolated sayings but on that character which the Spirit had
already acquired in the Old Testament. Already in the latter the Spirit
had been ethicized; it was the Spirit that inspired the prophets who
discerned between the precious and the vile: it was the Spirit that would
create in the revived Israel of Ezekiel's vision a new heart: it was the
Spirit that would inspire the ruler of Messianic times with counsel and
wisdom and righteousness.[5] It is unthinkable that when the Rabbis
described the Age to Come as an era of the Spirit they would not think
of the Spirit as bearing ethical fruit. We know that above all else the
Holy Spirit was for the Rabbis the inspirer of 'Scriptures', but this in
itself implied 'the ethicization of the Spirit' because it was through these
same Scriptures that Israel had come to know all ethical demands.[6]
Again we must insist that our Rabbinic sources would be much richer

[1] מביאה 'cause to come' has no suggestion of reward in a phrase like רוח הקדש מביא
לידי תחיית המתים
[2] A. Marmorstein, *The Doctrine of Merits in old Rabbinical Literature*, p. 177.
[3] Cf. M. J. Lagrange, *Le Judaïsme avant Jésus-Christ*, p. 444.
[4] *Yalkut on Gen.* 49. Lagrange dates this in the thirteenth century. But see Appendix C.
[5] Cf. F. Büchsel, *Der Geist Gottes im Neuen Testament*, p. 251.
[6] The mere fact that 'Israel' had the 'Torah' meant in some sense indeed that it
was never devoid of the Holy Spirit. F. Büchsel, op. cit. p. 130, writes: "Solange man
die Tora und die Propheten, die vom Geist eingegebene Schrift, besass, war man nicht
ohne Einwirkung des Geistes." See Moore, vol. I, pp. 235 f.: "The notion of inspired
scriptures grew naturally out of the nature of prophecy" (p. 238). Thus Emil Brunner
is justified in saying: "The giving of the Law on Mount Sinai is never...
abstract νόμος...for even the Law is a gracious revelation", in *Offenbarung und
Vernunft* (E.T.), p. 87.

in pneumatic references were it not for the dominance of the pneumatic element in Christianity. In any case it is probably right to contrast Rabbinic Judaism and Pauline Christianity not so much in that the one made the Spirit the reward for good works while the other made it the source of good works, but rather in that the one can only have had a faint awareness of the activity of the Spirit while the other was dominated by the conviction that the Age of the Spirit had come. The difference lay in the degree to which the Holy Spirit was felt to be experienced, not in the ethical or non-ethical nature of the Holy Spirit that was being experienced. At this point we may profitably refer to Büchsel's illuminating treatment of the significance of Paul's teaching on the Spirit in which he argues that that significance is to be found not in the so-called ethicization of the Spirit by Paul in itself, but in the emphasis which Paul places on all the Christian life as 'being in the Spirit'. It is the fact that for Paul Christianity is essentially 'pneumatic' (that he interprets Christianity through the category of Spirit) that makes it inevitable that he should also give a greater significance to the ethical aspect of the pneumatic life. We may quote Büchsel's own words: "Man verkleinert die Bedeutung des Paulus für den Geistgedanken, wenn man urteilt, Paulus habe den Geistgedanken versittlicht, er hat mehr getan, er hat den Geist zum beherrschenden Faktor der christlichen Frömmigkeit gemacht und deshalb, um den sittlichen Charakter der Frömmigkeit festzuhalten, die Heiligkeit des Geistes im einer ganz neuen Weise betonen müssen. Das zweite ist nur ein Folge des ersten und weiter nichts."[1] We need not, therefore, postulate that the idea of the Spirit as the source of the good life, which is so marked in the Pauline Epistles, was alien either to the early Church or to Rabbinic Judaism: for the latter the Age of the Spirit (as for Paul) would certainly be an age of moral dynamic. Nevertheless, one thing remains to be said in this connection. While it is true that it was not Paul who ethicized the Spirit as we have maintained, on the other hand it is clear that he did bring order into a very confused apprehension of the activity of the Spirit, which seems to have prevailed in the thought of the primitive Church. We cannot enlarge upon this subject here, but evidently the situation that confronted Paul at Corinth, for example, was that the glossolaly and ecstasy and other marks of enthusiasm in the life of the Church were given a status equal to that of the moral as expressions of the Spirit; and we cannot doubt that it was Paul who isolated the moral aspect of the activity of the Spirit and brought order into the con-fusion of popular Christian thought; it was he who introduced the idea

---

[1] F. Büchsel, *Der Geist Gottes im Neuen Testament*, p. 446.

that ἀγάπη was a more excellent way. In this again, so we believe, we are to trace the Rabbinic sobriety of the Apostle.[1]

Another aspect of Lagrange's discussion of the Holy Spirit leads us on naturally to our final section which will perhaps help us to understand the essential meaning of Paul's doctrine of the Spirit. Lagrange[2] refers to the fact that whereas in Paul the Holy Spirit is the result of Faith in Christ, in Rabbinic Judaism it is the reward of works.[3] That too much can be made of this contrast, however, is clear. Rabbinic Judaism, on the one hand, knew of a merit not only of the Torah but of Faith[4] (e.g. R. Eleazer of Modiim (c. A.D. 120) said that there is no need to provide for to-morrow, to gather wealth; have faith, and God will not forsake you)[5] and as Lagrange is constrained to point out there are passages connecting faith and the Holy Spirit.[6] On the other hand, Paul sometimes speaks of the gifts of the Spirit as things which come through striving, i.e. they are a reward. We read that we are to "set our heart on the higher talents".[7] A Christian may "advance to a higher gift by due exercise of his original endowments":[8] and again "a man who speaks with a tongue is to pray that he may gain the gift of interpreting".[9] There is an ἄσκησις in Pauline Christianity no less than in Rabbinic Judaism.[10] In the light of this, even if we could accurately characterize Rabbinic Judaism as entirely a religion of works we must deprecate that approach to our problem which exaggerates the antithesis between Pauline Christianity as a religion of Faith and the Spirit and Rabbinic Judaism as a religion of obedience and the Torah, and which has elevated the doctrine of Justification by Faith to the primary place in Paul's thought. In some contexts justification is merely one metaphor

[1] See 1 Cor. 12. 31. For a discussion of details see that of K. Lake in *Beginnings*, vol. v, pp. 111 ff. which clearly brings out the confusion in the early Church on this subject.

[2] *Le Judaïsme avant Jésus-Christ*, p. 443.

[3] Gal. 3. 2: "This only would I learn of you, Received ye the Spirit by the works of the Law or by the hearing of Faith?" Gal. 3. 14. For the connection of Spirit with Baptism in Paul, see H. G. Marsh, *The Origin and Significance of the New Testament Baptism*, pp. 136f. On the conception of Reward among the Rabbis see A. Marmorstein, *The Doctrine of Merits*, pp. 3, 4.

[4] A. Marmorstein, op. cit. p. 175. See especially J. Bonsirven, *Le Judaïsme Palestinien*, vol. II, p. 48. Str.-B. vol. III, pp. 186f.

[5] *Mekilta Vayassa'* 3; b. *Sotah* 48b; *Exod. R.* 25. 4. See C. G. Montefiore, *Rabbinical Literature and Gospel Teachings*, p. 201 and Appendix I, p. 377, by H. Loewe.

[6] *Mekilta Beshallah* 7; *Lev. Rabba* 35. 7; *Yalkut* on Exod. 14. 31.

[7] Cf. 1 Cor. 12. 31.

[8] Cf. J. Moffatt, *First Corinthians* (M.N.T.C.), p. 192.

[9] 1 Cor. 14. 1 f.

[10] See the remarks in F. Büchsel, *Der Geist Gottes im Neuen Testament*, p. 443.

among many others employed by Paul to describe his deliverance through Christ, and we are not justified in petrifying a metaphor into a dogma.[1] Moreover, in those contexts where the idea of Justification by Faith is central, we find that this is so only because of certain polemical necessities. It is only in those Epistles, namely, Galatians and Romans, where Paul is consciously presenting the claims of his Gospel over against those of Judaism that Justification by Faith is emphasized. Since Christ had replaced the Torah as the centre of his religious life, Paul in his controversy with those who insisted on the centrality of the old Torah and the necessity of obedience to it for all, had to find scriptural support for his position, the only kind of support that would carry conviction to his opponents. He did this by appeal to two passages from Gen. 15. 6[2] and Hab. 2. 14,[3] on the basis of which he could argue that faith rather than obedience was, according to Scripture itself, the basis of salvation. How little, however, Paul intended that Faith should be opposed to obedience will be clear when we recall his work as ethical διδάσκαλος and, in particular, how he had ascribed to Christ the significance of a New Torah to whose obedience he had been called. Not only so, even in regard to the old Torah we have seen that Paul practised obedience to it and urged other Jewish Christians to do likewise. Such an attitude, if the primary significance of Paul's thought is to be seen in his insistence on Justification by Faith over against the works of the Law, is inconceivable; it is only understandable when the doctrine of Justification by Faith is regarded not as the essential pivot of his thought but as a convenient polemic.[4] In addition to all this a doctrine such as Justification by Faith, which has always to be hedged about so as not to lead to antinomianism, a plague that Paul dreaded,[5] and which leads, as Schweitzer has rightly insisted, to an ethical cul-de-sac,[6] cannot have been the dominant factor in the thought of one who could never have separated religion and life.

It will, of course, be understood that when we relegate the doctrine of Justification by Faith to the periphery and not to the centre of Paul's thought, we do not thereby belittle its profound truth or its significance for Christian theology; we merely assign it to that proper place where it can be viewed in true perspective in its relation to the Pauline teaching as a whole. It is a simplification and even a falsification of the complexity of Paul's thought to pin down Justification by Faith as its quintessence,

---

[1] E.g. 1 Cor. 1. 30, 6. 11.   [2] Cf. Gal. 3. 6.
[3] Cf. Rom. 1. 17; Gal. 3. 11.
[4] Cf. W. Wrede, *Paul* (E.T.), pp. 122f.; A. Schweitzer, *The Mysticism of Paul the Apostle*, pp. 205f.
[5] Cf. above, chapter 6.   [6] *The Mysticism of Paul the Apostle*, p. 225.

and our work will have made it clear that the centre of that thought is to be found not in Paul's attack on the old Torah but in his awareness that with the coming of Christ the Age to Come had become present fact the proof of which was the advent of the Spirit; it lies in those conceptions of standing under the judgement and mercy of a New Torah, Christ, of dying and rising with that same Christ, of undergoing a New Exodus in Him and of so being incorporated into a New Israel, the community of the Spirit.[1]

Now it will be seen that in our attempt to understand Paul's thought we have had recourse to two conceptions that are usually set in opposition. We have insisted that to the totality of the teaching, life, death and Resurrection of Jesus, Paul had come to ascribe the significance of a New Torah. But we have also insisted that the advent of Christ meant for him the advent of the Spirit, and we have seen that for Paul the Risen Christ was closely associated if not identified with the Spirit. In short, Paul found in Christ both Torah and Spirit. If our interpretation be correct, there is found in Paul not only a 'Christifying' of the Spirit but also a 'Christifying'[2] of the Torah; Spirit and Torah for Paul are coincident as it were in Christ. This requires amplification.

We have already submitted evidence that the Age to Come which Paul believed to have arrived was regarded in Rabbinic thought as an Age of the Spirit. In a previous chapter, however, we saw that it would also be an age when the Torah would come into its own.[3] This twofold nature of the Age to Come, as the fulfilment of the expectation of an invasion of the Spirit and of a perfect conformity to the Torah can be traced back to the Old Testament. It will be remembered that whereas Ezekiel[4] had looked forward to the Age to Come as a time when the Spirit should reunite 'Israel' and renew its life, Jeremiah had looked forward to that age as the period when a New Covenant would be established between 'Israel' and Yahweh:

Behold, the days come, saith the Lord, that I will make a new covenant with the house of Israel, and with the house of Judah; Not according to the covenant

---

[1] That we are to find in those conceptions the essence of Paulinism rather than in the doctrine of Justification by Faith receives confirmation from a fact pointed out by Schweitzer. Referring to Paul's earliest treatment of Justification by Faith in Galatians, Schweitzer holds that "in order to carry through the conception required by his Scriptural argument Paul has recourse to the mystical doctrine of the being in Christ: *it is only in the Epistle to the Romans that Paul attempts to give to the doctrine of Justification by Faith a significance independent of the idea of being-in-Christ and therefore in the Spirit*". (Schweitzer, op. cit. pp. 209 f.) (our italics).

[2] Cf. C. A. A. Scott, *Christianity According to St Paul*, p. 144.

[3] See above, pp. 71 ff.   [4] Ezek. 37.

that I made with their fathers, in the day that I took them by the hand to bring them out of the land of Egypt; which my covenant they brake, although I was an husband unto them, saith the Lord: But this shall be the covenant that I will make with the house of Israel; After those days, saith the Lord, I will put my law in their inward parts, and write it in their hearts; and will be their God, and they shall be my people. And they shall teach no more every man his neighbour, and every man his brother, saying, Know the Lord: for they shall all know me, from the least of them unto the greatest of them, saith the Lord: for I will forgive their iniquity, and I will remember their sin no more.[1]

It is perhaps illegitimate to assume that when Jeremiah speaks of the inauguration of a New Covenant he also implies the promulgation of a New Torah,[2] but as we showed before there are not wanting passages in our Rabbinic sources that present the Messiah as the bearer of a New Torah.[3] Nevertheless, the Rabbis generally interpreted the passage in Jeremiah in reference to the old Torah; it meant that in this world only a few study the Law, one can know the Law only imperfectly or one learns it from fallible teachers or one learns and forgets, whereas in the Messianic world all know the Law perfectly, learning from God Himself, never forgetting. But whether Jeremiah's words be understood to imply a New Torah or merely a perfect conformity to the old Torah, the Age to Come would mark the triumph of obedience to the Law, it would be a time when the rebelliousness of the people of 'Israel' would cease. This was, however, in no wise incompatible with Ezekiel's vision of the Age to Come as that of the Spirit, because where the Spirit is poured forth there is fulfilled the hope of Jeremiah, that all would know God, every man, woman and child, that all would be prophets so that the exhortations of individual prophets, such as those of the 'ôlâm ha-zeh who, of course, spoke by the Spirit, would be unnecessary. Moreover, in the very chapter where Ezekiel looks to the coming of the life-giving Spirit he also speaks, like Jeremiah, of a New Covenant: "Moreover I will make a covenant[4] of peace with them, it shall be an everlasting covenant with them...." Our point is that for the Rabbis the Age to Come would be a period when Spirit and Law would be coincident and not opposed.

Let us return to Paul. He was convinced that he was living in the Age of the Spirit. Following his Lord, however, he had also described this Age as being marked by the New Covenant whose minister he

[1] Jer. 31. 31–4.
[2] See the discussion in J. Skinner, *Prophecy and Religion*, pp. 331 f.
[3] See above; also cf. I. Abrahams, *Studies in Pharisaism and the Gospels* (2nd ser.), pp. 125 f., especially p. 126, n.
[4] Ezek. 37. 26.

himself has become. To be a Christian for Paul, we wrote above, was to die and rise with Christ, to undergo a New Exodus, to stand at the foot of a New Sinai, and thereby to enter a New Covenant. What was the nature of this Covenant? Jeremiah, with an eye that had kept watch over countless failures to keep the Old Covenant, had envisaged and yearned for a New Covenant the essential characteristic of which was its 'inwardness'. "I will put my Law in their inward parts and write it in their hearts."[1] This mark of 'inwardness' in the New Covenant, however, does not seem to have been very influential in Rabbinic Judaism. We do, indeed, read of the Law being in the heart,[2] but the idea is not prominent; and we saw that in interpretations of Jer. 31 no emphasis is laid on this. We believe that it is at this point that Paul goes beyond anything that can be found in Rabbinic Judaism although, nevertheless, he is all the time drawing upon concepts derived from the latter. In the famous passage in 2 Corinthians where Paul is contrasting the Christian dispensation of the New Covenant with that of the Old, he claims that he himself has written Christ in the hearts of Christians, just as Moses had written his Law on tablets of stone. We read:

> Am I again beginning to commend myself? Do I need like some people to be commended by written certificates either to you or from you? Why you are my certificates yourselves, written on my heart, recognized and read by all men; you make it obvious that you are a letter of Christ which I have been employed to inscribe, written not with ink but with the Spirit of the living-God, not on tables of stone but on tablets of the human heart.[3] [Moffatt's translation.]

The thought in this passage suddenly changes from the idea of a letter of commendation to that of the inward spiritual nature of Paul's work. He is contrasting in the verses following the above the work of Moses and his own work as a Minister of Christ. He claims that he had been the means of planting a New Torah, so we may understand his words, in the hearts of Christians. Paul can speak in this way because for him the Torah has become 'Christified', as we suggested above; this further meant that it was Spirit because in Paul's thought Christ was almost identified with the Spirit. If we cannot go so far as to say that Christ,

[1] For the centrality of 'inwardness' in Jeremiah's conception cf. J. Skinner, *Prophecy and Religion*, p. 329.
[2] E.g. "The evil yetzer has no power over against the Law, and he who has the Law in his heart, over him the yetzer has no power." Anonymous: Midrash on Ps. 119. 10. See *R.A.* p. 125; cf. *Sifre Deut.* on 6. 6, §33. See also A. Büchler, *Studies in Sin and Atonement*, pp. 358 f.; 4 Ezra 9. 31: "For behold, I sow my Law in you, and it shall bring forth fruit in you and ye shall be glorified in it for ever." Cf. *Ap. and Ps.* vol. II, p. 602, n. 31.   [3] 2 Cor. 3. 1–3.

the New Torah, is Spirit and the Spirit is Torah we can at least say that by the Spirit Christ, who was the New Torah, could dwell in the hearts of Christians.[1] It is in the light of this thought that we are probably to understand his references to Christ being in him and living in him, the inwardness of the New Covenant of Jeremiah's hope is achieved for Paul through the indwelling Christ, the New Torah 'written in the heart'. The Law within him is Christ in him; the indwelling Christ has replaced the old Torah written on tablets of stone and has become a Torah written within. All this means that for Paul the true conditions of the Messianic Age when Spirit and Torah would coincide were established. To use Farmer's phrases, the absolute demands of the New Torah were, through the Spirit, an infinite succour also. In virtue of His twofold nature as Torah and Spirit Christ was for Paul both the goal and the means towards that goal. The obedience of the Christian man is loyalty to the promptings of the Spirit, but since this Spirit derives His character from a person, and is rooted in the words, life, death and resurrection of Christ, it is also for Paul a kind of Torah. We must not look for scientific precision in his use of terms, but Spirit and Torah are inextricable in his thought. So he can speak of the Law of the Spirit and of the obedience of the Spirit, and the Christian life becomes for him both *Gabe* and *Aufgabe*. Paul would have agreed with those words of Alice Meynell's when she says of Christ:

> Thou art the Way.
> Hadst Thou been nothing but the goal
> I cannot say
> If Thou hadst ever met my soul.

Perhaps we can best express the point at which Pauline Christianity departs from Rabbinic Judaism by saying that for the latter it was impossible to think of a new order that had arrived when Spirit and Law would both prevail, whereas for the former that new order was indeed a present fact 'in Christ', and our study drives us back to that impact which Jesus of Nazareth alive, crucified and risen made upon Paul's mind and on that of the early Church.

[1] Cf. A. E. J. Rawlinson, *The New Testament Doctrine of the Christ*, p. 159.

9

THE OLD AND THE NEW OBEDIENCE:
II. THE DEATH OF JESUS

MODERN biographical interest has often resulted in the effort to make the study of the life and character of Jesus the instigation of, or prelude to, faith in Him as Lord. To use a familiar antithesis we have been bidden to come to the Christ of experience through the contemplation of the Jesus of history. Our last chapter will have made it abundantly clear, however, that from such an approach Paul was very far removed. On the contrary, it was his experience of the living Christ, the Lord the Spirit, that compelled Paul to reconsider the significance of the Jesus of history. It was after he had stood beyond the Resurrection, had known the fellowship of the Spirit and from that point of vantage had looked back to the earthly life of Jesus that that life assumed for him a new meaning. So far from its being the case that Paul's preoccupation with the Risen Lord led him to the neglect of the life of Jesus in the flesh, a view which we have previously criticized,[1] it was this very preoccupation that necessarily demanded a new interest in that life and a new appraisal of it. Much as it is from the mountain top that the contours of the valley, its lights and shadows, become visible in true perspective, so it was from the height of his experience of the Lord the Spirit that Paul came to recognize the significance of the whole life of Jesus on earth and to reconsider it in such a way that it became credible as that of the Messiah of Jewish expectation.

It will be evident that, in any revaluation of the life of Jesus that his experience demanded, one aspect in particular, a dark shadow, its ending on the Cross, would compel Paul's scrutiny. It is notorious that for any Jew the manner of the death of Jesus would be doubly repulsive. Without entering into details we point out not only that crucifixion was the most abhorrent of all deaths because of its cruelty and its shame,[2] but for the Jew it also involved the curse of the Torah, the curse pronounced on "every one that hangeth on a tree".[3] He who was crucified defiled the

---

[1] See above, p. 195.

[2] Cf. J. Klausner, *Jesus of Nazareth*, pp. 349f.; *H.D.B.* vol. 1, pp. 528f. The shame of the Cross was due to its servile associations. As to its cruelty Klausner writes: "Crucifixion is the most terrible and cruel death which man has ever devised for taking vengeance on his fellow man." He refers to Cicero, *In Verrem*, v. 64; Tacitus, *Annales* iv. 3, 11. Klausner's whole chapter is illuminating.

[3] Cf. Deut. 21. 23; Gal. 3. 13. Although Christ died by Roman crucifixion Paul here (cf. Acts 5. 30, 10. 39) regards his death as on a tree—i.e. it was put in a Jewish

land. It is in the light of this that we are to imagine Paul's reaction
to the crucifixion of Jesus before his conversion. That the Messiah should
have suffered in any way may not have been wholly unexpected by him
because the Judaism of the first century may have conceived of a suffering
Messiah[1] (we shall discuss this later on), but that the Messiah should
have undergone the disgraceful and disgusting death of crucifixion and
thereby incurred the curse of the Torah, this was a σκάνδαλον, a σκάνδαλον that his experience of the Spirit alone enabled him to overcome.
It was only through the Spirit that the Cross was transformed for Paul
"from the wooden instrument of a dreamer's death to the supreme altar
of the Christian Faith".[2] Such a transformation demanded for its explanation all the resources of Paul's mind, but before we proceed to deal
with his distinctive contributions to the understanding of the Death of
Jesus it is well to recall briefly that Paul was not alone in seeking to
interpret that Death, and that this was a σκάνδαλον to the primitive
Church generally as, of course, we should expect.

It may be possible to over-emphasize the collapse of morale among the
disciples at the crisis of the Crucifixion, because it is clear that on the days
immediately following that event they were still in Jerusalem in expectant
mood,[3] and their readiness to accept the validity of the Resurrection
appearances points more to a wistful disappointment than to blank
despair.[4] What is certain, however, is that in the light of the Cross the
nature of their Messianic beliefs had to undergo a transformation. The
harsh truth, that Jesus had unsuccessfully sought to teach them by word
during His lifetime, that the Messiah should suffer according to a Divine
necessity[5] had now been placarded before them by the Cross and verified
for them in the Resurrection. The vindication of the Cross in the
Resurrection compelled them to find a place in the divine economy for
a crucified Messiah. The earliest attempts to do this are revealed to us
in the first chapter of the Book of Acts. The latter emphasized that the

context by him and emphasized as something due to the rejection by the Jews. For
the Jewish Law, see M. Sanhedrin, 5. See R. T. Herford, Christianity in Talmud and
Midrash, pp. 83 f., who writes: "The Talmud knows nothing of an execution of Jesus
by the Romans, but makes it solely the act of the Jews." The technical word for Cross
צלוב is not used. See also M. Goguel, The Life of Jesus (E.T.), pp. 70ff.

[1] Cf. Moore, vol. I, p. 551; vol. II, pp. 370f. Str.-B. vol. II, pp. 273 f. for the Messiah
ben David and the Messiah ben Joseph.
[2] H. Wheeler Robinson, The Christian Experience of the Holy Spirit, p. 78.
[3] Cf. W. Manson, Jesus the Messiah, p. 122.
[4] Cf. Luke 24. 13 f. especially. We must note, however, that the Markan account
disagrees with this.
[5] Mark 2. 19 f.; cf. Matt. 9. 15; Luke 5. 34; Mark 8. 31, 9. 12b, 31, 10. 33 f.
(cf. Matt. 17. 21b); Mark 10. 38; Matt. 20. 22.

death of Jesus was no mere regrettable accident but was in accordance with the purpose of God as it was revealed in Scripture, "it was by the determinate counsel and foreknowledge of God" and had been foreshadowed "by the mouth of all the prophets".[1] The act by which the Jewish nation had ignorantly rejected Jesus and handed Him over to be crucified by the Gentiles was an act of apostasy from the divine revelation.[2] While, however, it is clear that the Death of Jesus was connected in the minds of the earliest preachers with the remission of sins, the exact nature of this connection was not clarified by them.[3] On the whole, to judge from the Acts the primitive Church indeed in its earliest days was more enthused by the wonder of the advent of the Spirit than puzzled by the σκάνδαλον of the Cross, and at the beginning the disciples do not appear to have been acutely aware of what P. T. Forsyth has taught us to call "the cruciality of the Cross", and there is a certain truth in W. Manson's statement that "for the evidence of a more inward appreciation of the meaning of the Messiah's death we have. _ to look away from Acts to St Paul".[4]

Nevertheless, such a statement, justifiable as it is of the very earliest days of the Church, and also in maintaining the undoubted originality of Paul's contribution, would be misleading if it were taken to imply that in the development of his thought on the Death of Jesus Paul journeyed in isolation from his fellow Christians. On the contrary Paul himself has specially asserted that he owed to the Church a particular interpretation of the Death of Jesus: "For I delivered unto you first of all that which also I received how that Christ died for our sins according to the Scriptures."[5] We need not at this point stop to inquire into the full meaning of the interpretation that Paul here claims to have received; we are merely concerned to insist that, despite his originality, Paul shared in what might be called a treasury of thought on the Death of Jesus which was common in varying degrees to all Christians, and that he applied to that event certain interpretations that were current coin, as it were, in the primitive Church. To judge from the wealth of material presented to us on this subject by the various Epistles of the New Testament the Church must have become increasingly Cross-conscious, if such a term be permissible, and markedly individual as is much of Paul's thought on the Death of Jesus, it developed against the background of a Church that was wrestling with the same problem. To estimate precisely, even if this were possible, the extent to which Paul borrowed the interpretations of the contemporary Church, however, lies outside

[1] Acts 2. 23, 3. 18.   [2] Acts. 2. 22, 36, 3. 15, 17f.
[3] Acts 3. 19.
[4] *Jesus the Messiah*, pp. 123 f.   [5] 1 Cor. 15. 3.

our purpose, and it must suffice to refer to the convenient tabulation or the material in Dr Vincent Taylor's book, *The Atonement in New Testament Teaching*. Our purpose has been merely to recognize in passing that Paul's thought on the Death of Jesus is rooted in that of the primitive Church.[1]

As we should expect, however, Paul's profound consciousness of sin both personal, social and cosmic, and the depth of his spirituality revealed to him depths of meaning in the Death of Jesus that were hidden from his more prosaic brethren in the Faith. "Originality", it has been said, "consists in thinking for ourselves not in thinking differently from other people", and Paul was certainly original in this sense. We shall see that he was not the slave of a tradition but freely emphasized or modified any elements in it as he thought fit. He did not take anything over from the Church without making it his own. But Paul was original not merely in his manipulation of what he had received but also in the sense that he was an innovator. His Epistles make it clear that he introduced new categories into the interpretation of the Death of Jesus and that we are justified in speaking of a distinctive Pauline teaching on the Death of Christ. In this chapter we do not propose to deal with every aspect of Paul's interpretation of that Death, but we shall seek to establish that both in his handling of interpretations current in the Church of his day and in his introduction of novel conceptions he reveals his Rabbinic background.

We begin with Paul's treatment of the Death of Jesus as a sacrifice. This interpretation was familiar to the primitive Church and is to be traced back to the mind of Jesus Himself, and was clearly one element in the tradition that was received by Paul. We are now to inquire how Paul manipulated this, how far he made use of sacrificial terminology in his thinking on the Death of Jesus, and how, if in any way, he departed from that interpretation; was it central to his thought or did he find it uncongenial?

At this point it will be well to refute certain statements made by C. A. A. Scott[2] to the effect that the sacrificial system of necessity could not have much influenced Paul. He claims that for a Diaspora Jew such as Paul "the sacrificial ceremonial of the Temple could have only a distant and indirect bearing on personal religion". This, we feel, is merely another example of what Knox has called "the conventional dichotomy of Judaism into Palestinian and Hellenistic",[3] a dichotomy

[1] Cf. *The Atonement in New Testament Teaching*, pp. 83f.
[2] Cf. *Christianity According to St Paul*, p. 88.
[3] *Some Hellenistic Elements in Primitive Christianity*, p. 42. See Lecture II, pp. 30f.

which we have previously discussed.[1] Scott's view not only ignores the fact that Paul studied at Jerusalem, but also, as the Epistle to the Hebrews shows, that the appeal of the Temple and its sacrifices was not geographically limited to Jerusalem and its environs,[2] and that sacrificial forms could be vehicles for the expression of profound religious experience. Moreover, that absence makes the heart grow fonder is true in more spheres than one, and it is not impossible, as indeed Philo's idealization of the High Priest shows,[3] that the ceremonial of the Temple to whose upkeep he contributed was as significant, and possibly more so to a Diaspora Jew than to a Palestinian. Indeed, we shall later on even suggest over against C. A. A. Scott that it was Paul's very familiarity with the sacrificial system that possibly accounts for the comparatively little use that he makes of it in his theology. What must never be overlooked is what we may be permitted to call the 'actuality' of the sacrificial system, an actuality which we to-day find it difficult to realize. This is not the place to describe that system, but its impressive ceremonial and the innumerable victims necessary for the maintenance of its ritual would be a constant element in the religious milieu of first-century Jewry. Büchler has shown how scrupulous people in the decades before A.D. 70 often "longed for some special opportunities for bringing sin offerings and for that purpose undertook repeatedly the vow of the Nazarite".[4] He refers to the case of Baba b. Buta who "voluntarily brought every day a guilt offering for a doubtful sin, except on the day after the Day of Atonement and said, 'By this Temple I should bring one if they allowed me to do so; but they tell me to wait till I have come to a doubt'."[5] The daily distribution of hides among the priests points to a very large sacrificial activity. "The great number of hides given to the priests", writes Büchler, "proves in any case the considerable number of sin, guilt and burnt offerings brought by the Jews in the last decades of the Temple before its destruction."[6] In view of this we must

---

[1] See above, chapter 1.   [2] See Moore, vol. II, pp. 11f.

[3] See index of W. L. Knox, *St Paul and the Church of the Gentiles*, under 'High Priest'. The High Priest in Philo is used to symbolize the Logos: his emeralds symbolize the sky and his robes the cosmos. See J. Drummond, *Philo Judaeus*, vol. I, pp. 185, 272, 277; vol. II, pp. 171–2, 205, 210, 217, 219, 228–9, 237–8.

[4] *Studies in Sin and Atonement*, p. 429. The whole chapter, "Atonement of Sin by Sacrifice" (pp. 374f.) is important.

[5] Ibid. p. 427, and also *Types of Palestinian Piety*, p. 73. Moore, vol. I, pp. 498f.

[6] *Studies in Sin and Atonement*, p. 438. The importance of the cultus is seen in the remark of Simeon the Just in *P. Aboth* 1.2; cf. *P. Aboth* 1.18. Cf. J. Bonsirven, *Le Judaïsme Palestinien*, vol. II, pp. 114f., 118, and the whole of the chapter on pp. 106f. In a footnote, vol. II, p. 114, n. 5, Bonsirven writes: "Bertholet a calculé que les sacrifices publics comprenaient par an 1093 agneaux; 113 taureaux; 37 béliers; 32 boucs;

insist that the Temple, its ceremonial and its sacrifices were as much part of the religious milieu of Paul as were the Torah and the Synagogue.[1] Moreover, Paul's references to Christians as the Temple of God[2] and his very application to them of the term 'holy'[3] must be accepted as showing that his mind was influenced by Levitical concepts, and we have previously asserted with Carrington, that for Paul the Church was in a sense a neo-levitical community. We shall now seek to point out how Paul did actually make use of sacrificial concepts in his explanation of the meaning of the Death of Jesus.

An obvious starting-point will be the use which Paul makes of the term 'blood', a factor so familiar in sacrificial worship. Apart from passages connected with the Eucharist, with which we shall be concerned later, the following catena of passages falls to be considered.

Rom. 3. 25: Whom God hath set forth to be a propitiation through faith in his blood, to declare his righteousness for the remission of sins that are past, through the forbearance of God.

Rom. 5. 8, 9: But God commendeth his love towards us, in that, while we were yet sinners, Christ died for us. Much more then, being now justified by his blood, we shall be saved from wrath through him.

Eph. 1. 7: In whom we have redemption through his blood, the forgiveness of sins, according to the riches of his grace.

Eph. 2. 13: But now in Christ Jesus ye who sometimes were far off are made nigh by the blood of Christ.

Col. 1. 14: In whom we have redemption through his blood, even the forgiveness of sins.

Col. 1. 20: And having made peace through the blood of his Cross, by him to reconcile all things unto himself.

The interpretations offered of the use of the term 'blood' in such passages as the above are many. Deissmann would interpret it mystically. For him the expression is a "vivid way of realizing the living one who is also the Crucified and with whom we live in mystical—spiritual 'fellowship of blood'".[4] The expression 'in the blood of Christ' differs only slightly, if at all, from the phrase 'in Christ'.[5] It will, however,

5487 litres de farine fine; 2076 litres de vin et autant d'huile. Ajoutons les sacrifices offerts par les particuliers, sacrifices obligatoires, et dons volontaires. Tout cela vous donne quelque idée des dépenses considérables que représentait le culte du Temple."

[1] Cf. F. C. N. Hicks, *The Fullness of Sacrifice*, p. 105, for a discussion of the relation of Temple and Synagogue. See also pp. 192f. and Moore, vol. II, pp. 11f.

[2] 1 Cor. 3. 16.   [3] F. C. N. Hicks, op. cit. pp. 226, 229.

[4] Cf. *St Paul* (2nd ed.), p. 198.

[5] *St Paul*, p. 199, n. 2. Deissmann compares Dibelius' view, *H.Z.N.T.* on Eph. 2. 13, that there ἐν τῷ αἵματι τοῦ Χριστοῦ "is probably simply the repetition of ἐν Χριστῷ Ἰησοῦ"; cf. *H.Z.N.T., An die Kolosser, Epheser*, vol. XII, p. 52.

be agreed that it is impossible to import such a mystical meaning into any of the above passages, and Deissmann only specifically refers to the phrase in 1 Cor. 10. 16, κοινωνία τοῦ αἵματος τοῦ Χριστοῦ, in support of his view, but there the thought is to be understood sacrificially and not in terms of 'mysticism' as the whole context shows. On the other hand it has been claimed that in the passages under consideration the term 'blood' merely signifies the Death of Christ. J. Behm,[1] for example, has written that the phrase 'the blood of Christ' is only "a more vivid expression for the death of Christ in its redemptive significance". In his view we are to read into the phrase not sacrificial ideas derived from the cultus but, in accordance with the symbolism of late Judaism, the idea of a self-giving obedience culminating in death. Again, Ryder-Smith[2] has offered criticisms of the sacrificial interpretation of the references to the blood of Christ. First, since in passages not referring to Christ's death, e.g. Matt. 27. 24, Acts 5. 28, Heb. 12. 4, Rev. 19. 2, the term 'blood' refers to death not to life, we are to assume that in a phrase like the 'blood of Christ', the term 'blood' also refers to the same fact of death. Secondly, the sacrificial ritual does not express the idea of Resurrection at all, and the 'doctrine' of the Death of Jesus in Paul is inseparably connected with that of the Resurrection.[3] "It is not too much to say", writes Ryder-Smith, "that the emphasis on the Death of Christ in the New Testament is just as clear as the lack of emphasis on the death of the sacrifices in the Old."[4]

Let us deal with the statements of Ryder-Smith first. It has been claimed by Hicks that in one at least of the passages quoted above the Death of Christ is clearly distinguished from the blood of Christ. The passage is in Rom. 5. 8f.:

But God commendeth his love towards us, in that, while we were yet sinners, Christ *died* for us. Much more then, being now *justified by his blood*, we shall be saved from wrath through him.

Here Hicks believes that Paul brings out the backward look of death as death and the forward look of blood as life.[5] This interpretation,

---

[1] *Theologisches Wörterbuch*, vol. I, p. 173. "Das Interesse des N.T. haftet nicht an dem Blute Christi als Stoff, sondern an seinem vergossen Blut, dem ihm gewaltsam genommenen Leben; 'Blut-Christi' ist wie Kreuz nur ein anderer, anschaulicher Ausdruck für den Tod Christi in seiner Heilsbedeutung." Also *Die Religion in Geschichte und Gegenwart*, p. 1156.

[2] *The Bible Doctrine of Salvation*, pp. 211f.

[3] In his recital of the κήρυγμα that he had received Paul regards two themes as pivotal, the death and rising of Jesus. See 1 Cor. 15. 38; cf. Rom. 4. 25, 6. 10; 2 Cor. 5. 15; Acts 2. 23f.

[4] *The Bible Doctrine of Salvation*, p. 216.   [5] *The Fullness of Sacrifice*, p. 243.

however, is untenable. In Rom. 5. 8–10 we find that both the death and the blood of Christ have a backward look: the death, in verse 10, reconciled, and the blood, in verse 9, justified. The forward look is supplied by the idea of sanctification, the new kind of life following on justification.[1] Again Ryder-Smith[2] is fully justified in saying that there are "many passages in the New Testament where there is emphasis on the Death of Christ,. without the use of the term blood". But although this is the case it is surely significant that only in the above passages, Rom. 5. 8–9 and Col. 1. 20, do we find Paul connecting the Death strictly with the work of Redemption, and in both passages the correlative idea of blood is mentioned also. Apparently the term 'Death' by itself would not be used by Paul of the redemptive significance of the work of Jesus. We are justified then in saying that Paul's use of the term 'blood' implies more than death; it has the active connotation of life as well, as in the sacrificial system where the death of the victim was the necessary prelude, and no more, to the releasing of life.[3] Moreover, to revert to Ryder-Smith's second criticism, it seems to us that he verges on self-contradiction. In one and the same breath he insists both that the Death and Resurrection of Jesus are inseparably linked and that there is an emphasis on the Death *per se*. To judge from the longest treatment of the meaning of the Death of Jesus in Rom. 6. 1 f., we cannot but feel that for Paul the Death of Christ is never divorced from its counterpart the New Life, and we suggest that this twofold aspect of death and life is preserved for Paul in the term 'blood', which had this same twofold emphasis in the sacrificial system.

This brings us back to Behm's view and to Dr Vincent Taylor's criticism of it, a criticism that also applies to Ryder-Smith and C. A. A. Scott. Taylor has seen in the view of Behm the "marks of the revulsion of the modern man from the thought of blood sacrifices",[4] a revulsion that often indeed does influence modern scholars; for example the pupils of Dr T. H. Robinson will recall his frequent references to the revolting details of the sacrificial systems of India, with which he is familiar, in his treatment of the attitude of the prophets to the sacrificial system.[5] But whether Behm and the other scholars mentioned suffer from this

---

[1] *The Fullness of Sacrifice*, p. 243.

[2] *The Bible Doctrine of Salvation*, p. 215.

[3] Cf. Vincent Taylor, *Jesus and His Sacrifice*, p. 54; F. C. N. Hicks, *The Fullness of Sacrifice*, pp. 12, 177, 327; W. O. E. Oesterley, *Sacrifices in Ancient Israel*, p. 224; W. R. Smith, *The Religion of Semites* (3rd ed.), pp. 338, 377.

[4] Cf. Vincent Taylor, *The Atonement in New Testament Teaching*, p. 34.

[5] This does not lead Dr Robinson to say, however, that the prophets because they shared in this revulsion wholly repudiated the sacrificial system. Cf. *Hebrew Religion*, p. 201.

revulsion or not, despite the fact, which we shall discuss later, that the
sacrificial system was not of dominant significance in first-century
Judaism, it is a mistake to regard that system as having been spiritualized
through symbolism to such an extent as Behm suggests. It is doubtful
if there was any rationale of sacrifice in the first century.[1] In a religion
that took Revelation seriously, as did Judaism, it was not the part of
the worshipper to reason why, but merely to accept the fact that God
had ordained sacrifice as a means of communion with Him. Much in
the sacrificial system would be merely customary and to seek for
rationality in all its details is misleading. "Deep θεολογούμενα", it has
been written, "do not underlie the system: problems of salvation from
original sin, restitution and justification did not enter the minds of the
priests that ministered at the altar in Jerusalem."[2] The Rabbinic attitude
is well expressed in the words of Johanan b. Zakkai: "God has decreed.
A Statute I have ordained and an institution I have established and it is
not permitted to transgress the Law."[3]

It is unlikely then that any elaborate symbolism would be suggested
by the sacrificial system. It is not in that direction that we are to seek
for its importance for Paul. We have previously insisted on the actuality
of the system, that it must have filled a prominent place in the religious
environment of the Apostle. It is now pertinent to add that in all
sacrificial activity it was the blood that was central.[4] We need not here
enter into any discussion of the origins of sacrifice or seek to account
for the centrality of blood. We need only state that the principle laid
down in Lev. 17. 11, was fundamental. "For the life of the flesh is in
the blood: and I have given it to you upon the altar to make an atonement for your souls: for it is the blood that maketh an atonement for
the soul"; atonement comes through the blood—[5] אין כפרה אלא בדם
is another expression of the same truth. By the outpouring of blood life
was released, and in offering this to God the worshipper believed that
the estrangement between him and the Deity was annulled, or that the
defilement which separated them was cleansed. "Hence the sprinkling
of the blood", writes Büchler, "upon the altar was regarded as the
essential and decisive act of the offering up."[6] The sprinkling was the act

---

[1] Cf. Moore, vol. I, p. 500; Taylor, *Jesus and His Sacrifice*, p. 49.

[2] *J.E.* vol. x, pp. 615f.; the article on Sacrifice.   [3] *Num. Rabba* 19.

[4] For the place and meaning of blood in the sacrificial sphere, cf. F. C. N. Hicks,
The Fullness of Sacrifice, p. 12; W. R. Smith, *The Religion of the Semites*, pp. 344f.;
W. O. E. Oesterley, *Sacrifices in Ancient Israel*, p. 224. Also *J.E.* vol. II, pp. 275f. on
"Atonement" and pp. 137f., 53.   [5] *b. Yoma* 5a; *b. Zeb.* 6a; cf. Heb. 9. 12 ff.

[6] *Studies in Sin and Atonement*, pp. 418f. See also G. F. Moore, *Encyclopaedia Biblica*,
vol. IV, pp. 4217f.

of 'atonement' and was thus reserved for the priest.[1] The significance of blood will now be clear. Perhaps we may take R. Simeon b. Yoḥai's words as typical: "Though blood is despised and serves as food of dogs, God said that we should bring a sacrifice and apply its blood to the horns of the altar in order that the blood might atone for the blood of man"[2] [כדי שיכפר דם על הדם]. (For another translation see p. 338 (5).)

Bearing all the above in mind we must insist that for Paul the term 'blood' would inevitably have sacrificial connotations whatever symbolic meaning he may or may not have imported into it. The term would have none of the revolting associations it often has for us moderns, because, so Loewe[3] suggests, the sight of offal and blood from slain beasts was a commonplace in the first century, there being then no butchers' shops of the modern kind, and would indeed suggest sacred associations. In the light of all this we are justified in finding in the Pauline application of the term 'blood' to Christ the use of a sacrificial concept. Dr Vincent Taylor is surely right when he claims that "self-giving and complete obedience to God may certainly be included in the meaning of 'the blood of Christ', but the list of derivative ideas is hopelessly attenuated unless it also includes the thought of life through death, and an offering through which men may draw nigh to God".[4]

Nevertheless, before we leave this subject, we must issue one caveat. It has been pointed out by C. A. A. Scott that there is a great variety in the functions applied to blood by Paul. "By it or by the death men obtain justification, redemption, reconciliation; by it they are brought near, and peace is made; and at the same time reconciliation is traced to 'his flesh-body through death'." Scott goes on to say that "this very variety of expression suggests that we are in the presence not of a technical, but of a general idea. The efficacy which is thus assigned to the 'blood' goes far beyond the scope claimed for it in Leviticus, where its effect is only negative, the covering or neutralizing of that which forbids safe or acceptable worship of God."[5] Ryder-Smith[6] has also insisted on this point, and it is a real one. It warns us that though Paul used 'blood' in a sacrificial sense he was not bound to that sense; the sacrificial

---

[1] F. C. N. Hicks, *The Fullness of Sacrifice*, p. 12. "The victim is killed by the offerer, the sinner...the one person who does not kill the victim is the priest [except on the Day of Atonement when he kills a victim for his own sin, i.e. the High Priest]."

[2] Cf. A. Büchler, *Studies in Sin and Atonement*, pp. 418f.; *Pesikta R.* 194b.

[3] Cf. *R.A.* p. 643, for a very interesting discussion of this.

[4] *The Atonement in New Testament Teaching*, p. 35.

[5] *Christianity According to St Paul*, p. 86.

[6] *The Bible Doctrine of Salvation*, p. 215.

did not exhaust the meaning he applied to the 'blood' although it was included in it.

The sacrificial interpretation of the term 'blood' in Paul receives confirmation from one of the passages listed previously, namely, Rom. 3. 25, which reads: ἐν Χριστῷ Ἰησοῦ· ὃν προέθετο ὁ θεὸς ἱλαστήριον διὰ τῆς πίστεως ἐν τῷ αὐτοῦ αἵματι, εἰς ἔνδειξιν τῆς δικαιοσύνης αὐτοῦ, διὰ τὴν πάρεσιν τῶν προγεγονότων ἁμαρτημάτων ἐν τῇ ἀνοχῇ τοῦ θεοῦ. Into the complexity of the exegesis of all this passage we need not enter:[1] for our purpose the crux lies in the word ἱλαστήριον; what is involved in Paul's description of Christ as ἱλαστήριον? As for the essential idea underlying the word we are no longer in doubt. The traditional view that ideas of propitiation are implied[2] has been rendered untenable by the work of Dr Dodd. The latter has examined the meaning of the word ἱλάσκεσθαι and its cognates, and proved that these words which in classical Greek and in the Koine had the sense of 'to placate', or 'to propitiate', when used in the LXX both to translate the Hebrew *Kippêr* and its derivatives and otherwise are to be understood as conveying the meaning not of propitiating the deity but of "performing an act whereby guilt or defilement is removed". Of ἱλαστήριον in Rom. 3. 25, Dr Dodd has written: "The meaning conveyed (in accordance with LXX usage, which is constantly determinative for Paul) is that of expiation not of propitiation."[3]

Our difficulty, however, begins when we seek to penetrate behind the general idea of expiation to any particular aspect or expression of it, if there be any such, which may be in Paul's mind. Dr Dodd has been content with the translation 'a means of expiation', and in this he is followed by Dr Vincent Taylor.[4] Other scholars have sought a more specific reference. Thus some, both in the past and in the present, have translated ἱλαστήριον by 'mercy seat',[5] i.e. Christ is regarded as the Christian counterpart of the *kappôreth*, generally referred to in English as 'the propitiatory'.[6] The translating of *kappôreth* by 'mercy seat' is misleading in that it suggests a place where mercy is dispensed, whereas

---

[1] For this see Vincent Taylor, *Expository Times*, vol. L, pp. 295-300 (C. A. A. Scott, *Christianity According to St Paul*, pp. 59f., for a different view); C. H. Dodd, *Romans* (*M.N.T.C.*), pp. 48f.

[2] *The Bible and the Greeks*, pp. 82f. For the traditional view, cf. Str.-B.; *Romans* (*I.C.C.*); J. Denney, *Studies in Theology*, p. 116.

[3] *The Bible and the Greeks*, pp. 94f.

[4] *Expository Times*, vol. L, pp. 295-300. A. Deissmann's treatment in *Bible Studies*, although now superseded, should also be consulted.

[5] Cf. *H.D.B.* vol. IV, p. 665; especially also Str.-B. vol. III, pp. 165f.

[6] E.g. Ritschl, *Die Christliche Lehre von der Rechtfertigung und Versöhnung*, vol. II, p. 171.

the connotation of the word *kappôreth* is distinctly sacrificial. It is described for us in Exod. 25. 17-22:

17. And thou shalt make a mercy seat of pure gold: two cubits and a half shall be the length thereof, and a cubit and a half the breadth thereof. 18. And thou shalt make two cherubims of gold, of beaten work shalt thou make them, in the two ends of the mercy seat. 19. And make one cherub on the one end, and the other cherub on the other end; even of the mercy seat shall ye make the cherubims on the two ends thereof. 20. And the cherubims shall stretch forth their wings on high, covering the mercy seat with their wings, and their faces shall look one to another; towards the mercy seat shall the faces of the cherubims be. 21. And thou shalt put the mercy seat above upon the ark; and in the ark thou shalt put the testimony that I shall give thee. 22. And there I will meet with thee, and I will commune with thee from above the mercy seat, from between the two cherubims which are upon the ark of the testimony, of all things which I will give thee in commandment unto the children of Israel.

The importance of the *kappôreth* in Jewish ritual may be gauged from the fact that once a year, on the Day of Atonement [1] the High Priest entered alone into the Holy of Holies to bring the blood of the sin-offerings to be sprinkled on the *kappôreth* which was thus the innermost shrine of the sanctuary,[2] the point at which expiation was made on the most solemn of all occasions in the Jewish year. Although with the destruction of the first Temple the Ark and the *kappôreth* were lost, the ritual of the Day of Atonement was carried on as though they were still there, a stone having replaced the Ark and the *kappôreth*. "After the Ark was taken away a stone remained there from the time of the early prophets, and it was called *Shetiyah*.[3] It was higher than the ground by three finger-breadths...."

It is Büchsel[4] who has most recently restated the case for regarding the ἱλαστήριον of Rom. 3. 25 as the equivalent or rather the Christian counterpart of the *kappôreth*. He particularly emphasizes the fact that the conception of Christ as ἱλαστήριον is expressly connected with the Law and the Prophets as it is witnessed to by these.[5] Since this is the case, it is natural to turn to the central point at which the Law dealt with the expiation of sin, namely, the Day of Atonement, when the *kappôreth* would be sprinkled with 'blood', and to find there the cynosure of Paul's thought at this point. The Apostle is thinking of Christ in

[1] For this see J.E. vol. II, pp. 275 f.; M. *Yoma* (Danby, pp. 162 f.); W. O. E. Oesterley, *Sacrifices in Ancient Israel*, pp. 226 f.; Moore, vol. II, pp. 55 f.; Lev. 16. 1 f.
[2] Cf. H.D.B. vol. IV, p. 665.   [3] M. *Yoma* 5. 2; Danby, p. 167.
[4] *Theologisches Wörterbuch*, vol. III, pp. 321 f.
[5] Rom. 3. 21 f. ... μαρτυρουμένη ὑπὸ τοῦ νόμου καὶ τῶν προφητῶν.

terms of a spiritual ἱλαστήριον publicly set forth, not hidden away inaccessibly in the Holy of Holies and effective for atonement in virtue of His own blood, not that of any beast. Büchsel thus rejects the translation 'means of expiation' as too pale and boldly asserts the identity of ἱλαστήριον with the *kappôreth* in Paul's mind.

Criticisms of Büchsel's position have been offered by Dr Vincent Taylor.[1] The most relevant at this point are: (1) When ἱλαστήριον is used of the *kappôreth* it always has the definite article except in Exod. 25. 16, where the noun ἐπίθεμα is added to it. (2) Nothing in the context of Rom. 3. 25 suggests that St Paul is thinking of 'the propitiatory' (contrast Heb. 9. 5). (3) It is not St Paul's habit to allude to religious objects in the Levitical cultus, with the exception of the Temple itself (cf. 1 Cor. 3. 16, 6. 19). (4) The ideas of Rom. 3. 25 are unduly complicated if Christ is thought of as an offering ('by his blood') and as Himself 'the propitiatory'. Of these criticisms it does not seem to us that those numbered (2), (3), (4) can carry much weight. The second is surely mistaken. The preoccupation of Paul in Rom. 1–3 with the exceeding sinfulness of men would naturally suggest to him, even if it would not to us, the thought of that greatest of all days when this very fact would loom large for any Jew, especially a Rabbi—the Day of Atonement. Especially would this be true if, as T. W. Manson has suggested,[2] "Paul had very recently experienced a Day of Atonement" (this view we shall return to later). Again in answer to the third objection that Paul is not accustomed to allude to religious objects in the levitical cultus we may again recall the levitical element in Paul's thinking which we have previously discussed. He could regard the Christian life as a λογικὴ λατρεία;[3] he could treat the rite of circumcision as a spiritual reality [4] and it was not strange for him to contrast things Christian and things Jewish, the New and the Old Covenant, the New and the Old Israel, the New and the Old Torah; and it is not inconceivable that he should also have thought of a new ἱλαστήριον to be contrasted with the old *kappôreth*. As for the fourth objection we feel that it would only apply if Paul were writing a scientific treatise where terms would be precisely defined; and in any case what was possible to the author of the Epistle to the Hebrews, for whom Christ is both Priest and Victim,[5] might also be possible for Paul.

It is the first criticism that does, however, carry weight. The absence of the article does suggest that Paul is not referring to any such well-

[1] *Forgiveness and Reconciliation*, p. 46.
[2] *J.T.S.* (Jan.–April 1945), vol. XLVI.   [3] Rom. 12. 1.
[4] Phil. 3. 3; Col. 2. 11.   [5] Heb. 7. 27, 9. 12, 14.

known object as the *kappôreth*. But this objection is met by the theory advanced by T. W. Manson[1] to which we referred above. According to this, ἱλαστήριον stands not for the *kappôreth* in a strict sense but "for the locality at which the acts or events covered by the verb ἱλασκέσθαι take place". Büchsel[2] had rejected this view because of the use of ἱλαστήριον ἐπίθεμα in Exod. 25. 16–17 of the LXX to translate *kappôreth* (see footnote), but Manson has convincingly shown that the word ἐπίθεμα in Exod. 25. 16 (17) is highly suspect and to be rejected.[3] He has further adduced many examples to prove that ἱλαστήριον very often designates a place; thus in Ezekiel it is five times used to render ʾazârâh,[4] "a word whose exact meaning is uncertain though it is clear that it designates some part of the great altar in Ezekiel's temple".[5] This great altar would be the place where God would accept His people,[6] i.e. where expiation would be effected. In the Pentateuch, as we have seen, it denotes the *kappôreth* where on the Day of Atonement expiation would be made and in Gen. 6. 15, 16 Symmachus twice has ἱλαστήριον to translate *ha-têbâh* (LXX κιβωτός) because, says Manson, "Symmachus took the Ark to be what in the story it actually was, the only place in the world where man may seek and find the grace and mercy of God".[7] The interpretation of ἱλαστήριον as a place would clearly do away with the necessity for the article, and Manson seems justified in finding in Rom. 3. 25 the meaning that Christ crucified was "the place where God's mercy was supremely manifested".

Further than this Manson goes on to argue that it is the ritual of the Day of Atonement that lies at the back of Paul's mind. It would prolong our discussion too much to enumerate the details of Manson's argument in full, but the following table may serve to bring out broadly the antitheses which Paul, according to Manson, intends us to find between the old and the new place of expiation or ἱλαστήριον:

---

[1] *J.T.S.* (1945), vol. XLVI.

[2] *Theologisches Wörterbuch*, vol. III, pp. 321 f. Büchsel explained the appearance of the additional word ἐπίθεμα in LXX Exod. 25. 16 (17) by saying that the LXX: "fuhrt ihre Übersetzung von *Kappôreth* mit *hilasterion* dadurch ein, dass sie zum Adjectivum *hilasterion*, das sie im folgenden substantiviert braucht, an der ersten Stelle das im hebräischen Text nicht gegebene Substantivum *epithema* setzt. Daraus erhellt dass für sie τὸ ἱλαστήριον an sich nicht einem räumlichen Gegenstand, sondern: *das Sühnende ganz allgemein* bedeutet."

[3] Because, of twenty-one places where כַּפֹּרֶת is rendered by ἱλαστήριον in the Pentateuch, in twenty it is rendered by ἱλαστήριον alone: the reading itself is not sure in Exod. 25. 16 (17). For details see *J.T.S.* op. cit.

[4] Cf. Ezek. 43. 14, 17, 20.

[5] T. W. Manson, *J.T.S.* (1945), vol. XLVI.

[6] Cf. Ezek. 43. 27.   [7] Op. cit.

The Old ἱλαστήριον	The New ἱλαστήριον
1. Is hidden in the Holy of Holies.	1. Is displayed publicly (προέθετο).
2. Its benefits depend upon ritual.	2. Its benefits depend on faith.
3. Its expiation is effective through blood.	3. Its expiation is through His[1] blood.

In much of all this the difference between Manson and Büchsel will appear to be slight. Manson, however, carries his case still further in two directions which we briefly indicate. First, he would have us see in Rom. 1–3 an elaborate confession of sin for all mankind with the climax in 3. 23: "There is no distinction, for all have sinned and fallen short of the glory of God",[2] a confession corresponding to the threefold confession of sin in the ritual of the Day of Atonement; and in the reference to the 'blood' of Jesus in Rom. 3. 25 we are to see the exact counterpart to the sprinkling of the blood in the same ritual, the position of the former following immediately after the confession of Rom. 1–3. 23, being determined by the position of the sprinkling of the blood in the ritual. Secondly, Manson would also claim that it was a particular Day of Atonement, that following closely on his reconciliation with the Church at Corinth, that made Paul write in the way he does. In short, his thought in Rom. 3. 25 and the whole context is moulded by the ritual of a Jewish festival. This view of Rom. 1–3 is bound up also with the theory that "traces of the Jewish festival calendar" can be found throughout 1 and 2 Corinthians and the passages we have discussed in Romans.[3]

Accepting for the moment Manson's chronological reconstruction of the period during which 1 and 2 Corinthians and Romans were written, it may well be that at certain points in those epistles the Jewish festivals have influenced Paul's presentation of the Gospel, in particular we can accept the view that the thought of Rom. 3. 25 is to be understood against the background of the Day of Atonement. We hesitate, however, to endorse Manson's detailed application of the ritual of the latter to Rom. 1–3. Thus it is highly questionable whether the πρό in προέθετο in Rom. 3. 25 is strong enough to admit of Manson's emphasis when he interprets it to mean "to set forth publicly":[4] and equally

[1] The 'His' is emphatic.   [2] J.T.S. (1945), vol. XLVI.
[3] J.T.S. (1945), vol. XLVI.
[4] See Moulton and Milligan, Vocabulary of the Greek New Testament, p. 536. The evidence given there makes the emphatic use of πρό in προτίθημι very improbable. See also p. 554. προτίθημι is used commonly in the papyri='proclaim', 'set forth publicly' of an edict or notice. Both W. Sanday and A. C. Headlam, Romans (I.C.C.), ad loc. and A. Deissmann, Bible Studies, pp. 129 ff. accept this translation, i.e. 'set forth publicly' in Rom. 3. 25. It is rejected by Moulton, who renders προέθετο by 'offered' or 'provided'.

doubtful is it whether the αὐτοῦ is to be emphasized in the phrase ἐν τῷ αὐτοῦ αἵματι. The tones of confession may be audible in Rom. 3. 10f. but in the rather philosophical explanation of the origin and growth of human sinfulness, Rabbinic in thought but Stoic in expression, which we find in Rom. 1. 18f.; in the argumentative indictment of Rom. 2. 1f. and in the tortuous thought of Rom. 3. 1f. it is impossible to overhear them. Had Paul consciously or unconsciously based the form of these chapters on the ritual of the Day of Atonement we would expect to find more direct and recognizable traces of that ritual. In that case we would surely have had more of an approximation to that penetrating interpretation of the Death of Jesus in fully developed sacrificial terms which we find in the Epistle to the Hebrews: the bare reference in Rom. 3. 25 to two sacrificial terms, 'blood' and ἱλαστήριον, cannot bear the weight that Manson would put on it. The issue of all this is that, as in our treatment of Paul's use of 'blood' we had to close with a caveat, so in our treatment of ἱλαστήριον. While we go further than Dr Dodd and Dr Taylor in specifically reading ἱλαστήριον in Rom. 3. 25 in the light of the Day of Atonement, as do Büchsel and Manson, we are also constrained to point out that although in labouring to do justice to the significance of the Death of Jesus he uses sacrificial terms, Paul does not develop these but leaves them inchoate[1].

We next move to another point where Paul is clearly moving within the orbit of sacrificial ideas, namely, to 1 Cor. 5. 7:[2] "Purge out therefore the old leaven, that ye may be a new lump, as ye are unleavened. For even Christ our Passover is sacrificed for us." As will become evident as our argument proceeds, however, it is best to take this in conjunction with Paul's treatment of the Last Supper which also occurs in the same Epistle, and to this we will now turn. We shall ask how Paul interpreted the Last Supper, and seek to find out whether there are any particular emphases in his account of that Supper, which set it apart from other accounts preserved to us, and thereby reveal peculiarities of the Pauline interpretation of the Death of Jesus.

It is familiar that there are striking differences between the accounts of the Last Supper in Matthew, Mark, Luke, and 1 Corinthians. The Matthew version, however, closely follows the Markan except for the addition of the words εἰς ἄφεσιν ἁμαρτιῶν, which we may safely regard as an interpretative gloss.[3] As for the account in Luke the long form of

---

[1] Cf. G. F. Moore, *Encyclopaedia Biblica*, vol. IV, pp. 4229f.
[2] See especially on 1 Cor. 5. 7, and the possible place of a Christian Passover in the life of the Church, J. Weiss, Meyer, *Kommentar zum Neuen Testament, Der Erste Korintherbrief*, pp. 134f.   [3] Cf. V. Taylor, *Jesus and His Sacrifice*, p. 127.

the text clearly shows Pauline influence and is therefore possibly secondary. Otto,[1] however, has claimed that the text found in Luke 22. 15-19, 29 and 30, has historical priority over other accounts. On the other hand Taylor[2] has urged the priority of the Markan account, whilst Behm,[3] followed by Flew,[4] has placed the Pauline account before the Markan. The variety of views on this question reveals the difficulty of its solution and fortunately for our purpose we need not decide it. More relevant to our work is the fact that there was no single tradition about the nature of the Last Supper that was accepted by all; and not only so, but it appears that it was only very gradually that its significance for the understanding of Jesus' mind came to be recognized. At this point Dr Taylor's[5] treatment of the Eucharist in the primitive communities is especially helpful. He points out that in many parts of the New Testament writings, the Eucharistic teaching plays no part. This is so in the case of Acts, 1 Peter, the Pastoral Epistles, Hebrews and Revelation. This striking lack, he suggests, can only be accounted for on the assumption that the realization of the cruciality of the Death of Jesus was not universal. It was contrary to the method of Jesus to reveal bluntly to the disciples that in His words and actions at the Last Supper were the key to the meaning of His Death. Just as He made no explicit claim to be the Messiah but rather allowed the disciples of themselves to apprehend His Messiahship gradually, so on the night on which He was betrayed He did no violence to the disciples' minds by seeking to force them to comprehend what they were unprepared for, but allowed the meaning of His words and deeds to unfold itself gradually in the slow process of time.[6] It would not be surprising, therefore, that there should be communities which only partially understood the Last Supper and that any traditions that might emerge from such communities would bear the mark of the special emphasis that different communities might have placed on the Last Supper. It is in this light, for example, that we are probably to regard the tradition recorded for us in the Shorter Text of Luke.[7] It is evident that in the community from which the latter

---

[1] *The Kingdom of God and the Son of Man*, p. 268.

[2] Op. cit. pp. 203, 205.   [3] *Theol. Wörterbuch*, vol. II, p. 136.

[4] *Jesus and His Church*, p. 99, n. 1.

[5] See his "Detached Note on the Eucharist in the Primitive Communities" in *The Atonement in New Testament Teaching*, pp. 234f.

[6] Vincent Taylor, op. cit. p. 237. It is questionable, however, whether there is no reminiscence of the Eucharist in Revelation: surely it is at least suggested in for example, 3. 20: "Behold, I stand at the door, and knock: if any man hear my voice, and open the door, I will come in to him, and will *sup* with him, and he with me."

[7] Taylor, op. cit. p. 238. Luke 22. 14-18. According to Taylor, Luke added 19*a* to the previous verses.

emanated, the eschatological interest[1] in the words of Jesus predominated. Its emphasis would be on the anticipation of the joys of the future
kingdom. The fact that the Shorter Text has certain glaring omissions
must not necessarily be taken to mean that its author did not know of
other elements in the tradition of the Last Supper, but merely that those
elements had no significance for him; nor again should the fact that the
Shorter Text is so simple and apparently the least modified version of
the Last Supper be taken to imply that it is more primitive than the
Markan and Pauline accounts, but merely that its form has probably
been determined by a dominant eschatological interest.

When we turn to the Markan and Pauline accounts we find that both
are drawing upon traditions that have much in common. Only so can
we explain the marked similarity of the two accounts where the words
'covenant', 'blood', etc., obviously point to the same ideological background. This will be clear when the two accounts are set side by side.

Mark	Paul
καὶ ἐσθιόντων αὐτῶν λαβὼν ἄρτον εὐλογήσας ἔκλασεν καὶ ἔδωκεν αὐτοῖς καὶ εἶπεν· Λάβετε· τοῦτό ἐστιν τὸ σῶμά μου. καὶ λαβὼν ποτήριον εὐχαριστήσας ἔδωκεν αὐτοῖς, καὶ ἔπιον ἐξ αὐτοῦ πάντες. καὶ εἶπεν αὐτοῖς· Τοῦτό ἐστιν τὸ αἷμά μου τῆς διαθήκης τὸ ἐκχυννόμενον ὑπὲρ πολλῶν. ἀμὴν λέγω ὑμῖν ὅτι οὐκέτι οὐ μὴ πίω ἐκ τοῦ γεννήματος τῆς ἀμπέλου ἕως τῆς ἡμέρας ἐκείνης ὅταν αὐτὸ πίνω καινὸν ἐν τῇ βασιλείᾳ τοῦ θεοῦ.	ὁ Κύριος Ἰησοῦς ἐν τῇ νυκτὶ ᾗ παρε-δίδοτο ἔλαβεν ἄρτον, καὶ εὐχαρισ-τήσας ἔκλασε, καὶ εἶπε, Τοῦτό μου ἐστὶ τὸ σῶμα τὸ ὑπὲρ ὑμῶν. τοῦτο ποιεῖτε εἰς τὴν ἐμὴν ἀνάμνησιν. ὡσαύ-τως καὶ τὸ ποτήριον, μετὰ τὸ δειπ-νῆσαι, λέγων, Τοῦτο τὸ ποτήριον ἡ καινὴ διαθήκη ἐστὶν ἐν τῷ ἐμῷ αἵματι· τοῦτο ποιεῖτε, ὁσάκις ἂν πίνητε, εἰς τὴν ἐμὴν ἀνάμνησιν....

The above tabulation, however, reveals not merely an essential community of ideas but also differences of expression, and in these differences
in our submission we are to trace the Rabbinic mind of Paul. An examination of certain points will clarify this.

First of all we notice the different way in which reference is made to
the 'blood' in these two forms. In the Markan form the words τοῦτό
ἐστι τὸ αἷμά μου imply a direct equation of the cup with the 'blood',

---

[1] This will be clear from the text—καὶ ὅτε ἐγένετο ἡ ὥρα, ἀνέπεσε, καὶ οἱ ἀπόστολοι
σὺν αὐτῷ. καὶ εἶπε πρὸς αὐτούς, Ἐπιθυμίᾳ ἐπεθύμησα τοῦτο τὸ πάσχα φαγεῖν μεθ'
ὑμῶν πρὸ τοῦ με παθεῖν· λέγω γὰρ ὑμῖν ὅτι οὐ μὴ φάγω αὐτό, ἕως ὅτου πληρωθῇ
ἐν τῇ βασιλείᾳ τοῦ θεοῦ. καὶ δεξάμενος ποτήριον εὐχαριστήσας εἶπε, Λάβετε τοῦτο,
καὶ διαμερίσατε εἰς ἑαυτούς· λέγω γὰρ ὑμῖν, ὅτι οὐ μὴ πίω ἀπὸ τοῦ νῦν ἀπὸ τοῦ
γεννήματος τῆς ἀμπέλου, ἕως ὅτου ἡ βασιλεία τοῦ θεοῦ ἔλθῃ.

an equation which is avoided in the more refined Pauline form—τοῦτο τὸ ποτήριον ἡ καινὴ διαθήκη ἐστὶν ἐν τῷ ἐμῷ αἵματι. It is a commonplace that the Markan form has been deemed impossible on the lips of Jesus by some scholars on account of the Jewish aversion to the drinking of blood. The Torah specifically forbade the drinking of blood because it was 'the life' and had been ordained of God as a means of atonement; to drink blood was not only contrary to the Torah but a desecration of what was 'holy'. Thus in Lev. 17. 10f., we read:

And whatsoever man there be of the house of Israel, or of the strangers that sojourn among you, that eateth any manner of blood; I will even set my face against that soul that eateth blood, and will cut him off from among his people. For the life of the flesh is in the blood....Therefore I said unto the children of Israel, No soul of you shall eat blood, neither shall any stranger that sojourneth among you eat blood....

In view of this Montefiore has written:[1] "I would venture to suggest how difficult it is to believe that a Palestinian or Galilean Jew could have suggested that in drinking wine his disciples were even symbolically drinking blood." So too Klausner:[2] "The drinking of blood even if it was meant symbolically could only have aroused horror in the minds of such simple Galilean Jews."[3] The objection to the Markan account thus advanced by Montefiore and Klausner must be given its full weight and Dr Vincent Taylor has dealt seriously with it. He offers a criticism of the position of the above scholars on the four grounds: first, that Jesus was not an ordinary Jew but one who believed Himself to be the Son of Man destined to suffer for many; secondly, that the words of Jesus often aroused horror and intense opposition among the Jews; thirdly, that those to whom the words under discussion were addressed were not 'simple Galilean Jews' but disciples who had long been in the school of Christ learning of a Son of Man who had to suffer; fourthly, that the objection is only valid if the theory of transubstantiation is accepted. But "Jesus did not invite His disciples to drink blood or to drink blood symbolically, but to drink wine as representing His life surrendered for many.... What Jesus has in mind is a redemptive activity, not a transformation of substance."[4]

[1] C. G. Montefiore, *The Synoptic Gospels*, vol. i, p. 332.

[2] *Jesus of Nazareth*, p. 329; cf. also for the Jewish objection, H. Loewe, *R.A.* p. 647: "Jews shudder at the passages in Hebrews and Romans and the Gospel verses describing the constitution of the Eucharist...."

[3] For the place of blood in Jewish thought, see *Schriften des Institutum Judaicum in Berlin*, no. 14, "Der Blutaberglaube bei Christen und Juden von Hermann L. Strack".

[4] V. Taylor, *Jesus and His Sacrifice*, pp. 134f.

Nevertheless, whether we accept Taylor's view or not the significant fact remains that in the Pauline account of the Last Supper the offence of the 'blood' insisted upon by Montefiore and Klausner is absent, and scholars have been at pains to account for this. Dalman[1] has suggested that the substitution of "This cup is the New Covenant in my blood" for the Markan "This is my blood" arose in a Gentile environment in order to obviate the difficulties that the Markan form offered to Hellenists. It is difficult, however, to see how Paul's formula with its reference to an essentially Hebraic conception such as a covenant in blood would have been easier to understand than the more direct Markan form. This is borne out by the fact that it has been possible for some scholars to take a view exactly opposite to that of Dalman. Thus Flew,[2] following Behm, claims that "the Markan version has revised away the difficulties early felt in the Pauline form, especially the description of the cup as the Covenant". On the other hand again, Dibelius,[3] so far from thinking that the Pauline form arose under Gentile influences, has traced that form to Jewish sources. "A Jewish Christian Church," he writes, "with its dread of blood, would scarcely have made Jesus say 'This is my blood' (in the Cup), but This Cup means a New Covenant which is instituted by my blood, i.e. by my death", and he regards the Markan as later than the Pauline account.

When such divergent conclusions have been based upon the same evidence any dogmatism would be foolish. We incline to the view that the Markan form in its starkness is such as Jesus in His own arresting manner might well have used, and if we could ascribe priority to it, it would be very tempting to cut the Gordian knot by regarding the Pauline account as a modification of the Markan designed to obviate the objectionable way in which reference is made to the blood. The differences between the two accounts, however, compel us to recognize that it is safer to avoid the assumption that either is a considered variation of the other. The omission of the command to repeat the rite in the Markan account, its more emphatic eschatological note and other minor differences suggest that it is independent of the Pauline account.[4] We are probably to understand the emergence of the two accounts, as indeed of other accounts, as we have already suggested above, along lines proposed by Dr Taylor, and for the sake of clarity,

[1] *Jesus-Jeshua* (E.T.), p. 161.
[2] R. N. Flew, *Jesus and His Church*, p. 49, n. 1. Flew compares H. Lietzmann, *H.Z.N.T., An die Korinther*, p. 60.
[3] *From Tradition to Gospel*, p. 207.
[4] Cf. W. Manson, *Jesus the Messiah*, p. 136. See also V. Taylor, *Jesus and His Sacrifice*. See the whole discussion on pp. 203 f.

though at the risk of some repetition, it will be well to quote his words:

> I Cor. 11. 25 may be as original as Mark 14. 24 f. itself. It has already been suggested that the saying: "This is my blood of the Covenant, which is shed for many", may not have been fully understood at the time. While this admission is no argument against their genuineness, it suggests the possibility that Jesus may have expounded His own words. Is the saying found in I Cor. 11. 25 part of his interpretation? Criticism is rightly on its guard against harmonizing expedients, but when it can be shown that one saying is probably not derived from a second and that the second need not be a variant of the first, there is matter for reflection. It is especially important to avoid the delusion that different accounts of the Supper are self-contained and mutually exclusive. Form criticism reminds us that such narratives were merely the rounded residues of earlier stories from which much has fallen away and that the sayings they contain are those which attracted the interest of the narrators. Similar sayings in different narratives may be but need not be identical; on the contrary they may be original variations on the same theme. How far these principles can be applied to the present case, it may be impossible to decide, but there is certainly as much reason to explain I Cor. 11. 25 as an original interpretation of Mark 14. 24 as to adopt the hypothesis of modification.[1]

Particularly relevant in the present connection are the words in the above quotation which refer certain sayings to the interest of the narrators. We have already rejected that view which would make the Pauline account the deliberate modification or variation of the Markan in order to remove the offence of the 'blood', but, while rejecting this, we now advance another, namely, that the Pauline account in its treatment of the element of blood does reflect the interests of Paul the Rabbi. We may assume that if persons to whom Montefiore and Klausner referred as simple Galilean peasants would find the suggestion of drinking blood even symbolically repugnant, one who had been trained for the Rabbinate would have found it doubly so, so that Paul would hardly have found satisfaction in any form of words such as we find in Mark. We submit that in the refinement which the Pauline form undoubtedly presents we are to trace the mark of the Rabbi who has moulded what he has found in the tradition into a form palatable to his own delicate sensibilities.

The immediate and obvious criticism of such a view is that Paul in this passage expressly states that he is delivering to the Corinthian church what he had received, and Dr Taylor has been constrained to insist on the supreme objectivity with which Paul has dealt with his theme.[2] The

---

[1] V. Taylor, *Jesus and His Sacrifice*, p. 205.   [2] Ibid. p. 216.

crux of the matter, however, lies in the exact meaning of the sentence: "For I have received of the Lord that which also I delivered unto you." It has been suggested that we should take the ἐγώ in this sentence to imply that Paul is here consciously setting himself over against other leading Christians who had presented other traditions or interpretations of the Last Supper. Useful as this suggestion would be, however, in confirmation of our position, we cannot accept it. The significance of the ἐγώ in the above sentence is not to be emphasized, and it is not necessary to find any polemic motive in Paul's account of the Supper, and it is clear that Paul regards his version of the latter as consonant with the main apostolic tradition.[1] It is in our understanding of the words 'received' and 'delivered' that we are to find the true approach to the Pauline account. The obvious meaning of the phrase "I received from the Lord" is that Paul was directly informed in this matter by Jesus. Equally obviously, however, was this impossible because Jesus had died before Paul had come to acknowledge Him as Lord. How was it then possible for Paul to receive something directly from Him? That this difficulty was early felt is clear from the fact that some MSS. read παρά[2] instead of ἀπό. This easier reading, παρά, however, must be rejected: it is patently secondary. How then are we to understand "I received from the Lord"? Two views have been propounded: the first claims that Paul here refers to a direct revelation by vision from Jesus Himself of what happened at the Last Supper.[3] This is not convincing because as Otto[4] has pointed out Christ could not in a vision have referred to Himself in such words as "The Lord Jesus in the night in which he was betrayed", etc. Moreover, the terms employed by Paul—παραλαμβάνειν and παραδιδόναι—are certainly to be taken to refer to the reception and transmission of a tradition. They are in fact the Greek terms corresponding to two technical terms used in Rabbinical literature for the two activities mentioned, namely qibbêl and mâsar. Hence most scholars accept the second view that the sentence "I received from the Lord" refers to traditions that Paul had received from the Church in the days after his conversion. Although we incline to this view, however, it must be admitted that it is not wholly satisfactory because the term

---

[1] Cf. J. Moffatt, First Corinthians (M.N.T.C.), p. 163.

[2] παρά is read by D., ἀπο θεοῦ by G.

[3] So H. Lietzmann, H.Z.N.T., An die Korinther (3rd ed.), p. 57, who compares Gal. 1. 11, 12; he, however, thinks that Paul refers all that he heard about Jesus both before and after his conversion to the revelation on the way to Damascus.

[4] The Kingdom of God and the Son of Man, p. 276. The view is rejected by J. Moffatt, First Corinthians (M.N.T.C.), p. 167; V. Taylor, Jesus and His Sacrifice, p. 201; M. Goguel, The Life of Jesus (E.T.), p. 445.

qibbêl does imply the direct reception of specific words. It is only by blurring the obvious sense of παραλαμβάνω that we can make it here refer to the indirect reception of tradition.

It is the sentence, "I delivered unto you", however, that is our primary concern. For our purpose we would separate quite distinctly παραλαμβάνω and παραδίδωμι. Whereas if Paul had only written "I received from the Lord that the Lord Jesus on the night", etc., we would be in difficulty and compelled somehow to take him to mean that he was reproducing the *ipsissima verba* of Jesus, the fact that he speaks of his delivering a tradition means that he is possibly giving his own version of what he has received. It will help to clarify the issue if we cite an example of Rabbinical usage in this matter from the *Aboth*:

> Moses received the Torah from Sinai, and he delivered it to Joshua; and Joshua [delivered it] to the Elders; and the Elders [delivered it] to the Prophets; and the Prophets delivered it to the men of the Great Synagogue. These men said three things "Be deliberate in judgement"; and "Raise up many disciples"; and "Make a fence to the Torah" [1]

In the first part of the above, when it is written that Moses received the Torah from Sinai, what is meant is that he had a direct communication from God. But when he delivered the tradition to Joshua and Joshua delivered it to the Elders, etc., it is not implied that there was an exact verbal transmission of the Torah to each recipient. The whole history of the development of Torah shows that the 'delivery' of tradition was the explanation of what was implicit in, as well as the transmission of, a kind of fixed deposit. Oesterley's comment on the last sentence in the above quotation is relevant (i.e. the sentence: "These men said three things", etc., which might be paraphrased "These men delivered that we should be deliberate in judgement", etc.). He writes: "The three things said must not be regarded as having been formally uttered, they probably express three of the most important sayings which had been handed down, and represented precepts regarding which there was a general concensus among the earlier scribes...." [2]

Similarly we are not to understand from Paul's account of the Last Supper that he is quoting the *ipsissima verba* of Jesus, but we are to find there the precipitate of those words percolated through the mind of a Rabbi, much as the three words referred to above were the precipitate of much Rabbinical thought. This view receives confirmation from a fact that emerges from the Pauline account itself. Paul makes it clear

---

[1] P. *Aboth* I. I.

[2] *The Sayings of the Jewish Fathers*, p. 2. For קבלה see C. Taylor, *The Sayings of the Jewish Fathers*, p. 105.

that he had previously delivered to the Corinthian Church the essential tradition of the Lord's Supper before writing 1 Corinthians, but the Church had not understood it. In 1 Corinthians he is merely delivering in a more formulated or fixed form what he had 'delivered' before. This approach to Paul's account makes it possible for us to understand why it is, as has often been pointed out, that the essential meaning of the Markan and Pauline accounts is the same while it is the formulation that differs. In our view the Pauline formulation is a Rabbinization of the tradition in which the offence of the 'blood' is removed.

We now turn to another emphasis in the Pauline account of the Last Supper. Two conceptions have been discovered to underlie the Markan account, that of the Suffering Servant in the words 'shed for many' and that of the Covenant described for us in the book of Exodus.[1] In the Pauline account, on the other hand, we find no trace of any influence of the Servant conception. To understand the Pauline account we can conveniently turn again to the article by T. W. Manson already referred to. In the latter Manson has suggested that in his presentation of the work of Christ, it will be remembered, Paul has been deeply influenced by the festivals of the Jewish year, among others by the Passover, and that he has applied the ideology of these festivals to the work of Christ. It seems a justifiable assumption that 1 Corinthians was written before the Passover season and it is natural that the Passover ritual should be in the forefront of Paul's thought, and there is considerable evidence that this was so. Thus in 1 Cor. 15. 23 Christ is called the firstfruits,[2] an element in the Passover ritual, and there is a more specific reference still of course in 1 Cor. 5. 7. Perhaps it is strictly incorrect to claim that Paul in 1 Cor. 5. 7 is thinking of the Eucharist as the Christian equivalent of the Jewish Passover. Moffatt is to be followed in the view that Paul's thought in that passage is that the Christian life in its entirety is a festival. Nevertheless, we believe that Paschal ideas dominate his view of the Eucharist.[3] We have previously pointed out that the thought of Chris-

[1] Cf. V. Taylor, *Jesus and His Sacrifice*, p. 131.

[2] Cf. G. Buchanan Gray, *J.T.S.* vol. xxxvii, pp. 241 ff.; *Sacrifice in the Old Testament*, pp. 24 f., 46, 386, see index. See above, chapter 5.

[3] This is not the place to discuss the date of the Last Supper. According to Mark, Matthew and Luke it was the day of the Passover and the Last Supper was the Jewish Passover. There are difficulties in accepting this view and most scholars follow the Fourth Gospel which places the Last Supper before the Passover. One wonders whether it was through the influence of Paul that the Last Supper came to be looked on as the Passover meal. This does not, of course, affect the fact that in any case Paschal thoughts were in the mind of Jesus at the Last Supper. Cf. J. Moffatt, *First Corinthians (M.N.T.C.)*, ad loc.

tianity as a New Exodus, with its New Torah, was constantly in Paul's mind and it is fully consonant with this that the Last Supper should be regarded by him as the inauguration of the New Covenant that was to be contrasted with the old, this New Covenant being ratified in the blood of Jesus, and it is this aspect of the Death of Jesus that appears in his account of the Eucharist as central to Paul. The death of Jesus is viewed there almost exclusively in terms of the New Covenant. In this Paul is making explicit what was implicit in the tradition that he had received. That Jesus had thought in terms of a New Covenant instituted through His Death we cannot[1] doubt, and He may even have actually expounded His thought at the Last Supper to this effect. But we have seen that the significance of the Last Supper for the understanding of the mind of Jesus often passed unnoticed in early Christian circles. Thus, although the Markan account in our view does look back to Exod. 24. 8, the reference is not explicit and it has been possible for some to question this reference.[2] In any case the concept of the New Covenant is only implicit. It is the Pauline account that brings out clearly the significance of the Last Supper, and in thus bringing out into prominence the idea of the New Covenant Paul was not merely stating what he had 'received' in the literal sense but moulding what he had received in such a way as to reveal its inner meaning; and again we suggest the activity of a Rabbi's mind, because the covenantal idea would of course be central to such a mind.[3]

One further point in Paul's account of the Last Supper is highly significant from this point of view. The chief difference between the Markan and Pauline accounts of the Last Supper in addition to what has already been mentioned is that Paul presents words in which Jesus makes provision for the continuance of the rite, "Do this in remembrance of Me", and in no other account of the Supper is Jesus represented as envisaging the continued observance of the Eucharist. Dr Taylor has rejected the view that these words are not original.[4] To him the fact that Mark and Matthew omit them does not imply that the words were not part of the tradition of the Last Supper received by them but merely that they were assumed. Mark "may well have taken for granted a command which no one doubted". We agree with Dr Taylor that Paul is not innovating, that he is true to the mind of the Master, but

---

[1] Cf. T. H. Robinson, *Z.A.W.* (1925), Beihefte 40-41, pp. 232f.

[2] W. Manson, *Jesus the Messiah*, p. 146: "It is by no means certain that Jesus when He spoke of His sacrifice and of the institution of the New Covenant had Exod. 24. 8 in mind and not rather Deutero-Isaiah's language about the Servant."

[3] See the first chapter of A. Büchler's, *Studies in Sin and Atonement*.

[4] *Jesus and His Sacrifice*, pp. 206f. So J. Moffatt, *First Corinthians* (*M.N.T.C.*), p.166.

nevertheless it is again significant that Paul should have made explicit what was quiescent before. We suggest that the reason for this is that for Paul the Last Supper corresponds to the Passover of Judaism, it is the New Passover. Readers of the *Passover Haggadah* will recall how the element of memory is there emphasized. We read: "Now even though all of us were wise, all of us of great understanding, all of us learned as elders, all of us familiar with Scripture, it would still be our duty to tell again the story of the Exodus from Egypt...."[1] Memory of a deliverance was central in the Jewish Passover. Paul transfers this to the Eucharist, the New Passover, at which even the wise[2] of Corinth were again to remember the New Exodus. We do not doubt that εἰς ἀνάμνησιν is the equivalent of *l'zēker*[3] or *zēker* (in apposition) of the *Haggadah*, except that Christ has been substituted for "the day thou camest forth out of Egypt".

If our approach to the Pauline account of the Last Supper be correct, we should expect the idea of community to play a greater part in his thought of that Supper than that of the expiation of sin, as was the case in the Jewish Passover, and we find that this is so. That Christ's Death was a means of expiation Paul believed, as we have seen, but in his account of the Last Supper this idea is not very apparent; but just as in the Jewish Passover we have a memorial festival of thanksgiving for a past event that had led to the formation of the community of the old Israel so for Paul the Death of Jesus, when he thinks of the Eucharist, is primarily the means whereby the New Community is constituted. That he has in mind the Exodus of the old Israel and is thinking of the Christian dispensation as its counterpart comes out, finally, in 1 Cor. 10. 1-4. Moreover, in all the relevant passages for the understanding of Paul's thought on the Supper in 1 Cor. 10. 1-4, 14-22, 11. 20-34, the idea of community is prominent. Dr Vincent Taylor has written *a propos* of these sections that it is "inadequate to understand communion

---

[1] *Haggadah* (London, 1897), by Rev. A. A. Green, p. 27; cf. Deut. 16. 3.

[2] Cf. 1 Cor. 2.

[3] For this see also G. Buchanan Gray, *Sacrifice in the Old Testament*, p. 395, where he criticizes the sacrificial interpretation of εἰς ἀνάμνησιν as equivalent to the Jewish sacrificial term אַזְכָּרָה. As an example of the use of זֵכֶר we may refer to a sentence in the Qiddush: "For it (the Sabbath) is the first of the holy convocations, in remembrance of the departure from Egypt." זֵכֶר לִיצִיאַת מִצְרַיִם (*J.D.P.B.* p. 124). It is also noteworthy, as G. Buchanan Gray points out (op. cit. p. 395), that καταγγέλλω in 1 Cor. 11. 26 is the exact equivalent of the Hebrew הִגִּיד, and he goes on to write: "the recitation of the story of the death of the Lord, in other words of the act of redemption in which the Christian Church originates and on which it depends, corresponds exactly to the Haggadah at the Jewish Pascal meal, the recitation of the act of redemption from Egypt on which the Jewish nation depended."

(κοινωνία) of a fellowship of believers instituted by Christ", and that by κοινωνία of the Body and Blood of Christ Paul means "a vital relation with Christ Himself as the Crucified Saviour".[1] We need not disagree on the importance for Paul of the personal relation to Christ, but κοινωνία in the New Testament never departs from the primitive sense of sharing something in common, and in the passages under consideration the underlying idea is that of a common sharing in the Blood of Christ and this common sharing constitutes community.[2] In the above passages the idea of community is, therefore, central and in the immediate context of the Pauline account of the Last Supper it is the need of a proper awareness of the New Community to which Christ had given birth that makes it necessary for Paul to discuss the Supper at all.

It is not then as sacrificial and expiatory[3] but as covenantal that Paul chiefly thinks of the Death of Jesus in the context of the Last Supper, although of course everything covenantal had a sacrificial basis.

We have now dealt with the chief places where sacrificial concepts enter into Paul's thought on the Death of Christ. The other places where such concepts occur are not for our purpose important and can be safely ignored. Our study has revealed that Paul does use sacrificial terms and concepts, but at the end of each stage of our discussion we had to issue a caveat. We are compelled to recognize not only from the paucity of his use of such terms and concepts, but also from his obvious inability to enter into the full spiritual significance of the sacrificial system, as did the author of the Epistle to the Hebrews, that although his thought can move along the channels of sacrifice yet the latter are not fully native to him, as it were. We now go on to suggest that this is because he was a Rabbi and shared in the typical Rabbinic attitude to the sacrificial system. To understand what this means we shall have to examine further, and very briefly, the reactions of Rabbinic Judaism to that system.

Hitherto in our references to the sacrificial system we have emphasized its actuality and its acceptance by Jewry as a method revealed by God for the expiation of man's sin. Writing of the post-exilic period Oesterley has gone so far as to assert that "sacrificial worship, the means of approach to God, constituted after all the central and most important element of the Law";[4] and we recall the saying of *Aboth*:[5] "Simeon the Just

---

[1] Cf. V. Taylor, *Jesus and His Sacrifice*, p. 211.

[2] See C. H. Dodd, *The Johannine Epistles* (*M.N.T.C.*), pp. 6 f.

[3] G. Buchanan Gray, *Sacrifice in the Old Testament*, writes: "The Paschal victim was not a sin offering or regarded as a means of expiating or removing sins", p. 397. It is also significant that Paul does not say in 1 Cor. 5. 8 πενθῶμεν but ἑορτάζωμεν.

[4] *Sacrifices in Ancient Israel*, p. 215.

[5] *P. Aboth* 1. 2. עֲבוֹדָה is the Hebrew here: it might be translated 'worship'.

belonged to the last of the members of the Great Synagogue. He used to say: 'On three things the world stands, on the Torah, on the (Temple)-Service and on acts of love.'" The phrase 'temple-service' would here, of course, include sacrifice and although this saying is attributed to a high priest,[1] who might perhaps be suspected of over-emphasizing the significance of the cultus, there can be no doubt as to the recognized importance of the sacrificial system in Judaism. Nevertheless, the indications are unmistakable that that system, although accepted, was not fully satisfactory to the religious sensibilities of first-century Pharisaic Judaism, and we shall now point out how the sacrificial system was not the primary factor in Rabbinic thought on Sin and Atonement.

We may begin with the limited efficacy of the sacrificial system; the latter was concerned only with sins done unwittingly not with those done with a 'high hand', i.e. deliberate sins. Davidson writes: "The class of offences said to be done with a high hand were capital and followed by excision from the community. The sins of error and ignorance could be removed by sacrifice and offering.... In other words the Old Testament sacrificial system was a system of atonement only for the so-called sins of inadvertency."[2] Most scholars have so presented the distinction between sins done unwittingly and those done with a high hand as to leave the impression that the former were merely concerned with matters of ceremonial impurity, and that therefore the sacrificial activity of Jewry had little if any moral significance. Thus C. A. A. Scott has written: "As to the class of sins done with a high hand, which the sacrifices did not touch, upon the whole they were the sins forbidden by the moral law."[3] In the same way Schechter writes: "the great majority of sacrifices are largely confined to matters ritual and ceremonial and certain other transgressions relating to Levitical impurity",[4] and so Moore declares that the sin offering is "not an offering for sin in our sense at all" because for Judaism "sin is in fact a religious not primarily a moral conception".[5] It is, however, extremely doubtful whether we are to draw such a rigid distinction between what we should call moral offences and those dealt with by the sacrificial system; to do so is to over-simplify a complex issue. Büchler has shown that the defilement or taint which the sacrificial system was designed to remove was as much moral as ceremonial, and in Rabbinic Judaism no less than in

---

[1] Either Simeon II, High Priest in c. 226–198 B.C., or Simeon I, High Priest c. 300 B.C.; cf. W. O. E. Oesterley, *The Sayings of the Jewish Fathers*, p. 2.

[2] A. B. Davidson, *The Theology of the Old Testament*, p. 316.

[3] C. A. A. Scott, *Christianity According to St Paul*, p. 87.

[4] S. Schechter, *Some Aspects of Rabbinic Theology*, p. 296.

[5] Moore, vol. I, p. 461. See also pp. 463, 497 f.

the Old Testament the terms 'to be unclean' and 'to defile' have always a moral no less than a levitical connotation.[1] The case has been well put by Welch.[2] Pointing out that the Mosaic conception of sin as moral transgression had been superimposed on a more naïve type of religion, which conceived sin as ceremonial defilement, Welch shows how these two irreconcilable conceptions came to coexist in Judaism, so that the Torah came to include both ceremonial and moral demands. This persisted in Rabbinic Judaism, and in the light of this Welch has rightly criticized Moore's treatment of sin and atonement in the later Law. His words deserve to be quoted *in extenso*.

The weakness of Moore's discussion is that he has not allowed for the extent to which the idea of sin as moral transgression had lodged itself in Jewish thought, and has written at times as though only ceremonial impurity was recognized there. Now in the wealth of valuable and interesting material which he has collected, especially in the Notes, Vol. III, he has shown how persistently the early Rabbis discussed the value of repentance, and of the sin-offering respectively in relation to voluntary sins. But he has failed to explain why this particular question continually troubled the minds of thoughtful men in Jewry. They were recognizing the presence of two unreconciled elements in their ancestral faith and thus inconsistently showed that the faith was not homogeneous in its teaching on the subject. Nor has he recognized that the distinction in the post-exilic law between sins done *b'sh'gâgâh* or *per incuriam* and sins done *b'yâd râmâh*,[3] with the somewhat contradictory view as to whether sacrifice availed for both, proves how early the question forced itself on men's minds. Since, in my judgement, the distinction is not clearly drawn, nor is the validity of the sin-offering defined, I must conclude that the men of the Return left the fundamental contradiction unreconciled and handed it on to their successors.[4]

In the light of Welch's statement it is not justifiable to dismiss the sacrificial system as merely concerned with what has sometimes been too contemptuously called the solemn trifling of ceremonial impurity, and it must be recognized that a sin done unwittingly might have had a moral connotation. Nevertheless, it will be clear that a system which excluded

[1] *Studies in Sin and Atonement*: the whole book should be read, and especially in this connection §§ 3, 4. He finds the concept of sin as defiling in Rabbinic Judaism before A.D. 70. See pp. 288–92; *b. Pes.* 57a. On p. 306 we read: "...it is evident that the idea of the soiling nature of sin continued without any break from Biblical to the late Rabbinic times, and only the vocabulary expressing that character varied." See also p. 307.
[2] *Post-Exilic Judaism*, pp. 280f. and especially pp. 301f.
[3] For these, cf. Moore, vol. I, p. 463. Also S. Schechter, *Some Aspects of Rabbinic Theology*, p. 296. Cf. Lev. 4. 2f.; Num. 15. 22–31; Ps. 19. 13; Num. 15. 30; Deut. 17. 12.
[4] *Post-Exilic Judaism*, p. 304. Also *Prophet and Priest in Old Israel*, p. 142.

from its purview the sin, whether ceremonial or moral, which was the expression of man's deliberate rebellion or enmity against God failed at that point where the problem of atonement was most acute;[1] it is the recalcitrant will that is the crux of our moral problem, and it was just this with which the sacrificial system could not and indeed did not attempt to deal. It is a striking fact that the account of sin in Rom. 7: "For the good that I would I do not: but the evil that I would not that I do",[2] is the description of a soul divided against itself for which the sacrificial system did not profess to have a remedy. Despite its statutory character, therefore, which made its observance obligatory, it was inevitable that Judaism should not rest content with the sacrificial system and with the expiation that it offered; and first-century Judaism reveals clearly that in its thought on sin and atonement it was not sacrifice that was central but certain moral and spiritual realities. To enter into a full discussion of the attitude of first-century Judaism on this question is impossible here, but we may notice the following points.[3]

First, the folly of regarding sacrifice in itself as efficacious for the expiation of sin was often condemned. In this the Rabbis were the heirs of the prophets. The following words from Ecclesiasticus may safely be accepted as expressing a point of view that was generally recognized.

> 8. Bind not up sin twice; for in one [sin] thou shalt not be punished.
>
> 9. Say not, He will look upon the multitude of my gifts, and when I offer to the most High God, He will accept them.[4]

And again:

> 18. He that sacrificeth of a thing wrongfully gotten, his offering is made in mockery, and the mockeries of wicked men are not well-pleasing.
>
> 19. The Most High hath no pleasure in the offerings of the ungodly; neither is He pacified for sins by the multitude of sacrifices....[5]

Consonant with all this was the frequent reminder that it was not the costliness or weight of the sacrifice that mattered but the intention behind it.[6] This brings us to the second point: Büchler has shown how the priests officiating over the actual process of sacrifice made the latter the occasion for the inculcation of moral and spiritual truths: "How

---

[1] Cf. F. C. N. Hicks, *The Fullness of Sacrifice*. He accepts the view of the incompleteness of the sacrificial offerings but goes on to say that the amoral conception of the unclean is more profound than the moral conception, pp. 14f.

[2] Rom. 7. 19; cf. C. A. A. Scott, *Christianity According to St Paul*, p. 87.

[3] Throughout we are discussing Pharisaic Judaism, to which Paul belonged; certain other elements in Judaism would not be so critical of the sacrificial system. See T. W. Manson, "The Jewish Background", in *Christian Worship*, ed. N. Micklem, Oxford, 1936, pp. 35ff.

[4] Ecclus. 7. 8f. (Büchler's translation).   [5] Ecclus. 34. 18f.

[6] Cf. *Studies in Sin and Atonement*, p. 413; *Lev. R.* 3. 5; *Ps.* 50. 13.

much depended for the true understanding, and for a spiritual and moral concept, of the sacrifice in the mind of the average man on the conversation between him and the priest in front of the altar", writes Büchler,[1] "need hardly be emphasized." Moreover, confession of the nature of the sin for the expiation of which an offering was being brought was made part of the sacrificial act, this confession being made 'inaudibly and privately' in order not to put the person making it to shame.[2] In addition to this, before performing the actual act of sacrifice the priests made sure that the offerer of the sacrifice had, where necessary, made proper restitution to those who had been injured by his sin.[3] Whether very 'high' conceptions were read into the sacrificial system before A.D. 70 is, as we have seen previously, very doubtful, but from what we have already written it will be clear that although sacrifices were regarded as having been ordained of God, yet there was not ascribed to them any efficacy that was not conditioned by certain spiritual realities. The impression received is not so much that any profound symbolism was read into the sacrificial system but that the latter was hedged about so as to preserve it from becoming divorced from morality. But most important of all in this connection, however, is the emphasis placed on the efficacy of repentance for expiation, and indeed its necessity. We may quote Moore: "The important thing is that while the Temple was still standing the principle had been established that the efficacy of every species of expiation was morally conditioned—without repentance no rites availed...."[4] "Repentance is...the *conditio sine qua non* of the remission of sins."[5] It is not necessary to reproduce the evidence gathered by Moore and by Schechter.[6] We will be content with a familiar quotation. "The sin offering and the unconditional guilt offering effect atonement;[7] death and the Day of Atonement effect atonement if there is repentance. Repentance effects atonement for lesser transgressions against both positive and negative commandments in the Law; while for graver transgressions it suspends punishment until the Day of Atonement comes and effects atonement."[8]

---

[1] Ibid. p. 410.   [2] Ibid. pp. 416 f.   [3] Ibid. pp. 408 f. (cf. Lev. 5. 23), also p. 418.

[4] Cf. Moore, vol. I, p. 505.   [5] Cf. ibid. p. 498.

[6] *Some Aspects of Rabbinic Theology*, pp. 313 f. Repentance "is practically considered a necessary accompaniment of all other modes of atonement", p. 313.

[7] Moore's note is necessary here: the sin offering and the guilt offering effect atonement "in the particular case in which they are presented". Repentance is presumed from the bringing of the sacrifice.

[8] *M. Yoma* 8. 8. See also n. 210 in Moore, vol. III. In *b. Shebu.* 12 b–13 a the opinion is ascribed to Rabbi "that the Day of Atonement atones with or without repentance, for all sins except those of the man who כירק עול ומגלה פנים בתורה ומיפר ברית בבשר—for these it atones only on condition of repentance". This opinion did not prevail.

In our submission facts such as we have above enumerated justify
the view that it was not sacrifice *per se* that was central in the thought of
first-century Judaism on sin and atonement, and this view is also confirmed by the verdict of history. The destruction of the Temple in
A.D. 70, and the consequent cessation of the sacrificial system naturally
caused great sorrow among Jewry,[1] and there is evidence that many
traced the disasters that subsequently befell the nation to this cause.
Thus R. Joshua b. Hananiah said: "Since the destruction of the Temple
there has not been a day without some curse, the dew has not come down
as a blessing, and the taste of the fruits has been taken away." R. Jose
added: "Also the taste of the fruits has been taken away."[2] Nevertheless,
it is a significant fact that Judaism quickly and easily adjusted itself to
the new situation. The well-known story of Johanan b. Zakkai shows
how the best elements in Rabbinic Judaism faced the cessation of sacrifice.
At the sight of the temple in ruins R. Joshua b. Hananiah said: "Woe to
us, for the place where the iniquities of Israel were atoned for is destroyed!" Johanan b. Zakkai replied: "Do not grieve, my son, for we
have an atonement which is just as good, namely, deeds of mercy, as the
Scripture says, 'For I desire mercy and not sacrifice'." (Hos. 6. 6.)[3]
Schechter's statement of the case is admirably fair; he claims that while
there is no evidence that the Rabbis deprecated sacrifices, "on the other
hand the facility with which the Rabbis adapted themselves after the
destruction of the Holy Temple to the new conditions must impress
one with the conviction that the sacrificial system was not considered
absolutely indispensable".[4] We might perhaps even go further than
Schechter in this matter. We know that in the second century A.D.
Jewish Gnostics offered criticisms of sacrifices and of the God who
demanded them,[5] and that these criticisms compelled the Rabbis to offer
certain high interpretations or conceptions of the sacrificial system in
the attempt to refute them. It is doubtful if this was the case before
A.D. 70, but we do know that the Essenes[6] had wholly rejected animal
sacrifices and this fact in itself must have occasioned some questioning
at least. Moreover, it must not be overlooked that the Rabbis even

[1] Moore, vol. I, p. 503.
[2] R. Simeon b. Gamaliel in the name of R. Joshua, M. Soṭ. 9. 12, Tos. Soṭ. 15. 2,
p. 321.
[3] *Aboth de R. Nathan*, I. ז. סוף, p. 21.
[4] *Some Aspects of Rabbinic Theology*, p. 208, n. 3.
[5] A. Büchler, *Studies in Sin and Atonement*, p. 414.
[6] Cf. W. O. E. Oesterley, *A History of Israel*, vol. II (W. O. E. Oesterley and T. H.
Robinson), pp. 323 f. The evidence of Josephus and Philo differs on this point, but
Philo is to be followed. Cf. Josephus, *Antiquities*, 18. 1, 5, and Philo, *Quod omnis probus
liber sit*, 12, Cohn-Wendland, vol. VI, pp. 21 ff.

while they upheld the sacrificial system had also to study the prophetic passages criticizing that system.[1] In view of all this it is not inconceivable that the cessation of the sacrificial system was the occasion of much silent relief among the Rabbis, a relief that enabled them to find quickly a substitute for its observance in the study of the sacrificial system.[2]

In the above paragraphs we have sought to estimate the import of the sacrificial system in first-century Judaism, and we have assigned it to a secondary place. Our aim in doing this has been to appreciate the significance of Paul's tardiness in the use of sacrificial concepts in his interpretation of the Death of Jesus. These concepts, as we saw, formed part of the tradition that he had received and are not despised by Paul. With what we must feel to be a certain reserve he did interpret the Death of Jesus as expiatory after the analogy of the sacrificial system. But further than this he did not go. This was so, we suggest, because he was too strictly Pharisaic to make that system the core of his thought or indeed a dominant factor in his thought. His sparse use of its forms is just what we would expect of a first-century Rabbi. He was altogether too familiar with the sacrificial system and at the same time with its insufficiency to use it, as did the author of the Epistle to the Hebrews, who was not familiar with it, and wrote after its cessation, as the basis of his interpretation of the Death of Jesus.[3] Much as his sober Rabbinism had led Paul to curb the turbulent glossolaly of many of his converts, so too, if we may hazard the suggestion, it had led him at times perhaps to recoil from an over-emphasis on the 'blood' element in the primitive Christian presentation of the Death of Jesus.[4] We may perhaps cite as a parallel the way in which what we may loosely call the more 'rationalist' sections of the Christian Church have often been antagonized by certain 'Evangelical' presentations of the Cross of Christ.

Our discussion so far has led to the conclusion that for our understanding of Paul's interpretation of the Death of Jesus sacrificial categories are only of minor importance. In addition, however, it has further revealed again how much Paul carried over into his interpretation of

---

[1] See *R.A.* p. 647. H. Loewe writes: "the prophetical passages against sacrifice also received full consideration"; also p. xci, etc.

[2] Cf. *Pesikta* 60b (*R.A.* p. 25). R. Huna (A.D. 219–57): "If you study the laws about sacrifice, that is to me as if you had offered them." For substitutes for sacrifices see *J.E.* vol. II, pp. 275f. and vol. X, pp. 615f.

[3] Cf. V. Taylor, *The Atonement in New Testament Teaching*, p. 94; C. H. Dodd, *A Companion to the Bible*, p. 407, writes of the sacrificial element in Paul's teaching that "it has been given undue importance by his expositors"; C. A. A. Scott, *Christianity According to St Paul*, pp. 85f.

[4] A careful study of Luke will reveal a similar dislike or distrust of the 'blood' motif.

the Christian Dispensation the covenantal conceptions of Judaism. The Pauline account of the Eucharist, as we saw, presents the Death of Jesus as the inauguration of a New Covenant, and in our treatment of Paul's thought throughout the preceding chapters this concept has again and again emerged. It is not necessary for our purpose to enter into a detailed examination of all the connotations of the term 'covenant'[1] on the lips of Paul, but one of these will prove relevant to our understanding of the latter's thought on the Death of Jesus.

Always correlative with the idea of covenant in Judaism is that of obedience. The 'old' Israel was a covenant people: its redemption from Egypt, through the gracious intervention of Yahweh on its behalf, had been followed by the imposition upon it of a covenantal relationship with Yahweh; but this relation implied *ipso facto* the acceptance of the obligation to obey the demands made by Yahweh; the covenant was conditioned by obedience.[2] This is clarified for us in Exod. 19. 3 f.:

And Moses went up unto God, and the Lord called unto him out of the mountain, saying, Thus shalt thou say to the house of Jacob, and tell the children of Israel; Ye have seen what I did unto the Egyptians, and how I bare you on eagles' wings, and brought you unto myself. Now therefore, if ye will obey my voice indeed, and keep my covenant, then ye shall be a peculiar treasure unto me above all people: for all the earth is mine. And ye shall be unto me a kingdom of priests, and an holy nation....

In this passage 'to hear God's voice' and 'to keep His covenant' are synonymous terms: to be in the covenant is to obey. So much is this so, as Büchler[3] has pointed out, that in some places the covenant stands for the Decalogue itself. Thus in Deut. 4. 12, 13:

And the Lord spake unto you out of the midst of the fire: ye heard the voice of the words, but saw no similitude; only ye heard a voice. And he declared unto you his covenant, which he commanded you to perform, even ten commandments; and he wrote them upon two tables of stone.

Throughout the Old Testament passages could be quoted where the covenant stands for the Torah or for laws commanded by Yahweh;[4]

[1] For this, see *H.D.B.* vol. I, p. 509.
[2] For all the following, see especially A. Büchler, *Studies in Sin and Atonement*, § 1: "Obedience to the Torah, its source and its sanction."
[3] *Studies in Sin and Atonement*, p. 3.
[4] 2 Kings 17. 15: "And they rejected his *statutes* and his *covenant* that he made with their fathers...." Hos. 6. 7, 8. 1: "They have transgressed my *covenant* and trespassed against my *law*." In Joshua 23. 16, the covenant is 'commanded'; Judges 2. 19-20; Deut. 29. 1-7. In Num. 15. 31 מצוה is a synonym for ברית. See A. Büchler, op. cit. p. 11.

and when we turn to the Apocrypha and Pseudepigrapha the same is true. This is so, for example, in Ecclesiasticus,[1] 1 Macc.[2] the Psalms of Solomon,[3] Ass. Moses,[4] and 4 Ezra.[5] The Torah is the *sêpher ha-bᵉrîth*. Hence it comes about that to disobey the commandments is to break or transgress the covenant. "The deliberate, provocative transgression of one of God's laws is an open defiance of His authority and of God Himself, the Giver of the Law", writes Büchler, "the contempt involved is the breaking of a covenant imposed by God, the sovereign King of Israel."[6] The Rabbinic literature reveals the same outlook. Jews are *bᵉnê bᵉrîth* and Yahweh is *baʿal bᵉrîth*. A prayer that probably goes back to the first century reads: "On account of Thy love, O Lord our God, with which Thou hast loved Israel Thy people, and in Thy pity with which Thou, our king, hast pitied *the sons of Thy covenant*, Thou hast given us O Lord our God, this great and holy Sabbath in love";[7] and a saying attributed to R. Eliezer b. 'Arak reads: "Be watchful in the study of the Torah and know what answer to give to the unbeliever, and let not one word in the Torah be forgotten by thee, and know before whom thou toilest and who is *baʿal bᵉrithkâ*."[8] This *baʿal* demands implicit obedience, he is the sole master of Israel and to be within His covenant people implies absolute submission to His rule, the acceptance of the yoke of the Kingship of God, *ʿôl malkûth shâmaim*. The true spirit of a *ben bᵉrith* is well expressed by the zealot Eleaẓar: "We have resolved for a long time (δουλεύειν) to be subject neither to the Romans nor to anybody else, except to God alone, for He alone is the true and just Master (δεσπότης) of men."[9] But to acknowledge a master is to become an *ʿebed* and it is the duty of the *ʿebed* to obey. Hence it follows that to accept the *ʿôl malkûth shâmaim* is to accept the *ʿôl mitzwôth* or in other words the *ʿôl ha-tôrâh*. According to R. Simeon b.Yoḥai (A.D. 140–65) God said to the Israelites at Sinai: "Now that ye have accepted my kingship,

---

[1] 17. 11, 24. 23, 28. 7, 42. 2, 45. 5, 17, 39. 8.
[2] 1 Macc. 1. 15, 57, 2. 20, 27, 50. See A. Büchler, op. cit. p. 15.
[3] 10. 5.
[4] 1. 9, 3. 9, 11. 17, 12. 13. These passages speak of a Covenant. on these see A. Büchler, op. cit. p. 18: "The Covenant Law in 1. 14; cf. Gal. 3. 18, 19, where the mediator alluded to through whom came the Law is Moses" (Büchler, op. cit. p. 18). Cf. Charles, *Ap. and Ps.* vol. II, p. 415. In many of the references in nn. 1–3 above the equation of Covenant and Law or laws is implied in the parallelism.
[5] 4. 23, 7. 24, etc.
[6] A. Büchler, *Studies in Sin and Atonement*, p. 11.
[7] *Tos. Ber.* 3. 7, p. 6. It was a prayer said by the father of R. Eleazar b. R. Zadok (A.D. 80–120 or 140–65); cf. Acts 3. 25. See A. Büchler, op. cit. pp. 24f.
[8] Cf. *Aboth R. Nathan* I. יז, פרק, p. 65; cf. *P. Aboth* 2. 14.
[9] Josephus, *Wars*, 7, 6 (Whiston's translation, p. 600).

accept my decrees."[1] Again R. Joshua b. Korḥah (A.D. 140–65) says: "Why does (in the prayer) the recital of Deuteronomy 6. 4 ff. precede that of Deuteronomy 11. 13 ff.? In order that we should first accept upon us the yoke of the Kingship of God and then the yoke of the commandments."[2] One other quotation will suffice. The words of R. Joḥanan b. Zakkai, which we quote here again, are valid not only with reference to the question in reply to which they were uttered, but for the attitude of Rabbinic Judaism generally. According to him a decree issued by God is "a decree of the king of the King of Kings.... God said, I have ordered an ordinance and I have decreed a decree, and no mortal must transgress my decree, as it is written Numbers 19. 2. This is the ordinance of the Torah."[3] On this passage Büchler comments:

> First, the description of God's unchallenged and unquestioned position in the Universe should be noted: Vespasian, the Roman emperor is a mighty ruler over many kings and over vast territories of the earth, but there are other rulers like him in other parts of the earth, who also command the allegiance of numerous princes; but God is the king over the Roman emperor and the other equally mighty rulers and His dominion is the whole Universe. Just as the Roman emperor issues his edicts and orders to his subjects in Judaea and the Jews have to obey them whether they appeal to their understanding or not, so God as the Master of all living creatures issues decrees, most of them reasonable, to all humanity, including His people; and though He sometimes gives no reason for one or other of His ordinances, and it appears to be unintelligible, no human being disobeys it without exposing himself to God's resentment.[4]

We need not further elaborate what is a commonplace of Rabbinic Judaism: our purpose in going into the above details has been to insist on the centrality for the latter of the concept of obedience; and we have now, to avoid any misunderstanding, only to remind ourselves that the 'ebed is to have joy in this obedience.[5]

We are now in a position to proceed to the next point. It will be evident that implicit obedience to the demands of Yahweh revealed in the Torah would not always be unhampered, indeed we may assume that it was never so. From two directions in particular that obedience would be challenged. First, the Old Testament has familiarized us with the picture of the suffering of the righteous; obedience to the Torah

---

[1] *Mekilta Baḥodesh* 6.

[2] *M. Ber.* 2. 2. Although the two Rabbis quoted belong to the middle of the second century the thought expressed here is fundamental to Rabbinic Judaism from the beginning. On the 'yoke', see A. Büchler, *Studies in Sin and Atonement*, pp. 52 f.

[3] *Num. Rabba* 19.   [4] *Studies in Sin and Atonement*, p. 36.

[5] Cf. S. Schechter, *Some Aspects of Rabbinic Theology*, pp. 148 f.

did not secure immunity from the slings and arrows of outrageous fortune and the Book of Job and the Psalms[1] show that this constituted one of the 'problems' of Judaism. Secondly, however, in addition to the fact that all the pain to which flesh is heir made it difficult sometimes to submit to the *'ôl malkûth shâmaim*, there was another more terrible factor, made familiar to us in the pages of recent history, the frequent incompatibility between the yoke of the Torah and the yoke of the authorities of this world. The pre-Christian no less than the post-Christian history of Jewry is chequered with periods when to take upon oneself the yoke of the Torah was to court suffering and even death itself. Judaism had to come to terms with both these factors, with suffering and with persecutions that often issued in martyrdom. We need not enlarge upon the way in which the Rabbis dealt with the former. We need only point out that they inculcated the acceptance of suffering because it was sent by God in order to purge away sin;[2] suffering had atoning efficacy. The attitude of submission is revealed in the words of Akiba: "God judges men by Himself but to nothing in His judgements is objection to be raised as He judges all in truth and all in justice."[3] An anonymous passage reads: "His dealings with all human beings are perfect and we must not criticize the ways of God even so far as the slightest wrong to man."[4] Passages attesting the atoning efficacy of suffering are plentiful. We quote as examples: R. Akiba said: "Moreover man should rejoice at chastisements more than at prosperity, for chastisements bring forgiveness for his transgressions."[5] R. Nehemiah said: "Beloved are chastisements for just as sacrifices atone so also chastisements atone."[6]

Here, however, we are chiefly concerned with the other factor that challenged obedience to the Torah, the suffering unto death which was the lot of the martyr. There is evidence that for certain sections within first-century Judaism martyrdom for the sake of the Torah was considered to be the acme of obedience or, in other words, obedience to the Torah was being thought of in terms of death. To understand this, let us first look at the Maccabean revolt. The words with which Mattathias, the instigator of the revolt, summoned his adherents to follow him reveal the nature of that revolt. He cries out: "Whosoever is zealous for the Law and maintaineth the covenant let him come forth

---

[1] See W. O. E. Oesterley and T. H. Robinson, *Hebrew Religion*, pp. 308f.; A. S. Peake, *The Problem of Suffering in the Old Testament*.
[2] For the whole subject, see A. Büchler, *Studies in Sin and Atonement*, chapter II, pp. 119ff.; Moore, vol. I, pp. 546f.; vol. II, pp. 253f.
[3] *Mekilta Beshallah* 6.   [4] *Sifre Deut.* on 32. 4, § 307.
[5] *Mekilta Bahodesh* 10; *Sifre Deut.* on 6. 5, § 32.   [6] *Mekilta Bahodesh* 10.

after me":[1] the inspiration of the revolt was loyalty to the Torah.[2] Moreover, in its initial stages the revolt assumed the character of a movement of passive resistance;[3] devotion to the Law was carried to such an extent that the 'rebels' preferred to be slaughtered rather than break the Sabbath.[4] The picture of Eleazar and his seven sons may be taken as typical of a quietistic obedience to the Torah that inspired many in the Maccabean revolt.[5] True this passivity was soon replaced by an active militarism, but only so long was this so as the religious issue was in the balance. It is notorious that once religious freedom had been secured the Maccabean party lost the militant support of the *Chasidim*.[6] For our purpose what is important is that the obedience unto death to which the 'Maccabean' martyrs bore witness made a profound impression upon Jewry. In his introduction to the Assumption of Moses, which we are to date in the first three decades of the first century,[7] Charles has written words so relevant to our point that they deserve to be quoted at length.

The book was written by a Pharisaic Quietist and was designed by its author as a protest against the growing secularization of the Pharisaic party through its fusion with political ideals and popular Messianic beliefs. Its author sought herein to recall his party to the old paths, which they were fast forsaking, of simple unobtrusive obedience to the law.... The duty of the faithful was not to resort to arms, but simply to keep the Law, and prepare, through repentance for the personal intervention of God in their behalf. Accordingly, though he depicts in all its horrors the persecution under Antiochus, he leaves unmentioned the great achievements of the Maccabean leaders and only once refers to the entire dynasty from 165 to 37 B.C., and that in most disparaging terms. For him the true saints and heroes of the time were not Judas and his great brethren, but an obscure group of martyrs, Eleazar and his seven sons, who unresistingly yielded themselves to death on behalf of God and the Law.[8]

Although, with Rowley, we need not follow Charles in his identification of the figure of Taxo with the Eleazar of 2 Maccabees,[9] we are justified

[1] 1 Macc. 2. 23-8.
[2] For the Maccabean Revolt, see W. O. E. Oesterley and T. H. Robinson, *The History of Israel*, vol. II, pp. 217f.
[3] See T. Herford, *Pharisaism*, p. 38; W. O. E. Oesterley, op. cit. p. 225.
[4] 1 Macc. 2. 29-38.   [5] Cf. 2 Macc. 6. 18f.
[6] W. O. E. Oesterley and T. H. Robinson, *History of Israel*, vol. II, p. 239. Cf. 1 Macc. 7. 12f. See Edwyn Bevan, *Jerusalem under the High Priests*, pp. 97f.
[7] Cf. H. H. Rowley, *The Relevance of Apocalyptic*, pp. 86f. Rowley favours a date not long before A.D. 30.   [8] *Ap. and Ps.* vol. II, p. 407.
[9] H. H. Rowley, op. cit. pp. 87, 128. Note C: "The Figure of Taxo in the Assumption of Moses." Dr Rowley refers to a passage in Josephus where there is

in maintaining that, in view of the character of the Assumption of Moses, the idea of obedience unto death, a passive acceptance of death out of loyalty to the revealed will of God as the crown of loyalty to the Torah, was in the air in first-century Judaism, and that it played a great part in Rabbinic Judaism appears when we turn to the martyrdoms of the second century A.D. The story of the death of Akiba will illustrate this. Büchler relates the story as follows:

> When R. Akiba was apprehended in the act of teaching the Torah and, on sentence of a terrible death passed by the Roman governor Tineius Rufus was in the presence of the latter slowly done to death in Caesarea amid horrible tortures, it happened to be the time for the recital of the sh‘ma‘. While his flesh was being torn from his body with iron combs, R. Akiba accepted upon him the yoke of God's kingship over him. When his disciples who witnessed his sufferings expressed to him their astonishment at his recital amid his unspeakable pains, he said, "Throughout all my life I was anxious for an occasion to fulfil the enactment 'And thou shalt love the Lord thy God... with all thy soul', meaning, even if He take thy soul, and I considered whether, if it happened, I could fulfil it; should I not fulfil it now that it has come to me?"[1]

So too R. Simeon b. Azzai (A.D. 120–40) explained "with all thy soul" in Deut. 6. 5, thus: "Love Him to the pressing out of thy soul."[2] The view that death placed the seal on obedience and showed complete readiness for God's perfect will, clearly played a prominent part in the martyrdoms of the second century A.D. and throughout the first century.

In the light of what we have written Paul, we may assume, would be familiar with that view which saw in martyrdom the supreme act of obedience. Moreover, we should expect that in his thinking on the Death of Jesus he would apply to it this concept of obedience; the death of the Messiah could only have one meaning for him, it would be the expression of obedience to the demands of God. An examination of the Epistles reveals that this was the case. In two passages, Rom. 5. 13–18 and Phil. 2. 8, Paul refers to the obedience of Christ; and the centrality of the category of obedience in Paul's interpretation

---

"one curiously like Taxo who lived in the days of Herod". *Antiq.* 14, 15. 5 (Whiston's translation, pp. 310f.). But "there is no reason to identify him with Taxo" (Rowley, op. cit. p. 132). The figure of Taxo "remains completely obscure". It may be possible on the other hand that although Taxo was not identified with Eleazar by the author of the *Assumption of Moses*, nevertheless that figure may have influenced his delineation of Taxo. See also H. H. Rowley in *The Journal of Biblical Literature* (March 1945), vol. LXIV, Part I, pp. 141f. and C. C. Torrey, ibid. (Sept. 1945), vol. LXIV, Part III, pp. 395f.

[1] b. *Ber.* 61ʰ; A. Büchler, *Studies in Sin and Atonement*, pp. 151f.
[2] *Sifre Deut.* on 6. 5, § 32: ‏אוהבהו עד מיצוי הנפש‎.

of the Death of Jesus has been adequately recognized by C. A. A. Scott,[1] who drew attention to the above passages. When we go on to ask in what sense Jesus fulfilled the will of God or how he became aware of the demands of that will, we must answer that that will was revealed to him in Scriptures, the Death of Jesus was κατὰ τὰς γραφάς[2] and it was also revealed in the spiritual consciousness of Jesus Himself, because we have seen that for Paul, Jesus Himself in the totality of His being was a New Torah. There is therefore a duality or incongruity in the thought of Paul at this point; Christ is for him both the New Torah and also the example of a perfect obedience to that New Torah; such an incongruity, however, should not be regarded as a blemish in his thought but merely as a mark of its unresolved complexity.

We have sought to show that Paul's emphasis on the category of obedience as the clue to the Death of Jesus is essentially Rabbinic. Before we leave this point, however, it is well to point out that it was not confined to Paul. It goes back to the mind of Jesus Himself. It will also be remembered that Macleod Campbell[3] turned to the Epistle to the Hebrews to discover, "Lo, I come to do Thy will, O God", as the great keyword on the subject of the atonement. The author of the Epistle to the Hebrews "is manifestly occupied", so writes Macleod Campbell, "with that in the work of Christ which caused the shedding of His blood to have a virtue which was not in that of bulls and goats, which he represents as being the will of God done, the mind of God manifested, the name of the Father declared by the Son".[4] To Macleod Campbell, the author of the Epistle to the Hebrews was Paul and if we could accept this view it would add force to our contention that obedience was the essential category in Paul's understanding of the Death of Jesus. Modern scholarship, however, has made the Pauline authorship of the Epistle to the Hebrews untenable,[5] and we must regard the latter as a non-Pauline work in which the category of obedience is applied to the Death of Jesus, the latter being regarded as a sacrifice in which the essential element was the dedicated will. Of course, the depreciation of animal sacrifice such as we find in the Epistle to the Hebrews is familiar to us in Philo:

Again, sacred ministrations and the holy service of sacrifices is a plant most fair, but it has a parasitic growth that is evil, namely, superstition, and it is well to apply the knife to this before its green leaves appear. For some have imagined that it is piety to slaughter oxen, and allot to the altars portions of what they

---

[1] *Christianity According to St Paul*, p. 94.   [2] 1 Cor. 15. 3.
[3] *The Nature of the Atonement* (4th ed.), pp. 107f.   [4] Ibid. p. 108.
[5] See J. Moffatt, *Hebrews (I.C.C.)*—the Introduction; A. B. Davidson, *Hebrews*, pp. 25f.

have got by stealing, or by repudiating debts, or by defrauding creditors, or by seizing property, and cattle lifting, thinking, in their gross defilement, that impunity for their offences is a thing that can be bought. "Nay, nay," I would say to them, "no bribes, O foolish ones, can reach God's tribunal." He turns His face away from those who approach with guilty intent, even though they lead to His altar a hundred bullocks every day, and accepts the guiltless, although they sacrifice nothing at all. God delights in altars beset by a choir of Virtues, albeit no fire burn on them. He takes no delight in blazing altar fires fed by the unhallowed sacrifices of men to whose hearts sacrifice is unknown. Nay, these sacrifices do but put Him in remembrance of the ignorance and offences by the several offerers...."[1]

The author of the Epistle to the Hebrews must have been cognisant of that type of criticism of the sacrificial system that is represented for us in Philo[2] and it is therefore possible that his treatment of the sacrifice of Jesus as consisting essentially of obedience may be independent of Paul; indeed, he was probably drawing upon the common substratum of early Christian thought. But the category of obedience is far more integral to the whole of Paul's thought than it is to that of the author of the Epistle to the Hebrews. True as is Macleod Campbell's profound insight into the importance of that category for the understanding of the Atonement, his treatment is not wholly just to the text of the Epistle to the Hebrews, where although the idea of the obedience of Christ in chapter 10 "pervades...as an atmosphere",[3] yet, to quote Davidson:

The passage in the Epistle is far from saying that the essence or worth of Christ's offering of Himself lies simply in obedience to the will of God. It does not refer to the point wherein lies the intrinsic worth of the Son's offering, or whether it may be resolved into obedience unto God. Its point is quite different. It argues that the Son's offering of Himself is the true and final offering for sin, because it is the sacrifice which, according to prophecy, God desired to be made.[4]

The upshot of this is that it is the concept of sacrifice not of obedience that is primary for the Epistle to the Hebrews whereas, as we have shown above, the contrary is true for Paul, the Rabbi.

[1] Philo, *Plantat. Noe.* xxv. The Loeb Classical Library translation, vol. III, p. 267, by F. H. Colson and G. H. Whitaker.

[2] Cf. J. Moffatt, *Hebrews (I.C.C.)* on 10. 4: "The ringing assertion of verse 4 voices a sentiment which would appeal strongly to readers who had been familiar with the classical and contemporary protests against ritual and external sacrifice as a means of moral purification."

[3] T. C. Edwards, *The Epistle to the Hebrews (The Expositor's Bible)*, p. 177.

[4] *Hebrews*, p. 193. So J. Moffatt, *I.C.C.* ad loc., and T. C. Edwards, *The Epistle to the Hebrews (The Expositor's Bible)*, p. 177. Contrast C. H. Dodd, *The Gospel in the New Testament*, pp. 94f.

We have now established that Paul regarded the Death of Jesus primarily as the expression of His obedience; Jesus, the Messiah, had· rendered an obedience unto "the pressing out of his soul". Of the passages referred to above where the obedience of Jesus is emphasized there are two which need especial consideration, in order that we may see how Paul develops his thought on the significance of this obedience. The first passage is in Rom. 5. We quote verses 17–19:

> (...For if by one man's offence death reigned by one; much more they which receive abundance of grace and of the gift of righteousness shall reign in life by one, Jesus Christ.) Therefore as by the offence of one judgement came upon all men to condemnation; even so by the righteousness of one the free gift came upon all men unto justification of life. For as by one man's disobedience many were made sinners, so by the obedience of one shall many be made righteous.

In the above Paul ascribes to the obedience of Jesus an efficacy that avails for 'many'; he argues that just as the disobedience of Adam had involved all mankind in sin, so the obedience of Christ, the Second Adam, had the power to raise all men to righteousness. In verses 6 and 8 of the same chapter Paul had declared his conviction that "when we were yet without strength in due time Christ died for the ungodly (ὑπὲρ ἀσεβῶν)" and that "while we were yet sinners Christ died for us (ὑπὲρ ἡμῶν)", and elsewhere he wrote that "He loved me and gave Himself for me (ὑπὲρ ἐμοῦ)".[1] But this created a problem, how was it possible for the action of one man to be efficacious for others? It is to this problem that Paul addresses himself in the passage which we have quoted. The solution that he there offers, in our submission, has clearly grown out of that world of thought revealed to us in the Apocrypha and Pseudepigrapha and in the Rabbinic literature which gave birth to the Rabbinic doctrine of merit and of imputed sin. That doctrine derives from that vivid conception of the solidarity of all members of the community of Israel with which we have frequently dealt previously, and which need not therefore detain us here. At this point it will be our task to point out the way in which the concept of solidarity influenced the thought of Judaism on sin and righteousness and how this in turn supplied Paul with a means of interpreting the work of Christ.

It was a postulate of Rabbinic thought that a man by his obedience to the Torah could obtain merit.[2] In fact, according to some of the Rabbis the Torah had been expressly given in order that Israel might be given the opportunity of gaining merit. Thus R. Ḥananiah b. Akashya

---

[1] Gal. 2. 20.
[2] Cf. A. Marmorstein, *The Doctrine of Merits in the Old Rabbinical Literature*, p. 11.

(A.D. 140–65) says: "The Holy One, blessed is He, was minded to grant merit to Israel, therefore hath he multiplied for them the Law and the commandments, as it is written, It pleased the Lord for His righteousness' sake to magnify the Law and make it honourable."[1] These merits, however, benefited not merely the person who by his obedience had acquired them, but also his contemporaries, and in addition, because of that solidarity of all the members of the community both past, present and future to which we have referred, they would also avail for those who preceded him and those who would follow him both here and hereafter.[2] The idea that the good deeds of the pious man are stored up as treasures in heaven for his own benefit meets us in 2 Baruch[3] and the Testament of the Twelve Patriarchs,[4] but the first discussion on the question of merits in the Rabbinic literature occurred between two Rabbis of the first century B.C., namely, R. Shemaiah and R. Abṭalion.[5] The specific question with which they dealt was, "What merit did the Israelites possess that God divided the sea before them?" Shemaiah taught: "Sufficient is the faith, with which Abraham their father believed in Me that I should divide the sea before them, as it is said; And He believed in God and He counted it unto him (i.e. at the sea) for (doing) charity (with his children)."[6] (Gen. 15. 6.) Abṭalion says: "Worthy is the faith, they (the Israelites themselves) believed in Me so that I shall divide the sea before them, as it is said: 'And the people believed.'"[7] (Exod. 4. 31.) The difference between the views of these two Rabbis is significant and throughout the first century Rabbis were divided in the same way. It will be evident that the Doctrine of Merits which makes the merit of one available for others is open to the abuse of fostering moral laxity,[8] and we know from the New Testament,[9] and also from Jewish sources such as those cited in Strack-Billerbeck,[10] that there were many in Israel who were tempted to rely on the merit of their father Abraham for their salvation. The Rabbis were not unaware

---

[1] M. Makkoth 3. 16. Also P. Aboth 6. 11.

[2] See the whole of the discussion in the above work by Marmorstein; also Schechter, Some Aspects of Rabbinic Theology, pp. 170f. Schechter deals with the subject under the headings: (1) The Zakûth of a Pious Ancestry; (2) The Zakûth of a Pious Contemporary; (3) The Zakûth of the Pious Posterity.

[3] 2 Baruch 24. 1, 44. 14; cf. Matt. 6. 19–20.

[4] Test. Lev. 13. 5; Test. Napht. 8. 5.

[5] See A. Marmorstein, The Doctrine of Merits in the Old Rabbinical Literature, pp. 37f.

[6] Mekilta Beshallaḥ 4.   [7] Ibid. 4.

[8] See S. Levy, Original Virtue and Other Studies, pp. 38f.; A. Marmorstein, The Doctrine of Merits in the Old Rabbinical Literature, pp. 38f.

[9] Matt. 3. 9; cf. John 8. 33, 39.

[10] Str.-B. vol. 1, p. 116; cf. M. Baba Metzia 7. 1.

of this and, like John the Baptist, protested against it, and thus many
Rabbis only recognized the value of self-acquired merits, as did Abṭalion.
Hillel tried to take up a mediating position, which is, possibly, expressed
for us in the famous saying: "If I am not for myself, who is then for me?
And if I am for myself what am I?"[1] It was the view of people such
as Shemaiah, however, that was most prevalent and ultimately became
general, namely, that the merits of the righteous availed for others. With
the increasingly tragic development of events in the first and second
centuries of the Christian era for Jewry it was natural that appeal should
be made to the merits of the faithful in past ages. It is no accident that
the first Rabbi of the Tannaitic period to emphasize the Doctrine of
Merits was Eleazar of Modiim who lived in the period of the Bar Kokba
war.[2]

We shall now quote a few passages in order to illustrate the Doctrine
of Merits. Most prominent in the doctrine are the merits of the fathers
especially of the three patriarchs Abraham, Isaac and Jacob.[3] According
to one Rabbi the division of the sea at the Exodus was the result of the
merit of Joseph;[4] according to R. Nehemiah (A.D. 140–65) the redemption
from Egypt was for the merit of Moses and Aaron;[5] and a later Rabbi,
R. Naḥman, the son of R. Samuel b. Nahmani, explained the redemption from Egypt as a result of the merit of Abraham, Isaac, Jacob, Moses
and Aaron.[6] Marmorstein points out that the redemption from Egypt
naturally occupied the minds of the Rabbis in a period when resentment
at foreign domination was a perpetual sore.[7] There was in addition
what Schechter has called the zâkûth of a pious contemporary.[8] The
rather boastful words of R. Simeon b. Yoḥai (A.D. 140–65) are very
instructive. "If Abraham likes to justify [by his merits] all people from
his time up to my time, my merits will justify them from now up to the
time of the Messiah, if not I join with Achiah, ha-shîlônî, and we will

[1] P. Aboth 1. 14; see J.E. vol. IX, p. 560.
[2] See A. Marmorstein, The Doctrine of Merits in the Old Rabbinical Literature, p. 41.
[3] S. Schechter, Some Aspects of Rabbinic Theology, p. 171.
[4] Mekilta Beshallaḥ 4; Exod. Rabba 21. 8, mentions Abraham.
[5] Exod. Rabba 15. 3 ff. "The redemption from Egypt was for the merit of Moses
and Aaron. He compares the case with a king who wanted to marry a damsel. People
came and said: 'Do not do so. She is very poor indeed, she has really nothing but two
earrings. That is all.' The king said: 'Good, then I marry her for those two earrings.'
Likewise did God! It is sufficient that I redeem Israel for the sake of Moses and Aaron."
(A. Marmorstein, op. cit. p. 143.)
[6] Exod. Rabba 2. 5. It is not to be supposed that the views ascribed above to each
Rabbi were in any way peculiar to them. There was a very great variety of views.
[7] For these different views, see A. Marmorstein, op. cit. pp. 139f.
[8] Some Aspects of Rabbinic Theology, pp. 189f.

justify by our merits all creatures from Abraham up to the time of the Messiah."[1] More delightful, because of its true humility, is the story told of R. Ḥananiah b. Teradion (A.D. 120–40). His contemporary R. Jose b. Ḳisma was ill and R. Hananiah called on him.

> R. Jose b. Ḳisma said: "Hananiah, my brother, dost thou not know that to this nation [Rome] was given the rulership from heaven? A nation that has destroyed His house, burnt His temple, killed His pious ones and His best ones and still exists! Behold I heard of thee that thou art sitting and art engaged in the study of the law, and holdest the book in thy bosom." R. Ḥananiah said: "May heaven have mercy." R. Jose replied: "I told thee words of common-sense and thou sayest: May heaven have mercy. I wonder if they [the Romans] will not burn thee with the scrolls of Torah in fire." R. Ḥananiah, "Rabbi, am I going to have a share in the world to come?" R. Jose: "What hast thou done?" R. Ḥananiah: "Once I mistook my money put aside for the Purim meal for money of charity and distributed it among the poor." R. Jose: "I wish I had a share of thine; would that my lot were thine too."[2]

"That means to say", comments Marmorstein, "you have plenty of merits not merely for yourself, but also for others."[3] So far we have quoted passages in which the merits of certain righteous people are presented as redeeming and justifying others, but there are also passages which depict the merits of the righteous as atoning or forgiving the sins of men or affecting their reconciliation. Thus it was held that after the sin of making the golden calf at the foot of Mount Sinai God would have destroyed the people had not Moses referred to the merits of the Fathers. Thus R. Meir (A.D. 140–65) taught: "The dead ones of the Gentiles are dead, those of the Israelites are not dead, for through their merit the living exist; an instance for this is, when Israel did that deed, had Moses not mentioned the merits of the Fathers they surely would have perished from the world."[4] A later Rabbi compared the effect of referring to the merits of the Fathers to that of offering sacrifices. Thus R. Ḥaninah b. Ḥama (A.D. 279) says: "Had Moses known how appreciated the sacrifices are, he would have sacrificed all the offerings mentioned in the Torah at the time when Israel committed the deed, yet he ran and relied on the merits of the Fathers."[5] In this connection we may also refer to the famous passages in 2 and 4 Maccabees, where we have ideas very similar to those we have culled from Rabbinic sources. The

[1] *Gen. Rabba* 35. 2.
[2] b. *'Abodah Zarah* 18 a.
[3] *The Doctrine of Merits in the Old Rabbinical Literature*, p. 49.
[4] Cited freely by A. Marmorstein, ibid. p. 51; cf. *Tanḥuma Wayyera*, § 9, pp. 90–1.
[5] *Gen. Rabba* 1.

merits of the righteous Eleazar and his seven sons are believed to atone for Israel as a whole. We may quote these passages:

> We are suffering for our own sins, and though our living Lord is angry for a little, in order to rebuke and chasten us, he will again be reconciled to his own servants.... I, like my brothers, give up body and soul for our fathers' laws calling on God to show favour to our nation soon...and to let the Almighty's wrath, justly fallen on the whole of our nation, end in me and my brothers.[1]

And again:

> Be gracious to Thy people, being satisfied with our penalty on their behalf. Make my blood their purification, and take my life as the substitute for theirs.
> Because of them the enemy had no more power over our people, and the tyrant was punished, and the fatherland purified, inasmuch as they have become a substitute (for the life forfeited by) the sin of the people; and through the blood of these pious men and their propitiatory death, the divine Providence rescued Israel that before was afflicted.[2]

The thought in the above quotations goes beyond the Doctrine of Merits, but it belongs to the same genus as the latter, being governed by the same conceptions of solidarity. "The martyrs", writes H. W. Robinson, "do not complain that they, being personally innocent, are involved in the sufferings of guilty Israel; they accept Israel's corporate personality as involving themselves, and glory in the opportunity for this service to their brethren."[3]

It would be misleading to assert that the Doctrine of Merits and cognate ideas played a dominating part in first-century Judaism. We have already referred to criticisms that were made of that doctrine, and we must refer the reader who desires to view it in true perspective to the work of Schechter and Marmorstein. Nevertheless, it did form a well-defined element in the religious thought of that milieu into which Paul came, and that Paul was familiar with the Doctrine of the Merits of the Fathers would appear to be proved by his reference in Rom. 9. 5 and particularly in Rom. 11. 28.[4] The attempt made by Sanday and Headlam to deny the presence of the doctrine in the latter passage is unconvincing and irrelevant;[5] Dr Dodd's treatment of the passage is far

---

[1] 2 Macc. 7. 33, 37, 38.
[2] 4 Macc. 6. 28, 29, 17. 21, 22. Enough has been written above to justify the use of this Hellenistic work in this connection.
[3] *The Cross of the Servant*, pp. 59f., from which the above translations are taken.
[4] Cf. Moore, vol. I, p. 542.
[5] W. Sanday and A. C. Headlam, *Romans (I.C.C.)*, pp. 330f.

more convincing and correct; although he does not refer to the doctrine of merits by name he admits the presence of the idea.[1] Apart from the above references, however, the influence of the doctrine of merits comes out clearly in Paul's thought in Rom. 5, to which we referred at the beginning of this section, where he seeks to explain how the obedience of Jesus avails for others as we have already explained. Here he makes use of the concept of imputed sin in describing the consequences of Adam's sin, and of its opposite,[2] the concept of imputed righteousness or the doctrine of merits, in describing the effects of the obedience of Christ; and although in Rom. 5 Paul does not make use of any phrase that might be considered the equivalent of the term *zakûth*, nevertheless we cannot doubt that he is there governed by those conceptions of solidarity which the doctrine of merits implied. In seeking to express his awareness that the one man Jesus had in His exceeding love done that which benefited all men, Paul would naturally be helped by the fact that already in Judaism the belief that the merits of the righteous availed for others was a living one. Paul could think in terms of a 'merit' of Christ, gained through obedience, that was efficacious for all. He was saved from a false individualism and an atomistic interpretation of the Death of Jesus by that realistic emphasis on solidarity which we have found in Rabbinic thought. Moreover, one other factor remains to be noticed. The terms which Paul chiefly used to describe the results of the work of Christ are 'redemption', 'justification' and 'atonement'. It is not our task to examine what each of these terms signifies; we are merely concerned to point out that these are the conceptions most often found in the Rabbinical literature to describe the effects of the merits of the righteous, a fact which will be abundantly illustrated by the passages quoted above. The three terms referred to are such as would fall with great familiarity on the ears of the Rabbis of the first century and such as a Rabbi like Paul would naturally use in declaring the 'merits' of Christ and their benefits.

To recapitulate before we proceed to the next point, we have seen that Paul in true Rabbinic fashion interpreted the Death of Jesus as a triumph of obedience and that in Rom. 5 he employed categories rooted in ideas of solidarity familiar to Rabbinic Judaism to expound the efficacy of that obedience for others. There remains the application of the concept of obedience to the Death of Jesus in Phil. 2. 5 f.—a passage that emphasizes the element of death in the obedience of Christ.

[1] *Romans (M.N.T.C.)*, pp. 178 f.; Lietzmann's treatment in *H.Z.N.T., An die Römer*, p. 106, is unsatisfactory: he regards διὰ τοὺς πατέρας "als nur rhetorische Wort-parallele".

[2] Cf. S. Levy, *Original Virtue and Other Short Studies*, pp. 1–57.

In our previous treatment of this passage we argued that Paul was here thinking of Christ, as the Second Adam, who was to be contrasted with the first Adam, the obedience of the former being opposed to the disobedience of the latter. Combined with the Adamic conception we are to find here, however, the idea of the Suffering Servant of Deutero-Isaiah. In this passage, Christ the Second Adam is obedient *as Servant*. Dr Vincent Taylor[1] has complained of Paul's comparative neglect of the Servant-conception and, as a reason for this, has suggested that Paul could not bring himself to call his Lord a δοῦλος; this explains, for example, why in Phil. 2. 7 he speaks of Christ as taking μορφὴν δούλου not as a δοῦλος. But as Dr Taylor is compelled to admit, there are numerous indications of Paul's familiarity with the Servant-conception. We note the following passages: Rom. 4. 24–5, 8. 3; 1 Cor. 11. 23 ff., 15. 3; Eph. 5. 2, and above all the passage under consideration in Phil. 2. 5 f. The parallels between the latter and the Servant passages may be tabulated thus:

Servant Passages

Isa. 52. 13. He shall be exalted....	Phil. 2. 9. God hath highly exalted him.
Isa. 53. 7. He was oppressed, yet he opened not his mouth.	Phil. 2. 8. He humbled himself.
Isa. 53. 8. ἤχθη εἰς θάνατον (LXX).	Phil. 2. 8. ὑπήκοος μέχρι θανάτου.
Isa. 53. 12. He hath poured out his soul unto death.	Phil. 2. 6. ἑαυτὸν ἐκένωσε.

Compare also:

Isa. 45. 23. that unto me every knee shall bow, every tongue shall swear.	Phil. 2. 10. That at the name of Jesus every knee should bow...and every tongue should confess.

In view of the above we shall assume that Paul identified Jesus, the Messiah, with the Suffering Servant of Deutero-Isaiah. We shall also assume without discussion that this identification goes back to the mind of Jesus Himself. The question with which we are now confronted is whether that identification is alien to Rabbinic Judaism or one that was native to it. In short, did the idea of a Suffering Messiah originate with Christ or was it in some way part of His inheritance?

We begin with the fact that the New Testament presents the idea of a Suffering Messiah as constituting a σκάνδαλον to first-century Jewry,[2] and scholars have often drawn a complete contrast between the Messianic

---

[1] *The Atonement in New Testament Teaching*, pp. 95 f.

[2] Cf. Matt. 16. 21 f.; Mark 8. 31, 9. 31; Luke 24. 20 f.; Acts 17. 3; 1 Cor. 1. 23; Gal. 5. 11. Cf. Str.-B. vol. II, p. 274.

conceptions cherished by Jesus and those of his compatriots; we may refer to an article by J. B. Frey entitled *Le conflit entre le Messianisme de Jésus et le Messianisme des Juifs de son temps,*[1] in which this is emphasized. Moreover, it is urged that passages in the Rabbinic literature which refer to a Suffering Messiah are late and that the figure of the latter is either due to the desire to provide Judaism with a counterpart to the Crucified Lord of the Church or to the renewed interest in the Messianic problem that was naturally aroused by the Bar Kokba war.[2] As for the direct identification of the Messiah with the Suffering Servant of Deutero-Isaiah it is asserted that this is unknown in Judaism before Christ. The earliest explicit reference where Judaism interpreted Isa. 53 in terms of the Messiah is found in the Targum of Jonathan,[3] but here Isa. 53 is so interpreted that the picture of the Messiah which is derived from it is as unlike the Christian conception as it is almost possible for it to be. So much is this the case that it has been suggested that the Targum has been revised with the intention of refuting Christian exegesis.[4] To quote one example of the kind of Messiah presented in the Targum we quote:

Isa. 53. 7	The Targum
He was oppressed, and he was afflicted, yet he opened not his mouth: he is brought as a lamb to the slaughter,... he opened not his mouth.	He prayed and he was answered, and ere even he had opened his mouth, he was accepted: the mighty of the peoples he will deliver up like sheep to the slaughter...there shall be none before him opening his mouth or saying a word.

It has, therefore, been denied that pre-Christian Judaism knew a Suffering Messiah. Volz has summed up the position thus: "Von einem Leiden des Messias ist in unserer Periode noch nicht die Rede. Isa. 53 hat man erst später mit dem Messias in Verbindung gemacht."[5]

---

[1] J. B. Frey, in *Biblica* (1933), vol. xiv, pp. 133-49, 269-93.

[2] See Str.-B. vol. ii, p. 282.

[3] For this see Driver and Neubauer, *The Jewish Interpreters of Isaiah 53*, vol. ii, Translations, pp. 5f. Also W. O. E. Oesterley and G. H. Box, *The Religion and Worship of the Synagogue*, pp. 48f.

[4] It is not impossible, however, that it may also have been aimed at a Jewish tendency to believe in a suffering Messiah. Moreover, as Bonsirven points out, the Targum has not completely eliminated the elements of suffering. See verses 3 and 12; cf. J. Bonsirven, *Le Judaïsme Palestinien*, vol. i, p. 383.

[5] Paul Volz, *Judische Eschatologie von Daniel bis Akiba* (Tübingen and Leipzig, 1903), p. 237. Also, according to Dr H. H. Rowley, in the second edition of the above, *Eschatologie der Jüdischen Gemeinde im neutestamentlichen Zeitalter* (1934). See *The Relevance of Apocalyptic*, p. 130, n. 1.

The dismissal of the idea of a Suffering Messiah from Judaism in the pre-Christian period has not gone unchallenged. We may first notice attempts made to find a Suffering Messiah in the pre-Christian literature by King. The latter sought to establish that the germ of the belief in a Messiah b. Joseph, who is usually assigned to the second century A.D., "exists even in the Book of Genesis and that it runs through the whole of Jewish history, disappearing at times but always breaking out again in increased vividness."[1] In the course of his discussion of the origins of the Messiah b. Joseph, King refers to the fact that from the sixth century B.C. onwards up till the first century A.D. (the Psalms of Solomon), the hope of a Davidic Messiah had been eclipsed by that of a new Moses or Elijah.[2] In Ecclesiasticus the figure of Elijah has taken the place of the Messiah and there, in 48. 10, Elijah is given the functions of the Suffering Servant (καταστῆσαι φυλὰς 'Ιακώβ; cf. Isa. 49. 6, which forms part of one of the Servant passages). On the basis of this single quotation King goes on to infer that "if this quotation be admitted, we learn incidentally that the author of Ecclesiasticus (about 180 B.C.) already gave a personal interpretation to the prophecy respecting the Servant of the Lord in 2 Isaiah; so that the thought of a Suffering Messiah was not unknown before the days of Christ".[3] We cannot but feel, however, that the parallelism with the Servant poems is far too slight to admit of King's construction upon it. In the second place, however, like Strack-Billerbeck, King refers to the fact that already by A.D. 150 R. Judah and R. Nehemiah, who were disciples of R. Akiba, knew of the tradition of the Messiah b. Joseph, but on the evidence of b. Sukkah 52a, he goes further and traces that tradition back to the period before A.D. 70. There are two strands in his argument. First, one passage in b. Sukkah 52a reads, apropos of Zech. 12. 12, where there is a reference to the land mourning: "That mourning? What was it all about? R. Dosa and the (non-named) Rabbi differ on the point. The one says it is for Messiah the son of Joseph when he is killed, and the other says, It is for the Evil Yêtzer when it is killed." Accepting the reading of b. Sukkah over against that of the Yalkut, which has R. Jose, and that of the Jerusalem Talmud, which assigns the discussion to "two Amora teachers", King claims that R. Dosa was blind from old age before A.D. 70. Secondly, again in b. Sukkah 52a, there is a story in which God asks the Messiah b. David to ask what he will and it shall be done for him, "but when he saw that Messiah ben Joseph had been killed he said, O Lord of the Universe I ask of Thee nothing

---

[1] E. H. King, Yalkut on Zechariah (Cambridge, 1882), Appendix A, p. 85.
[2] Ibid. pp. 94f.   [3] Ibid. p. 97.

but life".[1] "This story", writes King, "is introduced by the formula
ת"ר 'our Rabbis have taught', which, according to Dr Schiller-Szinéssy,
is only used in the Talmud of the very oldest traditions, such indeed, as
by reason of their age, are unable to be traced to any known Rabbi."[2]
These two arguments, however, have not convinced Rabbinic scholars.
Strack-Billerbeck[3] place the date of R. Dosa at A.D. 180, and so do
Montefiore and Loewe.[4] Nevertheless, it must be admitted that it is
not impossible that figures familiarly known to Akiba and to his contemporaries might also have been known in the first century.

In another direction it has recently been suggested that we are to find
a pre-Christian Suffering Messiah in the figure of Taxo in the Assumption of Moses, who is to be explained in terms of the Suffering Servant
of Deutero-Isaiah. We owe the statement of this view, which is propounded by Lattey, to Dr H. H. Rowley's treatment of it in his book
The Relevance of Apocalyptic[5] and we need not here enter into a detailed
discussion of a theory that has been convincingly criticized by Dr Rowley.
The latter points out first, that the sole support of the equation of Taxo
with the Messiah is the assumed equation of Taxo and Shiloh in
Gen. 49. 10, an equation which rests on a series of textual and other
assumptions which are very questionable; secondly, that the action of
Taxo in his death does not resemble that of the Suffering Servant;
thirdly, that the reference to the seven sons of Taxo points to "a real
person already existing; nowhere else do we read of the sons of the
Messiah", and, fourthly, that Lattey's assertion that the death of Taxo
would usher in the Kingdom of God is not supported by the text. We
may quote Dr Rowley:

Moreover I find nothing in the text to indicate that the death of Taxo and
his sons would effect the coming of the Kingdom of God. It would be
followed by the coming of the Kingdom, which would avenge their innocent
death. But there is nothing in that to associate Taxo either with the Messiah
or with the Suffering Servant. The one was expected to establish the Kingdom
by His strength, and the other to serve and save by His vicarious suffering.
Taxo does neither....It may also be noted that the author of the Assumption

---

[1] Cf. *Yalkut on Zechariah*, p. 107.　　　　[2] Ibid. pp. 107–8.

[3] Cf. Str.-B. vol. II, p. 299.

[4] Cf. *R.A.* p. 700., where R. Dosa is relegated to the fifth generation of the Tannaites,
i.e. A.D. 165–200. See Ch. Guignebert, *The Jewish World in the Time of Jesus*, p. 144,
n. 3. Guignebert also claims that because the Messiah b. Joseph was destined to die
in battle he was not a suffering Messiah in the strict sense at all. Op. cit. p. 145: "The
Messiah b. Joseph is a fighting Messiah."

[5] See pp. 128–32.

of Moses supposed that Israel would find some special satisfaction in contemplating the sufferings of her foes in Gehenna after the establishment of the
Kingdom. This is a strange comment on the idea that he brought Isaiah 53 into
his conception of the means of establishment of the Kingdom. For nothing
could be in greater contrast to the spirit and message of that chapter.[1]

As we have pointed out above, what the Assumption of Moses points
to is the belief in the duty of a complete loyalty to the Torah even at
the price of death. It is this high estimation of obedience to the Torah
that we are to find there rather than any Messianic concepts; nevertheless,
it does elevate a Suffering hero!

We now come to the third place where it is possible that we are to
find traces of the merging of the Messianic with the Servant conceptions, namely, the Son of Man passages in the Similitudes of Enoch.
Charles placed the latter between the years 94 and 79 B.C.[2] and, although
some have regarded the Son of Man passages as Christian interpolations,
the weight of opinion assigns the Similitudes to the pre-Christian era.
The passages which come chiefly into consideration are the following:
46. 1, 3, 48. 4, 62. 2, 62. 6, 7, 62. 27-9. How are we to understand the
figure of the Son of Man in the above? It is clearly based on that of
the Son of Man in Daniel, and, as in the latter so in the Similitudes,
T. W. Manson has claimed that we are to regard the Son of Man as
the Faithful Remnant, the Community of the Righteous, and not an
individual person.[3] This view has been criticized by Dr Vincent Taylor,[4]
who points out that in Enoch 62. 13 the faithful remnant or the righteous
are "expressly distinguished from the Son of Man in a way which
emphasizes the personal character of the latter". Taylor has also asserted
that "the description of the Son of Man in the Similitudes is so full and
the functions of judgement are such that the personal interpretation is
much the more probable view". Otto[5] has accepted the personal inter-

[1] *The Relevance of Apocalyptic*, p. 131.
[2] Cf. *Ap. and Ps.* vol. II, p. 171. Also *The Book of Enoch* (Oxford, 1893), p. 30.
[3] *The Teaching of Jesus*, p. 228: "First it is not so clear as it once appeared that
'Son of Man' in Enoch is to be construed as the title of an individual Messiah. It is
only one of several names used. Besides 'Son of Man' we find 'the Righteous One',
'the Elect One', and 'the Anointed One'. Moreover, we find that beside 'the Elect
One' and 'the Righteous One' there are frequent references to 'the (my) Righteous
ones', and 'the (my) Elect ones' in the plural. It is at least arguable that the singular
term in these cases is the name for the body made up by the individuals included in
the plural term. The faithful Remnant may be personified as the Elect One and the
Righteous One, or regarded as the community of the Elect and the Righteous. Even
the title 'the Anointed One' need not be construed as a personal Messiah."
[4] *Jesus and His Sacrifice*, pp. 24f.
[5] *The Kingdom of God and the Son of Man*, pp. 201f.

pretation; he finds Enoch himself exalted to be the Son of Man. It is Dr Rowley's words that seem to us best to state the case: "The Son of Man in Enoch is no human figure but rather the personifying of the Danielic concept of the Son of Man in a supramundane person who should be the representative and head of the kingdom that concept symbolized, and who should come down to dwell with men."[1] We may then assume the personal character of the Son of Man in the Similitudes.

The question that now arises is whether the Son of Man is conceived as the Messiah. Dr Rowley[2] is emphatic in his denial of this. "It should be remembered, however," he writes, "that even though we accept all these passages and even though we equate all of these terms, and treat them as individual in their reference, that does not involve the equating of the Son of Man with the Messiah, in the technical sense of that term...." We differ with diffidence from Dr Rowley, but it seems that he draws too sharp a distinction between the concept of the Son of Man and that of the Messiah. We may agree that there is no technical equation of the Son of Man with the Messiah, but at the same time the two concepts cannot have remained in complete isolation. As Dr Rowley himself points out, those ideas which form the background of the future of the Son of Man are comparable with those associated with the Messiah,[3] and we think that Albright[4] is justified in his claim that already before the Christian era the ideas of the Messiah and of the Son of Man had been merged, although it would be incorrect to think of this merging as a precise identification. Thus in the description of the Son of Man in Enoch we find many parallels to the figure of the Messianic king. We note especially the following parallels: Enoch 46. 3, 48. 4, 62. 2, 71. 14, with Isa. 9. 7, 11. 4–5; Jer. 23. 5–6; Zech. 9. 9; Ps. of Sol. 17. 25, 28, 29, 31, 42, 46, 18. 8: with Enoch 46. 3, cf. Ps. 2. 6, 89. 27: with Enoch 46. 4, 62. 3, 9, cf. Ps. 2. 2, 10–12, 72. 10–11, 89. 27: with Enoch 48. 4, cf. Isa. 9. 2, etc. In the light of these references it is misleading to make too sharp a separation between the figure of the Messiah and the Son of Man in the Similitudes.

There is, however, a further factor; the Son of Man in the Similitudes shows many parallels not only to the Messiah but also to the Suffering Servant of Deutero-Isaiah. A comparison of the following passages will reveal this: with Enoch 46. 3, cf. Isa. 42. 1, 42. 6, 53. 11: with Enoch 46. 4, cf. Isa. 49. 7, 52. 15: with Enoch 48. 4, cf. Isa. 42. 6, 49. 3, 50. 4–5, 52. 13, 53. 11. From these references it is clear that the Son of Man in

---

[1] *The Relevance of Apocalyptic*, p. 57.
[2] Ibid. pp. 55 f.   [3] Ibid. p. 29.
[4] *From the Stone Age to Christianity* (1940), p. 292.

the Similitudes is merged to some extent at least into the concept of
the Suffering Servant, and as we saw previously this implies that the
concept of the Messiah has been mingled with the latter. In the references
given above we are indebted to W. Manson[1] and our conclusion may
be expressed in his words:

> Points of comparison might be indefinitely multiplied, but enough evidence
> has been adduced to show that the concepts of the Davidic Messiah, the
> Suffering Servant, and the pre-existent Heavenly Man, however disparate in
> origin they may have been, have in the religious thought of Israel been
> conformed to the same type, and are to be recognized, therefore, as far as the
> religion of Israel is concerned, as successive phases of the Messianic idea, which
> connect respectively with Israel as nation, Israel as Church, and Israel as the
> final, perfected elect of the supernatural Reign of God.

When we turn to other sources of a post-Christian date, although we
have been unable to prove conclusively that the figure of the Messiah
b. Joseph is that of a Suffering Messiah in the first century, we find much
evidence that in the second century the conception of a Suffering Messiah
was familiar. Particularly important is the evidence of the *Dialogue with
Trypho*.[2] Trypho does not know of any other possibility than that of

---

[1] *Jesus the Messiah*, Appendix C, pp. 173 f. In so far as the identification of the
Son of Man and the Messiah is concerned, Manson's conclusion is amply justified
when we turn to the Rabbinic literature. Thus R. Akiba (see *M. Hag.* 14. 9, *b. Sanh.* 38 b)
ascribed one of the thrones in Dan. 7. 9 to the Messiah and Joshua b. Levi applied
Dan. 7. 13 to the Messiah (see *b. Sanh.* 98 a). The human figure in Dan. 7. 13 coming
with the clouds of heaven was also interpreted of the Messiah, Sib. Oracles, 5. 414.
Cf. *b. Sanh.* 96 b, which reads: "R. Naḥman said to R. Isaac [late third century]:
'Have you heard when Bar Nafle will come?' 'Who is Bar Nafle?' he asked. 'Messiah',
he answered, 'Do you call Messiah Bar Nafle?' 'Even so', he rejoined, 'as it is written,
In that day I will raise up [97 a] the tabernacle of David ha-nofeleth [that is fallen]'."
Bar Nafle represents the Greek μετὰ τῶν νεφελῶν...ὡς υἱὸς ἀνθρώπου ἐρχόμενος.
'the Son of the clouds', Dan. 7. 13.
We shall be concerned with the Suffering Messiah above; but here it is noteworthy
that the Son of Man in Daniel was interpreted of the Messiah. But the Son of Man in
Daniel is a suffering figure—he represents the Saints of the Most High who are persecuted; cf. Dan. 7. 21, 25. The whole context points to a suffering Son of Man. Did not
then the Rabbis think of a Suffering Messiah? Moore gets over this difficulty by maintaining that the Rabbis "concerned themselves little about total contexts" (cf. Moore,
vol. II, p. 334, n. 3) and isolated Dan. 7. 9-14 "without concern about the beginning
of the chapter". This, however, is not very convincing. The fact that the Messiah =
the Son of Man and that the latter was a Suffering Son of Man should be borne in
mind when we discuss the idea of a suffering Messiah in first-century Judaism above.

[2] Probably Trypho is another name for Rabbi Ṭarfon (A.D. 120-40) a contemporary
of Justin Martyr. Schürer writes: "if then Trypho is ready to make these concessions,
he thereby only represented views held in the circles of his Palestinian colleagues."
Cf. Schürer, *The Jewish People in the Time of Jesus Christ*, Div. II, vol. II, p. 186,
n. 94.

a Suffering Messiah. It is the *manner* of Christ's death, not His suffering, that is the stumbling-block to Trypho.

Then Trypho remarked, "Be assured that all our nation waits for Christ; and we admit that all the scriptures which you have quoted refer to Him. Moreover, I do also admit that the name of Jesus, by which the Son of Nave (Nun) was called, has inclined me very strongly to adopt this view. But whether Christ should be so shamefully crucified, this we are in doubt about. For whosoever is crucified is said in the law to be accursed, so that I am exceedingly incredulous on this point. It is quite clear, indeed, that the scriptures announce that Christ had to suffer; but we wish to learn if you can prove it to us whether it was by the suffering cursed in the law."

I replied to him, "If Christ was not to suffer, and the prophets had not foretold that He would be led to death on account of the sins of the people, and be dishonoured and scourged, and reckoned among the transgressors, and as a sheep be led to the slaughter, whose generation, the prophet says no man can declare, then you would have good cause to wonder. But if these are to be characteristic of Him and mark Him out at all, how is it possible for us to do anything else than believe in Him most confidently? And will not as many as have understood the writings of the prophets, whenever they hear merely that He was crucified, say that this is He and no other?"

"Bring us, then," said Trypho, "on by the Scriptures, that we may also be persuaded by you, for we know that He should suffer and be led as a sheep. But prove to us whether He must be crucified and die so disgracefully and so dishonourably by the death cursed in the law. For we cannot bring ourselves even to think of this...."[1]

Guignebert dismisses the ideas expressed by Trypho in these passages by saying: "I am inclined to think that the Christian apologist was responsible for them himself, being already convinced that the Scriptures must necessarily have foretold the sufferings of Christ."[2] We cannot help feeling, however, that this is to make the wish father to the thought, and we must regard Trypho's evidence as very weighty. It is surely significant that a representative of the Jewish viewpoint regards it as an accepted fact that the Messiah should suffer.

In addition to this the Talmud often refers to the Suffering of the Messiah. Thus in *b. Sanh.* 93 *b* we read:

The Messiah—as it is written, 'And the spirit of the Lord shall rest upon him, the spirit of wisdom and understanding...and shall make him of quick understanding [*wa-hariḥo*] in the fear of the Lord'. R. Alexandri [*c.* A.D. 279] said: "This teaches that he loaded him with good deeds and suffering as a mill [is laden]!"[3]

[1] *Dialogue with Trypho*, chapters 89 and 90.
[2] Cf. *The Jewish World in the Time of Jesus*, p. 148, n. 1.
[3] This is a play of words on והריחו and ריחיים.

In *b. Sanh.* 98*a* we read that the Messiah sits at the gates of Rome attending to the wounds of lepers. Thus:

R. Joshua b. Levi [*c.* A.D. 219] met Elijah standing by the entrance of R. Simeon b. Yohai's tomb. He asked him: "Have I a portion in the world to come?" He replied, "If this Master desires it." R. Joshua b. Levi said, "I saw two, but heard the voice of a third." He then asked him, "When will the Messiah come?"—"Go and ask him himself," was his reply. "Where is he sitting?"—"At the entrance." "And by what sign may I recognize him?" —"He is sitting among the poor lepers: all of them untie [them] all at once, and rebandage them together, whereas he unties and rebandages each separately [before treating the next], thinking, should I be wanted [it being time for my appearance as the Messiah] I must not be delayed [through having to bandage a number of sores]."

Again, in *b. Sanh.* 98*b* we find the following where the Messiah is called 'the leper scholar':

What is his [the Messiah's] name?—The school of R. Shila [*c.* A.D. 350] said: "His name is Shiloh, for it is written, Until Shiloh come." The School of R. Yannai [*c.* A.D. 220] said: "His name is Yinnon, for it is written, His name shall endure for ever: e'er the sun was, his name is Yinnon." The School of R. Haninah [*c.* A.D. 220] maintained: "His name is Haninah, as it is written, Where I will not give you Haninah." Others say: "His name is Menahem the son of Hezekiah, for it is written, Because Menahem [the comforter] that would relieve my soul, is far." The Rabbis said: "His name is 'the leper scholar',[1] as it is written, Surely he hath borne our griefs and carried our sorrows: yet we did esteem him a leper, smitten of God and afflicted" [Isa. 53. 4].

It will be recognized that all the Talmudic passages quoted so far are third century and, therefore, too late to be used as evidence for our purpose. So also is probably the following passage which has been attributed to R. Jose the Galilean (A.D. 120–40), who is excellent evidence for the first half of the second century.

R. Jose the Galilean says: "King Messiah has been humbled and made contemptible on account of the rebellious, as it is said, He was wounded for our transgressions, etc. [Isa. 53. 5]. How much more will He make satisfaction therefore for all generations, as it is written, 'And the Lord laid on Him the iniquity of us all'" [Isa. 53. 6].[2] (See Appendix C, p. 335.)

Despite the late date of the Talmudic passages, however, in view of all the above it cannot be disputed that in the second century after Christ the idea of a Suffering Messiah, and indeed of a Messiah suffering as an atonement for human sin, was, at least in certain circles,

---

[1] חיורא: another reading is חוליא, 'the sick'.

[2] *Sifre.* See A. Wünsche, יסורי המשיח *oder Die Leiden des Messias*, pp. 65 f. I have been unable to find this quotation. See p. 335 (11).

a familiar one. How far are we justified in finding the same conception among the Rabbis of the first century? Two factors ought to be borne in mind when we think of this question. First, that a methodical consideration is involved. We find an idea well attested in the early second century, and we have pointed out that the concept of the Servant of Yahweh of Deutero-Isaiah had become associated with that of the Messiah before the first century. We are led to the feeling that if the idea of the Suffering Messiah were not a burning issue in Christian theology the evidence before us would have led naturally to the assumption that it existed in the first century despite the absence of specific evidence. Moreover, in the second place, we must presuppose that behind the punning interpretation of וַהֲרִיחוֹ in Isa. 11. 3, as the burden imposed on the Messiah, and of חוּלְיָא (the sick) and חִיוּרָא (the leper) in Isa. 53. 4, there was probably a very long development.

We are now in a position to state the result of our discussion. It has led us to the conclusion which, in view of those ideas of the value of suffering and particularly of the suffering of the righteous and of martyrs which we enumerated above, we should have expected, namely, that the assumption is at least possible that the conception of a Suffering Messiah was not unfamiliar to pre-Christian Judaism.[1] Before leaving this discussion finally, however, we have to point out that Strack-Billerbeck's treatment of the Son of Man in the Similitudes cannot be regarded as satisfactory. It is legitimate to hold that "the last word has perhaps not been said about the integrity of the Similitudes or upon the date of the Son of Man passages",[2] and withhold judgement on the issue under discussion, but if we do accept their pre-Christian date, and also that the Son of Man is merged with the Suffering Servant in the Similitudes, then to deny the emergence of the idea of the Suffering Messiah to pre-Christian Judaism is indefensible. But this is what Strack-Billerbeck do in their commentary. They claim that Messianic ideas in Judaism were wholly incompatible with the idea of a Suffering Messiah and then add in a footnote that there is one exception to this in the Similitudes where the Servant conception is applied to the Messiah.

If our thesis be correct, the suffering of Jesus as Messiah would not in itself be an insuperable difficulty for a Rabbi such as Paul, at least it would probably have been less difficult for him than for simpler folk who had perhaps less refined conceptions of the Messianic Kingdom than the Rabbis. Nevertheless, we do know that there was a σκάνδαλον for Paul in the Death of Jesus and we now suggest that even if Judaism did

[1] Contrast Schürer, Ch. Guignebert, Moore, M. J. Lagrange, *Le Judaïsme avant Jésus-Christ*, p. 385. See the discussion in J. Bonsirven, *Le Judaïsme Palestinien*, vol. 1, pp. 380ff.

[2] C. H. Dodd, *The Parables of the Kingdom*, p. 92, n. 2.

not expect a Suffering Messiah at all, the chief cause of the element of σκάνδαλον in the Death of Jesus for Paul was not the Death in itself but the form which it took; it was the death on the Cross that constituted the σκάνδαλον. To make this clear we refer again to the martyrdoms of the second century. Büchler's treatment of the latter is illuminating in this connection. He shows how the Rabbis in facing martyrdom were concerned not so much with their suffering as with the peculiar form that their deaths assumed. For example, there are several parallel accounts of the way in which two Rabbis, R. Ishmael and R. Simeon, who were probably well known in Jerusalem before the fall of the Temple, met their death. We quote from the account found in the *Mekilta*:[1]

> When R. Ishmael and R. Simeon were being led to be executed, R. Simeon said to R. Ishmael, "My Master, my heart goeth out, because I know not why I am to be slain." R. Ishmael replied, "Hast thou ever in thy life kept a man waiting who came to thee with a civil case or with a question [about a religious law] until thou hadst drunk thy cup or put on thy sandals or wrapped thyself in thy mantle, whereas the Torah says אִם עַנֵּה תְעַנֶּה, meaning delay whether long or short?" R. Simeon then said to him, "Thou hast comforted me, my Master."

It was the mode of his death, that he was 'to be slain' that worried R. Simeon. This comes out more clearly in the account in *Semaḥ. VIII.* Here R. Ishmael wept and R. Simeon b. Gamaliel comforted him, "...by two more steps thou shalt be in the bosom of the righteous men and thou weepest?" R. Ishmael said, "Do I weep because we are to be slain? No, but because we are to be slain in the same way as murderers, and as the desecrators of the Sabbath were...." Death by the sword implied a grievous sin; that was why it caused pain, not because it inflicted suffering.

It is in the light of stories such as the above that we are to understand how a Rabbi would regard a death by crucifixion; the latter was a death that according to the Torah implied that the victim was outside the pale of Israel; that he was *ḥêrem*. It is this that led Paul to say that Jesus by His death had become a curse for us and that He who knew no sin had been made sin on our behalf. We have been unable to find any material on the Rabbinic side to illumine the concepts of Christ as a 'curse' and as 'sin', and we must therefore here be content with seeing in these two concepts the strongest possible expression of Christ's suffering on our behalf wrung out of Paul's heart by the contemplation of Christ crucified; the specifically Rabbinic emphases in Paul's conception of the Death of Christ we have dealt with above.

---

[1] *Mekilta Nezikin* 18. See A. Büchler, *Studies in Sin and Atonement*, pp. 189 ff.

10

THE OLD AND THE NEW HOPE: RESURRECTION

IN his book, *Paul and his Interpreters*, Schweitzer[1] has criticized, with great justice, those writers who in their treatment of Pauline theology have assigned their discussion of Paul's eschatology to the last section of their work, as if eschatology were an aspect of the Apostle's thought which could be neatly isolated and treated as a kind of addendum, whereas in fact it is his eschatology that conditions Paul's theology throughout. With this criticism we largely agree and in the preceding chapters we have constantly emphasized that Paul's interpretation of the Christian dispensation becomes understandable only in the light of his conviction that Jesus of Nazareth was the Messiah of Jewish expectation, and it follows naturally from this that eschatology was an essential element in his thought and not merely an appendix to it. The encounter with the living Christ, the awareness of living in a new creation, the influx of the Gentiles into the true Israel, the experience of a new moral exodus, the discovery of a New Torah and the advent of the Spirit, all these were for Paul eschatological phenomena. It must, therefore, be understood when we turn in this last chapter to discuss certain aspects of Paul's teaching on the 'End' that we do so not because we have artificially confined his eschatology to a watertight compartment unrelated to the rest of his thought, but merely for the sake of clarity.

The complexity of the situation that confronted the early Church generally has been clarified for us by Dr Dodd. The earliest Christians recognized in the life of Jesus, in His wondrous works and teaching, in His death, resurrection and exaltation the advent of the powers of the Age to Come; for them "the eschaton, the final and decisive act of God, has already entered human experience":[2] it only remained for Jesus to come again on the clouds to complete that act. Dr Dodd has insisted that it was not an early but an immediate advent of Christ that was expected. He writes:

The more we try to penetrate in imagination to the state of mind of the first Christians in the earliest days, the more are we driven to think of resurrection, exaltation and second advent as being, in their belief, inseparable parts of a single divine event. It was not an *early* advent that they proclaimed

---

[1] *Paul and his Interpreters*, p. 53.
[2] *The Apostolic Preaching and its Developments*, p. 71.

but an immediate advent. They proclaimed it not so much as a future event for which men should prepare by repentance, but rather as the impending corroboration of a present fact.[1]

When, however, the Lord did not come on the clouds the Second Advent "came to appear as a second crisis yet in the future".[2] This demanded a readjustment in the Church's theology. We may again quote Dr Dodd:

> As the revelation still delayed the believers were driven to conclude that they had been mistaken in thinking that the Lord would return immediately, but a more attentive study of His teaching, and observation of the signs of the times, they thought, would enable them to divine the time of His coming, as well as the reason for its delay. The Church therefore proceeded to reconstruct on a modified plan the traditional scheme of Jewish eschatology, which had been broken up by the declaration that the Kingdom of God had already come. Materials for such a reconstruction were present in profusion in the apocalyptic literature.[3]

That Paul partook in this reconstruction of eschatology is clear from his Epistles. It is not necessary to find any elaborate reasons for Paul's evident interest in the Second Advent as Kennedy has sought to do. The latter explained the Apostle's expectation of an early return of Jesus as due, first, to the influence upon him of Old Testament prophecies, secondly, to the phenomenal success of his preaching in spreading the Gospel, and, thirdly, to his conviction that the forces of evil were ripening in preparation for the end;[4] these factors, so Kennedy argued, would suggest to Paul that the Lord was at hand. In view of what we have written above, however, such reasoning is superfluous. The belief in the Second Advent was integral to that eschatological faith which Paul shared with the early Church. It did not require any external factors to convince Paul that the Lord was at hand. On the contrary, as we saw was the case with early believers generally, it was the un-expected and continued delay of His coming that came to exercise Paul's thought, and it is to the postponement of the Second Advent that we owe Paul's elaboration of apocalyptic details in his description of the latter. Moreover, that the manner in which Paul, in common with other primitive Christians, pictured the Second Advent and its accompani-ments is throughout dependent upon the apocalyptic traditions of Judaism is self-evident when the eschatological details of his Epistles, e.g. 1 and 2 Thessalonians and 1 Corinthians, are compared with the

---

[1] *The Apostolic Preaching and its Developments*, p. 68.   [2] Ibid. p. 73.
[3] Ibid. p. 80.
[4] *St Paul's Conceptions of the Last Things*, pp. 184f.

relevant passages in the apocryphal and rabbinical literature.[1] It will not be our concern to present the details of such a comparison. This task has often been done elsewhere and we may well assume that Pauline eschatology is rooted in Judaism. Our purpose here will be to inquire whether in the course of the development of his thought Paul forsook or modified the essential Jewishness of his eschatological beliefs or remained true to his Rabbinic heritage; and since there is one point at which it has been claimed that Paul departs from Judaism in the direction of Hellenism, in his teaching on the Resurrection, this will form a convenient focus for our discussion.

The starting point of our treatment of Paul's teaching on Resurrection must be his interpretation of the Resurrection of Jesus. Is it possible for us to determine with exactitude the eschatological significance that he would be led to ascribe to such an event? At this point it is not necessary to deal exhaustively with the views of those scholars who have sought to do this; it will suffice to refer to Schweitzer's treatment of the question.[2] While protesting that Paul, like Jesus and the authors of Baruch and 4 Ezra, was not a slave to any apocalyptic convention, Schweitzer has nevertheless insisted on the extreme logicality of his eschatological thinking and has sought to unravel its intricacies with a precision that is mathematical. He points out that there were two main currents of eschatological thought in Judaism. First, there was the Messianic expectation of the prophets, both pre-exilic and exilic, according to which there would arise a scion of the House of David who would judge the nations and then allow the righteous who survived the sifting of the judgement to enter His Kingdom. This Messianic Kingdom would be the consummation of world history and its scene would be this earth, albeit an earth transformed in various ways. According to the earliest sources only those alive at the advent of the Messiah would be judged and could therefore participate in the blessings of the Messianic Kingdom, but later it was held that there would be a resurrection of the dead at the advent of the Messiah in order that they too might be judged and be partakers of the Kingdom. Secondly, on the other hand, there arose what we may conveniently call the Danielic eschatology, according to which the Kingdom of God is made manifest not through the advent of a Messiah but through that of the Son of

---

[1] H. St J. Thackeray, *The Relation of St Paul to Contemporary Jewish Thought*, pp. 98 f.; H. A. A. Kennedy, *St Paul's Conceptions of the Last Things*, pp. 38–76.

[2] *The Mysticism of Paul the Apostle*, pp. 75 f.: "For in this eschatology not only inspiration but thought is at work. Jesus, Paul and the authors of the Apocalypses of Baruch and Ezra do not simply take over traditional expectations of the future, but seek also to make out a logical satisfying whole."

Man, a supernatural being. The inauguration of this kingdom is marked
by a general resurrection of the dead, and their judgement. The kingdom
itself is of a supernatural character. We cannot here trace the various
vicissitudes of these two views of the end in order to show how now
one and then the other predominated; we merely point out that Judaism
had somehow to harmonize both. This harmonization was accomplished
ingeniously in the first century A.D., when we find that the Messianic
Kingdom comes to be regarded as one of temporary duration preceding
the final consummation of the historical process, which was supernatural, the Age to Come. Thus the eschatology of the first century falls
into the framework: this Present Age (*hâ-'ôlâm hâ-zeh*), the Messianic
Era, the Age to Come (*hâ-'ôlâm ha-bâ'*). This meant a change in the
incidence of the Resurrection. There was no compelling reason why
the dead should be raised to participate in a Messianic Age which itself
was 'but for a season', and so it came about that the Resurrection was
placed at the end of the Messianic Kingdom or at the beginning of the
Age to Come. This is the view taken in Baruch, 4 Ezra and the rabbinical
literature.[1]

So far we may well agree with Schweitzer's survey of the historical
development of apocalyptic thought in Judaism. It is when he attempts
to force the eschatological details of the Pauline Epistles into that
eschatological scheme which he finds in first-century Judaism that we
begin to question his procedure and conclusions. Schweitzer argues
that Paul had to face one factor which of necessity was not taken into
account by the traditional apocalyptists. The latter had not conceived
of a Messiah who should appear, die and rise again before the advent
of the Messianic Kingdom.[2] According to the traditional apocalyptic
convention only those alive at the Advent of the Messiah should participate in the Messianic Age. The situation confronting Paul, however,
was that many who were alive at the Advent of the Messiah, and who
had actually embraced Him as such, had died. Were these to be treated
on a par with believers who survived till the Second Advent or were
they to be left in their 'sleep' till the end of the Messianic Kingdom
when they would share in the general resurrection and thus enter the

[1] Cf. R. H. Charles, *Eschatology*, pp. 162, 305; Str.-B. vol. IV, pp. 799f.: "Diese
Welt, die Tagen des Messias, und die zukünftige Welt"; Moore, vol. II, pp. 323f.,
377f.; A. Schweitzer, *The Mysticism of Paul the Apostle*, pp. 75f. For the Rabbinic
references see Str.-B. vol. IV, pp. 816f.; e.g. *M. Sanh.* 10. 3 shows that the chief contrast
is not between this world and the Messianic Age but between this world and the Age
to Come; Str.-B. vol. IV, pp. 821f.; *Sifre Deut.* on 6. 5, § 32 (where, however, the
עולם הבא may mean the invisible realm to which souls go at death. See below,
pp. 314f.).
[2] *The Mysticism of Paul the Apostle*, p. 92.

Age to Come, i.e. were they to be denied participation in the Messianic Age? Schweitzer insists that in order to give those who had died before the Second Advent equality of treatment, as it were, Paul had to postulate for them a special resurrection in the Messianic Kingdom, a resurrection which he describes in 1 Thessalonians. It is in a similar way that Schweitzer understands the problem confronting Paul in Corinth. "The deniers of the resurrection", he writes, "were...no sceptics, but representatives of the ultra-conservative eschatological view that there was no resurrection. According to them only those have anything to hope for who are alive at the return of Jesus. They thus deny not only the resurrection to the Messianic Kingdom but that to eternal blessedness. Their position is the same as that of the Psalms of Solomon and the eschatology of the prophets."[1] The death of believers, therefore, compelled Paul to assume two resurrections: "a first in which believers in Christ attain to a share in the Messianic Kingdom, and a second in which all men who have ever lived upon earth, at the end of the Messianic Kingdom, appear for final judgement before the throne of God, to receive eternal life or eternal torment. In any case the creator of this doctrine of the two resurrections was Paul."[2] Accordingly Schweitzer propounds the following scheme of Paul's eschatology:[3]

1. The sudden return of Jesus. (1 Thess. 5. 1–4.)
2. The resurrection of believers who have already 'fallen asleep' and the transformation of those still alive into the resurrection mode of living. (1 Thess. 4. 14–15.)
3. All together are taken up into the clouds to be 'for ever with the Lord'. (1 Thess. 4. 16–17.)
4. The Messianic Judgement. (1 Thess. 4. 6.)
   (a) Held by Christ. (2 Cor. 5. 10; 1 Cor. 4. 4–5; 5. 2; 2 Cor. 1. 14; Phil. 1. 10; 2. 16.)
   (b) Held by God. (Rom. 14. 10; 1. 18; 2. 2–10; 3. 6.)
5. The Messianic Kingdom. (1 Cor. 15. 23–8.) Of this Schweitzer writes: "We have from Paul no description of the Messianic Kingdom."[4]
6. The last enemy, death, is overcome. (1 Cor. 15. 36.)
7. The Messianic Kingdom comes to an end.
8. The General Resurrection.
9. The Last Judgement.
10. God becomes all in all: the consummation. (1 Cor. 15. 28.)

On 8 and 9 above Schweitzer observes: "The general resurrection and the immediately following judgement upon all men and upon the defeated Angels, are not mentioned in the series of events enumerated

---

[1] *The Mysticism of Paul the Apostle*, p. 93.   [2] Ibid. pp. 93 f.
[3] Ibid. pp. 65–8.   [4] Ibid. p. 66.

by Paul in I Cor. 15. 23–8. All this falls for him under the general concept of 'the End' (εἶτα...τὸ τέλος) I Cor. 15. 24, and is taken for granted as well known."[1]

As we implied above, such an interpretation of Paul's eschatology as we have found in Schweitzer which ascribes to the Apostle a belief in a temporary Messianic Kingdom which was to precede the Age to Come had previously found favour with many scholars. Among the latter were Pfleiderer,[2] J. Weiss,[3] Lietzmann,[4] Thackeray[5] and Morgan,[6] although, with the exception of Pfleiderer, they do not always make it clear whether they also ascribe to Paul the belief in a twofold resurrection and judgement. In common with Schweitzer the assumption which they all make is that Paul would naturally borrow the contemporary Messianic categories and proceed to construct his specifically Christian eschatology on their basis. We must insist, however, that it is erroneous thus to make Paul conform too closely to current apocalyptic speculation. That, in his eschatology, the Apostle drew upon the latter for his terms will be obvious, but the character of that eschatology was determined not by any traditional scheme but by that significance which Paul had been led to give to Jesus. This is merely to affirm that his eschatology was subservient to his faith and not constitutive of it. To prove that this was so we shall now seek to show how the scheme of events which Schweitzer and others have imposed upon Paul's eschatology cannot be maintained. That scheme depends chiefly for its validity upon the interpretation of two passages with which we shall now deal.

(1) I Thess. 4. 13–18

13. But I would not have you to be ignorant, brethren, concerning them which are asleep, that ye sorrow not, even as others which have no hope. 14. For if we believe that Jesus died and rose again, even so them also which sleep in Jesus will God bring with him. 15. For this we say unto you by the word of the Lord, that we which are alive and remain unto the coming of the Lord shall not prevent them which are asleep. 16. For the Lord himself shall descend from heaven with a shout, with the voice of the archangel, and with the trump of God: and the dead in Christ shall rise first: 17. Then we which are alive and remain shall be caught up together with them in the clouds, to meet the Lord in the air: and so shall we ever be with the Lord. 18. Wherefore comfort one another with these words.

---

[1] *The Mysticism of Paul the Apostle*, p. 67.   [2] *Paulinism* (1877), vol. I, p. 269.
[3] Meyer, *Kommentar zum Neuen Testament, Der Erste Korintherbrief*, p. 358.
[4] H.Z.N.T., *An die Korinther*, p. 81. Lietzmann compares Rev. 20. 4; 4 Ezra 8. 53; Syr. Apoc. Baruch 21. 23; Test. Levi 18.
[5] *The Relation of St Paul to Contemporary Jewish Thought*, pp. 120f.
[6] *The Religion and Theology of Paul*, pp. 229f., especially pp. 234f.

Schweitzer's interpretation of this passage we have outlined above. There is, however, a far simpler explanation which does not necessitate his appeal to the logic of traditional eschatology. The Thessalonian Christians had quite clearly been taught that the transformation of those 'in Christ' into the resurrection mode of existence would soon take place and that without the experience of death. Not only so but, as passages such as Rom. 6. 1–14 show, the solidarity of Christians with their Lord was such that they had died but also risen with Christ to life; a second death was unthinkable; they had already passed from death to life. Referring to Rom. 6. 5, Héring writes:

> From this point it was not far to the idea that there was no reason why there should be a second death, and that Baptism also was an assurance against death (a φάρμακον ἀθανασίας if one should care to put it so, but certainly not in the Hellenistic sense) that guaranteed the prolongation of the terrestrial life until the moment when the Parousia of our Lord and the transfiguration of the surviving Christians should take place.[1]

In view of this, when certain Christians did die the survivors were naturally alarmed and the question inevitably arose why they had died: was their death a sign that they would not gain the blessing of the resurrection life owing to some sin of theirs? In one passage indeed Paul did suggest that the death of Christians was a mark of their moral failure,[2] but in 1 Thessalonians, writing to a Church that was strangely agitated by this problem, Paul has to reassure his fellow-Christians that at the advent of Christ those Christians who had died would be raised so as to share in the same privileges as those who had survived. There is no need to postulate that Paul here introduces the belief in a twofold resurrection under pressure from the logic of Jewish apocalyptic. On the contrary, the situation that confronted him at Thessalonica was the natural outcome of his own preaching.

(2) 1 Cor. 15. 22 f.

22. For as in Adam all die, even so in Christ shall all be made alive. 23. But every man in his own order: Christ the firstfruits; afterward they that are Christ's at his coming. 24. Then cometh the end (εἶτα τὸ τέλος), when he shall have delivered up the kingdom to God, even the Father; when he shall have put down all rule and all authority and power. 25. For he must reign, till he hath put all enemies under his feet. 26. The last enemy that shall be destroyed is death. 27. For he hath put all things under his feet. But when he saith all things are put under him, it is manifest that he is excepted, which did put all

---

[1] *Revue d'Histoire et de Philosophie religieuses* (1932), vol. XII, pp. 316f.; cf. J. Moffatt, M.N.T.C. p. 241.   [2] 1 Cor. 11. 27–34.

things under him. 28. And when all things shall be subdued unto him, then shall the Son also himself be subject unto him that put all things under him, that God may be all in all.

Let us first consider Schweitzer's view that those who denied the Resurrection at Corinth were ultra-conservative Christians who strictly applied to the problems of their Christian life the ancient apocalyptic view that only those living at the advent of the Messiah should share in the glories of the Messianic Age. It is unlikely in the first place that there should be Christians of such exceptionally conservative Jewish views in the Corinthian Church, which was chiefly, though indeed not entirely, Gentile in character.[1] Secondly, there are other more plausible interpretations of the anti-resurrectionists at Corinth. With one of these we shall be dealing later, with the view that the anti-resurrectionists were ultra-'spiritual' Hellenists. At this point we need only refer to J. Héring's view.[2] According to the latter Paul had probably at one period denied that there would be need of a resurrection for Christians since they had already risen with Christ, just as he had, as revealed in 1 Thessalonians, taught that Christians would not need to undergo the experience of death. Without further explanation we may quote Héring:

We do not err in affirming that Paul himself at an early period had expressly denied the future resurrection and that the anti-resurrectionists at Thessalonica and Corinth were after all only the representatives of the unchanged Pauline belief. It is no less true that their position was strongly placed in line with the fundamental conceptions of the Apostle—a fact which explains both their influence and the difficulty that Paul had to convince them.[3]

Besides that of Héring and that which we shall have occasion to describe later, Schweitzer's view of the anti-resurrectionists at Corinth is very artificial.

Apart from the above, however, let us now examine those details in 1 Cor. 15. 22f., which are thought to imply a Messianic Age. The verses 22-4 in Greek read as follows:

ὥσπερ γὰρ ἐν τῷ Ἀδὰμ πάντες ἀποθνήσκουσιν, οὕτω καὶ ἐν τῷ Χριστῷ πάντες ζωοποιηθήσονται. ἕκαστος δὲ ἐν τῷ ἰδίῳ τάγματι· ἀπαρχὴ Χριστός, ἔπειτα οἱ τοῦ Χριστοῦ ἐν τῇ παρουσίᾳ αὐτοῦ. εἶτα τὸ τέλος, ὅταν παραδιδοῖ τὴν βασιλείαν τῷ θεῷ καὶ πατρί, ὅταν καταργήσῃ πᾶσαν ἀρχὴν καὶ πᾶσαν ἐξουσίαν καὶ δύναμιν.

[1] See above, chapter 3, p. 50.
[2] "Saint-Paul a-t-il enseigné deux résurrections?" in Revue d'Histoire et de Philosophie religieuses (1932), vol. XII, p. 318.
[3] There were survivors who said that the resurrection was already past in the Church at a later date; cf. 2 Tim. 2. 18.

Two points arise:

1. It is claimed that the preposition εἶτα at the beginning of verse 24 implies a long interval of time during which we are to think of the Messianic Age. Thackeray writes:[1] "The sequence ἀπαρχή...ἔπειτα... εἶτα seems to require an interval between the second and the third points or stages alluded to, as there is undoubtedly an interval between the first and the second." Kennedy, however, has collected a number of instances where εἶτα does not imply "any interval of any duration between the preceding clause and that which it introduces". Cf. Jn. 13. 4, 5; 19. 26, 27; 1 Cor. 15. 5, 6, 7.[2]

2. The second point is the meaning of the term ...τὸ τέλος. The following interpretations are to be noted:

(a) Weiss[3] and Lietzmann[4] have argued that τὸ τέλος here signifies 'the rest of the dead' and refers to the general resurrection which precedes the final consummation. Weiss writes:

> In 1 Corinthians 15 three groups are differentiated at the resurrection. The firstfruits of those that slept, who come to life again in Christ; then follow those who belong to Christ; then—and now comes a word (τέλος) which can best be understood in this sense—then (will be made alive) the rest, i.e. the rest of the dead. In this case we should have the view of a double resurrection in Paul as well as in the Book of Revelation. There may perhaps also be assumed here a longer interval of time between the Parousia of Christ and the transfer of dominion to the Father.

This sense of τέλος would supply an obvious third τάγμα of the risen which would be more natural than the enumeration of only two, and would be in agreement with Rom. 11. 25-36, where Paul contemplates 'the universal sweep of redemption' and Lietzmann points out that the assumption of a βασιλεία τοῦ Χριστοῦ before the final consummation would supply that sphere where Christians are to reign with Christ.[5] There are only two examples which Weiss and Lietzmann adduce, however, where τὸ τέλος is said to mean 'the rest', one in Isa. 19. 15 (LXX) and the other in Aristotle, De generatione animalium I. 18. Héring[6] has examined both these passages. He points out that the meaning of

---

[1] *The Relation of St Paul to Contemporary Jewish Thought*, p. 121. See also J. Weiss and H. Lietzmann, ad loc.

[2] *St Paul's Conceptions of the Last Things*, p. 323. Also A. Robertson and A. Plummer, *First Corinthians (I.C.C.)*, p. 354.

[3] Meyer, *Kommentar zum Neuen Testament, Der Erste Korintherbrief*, p. 358.

[4] H.Z.N.T., *An die Korinther*, p. 80. Also J. Weiss, *The History of Primitive Christianity*, vol. II, p. 532.

[5] H.Z.N.T., *An die Korinther*, p. 81.

[6] *Revue d'Histoire et de Philosophie religieuses*, p. 304, n. 3.

Isa. 19. 15 is very obscure and that probably the LXX was led to translate with ἀρχὴν καὶ τέλος because it had rendered the Hebrew מעשׂה by ἔργον which would suggest something that had a beginning and an end, in which case τέλος in Isa. 19. 15 would mean 'end'. As for the Aristotelean passages, he finds that τέλος here has a teleological significance. We agree therefore with Moffatt[1] that the evidence produced by Weiss and Lietzmann is 'too remote and ambiguous' to support their hypothesis. Moreover, in addition, this hypothesis assumes, as we saw, that Paul taught the resurrection of all the dead, believers and non-believers. This assumption can be made, but it cannot certainly be deduced from 1 Cor. 15. It may be that πάντες in verse 22 implies that all mankind is 'in Christ' just as it was 'in Adam', but it may also mean that only those 'in Christ' are to be made alive.[2] Thus Schweitzer admits that there is no evidence for a general resurrection in Paul.[3]

(b) F. C. Burkitt[4] and also Karl Barth[5] have argued that τὸ τέλος is to be taken adverbially as meaning 'finally', and find the climax of the passage in the fact that death is put down as the last enemy. Burkitt would place a comma after verse 25 and compares the use of τὸ τέλος here to that in 1 Pet. 3. 8. He translates:

23. But every one in his own order: Christ as firstfruits, then those that are Christ's at his coming. 24. then finally... when he has abolished all rule and all authority and power (25. for he must reign till he put all the enemies under his feet), 26. death will be abolished as the last enemy, 27. for He hath put all things in subjection under his feet.

Burkitt does not make it clear whether he finds in the passage a Messianic Era of any duration, although he speaks of a further event after the Parousia and after the abolition of death when the Son becomes subject to the Father. Barth, however, does explicitly find a Messianic Era in Paul. This interpretation of τὸ τέλος cannot be accepted because it obviously makes what is mentioned almost in parenthesis, namely, the abolition of death, of paramount significance for the understanding of the passage.[6]

---

[1] *First Corinthians* (M.N.T.C.), p. 248.
[2] See especially the discussion in G. B. Stevens, *The Pauline Theology*, pp. 354f; cf. J. Weiss, *The History of Primitive Christianity*, vol. II, p. 532. See also R. H. Charles, *Eschatology*, p. 386, n. 1.
[3] *The Mysticism of Paul the Apostle*, p. 67.
[4] *J.T.S.* vol. XVII, pp. 384–5.
[5] *The Resurrection of the Dead* (1933), pp. 171f.
[6] Cf. J. Moffatt, *First Corinthians* (M.N.T.C.), p. 247.

(c) We now come to the third, and in our view the most probable, interpretation, which finds in τὸ τέλος a technical phrase denoting the final consummation. In the context in which τὸ τέλος appears it is natural that it should bear an eschatological sense and we are justified in so interpreting the word here. Schweitzer[1] and Moffat[2] also accept this view of translating τὸ τέλος by 'the End', but they take it to imply, on the analogy of current Messianic speculation, as we saw, a Messianic Age and a general resurrection and judgement. We have already questioned this and must again insist with Stevens[3] and Charles[4] that the text of 1 Cor. 15 means that the Parousia will be followed immediately, or at any rate with only a very short interval, by the Resurrection and the judgement which will usher in the final consummation. The following considerations confirm us in this view.[5]

In the first place, Paul very rarely speaks of a βασιλεία τοῦ Χριστοῦ. Whenever Paul speaks of a kingdom that is to come he thinks of a βασιλεία τοῦ θεοῦ. Thus:

1 Thess. 2. 12: That ye would walk worthy of God, who hath called you unto his kingdom and glory.

2 Thess. 1. 4, 5: So that we ourselves glory in you in the churches of God for your patience and faith in all your persecutions and tribulations that ye endure: 5. Which is a manifest token of the righteous judgment of God, that ye may be counted worthy of the kingdom of God, for which ye also suffer.

Gal. 5. 21: Envyings, murders, drunkenness, revellings, and such like: of the which I tell you before, as I have also told you in time past, that they which do such things shall not inherit the kingdom of God.

1 Cor. 6. 9–10: Know ye not that the unrighteous shall not inherit the kingdom of God? Be not deceived: neither fornicators, nor idolaters, nor adulterers, nor effeminate, nor abusers of themselves with mankind, 10. Nor thieves, nor covetous, nor drunkards, nor revilers, nor extortioners, shall inherit the kingdom of God.

1 Cor. 15. 50: Now this I say, brethren, that flesh and blood cannot inherit the kingdom of God.

Col. 4. 11: . . . These only are my fellowworkers unto the kingdom of God, which have been a comfort unto me.

The implication of all these passages is that the Christian is to enter the Kingdom of God, a kingdom that knows no end. There is no

---

[1] *The Mysticism of Paul the Apostle*, p. 68.
[2] *First Corinthians* (M.N.T.C.), p. 248.
[3] *The Pauline Theology*, p. 354.   [4] *Eschatology*, p. 390.
[5] Cf. J. Héring (*Revue d'Histoire et de Philosophie religieuses*, pp. 312f.), to whom we are indebted in all the above.

mention of a preliminary Messianic Age which they are to enter first.[1] A detail from 1 Thessalonians emphasizes this truth. At the coming of Christ a second time Christians will meet him in the 'air', i.e. in a super-terrestrial sphere and they shall be for ever with the Lord, i.e. they will enjoy the consummation which needs no further consummation in any future age.[2]

In the second place, the only text which explicitly makes mention of a βασιλέια τοῦ Χριστοῦ regards that kingdom as already a present fact. Thus Col. 1. 12–13 reads: "Giving thanks unto God the Father, which hath made us meet to be partakers of the inheritance of the saints in light: who hath delivered us from the power of darkness, and hath translated us into the Kingdom of His dear Son." The Resurrection had designated Christ the Son of God,[3] and from that moment the Kingdom of the Son was 'actualized'; the victory of the Cross was the beginning of that triumph of Christ over the evil powers mentioned in 1 Cor. 15. 24. It is not after but before the Parousia that the Messianic Kingdom lies in the mind of Paul:[4] and as we shall see it was already giving place to the final consummation.

In the third place, Paul clearly connects the Parousia of Christ with the day of judgement for the world. The following passages will reveal this:

1 Cor. 1. 7–8: So that ye come behind in no gift; waiting for the coming of our Lord Jesus Christ: 8. Who shall also confirm you unto the end, that ye may be blameless in the day of our Lord Jesus Christ.

2 Cor. 1. 14: . . . we are your rejoicing, even as ye also are our's in the day of the Lord Jesus.

---

[1] J. Héring, Revue d'Histoire et de Philosophie religieuses, pp. 312f. comments on the above texts: "Dans tous ces textes le privilège chrétien consiste à entrer un jour dans le royaume de Dieu, c'est à dire dans le royaume qui ne connaîtra pas de fin. Nulle part il n'est question d'une grâce supplémentaire qui ferait entrer les chrétiens ressuscités dans un royaume messianique préparatoire."

[2] Cf. J. Héring, op. cit. p. 314. Also J. Weiss, The History of Primitive Christianity, vol. II, p. 537.

[3] Cf. Rom. 1. 4.

[4] Cf. R. H. Charles, Eschatology, p. 390. It is important also to quote Charles further. He writes: "The character, moreover, of Christ's kingdom therein portrayed is wholly at variance with that of the temporary Messianic Kingdom of Apocalyptic and the Millenium of the Apocalypse; for the Messianic reign is here one of unremitting strife, whereas in the literature above referred to it is always one of peaceful dominion and blessedness. What the Apostle speaks of here is a Messianic reign of temporary duration from Christ's exaltation to the final judgement. In his later Epistles the Apostle conceives of this reign as unending." Perhaps we are to see in the Kingdom of Christ of Paul an approximation to the Matthaean conception of that Kingdom as the Church. Cf. for example, Matt. 13. 24–30.

Phil. 1. 6: Being confident of this very thing, that he which hath begun a good work in you will perform it until the day of Jesus Christ.

Phil. 1. 10: That ye may approve things that are excellent; that ye may be sincere and without offence till the day of Christ.

Phil. 2. 16: Holding forth the word of life; that I may rejoice in the day of Christ, that I have not run in vain, neither laboured in vain.

Charles observes that the judgement is "according to works (1 Cor. 4. 4; 3. 17; 6. 9, 10) that is, when the life is looked at from without and in its final consummation".

In view of what we have written above, Paul's eschatology is far simpler than Schweitzer would have us believe. It contains no reference to a Messianic Kingdom such as is contemplated in Baruch, 4 Ezra, and Revelation and can be briefly summarized as the early expectation of the Parousia when there would be a final judgement, a general resurrection of the righteous dead (and possibly of all the dead), the transformation of the righteous living and ensuing upon all this the final consummation, the perfected Kingdom of God when God would be all in all.[1] It will be readily admitted that this interpretation of Paul's eschatology brings the Resurrection of Jesus into closer proximity to the final consummation than does the schema of Schweitzer. Within the latter the Resurrection of Jesus can hardly be said to occupy anything but a minor place; the consummation is very far removed from the Resurrection of Jesus because there intervenes between the two events the Messianic Kingdom. In the thought of Paul, however, the Resurrection of Jesus is regarded as the firstfruits. This figure implies in the words of Johannes Weiss "that the full harvest will follow".[2] We cannot doubt that in the Resurrection of Jesus Paul saw the beginning of the End; already in that resurrection the powers of the Age to Come were at work.[3] Schweitzer,[4] as indeed did Johannes Weiss,[5] has seized upon this truth. At the conclusion of his chapter on 'Problems of the Pauline Eschatology' with great candour he has done full justice to it

[1] W. L. Knox has found here the popular philosophic notion of a reabsorption of all things in the divine (St Paul and the Church of the Gentiles, p. 128). But this is unnecessary; contrast. J.E. vol. XI, p. 86.

[2] Meyer, Kommentar zum Neuen Testament, Der Erste Korintherbrief, p. 356. On ἀπαρχή Weiss writes: "In dem kurzen Wort liegt eine These. Wenn von der Erste eine ἀπαρχή dargebracht wird (Lev. 23. 10 ἀπαρχὴν τοῦ θερισμοῦ, Rom. 11. 16) so zweifelt niemand, dass nun die Ernte selber folgen wird und muss; es liegt im Begriff der ἀπαρχή, dass der Rest nachfolgen muss."

[3] Cf. C. H. Dodd, "The Eschatological Element in the New Testament and its Permanent Significance", in The Interpreter (1923–4), vol. XX.

[4] The Mysticism of Paul the Apostle, pp. 97f.

[5] The History of Primitive Christianity, vol. II, p. 633.

although in fact he thereby invalidates the schematical position he had previously advocated. He writes:

> If Jesus has risen, that means, for those who dare to think consistently, that it is now already the supernatural age. And this is Paul's point of view. He cannot regard the Resurrection of Jesus as an isolated event, but must regard it as the initial event of the rising of the dead in general... powers of the supernatural world were already at work within the created order.[1]

In other words, the Age to Come has come.

Our study of Pauline eschatology has thus led us to that position which Dr Dodd has maintained in his work *The Apostolic Preaching and its Developments* in which, as we saw above, he has written that for Paul, as indeed for most of the New Testament writers, the *eschaton* has come. Paul shared in the reconstruction of eschatology to which the early Church had to address itself, but in this reconstruction he remained true to the central conviction that already in the Resurrection of Jesus the Age to Come had dawned. If it be asked what justification there is for the above very lengthy discussion, we now answer that it has been necessary for us thus to examine the detail of Paul's eschatology and to establish that he regarded the Resurrection of Jesus as a sign of the present activity of the powers of the Age to Come because it is our contention that this latter fact is the key to that problem with which we are occupied; namely, whether in the development of his thought on resurrection Paul was led to depart from his Rabbinic background and constrained to adopt Hellenistic conceptions. We are now in a position to turn to this question.

We have seen that for Paul the Resurrection of Jesus was the beginning of that general resurrection which should inaugurate the Age to Come. Since, however, the advent of the latter was already in process, as it were, we should expect that the mode of the resurrection and the nature of the resurrection life should occupy the minds of the early communities,

---

[1] *The Mysticism of Paul the Apostle*, p. 98. A passage in Romans seems to us weighty evidence in support of the view outlined above. In Rom. 11 where Paul deals with the problem of the relation of 'Israel' to Christ and to the Christian community he writes: "For if the casting away of them [i.e. Jewry] be the reconciling of the world, what shall the receiving of them be, but life from the dead" (Rom. 11. 15). Here Paul associates the ingathering of Israel into the Church with the final resurrection, so that he could not be contemplating a temporary Messianic reign. Cf. C. H. Dodd, *Romans* (*M.N.T.C.*), pp. 179f. Contrast. W. Sanday and A. C. Headlam, *Romans* (*I.C.C.*), p. 325, who regard the resurrection alluded to in Rom. 11. 15 as a sign of the inauguration of the Messianic Kingdom. So also H. Lietzmann, *H.Z.N.T.*, *An die Römer*, p. 103. Others refer the phrase 'life from the dead' to the greatest conceivable spiritual blessing.

and the Epistles of Paul supply us with evidence that this was indeed
the case. In this sphere again, however, the early Christians would not
be starting from a *tabula rasa*; Judaism had expended much thought
upon the problems involved in 'resurrection', and the early Church
would naturally be influenced by the contemporary Jewish speculation
in this field. It will be our first task at this juncture to inquire how
Pauline thought is related to the contemporary background.

One current of thought in first-century Judaism on the question
under discussion is clearly distinguishable. This is not the place to discuss
Hebrew anthropology or psychology but Wheeler Robinson[1] has long
since proved that any thought of a dualism of body and soul must be
excluded. Guignebert[2] has expressed this truth with admirable clarity.
"The Jews", he writes, "could only conceive of man in his totality,
as the vital union of flesh and soul. Their anthropological dichotomy
was not dualistic...a truly living being was always an embodied spirit,
soul and body having been created by God for a mutual interdependence
and being therefore incapable of genuine life apart from one another."[3]
Death, i.e. the separation of body and soul, for Judaism was not natural
to man but the consequence of sin, and this implied that the reunion of
soul and body in resurrection was involved in any doctrine of survival.[4]
It followed, therefore, both from the anthropology of the Hebrews and
from their conception of death that the life of the Age to Come came
to be considered as an 'embodied' life, and its manifestation as a resurrection into a 'bodily' form.

Apart from the first shoots of the belief in the Old Testament[5] it is
in the Maccabean period that the conviction of a future bodily resurrection took firm hold of Judaism. In 2 Maccabees it is recorded that
Judas commanded that sacrifices should be offered for the sins of the
dead, and the author remarks that therein he did "well and honestly in
that he was mindful of the resurrection: for if he had not hoped that
they that were slain should have risen again, it had been superfluous
and vain to pray for the dead".[6] That this resurrection was conceived
of with extreme literalness appears from the following and other passages.
The third of the martyred brothers "when he was required...put out
his tongue and that right soon, holding forth his hands manfully, and
said courageously, These I had from heaven; and for his laws I despise

[1] *The Christian Doctrine of Man*, pp. 20, 25, 27.
[2] *The Jewish World in the Time of Jesus*, p. 109.
[3] Ibid. p. 118.
[4] Cf. J. B. Frey, *Biblica* (1932), vol. XIII, p. 152; W. O. E. Oesterley, *Immortality and the Unseen World*, pp. 190ff., especially pp. 197f.
[5] Isa. 26. 19; Dan. 12. 1-3.　　　[6] 2 Macc. 12. 43f.

them: and from him I hope to receive them again".[1] We need not elaborate the historical development of the doctrine, but by the first century A.D., so Guignebert suggests, the belief had come fully into its own.[2] A few quotations illustrate for us the nature of this belief in pharisaic Judaism.

Two emphases in particular appear. There is, first, the insistence that the belief was scriptural. In *Mishnah Sanhedrin* 10. 1 we read: "All Israel have a portion in the world to come, for it is written, Thy people are all righteous; they shall inherit the land for ever, the branch of my planting; the work of my hands, that I may be glorified. But the following have no portion therein: He who maintains that resurrection is not a biblical doctrine...." Proof texts from the Law, the Prophets and the Hagiographa were adduced in support of the doctrine.[3] The fact that denial of the Resurrection carries an anathema[4] in itself reveals the weight attached to it while the insistence on the foundation in Scripture is probably due to a desire to confute Sadducees and Samaritans and other 'heretics' who contested it.[5] Secondly, and more to our purpose, is the studied emphasis on the bodily nature of the Resurrection, an emphasis which was present, as we saw, from the first. It was deemed fitting that as man had a twofold nature in this world so should he also be in the Age to Come. Thus the schools of Shammai and Hillel discussed whether there was a correspondence between the formation of the body in this world and of that formed in the Age to Come,[6] and there was much speculation as to the way in which the resurrection body was actually given form. For example, R. Ishmael (A.D. 120-40) said:

All the bodies crumble into the dust of the earth until nothing remains of the body except a spoonful of earthy matter. In the future life when the Holy One, blessed be He, calls to the earth to return all the bodies deposited with it, that which had become mixed with the dust of the earth, like the yeast which is mixed with dough, improves and increases and it raises up all the body. When the Holy One, blessed be He, calls to the earth to return all the bodies

[1] 2 Macc. 7. 10f.; cf. also 2 Macc. 4. 9, 14. 46.
[2] *The Jewish World in the Time of Jesus*, p. 120: "The opinion must be rejected that the idea of the resurrection was unknown to the majority of Jews in the time of Jesus. I believe on the contrary that the great mass of the Jewish population already adhered strongly to it, that only the somewhat sceptical aristocrats of the Temple staff, who professed to hold strictly to the teachings of the Torah openly denied it. The fact that the later Apocryphal books are well aware of the resurrection idea while the earlier ones are silent on the subject proves that it was about the time of Jesus that the new teaching came into its own."
[3] See *b. Sanh.* 90b.   [4] *b. Sanh.* 90b.
[5] Cf. A. Cohen, *Everyman's Talmud*, pp. 378f.
[6] *Gen. Rabba* 14. 5; Str.-B. vol. III, p. 473.

deposited with it, that which has become mixed with the dust of the earth improves and increases and raises up all the body without water.[1]

In the Apocalypse of Baruch we read that the dead are raised as they were buried in order that they might be recognizable:

And He answered and said unto me, "Hear, Baruch, this word, and write in the remembrance of thy heart all that thou shalt learn. For the earth shall then assuredly restore the dead (which it now receives, in order to preserve them). It shall make no change in their form, But as it has received so shall it restore them, And as I delivered them unto it, so also shall it raise them. For then it will be necessary to show to the living that the dead have come to life again, and that those who have departed have returned (again). And it shall come to pass, when they have severally recognized those whom they now know, then judgement shall grow strong and those things which before were spoken of shall come.[2]

The physical characteristics of the body in this life are thus perpetuated in the risen body, but defects and deformities are subsequently healed by God.[3] Two interesting practical details may be added; it is significant that, as proof of the reality of the belief that the dead were raised as they were buried, in some quarters great expense was often incurred to ensure that the dead were buried in appropriate clothes. So much was this the case that R. Gamaliel II (A.D. 80-120) thought it necessary to introduce the custom of burying the dead in cotton shrouds in order to counteract extravagance.[4] It is also noteworthy that the practice of cremation, except in cases where poverty threatened this or irreligion made it a matter of indifference, was not practised among the Jews in our period.[5]

We have now sufficiently illustrated the kind of Rabbinic speculation on resurrection with which Judaism abounded in the first century. It is notorious, however, that not only was there speculation on resurrection, which might have been the quiet occupation of the schools, but that there was also controversy on the subject, a fact which must have naturally given to the latter a certain prominence which it would otherwise have lacked.[6] There were two groups in particular, the Sadducees[7]

[1] Pirké de Rabbi Eliezer, § xxxiv, p. 258.
[2] 2 Baruch 50. 1-4.
[3] Cf. Moore, vol. II, p. 380; Ecc. Rabba 1. 4; Tanḥuma, Wayyigash, § 9, p. 203.
[4] Cf. J. H. Greenstone, The Messiah Idea in Jewish History, p. 89.
[5] J. B. Frey, Biblica (1932), vol. xiii, p. 154: "La vie de l'au-delà dans les conceptions juives au temps de Jésus-Christ."
[6] Cf. A. Cohen, Everyman's Talmud, p. 378.
[7] Cf. A. Schürer, The Jewish People in the Time of Jesus Christ, Div. II, vol. II, pp. 29 ff.

and the Samaritans,[1] who by their denial of resurrection provoked discussion. With the views of these two groups we need not trouble, because obviously they would have no influence on a person such as Paul who was prepared to stake his all on a resurrection from the dead. There is, however, another factor in first-century Judaism which closely concerns us. It is clear that there were those who under the influence of Hellenistic conceptions had either modified or abandoned the doctrine of resurrection in favour of the Hellenistic conception of the immortality of the soul. Again we need not enlarge upon Greek anthropology except to observe the familiar fact that here we are faced with a sharp dualism; the soul is imprisoned in the body and "the aim of the soul is finally to be delivered from the body and to depart into the realm of pure being, that is, of the divine, the invisible and the pure".[2] Hence it is the immortality of the disembodied soul not the reunion of soul and body in resurrection that is native to Hellenism. It is the influence of this concept that has been traced in the Book of Wisdom and in 4 Maccabees.[3] The following quotations will serve as illustrations:

(a) Wisd. 3. 1-4: "But the souls of the righteous are in the hand of God, and there shall no torment touch them. 2. In the sight of the unwise they seemed to die: and their departure is taken for misery, 3. And their going from us to be utter destruction: but they are in peace. 4. For though they be punished in the sight of men, yet is their hope full of immortality." (Cf. also 1. 15; 4. 1, 7, 10; 8. 13, 17; 15. 3.)

(b) 4 Macc. 9. 21 f. (of one of the martyrs): "But although the framework of his bones was now destroyed, the high minded and Abrahamic youth did not groan. But as though transformed by fire into immortality, he nobly endured the rackings...." (Cf. 10. 15; 14. 4 f.; 15. 2; 16. 13; 17. 18.)

It would be erroneous to conclude from the above references that the authors of the Book of Wisdom[4] and 4 Maccabees[5] have divested themselves entirely of Jewish conceptions; the fact is that in both these works the doctrine of the immortality of the soul is placed in uneasy juxtaposition with Jewish doctrines. Nevertheless, it is true of both works that Hellenistic conceptions have been assimilated as is the case with Philo.[6] Moreover, that it was not those only who were open to

[1] Cf. A. Schürer, op. cit. Div. II, vol. I, pp. 5f.
[2] Cf. R. H. Charles, *Eschatology*, p. 149. For references see J. Weiss, *The History of Primitive Christianity*, vol. II, p. 534, n. 18, and p. 535, n. 19; Meyer, *Kommentar zum Neuen Testament, Der Erste Korintherbrief*, p. 344.
[3] Cf. *J.E.* vol. VI, p. 566.
[4] Cf. Wisdom 3. 8. See C. V. Pilcher, *The Hereafter in Jewish and Christian Thought*, p. 147; *Ap. and Ps.* vol. I, p. 529.
[5] 4 Macc. 17. 18.   [6] J. Drummond, *Philo Judaeus*, vol. II, pp. 322f.

Alexandrian influences who were thus affected appears from the fact that in Palestine itself the Essenes accepted the doctrine of the immortality of the soul. We read of the Essenes in Josephus:[1]

> For their doctrine is this: "That bodies are corruptible, and that the matter they are made of is not permanent; but that the souls are immortal, and continue for ever; and that they come out of the most subtile air and are united to their bodies as in prisons, into which they are drawn by a certain natural enticement; but that when they are set free from the body of the flesh, they then, as released from a long bondage, rejoice and mount upward...."

In addition, traces of the doctrine have been found in the apocalyptic literature, e.g. in the Book of Jubilees 3. 4.

Having thus briefly indicated Paul's contemporary background of thought on 'resurrection' we can now go on to inquire how Paul's doctrine of resurrection is related to the two main branches of first-century Judaism which we indicated. Is Paul rooted throughout in the pharisaic tradition or has he succumbed to Hellenistic conceptions as did the author of 4 Maccabees and the Book of Wisdom and Philo?

There can be no question that in those earlier passages where Paul deals with resurrection he is thoroughly pharisaic. Passing by 1 and 2 Thessalonians, where the resurrection of the body does not directly come under scrutiny, we find that this is evident in 1 Cor. 15, where Paul discusses the question in detail. The position that confronted Paul at Corinth was that certain elements in the Church denied the Resurrection. Who these deniers of the Resurrection were it is difficult to establish.[2] They were not sceptics, since they were members of the Church.[3] Schweitzer's suggestion, that they were Christians who in their ultra-conservative adherence to the apocalyptic convention denied resurrection to the Messianic Age and confined the blessings of the latter to those who were alive at its advent, we have already rejected. More probable also than the view of Héring, which we outlined previously, is that the deniers of the Resurrection were Christians who being open to Hellenistic influences found in the idea of resurrection *per se* a source of difficulty. Resurrection implied that after death the soul departed to Hades or Sheol, and waited there till the day of judgement when it would be reunited to a body. To the educated Hellenistic world,

---

[1] *Wars of the Jews*, 2, 10. 11 (Whiston's translation, p. 478). W. O. E. Oesterley thinks the Essenes were confined to Palestine: *A History of Israel*, voi. II, p. 323.

[2] The best discussion is in J. Weiss, Meyer, *Kommentar zum Neuen Testament, Der Erste Korintherbrief*, pp. 343 f.

[3] 1 Cor. 15. 12.

however, such a view of the destiny of the soul was unacceptable on two grounds. First, as Knox has written: "No intelligent and educated person believed in a subterranean Hades; even the authority of Homer and Plato was unable to save it. . . ." And, secondly, as we saw above, it was escape from the body, not any future reunion with it in resurrection, that seemed desirable to the Hellenistic world owing to its particular anthropology. Hence it is not surprising that Corinthian Christians should "be sufficiently acquainted with the outlook of popular philosophy to refuse to believe in the resurrection of the dead" in the form in which Paul had preached it.[1] If it be asked what then these Christians thought of the Resurrection of Jesus Himself, we must admit our inability to answer. It is possible that they 'spiritualized' that event.[2] In any case Paul was faced with ultra-spiritualists, to use Moffatt's phrase, who were "satisfied with a hope of eternal life which sat loose to any future reunion of soul and body".[3] It is not necessary to accept Knox's view that it was only when Christianity left the shores of Palestine that this problem of resurrection would arise.[4] We have already referred to elements in Palestine itself which questioned it and adopted the Hellenistic alternative of the immortality of the soul. Nevertheless, it was in the Corinthian Church that the problem apparently most forcibly came to a head, and the way in which Paul dealt with it there reveals to us his thoughts on resurrection.

We have previously insisted that for Paul the Christian dispensation was a new creation which could be compared and contrasted with the old creation, and we had occasion to observe how this principle that 'the End' corresponds to 'the Beginning' governed Paul's thought also on the Resurrection of Jesus.[5] We need not again enter into a detailed description of the figures of the first and Second Adam in 1 Cor. 15. The thought of Paul fixes on a quotation from Gen. 2. 7. Just as the first Adam had introduced an order of life on the physical plane or the earthly plane, so Christ, the Second Adam, had introduced a new order of life in the Spirit. Hence it followed that even as the first Adam had needed a body suitable for existence on the earthly plane, so Jesus had need of a body suited for existence in the spiritual plane. Paul assumes that that latter plane will need a 'body' and that therefore the resurrection of believers would have to be a resurrection into 'bodies', similar to that which Jesus had assumed in the world of 'spirit'. Paul thus remains true

---

[1] Cf. W. L. Knox, *St Paul and the Church of the Gentiles*, pp. 125 f.

[2] J. Moffatt, *First Corinthians* (M.N.T.C.), p. 240.   [3] Ibid. p. 240.

[4] *St Paul and the Church of the Gentiles*, p. 126.

[5] Cf. also J. Weiss, Meyer, *Kommentar zum Neuen Testament, Der Erste Korintherbrief*, p. 356.

to his pharisaic background in that he insists on the embodied nature of the resurrection life. Further, the analogies which he uses in order to express this truth reveal the essentially Rabbinic cast of his thought. These are three in number:

(1) *The analogy of the grain of corn:*

35. But some man will say, How are the dead raised up? and with what body do they come? 36. Thou fool, that which thou sowest is not quickened, except it die: 37. And that which thou sowest, thou sowest not that body that shall be, but bare grain, it may chance of wheat, or of some other grain: 38. But God giveth it a body as it hath pleased him, and to every seed his own body.

(2) *The reference to the distinction between different kinds of flesh:*

39. All flesh is not the same flesh: but there is one kind of flesh of men, another flesh of beasts, another of fishes, and another of birds.

(3) *The reference to the different kinds of bodies—earthly and heavenly and their variations in 'glory' or 'splendour':*

40. There are also celestial bodies, and bodies terrestrial: but the glory of the celestial is one, and the glory of the terrestrial is another: 41. There is one glory of the sun, and another glory of the moon, and another glory of the stars: for one star differeth from another star in glory.

All the above analogies or figures are such as would come naturally to a Rabbi. Thus with (1) above we may compare the following:

(a) Rabbi Eliezer said: "All the dead will arise at the resurrection of the dead, dressed in their shrouds. Know thou that this is the case. Come and see from (the analogy of) the one who plants (seed) in the earth. He plants naked (seeds) and they arise covered with many coverings; and the people who descend into the earth dressed (with their garments), will they not rise up dressed (with their garments)?"[1]

(b) Queen Cleopatra asked R. Meir, "I know that the dead will revive, for it is written, And they (the righteous) shall (in the distant future) blossom forth out of the city (Jerusalem) like the grass of the earth. But when they arise, shall they arise nude or in their garments?" He replied, "Thou mayest deduce by an *a fortiori* argument (the answer) from a wheat grain: if a grain of wheat which is buried naked, shooteth forth in many robes, how much more so the righteous, who are buried in their raiment?"[2]

The analogy of the grain of corn used by Paul was thus probably a Rabbinic commonplace.

The second analogy, derived from different kinds of flesh, would, we feel, be such as a practising Jew familiar with making distinctions

---

[1] *Pirḳê de Rabbi Eliezer,* § XXXIII, p. 245.　　　　[2] *b. Sanh.* 90b.

between different kinds of flesh would be likely to use; we cannot imagine any Hellenist making use of such a 'fleshly' form in any discussion of the hereafter.[1] And again the reference to the varying degrees of glory of the heavenly bodies would be suggested naturally by the apocalyptic tradition; such a passage as Dan. 12. 2, 3:

And many of them that sleep in the dust of the earth shall awake, some to everlasting life, and some to shame and everlasting contempt.[2] 3. And they that be wise shall shine as the brightness of the firmament; and they that turn many to righteousness as the stars for ever and ever...

might easily lead to such a comparison as Paul makes in this connection, and we need not look for any Hellenic influence to account for it.[3]

We have then established that both in his insistence on the 'bodily' resurrection and in his use of analogies to expound this Paul was thoroughly pharisaic. At one point, however, he has been deemed in 1 Cor. 15 to have left his Rabbinic contemporaries far behind. Referring to R. Eliezer's use of the analogy of the seed, which we quoted above, Moffatt writes: "Paul soars above such matter of fact applications in his use of the seed analogy",[4] and he insists on the contrast between the crudely material conceptions of the risen body in current Rabbinic speculation and that 'spiritual' one found in Paul. Moffatt, however, in this matter has a long ancestry. Plummer described the Rabbinic conception of resurrection as 'gross'.[5] Kennedy[6] also remarked upon "the advance the Apostle has made beyond his early environment". It is to be doubted, however, whether this is just to Rabbinic Judaism. For the sake of emphasis in our present discussion we chose quotations above in which the physical nature of the resurrection body is prominent, and Weiss[7] is perfectly justified in holding that the *popular* pharisaic outlook was such as is illustrated by those quotations. Nevertheless, there are passages where a more 'spiritual' interpretation of the resurrection life is expressed. For example we read:

In the world to come there is neither eating nor drinking, no marital relations, no business affairs, no envy, hatred nor quarrelling; but the righteous sit with their garlands on their heads, enjoying the splendid light of the Divine Presence (*Shekinah*) as it is said: And they beheld God and they ate and drank (Exod. 24. 11).[8]

---

[1] Cf. Str.-B. vol. III, p. 475, who refer to *M. Ḥull.* viii. 1.

[2] Cf. W. L. Knox, *St Paul and the Church of the Gentiles*, p. 127; contrast J. Moffatt, *First Corinthians* (*M.N.T.C.*), p. 259.

[3] W. L. Knox, op. cit. p. 127; contrast J. Moffatt, op. cit. pp. 258 f.

[4] J. Moffatt, op. cit. p. 258.   [5] *First Corinthians* (*I.C.C.*), p. 368.

[6] *St Paul's Conceptions of the Last Things*, p. 242.

[7] *The History of Primitive Christianity*, vol. II, p. 537.   [8] *b. Ber.* 17 a.

Commenting on this passage, Abrahams[1] wrote: "This saying (parallel to Mark 12. 25) is cited by the Talmud in the name of Abba Arika (Rab) who died in A.D. 247. But the main ideas involved in his sentence are all much older, and are not inconsistent with the belief in the bodily resurrection." Again just as Paul described the life of the Age to Come by saying that "eye hath not seen, nor ear heard, neither have entered into the heart of man the things which God hath prepared for them that love him", so a saying of a first-century Rabbi is reported as follows: "R. Ḥiyya b. Abba said in R. Joḥanan's name: All the prophets prophesied (all the good things) only in respect of the Messianic Era, but as for the world to come 'the eye hath not seen, O Lord, beside thee, what he hath prepared for him that waiteth for him'."[2] The whole context from which this passage comes makes it clear that the life of the Age to Come, the resurrection life, was considered by some at least to be inexpressible in any terms of time and space. Whether or not Thackeray[3] is correct in assuming a Jewish anthology of Old Testament passages from which Paul has derived his quotation, the language that he used in 1 Cor. 2. 9 to describe the blessedness of the Age to Come was evidently traditional in Judaism. In addition to this Abrahams has reminded us that the bodily resurrection such as Hillel and Shammai believed in "was only regarded as one stage in the process of attaining to immortality". This comes out clearly in 2 Baruch.[4] In this passage, part of which we quoted above, the final stage of the resurrection act is described as follows:

> For in the heights of that world shall they dwell,
> And they shall be made like unto the angels,
> And be made equal to the stars,
> And they shall be changed into every form they desire
> From beauty unto loveliness
> And from light into the splendour of glory.

We may assume that it is this same 'splendour of glory' that Paul ascribes to the resurrection life. Moffatt[5] writes on 1 Cor. 15. 41 ("There is a splendour of the sun and a splendour of the moon and a splendour of the stars—for one star differs from another star in splendour"): "Probably... the remark about one star differing from another in glory

[1] *Studies in Pharisaism and the Gospels* (1st ser.), p. 168.

[2] *b. Sanh.* 99a.

[3] *The Relation of St Paul to Contemporary Jewish Thought*, pp. 244-5. See Meyer, *Kommentar zum Neuen Testament, Der Erste Korintherbrief*, p. 58; J. Moffatt, *First Corinthians* (M.N.T.C.), pp. 30f. The latter thinks it "a free adaptation of some words in the cry of a post-exilic prophet on Isaiah 64. 4".

[4] 2 Baruch 51. 10.   [5] *First Corinthians* (M.N.T.C.), p. 259.

is an echo not only of the apocalyptic idea that the stars were angelic beings, but also of his belief in the varying nature of recompense for the shining spirits of the faithful (3. 8) whose radiance, as again the Baruch Apocalypse has it,[1] varies, like that of the stars in the ageless upper world." In this we feel that Moffatt introduces an unnecessary idea and there is probably no reference in 1 Cor. 15. 41 to the varying recompense of the faithful: Paul is there merely concerned with the simple physical analogy afforded by the varying degrees of splendour in the heavenly bodies. Again the idea of 'glory' is associated with the righteous in their risen life in the Ethiopic Enoch 62. 15, 108. 11, 12. In view of all this Thackeray[2] is thoroughly justified when he writes: "The more spiritually-minded of Jewish thinkers in the time of St Paul were familiar with the conception of a transfigured resurrection body." "Paul", writes Charles,[3] "was not altogether an innovator but an able and advanced expositor of some current Jewish views." As we have written previously, Weiss[4] has argued that Paul is fighting on two fronts in 1 Cor. 15, not only against the Hellenistic denial of resurrection in favour of immortality, but also against a crass Jewish conception of a 'fleshly' resurrection. It seems probable that there were advocates of an extremely literal conception of the bodily resurrection in Corinth and against this 'popular' Jewish view Paul is led to assert that flesh and blood cannot inherit the Kingdom of God. In doing this he was not in any way departing from his pharisaic conceptions, because, as we have seen, there would be many Pharisees prepared to argue, as Paul does, for a transformed resurrection body. Moreover, as we have before asserted, we are not too hastily to assume that when Paul speaks of a 'spiritual' body he means thereby an 'immaterial one': the 'spirit' had a physical nuance for Paul such as it often had for his Rabbinic contemporaries.[5] In any case it should be admitted that the 'newness' of Paul's conception of a spiritual mode of resurrection body must not be over-emphasized: and the series of antitheses in 1 Cor. 15. 42–4 is not to be interpreted as un-Jewish; it would be the natural development of that contrast between hâ-'ôlâm ha-zeh and hâ-'ôlâm ha-bâ' which would be familiar to Rabbinic Judaism.[6]

It is on the next passage in which Paul deals with the hereafter, however, that those scholars have most fixed who claim that the Apostle

---

[1] 2 Baruch 51. 3, 4f.
[2] *The Relation of St Paul to Contemporary Jewish Thought*, p. 118.
[3] *Ap. and Ps.* vol. II, p. 508, n.
[4] Meyer, *Kommentar zum Neuen Testament, Der Erste Korintherbrief*, p. 345.
[5] See above, chapter 8.   [6] See Str.-B. vol. IV, pp. 799 ff. for this contrast.

substituted for the pharisaic doctrine of resurrection the Hellenistic doctrine of the immortality of the soul.[1] This passage in 2 Cor. 5. 1f. reads in Moffatt's translation:

I know that if this earthly tent of mine is taken down, I get a home from God, made by no human hands, eternal—in the heavens. It makes me sigh, indeed, this yearning to be under the cover of my heavenly habitation, since I am sure that once so covered I shall not be naked at the hour of death....

Two views of the relation of this passage to the thought of 1 Cor. 15 concern us here. Charles[2] has argued, in the first place, that 2 Cor. 5. 1 is a development upon 1 Cor. 15. He pointed out that there was an implied contradiction in Paul's discussion of the resurrection of the body in 1 Cor. 15. To the question, When does the resurrection take place? Paul replies in 1 Cor. 15. 51f.: "Here is a secret truth for you: not all of us are to die, but all of us are to be changed, changed in a moment, in the twinkling of an eye, at the last trumpet-call. The trumpet will sound, the dead will rise imperishable, and we shall be changed" (Moffatt's translation), i.e. it is at the Parousia that the new resurrection body comes into being. Should a Christian die, then, he would have to wait 'asleep' till the Parousia before he would be given this 'new' body. Clearly such a wait—so argues Charles, meant that there could be no continuity whatsoever between the old and the new bodies, whereas in fact they were to be "successive expressions of the same personality, though in different spheres". Continuity would demand that the new body should be given at death. Furthermore, the analogy of the seed, which Paul uses, "points in this direction", and Charles continues thus:

Seeing that with the corruption of the material husk the vital principle is set free to form a new body or expression of itself, the analogy urged by the Apostle leads to the inference that with the death of the present body the energies of the human spirit are set free to organize from its new environment a spiritual body—a body adapted to that environment. Thus in a certain sense the resurrection of the faithful would follow immediately on death, and not be adjourned to the Parousia. Of this variance between his living and growing thought and his inherited Jewish views the Apostle does not seem conscious in 1 Corinthians. In the second Epistle to the Corinthians we shall find that the Apostle has become conscious of the inherent inconsistencies of his former view, which was the traditional one, and abandoned it in favour of the doctrine of a resurrection of the righteous following immediately on death.[3]

It is doubtful, however, ingenious as is Charles' speculation, whether the thought of Paul in 1 Cor. 15 does really involve the assumption of the

[1] Cf. A. Schweitzer, *Paul and his Interpreters*, pp. 69f.
[2] Cf. *Eschatology*, pp. 394f.   [3] R. H. Charles, *Eschatology*, p. 395.

new body at death. An analogy should not be pressed to its logical issue as is the case in Charles' treatment of Paul's analogy of the seed in 1 Cor. 15. When R. Meir [1] used the analogy of the seed he was thinking most certainly of the glorious new body which would come into being at the resurrection and there is no reason to think that Paul also in 1 Cor. 15 was not thinking of the same event. Moreover, we cannot assume, as does Charles, that because the essential ego, as it were, is to persist there is, therefore, to be a continuity between the old and the new form which this ego assumes.[2] It is at least equally agreeable that such is the difference between the σῶμα ψυχικόν and the σῶμα πνευματικόν that no continuity need exist between them, and that therefore the interval during the 'sleep' of death, which intervened before the formation of the new body, would make no difference. It would be hazardous therefore to follow Charles in thinking that 2 Cor. 5 merely makes explicit what was implicit in 1 Cor. 15 or that it is the logical development from the latter.

Next we have to refer to the view of those scholars who have claimed that there is no change in Paul's thought in 2 Cor. 5. 1 f. Kennedy,[3] for example, has sharply criticized the theory that there is a change, as literalistic and pedantic. Emphasizing that Paul is not presenting a systematic theology in his Epistles, he claims in connection with 2 Cor. 5. 1, that "there is no reference here to the detail of time. He does not yet specify a period. The ἔχομεν ('we have') is simply equivalent to 'there awaits us as a sure possession'." [4] The Apostle's assertion is merely a repetition in another form of the statement in 1 Cor. 15. 38: "God giveth it a body." Kennedy goes on to suggest that "these words give a hint of Paul's earnest desire and hope of surviving to the Parousia, and so escaping the terrifying experience of death".[5] It is difficult,

---

[1] See above, pp. 272 f.

[2] For a discussion of this, see H. A. A. Kennedy, *St Paul's Conceptions of the Last Things*, p. 242. He writes: "How would St Paul in his thought connect the γυμνὸς κόκκος with its future σῶμα? What for him is the organic link between them? His answer is extraordinarily typical. It is the only one we can expect him to give, and it is given in the clause immediately following: 'The sovereign power of God.' 'He giveth it a body according as He willed (ἠθέλησε); the aorist denotes the final act of God's will determining the constitution of nature'—so Edwards, ad loc. admirably." Also J. Moffatt, *First Corinthians (M.N.T.C.)*, p. 261: "[Paul] repudiates any notion of a material identity between the present and future body."

[3] Op. cit. p. 263.

[4] Kennedy, op. cit. p. 265. The same position is maintained by L. S. Thornton, *The Common Life in the Body of Christ*, p. 284, additional note A.; A. Plummer, *Second Corinthians (I.C.C.)*, p. 161; J. Denney, *Second Corinthians (Expositor's Bible)*, ad loc.

[5] Kennedy, op. cit. p. 256; cf. A. Schweitzer, *Paul and his Interpreters*, p. 69.

however, to accept this view. There is nothing in the text to suggest Paul's hope of surviving to the Parousia.[1] Far more likely is it that two factors had constrained Paul to give more thought than he had previously done to what happened to the Christian at death; he himself had been at the gates of death[2] and the problem of Christians who died was becoming a pressing one; and Paul was thus led to state the fact that the Christian at death was not left naked but received a heavenly body.[3]

What we find in 1 Cor. 15 and 2 Cor. 5, then, is the juxtaposition of two different views, first, that the Christian waits for the new body, till the Parousia and, secondly, that immediately at death he acquires the heavenly body. How are we to explain this juxtaposition? It will be well first to expound the view of those who have found here at least a partial Hellenization of Paul's thought. Schweitzer has examined the views of Pfleiderer, Teichmann and Holtzmann in this connection and we may refer to his treatment in his book, *Paul and his Interpreters*.[4] The most convenient discussion of the subject for our purpose is that of Knox.[5] The argument of the latter scholar runs somewhat as follows. His experience at Athens had convinced Paul that the eschatological presentation of the Gospel would not avail with a Gentile world, and "from this point forward his Epistles show a progressive adaptation of the Christian message to the general mental outlook of the Hellenistic world".[6] Part of this process is visible in 1 Cor. 15, where we find a "spiritualization of the doctrine of the resurrection". This, however, did not go far enough. Knox writes: "It appears that Paul's admission of the immaterial nature of the risen body and his suggestion of some kind of reabsorption of all things unto God were not enough to satisfy the difficulties of the Corinthians. The Second Epistle is largely devoted to a complete revision of Pauline eschatology in a Hellenistic sense."[7] In support of this thesis Knox shows how the ideology of 2 Cor. 5. 1f. can be paralleled in Hellenistic sources. To summarize briefly, he suggests that in this passage: (a) Paul regards the body as a burden from which he longs to be delivered, although his intense Jewishness forbids his contemplating a bodiless existence in the hereafter and retains for him the conception that "the soul did not simply lay aside the body, but put on a new and glorious one".[8] The parallels drawn from Hellenistic literature to Paul's language in 2 Cor. 5. 1f., are many. The most striking is the reference to the earthly body as σκῆνος in Wisd. 9. 15:

---

[1] Cf. S. Cave, *The Gospel of St Paul*, p. 255, n. 1.   [2] 2 Cor. 1. 8–9.
[3] Cf. S. Cave, op. cit. p. 254; C. H. Dodd, *Ryl. Bull.* (Jan. 1934), vol. xviii, no. 1, pp. 28f.
[4] Pp. 69ff.   [5] *St Paul and the Church of the Gentiles*, pp. 128f.
[6] Ibid. p. 26.   [7] Ibid. p. 128.   [8] Ibid. p. 137.

φθαρτὸν γὰρ σῶμα βαρύνει ψυχήν, καὶ βρίθει τὸ γεῶδες σκῆνος νοῦν πολυφροντίδα (σκῆνος was a Pythagorean term).[1] (b) The conception of the spirit as being a present possession Knox explains in terms of the divine afflatus of Hellenistic belief.[2] (c) The idea that the Christian life in this world is an exile is essentially Hellenistic, "the only real reason why the soul was in exile in this life was that it, or the highest part of it, was of divine origin, and although a celestial being, imprisoned in the material world".[3] (d) The one element in the passage that is not Hellenistic is the idea of judgement. At this point we may be permitted a lengthy quotation.[4] Paul

was ready to abandon the apocalyptic tradition in favour of the ascent of the soul or spirit of man to the firmament which was the abode of God, and its transmutation into a radiant state of glory by the work of the Spirit; he was not prepared to abandon the eternal responsibility of man for his deeds. His discussion of the destiny of the soul of man ended with the statement that all must stand before the judgement seat of Christ (5. 10), a phrase borrowed from the traditional picture of the final judgement of mankind. This judgement, as in the book of Wisdom, retained a formal position in the scheme of things, though it had ceased to possess any real significance when the thought of the gradual transformation of the soul from the material to the spiritual during life, and the completion of the process at death, had been substituted for the final assize at the end of the world-process.

What shall we say to all this? Knox allows that there are two elements in 2 Cor. 5. 1f., that are essentially Jewish, namely the horror of 'nakedness'[5] at death, which is implied, and the retention of the judgement. It is in (a), (b) and (c) above that Knox finds Hellenistic influences. Let us take these in inverse order. The idea of this present life being an exile is surely so commonplace that we need not postulate any specifically Hellenistic influence to account for it; and our study of St Paul's conception of the spirit in a previous chapter made it clear that it is very far removed from Hellenistic ideas. It is the language of 2 Cor. 5 that seems to suggest Hellenistic influences most strongly. Let us look, however, at the passage again. In 2 Cor. 4. 7 Paul has compared himself to an

---

[1] Ibid. p. 136, n. 8, for parallels and see especially H. Windisch, in Meyer, *Kommentar zum Neuen Testament, Der Zweite Korintherbrief*, p. 158; H. St J. Thackeray, *The Relation of St Paul to Contemporary Jewish Thought*, pp. 131 f. Referring to Paul's connection with the Book of Wisdom, Thackeray writes: "The occurrence of the same expressions (γεῶδες, σκῆνος, βαρέω, βαρύνω, ἐπίγειος) in conjunction points to a literary connection...."

[2] *St Paul and the Church of the Gentiles*, p. 140.

[3] Ibid. p. 140.

[4] Ibid. p. 141.   [5] Cf. M. Ber. 3. 5.

earthen vessel, a figure which may have often been used. Thus a Rabbi living in the period A.D. 140–65 uses the figure:

There was a man in Sepphoris whose son had died. A heretic sat by his side. R. Jose b. Ḥalafta came to visit him. The heretic saw that he was smiling. He said unto him, "Rabbi, why do you smile?" He replied, "I trust in the Lord of Heaven that the man will see his son again in the world to come." Then that heretic said, "Is not his sorrow enough for the man that you should come and sadden him yet more? Can broken sherds be made to cleave again together? Is it not written, 'Thou shalt break them in pieces like a potter's vessel'?" [Ps. 2. 9]. Then R. Jose said, "Earthen vessels are made by water and perfected by fire; vessels of glass are both made by fire and perfected by fire; the former, if broken, cannot be repaired: the latter, if broken, can be repaired." The heretic said, "Why?" He replied, "Because they are made by blowing. If the glass vessel which is made by the blowing of a mortal man can be repaired how much more the being who is made by the blowing of God."[1]

Later on, in 2 Cor. 5. 1, Paul calls the earthly body a σκῆνος and although there are abundant parallels to this, as we saw, in Hellenistic literature, the term would also be quite natural to a Rabbi. We accept the suggestion made by T. W. Manson,[2] in an article to which we have previously referred, that Paul's thought is here influenced by the Feast of Tabernacles. The term σκῆνος is used in the LXX to translate the Hebrew sukkâh. Thus the LXX renders Lev. 23. 42, thus: Ἐν σκηναῖς κατοικήσετε ἑπτὰ ἡμέρας, πᾶς ὁ αὐτόχθων ἐν Ἰσραὴλ κατοικήσει ἐν σκηναῖς, ὅπως ἴδωσιν αἱ γενεαὶ ὑμῶν ὅτι ἐν σκηναῖς κατῴκισα τοὺς υἱοὺς Ἰσραήλ, ἐν τῷ ἐξαγαγεῖν με αὐτοὺς ἐκ γῆς Αἰγύπτου. We have previously emphasized that in 2 Cor. 3 f.[3] Paul is thinking of the Christian dispensation as a new Exodus and since in chapter 4 he has been dealing with the frailty and transitory nature of his life in the body of flesh, he would naturally be led to think of the latter in terms of the sukkâh which was essentially a temporary dwelling in which the Jew dwelt for seven days at the Feast of Tabernacles, a dwelling designed to recall "the time which our forefathers spent in the wilderness and of the life they led in tents and booths".[4] The Christian, so it might have occurred to Paul, would have to live in a booth before reaching the Promised Land. If, as Manson suggests, the Epistle was written near the time of the Feast, this

[1] Gen. Rabba 14. 7.
[2] J.T.S. (Jan.–April 1945), vol. XLVI, pp. 1–10.
[3] See above, p. 108.
[4] Cf. Tabernacle Services [The Book of Prayer or Order of Service According to the Custom of Spanish and Portuguese Jews (1906)]. See also Mishnah Sukkah (Danby. pp. 172f.); Sukkah, Mishnah and Tosefta (A. W. Greenup).

interpretation of σκῆνος carries added conviction.[1] Throughout the passage under consideration, therefore, the language of Paul can be explained without recourse to Hellenistic sources. Finally, according to Knox, the Hellenization of Paul's presentation of the hereafter arose out of a crisis of thought; it was the result of a need felt to restate the Gospel in terms understood by the Hellenistic world. We cannot elaborate our position at this point, but we have previously questioned both Knox's assumption that Paul's experience at Athens was of such profound significance for his thought, as he suggests,[2] and his view that 1 Cor. 15 implies the 'dematerializing' of the Resurrection.[3] In view of all this we cannot accept the interpretation of 2 Cor. 5 as the Hellenization of Paul's thought.

How then are we to account for the difference that we have found between 1 Cor. 15 and 2 Cor. 5? The solution to this question we believe lies in that conception of the Age to Come as having already dawned which we have found in Paul: indeed, it is this alone that justified us in discussing at such length, at the beginning of this chapter, the exact significance which Paul had ascribed to the Resurrection of Jesus. We shall now examine the relevance of this fact for the understanding of our problem.

We begin with the teaching of Judaism on the nature of the Age to Come. Frey[4] has quoted with approval the saying that "le trait le plus caractéristique du systeme théologique juif, c'est de n'avoir pas de système". This is especially true with reference to the conception of the 'ôlâm ha-bâ'. "There is in this sphere", writes Moore,[5] "not merely an indefiniteness of terminology, but an indistinctness of conception... there was not only no orthodoxy, but no attempt to secure uniformity in such matters." The general distinction between this age and the Age to Come has often been described and here we need only refer to the treatment of the subject in Strack-Billerbeck,[6] Bonsirven[7] and Moore, and remark only that this distinction was as familiar to the Rabbis as to the apocalyptists. For our immediate purpose the complexity arises when we ask when the Age to Come was to be experienced. There are two possible answers to this question which are to be very carefully noted.

[1] Manson also holds that "Paul's καταλυθῇ suits better the dismantling of the booth of Tabernacles than the striking of a tent". There is only doubtful support for this view in Liddell and Scott.
[2] See above, chapter 8.
[3] See above, chapter 8.
[4] Biblica (1932), vol. XIII, p. 130.
[5] Vol. II, p. 378.
[6] Str.-B. vol. IV, pp. 799f.
[7] Le Judaïsme Palestinien, vol. I, pp. 307f.

On the one hand, there are passages which clearly imply that the Age to Come always exists 'in heaven' or 'in the unseen'. Thus in a passage in the Book of Enoch, which Charles, although he regards it as an interpolation, nevertheless dates in the pre-Christian period,[1] we read:

> And he said unto me
> He proclaims unto thee peace in the name of the world to come.
> *For from hence has proceeded peace since the creation of the world.*
> And so shall it be for ever and for ever and ever.[2]

Further, there have always existed dwelling-places of the righteous:

> And there I saw another vision, the dwelling places of the holy,
> And the resting places of the righteous.
> Here mine eyes saw their dwelling places with his righteous angels,
> And their resting places with the holy.[3]

There is no need to find here with Charles that "the unities of time and place are curiously neglected";[4] there is here merely the recognition of a realm that always is. Into this Age to Come that always is the souls of the righteous enter at death. Thus this world is the vestibule of the Age to Come, i.e. it immediately precedes the latter.

R. Jacob (A.D. 140–65) said: "This world is like a vestibule before the world to come; prepare thyself in the vestibule that thou mayest enter into the banqueting hall."[5]

At death then the soul comes to experience *ha'ôlâm ha-bâ'*, and the initial experience in that sphere was judgement. This comes out clearly in a passage concerning R. Johanan b. Zakkai:[6]

> When R. Johannan b. Zakkai was ill, his disciples went in to visit him. On beholding them, he began to weep. His disciples said to him, "O lamp of Israel, right hand pillar [1 Kings 7. 21], mighty hammer, wherefore dost thou weep?" He replied to them, "If I was being led into the presence of a human king, who to-day is here and to-morrow in the grave, whose anger, if he were wrathful against us, would not be eternal, whose imprisonment, if he imprisoned me, would not be everlasting, whose death sentence, if he condemned me to death, would not be for ever, and whom I could appease with words and bribe with money—even then I would weep; but now, when I am being led into the presence of the king of kings, the Holy One, blessed be He, who lives and endures for all eternity, whose anger, if He be wrathful against me, is eternal, whose imprisonment, if He imprisoned me, would be

---

[1] See R. H. Charles, *The Book of Enoch* (Oxford, 1893), p. 33.
[2] 1 Enoch 71. 15.   [3] 1 Enoch 39. 4.
[4] *Ap. and Ps.* vol. II, p. 120; *The Book of Enoch*, pp. 114f., n. 4.
[5] *P. Aboth* 4. 16; cf. also for the same thought *Sifra Lev.* 85 d.; *J. Yeb.* 15. 14 d.
[6] *b. Ber.* 28 b.

everlasting, whose sentence, if He condemned me to death, would be for ever, and whom I cannot appease with words or bribe with money—nay, more, when before me lie two ways, one towards the Garden of Eden and the other towards Gehinnom, and I know not towards which I am to be led—shall I not weep?" They said to him, "Our master, bless us!" He said to them, "May it be His will that the fear of heaven be upon you [as great] as the fear of flesh and blood." His disciples exclaimed, "Only as great!" He replied, "Would that it be [as great]; for know, that when a man intends to commit a transgression, he says, 'I hope nobody will see me'."

Into the details of the way in which the soul was led to judgement we need not here enter. God Himself was most often the judge and His decisions were given according to works. Following the judgement, which was definitive in the sense that it pronounced God's final valuation of the soul's merits and demerits, the soul proceeded to Sheol. In the latter, however, the just and the unjust were not treated alike. According to the Book of Enoch there were four different compartments into which the souls were severally placed, two blessed compartments for the righteous and two designed for punishment. In other books Sheol was exclusively reserved for the wicked and became identified with Gehenna.

While the souls of the wicked were punished, those of the righteous received the reward of blessedness. The geography of this blessed state varied considerably from author to author. For our purpose the significant fact is that, as Strack-Billerbeck, Bonsirven and Moore point out, the 'ôlâm ha-bâ' was conceived of as eternally existent; it always IS in the heavens and we awake to it at death.[1]

On the other hand, however, the 'ôlâm ha-bâ' is said to come into being *after* the Messianic Age and the general resurrection; the Age to Come *follows* these latter events. The examples of this usage are legion and need not be given again at this point.

Obviously then there are two phases to the 'ôlâm ha-bâ'—it both IS and COMES, and in those passages where there is mentioned resurrection, the 'ôlâm ha-bâ' which we enter at death finds its consummation in that 'ôlâm ha-bâ' which follows the resurrection. The case has been well put by Strack-Billerbeck. They write:

...Yet the striking phenomenon that the Rabbinic teachers have used the expression hâ-'ôlâm ha-bâ' to designate both the heavenly world of the souls and also the future Age of Consummation would have made it clear to us, as it were, that the heavenly Aeon of the Souls and the future Aeon of consummation on earth were regarded as one and the same great 'ôlam ha-bâ'.

[1] For all the above see especially J. B. Frey, *Biblica* (1932), vol. XIII, pp. 135f.

This great 'ôlâm ha-bâ' at present had its place in heaven (1 Enoch 71. 14 ff.)
...into it the souls of the righteous entered at the hour of death for a preliminary
blessedness. That is their first phase in which it serves as the world of the souls
until it enters through the resurrection of the dead into its second phase in
order now to become the earthly sphere of the Aeon of full blessedness.[1]

This twofold conception of the 'ôlâm ha-bâ' which we have traced
would be familiar to Paul. We do not mean by this that he consciously
and precisely distinguished between the two phases of the 'ôlâm ha-bâ'
referred to, as we have done, but that the conceptions outlined would
be entertained by him without any sense of a possible contradiction.
In his pre-Christian days, Paul, like other Rabbis, would have thought
of the Age to Come as awaiting him at death and at the same time he
could and did conceive of it as a final consummation of all created being.
This unconscious ambiguity of his thought will help us to understand
the difference between 1 Cor. 15 and 2 Cor. 5. In the former Paul is
concerned with the impending advent of the Lord when the general
resurrection already in process would be consummated. His mind is
centred on the 'ôlâm ha-bâ' as the End of all history, and he can argue
eloquently, but nevertheless dispassionately, about the nature of the
resurrection body. In 2 Cor. 5. 1f., on the other hand, it is not resurrection as characteristic of 'the End' that concerns him. His experience
in Asia had made him recognize the possibility that he himself might die
before the Parousia as had many Christians around him; in chapter 4
he has been thinking of the strain and stress of his ministry; his outward
maɪ is perishing and thoughts of death crowd upon him; and the Apostle
is led naturally to think of what lies immediately beyond death.

We have seen what Paul the Pharisee would see beyond death. Death
would be for him the advent of the judgement, and then, as he would
have hoped, the entry into Paradise—he would be in the Age to Come.
But he would be in the Age to Come only in its first phase, so to speak,
he would still be disembodied until the resurrection, although participating in blessedness.

For Paul the Christian, however, things were different. Not only
would Paul believe that it was Christ and not Torah[2] that availed him
in death, but he would also have to consider another new factor. We
have seen that he now believed that the Age to Come eternally existent
in the Heavens had already appeared in its initial stages in the Resurrection of Jesus. Already the resurrection body, the body of the final Age
to Come was being formed. Paul had died and risen with Christ and

---

[1] Str.-B. vol. IV, pp. 819f. See also J. Bonsirven, *Le Judaïsme Palestinien*, vol. I,
p. 313.
[2] For the efficacy of Torah at death, cf. P. *Aboth* 6. 9.

was already being transformed. At death, therefore, despite the decay of his outward body, Paul would already be possessed of another 'body'. The heavenly body was already his.[1] Because the Age to Come had dawned in its second phase, both on this side of the grave and on the other Paul would be embodied. The final Act of God had transformed both this world and the world beyond death for Paul. To be 'in Christ' in this world and to be 'with Christ'[2] in the sphere beyond death was the final blessedness, the Age to Come in its second and last phase.

We have now seen that in 2 Cor. 5. 1f. Paul expresses the view that the dead in Christ would not be disembodied at death, the fate which awaited the righteous according to Rabbinic Judaism—and then undergo an intermediate period of waiting till the general resurrection. They would, on the contrary, be embodied, and there is no room in Paul's theology for an intermediate state of the dead.[3] It agrees with this that Paul in the later passages of his Epistles speaks not of the resurrection of Christians but of their revelation. In Rom. 8. 19 we read: "The earnest longing of the creation waiteth for the revelation of the sons of God": and in Col. 3. 4, we read: "When Christ who is our life shall be revealed then shall ye also be revealed with him in glory." There is no need to resurrect those who have already died and risen with Christ and received their heavenly body, but they may be revealed.[4] The final consummation would merely be the manifestation of that which is already existent but 'hidden' in the eternal order. All this is related, it will be recognized, with what has been called Paul's 'Christ-mysticism'. The unity of Christians with Christ their Lord is such for Paul that just as Christ Himself had already passed into the eternal order so had Christians also, although they still lived in the flesh. Thus the Colossians[5] had already risen with Christ and although still living in the flesh yet they are 'dead' and their "life is hid with Christ in God". In the words of Dr Dodd:[6] "The personality of Christ", which we note is now in the eternal world, "receives, so to speak, extension in the life of His Body on earth. Those 'saving facts', the death and resurrection of Christ, are not merely particular facts of past history, however decisive in their effect; they are re-enacted in the experience of the Church. If Christ died to this world, so have the members of His body; if He has risen into newness

---

[1] Cf. A. E. J. Rawlinson, *The New Testament Doctrine of the Christ*, pp. 154f.; cf. 2 Cor. 4. 16f.; Col. 3. 3; Rom. 8. 11.
[2] Cf. C. H. Dodd, *Romans* (M.N.T.C.), p. 89.
[3] See G. B. Stevens, *The Pauline Theology*, pp. 358f.
[4] Cf. R. H. Charles, *Eschatology*, p. 402.   [5] Col. 3. 1–4.
[6] *The Apostolic Preaching and its Developments*, pp. 147f.

of life, so have they;[1] if He being risen from the dead dieth no more, neither do they;[2] if God has glorified Him, He has also glorified them.[3] They are righteous, holy, glorious, immortal, according to the prophecies, with the righteousness, holiness, glory and immortality which are His in full reality, and are theirs in the communion of His Body— 'in Christ'."[4] This means that Christians are already partakers in the Age to Come 'in Christ' and that future events can only make this fact explicit.

If the above interpretation be correct, it will be seen that we need not go outside Rabbinic Judaism to account for Paul's thought in 2 Cor. 5. 1 f. This fact is, indeed, recognized by Knox despite his insistence on the Hellenization of Paul's thought. He writes on this passage: "It seems probable that Paul was employing a traditional argument, which would be recognized as entirely orthodox from the point of view of rabbinical learning, in which he had a solid advantage over his Jewish Christian opponents."[5] It was not a crisis of thought, no apologetic considerations that governed Paul's thought in 2 Cor. 5, as Knox suggests, rather was it a crisis in experience, the necessity to reconcile himself to death as a physical event. It is part of a process not of Hellenization but of what Dr Dodd has called 'reconciliation to experience'.[6]

The above discussion has revealed two diverse strains in Paul's conception of resurrection, that which we distinguished in 1 Cor. 15 and that of 2 Cor. 5. 1 f. These two strains continue to appear alongside each other throughout the Pauline Epistles. Thus, as Schweitzer[7] has rightly insisted, Paul's expectation of a Second Advent persists in the Epistles to the Romans and to the Philippians.[8] Nevertheless, without here entering into details, we must agree with Dr Dodd that in the Epistles which follow 1 Corinthians "the advent hope is in the background rather than in the foreground of his thought",[9] and Paul is more concerned with defining more clearly the full meaning of that coming of the Age to Come into his present experience which we have discussed above and with his desire to be 'with Christ' at death.[10] For our purpose,

---

[1] Rom. 6. 4.   [2] Rom. 6. 8–9.
[3] Rom. 8. 29–30.   [4] Cf. above, chapter 5.
[5] Cf. W. L. Knox, St Paul and the Church of the Gentiles, p. 143.
[6] See C. H. Dodd, "The Mind of Paul: Change and Development", in Ryl. Bull. (Jan. 1934), vol. XVIII, no. 1, pp. 38 f., 44.
[7] The Mysticism of Paul the Apostle, p. 53.
[8] Cf. Phil. 1. 6, 10, 2. 10, 3. 20–2, 4. 1–5; Rom. 8. 19, 13. 11, 12.
[9] C. H. Dodd in A Companion to the Bible (ed. T. W. Manson), p. 404.
[10] See especially C. H. Dodd, "The Mind of Paul: Change and Development", in Ryl. Bull. vol. XVIII.

however, what is significant is, if the interpretation we have offered above be accepted, that we have been able to account for both strains without going outside Rabbinic Judaism. The twofold conception of the 'ôlâm ha-bâ' both as a future event in time and as an eternally existing reality (which has already, in Christ, invaded the world of time for Paul) has provided us with a reconciling principle. In addition to this, however, this twofold conception drives us to the conclusion that it is misleading to separate too sharply Rabbinic and Hellenistic thought on the hereafter, and indeed both Strack-Billerbeck[1] and Bonsirven[2] have showed that already in the first century A.D. Judaism had been largely influenced and modified by Hellenistic conceptions of immortality. Readers will immediately recognize the import of all this for our understanding of the eschatology of the New Testament. We cannot enlarge on this here, but we recall that Dr Dodd suggested that the apocalyptists used language symbolically. Writing of the futurist element in the thought of Jesus Dr Dodd claimed that "these future tenses are only an accommodation of language. There is no coming of the Son of Man 'after' His coming in Galilee and Jerusalem, whether soon or late, for there is no before and after in the eternal order. The kingdom of God in its full reality is not something which will happen after other things have happened. It is that to which men awake when this order of time and space no longer limits their vision. . . ."[3] To this Dr Flew[4] has objected that it is far too Platonic to be valid and that "we have no other evidence that any of the sayings of Jesus implied that God's eternal order was beyond time". If, however, our discussion is not erroneous, such a conception of the Kingdom of God as is advocated by Dr Dodd in the above-quoted passage would be familiar to Palestinian Judaism. Similarly, the juxtaposition of eschatology and 'Platonic' elements in the Fourth Gospel need occasion no difficulty,[5] and 'mysticism' and eschatology such as has been found in Paul can both derive from Judaism. We close our study, therefore, with the assertion that it is wholly artificial to make too sharp a dichotomy between the Hebraic and the Hellenistic elements in Paul's thought, and that any Hellenistic elements which may be found in his thought do not imply that he was therefore outside the main current of first-century Judaism.

[1] Str.-B. vol. IV, p. 819. This was true of the first century B.C. also, as we saw in the Enochian passage. Cf. J. Bonsirven, Le Judaïsme Palestinien, vol. I, p. 317, n. 3.

[2] Op. cit. p. 315.

[3] The Parables of the Kingdom, p. 108; see also pp. 104 f.

[4] Jesus and His Church, p. 44, n. 1.

[5] See for a discussion of this W. F. Howard, Christianity According to St John, pp. 106 f.

CONCLUSION

OUR examination of the relevant aspects of the life and thought of Paul is now complete. In conclusion it will be well to consider very briefly the facts that have emerged.

We begin with the significant fact that throughout his life Paul was a practising Jew who never ceased to insist that his gospel was first to the Jews, who also expected Jewish Christians to persist in their loyalty to the Torah of Judaism, and who assigned to the Jews in the Christian no less than in the pre-Christian dispensation a place of peculiar importance. We have argued above that this 'preoccupation' of Paul with the significance and destiny of the Jewish nation as such is inconsistent with the declared universalism of his faith. We saw, however, that there were certain considerations of policy, which would inevitably incline Paul to the continued practice of the Law; any deviation from orthopraxy would irretrievably close the doors of Judaism against him. Moreover, we may reflect that Paul is not the only 'universalist' Christian who has charged his own nation with a special function in the providence of God; indeed, it was regarded as axiomatic in 'progressive' circles in the nineteenth century, and is still so regarded in certain quarters that every nation possesses a divine right to self-expression, a belief which logically differs little, except in degree, from Paul's insistence on the significance of 'Israel after the flesh'. Modern Christendom which has witnessed the growth of such phenomena as Nazism and British-Israelitism should not find it difficult to recognize that strict consistency in resolving the rival claims of 'nationalism' and religion is not easy of attainment.

There is also another factor to be noted. John Oman once wrote that "the stronger a person's natural quality, the more likely he is to remain racy of his native soil. A Scotswoman, it has been said", so Oman continues, "should never be trusted if she can keep her feet among the 'shalls' and 'wills', and the ability to pronounce the 'rr' in approved southern fashion might equally raise suspicion".[1] These words, playfully exaggerated though they be, suggest a profound truth. Even though we may not believe that the preservation of a man's peculiar nationality is integral to God's purpose for him, an issue which raises questions of race, history and culture which we cannot here discuss, nevertheless it will be readily agreed that a man's national heritage cannot be divested except at a heavy price. A Paul who when he became a Christian had

[1] *Concerning the Ministry*, pp. 117f.

ceased to be a 'Jew' would not be the Paul that we know; it was part of his very integrity as a man that he should retain his Hebrew accent, as it were, even in his new faith. We believe that Paul's concern for 'Israel after the flesh' is a tribute to the profundity of his thought no less than to the warmth of his affections, because, as we have previously asserted, it is a sublimation of nationalism in Christ such as Paul yearned for for his own people that must always be desired and not its suppression or extinction.

As we saw, however, it was not merely 'nationalism' in its customary connotation with which Paul was concerned. His 'national' heritage was not distinguishable from his religious heritage. It was the historic fact that the Old Israel had been chosen at the Exodus and had been, as a result, in a relation, if we may so express it, of peculiar intimacy throughout the ages with God, a relation that the whole tradition of Judaism, prophetic no less than legal, regarded as eternal; it was this that made Paul's 'nationalism' invade his Christianity. He found it difficult to admit that that Old Israel, which had in the past been the chosen people, should no longer act in that capacity, and so was led to ascribe to that Old Israel a significance even in the history of the New Israel. Dr Dodd has claimed with regard to Paul's insistence on the ultimate restoration of the Old Israel to the Church and its significance in Rom. 11. 1–32, that "from our standpoint with a far longer historical retrospect than Paul would have dreamt of the special importance here assigned to the Jews and their conversion in the forecast of the destiny of mankind appears artificial".[1] It may, however, be questioned whether our longer historic perspective does in fact confirm this judgement. One thing at least shines clear, that 'Israel after the flesh' persists as an enigma to the twentieth no less than to the preceding centuries. May it not be that the great hatred directed against Jewry in the modern world is a witness not only to man's inhumanity to man but also to the strange historical significance of 'Israel'? Paul thought of the incoming of the 'Old Israel' into the Church as life from the dead. Whether he was justified in this extreme claim, whatever its exact meaning, we cannot say, but it cannot be doubted that a Christendom which is almost entirely Gentile would gain by the incursion of the Old Israel, which is still the heir of the prophets.[2] In any case a truer understanding of Paul would at least have preserved the Church from the black stain of anti-Semitism.[3]

Whether we dismiss Paul's persistent emphasis on Jewry, however,

---

[1] *Romans* (M.N.T.C.), p. 182.
[2] Cf. Lev Gillet, *Communion in the Messiah*, pp. 191 ff.
[3] Cf. C. H. Dodd, *Romans* (M.N.T.C.), p. 181.

as an inconsistency unjustified at the bar of history or not, for our purpose, which is the understanding of Paul, the fact remains that his acceptance of Christ did not involve the rejection by him of the usages of his people nor a denial of community with them. "The most genuine characteristics of the Jewish nature were preserved by Paul when he became a Christian.... In opposition to mechanical divisions of the Jewish and the Christian elements in him, we need not hesitate to call him the great Jew-Christian of the earliest age."[1] Thus wrote Deissmann. In the light of all this, therefore, it would be erroneous to think that Paul regarded Christianity as the antithesis of Judaism as has so often been claimed. On the contrary, it appears that for the Apostle the Christian Faith was the full flowering of Judaism, the outcome of the latter and its fulfilment; in being obedient to the Gospel he was merely being obedient to the true form of Judaism. The Gospel for Paul was not the annulling of Judaism but its completion, and as such it took up into itself the essential genius of Judaism.

This latter fact came out most clearly when we dealt with the concept of the Torah and of obedience in relation to Paul's thought. Lev Gillet has recently written: "The religion of Paul became centred on a person, Jesus himself. This personality could by no means be expressed in terms of Torah."[2] But, if our thesis be correct, this is exactly what we do find in Paul, the application to the Person of Jesus of those concepts which Judaism had reserved for its greatest treasure, the Torah, so that we felt justified in describing the Pauline Christ as a New Torah. We found in Paul a 'Christifying' of the Torah and *ipso facto* a 'spiritualizing' of it. This last, however, does not mean that the concept correlative to that of the Torah in Judaism, namely, obedience, is absent from the Gospel of Paul; indeed, we saw that it was central to it. Paul was the preacher of a New Exodus wrought by the 'merit' of Christ who was obedient unto death, but this New Exodus like the Old was constitutive of community, it served to establish the New Israel; it also led to the foot of a New Sinai, and Paul appeared before us as a catechist, the steward of a New Didache that imposed new demands. 'Torah', 'Obedience' and 'Community' then are integral to Pauline Christianity no less than to Judaism. The source of Pauline Christianity lies in the fact of Christ, but in wrestling to interpret the full meaning and implications of that fact Paul constantly drew upon concepts derived from Rabbinic Judaism; it was these that formed the warp and woof if not the material of his thought. In this connection we may also be allowed to suggest that a truer appreciation of this fact might supply a reconciling

---

[1] *St Paul* (E.T.), p. 98.   [2] *Communion in the Messiah*, p. 7.

principle between much that is now divergent in Protestant and Roman Catholic theology.

Both in his life and thought, therefore, Paul's close relation to Rabbinic Judaism has become clear, and we cannot too strongly insist again that for him the acceptance of the Gospel was not so much the rejection of the old Judaism and the discovery of a new religion wholly antithetical to it, as his polemics might sometimes pardonably lead us to assume, but the recognition of the advent of the true and final form of Judaism, in other words, the advent of the Messianic Age of Jewish expectation. It is in this light that we are to understand the conversion of Paul. We have above referred cursorily to that interpretation of his conversion which depicts Paul in his pre-Christian days as suffering from agonies of discontent with the Torah, a discontent which was more particularly characteristic of Diaspora Judaism, as Montefiore has argued, and which Paul sought to suppress and hide by zeal in persecution. But, as we have previously written, there is little evidence that this was the case. Doubtless Paul, looking back on his pre-Christian days not only from the height of his Christian experience but also past many a bitter memory, could depict them as a period of dissatisfaction and frustration. Nevertheless, things are seldom in fact what they appear to be in retrospect. It is far more probable, as Branscomb[1] has cogently pointed out, that Paul's persecution of the Church was due not to his dissatisfaction with Judaism but to his zeal on its behalf. It was not the inadequacy of Judaism, not the fact that the Judaism which Paul knew was an inferior product of the Diaspora that accounts for Paul's conversion, but the impact of the new factor that entered into his ken when he encountered Christ. It was at this one point that Paul parted company with Judaism, at the valuation of Jesus of Nazareth as the Messiah with all that this implied. While, therefore, our study has led us to the recognition of Paul's debt to Rabbinic Judaism, it has also led us to that challenge which Pauline Christianity, and indeed all forms of essential Christianity, must issue to Judaism no less than to other religions: What think ye of Christ? Seldom have most of us pedestrian Christians seen in Christ what Paul saw in Him, and so to both Christians and Jews who have not found that in Christ the Age to Come has come and that in Him there is a New Creation, Paul would say

> 'Tis ye, 'tis your estrangéd faces
> That miss the many-splendoured thing.[2]

---

[1] *Jesus and the Law of Moses*, pp. 274 ff.
[2] Francis Thompson: "*In no strange land.*"

APPENDIX A

DR KARL BARTH'S INTERPRETATION OF
ROMANS I. 2

It is to be observed that our insistence on the presence of the Rabbinic conception of the Noachian commandments in Paul's thought in Romans I. 2 has an important bearing on current theological issues raised especially by Dr Karl Barth. While it would be impertinent on our part even to consider embarking upon a criticism of that great thinker's general theological position, we may be allowed to scrutinize his interpretation of the relevant sections of Romans I. 2 in the light of what we have written above, particularly in view of the fact that, in his famous commentary on the Epistle to the Romans, he explicitly states that it was his intention there not to theologize freely, but to *explain* the text.[1]

Barth's interpretation of Paul's thought in Romans I. 2, in so far as it concerns us here, we may briefly state as follows. God is essentially the Unknown; He is He whom man does not know. Now the created order—the things that are made—should have made man aware of that fact, namely, that God is the Unknown: it is this fact alone that can be known through the things that are made—that God is what man is not, that God is absolutely heterogeneous; and the created universe should have induced in man the only attitude which truly befits him, namely, that in which he recognizes his creatureliness over against God who is the Wholly Other. When Paul asserts that man has failed 'to know' God through the created order, what he means is that man has failed to acknowledge this creatureliness, not that he has missed what we may call a positive revelation of God through the natural world: he has missed not the knowledge of God, but the recognition of the impossibility of all knowledge of Him. The following may be taken as typical of Barth's exegesis:

> The insecurity and utter questionableness of all that is and of what we are, lie in the text-book open before us. What are all those enigmatic creatures of God—a zoological garden, for example—but so many problems to which we have no answer? But God only, God Himself, He is the answer. And so the boundary which bars us in and which nevertheless, points beyond itself, can *since the creation of the world* be clearly seen *through the things that are made* by God. By calm, veritable, unprejudiced religious contemplation the divine 'No' can be established and apprehended. If we do not ourselves hinder it, nothing can prevent our being translated into a most wholesome KRISIS by that which *may be known of God*. And indeed, we stand already in this KRISIS if we would but *see clearly*. And what is clearly seen to be indisputable reality is the invisibility of God, which is precisely and in strict agreement with the Gospel of the Resurrection—*His everlasting power and divinity*. And what does this mean but that we can know nothing of God, that the Lord is to be feared.[2]

[1] Cf. *The Epistle to the Romans* (E.T.), p. ix.   [2] Op. cit. pp. 46f.

All this implies that, according to Barth, Paul does not admit the possibility of a revelation of the nature of God in the created order or, in other words, lends no support to the possibility of a Natural Theology. This aspect of Barth's exegesis we have already criticized in chapter 7 above. It is with another related element in his exegesis that we are here concerned.

This failure to acknowledge his essential creatureliness over against God, man's loss of knowledge of the crevasse, the polar zone, as Barth expresses it, between himself and God, issues (cf. Rom. 1. 22-32) in idolatry in its multifarious forms; and, finally, the uncleanness of man's relation to God[1] submerges his life also in uncleanness until it leads to AGNOSIA (cf. 1 Cor. 15. 34), when man refuses to have God in his knowledge and becomes no longer capable of serious awe and amazement.[2] The full significance of this is made clear by Barth in his controversy with Brunner. The following summary of his position by Dr John Baillie[3] will suffice:

It is with him [Dr Barth] a fundamental premiss that no knowledge of God exists in the world save in the hearts of regenerate Christian believers. He stands, as did Ritschl and Herrmann in previous generations, in the tradition of that Lutheran christocentrism which made Christ the Mediator no less of knowledge than of salvation; the christocentrism which denies that except in His Incarnation in Jesus of Nazareth God has ever spoken to man at all; the christocentrism which seizes eagerly on the New Testament declaration that "neither knoweth any man the Father save the Son and he to whomsoever the Son will reveal Him" (Mat. 11. 27), and understands that to mean that not merely God's Fatherliness but His very reality was made known to men through Jesus alone. Except through revelation, he teaches, there is no knowledge of God, and there is no revelation except in Christ; "only the man who knows about Jesus Christ knows anything at all about revelation", so that "the confession becomes inevitable that Jesus Christ *alone* is the revelation".[4]

Further, Dr Baillie[5] writes:

Dr Barth does indeed accept the doctrine that man had once been created *ad imaginem et similitudinem Dei* (cf. Gen. 1. 27, 5. 1), but he holds that this image and likeness of God have been so totally defaced by the Fall as to leave not a trace behind, so that nothing but a wholly new act of creation will suffice. Man, it is true, still remains human—"he is still man and not cat" as he expresses it;[6] but his humanity has been so totally corrupted by sin that no more than a cat is he able to hear God's voice until, through faith in Christ, the image and similitude of God are created in him afresh....

In accordance with this, in his interpretation of Romans 2, Barth explains Paul's ascription of the Law to the Jews and a Law written within—on their hearts—to the Gentiles, as follows: "The possession of the Torah by the Jews means that 'they have in their midst the sign-post which points them to God, to the KRISIS of human existence, to the new world which is set at the barrier of this world.'"[7] This implies, if we understand Barth rightly, that

---

[1] Op. cit. p. 51.   [2] Op. cit. p. 53.
[3] *Our Knowledge of God*, pp. 17f.
[4] *Revelation* (ed. Baillie and Martin, 1937), pp. 48, 53.
[5] *Our Knowledge of God*, pp. 19f.
[6] *Nein!* p. 25.   [7] *The Epistle to the Romans*, p. 65.

its moral demand is not the primary significance of the Torah. Similarly when Paul refers to a Law written on the hearts of the Gentiles, he does not mean that the Gentiles are aware of certain ethical demands, which God has laid upon the conscience of all men, but that they know their creatureliness, that they are aware of "the negation by which the creation is distinguished from the Creator and of the affirmation which makes them His creatures".[1] A further quotation will make this clear:

Among the Gentiles there is, moreover, a shattering and disturbing awe; but God beholds it and knows its meaning. Whenever the Gentiles grow sceptical of the righteousness of men, there is exposed to them the righteousness of God. By nature and in the natural order they *do the law*. In their merry and worldly dependence upon the creation, in their simple, unpretentious, matter-of-fact behaviour, they are known of God and esteem Him in return. *They are not lacking in perception of the corruptibility of all things human....*[2] [Our italics.]

Again the law written on the heart, like the Torah of Judaism, does not find its primary significance in an ethical demand.

But is all this true to the mind of Paul? Does the significance of the Torah of Judaism and of the conscience of the Gentile for Paul reside in their capacity to act as sign-posts to the corruptibility of all things human? There are indeed passages where Paul seems to deny that there is any knowledge of God apart from Christ. Thus in 1 Cor. 1. 21 we read: "For after that in the wisdom of God the world by wisdom knew not God, it pleased God by the foolishness of preaching to save them that believe." Again in Acts 17. 30 we read that there has been a long-standing ignorance of God.

Nevertheless, it would be wrong to conclude from these two passages that Paul regarded the pagan world as being wholly without some awareness of God's moral demands. And if what we wrote above in chapter 6 be correct, then Barth's interpretation of Romans 1. 2 must be erroneous. In chapter 6 we suggested that the conception of the Noachian commandments underlies Paul's thought in Romans 1. 2. There Paul presupposes that God had entered into a covenant with all men prior to His covenant with Abraham and Moses, into a covenant with Noah, and that all men everywhere had been made aware of certain of His basic demands. In short, Paul presupposes throughout what is the Jewish equivalent of the Stoic doctrine of the Law of Nature: there had been a revelation of God's moral demands prior both to the giving of the Torah of Judaism and to the advent of the Christian Gospel.

This is also presupposed in other parts of the Epistle and elsewhere in Paul. Thus the Apostle assumes that there are certain actions that pagans no less than Christians and Jews will recognize as good. The capacity to judge that which is right has been given to them by nature as it were. The words in Romans 12, 17b, "...Provide these things honest in the sight of all men" imply a *communis sensus* which enables all men to recognize the good. Similarly Paul's valuation of the secular authorities rests upon the same truth:

<hr>

[1] Op. cit. p. 66.   [2] Op. cit. p. 66.

the secular authorities although outside the pale of Judaism and of Christianity nevertheless regulate society for good and thereby serve God (cf. Romans 13. 1ff.). Clearly they know how to do this apart from any special revelation, but simply in virtue of their 'human' capacity to make moral judgements. So too, as we saw, Paul can refer to what ἡ φύσις αὐτὴ διδάσκει (cf. 1 Cor. 11. 14).

A further consideration falls to be noticed. In Romans 2, Paul claims that men are without excuse for their moral depravity. But where there is complete *agnosia*, such as Barth refers to, there can be no responsibility, and, therefore, no relevance in claiming that men are without excuse for their condition. The argument of Paul that the Gentile can shame the Jew and that the Gentile is without excuse for his moral corruption implies that there had been given to the Gentile world apart from the Christian revelation a certain definite knowledge of God's moral demands—enough indeed to make that world responsible. We believe that it is in the light of his acceptance of the Noachian commandments that Paul can claim that the Gentiles are inexcusable and that they have a conscience, a law written in their hearts. The argument of Romans 1. 2 demands some such concept as we have found in the Noachian commandments.

It must be conceded in view of all the above, that Dr Barth's interpretation of Romans 1. 2, stimulating and suggestive though it is, fails to do justice to the Rabbinic core of Paul's thought at this point—a Rabbinic core which, as we pointed out, is clothed in Hellenistic terminology but nevertheless remains central for the understanding of Paul.

APPENDIX B

THE IMPERATIVE PARTICIPLE
IN *TANNAITIC* HEBREW

In view of Dr Daube's exhaustive treatment of this subject it will only be necessary here to give a few examples of the passages he quotes in support of his thesis.

Examples of the participle are (the participle is underlined):

Mishnah Berakoth 2. 4: האומנין קוראין בראש האילן

"Craftsmen may recite (the Shema) on the top of a tree."

Here the addressees are specified.

In other rules the addressees are not specified, e.g.

Mishnah Berakoth 1. 5: מזכירין יציאת מצרים בלילות

"One has to rehearse the going forth from Egypt (say the third section of the Shema) also at night."

Mishnah Taanith 4. 6: משנכנס אב ממעטין בשמחה

"When Ab comes in, one has to diminish gladness."

Dr Daube notes that the participle is never used for the imperative: (1) in a command addressed to a specific person on a specific occasion, nor (2) in the expression of an absolute, unquestioned and unquestionable law, nor (3) outside "codes and quotations from or allusions to codes".

As parallel to Romans 12. 17 Dr Daube quotes *Mishnah Shekalim* 3. 2:

בשלש קופות...תורמין...אין התורם נכנס...לפי שאדם צריך לצאת ידי הבריות
כדרך שצריך לצאת ידי המקום

"In three baskets one has to take up (lit. taking up) *Terumah* out of the Shekel-chamber. He that takes up *Terumah* may not go in (lit. not going in) either in a sleeved cloak or with shoes, lest if he becomes rich men should say that he became rich from the *Terumah*; for it is necessary for a man to satisfy mankind even as it is to satisfy God...and again Scripture says (Prov. 3. 4), 'So shalt thou find favour in the sight of God and man.'"

He also cites *Derek Eretz Zuta* 19b:

הוא היה אומר אין מעמידין מהם

"He (R. Jose) said, The barber and the tanner and the bath attendant one does not make any of them (lit. not making) head of the Congregation."

And *Derek Eretz Rabba* 19b:

הנכנס אומר יהי רצון וקודם שיכנס כיצד יעשה?...חולץ

"He that goes in to have a bath should say (saying), May it be Thy will that thou leadest me in peace and before he goes in how should he do? He should pull off his shoes."

APPENDIX C

PASSAGES REFERRED TO IN THE TEXT, OUTSIDE TALMUDIC SOURCES, THE *MIDRASH RABBAH,* AND THE *MEKILTA,* IN THE ORDER OF THEIR OCCURRENCE

I. PASSAGES FROM THE *TOSEFTA* (ed. M. S. Zuckermandel, 1880)

(1) *Soṭah* 15. 8 (see p. 6, n. 6):

של בית רבן גמליאל התירו ללמד יוונית מפני שהן זקוקין למלכות:

"They were allowed to teach Greek to those of the house of Gamaliel because they were associated with the authorities."

(2) *Sukkah* 2. 6 (see p. 13, n. 13):

בזמן שהמאורות לוקין סימן רע לכל העולם...ר' מאיר אומ' בזמן שהמאורות לוקין סימן רע לשונאי ישר' מפני שהן לימודי מכות:

"When the luminaries are eclipsed it is an evil sign for all the world...R. Meir said: 'When the luminaries are eclipsed it is an evil sign for the enemies of Israel because they are accustomed to taking knocks.'" [שונאי ישר' is probably to be taken as a circumlocution for Israel itself—a kind of euphemism.]

(3) *Soṭah* 13. 3 (see p. 207, n. 1):

שנכנסו חכמ' לבית גוריו ביריחו ושמעו בת קול אומ' יש כאן אדם שראוי לרוח הקודש אלא שאין דורו זכאי לכך ונתנו עיניהם בהלל הזקן וכשמת אמרו עליו הי עניו הי חסיד תלמידו של עזרא : שוב פעם אחת היו יושבין ביבנה ושמעו בת קול אומרת יש כאן אדם שראוי לרוח הקודש אלא שאין הדור זכאי לכך ונתנו עיניהם בשמואל הקטן וכשמת אמרו עליו הי עניו הי חסיד תלמידו של הלל...

"As the sages gathered at the house of Guryo in Jericho they heard a Bath Qol announce, 'One man is present here who is worthy of the Holy Spirit but his generation is not worthy of it'; and they gazed intently on Hillel the Elder. When he died they said concerning him, 'Alas for the pious, the disciple of Ezra'. Again once they were sitting in Jabneh and they heard a Bath Qol saying, 'There is a man present here who is worthy of the Holy Spirit but (his) generation is not worthy'. They gazed intently on Samuel the Small. When he died they said concerning him, 'Alas for the pious the disciple of Hillel'."

(4) *Soṭah* 13. 2 (see p. 209, n. 4):

משחרב בית הראשון בטל' מלכות מבית דוד ובטלו אורים ותומים ופסקו ערי מגרש שנ' ויאמר התרשתא להם אשר לא יאכלו מק' הק' עד ע' כ' לאורים ותומים כאדם שאומ' לחבירו עד שיבא אליהו או' עד שיחיו המתים משמת חגי זכריה ומלאכי נביאים האחרונים פסקה רוח הקודש מישראל ואף על פי כן היו משמיעין להן בבת קול:

"Since the destruction of the first temple the kingdom ceased from the house of David, and Urim and Thummim ceased, and the cities of refuge ceased, as it is said; 'And the Tirshatha said unto them, that they should not eat of the most holy things, till there stood up a priest with Urim and Thummim.' As a man says to his friend, 'Until the return of Elijah', or 'Until the rising of the dead'. From the death of Haggai, Zechariah and Malachi, the latter prophets, the Holy Spirit ceased from Israel. But in spite of that it was allowed them to hear messages from God by a Bath Qol."

(5) *Soṭah* 13. 5 (see p. 211, n. 3):

יוחנן כהן גדול שמע מבית קודש הקדשים נצחו טליא דאזלו לאגחא קרבא באנטוכיא
וכיונו את אותה השעה וכיונו שנצחו אותה שעה:

"Johanan the High Priest heard from the house of the Holy of Holies 'The young men who went forth to wage war against Antioch have conquered'. They marked that hour and determined exactly that they had the victory on that hour."

(6) *Pesahim* 1. 27 (see p. 211, n. 6):

כיון רבן גמליאל ברוח הקדש...

"Rabban Gamaliel saw directly by the Holy Spirit." [This refers to the fact that he had been able to call a person whom he had never seen before by his name.]

(7) *Berakoth* 3. 7 (see p. 261):

אמר ר' אלעזר בר צדוק אבא היה מתפלל תפלה קצרה בלילי שבתות מאהבתך יי' אלהינו
שאהבת את ישראל עמך ומחמלתך מלכנו שחמלת על בני בריתך נתת לנו יי' אלהינו את יום
השביעי הגדול והקדוש הזה באהבה ועל הכוס אומר אשר קידש את יום השבת ואינו חותם:

"R. Eliezer the son of Zadok said, 'My father used to pray a short prayer on the Sabbath eve, namely, 'Out of thy love Yahweh our God with which thou hast loved Israel thy people and out of thy compassion, our king, with which thou didst have compassion upon the sons of thy covenant, thou didst give to us, Yahweh our God, this great and holy seventh day in love'. And over the cup he used to say, 'Who sanctified the Sabbath', and he did not use a concluding formula of blessing.'"

(8) *Soṭah* 15. 2 (see p. 258 for translation):

שמעון בן גמליאל אומ' משום ר' יהושע מיום שחרב בית המקדש אין יום שאין בו קללה
ולא ירד טל לברכה וגוטל טעם הפירות:

"R. Simeon b. Gamaliel said in the name of R. Joshua, 'Since the day of the destruction of the Temple there has not been a day without some curse, the dew has not come down as a blessing and the taste of the fruits has been taken away'."

II. PASSAGES FROM *SIFRA* ON LEVITICUS (J. H. Weiss and J. Schlossberg; Wien, 1862)

(1) 89b פרק ד (see p. 55 for translation):

ואהבת לרעך כמוך. רבי עקיבא אומר זה כלל גדול בתורה. בן עזאי אומר זה ספר
תולדות אדם. זה כלל גדול מזה:

(2) On 13. 5. 85d. פרק יג (see p. 315, n. 5):

ושמרתם את חוקותי ואת משפטי אשר יעשה אותם האדם. ליתן שמירה ועשייה לחוקים
ושמירה ועשייה למשפטים. וחי בהם לעולם הבא. ואם תאמר בעולם הזה והלא סופו מת
הוא הא מה אני מקיים וחי בהם לעולם הבא. אני ה' נאמן לשלם שכר:

"'And ye shall keep my statutes and my judgements, which if a man perform,' i.e. observe and perform the statutes and observe and perform the judgements. 'Then he will live by them,' i.e. in the Age to Come. And if thou shalt say—'In this Age; surely the end of him is that he shall die', well then how do I fulfil the promise (that he may live by them to the Age to Come?). I am the Lord, i.e. am to be trusted to pay a reward."

For this idea concerning the Age to Come compare also the following: J. *Yebamoth* 15. 14*d* (see p. 315, v. 5):

ביום נשק...ד"א ביום ששני עולמות נושקין זה את זה העולם הזה יוצא והעולם הבא
נכנם:

"'In the day of battle' [Ps. 140. 8]...another interpretation is—on the day when two ages kiss one another; this age making its exit and the Age to Come entering."

III. PASSAGES FROM *SIFRE* ON NUMBERS AND DEUTERONOMY.

(References are to the Biblical chapter and verse and the chapter in the *Sifre*; Wilna, 1866)

(1) Numbers 6. 25, § 41 (see p. 148, n. 2):

יאר ה' פניו אליך...ד"א יאר זה מאור תורה שנאמר כי נר מצוה ותורה אור .

"'The Lord make his face to shine upon thee.'...Another interpretation [runs]: 'make to shine'—this is the light of the Torah, as it is said, 'For the commandment is a lamp and the Torah a light.'"

(2) Deuteronomy 6. 5, § 32 (see p. 21, n. 7; also p. 263, n. 5):

בכל לבבך · בשני יצריך ביצר טוב וביצר רע...ד"א שמעון בן יוחאי אומר חביבים
יסורים ששלש מתנות נתן הקב"ה להם לישראל שעובדי כוכבים מתאווים להן ולא נתנוהו
לישראל אלא על ידי יסורים ואלו הן תורה וארץ ישראל והעולם הבא...העולם הבא מנין
שנא' כי נר מצוה ותורה אור ודרך חיים תוכחות מוסר . איזהו דרך שמביא לעולם הבא
הוי אומר זה יסורים .

"'With all thy heart'...with thy two *yétzers*: with the good *yétzer* and with the bad *yétzer*....

R. Simeon b. Yohai used to say, 'Blessed are sufferings, for three gifts did the Holy One, Blessed be He, give to them—to Israel, which gentiles desire. And He gave them not to Israel except through sufferings. These are they—Torah, the land of Israel, and the Age to Come.... Whence is the Age to Come known to be such? From the verse [Prov. 6. 23], 'For the commandment is a lamp; and the law is light; and reproofs of suffering [A.V. instruction] are the way of life.' Which then is the way leading to the Age to Come? Surely, you must say, it is suffering.'"

(3) Deuteronomy 11. 18, § 45 (see p. 22, n. 4):

ושמתם את דברי אלה על לבבכם ועל נפשכם ' מגיד הכתוב שנמשלו דברי תורה בסם
החיים. משל לאב שהכה את בנו מכה גדולה והניח לו רטיה על מכתו אמר לו בני כל זמן
שרטיה זו על מכתך אכול ושתה מה שהנאתך ורחוץ בין בחמין בין בצונן ואין אתה נזוק
ואם אתה מעבירה הרי אתה מעלה נומי כך אמר להם הקב"ה לישראל בני בראתי לכם
יצר הרע בראתי לכם תורה תבלין: כל זמן שאתם עוסקים בה אינו שולט בכם שנאמר הלוא
אם תיטיב שאת' ואם אין אתם עסקים בתורה הרי אתם נמסרים בידו שנא' ואם לא תיטיב
לפתח חטאת רובץ...

"'Therefore shall ye lay up these my words in your heart and in your soul.' That
which is written declares how the words of Torah are like a medicine of life, like to
a father who smote his son a great wound and placed a plaster on his wound for him,
(and) said to him. 'My son, so long as this plaster is on your wound eat and drink
what you like and wash in cold or warm water, and you will suffer no harm. But
if you remove it, you will get a bad boil.' So God says to the Israelites, 'My son,
I have created within you the evil *yêtzer*, but I created the Torah as a medicine. As
long as you occupy yourselves with the Torah, the *yêtzer* will not rule over you,
as it is said, 'If thou wilt be good thou wilt be able to withstand.' But if you do not
occupy yourselves with the Torah, behold you will be delivered into the power of
the *yêtzer*, as it is said, 'If thou dost not do good, sin croucheth at the door.'...'"

On the above *R.A.* pp. 125 f; also G. R. Driver, *J.T.S.* 1946, vol. XLVII,
p. 158.

(4) Deuteronomy 6. 6, § 33:

והיו הדברים האלה אשר אנכי מצוך היום על לבבך:...שלא יהו בעיניך כדיוטגמא ישנה
שאין אדם סופנה [אלא] כחדש שהכל רצים לקראתה: על לבבך ' מכאן היה ר' יאשיה
אומר צריך להשביע את יצרו שכך אתה מוצא בכל הצדיקים שהשביעו את יצרם ' באברהם
הוא אומר הרימותי ידי אל ה' אל עליון קונה שמים וארץ אם מחוט ועד שרוך נעל ואם אקח
מכל אשר לך...

"'And these words which I command thee this day, shall be in thine heart.'...They
shall not be in thine eyes like an antiquated edict which no man respects, but like
a new one which all run forward to read. 'In thine heart': R. Joshua used to say,
'One should adjure his *yêtzer*, for that is what you find with all the righteous, namely,
they adjured their *yêtzers*. With regard to Abraham Scripture says, 'I have lift up mine
hand unto the Lord, the most high God, the possessor of heaven and earth, that I will
not take from a thread even to a shoe-latchet, and that I will not take anything that is
thine.'...'"

(5) Deuteronomy 32. 32, § 323 (see p. 46, nn. 1, 11):

ר' יהודה אומר...בניו של אדם הראשין אתם שקנס עליכם מיתה ועל כל תולדותיו
הבאים אחריו עד סוף כל הדורות.

"R. Judah used to say...'You are the sons of the first man upon whom he decreed
the penalty of death and upon all his generations that came after him unto the end of all
generations.'"

(6) Deuteronomy 33. 2, § 343 (see p. 65, n. 1):

ה' מסיני בא כשנגלה הקב"ה ליתן תורה לישראל לא בלשון אחד נגלה אלא בארבע
לשונות ' ויאמר ה' מסיני בא זה לשון עברי ' וזרח משעיר למו זה לשון רומי ' הופיע מהר
פארן זה לשון ערבי ' ואתה מרבבות קודש זה לשון ארמי '...ד"א ה' מסיני בא כשנגלה
המקום ליתן תורה לישראל לא על ישראל בלבד הוא נגלה אלא על כל האומות...

"'The Lord came down from Sinai.' When God revealed Himself to give the Torah,
He did so in four tongues. 'He came from Sinai', that is Hebrew. 'He rose up from
Seir', that is Latin (Seir = Edom = Rome). 'He shone forth from Mount Paran', that is
Arabic (Paran is said to be Arabia). 'He came from Kadesh', that is Aramaic. [So
far the translation of the R.A. pp. 78 f.]....Another interpretation is...'God came
down from Sinai.' When God was revealed to give the Torah to Israel, He was not
revealed to Israel alone but to all the peoples...."

(7) Deuteronomy 6. 6, § 33 (see p. 104, n. 2 and see (4) above):

(8) Deuteronomy 32. 1, § 306:

אמר לו הקב"ה למשה אמור להם לישראל הסתכלו בשמים שבראתי לשמשכם שמא שינו
את מדתם או שמא נלגל חמה אינו עולה מן המזרח ומאיר לכל העולם כולו (ולא) כענין
שנאמר וזרח השמש ובא השמש ' ולא עוד אלא שמח לעשות לי רצוני שנאמר והוא כחתן
יוצא מחופתו ישיש כגבור לרוץ אורח: ותשמע הארץ אמרי פי ' הסתכלו בארץ שבראתי
לשמשכם שמא שינתה את מדתה שמא זרעתם ולא צמחה שמא זרעתם חטים והעלתה
שעורים או שמא פרה אינה דשה ואינה חורשת היום או שמא חמור זה אינו טוען ואינו
הלך ' וכן לעניין הים הוא אומר האותי לא תיראו נאם ה' אם מפני לא תחילו אשר שמתי
חול גבול לים שמשעה שגזרתי על הים שמא שינה את מדותיו ואומר אעלה ואציף את
העולם לא כענין שנאמר ואשבור עליו חוקי ואומר עד פה תבוא ולא תוסיף ולא עוד אלא
שמצטער ואין יכול מה לעשות כענין שנאמר והמו גליו ולא יוכלו והרי דברים ק"ו ומה אלו
שלא נעשו לא לשכר ולא להפסד אם מקבלים אין זוכים אם מקבלים שכר ואם חוטאים אין מקבלים
פורענות ואין חסים על בניהם ועל בנותיהם לא שינו את מדתם אתם שאם זכיתם אתם
מקבלים שכר ואם חטאתם אתם מקבלים פורענות ' ואתם חסים על בניכם ובנותיכם
עאכ"ו שאתם צריכים שלא תשנו את מדותיכם '

This is rendered as follows in the R.A. pp. 207 f.:

"God said to Moses, 'Say unto Israel; consider the heavens which I made to serve
you, have they ever failed in their duty?' [lit. changed their nature]. Does not the
sun rise in the east and give light to the inhabitants of the earth? It rises and it sets
with regularity (Eccles. 1. 5) nay, more, it rejoices in doing its Creator's will (Ps. 19. 5).
'And let the earth hear my mouth's words' (ibid.). Consider the earth which I created
for your service. Has it ever changed its nature? Have you ever sown without its
sprouting forth? Have you ever sown wheat, and has it produced barley? Or does
the cow not thresh and plough? Or the ass not bear his load and walk? Does not the
sea observe the limits which I have assigned to it? (Jer. 5. 22). If these have not changed
their nature, these which, unlike you, were created neither for profit nor for loss;
if, unlike you, when they do well, they receive no reward, if when they sin, they are
not punished: they have no care for their sons or their daughters, yet these have not
changed their nature: but you if you do well you receive reward, if you do evil, you
receive punishment, and you have care for your sons and daughters. How much
more ought you in no wise to change your characters?"

(9) Deuteronomy 11. 10, § 37 (see p. 170):

תורה לפי שהיא חביבה מכל נבראת קודם לכל שג' ה' קנני ראשית דרכו קדם מפעליו
מאז :

"The Torah, because it was beloved more than all things, was created before all,
as it is said, 'The Lord created me in the beginning of his way, before his works
of old.'"

(10) Deuteronomy 18. 12, § 173:

כשהיה ר' אלעזר מגיע לפסוק זה, היה אומר חבל עלינו מה אם מי שמדבק בטומאה רוח
טומאה שורה עליו המדבק בשכינה דין הוא שתשרה עליו רוח הקדש ׳ ומי גרם כי אם
עונותיכם היו מבדילים ביניכם לבין אלהיכם :

For translation see p. 206.

(11) The passage which we quoted on p. 282 is derived according to Schürer,[1]
who follows Wünsche,[2] from *Sifre*. Wünsche gives the Hebrew context in
full as follows:

אמר רבי יוסי הגלילי צא ולמד זכות מלך המשיח ושכרן של צדיקין מאדם הקדמוני שלא
נצטווה לו אלא מצוה אחת בלא תעשה ועבר עליה . ראה כמה מיתות נקנסו לו ולדורותיו
ולדורות דורותיו עד סוף כל הדורות . וכי איזה מדה מרובה מדת הטוב או מדת הפורעניות ֹ
הוי אומר מדת הטוב מרובה ומדת הפורעניות מעוטה . ומלך המשיח המתענה והמצטער בעד
הפושעים שנאמר והוא מחולל מפשעינו וגו' על אחת כמה וכמה, שידכה לכל הדורות כלן
הרא דכתיב ויהוה הפגיע בו את עון כלנו...

"Rabbi Jose the Galilean said, 'Go and learn the merit of King Messiah and the reward
of the righteous from Adam Qadmon who was given only one command—a negative
one, and he transgressed it. See to how many death penalties he and all his generations
succeeding unto the end of all generations became condemned. Now which attribute
is the more abundant, the attribute of good or the attribute of punishment? You must
say the attribute of good is the more abundant, and the attribute of punishment the
lesser.' . . ."

If genuine, this passage would supply us with excellent evidence of the
concept of a Suffering Messiah in the early second century. Unfortunately,
we have been unable to trace the passage in *Sifre* and therefore cannot use
it as evidence. Schürer recognized this in his 4th edition (German) (1907).
See also Moore, ad loc.: we cannot enlarge on the problem here.

[The work of H. F. Fischel in the *Hebrew Union College Annual*, 1944,
where he finds the figure of a suffering Phinehas, a Messianic figure, going
back to an early date, came too late into our hands for us to examine it fully,
but it would seem to help to confirm the position we have taken in the
text.]

[1] *The Jewish People in the time of Jesus Christ*, Division II, vol. II, p. 185.
[2] *Die Leiden des Messias* (Leipzig, 1870), pp. 65 f.

(12) Deuteronomy 32. 4, § 307 (see p. 263, n. 4):

תמים פעלו. פעולתו שלימה על כל באי העולם ואין להרהר אחד מדותיו אפילו [שנה] של
כלום ואין אחד מהם שיסתכל ויאמר אלו היו לי שלשה עינים אלו היו פני הפוכים לאחורי
כמה היה נאה תלמוד לומר תמים פעלו...

"'His work is perfect' [32. 4]. His work is final upon all that comes into the world
and it is impossible to criticize his ways even to the extent of a small 'injustice'. There
is no one to ponder to himself and say, If I only had three eyes or if my face were
turned backwards, how nice it would be. The Torah therefore teaches us: 'His work
is perfect.'" [Note: The translation 'injustice' is after Friedmann's edition.]

IV. PASSAGES FROM PESIKTA (die älteste Hagada redigirt in Palestina von Rab Kahana, ed. Salomon Buber; Lyck, 1868)

(1) 165a (see p. 25, n. 5):

א"ר סימאי לצור גבוה שהיה עומד בפרשת דרכים והיו בני אדם נכשלין בו, אמר להם
המלך סתתו קימעה קימעה, עד שתהא תבא חשעה ואני מעבירו מן העולם...

"Rabbi Simai said: 'The evil *yêtzer* is like a big rock which stands at the cross-roads,
and people stumble against it. The king said to them, Crush it little by little till I come
and remove it altogether. So God says, 'The evil *yêtzer* is a great stumbling-block;
crush it little by little till at the last I remove it from the world'.'" [Cf. *R.A.* p. 296.]

(2) 36b (see p. 38, n 10 and (5) below).

(3) 36b (see p. 45, n. 4):

ד'א מי כחכם (קהלת שם) זה אדם הראשון דכתיב ביה, אתה חותם תכנית מלא חכמה
(יחזקאל כ"ח י"ב).

"Another explanation: 'Who is as the wise?' (Eccles. 8. 1). This means the first
man of whom it is written, 'Thou sealest up the sum full of wisdom'" (Ezek. 28. 12).

(4) 1b (see p. 45, n. 9):

אמר רבי אייבו, באותה שעה גדעה קומתו של אדם הראשון ונעשית של ק' אמה:

"Rabbi Aibu said, 'At this time the stature of the first man Adam was shortened and
it was made a hundred ells.'"

(5) 36b (see p. 46, n. 4 and p. 38, n. 10):

ר' לוי בשם ר' שמעון בן מנסיה אמר תפוח עקיבו של אדם הראשון היה מכהה גלגל חמה,
ואל תתמה על זה כי מנהגו של עולם, אדם עושה לו שני קיטונין אחד לו ואחד לבן ביתו למי
הוא עושה נאה לא שלו כך הקב"ה ברא אדם הראשון לתשמישו, וגלגל חמה לתשמישן של
בריות, דין הוא שיכהה גלגל חמה, ומה תפוח עקיבו כך קלסתר פניו אעכ"ו:

"Rabbi Levi said, in the name of Rabbi Simeon b. Menasya, 'The heel of the first man
made the sun look dark, and do not be surprised at this, for it is usual among men
that one makes for oneself two vessels one for one's own use and one for that of some
member of his household. For whom would he make a more beautiful one? Surely
for himself. Even so, the Holy One, Blessed be He, created the first man for His own
purposes, and the circle of the sun for the use of the creatures: by analogy He would
make the sun the darker; and seeing that the heel is such, how much brighter will be
the face of the first man?'"

(6) 34a (see p. 63, n. 8):

ויחכם מכל האדם...זה אדם הראשון, ומה היתה חכמתו, את מוצא בשעה שביקש
הקב"ה לבראות את האדם נמלך במלאכי השרת, ואמר להם, נעשה אדם בצלמנו (בראשית א'
כ"ו) אמרו לפניו, מה אנוש כי תזכרנו וגו'...אמר להם אדם זה שאני רוצה לבראות בעולמי,
תהא חכמתו מרובה משלכם, מה עשה, כנס כל בהמה חיה ועוף והעבירן לפניהם, אמר להם
מה שמותם של אלו, ולא היו יודעין, כיון שברא אדם הראשון, כינס כל בהמה חיה ועוף,
והעבירן לפניו, אמר ליה מה שמותם של אלו, אמר לזה נאה לקרותו שור, ולזה נאה לקרותו
סום, ולזה גמל, ולזה נשר, ולזה ארי, וכן כלם, ויקרא אדם שמות לכל הבהמה וגו'...

"'And he was wiser than all' [1 Kings 4. 31]—this means than the first man: and what
was his wisdom? You find that when the Holy One, Blessed be He, sought to create
man, He took counsel with the ministering angels. He said to them, 'Let us make
man in our own image' (Gen. 1. 26). They said before Him, 'What is man that thou
art mindful of him?' He said to them, 'The wisdom of man whom I desire to create
in my world will be greater than yours'. What did He do? He gathered all the living
beasts and birds and caused them to pass before them. He said to them, 'What are the
names of these?' and they did not know. When God had created the first man he
gathered all the living beasts and birds and caused them to pass before him. He said
to him, 'What are the names of these?' He answered, 'This is to be called an ox, this
a horse, this a camel, this an eagle, this a lion,' and so for all; and man gave the names
to all the beasts...."

(7) 60b (see p. 259, n. 2 for translation):

אמר הקב"ה הואיל ואתם מתעסקים בהם כאלו מקריבים קרבנות.

(8) 176b (see p. 211, n. 7):

צפה ר'עקיבא ברוח הקודש..

"Rabbi Akiba saw by the Holy Spirit."

(9) 90a (see p. 211, n. 8):

צפה רשב"י ברוח הקודש..

"Rabbi Simeon b. Yoḥai saw by the Holy Spirit."

V. PASSAGES FROM PESIḲTA RABBATI (ed. M. Friedmann; Wien, 1880)

(1) 115a (see p. 45, nn. 7, 8):

גלמי ראו עיניך ועל ספרך כולם יכתבו ימים יוצרו ולא אחד בהם. ר"ש בן לקיש בשם
רבי אלעזר בן עזריה בשעה שברא הקב"ה את אדם הראשון גולם בראו. והיה מוטל מסוף
העולם ועד סופו. והיה הקדוש ברוך הוא מעביר לפניו דור ודור וצדיקיו [דור ודור ורשעיו]
דור ודור ודורשיו דור ודור ומנהיגיו. ואמר לו גולם מה ראו עיניך. מה תלמוד לומר ועל
ספרך כולם יכתבו איזה זה ספרו של אדם הראשון זה ספר תולדות האדם:

"'Thine eyes did see my substance...and in thy book all (my members) were
written' [Ps. 139. 17]....Rabbi Simeon ben Laḳish said in the name of Rabbi Eliezer ben
Azariah. 'When the Holy One, Blessed be He, created the first man, He created Him
as a mass and he lay from one end of the earth to the other. And the Holy One, Blessed
be He, caused to pass before him each generation and its righteous ones (each generation
and its wicked ones), each generation and its teachers and leaders; and He said to him:
'Formless mass, what have thine eyes seen?' What does Scripture mean to teach us by
'And upon thy book all of them are written?' What book is meant? This is the book
of the first man, referred to in the verse [Gen. 5. 1] 'This is the book of the
generations of Adam'."

(2) 161 a (see p. 65, n. 6):

דבר אחר רני ושמחי [וגו' ונלוו גוים רבים אל ה'] אמר רבי חנינא בר פפא אין הכתוב
מדבר אלא כנגד אותה שעה שהקב"ה דן את כל אומות העולם לעתיד לבא. באותה השעה
מביא הקדוש ברוך הוא את כל הגרים שנתגיירו בעולם הזה ודן את בל האומות בפניהם.
ואומר להם מפני מה הנחתם אותי ועבדתם את ע"ז שאין בה ממש. ואומרים לפניו רבונו
של עולם אם באנו לפתחך לא קבלתנו. אמר להם יבואו הגרים שנתגיירו מכם ויעידו בכם.
מיד מביא הקדוש ברוך הוא את כל הגרים שנתגיירו והם דנים אותן ואומרים לפניהם מפני
מה הנחתם אותי...ועבדתם ע"ז שאין בהם ממש. יתרו לא כומר של ע"ז היה. וכיון שבא
לפתחו של הקדוש ברוך הוא קיבלו. מיד מתביישים כל הרשעים מתשובה הגרים:

See translation, p. 65 above; R.A. p. 576.

(3) 74 a (see p. 84, n. 5; cf. Cant. R. 2. 13):

התאנה חנטה פגיה אילו שלשת ימי אפילה שבהם כלו רשעי ישראל:

"'The fig tree putteth forth her green figs': this refers to the three days of darkness
during which the wicked of Israel perished." [The explanation of this section given
by Strack-Billerbeck is possible but not entirely convincing: there is no specific
reference to resurrection here at all.]

(4) 160 a (see p. 207, n. 4):

שבשעה שנגנזה הבית האחרון לא שרתה [בו] שכינה. שכך אמר הקדוש ברוך הוא אם
עולים ישראל כולם תשרה שכנה...

See p. 207 for the translation.

(5) 194 b (see p. 236, n. 2):

א"ר שמעון בן יוחי בא וראה הדם דבר בזוי הוא ומאכל כלבים הוא ואמר הקב"ה שיהא
קרב על המזבח. אלא כביכול אמר הקב"ה הבא לפני קרבן וטול דמו ותן על קרנותיו של
מזבח כדי שיכפר דם על דם:

"Rabbi Simeon ben Yoḥai said, 'Come and see, blood is a thing despised and eaten
of dogs but the Holy One, Blessed be He, said that it should be offered on the altar.
Nevertheless, if one might say so, the Holy One, Blessed be He, said, 'Bring before me
a gift and take its blood and put it upon the horns of the Altar in order that blood
should atone for blood'.'"

VI. PASSAGES FROM *TANḤUMA* (ed. Salomon Buber; Wilna, 1885)

(1) *Bereshith*, p. 25, § 38 (see p. 23, n. 2):

אמר הקב"ה ראו מה עשו הרשעים הללו שתי בריות אני עשיתי באדם יצר טוב ויצר הרע
שנא' עיר קטנה ואנשים בה מעט...עיר קטנה זה הגוף ואנשים בה מעט אילו אברים ובא
אליה מלך גדול...זה יצר הרע ובנה עליה מצודים גדולים...אלו חטאות ומצא בה איש מסכן
וחכם [חכם]...זה יצר טוב ומלט הוא את העיר בחכמתו...שהוא מביא את האדם לחיים ואדם
לא זכר וגו...זה דור המבול שלא קבלו עליהם יצר טוב:

"The Holy One, Blessed be He, said, 'See what the wicked people have done. Behold two creations have I made in man—a good *yêtzer* and a bad *yêtzer*, as it is said, 'There was a little city and a few men, within it.' 'A little city'—this is the Body; 'and a few men within it'—these are the members. 'And there came a great King against it'—this is the bad *yêtzer*; 'and built great bulwarks against it'—these are the sins. 'And there was found in it a poor wise man'—this is the good *yêtzer*. 'And he by his wisdom delivered the city'—it is he that brings the man to life.—'Yet no one remembered that same poor man', this refers to the generation of the flood which did not accept the good *yêtzer*'."

(2) **וארא**, p. 17, § 1 (see p. 65, n. 1):

אמר ר'יוסי ב"ר סימון עד שלא עמדתם על הר סיני וקיבלתם את תורתי ישראל הייתם נקראים כשם שאומות העולם נקראים סבתכא ורעמה, אבל כשעמדתם על הר סיני וקבלתם את תורתי נקראתם עמי, שנאמר שמעה עמי ואדברה:

For translation see p. 65 above; *R.A.* p. 81.

(3) *Yitro*, p. 73, § 7 (see p. 104, n. 3):

ביום ההוא [אין כתיב כאן, אלא ביום הזה] כאילו ביום הזה באו מדבר סיני כל יום שאתה עוסק בתורה הוי אומר כאילו ביום הזה קיבלתיה מסיני ואומר היום הזה ה' אלהיך מצוך לעשות וגו':

"'In this day'—it does not say on that day but it says on this day, as if on this day they came to the wilderness of Sinai. Every day that you study the Torah say: 'It is as if this day I have received it from Sinai'; and it further says, 'This day the Lord thy God commanded thee to do it.'..."

(4) *Wayyera*, pp. 90f., § 9 (see p. 271, n. 4):

אמר חזקיה בר חייא לא ערב להקב"ה עד שהזכיר משה זכות אבות אמר לו הקב"ה משה אילולי שלא היה להם זכות אבות הייתי מאבדן...

"R. Hezekiah b. Ḥiyya said, 'It was not pleasing to the Holy One, Blessed be He, till Moses recalled the merit of the Fathers. The Holy One, Blessed be He, said, 'Moses were it not that they had merit of the Fathers I would have destroyed them'."

(5) *Wayyigash*, p. 208, § 9 (see p. 301, n. 3):

בא וראה שכל מה שהכה הקב"ה בעולם הזה מתרפאין לעולם הבא.... העורים מתרפאין שנאמר אז תפקחנה עיני עורים והפסחים מתרפאין שנאמר אז ידלג כאיל פסה...ואלמים מתרפאין שנאמר ותרון לשון אלם הכל מתרפאין...אלא כשאדם הולך כך הוא בא...הולך עור ובא עור הולך חרש ובא חרש הולך פסח ובא פסח הולך אלם ובא אלם...כשם שהולך לבוש כך בא לבוש...

"Come and see how that all that the Holy One, Blessed be He, smote in this world, He healed in the Age to Come. The blind are healed, as it is said, 'Then shall the eyes of the blind be opened.' And the lame shall be healed, as it is said, 'Then shall the lame man leap as a hart.' And the dumb shall be healed, as it is said, 'And the tongue of the dumb shall sing.' All shall be healed. But as a man departs so shall he return: he departed blind, and he will return blind, he departed lame, and he will return lame, he departed dumb, and he will return dumb. In the manner which he departed he will return—he that departed clothed will return clothed."

VII. PASSAGES FROM *ABOTH DE RABBI NATHAN*
(ed. Salomon Schechter; London, 1887)

(1) I. פרק טז, p. 62 (see p. 25, n. 3):

שלש עשרה שנה גדול יצר הרע מיצר טוב. ממעי אמו של אדם הוא גדל...

"By thirteen years is the evil *yêtzer* older than the good *yêtzer*. From his mother's womb does it grow up with a man."[1]

(2) I. פרק טז, p. 63 (see p. 27, n. 2):

בזמן שאדם מחמם את עצמו והולך לדבר זימה כל אבריו נשמעין לו מפני שיצר הרע
מלך הוא על מאתים וארבעים ושמונה אברים.

"When a man inflames his passions [lit. himself] and goes to commit an act of unchastity, all parts of his body obey him [i.e. the evil *yêtzer*] for the evil *yêtzer* is king over his 248 organs."

[The passage goes on to state that when man goes to perform a *mitzwâh* all his organs begin to grow lazy with him because his evil *yêtzer* reigns over the 248 organs of the body.]

(3) I. פרק לא, p. 91 (see p. 54, n. 4):

למדת שאדם אחד שקול כנגד מעשה בראשית כולו. רבי נחמיה אומר מנין שאדם אחד
שקול כנגד כל מעשה בראשית שנאמר זה ספר תולדות אדם [וגו'] ולהלן הוא אומר אלה
תולדות השמים והארץ בהבראם וגו מה להלן בריה ועשייה אף כאן בריאה ועשייה:

"You must conclude that one man is equal to the whole creation. R. Nehemiah used to say, 'Whence do we know that one man was equal to all creation, for it is said, 'This is the book of the generations of Adam' [Gen. 5. 1]. And in another passage Scripture says [Gen. 2. 4]: 'These are the generations of the heavens and of the earth when they were created, in the day that the Lord God made the earth and the heavens.' Seeing that in regard to heaven and earth and likewise in regard to man the terms create and make are used, the deduction is that both are of equal weight in the eyes of the Maker.'"

(4) I. פרק ד, p. 21 (see p. 258 for translation):

פעם אחת היה רבן יוחנן בן זכאי יוצא מירושלים והיה ר' יהושע הולך אחריו
וראה...בית המקדש חרב אמר ר' יהושע אוי לנו על זה שהוא חרב...מקום שמכפרים בו
עונותיהם של ישראל. א"ל בני אל ירע לך יש לנו כפרה אחת שהיא כמותה ואיזה זה גמילות
חסדים שנאמר כי חסד חפצתי ולא זבח:

(5) I. פרק יז, p. 66 (see p. 261 for translation):

רבי אליעזר אומר הוי שקוד ללמוד תורה ודע מה שתשוב לאפיקורוס ודבר אחר בתורה אל
תשתכח ממך דע לפני מי אתה עמל ומי הוא בעל בריתך:

---

[1] On the view that the evil *yêtzer* enters a man when he is still in the embryonic state, see S. Schechter, *Some Aspects of Rabbinic Theology*, p. 253.

VIII. PASSAGE FROM *AGADATH BERESHITH*

(ed. Buber; Chapter 47, p. 68)

וכן דניאל אוטר ואני שמעתי ולא אבין ואמרה אדוני מה אחרית אלה אמר לו הקב״ה כבר
הנביא קדטך ואטר והיה באחרית הימים נכון יהיה וגו׳ ...

"And thus Daniel was speaking: 'And I heard but I understood not and then I said,
O my Lord, what shall be the end of these things?' The Holy One, Blessed be He,
said to him, 'The prophet has answered your question in advance when he said:
'And it shall be in the last days,' etc....'"

IX. *YALKUT*

(1) On Gen. 49 (see p. 219, n. 4):

כל מה שהצדיקים עושין ברוח הקודש הן עושין

"All that the righteous do, they do in the Holy Spirit." [There is a parallel in
Tanḥuma, see *R.A.* p. 677.]

(2) On Psalm 119. 11 (see p. 225, n. 2):

אין יצר הרע שולט אצל התורה ומי שהתורה בלבו אין יצר הרע שלט בו:

For translation see p. 225, n. 2.

APPENDIX D

A REVIEW OF H. J. SCHOEPS
PAULUS; DIE THEOLOGIE DES APOSTELS IM LICHTE DER JÜDISCHEN RELIGIONSGESCHICHTE[1]

Contributed to New Testament Studies, 10, 1963-4

This work, it can be safely claimed, is the most significant contribution to Pauline studies since the appearance of J. Munck's *Paulus und die Heilsgeschichte* (1954). And, like that volume, it is difficult to assess with precision, because it commands deep admiration and dissent. In particular, it is exceedingly complex. Like Munck, Professor Schoeps emphasizes eschatology as the clue to Paul. But his total interpretation of primitive Christianity turns out to be almost the exact opposite of that of Munck, whom, at one point, he accuses of turning history on its head (p. 63). Munck's removal of any gulf between Paul and certain Judaistic elements in the *Urgemeinde* is rejected outright. Again while, with Bultmann, Professor Schoeps claims that Paul interpreted Jesus in terms of a Hellenistic myth of a Divine Saviour, he dismisses Bultmann's assumption of a pre-Pauline Hellenistic-Christianity, upon which Paul drew, as a figment of scholarship. It is to Schweitzer that Schoeps owes his greatest debt for his understanding of Paul and he frequently refers to the work of Werner and Buri, the two leading present-day "thoroughgoing eschatologists," with marked approval. In his assessment of the cultural and religious background of the Apostle he stands nearest to the present reviewer's work on *Paul and Rabbinic Judaism*, but again with significant differences. Most characteristic, therefore, is the comprehensive complexity of Professor Schoeps's work. Like his other major contributions, *Theologie und Geschichte des Judenchristentums*, the present volume is massive in its scope and, in parts, bold in its conclusions. Especially as it bears upon the background of Paul in its various ramifications, and particularly in Judaism, but also in its whole range, this study is in itself an education in the world of the Apostle. Is it an education in Paulinism?

I

To judge the work aright full weight must be given to the sub-title. Professor Schoeps approaches Paul from the standpoint of what used to be called "Comparative Religion" but is now usually referred to as the "History of Religions."

[1] Tübingen: J. C. B. Mohr, 1959. I dedicate this review to Professor Ethelbert Stauffer of The University of Erlangen, in gratitude for his warm kindness in the summer of 1957, because I was unable to contribute to the *Festschrift* in his honour, ed. by E. Bammel, when invited to do so. An English translation by H. Knight has been published by the Lutterworth Press, 1961; page references are to this translation.

And he accordingly devotes 50 packed pages to a survey of the various approaches that have been taken to "Paulinism." He deals in turn with the Hellenistic approach (the Mystery Religions, the Kyrios-cult theory of Bousset and others, Gnosis), the Hellenistic-Judaistic (Diaspora-Judaism, the LXX, Philo, Greek Philosophy, the Palestinian-Judaic approach (Rabbinical exegesis, Apocalyptic), and, finally, the eschatological approach associated especially with Schweitzer's *The Mysticism of Paul the Apostle*. Comparable to the recent surveys by Rigaux[1] and Earle Ellis,[2] with which it should be compared, the material assessed by Schoeps on pp. 1–50 constitutes a sound and thorough guide to the literature in this field. Especially satisfying is the treatment of the Septuagintal element in Paul on pp. 27–32 and, for the reviewer at least, the clear recognition on p. 40 that a "Rabbinic" explanation of Paul, where demonstrable, "deserves *a limine* preference over all other explanations". Two things are particularly, and we think rightly, insisted upon, first that *all* the various approaches are relevant, because of the immense complexity of Paul's background, and secondly, that Paul is more than the sum of the various influences that went into his making; he is a personality unique and "new". To understand his world is not to exhaust him (pp. 47–8).

Following his rich discussion of Pauline research, Professor Schoeps deals in chapter 2 with the position of the Apostle in primitive Christianity. Here the contrast with Munck's work is very marked in two ways. First, Munck devotes to the "conversion" of Paul a lengthy and dominant chapter and derives from it Paul's crucial understanding of himself as *the* decisive eschatological figure who had a unique role to play in the eschatological events inaugurated by the coming of Jesus. But Professor Schoeps is content to discuss the "conversion" in two pages, 53–5. Like Munck, he dismisses any psychological approach to that "event" but, in a tantalizingly brief statement, he categorically states: "If we wish to understand what happened at this point in the life of the apostle, and what were its consequences, then we must accept fully the real objectivity of the encounter as it is testified in the letters and in Acts. . . . The historian of religion is expected to recognize the faith of Paul in the manifested Son of God to be the factual result of his encounter with the crucified and exalted Jesus of Nazareth" (p. 55). He reiterates this very forcibly on p. 279. And although the "conversion", in the sense indicated, is given absolute centrality by Professor Schoeps, at no point does he enlarge upon it: he accepts it as a "fact" (shall we say?) from "the blue".

It agrees with this that, secondly, he differs radically from Munck in his understanding of the relation of Paul to the *Urgemeinde*.[3] In the light of his understanding of the "conversion", Schoeps necessarily insists that the "Jesus of history", that is, Jesus as a man who acted and taught in Galilee and Judaea, was of little significance for Paul. In this he is in an eminent company that includes Schweitzer, Bultmann and Kümmel. It also follows that he does not need to

[1] In *Recherches Bibliques*, vol. v (1960).
[2] *Paul and His Recent Interpreters* (Grand Rapids, Michigan, 1961).
[3] See my *Christian Origins and Judaism* (1962), pp. 179 ff.

minimize (or exaggerate) the separation between Paul and the *Urgemeinde*, and his treatment of the relationship between the Apostle and the Jewish–Christianity of Jerusalem and to the "pillars" of the Church is highly discriminating and satisfying. Unlike Munck, he rightly recognizes that while "the pillars", Peter, James and John, were not fundamentally opposed to Paul, there *was* a Judaistic–Pharisaic element in the primitive Jerusalem Church antagonistic to Paul and doggedly seeking to undermine his influence.[1] From this element Jewish–Christianity later emerged, and from this mainly (although according to Schoeps there was also "Gnostic" opposition to the Apostle) arose the criticisms of Paul's claims to be an Apostle. Professor Schoeps reiterates in this volume (but with more caution and fairness in his treatment of the "pillars", as we have implied above) the position he made familiar in his *Theologie und Geschichte des Judenchristentums*, that the Pseudo-Clementines illumine the anti-Pauline currents in primitive Christianity (pp. 82 ff.). But despite his recognition of the presence of Judaistic opponents of Paul, Professor Schoeps, rightly we think, roots the Apostle in the primitive *Gemeinde* and rejects the claim made by Heitmüller, Bousset and, latterly especially by Bultmann, that the development of early Christianity is to be traced through the line—Jesus–Primitive Church–Hellenistic-Christianity–Paul. For Schoeps all pre-Pauline groupings alleged to have existed in the Church, for example, the Galilean Christianity postulated by Lohmeyer and the Hellenistic postulated by Bultmann, must remain, at best, problematic. The only point where we are uneasy in this section, pp. 59–87, lies in the treatment of Paul's assessment of "visions" in II Cor. xii. Is the thrust of the discussions there to rebut those who criticized Paul for appealing too strenuously to visions, not only that on the way to Damascus but others (p. 85)? This is unlikely. Paul seems to have differentiated radically between his "eschatological" experience on that way and other "visions" which he himself seems to discount.

And, in the third chapter, Professor Schoeps takes up the pivotal question of Paul's eschatology. He introduces his treatment with a valuable survey of this theme in Judaism in which he draws illuminatingly on Buber and others not always sufficiently consulted by Christian New Testament scholars. He finds in the first century a fusion of Davidic Messianology, Son of Man ideology and the concept of "The Two Ages". (One may here ask whether footnote 4 on p. 96 is to be accepted. Did Akiba reject Apocalyptic?) Paul moves within the framework of this variegated eschatology. Following Schweitzer (see p. 101), Schoeps insists that this fact deserves greater weight than is customarily given to it in Pauline studies. One thing alone differentiates Paul from the Jewish Apocalyptists of his day—the conviction that in the Resurrection of Jesus the eschaton was already in process. Although on p. 101 Professor Schoeps asserts that Paul contemplated a very brief Messianic period, inaugurated by Jesus, which was to lead on immediately to "The Age to Come", as in the case of Schweitzer, the *precise* significance of the Resurrection in his work is hard to disentangle—did it

[1] G. Johnston, *The New Peake Commentary* (1962), p. 725 (631 e) has some very balanced words on this.

inaugurate the preliminary Messianic Age or "The Age to Come" itself (compare pp. 101 and 106)? In any case Professor Schoeps claims that "We should misunderstand the apostle's letters as a whole, and the governing consciousness from which they spring, if we failed to recognize that Paul only lives, writes, and preaches in the unshakeable conviction that his generation represents the last generation of mankind" (p. 102). In the Resurrection of Jesus believers are resurrected. Suffice it to say that Schoeps here gratefully endorses Schweitzer's cosmic "mysticism". But, if Jesus in his Resurrection had such cosmic significance, "the figure of the Messiah must undergo a transformation in Paul's thought" (p. 108). Jesus as resurrected becomes different from him who walked on earth. He belongs no more to the fleshly sons of Adam: he has become *Kyrios*. The way was open to the developed Pauline Christology for which, Professor Schoeps does not tire to insist, the earthly life of Jesus is no longer relevant (see, for example, p. 108). And, since it was possible for each individual Christian to enter into a relation with the Kyrios, there developed the sacramental teaching of Paul. Schoeps recognizes that the Sacraments are originally eschatological in their significance for Paul (pp. 111 ff.), but he urges that, in order to bring home their meaning to Greeks, the Apostle used concepts familiar to them in the Mysteries. Despite his eschatological intent in interpreting the Sacraments, their "similarity to the mysteries, a fact to which Schweitzer closes his eyes, remains nevertheless fatal" (p. 113). In his sacramental teaching Paul introduced into Christianity "something which did not before exist in Judaism, and something which Paul could have derived neither from rabbinism nor from Hellenistic Judaism" (ibid.). Professor Schoeps shares Bultmann's view at this point despite his earlier repudiation of his pre-Pauline Hellenistic-Christianity. Both Baptism and the Eucharist have become part "of the class of mystery cults. The sacramental teaching of Paul is, therefore, an amalgamation of ideas and traditions of heterogeneous origin . . . a piece of Jewish-pagan syncretism" (p. 118). Later the ecclesiastical Sacraments came to compensate for the delay in the Parousia. Professor Schoeps joins the company of Schweitzer, Werner, Buri. While he admits elements of "realized eschatology" in the teaching of Jesus, so that he can even write that the "whole system of apocalyptic calculations did not interest Jesus (Luke xvii. 20 ff.)" (p. 122), he refuses to recognize such in Paul, who was governed by a futuristic eschatology. The Apostle's expectations did not materialize—the End delayed. But, if we understand Professor Schoeps aright, the sacramental teaching of Paul made possible the genesis of the Catholic Church, despite the collapse of the hope of the Parousia. Nevertheless, because Paul's theology was wholly governed by this hope, it was Peter and not the man from Tarsus who was *recognized* as the founder of that Church. Such is the irony of history.

Professor Schoeps next deals, in the fourth chapter, with Paul's soteriology, that is, his claim that through the death and resurrection of the Son of God man's reconciliation to God was effected. Paul's doctrine of the dying Son of God, effecting the redemption of the cosmos, has no analogies in Jewish sources (p. 127): it takes us outside Judaism; in fact, claims Professor Schoeps, to Hellenism. Despite this, he devotes pp. 126–67 to showing that certain Jewish ideas lie at the base of Paul's Soteriology although its developed form takes us, as we have seen, outside Judaism. He deals with the material under three heads: (1) The meaning of suffering and of a vicarious atoning sacrifice; (2) the picture of the suffering servant of God in Isaiah 53 and the idea of a dying Messiah arising therefrom; and (3) the *Aqedath Isaac* and its problems as the ultimate pattern of thought (see p. 127). In dealing with items (1) and (2), Professor Schoeps provides rich surveys of the pertinent sources and discussions. In the light of recent work by Hooker and others, perhaps greater caution should have been observed in dealing with the role of Isa. 53 in the New Testament (p. 137), and more emphasis might well have been placed on the Merits of the Fathers, mentioned briefly on p. 140; but, these things apart, the whole discussion is illuminating and indispensable.

It is in the third section, (3), that Professor Schoeps is most original. He regards the *Aqedath Isaac* as "the very model for the elaboration of Pauline Soteriology". The explicit Christian references to which he appeals are late, as are most of the Rabbinic ones (pp. 142-3), but Professor Schoeps claims an ancient traditional development for the motif in the Synagogue liturgy (pp. 142-5, especially the footnotes). The specific passages in the New Testament understood as referring to the *Aqedath Isaac*, Rom. 8. 32, τοῦ ἰδίου υἱοῦ οὐκ ἐφείσατο, cf. Gen. 22. 16 (LXX); Rom. 3, 25, προέθετο recalling ראה in Gen. 22. 8—and the Patristic exegesis of these, are not sufficiently cogent, in view of the absence of any explicit reference to the *Aqedath Isaac* in Paul, to be convincing. But the position put forward demands a full examination such as cannot be attempted here.

In any case, Professor Schoeps insists that it is not even here, in the use of the *Aqedath Isaac*, as he understands the evidence, that Paul is most daring, nor even in his combination of the sufferings of the righteous, the suffering of the Messiah and the *Aqedath Isaac*, and not even in the ascription of soteriological significance to Jesus as the Messiah. Where, then, does Paul make a radical innovation? It is in his exaltation of Jesus as Messiah "beyond all human proportions to the status of real divinity" (p. 149): "this is the radically un-Jewish element in the thought of the Apostle" (ibid.). Here "it is impossible not to link Paul with" heathen mythological conceptions: he has introduced the Hellenistic myth of a Heavenly Man: "the acute Hellenization of Christianity" is begun. Professor Schoeps's position is exceedingly complicated. This idea of Jesus as Divine Son, the most Hellenistic element in Paul's thought, he traces also to a very unexpected source, namely, to Jesus Himself as he is revealed in the Synoptics. He recognizes "anticipations" for such an elevation of Jesus in Rabbinic speculation about the Torah (p. 155), in the idea of the Messiah as Son (p. 156), in that of the בני אלהים of the Old Testament. Nevertheless, the Divine Sonship of Jesus is ultimately only explicable in terms of the Hellenistic myth. We meet here with complexity within complexity: a Palestinian Jesus, about whom Paul knew little, supplies him with his most Hellenistic concept.

In the fifth chapter, "Paul's teaching on the Law", we again meet boldness of conception. Here it is claimed that Paul, whose Rabbinic connexions, as we have seen, are fully recognized, suffered from an inadequate appreciation of the most fundamental aspect of Judaism, the Torah. We may summarize the author's case crudely as follows. The Pauline understanding of the Torah is determined by the Apostle's eschatology. He remains true to a Jewish expectation that, with the coming of the Messianic Age, according to some rabbis at least, the Torah would come to an end (see my *Torah in the Messianic Age*, 1952). This is the meaning of Τέλος γὰρ νόμου Χριστὸς (Rom. 10.4). "The validity of the Law as a divine way of salvation has finished since the resurrection of Jesus from the dead which proves both his Messianic status and the inbreak of the last age" (p. 171). It cannot be sufficiently emphasized that Schoeps here recalls us forcibly, as he has done earlier in his *Aus frühchristlicher Zeit*—to the fundamental relation between the Law and Messianic speculation in Judaism. His references to Scholem's work on Sabbatai Sebi are most pertinent. Similarly the treatment of the Law and "the curse" in Gal. 3. 10–13 and the problem of the fulfillability of Torah (where Professor Schoeps could also have appealed to Schechter) is important. We welcome especially the point that Paul had first taken offence at the manner of Jesus' death, and the light which he sheds on Gal. in Deut. 27. 26 in terms of Deut. 21. 23 (p. 179).

Even more striking is the insistence that Paul, unaware of the idea of the "fear of God" and its significance for Judaism as the presupposition of the Torah (p. 188), "simply understood the Law as a sum of prescriptions and has played off the fact of sin as offence against the commandments" (ibid.). Ignorant of the power of repentance and its value for Judaism, and, because of his dependence on the LXX, unable to appreciate the fullness of the Covenantal relation (ברית he translates as διαθήκη), Paul understood Torah as a one-sided declaration of the will of God, an arrangement which God has made and authorized, so that "the תורה קדשה was reduced (by Paul) to the scope of the ethical law, which he understands as a law intended to make righteous. . . . This moralization of the Torah, this legalistic emphasis which is already found in the LXX, must have been a special characteristic of Hellenistic Judaism" (p. 198). It is this moralization, revealing a radical misunderstanding of Torah, which lies at the root of Paul's attack on the Law. Here again he turns out to be Hellenistic. Similarly, although his discussion of "sin" and "flesh" are admirably cautious (full weight is allowed to the "Evil Yetzer"), Professor Schoeps finally places Paul, in his understanding of sin, outside the optimism of Judaism and (testily it is true) roots him in Hellenistic pessimism.

There follows a chapter on "Paul's understanding of Saving History". The thoroughness and scope are again admirable. There is an excellent survey of the Gentile question in Judaism on pp. 220–8, and of the Judaism out of which Paul came in its eschatological concern. Professor Schoeps helps us to see with fresh force how Paul, the *Christian* missionary, was part and parcel of a proselytizing movement within Judaism itself. But Paul's missionary activity was determined by his eschatological convictions throughout. Unlike Munck, who postulated, as an immediate cause of the mission to the Gentiles, the failure of a well-defined, early mission to the Jews, the author rejects any such mission. Not the sour grapes of a futile mission to Israel led to Paul's mission to the Gentiles but the logic of his eschatology. The Messiah had appeared, therefore, the time of the ingathering of the Gentiles had come (p. 230). Nevertheless, the rejection of Jesus by Jewry did constitute a problem. In wrestling with this, Paul, in Rom. 9–11, was led beyond all customary Jewish speculation on the Gentiles: he developed his own peculiar understanding of the role of Israel even in the post-Messianic era. Professor Schoeps discusses this understanding in a masterly fashion on pp. 237–43. He points out how Jewish-Christianity differed in its interpretation of history from Paul. In his form of universalism, Paul departed from Jewish expectations: in theirs, Jewish-Christians did not. Instead of accounting for Israel's failure to receive Jesus as the Christ by the concept of the "hardening of Israel," as did Paul, they urged the recognition that the revelation in Moses was one especially fitted for Israel and that in Jesus for Gentiles. Jewish- and Gentile-Christianity (and even Judaism?) could be reconciled in a higher unity which recognized this.

Here Professor Schoeps writes very movingly. On pp. 249 ff. he contrasts the Pauline view of Salvation History (*Heilsgeschichte*) with the Rabbinic. Even in his treatment of the Gentiles Paul was not wholly without precedence within Judaism itself, not only in its view of the Noachian commandments (the significance of these is found, as by Daube, to be the recognition by Judaism that the whole of the Law should not be demanded of the Gentiles), but also in its view that Gentiles who kept those commandments were equal to Jews. Professor Schoeps reminds us how even in the sacrificial system itself the Gentiles were not forgotten. In fact, he urgently points out that Judaism has often understood the relation between itself and Christianity in the same way as did Jewish-Christianity. He suggests that such a philosophy of history as Rabbinism and Jewish-Christianity often shared, speculative as it is, is no less so than the Pauline, and is, in his view, superior to the latter and deserving of serious consideration today (p. 258).

And, finally, in his last chapter, Professor Schoeps discusses "Perspectives of the History of Religion in Paulinism", and traces illuminatingly the way in which Paul has been understood (and more frequently misunderstood) in Christendom and how he might be of great significance to Judaism itself by raising for it the problem of the value of the Law, the centrality of the fear of God which the Law presupposes, and which, for Professor Schoeps, is its true end, the character of the Law as not itself the "word" of God but the "representative" thereof, and, finally, the relevance of the Law for all mankind. In this section Professor Schoeps passes outside history to speculation and, as he himself admits, he may well seem to Jewish readers at least to be concerned with "the rescue of the heretic" (p. 294). His study, at this point, passes into the realm of belief, and there, in this connexion, we must leave it.

This major interpretation of Paul prompts certain questions, even while it evokes unlimited gratitude for the encyclopaedic learning and largesse of spirit which lies behind it. We may gather up these questions as follows.

II

Has Professor Schoeps sufficiently liberated himself from the customary, but now highly questionable, dichotomies made within Judaism in the first century?

True the distinction between Palestinian or Rabbinic and Hellenistic Judaism is more than a convenience of scholars. There *is* a difference between Philo and, let us say, R. Joshua b. Hananiah or R. Simeon b. Gamaliel. And yet it is now also apparent that to make a rigid distinction between them is erroneous. Does Professor Schoeps still operate with categories which were more fluid and inter-penetrating than he would seem to allow? At crucial points he suddenly has recourse to "Hellenistic" categories right in the midst of discussions of Palestinian ones, for example, on the "Sonship" of Jesus, on the Law, on the Sacraments. The sudden change of reference does not seem true to the muted contrasts and ambiguities of first-century Judaism.

Related to this are two points to note. Except incidentally and illustratively, Professor Schoeps does not deal with the Dead Sea Scrolls either in his discussion of the major divisions of the background studies or in the body of his work on the great Pauline motifs. This is to be regretted because the Scrolls have reinforced our suspicion of the rigid dichotomies to which we referred above and supplied us with material highly pertinent to any discussion of Paul's background and theology. For example, any discussion of "sin" and of "flesh" in Paul must now take into account the Dead Sea Scrolls; and there can be little question, as Professor Dahl and others have recently insisted, that the most illuminating material for the understanding of "justification by faith" in Paul comes from the same documents. Professor Schoeps has written extensively on the material from Qumran, but has he sufficiently integrated his Pauline studies with those on the Scrolls? In his preface he mentions that this volume has been in formation for twenty years: one has the feeling that the Scrolls entered into his ken when it had already fallen into a significant structure, and that they could only be fitted in as addenda.

Similarly, while Professor Schoeps does refer to Professor Van Unnik's argument, mainly on the basis of Acts 23. 3, that while Paul was born in Tarsus he had been brought up in Jerusalem, he does not seem to us to deal with it with sufficient thoroughness. Van Unnik's thesis, if correct, has very important consequences for any attempt to understand Paul's background, and especially for such as is undertaken by Professor Schoeps (see pp. 5 ff.).

III

As we have seen, Professor Schoeps accepts the "conversion" of Paul as a central datum, determinative for Pauline Theology; but he does not seek to explain it. But is it adequate, even for the historian of religion, merely to record a fact of such momentous significance for his theme? Must he not also (as E. H. Carr has recently urged in *What is History?*) seek to understand it and give reasons for it? Should he be content with a bare statement of a fact from "the blue"? The reaction against psychological interpretations of Paul's conversion seen in the work of Munck, Schoeps, and others, has gone too far. However discontinuous the life of Paul as a Christian may have been with that of his life as a Jew, however sudden his experience on the road to Damascus, and however unprepared for it on the conscious level Paul had been, his conversion must have been integrally related to his previous experience to have had any meaning for him at all. To deny this is to reduce the constraint of the Risen Lord upon him in his "conversion" to a specimen of magic. (Just as the mere experience of a Risen Christ unrelated to the Jesus whom they had previously known would have been meaningless for the Apostles.)

The results of Professor Schoeps's "uncritical" approach to the "conversion", which is dictated, we must in fairness note, by his fine sensitivity in dealing with a Christian theme, are serious. It makes it impossible for him to do justice to two things: (*a*) the significance of the "historical Jesus" for Paul (with this we deal below); and (*b*) the role of the Church in the "conversion". According to Galatians and Acts it was as he was persecuting the Church that Paul was apprehended. This is a fact of basic significance for the whole of Paul's theology, and it is not brought out in this volume.[1]

IV

The concentration on "eschatology" in Paul, made familiar to us especially by Schweitzer and recently by Munck and now in this work, salutary as it is, has to be carefully assessed. Oddly enough, as we saw, Professor Schoeps allows a degree of "realized eschatology" in Jesus, but refuses to contemplate any such in the Apostle, who, in his judgement, is dominated throughout by an eschatology that is futuristic. But, despite the continuance of "futurism" even in the latest of the Pauline epistles, there is in them a change of emphasis. There emerges a concentration on what has already been achieved "in Christ". A specifically Christian understanding of existence begins to appear. Significantly there is no reference made to the well-known essays by C. H. Dodd, first published in the *Bulletin of the John Rylands Library* (1933, 1934), on the change and development that took place in Paul's thought. But as we wrote in a previous critique of Munck, while the whole of Paulinism is eschatological, eschatology is not the whole of Paul. It is possible to introduce so great a mathematical precision into the treatment of Pauline eschatology as to make the Christ of Paul subordinate to an eschatological dogma instead of its fulfilment, and, therefore, one who bursts its bounds. For example, while the treatment of the Law in Paul is to be understood within an eschatological context, nevertheless, if it is completely determined by that context, it is odd that at no point is the connexion between the end of the Law and Rabbinic speculation explicitly made. Rom. 7. 1 ff. is at least ambiguous, and cannot certainly be connected with such. Eschatological speculation was more prolific than systematic and the extreme logicality in its application which Professor Schoeps employs is suspect. The outcome of it is to make such speculation rather than the fact of Christ normative for Paul. This leads us to the next point.

V

The treatment of Paul in this work, brilliant as it is, somehow does not bring to the fore the central moral and Christian realities of Paulinism in their religious

---

[1] J. A. T. Robinson, *The Body* (1952), p. 58; Dibelius-Kümmel, *Paul*, p. 56.

dimension. This is due perhaps to the last point made: Paul is placed in a "strait-jacket" of eschatological speculation. Paul's conversion, as we saw, Professor Schoeps does not attempt to explain: insisting on its eschatological significance for Paul, he removes it from historical investigation and *ipso facto* strikes out the possibility of doing justice to the impact of the historical figure of Jesus of Nazareth on the Apostle's thought. The result of this is to mechanize the Christ of Paul. Christ here becomes an eschatological pivot without moral or spiritual content. The intensity of Paul's devotion to Christ, whom he imitates (and imitation implies knowledge of and devotion to Jesus), the depth of the "being in Christ"—these are not felt. It would be unfair perhaps not to expect this, because Professor Schoeps himself recognizes fully the limitations of the "History of Religions" approach at this point (see the introduction). Nevertheless, Professor Schoeps's work does prompt the question whether a due appreciation of the place of the historical Jesus is as important for the true appreciation of Paul, as for Christian theology generally.

VI

The question raised above is related to the last point we make. The recognition that Paul came to be dominated by Jesus Christ—a historical figure who had been raised from the dead—would have enabled Schoeps to do even more justice than he does to the strictly Rabbinic or Judaistic elements in Paul. We have seen that at crucial points he turns abruptly to Hellenistic influences for the explanation of Paul. At three points especially is this the case—Christology, the Sacraments, the Law. Christologically the factors in Judaism, for example, the quasi-personification of wisdom, the personalized Torah, etc., are more convincing as the soil from which the developed Pauline interpretation of Christ grew than the mysteries. Professor Schoeps still does not recognize that, so far, the figure of the Redeemer in the Mysteries is post-Christian. And the great Pauline affirmations of being "in Christ" as are the ideas of dying and rising with Christ in Baptism and participating in him in the Eucharist are better understood, in our view, in terms of the concepts of solidarity, memory, re-enactment which have become familiar to us in recent interpretations of Judaism than in those of the Hellenistic Mysteries.[1] To repeat, a closer attention to "Jesus" as a Messianic figure within Judaism, who came to influence Paul in his risen life and in the life of his community, would have saved Professor Schoeps from the necessity of using Hellenistic concepts at crucial points as a *Deus ex machina* to explain the peculiarities of Paul mostly explicable in terms of Judaism. On the Law, we can only ask whether Professor Schoeps is not involved in an inconsistency. If Paul's understanding of the Law was moralistic and Hellenistic, can he, as Professor Schoeps claims, be really pertinent in the dialogue with Judaism? But this question we cannot pursue here.[2]

We may state the significance of this last point—that Schoeps does not exploit

---

[1] On this compare *Paul and Rabbinic Judaism*, for example, on pp. 102 ff.

[2] See P. Démann, *Das Judentum* (1962), p. 71.

the Judaism of Paul enough, despite his clear and forceful recognition of it, as follows. The Paul whom Schoeps presents is a split-personality. Judaistic and Hellenistic concepts jostle each other in his mind and never come to terms. We may ask, does Professor Schoeps belong to those scholars who have produced a Paul who is psychologically incredible? Does he not despite his vast admiration of Schweitzer, really stand, in some ways, nearer to Holtzmann and Pfleiderer and others who shared their position? May we say of him that he has introduced a duality into Paul himself which creates many more difficulties than the problems it was intended to solve or is it that the "History of Religions" approach is here employed to the limits of its applicability and found wanting?

BIBLIOGRAPHY

A. DICTIONARIES AND ENCYCLOPÆDIAS
AND SOURCE BOOKS

1. *The Apocrypha and Pseudepigrapha of the Old Testament* (ed. R. H. Charles, 2 vols.). Oxford, 1913.
2. *Biblia Hebraica* (ed. R. Kittel, 2 vols.). Stuttgart, 1925.
3. COHN and WENDLAND, ed. Philo Judaeus, 1896–8. Index vol. by H. Leisegang, 1926; E.T. by F. H. Coulson (Loeb, 1929).
4. *Dictionary of the Bible* (ed. J. Hastings, 5 vols.). Edinburgh, 1900.
5. *Dictionary of the Targumim, the Talmud Babli and Yerushalmi and the Midrashic Literature* (Marcus Jastrow, 2 vols.). London and New York, 1903.
6. *Die Religion in Geschichte und Gegenwart*, hrsg. von Hermann Gunkel und D. Leopold Zscharnack (5 vols.). Tübingen, 1927.
7. *Encyclopædia Biblica* (ed. T. K. Cheyne and J. Sutherland Black). London, 1899.
8. *Encyclopædia Judaica, Das Judenthum in Geschichte und Gegenwart* (10 vols.). Berlin, 1927.
9. *Encyclopædia of Religion and Ethics* (ed. J. Hastings, 13 vols.). Edinburgh, 1908.
10. *Griechische und Lateinische Lehnwörter im Talmud, Midrasch und Targum*, von Samuel Krauss. Berlin, 1898.
11. HATCH, E. and REDPATH, H. A. *A Concordance to the Septuagint and other Greek Versions of the Old Testament including the Apocryphal Books*. Oxford, 1897–1907.
12. *Jewish Encyclopedia* (ed. Isidore Singer, 12 vols.). New York and London, 1901.
13. PAULY. *Realencyclopaedie der Classischen Altertumswissenschaft*, hrsg. von Georg Wissowa. Stuttgart, 1894.
14. *Theologisches Wörterbuch zum Neuen Testament*, hrsg. von Gerhard Kittel (vols. I–III). Stuttgart, 1933.
15. *The Vocabulary of the Greek Testament* (J. H. Moulton and G. Milligan). London, 1914–29.
16. *The Works of Flavius Josephus* (E.T. by W. Whiston). Edinburgh. [No date.]
17. *The Babylonian Talmud* (E.T. ed. by Rabbi Dr I. Epstein, not completed). London: Soncino Press, 1935.
18. *Mekilta* (E.T. and Hebrew Text, ed. by J. Z. Lauterbach). Philadelphia, 1933–5.
19. *Midrash Rabbah* (E.T. ed. by H. Freedmann and M. Simon, 9 vols.). London: Soncino Press, 1939.
20. WÜNSCHE, AUG. *Bibliotheca Rabbinica*. Leipzig, 1881.
21. *The Babylonian Talmud* (the ordinary pagination is followed): *Jerusalem Talmud* (ed. Krotoschin, 1866).
22. *Jewish Authorized Daily Prayer Book* (Hebrew and English, 13th Ed.). London, 1925.

Other Rabbinic Sources are indicated in Appendix C.

B. BOOKS BY MODERN AUTHORS (ONLY THOSE CITED IN THE TEXT ARE INSERTED)

ABELSON, J. *The Immanence of God in Rabbinical Literature.* London, 1912.
—— *Jewish Mysticism.* London, 1913.
ABRAHAMS, I. *Studies in Pharisaism and the Gospels, First and Second Series.* Cambridge, 1917.
ALBRIGHT, W. F. *From the Stone Age to Christianity.* Baltimore, 1940.
BACHER, W. *Die Agada der Tannaiten* (Erster Band, 1884; Zweiter Band, 1890). Strassburg.
—— *Die exegetische Terminologie der jüdischen Traditionsliteratur.* Leipzig, 1899–1905.
BARTH, K. *The Epistle to the Romans* (E.T. by E. C. Hoskyns). Oxford, 1933.
—— *The Resurrection of the Dead* (E.T. by H. J. Stenning). London, 1933.
BELL, G. K. A. and DEISSMANN, A. (ed.). *Mysterium Christi.* London, 1930.
BENNETT, W. H. *The Post-Exilic Prophets.* Edinburgh, 1907.
BENTWICH, N. *Hellenism.* Philadelphia: The Jewish Publication Society of America, 1919.
BERNARD, J. H. (ed.). *The Odes of Solomon.* Cambridge, 1891.
BEVAN, E. R. *Hellenism and Christianity.* London, 1921.
—— *Jerusalem under the High Priests.* London, 1904.
—— *The Hellenistic Age* (with J. B. Bury, E. A. Barber and W. W. Tarn). Cambridge, 1923.
—— *The Legacy of Israel* (Essay on 'Hellenistic Judaism'). Oxford, 1927.
—— *Sibyls and Seers.* London, 1928.
—— *Stoics and Sceptics.* Oxford, 1913.
—— *Symbolism and Belief.* London, 1938.
BIGG, C. *A Critical and Exegetical Commentary on the Epistles of St Peter and St Jude.* Edinburgh, 1902.
BONSIRVEN, J. *Le Judaïsme Palestinien au temps de Jésus-Christ* (2 vols. Bibl. de théol. hist.). Paris, 1934–5.
BOUSSET, W. *Die Religion des Judentums im späthellenistischen Zeitalter*, Berlin, 1903; in dritter Auflage, hrsg. von H. Gressmann, Tübingen, 1926.
—— *Hauptprobleme der Gnosis.* Göttingen, 1907.
—— *Jesus der Herr.* Göttingen, 1916.
—— *Kyrios Christos.* Göttingen, 1st Ed. 1913; 2nd Ed. 1921.
BOX, G. H. *The Ezra Apocalypse.* London, 1912.
—— (With W. O. E. Oesterley). *The Religion and Worship of the Synagogue.* London, 1907.
BRANSCOMB, B. H. *Jesus and the Law of Moses.* London, 1930.
BRAUDE, W. G. *Jewish Proselytizing in the First Five Centuries of the Common Era, the Age of the Tannaim and Amoraim* (Brown University Studies 6). Providence, R.I., 1940.
BRIGGS, C. A. *Messianic Prophecy.* Edinburgh, 1886.
BRIGGS, C. A. and BRIGGS, E. G. *A Critical and Exegetical Commentary on the Book of Psalms* (2 vols.). Edinburgh, 1907–9.
BROWN, L. E. *Early Judaism.* Cambridge, 1929.
BRUNNER, H. E. *Man in Revolt* (E.T. by O. Wyon). London, 1939.

BÜCHLER, A. *Studies in Sin and Atonement in the Rabbinic Literature of the First Century* (Jews' College Publications, No. 11). London, 1928.
—— *Types of Jewish Palestinian Piety from 70 B.C.E to 70 C.E.* (Jews' College Publications, No. 8). London, 1922.
BÜCHSEL, F. *Der Geist Gottes im Neuen Testament.* Gütersloh, 1926.
BURKITT, F. C. *Christian Beginnings.* London, 1924.
BURNETT, J. *Greek Philosophy.* London, 1914.
BURNEY, C. F. *The Aramaic Origin of the Fourth Gospel.* Oxford, 1926.
CAMPBELL, J. McL. *The Nature of the Atonement* (4th Ed.). London, 1873.
CARRINGTON, P. *The Primitive Christian Catechism.* Cambridge, 1940.
CAVE, S. *The Gospel of St Paul.* London, 1928.
CHARLES, R. H. *A Critical History of the Doctrine of a Future Life in Israel, in Judaism, and in Christianity.* London, 1899.
—— *Religious Development between the Old and the New Testaments.* London, 1914.
—— *The Book of Enoch.* Oxford, 1893.
CHEYNE, T. K. *The Origin and Religious Contents of the Psalter.* London, 1891.
COCKS, H. F. L. *By Faith Alone.* London, 1943.
COHEN, A. *Everyman's Talmud.* London, 1932.
COOK, S. A. *The Old Testament: a Reinterpretation.* Cambridge: Heffer, 1936.
—— *The 'Truth' of the Bible.* Cambridge: Heffer, 1938.
COOKE, G. A. *A Critical and Exegetical Commentary on the Book of Ezekiel.* Edinburgh, 1936.
CREED, J. M. *The Gospel according to St Luke.* London, 1930.
CUMONT, F. *Les Réligions Orientales dans le Paganisme Romain.* Paris, 2nd Ed. 1909; 4th Ed. 1929. (E.T. by G. Showerman, Chicago, 1911.)
DALMAN, G. *Jesus-Jeshua* (E.T. by P. P. Levertoff). London, 1929.
DANBY, H. *The Mishnah.* Oxford, 1933.
DAVIDSON, A. B. *The Theology of the Old Testament.* Edinburgh, 1904.
—— *The Book of Job:* in *The Cambridge Bible for Schools and Colleges.* Cambridge, 1889.
DAVIDSON, W. L. *The Stoic Creed.* Edinburgh, 1907.
DEISSMANN, A. *Bible Studies* (E.T. by A. Grieve). Edinburgh, 1901.
—— *Paul: A Study in Social and Religious History* (E.T. by W. E.Wilson). London, 1926.
DIBELIUS, M. *A Fresh Approach to the New Testament and Early Christian Literature* (E.T.). London, 1937.
—— *From Tradition to Gospel* (E.T. by B. L. Woolf). London, 1934.
DIETRICH, A. *Eine Mithrasliturgie.* Leipzig, 1903.
DODD, C. H. *The Apostolic Preaching and its developments.* London, 1936.
—— *The Bible and the Greeks.* London, 1935.
—— *The Johannine Epistles* (M.N.T.C.). London, 1946.
—— *The Epistle to the Romans* (M.N.T.C.). London, 1932.
—— *The Gospel in the New Testament.* London: National Sunday School Union.
—— *History and the Gospel.* London, 1943.
—— *The Parables of the Kingdom.* London, 1935.
—— *The Mind of Paul:* (1) *Psychological Approach,* (2) *Change and Development* (Ryl. Bull. vols. XVII, XVIII). Manchester, 1933.
DRIVER, S. R. and NEUBAUER, AD. *The 53rd Chapter of Isaiah According to the Jewish Interpreters* (Texts and Translations, vols. I, II). Oxford, 1876.
DRUMMOND, J. *Philo Judaeus of the Jewish Alexandrian Philosophy* (vols. I, II). London, 1888.

DUNCAN, G. S. *The Epistle to the Galatians* (*M.N.T.C.*). London, 1934.

EDERSHEIM, A. *The Life and Times of Jesus the Messiah* (vols. I, II). London, 1901.

EDWARDS, T. C. *A Commentary on the 1st Epistle to the Corinthians.* London, 1885.

—— *The Epistle to the Hebrews* (*The Expositor's Bible*). London, 1888.

ETHERIDGE, J. W. *The Targums of Onkelos and Jonathan ben Uzziel on the Pentateuch* (2 vols.). London, 1865.

FRIEDLANDER, G. *Pirkê de Rabbi Eliezer.* London, 1916.

FLEW, R. N. *Jesus and His Church.* London, 1938.

GAVIN, F. *The Jewish Antecedents of the Christian Sacraments.* London, 1928.

GILLET, LEV. *Communion in the Messiah.* London, 1942.

GLOVER, T. R. *Paul of Tarsus.* London, 1925.

GOGUEL, M. *The Life of Jesus* (E.T. by O. Wyon). London, 1933.

GOODENOUGH, E. R. *By Light, Light: The Mystic Gospel of Hellenistic Judaism.* Newhaven, 1935.

GRAY, G. B. *Sacrifice in the Old Testament.* Oxford, 1925.

GREEN, A. A. *The Revised Hagada.* London, 1897.

GREENSTONE, J. H. *The Messiah Idea in Jewish History.* Philadelphia: The Jewish Publication Society of America, 1906.

GREENUP, A. W. *Sukkah, Mishna and Tosefta* (in *Translations of Early Documents*). London: S.P.C.K., 1925.

GUIGNEBERT, C. A. H. *Le monde juif vers le temps de Jésus* (E.T. by S. H. Hooke). London, 1939.

GUNKEL, H. *Die Wirkungen des heiligen Geistes.* Göttingen, 1888.

—— *Schöpfung und Chaos in Urzeit und Endzeit.* Göttingen, 1895.

HARNACK, A. *The Sayings of Jesus.* (E.T. by J. R. Wilkinson.) London, 1908.

HARRIS, J. R. and BURCH, V. *Testimonies.* Cambridge, 1916.

HERFORD, T. R. (*Pirqê*) *Aboth* (2nd Ed.). New York, 1925.

—— *Christianity in Talmud and Midrash.* London, 1903.

—— *Pharisaism.* London, 1912.

HICKS, F. C. N. *The Fullness of Sacrifice* (1st Ed.). London, 1930.

HOLTZMANN, H. J. *Lehrbuch der neutestamentlichen Theologie* (2 vols.; zweite neu bearbeitete Auflage). Tübingen, 1911.

HOOKE, S. H. (ed.). *Myth and Ritual.* London, 1933.

HOSKYNS, E. C. and DAVEY, F. N. *The Riddle of the New Testament* (1st Ed.). London, 1931.

HOWARD, W. F. *Christianity according to St John.* London, 1943.

—— *The Fourth Gospel in Recent Criticism and Interpretation.* London, 1931.

HUNTER, A. M. *Paul and His Predecessors.* London, 1940.

JOHNSON, A. R. *The One and the Many in the Israelite Conception of God.* Cardiff: University of Wales, 1942.

JOHNSTON, G. *The Doctrine of the Church in the New Testament.* Cambridge, 1943.

JUSTER, J. *Les Juifs dans l'Empire Romain* (Librairie Paul Geuthner). Paris, 1914.

KAUTZSCH, E. (ed.). *Die Apokryphen und Pseudepigraphen des Alten Testaments* (2 vols.). Tübingen, 1900.

KENNEDY, H. A. A. *Philo's Contribution to Religion.* London, 1919.

—— *St Paul and the Mystery Religions.* London, 1913.

—— *St Paul's Conceptions of the Last Things.* London, 1904.

—— *The Theology of the Epistles.* London, 1919.

KENYON, F. G. *Greek Papyri in the British Museum.* London, 1893.

KING, E. G. *Simeon ben Chelbo Kara; The Yalkuṭ on Zechariah.* Cambridge, 1882.

KIRK, K. E. *The Epistle to the Romans (Clarendon Bible).* Oxford, 1937.

KITTEL, G. *Die Probleme des palästinischen Spätjudenthums und des Urchristentums.* Stuttgart, 1926.

KLAUSNER, J. *From Jesus to Paul* (E.T. by W. F. Stinespring). London, 1942.

—— *Jesus of Nazareth* (E.T. by H. Danby). New York, 1927.

KLEIN, G. *Der älteste christliche Katechismus.* Berlin: Georg Reimer, 1909.

KLOSTERMANN, E. *H.Z.N.T. Das Matthäusevangelium* (2nd Ed.). Tübingen, 1927.

KNOX, W. L. *St Paul and the Church of the Gentiles.* Cambridge, 1939.

—— *St Paul and the Church of Jerusalem.* Cambridge, 1925.

—— *Some Hellenistic Elements in Primitive Christianity* (Schweich Lectures, 1942). London, 1944.

LACEY, T. A. *The One Body and the One Spirit.* London, 1925.

LAGRANGE, M.-J. *Le Judaïsme avant Jésus-Christ.* Paris, 1931.

—— *Évangile selon S. Matthieu.* Paris, 1923.

LAKE, K. *The Earlier Epistles of St Paul* (2nd Ed.). London, 1919.

LAKE, K. and FOAKES JACKSON, H. *The Beginnings of Christianity* (5 vols.). 1920–33.

LEBRETON, J. *Histoire du dogme de la Trinité* (7th Ed.). Paris, 1927. (E.T. from 8th Ed. by A. Thorold, London, 1939.)

LEVEEN, J. *The Hebrew Bible in Art* (Schweich Lectures, 1939). London, 1944.

LEVERTOFF, P. P. *Midrash Sifre on Numbers.* London, 1926.

LEVY, S. *Original Virtue and Other Studies.* London, 1907.

LIETZMANN, H. *H.Z.N.T. An die Römer* (4th Ed.).

—— *H.Z.N.T. An die Korinther* (3rd Ed.).

LIGHTFOOT, J. B. *The Epistle to the Galatians* (5th Ed.). London, 1876.

—— *The Epistles to the Colossians and to Philemon* (9th Ed.). London, 1890.

—— *The Epistle to the Philippians* (1st Ed.). London, 1890.

LODS, A. *Les Prophètes d'Israel et les débuts du Judaïsme.* Paris, 1935.

MACDONALD, D. B. *The Hebrew Philosophical Genius.* Princeton, N.J., 1936.

MACGREGOR, G. H. C. *Eucharistic Origins* (Bruce Lectures). London, 1929.

MACGREGOR, G. H. C. and PURDY, A. C. *Jew and Greek Tutors unto Christ.* London, 1936.

MACKINTOSH, H. R. *The Doctrine of the Person of Jesus Christ* (2nd Ed.). Edinburgh, 1913.

MANSON, T. W. *The Teaching of Jesus.* Cambridge, 1931.

—— (ed.). *A Companion to the Bible.* Edinburgh, 1939.

—— *St Paul in Ephesus: (2) The Problem of the Epistle to the Galatians* (Ryl. Bull. vol. XXIV, No. 1, 1940).

MANSON, W. *The Gospel According to St Luke* (M.N.T.C.). London, 1930.

—— *Jesus the Messiah.* London, 1943.

MARMORSTEIN, A. *The Doctrine of Merits in the Old Rabbinical Literature* (Jews' College Publications, No. 7). London, 1920.

—— *The Old Rabbinic Doctrine of God* (Jews' College Publications, Nos. 10, 14). London, 1927.

MARSH, H. G. *The Origin and Significance of the New Testament Baptism.* Manchester, 1941.

McGIFFERT, A. C. *A History of Christian Thought* (2 vols.). New York, 1932–3.

McNEILE, A. H. *The Gospel According to St Matthew.* London, 1917.

MEYER, E. *Ursprung und Anfänge des Christentums* (3 vols.). Stuttgart, Berlin, 1921–3.

MICHAEL, J. H. *St Paul's Epistle to the Philippians (M.N.T.C.).* London, 1928.

MOFFATT, J. *The First Epistle to the Corinthians (M.N.T.C.).* London, 1938.

MONTEFIORE, C. J. G. *Lectures on the Origin and Growth of Religion as Illustrated by the Religion of the Ancient Hebrews* (Hibbert Lectures). London, 1892.

—— *IV Ezra: a Study in the Development of Universalism.* London, 1929.

—— *Rabbinic Literature and Gospel Teachings.* London, 1930.

—— *Judaism and St Paul.* London, 1914.

—— *The Synoptic Gospels* (2 vols.; 2nd Ed.). London, 1927.

MONTEFIORE, C. J. G. and LOEWE, H. M. *Rabbinic Anthology.* London, 1938.

MOORE, G. F. *Judaism* (3 vols.). Oxford, 1927–30.

MORGAN, W. *The Religion and Theology of Paul.* Edinburgh, 1917.

MOULTON, J. H. *A Grammar of New Testament Greek* (vols. I–II). London, 1906–20.

MURRAY, G. *The Five Stages of Greek Religion.* Oxford, 1925.

NIEBUHR, R. *The Nature and Destiny of Man* (2 vols.; Gifford Lectures). London, 1943.

NOCK, A. D. *Conversion.* Oxford, 1933.

—— *St Paul.* London, 1938.

NORDEN, E. *Agnostos Theos.* Leipzig, Berlin, 1913.

OESTERLEY, W. O. E. *The Books of the Apocrypha.* London, 1914.

—— *The Sayings of the Jewish Fathers.* London, 1919.

—— *Sacrifices of Ancient Israel.* London, 1937.

—— *The Evolution of the Messianic Idea.* London, 1908.

—— *II Esdras (Westminster Commentaries).* London, 1933.

—— (ed.). *Judaism and Christianity* (2 vols.). London, 1937.

OESTERLEY, W. O. E. and ROBINSON, T. H. *Hebrew Religion.* London, 1930.

—— —— *A History of Israel* (2 vols.). Oxford, 1932.

—— —— *An Introduction to the Literature of the Old Testament.* London, 1934.

OTTO, R. *The Kingdom of God and the Son of Man* (E.T. by F. V. Filson and B. L. Woolf). London, 1938.

PARKES, J. W. *Jesus, Paul and the Jews.* London, 1936.

PEAKE, A. S. (ed.). *The People and the Book.* Oxford, 1925.

—— *The Problem of Suffering in the Old Testament.* London, 1904.

—— *The Servant of Yahweh.* Manchester, 1931.

PEDERSEN, J. *Israel, its Life and Culture,* I–II. Oxford, 1926.

PFLEIDERER, O. *Paulinism* (2 vols.; E.T. by Edward Peters). London, 1877.

PILCHER, C. V. *The Hereafter in Jewish and Christian Thought.* London, 1940.

PLUMMER, A. *A Critical and Exegetical Commentary on the Second Epistle of St Paul to the Corinthians.* Edinburgh, 1915.

PLUMMER, A. and ROBERTSON, A. *A Critical and Exegetical Commentary on the First Epistle of St Paul to the Corinthians* (2nd Ed.). Edinburgh, 1914.

PORTEOUS, N. W. *In Record and Revelation* (ed. H. W. Robinson). Oxford, 1938.

PORTER, F. C. *The Mind of Christ in Paul.* New York, 1930.

RABBINOWITZ, J. *Mishnah Megillah.* Oxford, 1931.

RAMSEY, W. M. *Cities and Bishoprics of Phrygia.* Oxford, 1895.

RANKIN, O. S. *Israel's Wisdom Literature.* Edinburgh, 1936.

RAVEN, C. E. *The Creator Spirit.* London, 1927.

—— *Science, Religion and the Future.* Cambridge, 1943.

RAWLINSON, A. E. J. *The New Testament Doctrine of the Christ.* London, 1926.

—— (ed.). *Essays on the Trinity and the Incarnation.* London, 1928.

REES, T. *The Holy Spirit.* London, 1915.

REITZENSTEIN, R. *Die Hellenistischen Mysterienreligionen* (3. Aufl.). Leipzig, Berlin, 1927.

RESCH, J. A. *Jesus Christ Agrapha*, in *Texte und Untersuchungen*, hrsg. von O. von Gebhardt und A. Narnack (No. 5). Leipzig, 1889.

—— *Der Paulinismus und die Logia Jesu*, in *Texte und Untersuchungen*. Leipzig, 1904.

ROBINSON, H. W. *The Christian Doctrine of Man*. Edinburgh, 1911.

—— *The Cross of the Servant*. London, 1926.

—— *The Christian Experience of the Holy Spirit*. London, 1928.

—— *The Hebrew Psychology in Relation to Pauline Anthropology* in (Mansfield College Essays, 1909). (See also *The People and the Book*, ed. A. S. Peake.)

—— *The Religious Ideas of the Old Testament*. London, 1913.

—— *Redemption and Revelation*. London, 1942.

ROBINSON, J. A. *St Paul's Epistle to the Ephesians* (2nd Ed.). London, 1904.

ROBINSON, T. H. *Prophecy and the Prophets*. London, 1923. See under OESTERLEY, W. O. E.

ROWLEY, H. H. *The Relevance of Apocalyptic*. London, 1944.

RYLE, H. E. and JAMES, M. R. ΨΑΛΜΟΙ ΣΟΛΟΜѠΝΤΟΣ: *Psalms of the Pharisees*. Cambridge, 1891.

SANDAY, W. and HEADLAM, A. C. *A Critical and Exegetical Commentary on St Paul's Epistle to the Romans* (*I.C.C.*) (5th Ed.). Edinburgh, 1902.

SCHECHTER, S. *Some Aspects of Rabbinic Theology*. London, 1909.

SCHOLEM, G. G. *Major Trends in Jewish Mysticism*. Jerusalem: Schocken Pub. House, 1941.

SCHULTZ, H. *Old Testament Theology* (E.T. from 4th German Ed., J. A. Paterson). Edinburgh, 1892.

SCHÜRER, E. *The Jewish People in the Time of Jesus Christ* (5 vols. and Index; E.T. by Sophia Taylor and Peter Christie). Edinburgh, 1885.

SCHWEITZER, A. *The Mysticism of Paul the Apostle* (E.T. by W. Montgomery). London, 1931.

—— *Paul and His Interpreters* (E.T. by W. Montgomery). London, 1912.

SCOTT, C. A. A. *Christianity According to St Paul*. Cambridge, 1932.

—— *The Fellowship of the Spirit*. London, 1921.

SCOTT, E. F. *The Spirit in the New Testament*. London, 1923.

—— *The Epistles to Colossians, Philemon, Ephesians* (*M.N.T.C.*). London, 1923.

SCOTT, W. *Hermetica* (4 vols.). Oxford, 1924.

SELWYN, E. G. *The First Epistle of St Peter*. London, 1946. (D. Daube, Appended Note, "Participle and Imperative in 1 Peter", pp. 467ff.)

SKINNER, J. *A Critical and Exegetical Commentary on Genesis* (*I.C.C.*). Edinburgh, 1930.

—— *Isaiah XL–LXVI* (*Cambridge Bible for Schools and Colleges*). Cambridge, 1902.

—— *Prophecy and Religion*. Cambridge, 1922.

SMITH, C. A. R. *The Bible Doctrine of Salvation*. London, 1941.

SMITH, J. N. P. *A Critical and Exegetical Commentary on Micah, Zephaniah, etc.* (*I.C.C.*). Edinburgh, 1912.

SMITH, W. R. *The Religion of the Semites* (3rd Ed. with Introduction and Notes by S. A. Cook). London, 1927.

SNAITH, N. H. *The Distinctive Ideas of the Old Testament*. London, 1944.

SNEATH, E. H. (ed.). *The Evolution of Ethics*. Newhaven, 1927.

STEVENS, G. B. *The Pauline Theology*. London, 1892.

STRACHAN, R. H. *The Historic Jesus in the New Testament*. London, 1931.

—— *The Second Epistle to the Corinthians* (*M.N.T.C.*). London, 1935.

STRACHAN, R. H. *The Fourth Gospel, its Significance and Environment* (3rd Ed.). London, 1941.

STRACK, H. L. *Der Blutaberglaube bei Christen und Juden* (Abdruck 2). München, 1891.

—— *Introduction to the Talmud and Midrash* (E.T. from 5th German Ed.). Philadelphia: Jewish Publications Society, 1931.

STREETER, B. H. *The Four Gospels*. London, 1930.

—— *The Primitive Church*. London, 1929.

SWETE, H. B. *The Holy Spirit in the New Testament*. London, 1909.

TAYLOR, C. *The Sayings of the Jewish Fathers* (2nd Ed.). Cambridge, 1897.

TAYLOR, V. *The Atonement in New Testament Teaching*. London, 1940.

—— *Jesus and His Sacrifice*. London, 1937.

—— *Forgiveness and Reconciliation*. London, 1941.

TENNANT, F. R. *The Sources of the Doctrines of the Fall and Original Sin*. Cambridge, 1903.

THACKERY, H. ST J. *St Paul and Contemporary Jewish Thought*. London, 1900.

THORNTON, L. S. *The Common Life in the Body of Christ*. Westminster, 1941.

TOY, C. H. *A Critical and Exegetical Commentary on the Book of Proverbs (I.C.C.)*. Edinburgh, 1904.

VOLZ, P. *Jüdische Eschatologie von Daniel bis Akiba*. Tübingen und Leipzig, 1903.

WEISS, J. *The History of Primitive Christianity* (E.T. by R. Knopf, completed by four friends; ed. F. C. Grant, 2 vols.). London, 1937.

—— Meyer, *Kommentar: Der Erste Korintherbrief* (9th Ed.). Göttingen, 1910.

WELCH, A. C. *Post-Exilic Judaism*. Edinburgh, 1935.

—— *Prophet and Priest in Ancient Israel*. London, 1936.

WENDLAND, P. *Die Hellenistische-römische Kultur*. Tübingen, 1912.

WILLIAMS, N. P. *The Ideas of the Fall and of Original Sin*. London, 1927.

WINDISCH, H. *Der Sinn der Bergpredigt (Untersuchungen z. Neuen Testament, 16)*. Leipzig, 1929.

—— *Untersuchungen z. Neuen Testament*, hrsg. von H. Windisch. Leipzig, 1912.

—— Meyer, *Kommentar: Der Zweite Korintherbrief*. Göttingen, 1924.

WOOD, I. F. *The Spirit of God in Biblical Literature*. London, 1904.

WREDE, W. *Paul* (E.T. by E. Luminis). London, 1907.

WÜNSCHE, A. *Die Leiden des Messias*. Leipzig, 1870.

PERIODICALS REFERRED TO IN THE TEXT

J.T.S.

(1909), vol. x.   (C. F. Burney), p. 580.
(1916), vol. xvii.   (F. C. Burkitt, "On I Corinthians 15. 26"), pp. 384 f.
(1924), vol. xxvi.   (C. H. Dodd, "Notes from Papyri"), pp. 77 f.
(1925), vol. xxvi.   (J. M. Creed, "The Heavenly Man"), p. 113.
(1926), vol. xxvii.   (C. F. Burney, "Christ as the ἀρχή of Creation"), p. 160.
(1931), vol. xxxii.   (C. H. Dodd, "ΙΛΑΣΚΕΣΘΑΙ", etc.), p. 352.
(1936), vol. xxxvii.   (G. B. Gray, "Passover and Unleavened Bread"), pp. 241 ff.
(1936), vol. xxxvii.   (D. Winton Thomas), p. 85.
(1936), vol. xxxvii.   (T.W. Manson, "A Parallel to the N.T. use of σῶμα"), p. 385.
(1937), vol. xxxviii.   (G. C. Richards, "Parallels to the N.T. use of σῶμα"), p. 165.
(1937), vol. xxxviii.   (W. L. Knox, "The Divine Wisdom"), pp. 230 ff.
(1938), vol. xxxix.   (D. Daube, "ἐξουσία in Mark 1. 22, 27"), p. 45.
(1938), vol. xxxix.   (W. L. Knox, "Parallels to the N.T. use of σῶμα"), p. 243.
(1938), vol. xxxix.   (H. Danby), p. 178.
(1940), vol. xli.   (A. D. Nock), p. 292.
(1942), vol. xliii.   (D. Daube), p. 127.
(1945), vol. xlvi.   (T. W. Manson, "ΙΛΑΣΤΗΡΙΟΝ"), p. 1.
(1946), vol. xlvii.   (G. R. Driver), p. 158.

Expository Times

(1916), vol. xxvii.   (C. W. Emmet, "Esdras and St Paul"), pp. 551 ff.
(1939), vol. l.   (V. Taylor, "Great Texts reconsidered, Rom. 3. 25"), pp. 295 ff.
(1943), vol. lv.   (D. R. Griffiths, "The Lord is the Spirit"), p. 81.

Biblica (Rome)

(1932), vol. xiii.   (J. B. Frey, "La vie de l'au-delà, dans les conceptions juives au temps de Jésus-Christ"), p. 129.
(1933), vol. xiv.   (J. B. Frey, "Le conflit entre le messianisme de Jésus et le messianisme des juifs de son temps"), pp. 139–149; 269–293.

Revue d'Histoire et de Philosophie religieuses (Strasbourg) (1932), vol. xii. (J. Héring, "Saint Paul a-t-il enseigné deux résurrections"), p. 300.

Archiv fur Religionswissenschaft (1930), vol. xxviii.   (A. Marmorstein, "Der heilige Geist in der rabbinschen Legende"), p. 286.

J.Q.R.

Vol. xx.   (H. Parzen, "The Ruaḥ Haḳodesh in Rabbinical literature"), p. 51.
Vol. xxxv.   (D. Daube, "The Interpretation of a Generic Singular"), pp. 227 ff.

Revue des Études Juives

(1903), vol. xlvii.   (S. Krauss, "Les Préceptes des Noachides"), pp. 34 ff.
(1928), vol. lxxxvi.   (A. Marmorstein, "Conceptions Théocentriques de l'Agada"), pp. 36 ff.

Gnomon (March 1937).   (A. D. Nock), p. 156.

The Journal of Religion, vol. viii, No. 1.   (F. C. Porter, "Judaism in New Testament Times."), pp. 30 ff.

The Hibbert Journal (Oct. 1911).   (A. Loisy, "The Christian Mystery"), pp. 45 ff.

Z.A.W. (1925), Beihefte xl, xli.   (T. H. Robinson, "My Blood of the Covenant"), pp. 232 ff.

The Interpreter (1923–4), vol. XX. (C. H. Dodd, "The Eschatological Element..."), pp. 14 ff.

The Catholic Biblical Quarterley (1942) (following Dr H. H. Rowley), C. Lattey, "The Messianic Expectation in the Assumption of Moses", p. (not available).

Zeitschrift für die Neutestamentliche Wissenschaft (1903). (A. Bugge, "Das Gesetz und Christus"), p. 89.

H.T.R.
  (1921), vol. XIV. (G. F. Moore, "Christian Writers on Judaism"), p. 197.
  (1936), vol. XXIX. (C. Roberts, T. C. Skeat and A. D. Nock, "The Gild of Zeus Hypsistos"), p. 39.

Revue d'histoire et de littérature religieuses (1913). (A. Loisy, cited by C. J. G. Montefiore.) See p. 2.

J.B.L.
  (1945), vol. LXIV. (H. H. Rowley on the figure of Taxo), p. 141.
  (1945), vol. LXIV. (C. C. Torrey on the figure of Taxo), p. 395.

Transactions of Dr Dodd's Seminar
  (1) On Mark and Form Criticism (1938).
  (2) J. Macpherson on John 13 ff. (1939).

COMMENTARIES CONSULTED

LIETZMANN, H. (ed.). *H.Z.N.T.* Tübingen, 1926 etc.

MEYER. *Kommentar zum Neuen Testament*. Göttingen. Various dates.

PEAKE, A. S. *Commentary on the Bible*. Edinburgh, 1929. Supplement (ed. A. J. Grieve). 1936.

GORE, C., GOUDGE, H. L. and A. GUILLAUME. *A New Commentary on Holy Scripture including the Apocrypha*. London, 1928.

NICOLL, W. R. *Expositor's Greek Testament*. London, 1897.

I.C.C. Edinburgh. Various dates.

M.N.T.C. London. Various dates.

For other commentaries see bibliography.

ADDITIONAL NOTES[1]

I. General Note on the *D.S.S.* and Paulinism

The date of the *D.S.S.* is still a matter of debate, but perhaps the majority of scholars in the field favour one prior to the first century. Affinities between them and the New Testament have been pointed out by W. H. Brownlee in scattered notes in *B.A.S.O.R.*, Supplementary Studies, 10–12, 1951; W. Grossouw, "The *D.S.S.* and the New Testament", in *Studia Catholica,* (1) Dec. 1951, pp. 289ff.; (2) Jan. 1953, pp. 1ff.; K. G. Kuhn, "Πειρασμός, ἀμαρτία, σάρξ im Neuen Testament und die damit zusammenhängenden Vorstellungen", in *Zeitschrift für Theologie und Kirche*, 1952, Heft 2, pp. 200ff.; and others; for all bibliographical details consult the masterly survey by H. H. Rowley, *The Zadokite Fragments and the Dead Sea Scrolls*, Oxford, 1952. If the pre-Christian dating of the *D.S.S.* be accepted, they can be claimed at least to impinge on Paulinism chiefly at the following points:

1. They further confirm that such terms as μυστήριον, τέλειος, etc., in Paul need not be traced to any extra Palestinian influences related to Hellenistic Mysteries. In the *D.S.S.* the terms *rz* and *swd* occur frequently with an eschatological meaning as in Paul. See *D.S.D.* II: 23; III: 15; IV: 6, 18; XI: 3–6; *D.S.H.* VII: 5, etc.; also *D.S.D.* I: 3; *D.S.H.* II: 9; VII: 5. Compare p. 91 above. In addition see W. D. Davies, " 'Knowledge' in the D.S.S. and Matthew 11. 25–30", in *The Harvard Theological Review*, July 1953.

2. They reveal anticipations of the Pauline doctrine of Justification by Faith. This was indicated by W. H. Brownlee, op. cit., pp. 43, n. 5, 45, n. 20 (who cites M. Burrows also), and W. Grossouw, op. cit., 2, pp. 4f., who regards the similarity in the terminology and teaching regarding justification as the most important item in the affinity between the *D.S.S.* and Paul. This further perhaps helps to confirm what we noted on pp. 221ff. that not Justification by Faith as such so much as the significance of Jesus of Nazareth as the Messiah is pivotal for Paul. See *D.S.D.* XI: 3, 14f., *D.S.H.* VIII: 1f.

3. Most important is the comparison made by K. G. Kuhn, op. cit., pp. 209ff., between the Pauline understanding of the flesh and that found in the *D.S.S.*, where among other more usual connotations, the flesh stands for man as opposed to God. The similarity between the interpretation of the flesh in Paul offered by J. A. T. Robinson in *The Body*, 1952, pp. 17ff. *et passim*, and that revealed by K. G. Kuhn in the *D.S.S.* is most striking. We claimed on pp. 19f. that Paul's use of σάρξ is "an accentuation of the ethical connotation that the term already had in certain late documents of the Old Testament". This need not be modified in the light of the *D.S.S.*

[1] References to texts, authors, etc., in this section are not included in the indexes.

except that we have now to recognize that this accentuation is more radical than we recognized in the text. Moreover this modification is not peculiarly Pauline; it had already clearly developed in certain circles in pre-Christian Palestinian Judaism. In the light of chapter I above we need not cavil at recognizing that this accentuation may have occurred under Hellenistic influences and possibly also under Persian ones (see K. G. Kuhn, *Zeitschrift für Theologie und Kirche*, vol. XLII, 1950, p. 211; A. Dupont-Sommer, *Revue de l'Histoire des Religions*, CXLII, No. 1, July-Sept. 1952, pp. 5ff., on "L'instruction sur les deux Esprits dans le 'Manuel de Discipline'."). The significant factor is that the Pauline concept of the "flesh" could be native to Palestinian Judaism. See also R. Bultmann, *Theology of the New Testament*, vol. 1, (E.T.), 1951, p. 235. On the D.S.S. and the origins of Christianity, see A. Dupont-Sommer, *The Jewish Sect of Qumrân and the Essenes* (E.T.), London, 1954, pp. 147ff.

II. Detailed Notes

P. 3, n. 3   Add: B. J. Bamberger, "The Dating of Aggadic Materials", in *J.B.L.*, LXVIII (1949), pp. 115-23; Samuel Sandmel, "Judaism, Jesus and Paul", *Vanderbilt Studies in the Humanities*, vol. I, 1951, pp. 220-50.

P. 9   On the relation between Apocalyptic and Pharisaism, see W. D. Davies, "Apocalyptic and Pharisaism, Unsolved New Testament Problems" in *The Expository Times*, vol. LIX, pp. 233ff. There is a penetrating study by T. W. Manson, "Some Reflections on Apocalyptic", in *Aux Sources de la Tradition Chrétienne: Mélanges offerts à M. Maurice Goguel*, Paris, 1952, pp. 139ff., "Apocalyptic is really an attempt to rationalize and systematize the predictive side of Prophecy as one side of the whole providential ordering of the Universe. The other side of the systematizing process is the scribal treatment of the Law leading to the codification of the Mishnah" (p. 142). (With this compare Santayana's understanding of the relation between religion and poetry noted by A. N. Wilder, *Modern Poetry and the Christian Tradition*, New York, 1952, p. 3, n. 1.) See also E. Stauffer, *Die Theologie des Neuen Testaments*,[4] 1948, pp. 3ff., where he refers to the evidence found at Dura-Europos (p. 238, n. 52) for the "lebendige Anfangszeit der Synagoge, in der Apokalyptik und Rabbinat in fruchtbarer Wechselbeziehung standen (cf. 4 Esr; Hb. Hen; Dura)"; see J. Bloch, *On the Apocalyptic in Judaism*, Philadelphia, 1953, who shows how Apocalyptic penetrates the main stream of Judaism.

P. 15, n. 1   Add S. Liebermann, *J.B.L.*, vol. LXXI, December 1952, pp. 199ff. (on this, see S. Zeitlin, *J.Q.R.*, vol. 43, 1952–3, pp. 297ff.) J. Sanhedrin 10. 5 (there were twenty-four sects in Israel at the destruction of the second Temple).

P. 16   On the falsity of the sharp distinction between Palestinian and Diaspora Judaism, see further S. Liebermann, *Greek in Jewish Palestine*, 1942. Even Rabbinic methods of exegesis have been claimed to be largely Hellenistic, see especially D. Daube, *Hebrew Union College Annual*, vol. xxii, pp. 239ff.; cf. W. F., Albright, *From the Stone Age to Christianity*,[2] Baltimore, 1946 pp. 274f., 337, n. 26. This last study discusses the cultural interactions of the first century and reinforces our thesis in chapter 1 at every point, as does also the archaeological material which is exhaustively surveyed by E. R. Goodenough, *Jewish Symbols in the Greco-Roman Period*, Bollingen Series, Pantheon Books, 1953. See also G. D. Kilpatrick, *The Gospel According to St. Matthew*, 1946, pp. 105ff. We have already indicated in Note 1 the relevance of the *D.S.S.* at this point; see, e.g., W. F. Albright's appendix to W. H. Brownlee, *op. cit.* For the penetration of Hellenistic Gnosis into the Haggadah, see A. Altmann, "Gnostic Themes in Rabbinic Cosmology", in *Essays in honour of J. H. Hertz*, London, 1942, pp. 19ff. "The early stages of Tannaitic thought are already under the spell of Gnostic ideas" (p. 20). On Mysteries and Judaism, see A. D. Nock, *Mnemosyne*, S. iv, vol. v, 1952, pp. 190ff. See also further, D. Daube, "Alexandrian Methods of Interpretation and the Rabbis", in *Festschrift Hans Lewald*, Basel, 1953, pp. 27ff.

P. 18   See note 1 on the flesh in the *D.S.S.*

P. 20   On the contrast between the ψυχικοί and the πνευματικοί see Dom J. Dupont, *Gnosis, La Connaissance religieuse dans les Épitres de Saint Paul*, Louvain, 1949, reviewed by R. Bultmann, *J.T.S.*, N.S., vol. iii, April 1952, pp. 10ff., where, as in *New Testament Theology* also, R. Bultmann insists on the Hellenistic character of the contrast (contrast J. Dupont). K. G. Kuhn finds the contrast between the χοϊκός and the 'επουράνιος and πνευματικός in the *D.S.S.*, where however he finds no reference to the ψυχικός. See K. G. Kuhn, *Zeitschrift für Theologie und Kirche*, 1950, pp. 203ff., especially 210.

The term *yêtzer* occurs in *D.S.D.* v: 1, etc. W. H. Brownlee points out that "the phrases yetzer hara and yetzer hattov known from Test of B. 6: 4 and Pirqe Aboth 2: 15 and current in later Rabbinic literature do not occur in D.S.D. or C.D.C." He refers to the occurrence of *yêtzer 'ashmâh* in C.D.C. 11: 16 (3: 2). E. Kautzsch, *op. cit.*, ad loc., does not find the *yêtzer* in Sirach 15. 11–14.

P. 21, n. 8   The term *yêtzer* occurs in a context where the heart is prominent in *D.S.D.* v: 4.

P. 28   Contrast Stig Hanson, *The Unity of the Church in the New Testament, Colossians and Ephesians*, Uppsala, 1946, p. 59.

P. 32   For Paul's side-glance at Adam in Rom. 7, see also A. S. Peake, "The Quintessence of Paulinism", *Ryl. Bull.*, vol. 4, No. 2, Sept. 1917–Jan. 1918, p. 24.

P. 37, n. 3   Dr Otto Piper informs me that perhaps the earliest to support a definite semantic differentiation between the two words καινός and νέος is J. H. Tittmann, *Remarks on the Synonyms of the New Testament*, Eng. Trans., vol. I, pp. 106–9 (Biblical Cabinet, Edinburgh, 1838, vol. III). See the excellent statement by J. Behm, *Theologisches Wörterbuch*, III, p. 450f., which fully substantiates the differentiation.

P. 37, n. 7   W. H. Brownlee finds traces of *Ma'aseh Bereshith* in *D.S.D.* x, see op. cit., pp. 38, n. 3, 50, Appendix E.

P. 39, n. 6   Add P. Volz, *Eschatologie der Jüdischen Gemeinde im neutestamentlichen Zeitalter*, 1934, pp. 359ff.; H. J. Schoeps, *Theologie und Geschichte des Judenchristentums*, Tübingen, 1949, pp. 91ff.; N. A. Dahl, *Das Volk Gottes*, Oslo, 1941, pp. 38, 84, 113; also in *Aux Sources de la Tradition Chrétienne* where he discusses the Epistle of Barnabas 6. 8–19; O. Cullmann, *Christus und die Zeit* (English trans.), 1950, pp. 92–9, but he warns against pressing the principle that "the End is as the Beginning" too far theologically, see pp. 67, 91. There is a "how much more" always in the End. Cf. E. Brunner, *The Christian Doctrine of Creation and Redemption*, London, 1952, (E.T.), pp. 101–2, 128–9, 157, 374f.

P. 40   For a convenient summary of much recent discussion on cosmic mythology in the Old Testament, see a forthcoming paper by H. G. May in the *J.B.L.*

P. 41   H. Lietzmann, *Zeitschrift für die neutestamentliche Wissenschaft*, XXII, 1923, p. 265, and E. Lohmeyer, *Kyrios Jesus*, 1927–8, p. 65f., have argued that Phil. 2. 6–11 formed part of some primitive eucharistic liturgy, but this is mere conjecture. J. N. D. Kelly, *Early Christian Creeds*, 1950, p. 18, takes it to be a pre-Pauline Palestinian hymn. The motifs that enter into the passage are varied. See J. Jeremias, *Theologisches Wörterbuch*, v, p. 708, who takes the passage as cultic and pre-Pauline. Cf. S. G. F. Brandon, *The Fall of Jerusalem and the Christian Church*, London, 1951, p. 82.
               The Roman Emperor, The Servant of the Lord, (perhaps Lucifer), and the Adamic motif have all contributed to the theme. See also F. Pratt, op. cit., vol. I, p. 456.

P. 42   That Mark 1. 13 casts a side-glance at Adam is noted by

J. Jeremias, *Theologisches Wörterbuch*, I, p. 141 (he takes the Lukan genealogy to have been influenced by Paul's speculation on Adam). So also E. Lohmeyer, *Markusevangelium*, ad loc.; V. Taylor, *The Gospel According to St. Mark*, 1952, p. 146b; R. Bultmann, op. cit., pp. 235, 250. For Adamic speculation in Jewish-Christianity, see H. J. Schoeps, op. cit., pp. 100ff.; for its origin p. 104, n. 1; also his *Ausfrühchristlicher Zeit*, Tübingen, 1950, pp. 7ff.

P. 43, n. 5 T.W. Manson, *J.T.S.*, April 1950, holds "that the upper ranks of the hierarchy, the High Priest and his immediate entourage, belonged to the Sadducean party, but the great mass of the rank and file priests, who were only in residence for a couple of weeks in the course of the year, were in a different category". S. W. Baron, *A Social and Religious History of the Jews*, vol. II, pt. II, p. 117, points out the significance of the priestly background of leaders in both the post-exilic and Jamnian periods. On the priesthood, see J. Jeremias, *Jerusalem zur Zeit-Jesu*, ad loc., and on the genius of the Pharisees, L. Finkelstein, *The Pharisees*, 1938–40. For the rôle of the priests, see J. L. Lauterbach, *Rabbinic Essays*, Cincinnati, 1951, pp. 196ff. After the days of the Soferim there were "democratic" tendencies "against the monopolization of the knowledge by the priests and in favor of spreading the knowledge of the Law among the people at large" (p. 197, n. 40). For a convenient survey see R. Marcus, *The Journal of Religion*, vol. XXXII, July 1952, pp. 153ff.

P. 44 C. H. Dodd, *According to the Scriptures*, 1952, rejects Rendel Harris' view and argues that "there were some parts of scripture which were early recognized as appropriate sources from which testimonia might be drawn" (p. 60).

P. 45, n. 2 Compare with C. H. Dodd, A. D. Nock, *Nuntius*, no. 5, 1951, p. 38.

P. 46, n. 3 W. H. Brownlee, op. cit., pp. 16f. translates *D.S.D.* IV: 22b-3 thus: "For God has chosen them for an eternal covenant so that theirs is all the glory of Adam [or man]." He renders אדם as Adam. A. Dupont-Sommer, op. cit., has seen here the *Ur-mensch* of Persian speculation, but most scholars have preferred to translate simply "man". See translations by Bo Reicke, Malik, Lambert, Van der Ploeg: bibliography in H. H. Rowley, op. cit. But in view of the probability that the Dead Sea Sect indulged in speculation on the *Ma'aseh Bereshîth* and of the frequent references to the glory of Adam to which we refer, W. H. Brownlee's rendering seems preferable. His reference is to the sinlessness of Adam. It should also be noted that the glory of Adam refers not only to his sinlessness as appears from the passages cited. Vermès and Molin now translate "Adam".

P. 51, n. 1   The date of the Clementines is treated by H. J. Schoeps in his monumental study, *Theologie und Geschichte des Judenchristentums*, Tübingen, 1949. Much material therein he traces to the last decades of the first century, but see G. Kümmel, *Theologische Rundschau*, Heft 2, 1954, pp. 147ff.

P. 52   For a similar interpretation of 1 Cor. 15. 44f. see J. Héring, *La Première Épitre de Saint Paul aux Corinthiens*, Paris, 1949, pp. 148f., who states that the doctrine of the twofold Adam is absent from Jewish Apocalyptic, the Talmud, and Hellenistic and Mandaean speculation. Hippolytus contains a slight parallel (*Philosophoumena*, v: 6: 11). Héring does not mention the polemic motif in Paul but does point out the significant differences between him and Philo. See also J. Jeremias, *Theologisches Wörterbuch*, 1, pp. 142ff.; he refers to the targumic treatment of Gen. 2. 7 and the use of *qal w^{a}hômer* in the passage. But he does not find here any emphasis on the fact that Christ is born *after* the first Adam as does J. Héring and as we did and as O. Cullmann, *Christ and Time*, p. 95, has emphasized. Jeremias refers 1 Cor. 15. 46 not to the two Adams but to the embodied states of Christians who first bear a physical and later, at the Parousia, a spiritual form. J. Héring's treatment of the text agrees with our understanding of the resurrection body noted on pp. 318f. In 1 Cor. 15. 49 there are two readings φορέσομεν and φορεσώμεν. It is the latter which has the weightiest attestation as J. Héring points out, but J. Jeremias accepts, by implication, the future. To read φορεσώμεν is to recognize that Christians are "in Christ" already ἐπουράνιοί and that the reference to the appearance of the Second Adam in 1 Cor. 15. 45 refers not to the Parousia but to the Incarnation. So J. Héring, op. cit., p. 149. Cf. R. Bultmann, op. cit., pp. 347ff.

P. 56, n. 1   Add to those who interpret "body" in 1 Cor. 11. 27f. of the Church, A. J. B. Higgins, *The Lord's Supper in the New Testament*, 1952, pp. 72ff. Contrast C. T. Craig in *The Joy of Study*, New York, 1951, p. 82.

P. 57, n. 1   Add: Cf. Traugott Schmidt, *Der Leib Christi*, 1919. Note that H. Schlier, *Christus und die Kirche in Epheserbrief*, 1930; E. Käsemann, *Leib und Leib Christi*, 1933, R. Bultmann, op. cit., pp. 199ff.—turn to Gnosticism for the background of the "Body".

P. 57, n. 5   See Stig Hanson, op. cit.; A. S. Peake, op. cit., p. 23, finds in the Adamic the fundamental doctrine of Paul; M. Black, *The Scottish Journal of Theology*, vol. vii, June, 1954, pp. 170–9.

Craig, op. cit., ignores the significance of Adamic speculation for understanding the term "body".

P. 61.   On the struggle between Universalism and Particularism add R. Marcus, *Law in the Apocrypha*, (1927), pp. 35f.; E. Lohmeyer, *Kultus und Evangelium*, (1942), pp. 21f.

P. 64   See also B. J. Bamberger, *Proselytism in the Talmudic Period*, Cincinatti, 1939. His conclusions agree with those of W. G. Braude, op. cit. Contrast J. Munck, *Paulus und die Heilsgeschichte*, Copenhagen, 1954, pp. 259ff.

P. 68, n. 5 J. Munck, op. cit., pp. 112f., insists that the Epistles agree with Acts in this.

P. 72   See W. D. Davies, *Torah in the Messianic Age and/or the Age to Come*, 1952; H. J. Schoeps, *Ausfrühchristlicher Zeit*, 1950, pp. 221ff.

P. 73   On Elisha b. Abuyah see R. T. Herford in *Essays in Honour of J. H. Hertz*, 1942, pp. 215f. That the ride through Jerusalem on a Sabbath is legendary makes it no less significant for our purpose.

P. 73, n. 1 It has been customary to take the "But I say unto you" of Mt. 5. 22, 28, 32, 34, 39 as the Messianic "I" of Jesus in which he repudiated the principle of the Halakah. See for bibliographical details, and criticism of the *linguistic* basis for the view, Morton Smith, *Tannaitic Parallels to the Gospels*, Philadelphia, 1951, pp. 27f.

P. 75   H. H. Rowley has surveyed the question in *The Biblical Doctrine of Election*, 1950; see also N. A. Dahl, *Das Volk Gottes*, Oslo, 1941, pp. 209ff. For later developments M. Simon, *Verus Israel*, Paris, 1948, pp. 100ff. He connects the concept of a new law in Christianity with that of the New Israel.

P. 76   On "the land" see N. A. Dahl, op. cit., pp. 17ff.

P. 79   That the idea of the "Remnant" should only be carefully used in the discussion of Old Testament Theology appears from E. W. Heaton, *J.T.S.*, N.S., vol. III, pt. 1, pp. 27ff. See Herntrich, *Theologisches Wörterbuch*, IV, 200ff., and Schrenk, ibid., p. 218, for the way in which for Paul "Das λεῖμμα ist nicht der Endzweck, sondern das Ziel ist Wiederannahme, Rettung von ganz Israel."

P. 83   T. W. Manson pointed out to me that Moore is not strictly right in connecting the Greek concept of immortality with the value of the individual personality in Greek thought. It was connected rather with the notion of some kind of indestructible substance which constituted the soul. See C. H. Dodd's first Ingersoll Lecture on the Immortality of Man, Harvard University, for a brilliant treatment of the problem concerned.

P. 84   See *Theologisches Wörterbuch*, I, p. 572.

P. 87, n. 6 On "in Christ", see F. Büchsel, and J. A. T. Robinson, op. cit.

P. 89, n. 6 Add: A. D. Nock, "Hellenistic Mysteries and Christian Sacraments", in *Mnemosyne*, S. iv, vol. v, 1952, pp. 12ff.: he shows how metaphors derived from the mysteries came to be used in the experience of philosophic discipleship (p. 189), and in Judaism.

P. 91   See above note on the *D.S.S.* and Paulinism, on μυστήριον; also W. D. Davies, "'Knowledge' in the D.S.S.", *H.T.R.*, July, 1953.

P. 91, n. 3 Add: W. F. Flemington, *The New Testament Doctrine of Baptism*, 1948, pp. 76f.; G. W. H. Lampe, *The Seal of the Spirit*, 1951, p. 93. Contrast R. Bultmann, op. cit., p. 298, *et passim*. O. Cullmann, *Baptism in the New Testament*, (Eng. Trans.), 1950, p. 14, n. 2, writes: "The affinity with analogous rites of the mystery religions cannot be denied." But he does not enlarge. C. H. Kraeling, *John the Baptist*, 1951, dismisses Mystery explanations of the Baptist's rite, pp. 106ff.; he has no occasion to deal with Paul. The *D.S.S.* may throw light on the background of the Baptist, see W. H. Brownlee, *Interpretation*, vol. IX, No. 1 (Jan., 1955), pp. 71–80.

P. 98   Others who reject E. R. Goodenough's position are N. A. Dahl, op. cit., p. 301, n. 181; W. Völker, *Theologische Blätter*, 1937, pp. 297–301; A. D. Nock, *Mnemosyne*, op. cit. But see G. D. Kilpatrick, *The Expository Times*, vol. LXIV, Oct. 1952, pp. 4ff.

P. 98, n. 1 For a brilliant statement of the situation see A. D. Nock, *Nuntius*, op. cit., p. 38f.; review of R. Bultmann, *Das Urchristentum im Rahmen der antiken Religionen*, Zürich, 1949.

P. 99   Cf. C. H. Dodd, *According to the Scriptures*, 1952, pp. 113f. J. A. T. Robinson, op. cit., p. 58, makes striking use of this idea of solidarity in Acts 26. 14f.; cf. 9. 4f.; 22. 7f. Cf. Dibelius-Kümmel, *Paul* (E.T.), Philadelphia, 1953, pp. 55f.

P. 100   G. S. Duncan urges the dependence of Jesus on Ezekiel for the Son of Man concept, *Jesus, Son of Man*, 1949, pp. 145f. C. H. Dodd, op. cit., p. 117, n. 1, rejects this. He refers to Pss. 8, 80, And Daniel 7 as those passages containing the term Son of Man which can be proved to have been used as *testimonia*. See M. Black, *Scottish Journal of Theology*, vol. VI, no. 1, 1953, pp. 10f. for 1 Enoch and N.T.

P. 100, n. 8 R. Bultmann, op. cit., pp. 26ff., re-examines the problem of the Messianic consciousness of Jesus only to reject any such. The Messiahship of Jesus has been superimposed upon him by the Church. Jesus neither reinterpreted the traditional concept of the Messiah nor regarded Himself as the future Messiah. (Bultmann even doubts the choice of the Twelve by Jesus, p. 37. See the convincing refutation of this in J. Wagennmann, *Die Stellung des Apostels Paulus neben den Zwolf in den ersten zwei Jahrhunderten*, 1926, p. 6. Wagennmann examines the views of Johannes Weiss and R. Schütz and others). The answer to R. Bultmann is still that given by A. E. J. Rawlinson, *The New Testament Doctrine of the Christ*, 1926, pp. 11f., this apart from R. Bultmann's extreme historical pessimism in dealing with the New Testament documents. Cf. O. Cullmann, op. cit., p. 111.

P. 101   For the centrality of Jerusalem, see J. Jeremias, *Bulletin of Society for New Testament Studies*, III, Oxford, 1952; R. H. Lightfoot, *The Message of St. Mark*, 1950, p. 64; for Paul and Jerusalem, J. Munck, op. cit., pp. 277ff.

P. 103   For the Messianic Age as a New Exodus, see N. A. Dahl, op. cit., pp. 38f., 284 n., 46f.; also W. D. Davies, *Torah in the Messianic Age and/or the Age to Come*.

P. 108   Compare from another point of view O. Cullmann, *Christ and Time*, pp. 218ff. At the same time, see his criticism of S. Kierkegaard's insistence on contemporaneity, p. 168.

P. 109, n. 1 For an interesting sidelight on the relation of this to pseudepigraphic writing see L. Finkelstein, *Akiba*, ad loc.

P. 109, n. 2 Add: 1 John 1. 1-4 where "we" stands for the group. See C. H. Dodd, *The Johannine Epistles*, 1946, pp. 9f.; on "we" in contemporary literature, see A. D. Nock, *Gnomon*, Band 25, 1953, p. 503, n. 2.

P. 110, n. 1 On the Passover and the Last Supper see the important work of J. Jeremias, *Die Abendmahlsworte Jesu*,[2] 1949. The literature is admirably surveyed in A. J. B. Higgins, *The Lord's Supper in the New Testament*, London, 1952. See especially pp. 45ff. But see G. D. Kilpatrick, "The Last Supper", in *Expository Times*, vol. LXIV, Oct. 1952, pp. 4f. Jacob Z. Lauterbach, *Rabbinic Essays*, Cincinnati, 1951, throughout emphasizes the impact of Greek rule on Palestine. He connects the emergence of the Mishnah-form with the change from Persian to Greek rule, pp. 182ff. For the way in which festal practices of the Graeco-Roman world may have impinged upon Jewish and early Christian practice, see the interesting study by P. Carrington, *The Primitive Christian Calendar*, Cambridge, 1952, pp. 72f., 78; but see W. D. Davies, *H.T.R.* (forthcoming), on this work.

P. 111, n. 4 Add: T. F. Glasson in *The Second Advent*, also "The Kerygma: is our version correct" in *The Hibbert Journal*, vol. LI, Jan. 1953, pp. 129ff.

P. 113, n. 3   Add: B. J. Bamberger, op. cit., 134ff.

P. 116   See also R. Bultmann, *Der Stil der paulinischen Predigt und die Kynisch-stoische Diatribe*, Göttingen, 1910; *New Testament Theology*, pp. 216ff.

P. 120, n. 4   Add: See also H. G. W. Lampe, op. cit., pp. 93f.

P. 121   On Jewish Proselyte baptism and the New Testament, see W. F. Flemington, op. cit., pp. 3f.; bibliography C. H. Kraeling, op. cit., pp. 95ff., 202ff.; H. H. Rowley, *The Unity of the Bible*, 1953, p. 151, n. 1 and 2.

P. 131   The *D.S.S.* have greatly enriched us in our understanding of the sect life of pre-Christian Judaism. Thus *D.S.D.* in particular shows us an example of the discipline imposed on such.

P. 137, n. 4   Add: V. Taylor, *The Gospel According to St. Mark*, 1952, pp. 125ff. On Matthew and Paul see C. H. Dodd, *The Expository Times*, vol. LVIII, 1947, pp. 294ff.

P. 143, n. 4   Add: R. Bultmann, *Jesus the Word* (Eng. Trans.), pp. 55f.; J. Weiss, *Paulus und Jesus*, p. 38, Rengenstorf, *Theologisches Wörterbuch*, II, pp. 155ff.; T. W. Manson, *The Teaching of Jesus*,[2] p. 48.

P. 144   On the term *talmíd* see T. W. Manson, op. cit., pp. 237ff.: he argues that Jesus did not use this term for his disciples but rather שׁוּלְיָא, the choice of which indicates Jesus' definite opposition to the whole scribal system. He favours this on the ground that μου ἄξιος in Matt. 10. 37f. is equivalent to שָׁוֵי לִי which was corrupted to שׁוּלְיָא. But see the usage of the *D.S.S.* as treated by Krister Stendahl, ΑΞΙΟΣ *im Lichte der Texte der Qumran Höhle, Nuntius*, no. 7, 1952, pp. 53f. "Die 'Würdigkeit' ist hier also *grundsatzlich ethisch* gedacht, umfasst aber auch das rechte Verstandnis des Gesetzes . . ." (our italics).

P. 145   See further C. H. Dodd, *Law and Gospel*, 1951, p. 65, whose treatment is largely like that of O. Cullmann, *Christ and Time*, pp. 222ff., except that it allows for a more just place to the *words* of Jesus. R. Bultmann, op. cit., p. 260, fails to recognize Paul's familiarity with the words of Jesus. T. F. Torrance, *The Doctrine of Grace in the Apostolic Fathers*, 1948, overemphasizes the distinction between Law and Gospel in the New Testament.

P. 148, n. 2   Add: See also H. Odeberg, *The Fourth Gospel, Interpreted in its Relation to Contemporaneous Religious Currents*, Uppsala, 1929, pp. 286ff.

P. 149, n. 4   Add: see especially Morton Smith, op. cit., p. 159; O. Cullmann, *Revue d'histoire et de philosophie religieuses*, no. 1 (1950), pp. 12ff.

P. 150, n. 3   For the concept of a new law in later Judaism see M. Simon, op. cit., p. 100.

P. 152   O. Cullmann, *Christ and Time, passim,* fully recognizes the work of Christ both in creation and redemption. See a forthcoming study by N. A. Dahl, *Christ, Creation and Church.*

P. 156   On Matt. 11. 25–30 see T. Arvedson, *Das Mysterium Christi,* Uppsala, 1937; W. D. Davies, *H.T.R.,* July, 1953, " 'Knowledge' in the D.S.S. and Matt. 11. 25–30".

P. 162   On pre-existence in the New Testament see A. Harnack, *The History of Dogma* (Eng. Trans.), vol. i, pp. 318ff.

P. 163   On W. L. Knox's thesis see W. F. Albright, op. cit., pp. 282ff., 338, n. 48, who claims that "the original Canaanite text of Prov. 8–9 can hardly be later than the seventh century B.C." The glorification of wisdom he finds in the fifteenth century B.C.: it is originally a Canaanite-Aramaean figure.

P. 170, n. 4   Add: Gutbrod, *Theologishes Wörterbuch,* IV, p. 1048.

P. 171, n. 4   Such verses as Isa. 49. 16 are not far removed from a kind of "Platonism". See N. A. Dahl, op. cit., pp. 78f.; also a forthcoming study by C. K. Barrett on *The Eschatology of Hebrews,* where the possibility of reconciling Platonic and Apocalyptic concepts is recognized.

P. 175   Contrast sharply O. Cullmann, op. cit., pp. 179–84, who like R. Bultmann, whom he cites, denies that we are to find any basis for a Natural Theology in Rom. 1. 18ff. His exegesis here seems, however, forced.

P. 177   See R. Bultmann, op. cit., pp. 229f., on the relation between cosmology and soteriology in Paul.

P. 182, n. 1   J. A. T. Robinson, *The Body,* p. 12, n. 1, rejects this, as he does R. Bultmann's interpretation of the "body" "as the self as the object of its own consciousness or action". See R. Bultmann, op. cit., pp. 202f.

P. 182, n. 6   Contrast with C. H. Dodd, W. L. Knox in *Theology,* vol. LII, July 1949, p. 33, who cites Diog. Laert., VII, 7, 143, to show that the divine element pervading all things in Stoicism had already been described as νοῦς by Posidonius.

P. 183   R. Bultmann, op. cit., pp. 333ff., though allowing the materiality of the Spirit in Paul, concludes that "the sporadically occurring notion of the Spirit as material is not one that is really determinative for Paul's concept . . . "

P. 188f.   Compare C. K. Barrett, *The Holy Spirit and the Gospel Tradition,* 1947, pp. 18ff., whose conclusions are essentially like ours, as to the rôle of the Spirit in and on creation.

P. 191, n. 6   Add: R. Bultmann, op. cit., pp. 164–8; A. J. Festugière, "Cadre de la Mystique Hellénistique" in *Aux Sources de la Tradition Chrétienne,* pp. 74ff.

P. 193   R. Bultmann, who throughout emphasizes gnostic motifs in

Paul, pp. 172, 182, treats πνευματικός and τέλειος as of gnostic derivation. K. G. Kuhn has discovered the term πνευματικός in a Hebrew dress in the D.S.S.

P. 195, n. 2 R. Bultmann's understanding of Paul is essentially similar, op. cit., p. 188.

P. 195, n. 4 Add the excellent discussion of 2 Cor. 5. 16 by F. C. Porter, *The Journal of Biblical Literature*, vol. xlvii, (1928), pp. 257-75.

P. 198 Here Bultmann is equally emphatic. The Spirit does not mean for Paul the capacity for mystical experiences, op. cit., 335, 339f., 160f.

P. 199, n. 4 Add: F. Cumont, *H.T.R.*, vol. xxvi, (1933), p. 158: "La fameuse 'Mithrasliturgie' qui n'est pas une liturgie et n'est pas mithriaque." See also A. D. Nock's warning against regarding *Gnosis* as "a specific entity", in *Nuntius*, op. cit., p. 37.

P. 200, n. 3 Add: F. C. Burkitt, *The Church and Gnosis*, 1932, pp. 35f.

P. 212 A. Guttmann in *The Hebrew Union College Annual*, vol. xx, Cincinnati, 1947, pp. 363ff., has examined miracles in Talmudic Judaism: he found an increasing disinclination to rely on miracle, especially in the decision of legal matters. This disinclination finally found expression in an anonymous Tannaitic principle אין מזכירין מעשה נסים, "one should not mention miracles," i.e., as evidence in deciding any controversy involving a legal decision. A. Guttmann explains this in the light of the fact that miracles were often regarded in the first century as evidence for the truth; they played, therefore, a prominent place in the proclamation of Christianity and accounted much for its advancement. This in turn engendered, by way of reaction, an unfavourable attitude towards miracle among the Rabbis. (See A. Guttmann, op. cit., pp. 391ff. He traces the above-mentioned principle back to the third Tannaitic generation; he refers to Ber. 60a, Yeb. 121b, Yer. Yeb. 16. 4; 15d; Hul. 34a; Yer. Shek. 4. 3; 50a.) (The distinction drawn by A. Guttmann between miracles which have already happened and are used as evidence in halakic discussions and "potential" miracles does not here concern us.) Connected with this was the sudden change in the attitude taken towards the *bath qôl*. The famous halakic controversy between the House of Hillel and Shammai was resolved by the advent of a *bath qôl* (see p. 262). A. Guttmann forcibly argues for dating this event very shortly after A.D. 70 (pp. 371ff.). But this poses a problem. Why did the *bath qôl*, which immediately after A.D. 70 could play such a crucial part in settling one of the most important problems of Jewish unity, cease to exert any further influence on the development of the Law? Guttmann, following Goodspeed, refers to the upsurge of Pauline influence between A.D. 90–100 as witnessed in the emergence of the Pauline corpus. He connects with this an awakening on the part of Rabbinic leaders to the menace of Christianity. One result of this awakening—which others too date about this time, as we saw above—was the rejection of the *bath qôl* in halakic discussions, in favour of the majority decision, because of its popularity with Christians.

One may question the necessity of connecting Pauline Christianity specifically with this rejection; Christian forces in general may have been responsible. But, in any case, A. Guttmann's article throws much light on Jewish-Christian interactions in the first century, light which need not, however, be confined necessarily to the last decade. Morton Smith has examined P. Fiebig's book *Jüdische Wundergeschichten des neutestamentlichen Zeitalters*, 1911. He admits the presence of miracles among the Tannaim but "[in the matter of miracles] the parallels between the Gospels and T.L. [Tannaitic literature] are not so important as the differences between them, and that difference is that stories like these [i.e., miraculous ones] are very frequent in the Gospels and almost totally lacking in T.L." (op. cit., p. 84). A heightening of the miraculous would naturally be expected in the literature of the Messianic community and a corresponding reaction against it in the relevant literature of the old Israel.

P. 216   For other instances of the way in which elements prominent in Christianity were suppressed in Rabbinic sources, see H. J. Schoeps, *Theologie und Geschichte des Judenchristentums*, p. 90; J. Bonsirven, op. cit., vol. I, pp. 79f.

P. 218   The teaching of the *D.S.S.* on the Spirit should further make it impossible to regard the Spirit as ethically neutral. See *D.S.D.* IV: 2, etc.

P. 220f.   See R. Bultmann, op. cit., pp. 160, 337.

P. 224   See W. D. Davies, *Torah in the Messianic Age and/or the Age to come*; C. H. Dodd, *According to the Scriptures*, pp. 44ff., 85, 124; Quell, *Theologishes Wörterbuch*, II, p. 127; Behm, ibid., pp. 132ff. G. Ostborn, *Tōrā in the Old Testament*, Lund, 1945, pp. 157ff., has, independently, treated the Christian Dispensation in the same light as we do here. See also O. Cullmann, *Revue d'histoire et de philosophie religieuses*, op. cit.

P. 226   For obedience in Paul, see Rom. 16. 19; 1. 5; 2 Cor. 9. 13; 10. 5f.

P. 229   See C. H. Dodd, op. cit., pp. 123ff.

P. 231f.   On the Temple in Judaism, see E. Lohmeyer, *Kultus und Evangelium*, 1942, ad loc.

P. 233, n. 1 Behm's position is accepted by L. Morris, *J.T.S.*, N.S., vol. III, October 1952, pp. 216–27.

P. 234 See the debate between H. H. Rowley and C. J. Cadoux, *The Expository Times*, vol. 58, pp. 43ff., 69ff., 305ff.

P. 237 R. Bultmann constantly uses the term propitiation although he does not regard the propitiatory as the characteristic Pauline view of Christ's death. See op. cit., pp. 289, 296. On p. 298 he interprets Paul's concept of the Death of Christ in terms of the Mysteries. Against C. H. Dodd's understanding of ἱλαστήριον, see Leon Morris, *Expository Times*, May, 1951, pp. 227–33.

P. 241 There is an increasing tendency to connect the Pauline Epistles as other New Testament documents with the Jewish-Christian year. See P. Carrington, *The Primitive Christian Calendar*, Cambridge, 1952, pp. 37ff., 43. But see R. P. Casey, *Theology*, vol. LV, October 1952, pp. 362ff. For the way in which early Christians may have drawn up catechisms in anti-cultic terms, see C. F. D. Moule, *J.T.S.*, N.S., vol. I, April 1950, pp. 29–41.

P. 248f. On 1 Cor. 11. 25, see O. Cullmann, op. cit., who argues that κύριος is here and elsewhere equivalent to the *tradition* of the Apostolic Church regarded as the voice of the living Christ. He too emphasizes the parallelism between the transmission of Christian and Rabbinic tradition. See A. J. B. Higgins, op. cit., pp. 24ff. According to Higgins, J. Jeremias' attempt to interpret the words εἰς τὴν ἐμὴν ἀνάμνησιν as meaning that "God may remember me" has been proved untenable by W. C. van Unnik, "Kanttekeningen bij een nieuwe verklaring van de Anamnese-woorden" in *Nederlands Theologisch Tijdschrift*, IV, 6 (Aug. 1950), pp. 369–77. For H. Lietzmann's view that Paul is responsible for the commandment "Do this in remembrance of me", see *Messe und Herrenmahl*, 1926, p. 255. See A. J. B. Higgins, op. cit., for bibliographical details.

P. 260 On Covenant, see Quell and Behm, *Theologisches Wörterbuch*, II, pp. 106–27, 127–37. On the comparative neglect of the idea of the covenant among the Rabbis, J. Bonsirven, op. cit., vol. I, pp. 79f.

P. 262, n. 2 Add: T. Arvedson, op. cit., p. 179.

P. 262, n. 5 Add: L. Ginzberg, *Hebrew Union College Annual*, vol. I, 1924, pp. 219f.

P. 264 For the liveliness of the Maccabbaean tradition in the first century, see W. R. Farmer, *J.T.S.*, N.S., vol. III, April 1952, pp. 62ff. See also E. Lohmeyer, *Revue d'Histoire et de Philosophie religieuses*, 1927, pp. 316–29, on "L'idée du martyre dans le judaisme et dans le Christianisme primitif".

P. 267, n. 4 Add: *According to the Scriptures*, 1952, p. 125.

P. 269   On the merits of the Fathers in the Apocrypha, see R. Marcus, *Law in the Apocrypha*, p. 14ff.

P. 274, n. 1   Compare for the New Testament generally C. T. Craig, *The Journal of Religion*, vol. XXIX, 1944, pp. 240–5; R. Bultmann, op. cit., pp. 31, 46f., 50f. Contrast T. W. Manson, *The Teaching of Jesus*,[2] pp. 230ff.; C. H. Dodd, *According to the Scriptures*, 1952, pp. 118ff., 123ff.; J. Jeremias, *Theologisches Wörterbuch*, v, pp. 653ff.

P. 275, n. 5   Add: R. Bultmann, op. cit., p. 47.

P. 283   H. H. Rowley has exhaustively re-examined the question whether pre-Christian Judaism knew a suffering Messiah in a masterly essay, "The Suffering Servant and the Davidic Messiah", in the *Servant of the Lord*, 1952, pp. 61ff. He rejects very forcibly the position taken in the text but recognizes that the Davidic Messiah and the suffering servant of the Lord "are drawn from common roots" and "had many points of connexion with one another" (pp. 86, 88). Since H. H. Rowley's work J. Jeremias has reiterated his view in *Theologisches Wörterbuch*, ibid. Particular attention should be given to the work of Scandinavian scholars (see, e.g., A. Bentzen, *Messias, Moses Redivivus, Menschensohn*, 1948): details are found in H. H. Rowley's work. It has not been possible to recast our treatment in the light of this. See further M. Black, *Scottish Journal of Theology*, vol. 6, no. 1, pp. 1ff.; Brownlee, *B.A.S.O.R.*, December, 1953, October, 1954.

Fragments of the original book of Enoch are among the D.S.S.

P. 307, n. 2   Cf. T. W. Manson, op. cit., p. 277, n. 2.

P. 310, n. 4   Add: A. M. Ramsey, *The Resurrection of Christ*,[2] 1946, p. 108.

P. 315, n. 2   Add: see further R. Otto, *The Kingdom of God and the Son of Man* (Eng. Trans.); J. Bonsirven, op. cit., vol. I, p. 314. Note must be taken in connection with all this of the important work of O. Cullmann, *Christ and Time*, in which the problem of Hellenism and Hebraism in the New Testament is brought to a head with brilliant clarity. Cullmann objects to the use of such phrases as "an eternally existent kingdom", insisting that the concept of time in the New Testament is a linear one: "the Greek manner of distinguishing between time and eternity is foreign to it". (See F. V. Filson in an unpublished paper summarized in *J.B.L.*, vol. LXXI, March 1952, p. xvi.) But if our treatment be sound, Greek conceptions of time, as of other things, had already invaded Judaism, and it would appear that O. Cullmann's work suffers from an extreme logicality. For a criticism of O. Cullmann, see John Marsh, *The Fulness of Time*, 1952, Appendix.

P. 319   The whole discussion on pp. 308–19 should be compared and contrasted with that of O. Cullmann, op. cit., pp. 237–42. He resolves the apparent contradiction between 1 Cor. 15 and 2 Cor. 5 by urging that "the being with Christ" which is the Christian's lot in death "does not yet signify resurrection of the body but does signify a closer connection with Christ which is already effected through the resurrection power of the Holy Spirit" (p. 240; cf. pp. 88, 143). At many points O. Cullmann's position agrees with ours. He finds no essential contradiction between 1 Cor. 15 and 2 Cor. 5: he emphasizes that already Christians through the Spirit have a possession which cannot be lost. He denies, however, what we have argued above, that already a "spiritual body" is being formed. His treatment provides us therefore with a hiatus: he fails to explain the nature of the possession which the Spirit gives, this because his treatment is vitiated by his refusal to recognize that there is a two-fold aspect to the Age to Come. The same applies to P. Menoud, *Le Sort des Trépassés*, Paris, 1945, pp. 32ff. Neither O. Cullmann nor P. Menoud explains what that Christian entity is which is "with Christ" before the final Resurrection. It is not enough with Cullmann merely to define the Spirit as "the partial anticipation of the end" in the present (p. 236). That "with Christ" speaks of "no external occurrence ... but of a common organic functioning" is shown by J. A. T. Robinson, op. cit., p. 63, who interprets resurrection in 2 Cor. 5. 1 of the Church, op. cit., pp. 76ff. See also J. Dupont, *L'union avec le Christ*, p. 150, n. 1; W. C. van Unnik in *Studia Paulina*, 1953, pp. 202ff. Both of these criticize the position taken in the text.

P. 324   On the "psychological" interpretation of Paul's conversion see especially E. Stauffer, *Die Theologie des Neuen Testaments*,[5] pp. 21, 238, n. 53, who takes the position adopted in our text.

P. 329   On the imperative participle see further C. F. D. Moule, *An Idiom Book of New Testament Greek*, Cambridge, 1953, pp. 179ff. He refers to W. Bauer's claim that the imperatival use of the participle is found in pre-Christian *Koine*, with which compare H. G. Meecham, *E.T.*, vol. LVIII, May, 1947, p. 204f. The *D.S.S.* present us with evidence probably of the way in which the Hebrew usage developed. See *D.S.D.* 1, 18ff. on which W. H. Brownlee, *Bulletin of the American Schools of Oriental Research*, Supplementary Studies, Nos. 10–12, p. 9, comments that "The force of the verb is carried forward from line 18 to the participles which follow, giving to them the sense of the imperative." One can easily see how the separation of the verb from the participle in this way could and did easily lead to the emergence of the imperatival participle

INDEXES

I. QUOTATIONS FROM THE OLD TESTAMENT

Figures in black type refer to pages

Gen. I.   37, 44, n. 2, 47, 166, 182, n. 6,
  I. I   152   [217, n. 4
  I. 2   40, 41, 44, n. 2, 47, 48, 188, n. 7,
    189, 189, n. I
  I. 26   54
  I. 27   48, 326
  I. 31   22
  2.   37, 47, 217, n. 4
  2.   37, 44, n. 2, 47, 217, n. 4
  2. 15   48
  2. 18 f.   42, n. 4
  3.   38, 44
  3. 8   164, n. 3
  4. 7   25, n. 2
  5. I   54, 55, 326
  6. 1–4   38
  6. 5   26, n. 3
  6. 15   240
  6. 16   240
  8. 21   26, n. 3
  9. 4   115, n. I
  15. 6   222, 209
  17. 9   104
  17. 12   104
  17. 13 f.   104
  18. 18   164, n. 4
  49. 10   277
Exod. 4. 31   269
  12. I   206, n. 6
  12. 18 f.   114, n. 7
  12. 26   103
  13. 8   102, 103
  19. I   104
  19. 3 f.   260
  20. 10 f.   114, n. 5
  23. 2   215
  24. 8   251
  24. 11   306
  25. 16   239, 240
  25. 16 (17)   240, n. 2
  25. 17   240
  25. 17–22   238
  31. 16   104
  32. 31 f.   83, n. 6
Lev. 4. 2 f.   255, n. 3
  16. I f.   238, n. I

17. 7–9   114, n. 3
17. 10 ff.   114, n. 6, 245
17. 11   235
18. 6–26   114, n. 4
19. 18   55
23. 10   297, n. 2
23. 42   313
24. 10–12   184
24. 11–16   164, n. 8
25. 23   77, n. 2
Num. II. 29   204, n. I
  15. 22–31   255, n. 3
  15. 30   255, n. 3
  15. 31   260, n. 4
  19. 2   262
  24. 16   164, n. 8
Deut. 4. 6   109, n. 2
  4. 12   260
  4. 13   260
  6. 4 ff.   262
  6. 23   103
  6. 30   103
  8. 15   153
  10 ff.   104
  10. 16   75, n. 3
  11. 10   170
  11. 13 ff.   262
  16. 3   252, n. I
  17. 12   255, n. 3
  18. 12   206
  21. 23   227, n. 3
  26. 1–11   106, n. 2
  26. 5 f.   109, n. 2
  29. 1–7   260, n. 4
  30. 6   75, n. 3
  30. 11–14   153
  30 12–14   154, n. 2
  31. 16   104
  31. 20   104
  31. 21   26, n. 3
  32. 20   84, n. 6
  34. 10   157, n. 4
Joshua 23. 16   260, n. 4
  24.   109, n. 2
Judges 2. 19–20   260, n. 4
  6. 34   203, n. 5

Judges 14. 6.   203, n. 4
    15. 14   203, n. 5
Ruth 2. 10   114, n. 1
1 Sam. 10. 6   203, n. 6
    19. 20 f.   203, n. 4
    26. 19   77, n. 2
2 Sam. 6. 12 f.   203, n. 6
1 Kings 7. 21   315
2 Kings 5. 17   77, n. 2
    17. 15   260, n. 4
    17. 26 f.   77, n. 2
1 Chron. 28. 9   26, n. 3
    29. 18   26, n. 3
Neh. 1. 9   81, n. 7
Job 4. 17   18
    10. 4   18
    15. 7 ff.   45
    25. 4 f.   18
    26. 13   188, n. 7, 189
    27. 3   188, n. 7
    28. 23   167
    28. 25-7   167
    33. 4   165, 188, n. 7
Ps. 2. 2   279
    2. 6   279
    2. 9   313
    2. 10-12   279
    9. 5   55, n. 5
    9. 17   59, n. 5
    10. 2-4   59, n. 5
    19. 8   174, n. 1
    19. 13   255, n. 3
    22.   60, n. 6
    33. 6   166, 188, n. 7, 189
    33. 8-9   166
    34. 12 ff.   133, n. 1
    34. 15   133, n. 1
    46. 4   279
    50.   165
    50. 13   256, n. 6
    56. 5   18
    58. 10   59, n. 5
    62. 3   279
    62. 9   279
    64. 8   40
    65.   60, n. 6
    68. 2   59, n. 5
    72. 10-11   279
    72. 11   62, n. 6
    74. 9   209, n. 2
    78. 39   18
    86.   60, n. 6
    87.   60, n. 6
    89. 27   279

    93. 3 f.   40
103. 14   18, 26, n. 3
104. 29 f.   189
104. 30   188, n. 7, 189
107. 20   165
110. 1   161
110. 1-3   161
110. 3   162
113. 3 f.   40
119. 10   225, n. 2
119. 50   165
123. 6   189
125. 3   59, n. 5
139. 5   48
139. 16   53
Prov. 4. 2   171
    8.   152
    8. 22   151, 160, 161
    8. 22 f.   152, 170
    8. 30   172
    8. 35 a f.   168
    10. 30   77, n. 2
Eccles. 4. 4   22
Isa. 1. 4   203, n. 7
    2. 2-4   60
    4. 3-5   78, n. 2
    4. 4   84, n. 6
    5. 30   40
    6.   164, n. 5
    9. 2   279
    9. 7   279
    11. 2   281
    11. 2 f.   204, n. 4
    11. 3   283
    11. 4-5   279
    11. 6   37, n. 6
    11. 9   72, n. 3, 160
    11. 12   82, n. 3
    19.   60
    19. 15   293, 204
    20. 3   20, n. 3
    26. 10   59, n. 5
    26. 19   299, n. 5
    27. 13   82, n. 1
    29. 16   26, n. 3
    31. 3   18
    40. 6   18, 20
    40. 13   189
    40. 20 f.   164, n. 6
    42. 1   204, n. 5, 279
    42. 6   279
    43. 5   81, n. 6
    43. 10   165
    43. 23   274

Isa. 44. 3 204
44. 3–4 788, n. 7
45. 23 274
46. 3f. 279
48. 4 279
49. 3 279
49. 6 60, n. 5, 276
49. 7 279
49. 15–16 82, n. 7
50. 45 279
52. 13 274, 279
53. 100, 275, 278
53. 4 282, 283
53. 5–6 282
53. 7 274, 275
53. 8 274
53. 11 279
53. 12 274
54. 7 81, n. 6
56. 62, n. 6
59. 2 206
59. 21 204, n. 4
64. 4 307, n. 3
65. 25 37, n. 6
66. 24 20
Jer. 1. 1 80, n. 3
1. 2 789
1. 4 207, n. 7
1. 32 80, n. 3
3. 12f. 80, n. 6
4. 4 75, n. 3
4. 22 84, n. 6
5. 22 40
11. 7 82, n. 4
11. 10 104
12. 16f. 60, n. 2
16. 19 60, n. 2
17. 5 18
20. 34 82, n. 4
20. 41 82, n. 4
23. 5–6 279
31. 2–6 80
31. 18–20 80
31. 21–2 80
31. 25f. 80
31. 31–4 158, n. 3, 224, n. 1
31. 33 72, n. 2, 104
31. 34 157, n. 4
31. 35 40
32. 6ff. 80, n. 7
38. 36 40
Ezek. 1. 3 206, 206, n. 4
1. 4ff. 37
1. 28 164, n. 5

2. 2 186
3. 1 203, n. 7
5. 13 81, n. 3
13. 1f. 207
16. 82, n. 6
16. 38 81, n. 2
17. 20 240, n. 4
20. 9 81, n. 2
20. 22 81, n. 2
28. 45
28. 25 77, n. 2
36. 5f. 81, n. 2
36. 16–38. 81, n. 5
37. 183, n. 6, 223, n. 4
37. 5f. 186
37. 10 188, n. 7, 189
37. 11–14 204, n. 1
37. 12–14 78, n. 2
37. 24 81, n. 5
37. 26 82, n. 5, 224, n. 4
39. 25 81, n. 2
39. 25f. 81, n. 4
43. 14 240, n. 4
43. 27 240, n. 6
Dan. 7. 100
7. 9 280, n. 1
7. 9–14 280, n. 1
7. 13 280, n. 1
7. 13–14 78, n. 2
7. 14 62, n. 6
7. 21 280, n. 1
7. 22–7 78, n. 2
7. 25 280, n. 1
8. 2 207
10. 4 207
12. 1–3 299, n. 5
12. 2 306
Hos. 1. 2 77, n. 2
2. 1 84, n. 6
2. 23 77, n. 2
4. 1 157, n. 4, 203, n. 7
5. 1 203, n. 7
6. 6 157, n. 4, 258
6. 7 260, n. 4
8. 1 260, n. 4
9. 1 203, n. 7
14. 1 203, n. 7
Joel 2. 28 216
2. 28–9 204
Amos 3. 1 203, n. 7
3. 2 78, 109
3. 3 157, n. 4
4. 1 203, n. 7
5. 1 203, n. 7

Amos 9. 1–15   81, n. 7
      9. 15   77, n. 2
Mic. 2. 12   81, n. 7
      4. 1–3   60
      4. 6f.   81, n. 7
      5. 1   160, 161
Hab. 1. 4   59, n. 5
      1. 13   59, n. 5
      2. 4   222
      2. 18   26, n. 3
Zeph. 3. 19   81, n. 7
Zech. 2. 11   65

2. 12   77, n. 2
2. 13   20
4. 10   53
9. 9   279
9. 14   82, n. 1
10. 8–10   81, n. 7
12. 10   205, n. 1
12. 12   276
14.   62, n. 6
Mal. 1. 11   60, n. 8
      3. 16–17   78, n. 2

II. QUOTATIONS FROM THE APOCRYPHA AND PSEUD-EPIGRAPHA OF THE OLD TESTAMENT

1 Macc. 1. 15   261, n. 2
        1. 57   261, n. 2
        2. 20   261, n. 2
        2. 23 f.   264
        2. 50   261, n. 2
        2. 57   261, n. 2
        4. 46   209
        7. 12   264
        9. 27   209
        14. 41   209
2 Macc. 1. 6   82
        1. 18   82
        4. 9   300, n. 1
        6. 18   264
        7. 10f.   300, n. 1
        7. 32   83, n. 2
        7. 33   272, n. 1
        7. 37   272, n. 1
        7. 38   272, n. 1
        12. 43f.   299, n. 6
        14. 15   83, n. 2
        14. 46   300, n. 1
3 Macc. 6. 3   83, n. 2
        6. 11   30, n. 2
Tobit 13. 6f.   81, n. 9
      13. 11   61, n. 1
      14. 7   81, n. 9
Judith 7. 30   82, n. 10, 83, n. 2
       8. 18f.   30, n. 3
Ecclus. 3. 21–4   37, n. 7
        7. 8f.   256, n. 4
        15. 11–14   20, n. 3
        15. 24   32, n. 1
        17. 7f.   83, n. 2
        17. 11   261, n. 1
        17. 17f.   83, n. 8

23. 3 ff.   169
24. 4–10   82, n. 9, 83, n. 2, 169
24. 9   161
24. 23   169, 261, n. 1
24. 24   38, n. 5
25. 24   32, n. 1
28. 7   261, n. 1
34. 18f.   256, n. 5
36. 11   81, n. 9
39. 8   261, n. 1
42. 2   261, n. 1
45. 5   261, n. 1
45. 17   261, n. 1
47. 22   82, n. 10, 83, n. 2
48. 10f.   81, n. 9, 276
49. 16   46, n. 3
51.   156, 157, 158
51. 1–12   156
51. 13–22   156
51. 23 f.   157
51. 23–30   156
Wisd. of Sol. 1. 7   165
             1. 15   302
             2. 4   153, n. 4
             2. 23f.   32, n. 1
             3. 1–4   302
             3. 8   302, n. 4
             4. 1   302
             4. 7   302
             4. 10   302
             8. 13   302
             8. 17   302
             9. 4   161, n. 4
             9. 10   161, n. 4
             9. 15   311
             13–15.   30, n. 2

Wisd. of Sol. 13. 1–7 116
       15. 3 302
1 Baruch 3. 29 ff. 154
    3. 37 f. 170, n. 2
    21. 23 290, n. 4
    23. 5 165
    59. 2 148, n. 2
    72. 62, n. 6
    77. 16 148, n. 2
    83. 3 62, n. 7
    83. 6 62, n. 7
    83. 7 62, n. 7
Epistle of Jeremy vv. 4–73 30, n. 2
Prayer of Azariah v. 15 210, n. 7
Song of the Three Children 1. 12 83, n. 2
Susanna 6. 23 83, n. 2
    16. 5 82, n. 11
    16. 5 f. 83, n. 2
    19. 29 82, n. 12
Jubilees 1. 15 82
    1. 17 83, n. 2
    2. 19 ff. 83, n. 2
    2. 23 46, n. 2
    3. 1–35 39, n. 1, 46, n. 8
    3. 4 303
    3. 28–9 38, n. 6
    9. 4–7 30, n. 2
    15. 1 83, n. 2
    19. 18 83, n. 2
    19. 28 83, n. 2
    22. 9 83, n. 2
    23. 29 62, n. 7
    33. 20 83, n. 2
Letter of Aristeas §§ 134 f. 30, n. 2
Adam and Eve 12. 1 46, n. 6
1 Enoch 10. 21 61, n. 2
    39. 4 315, n. 3
    42. 160
    46. 1 278
    46. 3 278, 279
    48. 1–7 159
    48. 4 61, n. 2, 278, 279
    49. 1–3 72
    49. 2 159, 160
    51. 3 72, n. 3
    57. 82
    62. 2 205, 278, 279
    62. 6 278
    62. 7 278
    62. 13 278
    62. 15 308
    62. 27–9 278
    71. 14 279
    71. 14 ff. 317

    89. 51 80, n. 2
    90. 30 82
    108. 11 308
    108. 12 308
Test. Reuben 6. 8 82
Test. Simeon 6. 5 61, n. 3
Test. Levi 2. 11 61, n. 3
    4. 4 61, n. 3
    8. 14 61, n. 3
    13. 5 269, n. 4
    14. 3 83, n. 2
    16. 5 82
    18. 290, n. 4
Test. Judah 23. 83, n. 2
    25. 84, n. 3
    25. 5 61, n. 3
Test. Zebulun 9. 1 f. 80, n. 2
    10. 2 84, n. 3
Test. Dan 6. 7 61, n. 3
Test. Naphtali 2. 5 61, n. 3
    3. 2 28 f.
    8. 3 61, n. 3
    8. 5 269, n. 4
Test. Asher 1. 6 21
    7. 3 61, n. 3
    7. 4 82
Test. Benjamin 9. 2 61, n. 3, 82
    10. 5 61, n. 3
    10. 7 84, n. 3
Sib. Oracles 3. 11 180, n. 7
    3. 24–6 55, n. 2
    3. 772 60, n. 9
    3. 773 60, n. 9
    4. lines 24–34 134, n. 1
    5. 414 280
Ass. Moses 1. 9 261, n. 4
    1. 14 261, n. 4
    3. 9 261, n. 4
    10. 7–10 62, n. 7
    11. 17 261, n. 4
    12. 13 261, n. 4
2 Enoch 10. 6 30, n. 2
    30. 10–18 48, n. 1
    30. 13 55
    31. 3 42, n. 5
    43. 6 52, n. 4
2 Baruch 3. 7 39, n. 5
    14. 18 83, n. 1
    14. 19 83, n. 1
    15. 7 83, n. 1
    17. 3 46, n. 1, 46, n. 11
    21. 23 290, n. 4
    21. 24 83, n. 1
    23. 4 46, n. 1, 46, n. 11

2 Baruch 24. 1   269, n. 3
        44. 14   269, n. 3
        48. 20   83, n. 2
        50. 1–4   301, n. 2
        51. 3–4f.   308, n. 1
        51. 10   307, n. 4
        54. 15–19   32
        77f.   82
        78. 4f.   82
        78. 7f.   82, n. 2
4 Ezra (2 Esdras) 3. 7   32, n. 1, 46, n. 1,
                        46, n. 11
        3. 17   82, n. 3
        3. 19f.   11, n. 2
        3. 21   21, n. 1
        3. 21–2   33
        4. 23   261, n. 5
        4. 25   83, n. 3
        4. 30f.   21, n. 1
        4. 30–2   33
        5. 23   83, n. 3
        5. 23–7   62, n. 7
        5. 32   83, n. 3
        5. 41   82, n. 3
        5. 41f.   109, n. 1
        5. 55   13, n. 3
        6. 45   38, n. 10
        6. 55   38, n. 9, 83, n. 1,
                83, n. 3
        6. 58   83, n. 3
        6. 59   38, n. 9, 83, n. 1
        7. 11   38, n. 9, 83, n. 1
        7. 24   261, n. 5
        7. 29   39
        7. 32   39
        7. 62f.   63, n. 3
        7. 72   64, n. 5
        7. 116f.   33
        7. 116–31   11, n. 4
        7. 127–9   33
        8. 1   38, n. 9
        8. 11   38, n. 11
        8. 29–32   39, n. 5

        8. 41f.   63, n. 4
        8. 44   38, n. 9
        8. 53   290, n. 4
        8. 56   33
        9. 21   63, n. 4
        9. 31f.   11, n. 2
        13. 37   62, n. 7
        14. 20f.   148, n. 2
Psalms of Sol. 7. 5f.   83, n. 2
        8. 27   82
        9. 17   83, n. 2
        9. 17f.   82, n. 13
        10. 5   261, n. 3
        11. 1   82
        17. 1f.   82
        17. 25   279
        17. 28   279
        17. 28f.   81, n. 8
        17. 29   279
        17. 31   279
        17. 32   62, n. 6
        17. 35   72, n. 3
        17. 37f.   205
        17. 42   279
        17. 46   279
        17. 48   72, n. 3
        17. 56   82
        18. 8   279
4 Macc. 1. 17   170, n. 3
        6. 28   272, n. 2
        6. 29   272, n. 2
        7. 21–3   170, n. 3
        8. 7   170, n. 3
        9. 21f.   302
        10. 15   302
        14. 4f.   302
        15. 2   302
        16. 13   302
        17. 18   302, 302, n. 5
        17. 21   272, n. 2
        17. 22   272, n. 2
Zadokite Fragment 9 (B) v. 11   131
                    9 (B) v. 15   131

III. QUOTATIONS FROM THE NEW TESTAMENT

Matt. 1. 23   40
        2. 16–19   155
        2. 25–30   156
        3. 9   269, n. 9
        5.   73, n. 1
        5. 11–12   99, n. 8

        5. 13   139
        5. 29f.   139
        5. 48   140
        6. 19–20   269
        6. 24   100, n. 6
        6. 26   175

Matt. 6. 30 175
   7. 1 138
   7. 13 100, n. 6
   9. 15 228, n. 5
   10. 10 140
   10. 14–15 99, n. 5
   10. 19 139
   10. 40 99, n. 4
   11. 16–19 157
   11. 25 137, n. 2, 156
   11. 25–30 156, 157
   11. 27 106
   11. 28f. 157, 326
   11. 28–30 156
   11. 29f. 150
   13. 11 139
   13. 24–30 296, n. 4
   15. 11 138
   15. 24 101
   16. 21f. 274, n. 2
   17. 21b 228, n. 5
   18. 5–6 99, n. 6
   18. 7 138
   18. 8f. 139
   18. 20 150
   19. 28 100, n. 8
   20. 22 228, n. 5
   22. 15ff. 138
   22. 34–40 138
   23. 15 63, n. 6
   23. 34f. 155
   24. 42f. 139
   25. 31–45 99, n. 7
   26. 1f. 261, 274, n. 1
   26. 41 139
   26. 60b–1 101, nn. 5, 7
   27. 24 233
Mark 1. 12–13 42
   1. 13 42, n. 4
   1. 15 36, n. 13
   1. 21–8 144, n. 2
   1. 22 144, n. 2
   1. 27 144, n. 2
   2. 19f. 228, n. 5
   4. 11 139
   4. 35 41
   4. 35f. 40
   5. 1–20 40, 41
   7. 15 138
   8. 31 228, n. 5, 274, n. 2
   8. 33 42
   9. 12b 228, n. 5
   9. 31 228, n. 5, 274, n. 2
   9. 42 138

   9. 43 139
   9. 47 139
   9. 49 139
   9. 50 139
   10. 12 140
   10. 33f. 228, n. 5
   11. 5 101, n. 3
   11. 13 101, n. 6
   12. 1f. 101, n. 6
   12. 13f. 138
   12. 25 307
   12. 28–34 138, 143, n. 5
   13. 2 101, n. 5
   13. 11 139
   13. 37 139
   14. 22 101, n. 4
   14. 24 247
   14. 38 139
   14. 58 101, n. 7
   15. 58 101, n. 5
Luke 1. 35 40
   1. 78f. 40
   2. 32 40
   3. 38 46, n. 3
   5. 34 228, n. 5
   6. 23 139
   6. 37 138
   6. 38 139
   7. 31–5 155
   8. 10 139
   10. 7 140
   10. 16 139
   10. 20 139
   10. 21 137, n. 2
   10. 21–2 156
   10. 25–8 138, 143, n. 5
   11. 49 155
   12. 12 139
   12. 24–8 175
   12. 39ff. 139
   13. 24 140
   13. 33 101, n. 2
   14. 34f. 139
   17. 1–2 138
   20. 20–6 138
   21. 14 139
   21. 25 40, 41
   21. 34 139
   21. 36 139, 140
   22. 14–18 243, n. 7
   22. 15–19 243
   22. 29f. 243
   22. 40 139
   22. 46 139

Luke 24. 13f.　**228. n.** 4
　　24. 20f.　**274, n.** 2
John 2. 19　**101,** n. 7
　8. 33　**269,** n. 9
　8. 39　**269,** n. 9
　12. 20　**101**
　13–17.　**110,** n. 1
　13. 4–5　**293**
　19. 26　**293**
　27. 1　**293**
Acts 2. 16f.　**185,** n. 7
　2. 22　**229,** n. 2
　2. 23　**229,** n. 1
　2. 23 f.　**233,** n. 3
　2. 36　**229,** n. 2
　2. 44–6　**202,** n. 1
　3. 15　**229,** n. 2
　3. 17 f.　**229,** n. 2
　3. 18　**229,** n. 1
　3. 19　**229,** n. 3
　3. 25　**261,** n. 7
　4. 32–7　**202,** n. 1
　5. 28　**233**
　5. 30　**227,** n. 3
　5. 33 ff.　**66,** n. 6
　5. 34 f.　**73,** n. 4
　6. 7　**43, 43,** n. 4
　6. 9　**6,** n. 3
　6. 14　**101,** n. 5
　9. 1　**66,** n. 3
　9. 1 f.　**67,** n. 9
　9. 3　**185,** n. 1
　9. 3 f.　**197,** n. 5
　9. 15　**68,** n. 4
　10. 39　**227,** n. 3
　11. 22 f.　**68,** n. 1
　13. 5　**68,** n. 5
　13. 14　**68,** n. 5
　13. 15　**7,** n. 3
　13. 45 f.　**69,** n. 1
　13. 46　**68,** n. 6
　14. 1　**68,** n. 6, **69,** n. 2
　15.　**117, 118**
　15. 5　**43,** n. 5
　16. 3　**70,** n. 2
　17.　**188**
　17. 1　**68,** n. 5
　17. 2　**7,** n. 3
　17. 3　**274,** n. 2
　17. 7–8　**36,** n. 14
　17. 17　**68,** n. 5
　17. 28　**188,** n. 1
　17. 30　**327**
　18. 4　**7,** n. 3, **68,** n. 5

　18. 6　**69,** n. 1
　18. 9　**179,** n. 7
　18. 18　**73**
　18. 24f.　**51,** n. 6
　18. 24ff.　**68,** n. 5
　19. 1　**51,** n. 6
　20. 35　**140**
　21. 21f.　**70**
　21. 23f.　**73**
　21. 26　**70,** n. 2
　21. 39　**66,** n. 2
　22. 3　**2, 2,** n. 4
　22. 4–16　**67,** n. 9
　22. 11　**185,** n. 1
　22. 17　**197,** n. 7
　23. 6　**70,** n. 2
　26. 12–18　**76,** n. 9
　26. 17　**68,** n. 4
　28.　**69**
　28. 17f.　**69,** n. 3
Rom. 1.　**23, 27, 28, 29, 30, 109, 117, 325ff.**
　1. 2　**177,** n. 2
　1. 4　**182,** n. 6, **296,** n. 3
　1. 17　**222,** n. 3
　1. 18　**289**
　1. 18f.　**58,** n. 5, **242**
　1. 18–23　**116**
　1. 20　**27,** n. 4, **29**
　1. 26　**27,** n. 4
　1. 26f.　**116,** n. 2
　2.　**23, 58, n. 5, 109, 117, 239, 241, 325ff.**
　2. 1f.　**242**
　2. 2–10　**289**
　2. 7　**90,** n. 7
　2. 14　**116,** n. 1
　2. 15　**25,** n. 3
　2. 16　**111,** n. 3
　2. 28–9　**75,** n. 3
　3.　**239, 241**
　3. 1f.　**76,** n. 1, **242**
　3. 6　**289**
　3. 20　**11,** n. 3
　3. 21f.　**36,** n. 4, **67,** n. 2, **238,** n. 5
　3. 23　**241**
　3. 25　**232, 237, 238, 239, 240, 241**
　　　　　241, n. 4, **242**
　3. 31　**69,** n. 8
　4.　**97**
　4. 25　**233,** n. 3
　4. 24–5　**274**
　5.　**18,** n. 2, **273**
　5. 1　**86,** n. 1
　5. 5　**201,** n. 6
　5. 6　**268**

Rom. 5. 8 232, 268
5. 8–9 233, 234
5. 8–10 234
5. 9 232
5. 12 32
5. 12f. 23, 31, 34, 41, n. 2
5. 12–21 41, 52, n. 3, 265
5. 17–19 268
5. 19 31, n. 3, 32, 34
6. 107, 111, 122, 178
6. 1–14 234, 291
6. 3 122, n. 1
6. 4 88, 319, n. 1
6. 5 87, 291
6. 6 36, n. 7, 88
6. 8–9 319, n. 2
6. 10 233, n. 3
6. 11 122, n. 2
7. 19,, n. 7, 23, 25, 26, 27, 30, 32, 34.
34. n. 2, 58, n. 5, 109, 141, 256
7. 6 69, n. 6
7. 7 25, n. 4
7. 8 24, nn. 3, 4
7. 9 24, nn. 3, 4
7. 11 32
7. 15f. 24, n. 5
7. 18 19, n. 5
7. 19 256, n. 2
7. 24 31, n. 1
7. 25f. 24, n. 6
8. 24, n. 6, 36, n. 10
8. 2 178, n. 4, 181, n. 8, 182, n. 5,
201, n. 1
8. 3 19, n. 3, 36, n. 1, 91, n. 1
8. 4 274
8. 6 24, n. 1
8. 9 182, n. 6
8. 9f. 177, n. 4, 178, n. 1
8. 10 177, n. 5, 178, nn. 2, 4
8. 11 181, n. 9, 186, n. 5, 318,
n. 1
8. 15 36, n. 3, 139, n. 1
8. 16 185, n. 4, 186, n. 5
8. 17 88, 88, n. 2
8. 19–23 58, n. 3, 318, 319, n. 8
8. 20f. 38f.
8. 22 37, n. 5
8. 22f. 40, n. 2
8. 23 37, n. 5
8. 26 37, n. 5, 186, n. 5
8. 27 186, n. 5
8. 29–30 319, n. 3
8. 49 195
9. 1–5 75, n. 5, 76, n. 1

9. 5 272
10. 1 75, n. 5
10. 3 36, n. 2
10. 6ff. 153
10. 12 67, n. 6, 201, n. 16
11. 298, n. 1
11. 1–32 322
11. 15 298, n. 1
11. 16 297, n. 2
11. 25–36 181, 293
11. 28 272
11. 32 58, n. 4
11. 33f. 181
11. 35f. 181, n. 2
11. 34 194, n. 4
12. 1 239, n. 3
12. 1f. 122, 133, n. 1
12. 3 141, n. 1
12. 4 56, n. 5
12. 4f. 178, n. 5
12. 9–19 130
12. 13 202, n. 1
12. 14 138
12. 17 138, 327
12. 21 138
13. 1 141, n. 1, 328
13. 7f. 138
13. 11 130, 319, n. 8
13. 12 319, n. 8
14. 10 138, 289
14. 13f. 138
15. 3 147, n. 1
15. 8 101
1 Cor. 1–3. 193
1. 7–8 296
1. 8 112, n. 4
1. 13 147, n. 5
1. 17 129, n. 4
1. 18f. 50, n. 3, 327
1. 23 274, n. 2
1. 24 154, 172
1. 30 154, 155, n. 1, 173, n. 4,
222, n. 1
2. 188, 252, n. 2
2. 1f. 187
2. 4 197, n. 8, 201, n. 2
2. 9 307
2. 11 185, n. 3
2. 11f. 186, n. 4
2. 14 20, n. 2
2. 16 182, n. 6, 183, 194, n. 4
3. 3 20, n. 2, 22, n. 4, 50, n. 4
3. 4f. 51, n. 6
3. 8 308

1 Cor. 3. 10 187
3. 16 178, n. 1, 232, n. 2, 239
3. 16 201. n. 13
3. 17 297
4. 1 92
4. 4–5 289, 297
4. 6 141, n. 1
5. 1f. 131, n. 4
5. 2 289
5. 6 141, n. 1
5. 6–8 105
5. 7 200, 242, 242, n. 2, 250
5. 8 253, n. 3
5. 10 29, n. 6
6. 1 107, n. 2
6. 4 118, n. 1
6. 9 29, n. 6, 297
6. 9–10 118, n. 1, 295, 297
6. 11 122, n. 1, 222, n. 1
6. 17 201, n. 7
6. 19 178, n. 1, 239
6. 19f. 201, n. 8
7. 1–3 49, n. 4
7. 3 107, n. 2
7. 3–5ff. 71
7. 6 194, n. 5
7. 10 140
7. 14 56, n. 3
7. 18 70, 70, n. 3
7. 21–2 71
7. 23 107, n. 2
7. 25 140, 141, 194, n. 5
7. 26 112, n. 4
7. 29 112, n. 4
7. 40 201, n. 3
8. 5 107, n. 2
8. 6 181, 181, n. 2
9. 50, n. 5
9. 7 112, n. 6
9. 10 141, n. 1
9. 11 20, n. 2
9. 14 140
9. 21 69, n. 7, 70, n. 3
10. 1f. 105
10. 1–4 110, n. 1, 152, 252
10. 1–5 105
10. 3f. 182, n. 6
10. 14–22 252
10. 16 233
10. 24 141, n. 1
10. 27 119, n. 1
10. 33 141
11. 1 147, n. 6, 148
11. 14 114, 118, n. 9, 328

11. 20–34 252
11. 23 101, n. 4
11. 23ff. 140, 274
11. 25 247 .
11. 26 252, n. 3
11. 27f. 56, n. 1
11. 27–34 291, n. 2
11. 29 55
12–14 111, n. 1, 201, n. 9
12. 1f. 198, n. 2
12. 11f. 56, n. 5
12. 12 86, n. 5, 178, n. 5
12. 13 201, n. 12
12. 14f. 201, n. 14 .
12. 20f. 201, n. 11
12. 31 221, nn. 1, 7
13. 147, n. 3, 201, n. 15
13. 1f. 198, n. 2
13. 5 141
14 1f. 221, n. 9
14. 6 197, n. 6
14. 18 197, n. 6
14. 34f. 141
14. 37 140, 141, 141, n. 5
15. 49, 52, 194, 293, 294, 295, 304,
306, 308, 309, 310, 311, 314,
317, 319
15. 3 229, n. 5, 266, 274
15. 5f. 293
15. 7 293
15. 12 303, n. 3
15. 20 106
15. 22 41, n. 2, 294
15. 22f. 291, 292
15. 22–4 292
15. 23–4 58, n. 2, 250
15. 23–8 58, n. 2, 289, 290
15. 24ff. 43ff., 141, 177, n. 3, 178,
n. 9, 182f., 233, n. 3, 290,
293, 295, 296, 305ff.,
326
2 Cor. 1. 5f. 88, n. 2
1. 8–9 311, n. 2
1. 14 289, 296
1. 22 181, n. 8
2. 17 133, n. 1
3. 107, n. 2
3 f. 313
3. 1–3 225, n. 3
3. 1–11 106
3. 6 33, n. 3
3. 16–18 182, n. 6
3. 17–18 196, n. 1
3. 18 195, n. 3

2 Cor. 4. 6   37, n. 4, 58, n. 6
4. 7   312
4. 16f.   181, n. 8, 318, n. 1
5.   310, 311, 312, 314, 317
5. 1f.   309, 310, 311, 312f., 317,
318f.
5. 5   181, n. 8
5. 10   289, 312
5. 15   233, n. 3
5. 16   195, 195, n. 2
5. 17   37, n. 3, 40, n. 2, 119, n. 4
5. 18   36, n. 6
5. 19   58, n. 3, 74, n. 4
6.   66, n. 4
6. 14   19, n. 6
7.   66, n. 4
7. 1   19, n. 6
8. 7f.   202, n. 1
8. 8   195, n. 5
8. 9   147, n. 4
10. 1   147, n. 2
10. 3–6   112, n. 6
11. 3   32
11. 22   2
12.   198
12. 2   87, n. 1
12. 2–4   197, 197, n. 1
12. 9   197, n. 7
12. 11   197, n. 8
13. 13   178, n. 6
Gal. 1. 4   36, n. 12
1. 11f.   248, n. 3
1. 13f.   66, n. 3
1. 14   2, n. 5, 87, n. 4
1. 15   195, n. 4
1. 16   68, n. 4
2. 2   112, n. 6
2. 7   68, n. 4
2. 11–14   118
2. 20   87, n. 5, 88, 88, n. 1, 91, n. 6,
177, n. 5, 197, 197, n. 4,
268, n. 1
3. 2   221, n. 3
3. 6   222, n. 2
3. 11   222, n. 3
3. 13   36, n. 2, 227, n. 3
3. 14   221, n. 3
3. 18f.   261, n. 4
3. 26–9   76, n. 6
3. 28   58, n. 1, 201, n. 16
4. 3   36, n. 9
4. 6   182, n. 6, 185, n. 7, 201, n. 6
4. 9   36, n. 9
5.   27

5. 1   36, n. 9, 67, n. 8, 69, n. 6
5. 9   141, n. 1
5. 11   274, n. 2
5. 20   29
5. 21   295
5. 22f.   186, n. 6, 217, n. 5
6. 2   73, n. 3
6. 8   178, n. 4
6. 15   37, n. 2, 40, n. 2, 119, n. 4
6. 15–16   75
6. 18   185, n. 2
Eph. 1. 7   232
1. 9   67, n. 7
1. 10   57, n. 5
1. 13   181
2.   67, n. 3, 67, n. 8
2. 3   23, n. 5
2. 11f.   113, n. 2
2. 12   113, n. 4
2. 13   232, 232, n. 5
2. 18f.   201, n. 11
3. 3f.   67, n. 7
3. 16f.   201, n. 6
4. 1   112, n. 4
4. 2f.   130
4. 3f.   201, n. 11
4. 4   178, n. 5
4. 5f.   181
4. 20–6   19, 122
4. 22–6   132
4. 24   119, n. 4
4. 30   201, n. 6
5. 2   274
5. 14   42, n. 2, 129
6. 10–16   36, n. 3
6. 10–17   112, n. 6
19.   122
Phil. 1. 6   297, 319, n. 8
1. 10   289, 297, 319, n. 8
1. 23   19, n. 4, 178, n. 8
2. 1   178, n. 6
2. 5f.   88, n. 7, 147, n. 3, 273, 274
2. 6   274, 297
2. 6f.   41, 265
2. 7ff.   274
2. 12   99, n. 1
2. 16   289, 297
2. 25   112, n. 6
3. 1   88
3. 2–3   69
3. 3   239, n. 4
3. 5ff.   2
3. 10   88, n. 2
3. 13   99, n. 1

Phil. 3. 14   **112**, n. 6
3. 20–2   **319**, n. 8
4. 1–5   **319**, n. 8
Col. 1. 12–13   **296**
1. 13   **36**, n. 11
1. 14   **36**, n. 5, **232**
1. 15   **151**, **173**, n. 5
1. 15f.   **150**, **181**, **181**, n. 2
1. 16f.   **181**
1. 20   **58**, n. 3, **232**
1. 22   **19**, n. 3, **90**, n. 3, **234**
1. 27   **177**, n. 5
2. 3   **173**, n. 6
2. 11   **239**, n. 4
2. 12   **88**
2. 15   **36**, n. 3
2. 16   **172**, n. 1
3. 1   **88**, **136**
3. 1f.   **112**, n. 5
3. 1–4   **318**, n. 5
3. 3   **318**, n. 1
3. 3f.   **181**, n. 8
3. 4   **178**, n. 4, **318**
3. 5   **29**, n. 6, **139**
3. 8–4. 12   **122**f.
3. 9   **120**, n. 6
3. 10   **36**, n. 8, **37**, n. 3, **119**, n. 4
3. 11   **58**, n. 1, **58**, n. 3
3. 12   **139**
3. 12f.   **130**
3. 13   **139**
3. 16   **130**
3. 18   **141**, n. 1
3. 18–4. 1   **136**
3. 22   **136**
4. 2f.   **139**
4. 6   **139**
4. 11   **295**
4. 12   **140**
17. 21f.   **172**, n. 1
1 Thess. 1. 5   **201**, n. 2
1. 6   **147**, n. 6, **148**, **201**, n. 4
1. 9   **31**, n. 3
1. 10   **111**, n. 3
2. 12   **295**
4. 1   **112**, n. 2
4. 1–12   **130**, n. 1

4. 5   **112**, n. 1
4. 6   **289**
4. 8   **139**
4. 9b   **139**
4. 11f.   **111**, n. 5
4. 13–18   **290**
4. 14–15   **289**
4. 15f.   **140**
4. 16   **141**, n. 1
4. 16f.   **139**
4. 16–17   **289**
4. 17   **178**, n. 8
5. 1–4   **289**
5. 2f.   **139**
5. 3f.   **201**, n. 5
5. 6   **139**
5. 8   **112**, n. 6
5. 13   **139**
5. 15f.   **139**
2 Thess. 1. 4f.   **295**
3. 3   **139**, n. 1
2 Tim. 2. 18   **292**
4. 7   **112**, n. 6
Philemon *v.* 2   **112**, n. 6
Heb. 4. 15   **43**, n. 1
7. 27   **239**, n. 5
9. 5   **239**
9. 12   **235**, n. 5, **239**, n. 5
9. 14   **239**, n. 5
10.   **267**
12. 1f.   **122**
12. 4   **232**
Jas. 1. 1–4. 10   **122**, **127**
2. 18   **120**, n. 3
1 Pet. 1. 1–4. 11   **122**
1. 3   **120**, n. 2
1. 3–4. 11   **122**
1. 4   **127**
2. 2   **120**, n. 2
3. 8   **294**
4. 12–5. 14   **122**
5. 5f.   **128**
11.   **127**
2 Pet. 3. 8   **46**, n. 2
Rev. 3. 20   **243**, n. 6
19. 2   **233**
20. 4   **290**

IV. QUOTATIONS FROM THE TARGUMS

Onkelos
  On Gen. 2. 7   44, n. 1
Jonathan
  On Gen. 1. 2   189f.
  On Isa. 12. 3   72
  On Isa. 53.   275

On Ezek. 1. 3   206
Jerusalem
  On Gen. 2. 7   54, n. 2
  On Isa. 40. 6   20
  On Isa. 66. 23   20
  On Zech. 2. 17   20

V. QUOTATIONS FROM RABBINICAL LITERATURE

I. THE MISHNAH. (Tractates alphabetically arranged)

Aboth or (*Pirke Aboth*) 1. 1   249, n. 1
  1. 2   171, n. 3, 231, n. 6, 253, n. 5
  1. 12   64
  1. 14   270, n. 1
  1. 17   37, n. 7
  1. 18   231, n. 6
  2. 14   261, n. 8
  2. 18   8, n. 2
  3. 6   150, n. 2
  3. 7   150, n. 1
  3. 23   171, n. 1
  4. 16   315, n. 5
  5. 19   75, n. 3
  5. 24   24, 25, n. 1
  6. 9   317, n. 2
  6. 11   269, n. 1
Baba Metzia 4. 10   64, n. 2
  71. 1   269, n. 10

Berakoth 2. 2   262, n. 2
  3. 5   312
  9. 5   21, n. 7
  11. 2   150, n. 2
Hagigah 2. 1   37, n. 7
Hullin 8. 1   306, n. 1
Makkoth 3. 16   269, n. 1
Megillah 1. 8   6, n. 5
Pesahim 5. 5   102, n. 3
  10.   102, n. 4
  10. 6   103, n. 2
Sanhedrin 4. 5   38, nn. 9, 10, 53, 55
  10. 1   84
Sotah 9. 12   209, n. 4
  9. 15   209, n. 8, 218, n. 2
Yadaim 4. 6   7, n. 4
Yoma 5. 2   238, n. 3
  8. 8   257, n. 8

2. THE BABYLONIAN TALMUD

'Abodah Zarah 16b–17a   143, n. 3
  18a   271
  20b   209, n. 8, 218, n. 2
  55a   117, n. 1
  64b   115, n. 1
Baba Bathra 12a   211, n. 1, 216, n. 1
  58a   46, n. 4
Baba Metzia 59b   212, n. 3, 214, n. 6
Berakoth 17a   306
  28b   315, n. 6
  61a   21, n. 6, 54, n. 3
  61b   265, n. 1
Gittin 56a   211, n. 4
'Erubin 13b   13, n. 5, 212, n. 2
  18a   54, n. 3
  64b   211, n. 6

Hagigah 13a   37, n. 7
  13b   198, n. 1
  14b   15, 213, n. 4
  15a   184
Kiddushin 30b   22, n. 4
  36a   84, n. 6
  81a   22, n. 4
Makkoth 23b   184
Megillah 3a   144, n. 2
  14a   184
  17b–18a   82, n. 3
Nedarim 39b   170, n. 5
Pesahim 54a   170, n. 5
  57a   255, n. 1
  87b   63, n. 8
Sanhedrin 11a   207, n. 1, 209, n. 4

Sanhedrin 38 *a* 53, n. 4, 54, n. 1
    38 *b* 280, n. 1
    39 *a* 214, n. 2
    56 *a* 111, n. 1
    56 *b* 115, n. 1
    59 *b* 42, n. 5, 46, n. 7
    65 *b* 213, n. 5
    68 *a* 211, n. 5
    90 *a* 213, n. 3
    90 *b* 300, n. 3
    91 *b* 25, n. 2
    93 *b* 281
    96 *b* 280, n. 1
    97 *a* 280, n. 1
    98 *a* 282
    98 *b* 282
    99 *a* 307
    107 *b* 22, n. 3
Shabbath 31 *a* 63, n. 10, 64, n. 2

    88 *b*–89 *a* 170, n. 5
    105 *b* 30, n. 1
    156 *a* 13, n. 2
Shebu'oth 12 *b*–13 *a* 257, n. 8
Soṭah 17 *a* 214, n. 2
    47 *b* 144, n. 2
    48 *b* 207, n. 1, 209, n. 4, 221, n. 5
    49 *a* 6, n. 7
Sukkah 5 *a* 214, n. 2
    52 *a* 23, n. 3
    52 *b* 22, n. 2
Yebamoth 47 *a* 121
    48 *b* 119
    62 *a* 120, n. 1
Yoma 5 *a* 235, n. 5
    9 *b* 209, n. 4
    21 *b* 208, n. 3
Zebaḥim 6 *a* 235, n. 5
    116 *a* 170, n. 5

3. JERUSALEM TALMUD. (Ed. Krotoschin, 1866)

'*Abodah Zarah* 3. 42 *c* 207, n. 2
Megillah 1. 71 *a* 6, n. 5
Nedarim 9. 41 *b* 13, n. 2

Soṭah 1. 16 *b* 211, n. 8
    9. 24 *b* 207, n. 1
Yebamoth 15. 14 *d* 332

4. EXTRA-CANONICAL TRACTATES

Aboth de Rabbi Nathan (ed. Salomon
  Schechter, London 1887):
    p. 21 258, n. 3
    p. 62 25, n. 3
    p. 62 27, n. 2

    p. 66 261
    p. 91 54, n. 4
Derek Eretz Rabba 19 *b* 329
Derek Eretz Zuta 19 *b* 329
Semaḥoth VIII. 284

(For *Pirké de Rabbi Eliezer* see index for Rabbis)

5. MEKILTA. (Ed. J. Z. Lauterbach, Philadelphia, 1933–5)

Pisha 1 206, nn. 1, 6, 208, n. 4
Beshallah 2 64, n. 4
    4 270, n. 4
    6 263, n. 3
    7 209, n. 7, 221, n. 5
    10 263, nn. 5, 6

Vayassa 3 221, n. 6
Baḥodesh 4 206, n. 5
    6 262, n. 1, 263, n. 3
Nezikin 17 22, n. 1
    18 64, nn. 1, 2

6. TOSEFTA. (Ed. M. S. Zuckermandel, Pasewalk, 1880)

Berakoth 3. 7 261
Pesaḥim 1. 27 211, n. 6
Soṭah 13. 2 209, n. 4
    13. 3 207, n. 1

    13. 5 211, n. 3
    15. 2 258
    15. 8 6, n.5
Sukkah 2. 6 13, n. 13

7. MIDRASH RABBAH. (Ed. Wilna, 1876)

Genesis Rabbah 1. 7, n. 4, 166, n. 3
1. 4   170, n. 5
8 on 1. 26   38, n. 10
8. 1   45, n. 8, 46, n. 5,
    48, n. 7, 53, n. 4,
    54, n. 3
9. 7   22, n. 3
10 on 2. 1   7, n. 4
12. 2   171, n. 2
14. 5   300, n. 6
14. 7   313
16. 6   115, n. 1
22 on 4. 6   25, n. 2
24. 1   54, n. 4
24. 7   55, n. 3
28. 6   38, nn. 9, 11
38. 13   29, n. 1
39. 4   119
44. 4. 5   13, n. 2
70. 8   184
85. 9   184
91. 6   184
Exodus Rabbah 2. 5   270, n. 6
15. 3   270, n. 5
21. 8   270, n. 5

25. 4   221, n. 5
35. 2   271, n. 1
40. 3   55, n. 1
48 on 35. 30   13, n. 5
Leviticus Rabbah 1. 1   184
2. 9   65, n. 5
3. 5   256, n. 6
8. 2   184
9. 9   184
13 on 11. 1   72, n. 5
15. 2   185
32. 4   184
35. 7   221, n. 6
Numbers Rabbah 14. 10   65, n. 1
15. 10   208, n. 3
15. 25   216, n. 4
19 on 19. 2   262, n. 3
22. 9   21, n. 5
Deuteronomy Rabbah 7. 3   148, n. 2
Ecclesiastes Rabbah 1. 8   64, n. 1
Canticles Rabbah (or *Song of Songs Rabbah*)
1 on end of v. 2 (Warsaw Ed. 1. 19) 64, n. 1
1. 8   209, n. 6
2. 13   84, n. 5
8.   208, n. 3

8. SIFRA ON LEVITICUS. (Ed. J. H. Weiss and J. Schlossberg, Wien, 1872)

85 d   315, n. 5   89.   55

9. SIFRE ON NUMBERS AND DEUTERONOMY. (Wilna, 1866)

Num. 6. 5, § 41   148, n. 2
Deut. 6. 5, §. 32   21, n. 7
6. 6, § 33   23, n. 1, 104, n. 2
6. 6, § 33   225, n. 2
11. 10, § 37   170
11. 18, § 45   22, n. 4

18. 12, § 173   206, n. 3, 213, n. 5
32. 1, § 306   174, n. 1
32. 4, § 307   263, n. 4
32. 32, § 323   46, nn. 1, 11
32. 2, § 343   65, n. 1

10. PESIKTA KAHANA. (Ed. Salomon Buber, Lyck, 1868)

1 b   45, n. 9
34 a   46, n. 8, 63, n. 8
36 b   38, n. 10, 45, n. 4, 46, n. 3
60 b   259, n. 3

90 a   211, n. 8
165 a   25, n. 5
176 b   211, n. 7

11. PESIKTA RABBATI. (Ed. Salomon Buber, Wilna, 1885)

74 a   84, n. 5
115 a   45, nn. 7, 8
160 a   207, n. 4

161 a   65, n. 6
194 b   236, n. 2

12. TANḤUMA. (Ed. Salomon Buber, Wilna, 1885)

Bereshith, § 38, p. 25 23, n. 2   *Wayyera*, § 9, p. 90 271, n. 4
וארא § 1, p. 17 65, n. 1   *Wayyigash*, § 9, p. 208 301, n. 3
Yitro, § 7, p. 73 104, n. 3

13. AGADATH BERESHITH. (Ed. Salomon Buber)
§ 47, p. 68 215, n. 3

14. YALḲUṬ

On Gen. 49 219, n. 4   On Ps. 119. 11 225, n. 2
On Exod. 14. 31 221, n. 6

VI. REFERENCES TO CLASSICAL AND HELLENISTIC AUTHORS AND TO EXTRA-CANONICAL CHRISTIAN WRITINGS

Apuleius 90, 92
Antipater 179, n. 11
Aratus 187, n. 2
Aristotle 24, n. 5, 293
Athenodorus 179, n. 11

Athenodorus Cananites 179, n. 11
Chrysippus 179
Cicero 227, n. 2
Cleanthes 179, 187, n. 2

(References to *The Clementine Homilies*, Ante-Nicene Christian Library, Vol. XVII, Edinburgh, 1870)

3. 7 51, n. 2   3. 20 51, n. 5
3. 18 51, n. 3   13. 14 51, n. 5

References to *Hermetica*
1. 6 194, n. 5
1. 26 191, n. 7
4. 193, n. 6
10. 5 192
12. 9 191, n. 5
13. 15 195, n. 1
Flavius Josephus
(a) *Antiquities*
13. 1. 1 209, n. 3
14. 7. 2 6, nn. 10, 11
17. 11. 4 9, n. 1
18. 1. 5 258, n. 6
20. 2. 3 133, n. 1
20. 11 5, n. 9
(b) *Wars of the Jews*
6. 11. 3 6, n. 10
7. 6 261, n. 9
2. 10. 11 303
Heracleitus 28, 179
Homer 7, n. 4, 304
Marcus Aurelius 180
Philo of Alexandria 7, n. 4, 8, 11 f., 18,
46 ff., 51 f., 94 ff., 151, 153, 171, 173, 180,
231, 258, n. 6, 267, 302, 303
De opificio Mundi
§ 21 18, n. 4
§ 69 47
§ 139 48

Legum Allegoriae
1. 30 48, n. 4
1. 31 47 '
2. 21 163, n. 3
De Migratione Abrahami
§ 92 96, n. 4
De Exsecrationibus
§§ 138 f. 96, n. 4
De Specialibus Legibus
1, §§ 319 ff. 97, n. 1
De vita contemplativa 97
Quod omnis probis liber sit
12 258, n. 6
75 ff. 97
De Monarchia
§§ 34 f. 116
Plato 7, n. 4, 8, 28, 30, 48, 97, 162, n. 2,
171, 304
Plutarch 18, n. 3
Posidonius 179
Pseudo-Phocylides 134
Sophocles 114
Stobaeus 179
Strabo 6, n. 11
Symmachus 240
Tacitus 227, n. 2
Zeno 179

VII. REFERENCES TO RABBIS CITED

Abba Arika (Rab), 307
R. Abba, 212
R. Abdimi of Haifa, 211, 212
R. Abtalion, 269, 270
R. Aibu, 336
R. Aha, 54
R. Akiba, 132, 170, 211, 213, 216, 263, 265, 276, 277, 280, n. 1, 337
R. Alexandri, 281
R. Azariah, 210
Ben Zoma, 184
R. Dosa, 276, 277
R. Eleazar of Modiim, 63, 221, 270
R. Eleazar b. Zadok, 261, 331
R. Eliezer (Pirke d.), 42, n. 5; 46, n. 8; 54, 206, 305, 306
R. Eliezer b. 'Arak, 261
R. Eliezer b. Azariah, 45, nn. 7, 8; 337
R. Eliezer b. Hyrkanos, 63, 116, 121, 133, 211, 212, 214, 219
R. Elisha b. Abuyah, 6, 73
R. Gamaliel II, 102, 211, 301, 331
R. Haninah b. Dosa, 211
R. Hana b. Aha, 22, n. 2
R. Hananiah, 119
R. Hananiah b. Akashya, 268 f.
R. Hananiah b. Teradion, 271
R. Haninah, 282
R. Haninah b. Hama, 271
R. Haninah b. Papa, 65
R. Hezekiah b. Hiyya, 339
Hillel, 63, 64, 66, 207, 212, 270, 300, 307
R. Hiyya, 209, 307
R. Hiyya b. Abba, 307
R. Hoshaiah, 172
R. Huna, 259, n. 2
R. Ishmael, 22, n. 4; 284, 300
R. Isaac, 280, n. 1
R. Jacob, 315
R. Judah, 46, n. 1; 276
R. Jeremiah, 214
R. Johanan b. Zakkai, 3, 211, 213, 235, 258, 262, 315 f.

R. Johanan b. Nuri, 30, n. 1
John Hyrkanos, High Priest, 211
R. Jose, 119, 276
R. Jose the Galilean, 282, 335
R. Jose b. Halafta, 313
R. Jose b. Kisma, 271
R. Jose b. Simeon, 63, 258, 339
R. Joshua b. Hananiah, 121, 184, 258, 212, 214, 331, 333
R. Joshua b. Levi, 280, n. 1; 282, 336
R. Joshua b. Karhah, 262
Judah the Prince, 6, 23
R. Judah b. Tema, 24, 46, 206
R. Meir, 22, n. 4; 45, 53, 84, 184, 271, 305, 310, 330
R. Nahman, 270, 280, n. 1
R. Nathan, 258, n. 3; 261, n. 8
R. Nehemiah, 206, 209, 263, 270, 276, 340
R. Phinehas b. Jair, 209, 210, 218, 219
R. Samuel, 212
R. Samuel b. Nahman, 22, 270
Samuel the Small, 207
Shammai, 63, 64, 66, 212, 300, 307
R. Shemaiah, 269, 270
R. Shila, 282
R. Simai, 25, n. 5, 336
R. Simeon b. Azzai, 55, 208, 265
R. Simeon b. Eleazar, 22, n. 3
R. Simeon b. Gamaliel, 65, 258, n. 2; 284
R. Simeon b. Gamaliel II, 6
R. Simeon b. Lakish, 337
R. Simeon b. Menasya, 46, n. 3, 336
R. Simeon b. Yohai, 211, 236, 261, 270 f., 282, 332, 337, 338
R. Simeon, 284
Simeon the Just, 171, 231, n. 6
R. Tanhuma, 216
R. Tarfon (Trypho), 280, n. 2; 281
R. Yannai, 30, n. 2; 282
R. Yudan (or R. Judan), 171, 209
R. Zadok, 213, 261

VIII. INDEX OF AUTHORS

Abelson, J., 11 f., 14, 15, n. 2; 184 f., 209, n. 1; 210, 211, n. 10; 212
Abrahams, L., 12, 209, n. 1; 210, 211, n. 1; 213, n. 2; 215, n. 1; 216, 224, n. 3; 307
Albright, W. F., 279

Bacher, W., 23, n. 1; 55, n. 3; 210, n. 3

Baillie, J. 326
Barth, K., 175, 294, 325 ff.
Baur, F. C., 150
'Beginnings', 7, nn. 1, 2; 63, n. 7; 67, n. 9; 113, n. 3; 114, n. 2; 121, nn. 5, 6, 7; 134, n. 3; 159, n. 2; 188, n. 3; 221, n. 1
Behm, J., 233, 234, 243, 246

Bennett, W. H., 164
Bentwich, N., 5, n. 11; 7, n. 4; 8, n. 4; 12
Bergson, H., 190, n. 3
Bernard, J. H. 173, n. 7
Bevan, E. R., 6, n. 11; 8, n. 7; 12, 90, 169, 178f., 180, 183, n. 2; 198, n. 3; 204, n. 3; 264, n. 6
Bonsirven, J., 3, n. 3; 4, n. 3; 5, n. 8; 5, n. 10; 6, nn. 4, 5, 7; 7, n. 4; 8, 10, 29, n. 4; 73, n. 6; 149, n. 2; 159, n. 2; 162, n. 2; 164, nn. 7, 8; 166, n. 3; 170, n. 5; 171, nn. 1, 4; 221, n. 4; 231, n. 6; 275, n. 4; 283, n. 1; 314, 316, 317, n. 1; 320
Bousset, W., 1, 2, 17, 42, n. 5; 45, n. 1; 46, n. 5; 47, 51, n. 5; 89, 191, 195, n. 4; 216
Box, G. H., 11, 13, n. 4; 63, n. 3; 109, n. 1
Branscomb, B. H., 9, n. 1; 324
Braude, W. G., 64, nn. 1, 4; 66, n. 7; 113, n. 3; 133, n. 1
Briggs, C. A., 160, n. 3; 161
Browne, L. E., 61, nn. 3, 5
Brunner, H. E., 175, 219, n. 6, 326
Büchler, A., 104, 206, n. 6; 210, 225, n. 2; 230, 235, 236, n. 2; 251, n. 3; 254, 256f., 258, n.5; 260f., 262, 263, n. 2; 265, n. 1; 284
Büchsel, F., 179, n. 2; 182, 187, n. 1; 195, n. 4; 199, nn. 4, 5; 200, nn. 1, 2; 204, n. 1; 205, n. 3; 207, n. 3; 211, nn. 1, 2; 213, nn. 1, 5; 218, n. 4; 219, nn. 4, 5; 220, 221, n. 10; 238f., 240f., 242
Bugge, A., 153, n. 2
Bultmann, R. K., 143, n. 4; 158, n. 3
Burkitt, F. C., 117f., 119, n. 5; 120, n. 4; 294
Burnet, J., 179, n. 2
Burney, C. F., 40, 43f., 151f., 160, n. 3; 172

Campbell, Macleod, 266, 267
Carlyle, T., 208
Carrington, P., 106f., 118, n. 2; 121, n. 5; 122ff., 128, n. 1; 129, n. 1; 130, 134, n. 4; 145, 232
Cave, S., 311, nn. 1, 3
Charles, R. H., 9, n. 2; 21, n. 3; 28, nn. 1, 3; 30, n. 2; 32, n. 5; 42, n. 4; 46, nn. 1, 3, 6; 59, nn. 2, 3, 4, 6; 60, nn. 1, 5, 9; 61, n. 3; 62 n. 6; 64, n. 4; 72, n. 1; 77, n. 5; 78, n. 3; 81, n. 9; 82, n. 8; 83, nn. 1, 5; 109, n. 1; 131, nn. 1–4; 160, n. 2; 225, n. 2; 261, n. 4; 278, 288, n. 1; 294, n. 2; 295, 296, n. 4; 297, 302, nn. 2, 4; 308, 309f., 315, 318, n. 4

Cheyne, T. K., 60, n. 7
Cocks, H. F. L., 197, n. 4
Cohen, A., 6, n. 8; 25, n. 1; 28f., 29, nn. 4, 5; 37, n. 7; 61, 83, n. 4; 215, 300, n. 5; 301, n. 6
Cook, S. A., 61, n. 5; 77, n. 2; 78, 80, n. 4; 100, n. 6; 109, n. 3; 163, 168, n. 3
Cooke, G. A., 81, nn. 5, 7; 82, n. 5
Creed, J. M., 45, n. 1; 89, n. 8; 155, n. 2; 199, n. 3
Cudworth, R., 190, n. 3
Cumont, F., 199, n. 3

Dalman, G., 246
Danby, H., 3, nn. 4, 5, 7; 21, n. 7; 53, n. 3; 132, n. 2; 238, nn. 1, 3; 313, n. 4
Daube, D., 44, n. 1; 57, n. 4; 64, n. 4; 130f., 132, 135, 144, n. 2; 213, n. 1
Davidson, A. B., 167, 188, 254, 266, n. 5; 267
Davidson, W. L., 179, n. 2
Deissmann, A., 86, n. 2; 87, 232, 241, n. 4; 323
Denney, J., 310, n. 4
Dibelius, M., 112, n. 4; 129, 136, nn. 1, 3; 138, n. 1; 140f., 150, n. 5; 152, 232, n. 5; 246
Dodd, C. H., 10, 19, n. 3; 24, nn. 3, 4, 5; 28, n. 1; 32, 37, n. 5; 38, n. 8; 39, n. 6; 41, 42, n. 3; 45, n. 2; 49, nn. 1, 2; 52, n. 3; 53, n. 2; 56, 58, nn. 4, 7; 63, n. 3; 66, n. 5; 67, nn. 1, 9; 68f., 70, 75, 76, n. 1; 85, n. 1; 86, n. 6; 87, n. 1; 88, n. 5; 91, n. 1; 100, nn. 6, 7, 8; 101, nn. 1, 8; 108, 110, n. 1; 111, n. 3; 112, 115, n. 3; 116, nn. 4, 5; 129, n. 3; 136, n. 3; 138, 141, 142, n. 4; 143, 144f., 147, nn. 4, 5; 149, n. 2; 154, n. 2; 158, n. 3; 164, n. 11; 166, 174, 179, 182, nn. 1, 3, 6; 196, 199, 217, 237, 242, 253, n. 2; 259, n. 3; 267, n. 4; 272, 283, n. 2; 285f., 297, n. 3; 298, 311, n. 3; 318, nn. 2, 6; 319, 320, 322
Driver, G. R., 333
Driver, S. R. and Neubauer, Ad., 275, n. 3
Drummond, J., 18, n. 2; 48
Duncan, G. S., 197, n. 4

Edersheim, A., 6, nn. 4, 9
Edwards, T. C., 155, n. 1; 267, nn. 3, 4; 310, n. 2
Emmett, C. W., 11, n. 1
Encyclopaedia Judaica, 10, n. 5
Epstein, I., 53f.

Farmer, H. H., 226
Fischel, H. F., 335
Flew, R. N., 56, n. 6; 75, n. 2; 86, n. 6; 100,
  101 f., 112, n. 1; 178, n. 6; 203, 204, n. 3;
  217, n. 6; 218, 243, 246, 320
Freedman, H., 22, n. 3; 133
Frey, J. B., 275, 299, n. 4; 301, n. 5; 314
Friedlander, G., 54, n. 2

Gavin, F., 120, n. 1; 121, nn. 3, 4, 7
Gillet, L., 43, n. 5; 322, n. 2; 323
Glover, T. R., 66, nn. 4, 8
Goguel, M., 227, n. 3; 248, n. 4
Goodenough, E. R., 94 ff.
Gray, G. B., 106, n. 1; 250, n. 2; 252, n. 3;
  253, n. 3
Green, A. A., 103, n. 2; 252, n. 1
Greenstone, J. H., 301, n. 4
Greenup, A. W., 313, n. 4
Griffiths, D. R., 196, n. 1
Guignebert, Ch. A. H., 15, nn. 1, 4;
  277, n. 4; 281, 283, n. 1; 299, 300
Gunkel, H., 41, 122, 183, 197, n. 9; 203,
  216, 217 f.

Harnack, A., 157, n. 5
Harris, J. R., 43
Hatch, E. and Redpath, H. A., 161, n. 1
Herford, T. R., 25, n. 1; 73, n. 7; 227, n. 3
Héring, J., 291, 292, 293 f., 295, n. 5;
  296, nn. 1, 2; 303
Hicks, F. C. N., 232, n. 1; 233, 234, n. 1;
  235, n. 4; 236, n. 1; 256, n. 1
Holland, H. S., 112, n. 1
Holtzmann, H. J., 1, 17, 150, 196, n. 2; 311
Hooke, S. H., 90, n. 5
Hoskyns, E. C. and Davey, N., 40, n. 4;
  44, n. 2
Howard, W. F., 17, n. 6; 120, n. 4; 157,
  172 f., 320
Hügel, F. von, 185, n. 1; 196, n. 2
Hunter, A. M., 41 f., 42, n. 2; 129, n. 3;
  136, 139, n. 1; 217, n. 6

J.D.P.B., 84, n. 4
J.E., 9, n. 4; 14, n. 6; 15, n. 4; 53, n. 4;
  54, n. 1; 57, n. 4; 63, n. 7; 73, n. 7; 96, n. 5;
  102, n. 2; 113, n. 1; 117, n. 2; 132,
  210, n. 4; 213, n. 1; 235, nn. 2, 4; 238, n. 1;
  270, n. 1; 297, n. 1; 302, n. 3
Johnson, A. R., 109, n. 3
Johnston, G., 56, n. 6; 62, n. 2; 75, n. 2;
  101, nn. 4, 9; 135, n. 2; 178, n. 7

Jones, F. W., 163, n. 5
Juster, J., 67, n. 5
Justin Martyr, 280, n. 2

Kautzsch, E., 10
Kennedy, H. A. A., 12, n. 3; 88, n. 4;
  89, nn. 3, 4, 5, 6; 90, nn. 1, 3, 5; 91, 98,
  137, n. 3; 138, n. 1; 191, n. 6; 192, n. 1;
  194, nn. 2, 4; 197, 286, 287, n. 1; 293,
  306, 310
Kenyon, F. G., 193, nn. 3, 4
Kierkegaard, S., 87, 100
King, E. G., 276
Kirk, K. E., 31, n. 3
Kittel, G., 5, n. 9
Klausner, J., 1, n. 3; 6, 13, n. 5; 149, n. 4;
  227, n. 2; 245, 247
Klein, G., 116, 117, n. 3; 121, n. 5; 132 ff.
Klostermann, E., 156, n. 3
Knox, W. L., 2, n. 4; 7, nn. 2-4; 8, nn. 2, 3, 7;
  13, 36, n. 14; 46, n. 2; 50, n. 2; 50, n. 6;
  57, 61, n. 3; 63, nn. 1, 5, 7; 66, n. 7;
  68, nn. 2, 7; 70, n. 3; 74, nn. 1, 2; 96 f.,
  107 f., 111, n. 4; 120, n. 4; 149, 157, n. 2;
  159, n. 1; 162 f., 169, 170, n. 1; 172 f., 174,
  179, 181, 185, 188, n. 4; 200, n. 3; 230,
  297, n. 1, 304, 306, nn. 2, 3; 311 f., 314,
  319
Kohler, K., 48, n. 5
Krauss, S., 5, n. 10; 115, n. 1
Kroll, W., 199, n. 3

Lacey, T. A., 187 f.
Lagarde, P. de, 156, n. 2
Lagrange, M. J., 3, n. 3; 5, n. 8; 6, n. 2;
  9, n. 2; 14, n. 4; 211, n. 10; 214, n. 1; 218,
  219, n. 3; 221, 283, n. 1
Lake, K., 88, 134, 188, n. 3; 221, n. 1
Lattey, C., 277
Lebreton, J., 168   96, n. 1
Leveen, J., 95, n. 1
Levy, S., 269, n. 8; 273, n. 2
Liddell and Scott, 18, 314, n. 1
Lietzmann, H., 32, nn. 1, 2; 106, n. 1; 141,
  n. 5; 155, n. 1; 195, n. 4; 248, n. 3; 273,
  n. 1; 290, 293, 294, 298, n. 1
Lightfoot, J. B., 37, n. 3; 151, 172, n. 1;
  197
Lods, A., 164, n. 9; 166
Loewe, H., 65, n. 3; 174, n. 1; 245, n. 2;
  259, n. 1; 277
Loisy, A., 2, 88 f.

Macdonald, D. B., 168, n. 4

Macgregor, G. H. C., 91, n. 3; 110, n. 1
Macgregor, G. H. C. and Purdy, A. C., 4, n. 1; 7, n. 1; 9, n. 1; 10, n. 5; 11, 12, n. 7
Mackintosh, H. R., 152, n. 2; 175, n. 3
Maclean, A. J., 121, n. 5
Macpherson, J., 110, n. 1
Manson, T. W., 39, n. 6; 57, 59, n. 4; 79, n. 1; 100, n. 2; 118, 119, n. 3; 239 ff., 250, 278, 313
Manson, W., 45, nn. 1, 2; 89, n. 8; 91, 142 f., 144, n. 1; 155, n. 2; 156, n. 3; 157, n. 5; 228, n. 3; 229, 246, n. 4; 251, n. 2; 280
Marmorstein, A., 8, n. 5; 208, n. 2; 210 ff., 214, 215, n. 3; 219, n. 2; 221, nn. 3, 4; 268, n. 2; 269, nn. 2, 5, 8; 270 ff.
Marsh, H. G., 91, n. 3; 121, n. 7; 221, n. 3
McGiffert, A. C., 145, nn. 3, 4
McNeile, A. H., 156, nn. 1, 3; 158, n. 1
Menzies, A., 148, n. 2
Meyer, E., 132, n. 1
Moffatt, J., 49, n. 4; 50, nn. 5, 6; 56, 71, nn. 4, 5; 105, 106, n. 1; 153, 155, n. 1; 182, n. 2; 187, 221, n. 8; 248, nn. 1, 4; 250, 251, n. 4; 266, n. 5; 267, nn. 2, 4; 291, n. 1; 294 f., 304, 306 f., 310, n. 2
Montefiore, C. J. G., 1–5, 11 ff., 15 f., 17, 59, 60, n. 7; 62, n. 1; 63, 66, 213, n. 3; 245, 247, 277, 324
Moore, G. F., 3, nn. 3, 6; 9, n. 3; 11, n. 6; 12, n. 4; 22, nn. 2, 3; 23 f., 25, n. 2; 30, n. 3; 34, 37, n. 7; 39, n. 5; 63, nn. 5, 9; 64, n. 3; 65, n. 2; 67, nn. 4, 5; 72, n. 4; 73, n. 5; 83, nn. 4, 5; 84, 94, n. 4; 102, n. 2; 104, 113, n. 1; 114, n. 2; 115, n. 2; 121, n. 2; 149, 150, n. 2; 159, n. 2; 162, n. 2; 165, n. 1; 170, nn. 5, 6; 171, 211, n. 10; 213 f., 214, n. 3; 219, n. 6; 228, n. 1; 231, nn. 2, 5; 235, nn. 1, 6; 238, n. 1; 254 f., 257, 258, n. 1; 263, n. 2; 272, n. 4; 280, n. 1, 283, n. 1; 288, n. 1; 301, n. 3; 314, 316
Morgan, W., 1, 290
Moulton, J. H., 130, 195, n. 4
Moulton-Milligan, 31, n. 3; 241, n. 4
Murray, G., 13, 192, n. 3

Niebuhr, R., 34 f.
Nock, A. D., 68, n. 2; 89, nn. 5, 6; 90, nn. 2, 3; 91, n. 3; 92 f., 94, n. 4; 96, n. 3; 97, 98, n. 1; 188, n. 4
Norden, E., 151, n. 6; 156, 158, 180

Oesterley, W. O. E., 5, n. 8; 25, n. 1; 32, n. 4; 41, n. 1; 44, n. 3; 83, n. 3; 171, n. 1; 234, n. 3; 235, n. 4; 238, n. 1; 249, 253, 254, n. 1; 299, n. 4; 303, n. 1
Oesterley, W. O. E. and Box, G. H., 275, n. 3
Oesterley, W. O. E. and Robinson, T. H., 38, n. 1; 62, n. 4; 77 f., 79, 80, n. 1; 163, n. 4; 258, n. 6; 263, n. 1; 264, nn. 2, 3, 6
Oman, J., 321
Otto, R., 100, n. 1; 243, 248, 278

Parkes, J. W., 1, n. 3; 68, n. 6
Parzen, H., 206, 211, n. 1
Peake, A. S., 4, n. 2; 263, n. 1
Pederson, J., 108, 208
Perdelwitz, R., 122
Pfleiderer, O., 17, 290, 311
Pilcher, C. V., 302, n. 4
Plummer, A., 37, n. 2; 50, n. 3; 155, n. 1; 156, n. 3; 306, 310, n. 4
Porteous, N. W., 78, n. 6
Porter, F. C., 9, 17, n. 1; 20, n. 3; 21, nn. 2, 7, 8; 26, nn. 1, 3; 33, 150 f., 152, n. 2; 177, n. 1

Rabbinic Anthology (R.A.), 11, n. 8; 13, n. 5; 20, n. 1; 21, n. 9; 22, nn. 2, 4; 25, n. 5; 63, n. 8; 64, n. 3; 65, nn. 1, 2, 3; 66, n. 1; 83, 150, n. 2; 170, n. 4; 174, n. 1; 213, n. 3; 225, n. 2; 236, n. 3; 245, n. 2; 259, nn. 1, 2; 277, n. 3
Rabbinowitz, J., 6, n. 5
Ramsay, W. M., 7, n. 2; 179, n. 11
Rankin, O. S., 163, nn. 2, 3, 4; 165, 167, nn. 1, 2; 168, n. 4
Raven, C. E., 163, 190
Rawlinson, A. E. J., 2 f., 11, n. 7; 12, n. 6; 41, 49, 56, 87, n. 5; 88, n. 4; 89, nn. 1, 9; 90, n. 5; 91, n. 8; 151, n. 6; 157, n. 3; 159, n. 2; 182, 191, n. 3; 195, 196, n. 1; 199, 217, n. 2; 226, n. 1; 318, n. 1
Ray, J., 190
Rees, T., 183, n. 3; 188, nn. 5, 7; 189, 196, n. 1; 205, n. 3; 217, n. 6
Reitzenstein, R., 1, 89, 191 ff., 194 ff., 200
Resch, J. A., 137, 141, n. 1
Richards, G. C., 57, n. 1; 96, n. 3; 97, n. 1
Ritschl, A., 237, n. 6
Roberts, C., Skeat, T. C. and Nock, A. D., 7, n. 2
Robertson, A. and Plummer, A., 293, n. 2

Robinson, H. W., 17, n. 4; 18 f., 19, nn. 1, 2; 21, n. 8; 31, n. 3; 32, n. 3; 44, n. 3; 59, nn. 2, 3; 78, n. 5; 109, n. 3; 182, n. 6; 185, 186, nn. 2, 3; 191, n. 1; 193 f., 228, n. 2; 272, 299

Robinson, J. A., 91, n. 8; 121, n. 5; 173, n. 7

Robinson, T. H., 59, n. 2; 77, n. 2; 156, nn. 1, 4; 163, 234, 251, n. 1

Rowley, H. H., 10, n. 5; 12, n. 7; 132, n. 1; 264, nn. 7, 9; 265, 275, n. 5; 277 f., 279

Ryder-Smith, C. A., 233 f., 236

Ryle, H. E. and James, M. R., 62, n. 6

Sanday, W. and Headlam, A. C., 17, n. 4; 28, 53, n. 1; 76, n. 1; 130, n. 3; 153, 241, n. 4; 272, 298, n. 1

Schechter, S., 14, n. 4; 64, n. 5; 83, n. 3; 149, n. 2; 162, n. 2; 170, 254, 255, n. 3; 257, 258, 262, n. 5; 269, n. 2; 270, 272

Schiller-Szinessy, 277

Schmidt, P. W., 157 f.

Scholem, G. G., 14, 15, n. 1; 37, n. 7

Schultz, H., 160, n. 3

Schürer, E., 5, n. 8; 39, 63, n. 7; 72, n. 4; 280, n. 2; 283, n. 1; 301, n. 7

Schweitzer, A., 1, 8, n. 10; 10, 14 f., 56, 58, nn. 4, 7; 63, n. 5; 69, n. 5; 70, n. 1; 71, 73, n. 2; 91, n. 2; 98 f., 120, 188, 222, nn. 4, 6; 223, n. 1; 285, 287, 288 ff., 295, 297 f., 303, 309, n. 1; 310, n. 5; 311, 319

Scott, C. A. A., 70 f., 85, nn. 2, 5, 6; 90, nn. 1, 2; 91, 108, n. 2; 147, n. 7; 178, n. 6; 183, n. 1; 195, n. 4; 196, n. 1; 202, 223, n. 2; 230 f., 234, 236, 237, n. 1; 254, 256, n. 2; 259, n. 3; 266

Scott, E. F., 139, 151, 196, n. 1; 201, n. 10; 202, 205

Scott, W., 179

Simpson, D. C., 166, n. 4

Singer, I., 64, n. 2

Skinner, J., 78, n. 3; 79, n. 3; 80, 166, n. 3; 204, 224, n. 2; 225, n. 1

Smith, J. M. P., 160, n. 3

Smith, W. R., 76 f., 77, n. 5; 79, 234, n. 3; 235, n. 4

Snaith, N. H., 43, n. 5; 165, n. 1; 183, n. 7; 185

Stade, B., 60, n. 7

Stevens, G. B., 31, n. 3; 32, nn. 2, 3; 294, n. 2; 295, 318, n. 3

Strachan, R. H., 107, n. 2; 121, n. 1; 143, 148, n. 2; 195, n. 4; 196, n. 1

Strack, H. L. and Billerbeck, P., 7, n. 4; 20, 21, nn. 2, 5, 6, 7; 22, nn. 1, 4; 23, n. 3; 25, nn. 3, 5; 27, n. 2; 30, n. 3; 37, n. 1; 38, 39, nn. 1, 2, 3; 42, n. 4; 44, n. 1; 45, nn. 4, 7, 8, 9; 46, nn. 1, 2, 3, 5, 7, 8, 10; 48, 53, nn. 1, 4; 54, nn. 1, 2, 3, 4; 55, n. 1; 72, nn. 3, 5; 75, n. 3; 84, n. 7; 102, n. 2; 107, n. 2; 119, n. 6; 120, 148, n. 2; 149, n. 5; 153, nn. 1, 3; 190, n. 1; 207, n. 1; 209, n. 1; 212, n. 1; 221, n. 4; 237, n. 5; 269, 274, n. 2; 275, n. 2; 276 f., 277, n. 2; 283, 288, n. 1; 300, n. 6; 306, n. 1; 308, n. 6; 314, 316, 317, n. 1; 320

Streeter, B. H., 121, n. 5; 122, 142

Swete, H. B., 201, n. 9; 202, n. 2

Taylor, C., 121, n. 5; 249, n. 2

Taylor, V., 86, n. 6; 87, nn. 2, 6, 7; 88, n. 6; 91, 99, 110, n. 1; 137, n. 4; 158, 230, 234, 235, n. 1; 236, 237, 239, 242 f., 245 ff., 248, n. 4; 250, n. 1; 251 f., 259, n. 3; 274, 278

Teichmann, 311

Tennant, F. R., 23, n. 5; 27, 31, n. 3; 32, nn. 2, 3; 38, 39, n. 2; 45, nn. 3, 5; 46

Thackeray, H. St J., 32, n. 2; 52, n. 1; 287, n. 1; 290, 293, 307 f., 312, n. 1

Thomas, D. W., 73, n. 6; 171, n. 4

Thornton, L. S., 87, n. 3; 105, n. 2; 108, n. 1; 310, n. 4

Torrey, C. C., 9, n. 4; 10, 264, n. 9

Volz, P., 183, n. 7, 275

Weber, F., 17, n. 1

Weiss, J., 49, n. 5; 52, n. 1; 69, n. 4; 70, nn. 1, 4; 105, nn. 1, 2; 112, n. 4; 116, 118, 119, n. 2; 133, n. 1; 141 f., 144, n. 4; 147, n. 7; 151, 175, n. 2; 181, 195, n. 4; 242, n. 2; 290, 293 f., 296, n. 2; 297, 302, n. 2; 303, n. 2; 304, n. 5; 306, 307, n. 3; 308

Welch, A. C., 61, n. 5; 255

Wells, H. G., 61, n. 4

Wendland, P., 8, n. 9

Williams, N. P., 17, n. 6; 18, 21, n. 4; 22, n. 3; 26, 27, n. 1; 31, n. 3; 32, n. 1; 34, n. 3; 38, 45, nn. 5, 6

Windisch, H., 149, n. 5; 150 f., 154, 159 ff., 312, n. 1

Wood, I. F., 189, 203

Wrede, W., 222, n. 4

Wünsche, A., 282, n. 2

IX. SUBJECT INDEX

Aaron, 270, 273

Abraham, 95, 97, 269

Acts, credibility of, 2 f.; missionary practice of Paul in, 68

Adam, (a) First Adam: sin of and its consequences, 31; its representative character, 32; cosmic consequences of, 38; glory of, before his Fall, 45; and temptation of Christ, 42; in Philo, 47 f., 52; in *Clementine Homilies*, 50 ff.; unity of mankind in, 53; formation of his body, 53; his bi-sexuality, 48, 54; his name, 54; Adamic speculation, and Paul's doctrine of the Church, 53; relation to *Ur-mensch* and Heavenly Man, 45, 49; disobedience of, 268; Adamic commandments, 114. (b) Second Adam: 41, 43, 49; concept of, originated by Paul, 41 ff., 151; First and Second Adam, 120, 268, 274, 304

Age to Come, follows the Messianic Age, 288; has come, 298; Christians already partake in, 319; two phases of, 314; entered at death, 315; in Paul, 317; this age as vestibule to, 315; character of, 307

Alexandria, Alexandrian influence on Paul, 28, 151

Antinomianism, 111

Apocalyptic, relation to Rabbinic Judaism, 9 f.; importance for the understanding of Paul, 10 f.

Apostolic decree, 117 ff.; and Paul, 118 f.

Ark, 208, 238, 240

Athens, Paul at, 187, 311; missionary tactics at, 68, n.

Atonement, 273

Baptism, 91, 98, 198, 221; proselyte baptism, 121; and dying and rising with Christ, 122; baptismal catechisms, 122 ff., 129; baptismal hymn, 129

Bar-Mitzwâh, and different periods of a man's life, 24 ff.

Basileia, term avoided by Paul, 36

Blood, various meanings of term in Paul, 232; revulsion against, amongst scholars, 234; central in sacrifice, 235; sacrificial connotation of, in Paul, 236 f.; Jewish objection to drinking blood, 245; Paul's treatment of, in Eucharist, 244 f.

Body, heavenly, 315; *see under* Christ

Chasidim, 264

Christ, body of, 56, 318; as teacher, 143; Law of, 142; as Rabbi, 143; as New Torah, 147 ff., 266; as Second Adam, *see under* Adam; solidarity of all Christians with, 101, 291, 318; 'in Christ', 86, 112, 178, 188, 197, 318; dying and rising with, 87 ff., 98 ff., 198 ff., 318; 'with Christ', 318; Messiah, 324; obedience of, 265; in Epistle to Hebrews, 267; as Rock, 168 ff.; pre-existence of, 162, 174; as agent in Creation, 174; as Wisdom, 150 ff.; words of, 136 ff., 140 ff.; imitation of, 88, 147

Christians, as strangers and foreigners, 113 ff.

Church, as New Israel, 75, 100 ff., 201, 308; constituted by the Death of Christ, 252; as body of Christ, 53 ff., 318; home of Spirit, 178; as neo-levitical community, 130

Circumcision, in Philo, 96, 121

Codes, Jewish Codes, possibly used by Paul, 130 ff.

Community, emphasis on, in Paul, 253, 323; Christians as new community, 102 ff.

Conversion of Paul, 67, 197, 324

Corinth, 50

Cosmological speculation, in Judaism, 37 f., 165 ff.

Covenant, 148, 260, 261

Creation, Christian Dispensation as New Creation, 37 ff.; Incarnation as New Creation, 40; Christian as New Creation, 119 f., 127; proselyte as New Creation, 129; Messianic Age corresponds to Creation, 39, 49, 304; as witness to God, 28 f., 175; Jesus as Lord of, 40; problem of, 166; Christ as agent of, 174

Cross, as an act of obedience, 265 f.; constitutive of new community, 252; as expiatory, 259; in Early Church, 228, 229 f.; as sacrifice, 230; as scandal, 283

Day of Atonement, 238 ff., 240 ff., 257

Death, of Jesus, *see under* Cross; of Christians unthinkable, 291

Decalogue, as Covenant, 260

Derek Eretz literature, 126, 132

Didache, 90, n. 2, 121, 133, 150

Dying and rising with Christ, *see under* Christ; and the mysteries, 89; interpretation of, 98 f., 198, 199

Ecstatic experiences, of Paul, 197; of Rabbis, 198, 211; Paul's valuation of, 198
Eleazer, 272
Election, 71, 100
Elijah, 276
Epicureanism, 8
Eschatology, 111; in Paul, 285; realized eschatology, 286, 320; possible revision of Pauline eschatology, under Hellenistic influence, 311; futurist element in, 320
Essenes, 303
Eucharist, 55; in Early Church, 243; in Matthew, Mark and Luke, 242; Marcan and Pauline accounts of, 245; Paul's treatment of blood in, 244 f.; Pauline account of, is Rabbinized, 246 ff.; as remembrance, 251; and Passover, 250; and Suffering Servant, 250; and New Covenant, 260
Exile, 38, 166

Faith, 5, 91; Schweitzer and Pauline faith, 98 f., 269, 270; and Works, 221; Justification by, 221
Festivals, Paul and Jewish Festivals, 239, 241
Firstfruits, Christ as, 106, 250; Resurrection as, 297
Flesh, 5; opposed to Spirit, 17; Paul's doctrine of, not Hellenistic, 18 ff.; O.T. basis of Pauline doctrine of, 18; morally indifferent, 19

Gentiles, uneasy conscience of Judaism about, 63; given same chance as Israel, 64; given the Adamic and Noachian Laws, 65; given Prophets, 65; Paul and Gentiles, 66 f.; Gentiles as strangers and foreigners, 113
Gnosis, 191
God, idea of, in Diaspora Judaism, 11 f.; unique relation of to Israel, 82; transcendance of, 164, 165, n. 1, 175; knowing God, 157
Grace, and Nature, 174 f.

Hermetic writings, 18, 129, 199; and mysteries, 199
High Priest, 231; and Holy Spirit, 95, 211, 213

ἱλαστήριον, in Rom. 3. 25, 237 ff.
Immortality, 302
Intermediate state of the dead, not found in Paul, 318
Isaac, 95, 270
Israel, 78 f.; New Israel, *see under* Church; hope for ingathering of dispersed of, 79 f.; eternal relation of God and, 82 f.; solidarity of, 83 f.

Jacob, 95, 270
Jerusalem, open to Greek influences, 6
John the Baptist, 270
Judaism, of Diaspora, 1, 4 f., 324; contacts of Diaspora with Palestinian, 6 f.; Palestinian, 3 f.; Greek influence on latter, 5 f.; variety within first century, 4; religion of Torah, 67; Orthopraxy in, 74; fulfilled in Christianity, 322; tolerance of, 74
Judgement, 296 f., 316
Justification, 273; by Faith, 221 f.

Kingdom of Christ, 287, 289 f.; did Paul teach temporary Messianic Kingdom?, 292, 296 ff.
Kingdom of God, 287, 295
Kokba, Bar, 216, 217, 275

Law or Torah, yoke of, 150, 262; Christ as Torah, *see under* Christ; given in order to give Israel a chance to gain merits, 268; observed by Paul, 321; despair of, 11; symbolic interpretation of, 11, 96, 146; as Light, 148; attitude of Paul to Torah, 69 ff.; inconsistency of Paul in attitude to Torah, 69 ff.; New Torah in Messianic Age, 72; emphasis on observance of, 73; centrality of, in Judaism, 215; Law of Christ, *see under* Christ; efficacious at death, 317; New Torah, 223 ff.; Christifying of Torah, 223; and Wisdom, 168 ff.; pre-existent, agent in creation, world created for its sake, 170; and Platonism, 171
Logos, 45, 151, 173

Ma'aseh Bereshith and Ma'aseh Merkabah, 7, n. 4
Maccabean Revolt, 263
Magical texts, 199
Mattathias, 263
Matthew, Gospel of Christian Rabbinism, 137, 149 f.

Merits, 268 f.; stored up as treasure, 269; danger of doctrine of, 269; in Paul, 272; and Death of Christ, 273; of Patriarchs, 270

Messiah, b. David, 276; b. Joseph, 276; and Son of Man, 278 f., 283; and Suffering Servant, 279; Suffering Messiah; a scandal, 274; theories of pre-Christian Suffering Messiah, 276 ff.; in Talmud, 281; *Dialogue with Trypho*, 281; of House of David, 287, 288; death of as act of obedience, 265 f.; Jesus as, 324, see Wisdom

Miracles, 213

Mishnah, 3

Moses, 148, 162, 270, 271, 255

Mysteries, criticism of view that Paul is dependent on, 89 f.; Lucius's experience, 72; Goodenough's theory of a Hellenistic Jewish mystery and criticism thereof, 93 ff.; three classes in mysteries, 193 ff.; and Hermetic literature, and magical texts, 199

Mysticism, (a) 'Christ Mysticism', 88 f., 102, 146, 318, 320; Schweitzer and, 99. (b) Mysticism, general, 5, 13 ff.; Pauline mysticism not Hellenistic, 15; evidence of, suppressed in *Mishnah*, 14, 56

Nationalism, 57 ff., 61, 321 f.; growth of particularism in first century, 62; in Paul, 75, 85

New Birth, 120

New Covenant, 131, 148, 223, 225; and Eucharist, 251, 26c

New Creation, see under Creation

New Exodus, 146, 251, 252, 313

New Torah, 53 f.; relation to Spirit, 223, 323; Christ as, 147–76

Noachian commandments, 114 ff.; in Romans, 115 f.; and Apostolic decree, 117 ff.; see also 325 ff.

νοῦς, 182, 193 f.

Obedience, 260 f.; and persecution, 263; and suffering, 263; unto death, 263; and Christ, 265 ff.; in Hebrews, 267

Ordination, in Rabbinic Judaism, 211, 213

Parousia, see Second Advent

Participial imperative, 130 f., 329

Passover, 102 ff., 242, 250

Paul, relations to Jerusalem, 2; inconsistencies of, 68 f.; attitude to Gentiles, 66 f.; conversion, 67; missionary tactics, 68; attitude to Torah, 69 ff.; to Noachian laws, 115 ff.; as *Tanna*, 145; his philosophy of history, 77; and Old and New Israel, 75 ff., 102 ff.; and Festivals, 239, 241; and the pneumatic, 192 ff.; and historic Jesus, 143, 195, 227; double personality in, 196 ff.; as ecstatic, 197; and ethicization of the Spirit, 217 ff.; Paul and Philo, 52

Paulinism, in Mark and Luke, 137

Pessimism, 5, 13

Pharisees, 3, 43 n., 264

Pneumatic experiences among Rabbis, 211; see under Paul

Promised Land, 206, 313

Prophecy, degenerated in Judaism, 210

Proselytes, divergent views on, 63 f., 113 ff.

Q, Paul and, 142, 157

Rabbis, and power of prediction, 211, 213

Reception and delivery of tradition, 248 f.

Resurrection, of nation, 83; of body, 299; importance of, in Judaism, 300; controversy on, 301 f.; Hellenistic influences on doctrine of, 302; Paul and, 303 ff.; spiritual interpretation of Resurrection of Jesus, 304; denial of, 303; analogies used to explain, 305; popular view of, 306 ff.; glory of, 307; alleged contradiction in Paul's teaching, 309; Paul's view of, Hellenized, 311; varying incidence of, 288; Schweitzer's scheme on, 289; as firstfruits, 297; at Corinth, 291; twofold resurrection, 289, 291; no general resurrection in Paul, 294; Charles, R. H. on, 309; Kennedy, H. A. A. on, 310; dematerialized, 314

Sabbath, 264

Sacrifice, not efficacious unless properly motivated, 256; occasion for ethical teaching, 257; and restitution, 257; and repentance, 257; sorrow at cessation of, 258; substitutes for, 259; inferior to merits of the Fathers, 271

Sacrificial system, little influence on Paul, 230; and the Diaspora Judaism, 231; its scale, 231; symbolism in, 235; not central in first-century Judaism and limited efficacy of, 254; Philo's criticism

Sacrificial system *continued*
of, 266; in Epistle to the Hebrews, 267;
Rabbinic criticism of, 258 f.; and Paul,
259
Second Advent, delay of, influences
theology, 286, 288; *see also* 296, 319
Sermon on the Mount, 149
Servant (Suffering), and Eucharist, 250;
in Paul, 274 ff.; and Son of Man, 279
Shekinah, 211, 213 f.; and Holy Spirit,
213 f.
Sin, doctrine of, in Rom. 7, 24 ff.; in
Rom. 1. 2, 27 ff.; with high hand and
inadvertent, 254; moral and ritual, 255;
see also Adam and *Yêtzer*
σκῆνος, 311
Solidarity, of all Christians in Christ,
101; of community, 253; of God and
worshipper, 77; of Nation of Israel, 83 f.,
108 ff., 201, 268, 272; *see also* Adam
Son of Man, 159, 245, 288; and Messiah,
279; and Suffering Servant, 279
Spirit, Holy Spirit and Second Adam, 304;
and Scriptures, 219; suppression of
references to, in Rabbinic literature, 216,
220; and morality, 219 ff.; alleged
ethicization of, by Paul, 217 ff.; and
present possession of, 144, 312; in Paul,
177 f.; Stoic conception of Spirit, 179;
materially interpreted, 181 ff.; relation to
Christ, 182, 196; in O.T., 183; in
Rabbinic literature, 184; Paul's doctrine
of, not Stoic, 186 ff.; relation to Cosmos,
in Stoicism, 187 f.; in Judaism and O.T.,
188 ff.; Reitzenstein on, 193; Rabbinic
concept of, 205 ff.; and Prophets, 193,
206; and individual in Paul, 200 f.; and
community, 201 ff.; and Paul's missionary
experience, 202; and Palestine, 206; and
age of Spirit, 208; ceased with destruction of First Temple, 208; with cessation

of Prophets, 209; still active in Israel,
209 f.; and the Sages, 211 f.; arid Shekinah,
211 f.; mark of Messianic Age, 215 f.;
and morality, 217
Stoicism, 8, 28, 116, 144, 151 f., 169, 174;
and Paul's doctrine of the Spirit, 178 ff.;
at Tarsus, 179; in Acts 17, 188
Suffering, 263; *see also* Messiah
Sukkâh, 313
Synagogue, 7, 232

Taxo, 277
Temple, 162, 257 f., 238
Testimonia, 43

Universalism, 57 f.
Urim and Thummim, 208, 331

Wisdom, as *rêshîth* of Creation, 151 f.; in
Philo, 153; in the mind of Jesus, 155 f.;
relation to Messiah, 158 ff.; identified
with Torah, 168 ff.; in O.T., 163 ff.;
Book of, 28
Words of Jesus, reminiscences in Paul,
136 ff.; collections of, possibly used
by Paul, 140; as Law of Christ,
142 ff.

Yêtzer, doctrine of good and evil *yêtzer*,
20 ff.; predominance of concept of evil
yêtzer, 21; associated with sex and the
heart, 21; with unchastity and immorality, 22, 29; not intrinsically evil,
22; cured by study of Torah, 22, 25 f.;
by repentance, 23; uprooted in Age to
Come, 23; and Paul, 23 ff.; neglect of
good impulse in Paul, 26; evil *yêtzer*
located by Paul in flesh, not heart, 27

Zadokite Fragment, 131